AMERICAN FOREIGN POLICY
PATTERN AND PROCESS

THIRD EDITION

AMERICAN FOREIGN POLICY
PATTERN AND PROCESS

THIRD EDITION

CHARLES W. KEGLEY, JR.
University of South Carolina

EUGENE R. WITTKOPF
Louisiana State University

St. Martin's Press   New York

ACKNOWLEDGMENTS

Table 4-1, "A Balance Sheet on Strategic Arms and Arms Proposals, 1985," Copyright © 1985 by The New York Times Company. Reprinted by permission.

Figure 4-2, "Star Wars: Scenario for Space Defense," *The Washington Post Weekly Edition*, March 18, 1985; 6. Reprinted by permission.

Figure 6-1, "The Distribution of Global Gross Domestic Product, 1960, 1970, and 1980," Reprinted with permission from *U.S. Foreign Policy and the Third World: Agenda 1985-86*, edited by John W. Sewell, Richard E. Feinberg, and Valeriana Kallab, U.S.-Third World Policy Perspective, No. 3 (New Brunswick, NJ: Transaction Books for the Overseas Development Council, 1985). © Overseas Development Council, 1985.

Figure 6-2, "Per Capita Gross National Product in Developed and Developing Countries, 1975-1981," Reprinted with permission from *U.S. Foreign Policy and the Third World: Agenda 1985-86*, edited by John W. Sewell, Richard E. Feinberg, and Valeriana Kallab, U.S.-Third World Policy Perspective, No. 3 (New Brunswick, N.J.: Transaction Books for the Overseas Development Council, 1985). © Overseas Development Council, 1985.

Table 7-1, "Current Account Balances of Industrial and Developing Countries, 1970-1985," From *World Development Report 1985*. Copyright © 1985 by The International Bank for Reconstruction and Development/The World Bank. Reprinted by permission of Oxford University Press, Inc.

Box 7-1, "The Bretton Woods Conference and Its Twin Institutions," From *World Development Report 1985*. Copyright © 1985 by The International Bank for Reconstruction and Development/The World Bank. Reprinted by permission of Oxford University Press, Inc.

Box 7-2, "The United States as a Debtor Nation," *The Washington Post National Weekly Edition*, October 7, 1985. Reprinted by permission.

Box 7-3, "Sovereign Risk and Its Implications for International Lending," From *World Development Report 1985*. Copyright © 1985 by The International Bank for Reconstruction and Development/The World Bank. Reprinted by permission of Oxford University Press, Inc.

Box 10-1, "The National Security Assistant: The Professionals' Job Description," by I.M. Destler, 1983. Reprinted by permission of the author and The National Academy of Public Administration.

Figure 12-1, "Presidential Success on Congressional Votes, 1953-1985," *Congressional Quarterly Weekly Report*, January 11, 1986: 69. Copyright © 1986 Congressional Quarterly, Inc. Reprinted with permission.

For Pamela and Barbara

PREFACE

Has American foreign policy changed since 1945? If so, how, and with what consequences? What are the sources of American foreign policy? Do these sources promote policy change or inhibit it? These are the principal questions we seek to answer in *American Foreign Policy: Pattern and Process*.

The years since publication of the first edition of this book in 1979 have been turbulent ones for the United States. Many of the challenges the nation has faced seemed to call into question the wisdom of the conventional assumptions that have governed America's approach to the world since World War II. Yet, despite these challenges and the policy debates and adjustments they have stimulated, American foreign policy continues to be characterized by continuity. The thesis of the first edition of the book—that both the ends sought by American foreign policy makers and the means through which they have been pursued have become deeply entrenched patterns that have undergone only remedial adjustments over the course of several decades—remains a compelling interpretation. Indeed, time continues to deal generously with it.

How does one account for such policy continuity? To probe this question, we continue in this edition of *American Foreign Policy: Pattern and Process* to utilize the pre-theoretical framework of the previous editions, which maintains that five factors—international, societal, governmental, role, and individual—collectively influence foreign policy objectives and the means chosen to realize them. The pre-theoretical framework organizes examination of both the international and domestic sources of American action abroad, and explores the linkages between political institutions and policy formulation processes, on the one hand, and policy outcomes, on the other. The framework thus facilitates an examination of the past diplomatic record and provides a basis for anticipating the future. In speculating about the future in the concluding chapter of the book, we are encouraged by the fact that many of the predictions advanced in the first and second editions have proven accurate, including especially the evidence that the foreign policy of the Reagan administration has reaffirmed the postwar pattern of American foreign policy rather than deviating from it. Indeed, the events of the past decade have lent credence to the book's thesis and attest to the utility of the theoretical framework which structures and informs the analysis.

Although the thematic thrust and organizational framework of the earlier editions have been preserved, numerous changes have been made in this edition. The evidence has been thoroughly updated and new literature incorporated, and the coverage of several topics has been revised and expanded, while that of others has been shortened or dropped. Readers familiar with the first two editions of the book will quickly notice that the discussion of the instruments of American foreign policy has been expanded with the addition of a new chapter focused on national security policy (chapter five). We continue to maintain the sixteen chapter format by merging into a single chapter (thirteen) the treatment of role sources of American foreign policy. Other changes are spread throughout the book. They include examination of the challenge of international terrorism; the American foreign policy response to the Third World debt crisis; and treatment of the impact of the electronic media on public attitudes toward foreign policy. The role of the United States in the global food regime has been elaborated, while the coverage of its role and stake in the global oil regime, so prevalent an issue demanding of detailed analysis when the previous editions of the book were published, has been reduced. The retreat from multilateralism evident in the policies of the Reagan administration is addressed in a variety of contexts, and the discussion of alternative interpretations of American foreign policy patterns has been sharpened and focused more clearly. Other changes are evident throughout, but undiminished is our commitment to relate the five sources of American foreign policy to its durable tenets captured in the themes of globalism, anticommunism, containment, military strength, and interventionism.

Many people have contributed to the development of the book and its evolution over nearly a decade. As the list of those to whom we are indebted continues to grow beyond those who were explicitly acknowledged in the first and second editions, we run the risk of slighting some in our desire to thank all. William A. Clark, Mark J. DeHaven, Lucia Wren Rawls, and Barry Rich deserve special thanks for their contributions to the onerous technical tasks associated with production of this edition. Others who have contributed in some special way to our thinking or who have otherwise made important contributions to the book as it has evolved over a decade now number in the dozens. We thank you collectively. Our appreciation is in no way diminished by this impersonal expression of our gratitude.

We also express our appreciation to Jean Smith, Peter Dougherty, Richard Steins, and Emily Berleth, our taskmasters at St. Martin's Press, for their continued enthusiasm for the book; to James B. Holderman and Alfred B. Clubok, our valued colleagues and friends at our respective institutions, for their personal support for our scholarly endeavors; and to our wives, Pamela and Barbara, to whom the book is dedicated.

CONTENTS

IV. SOCIETAL SOURCES OF AMERICAN FOREIGN POLICY

V. GOVERNMENTAL SOURCES OF AMERICAN FOREIGN POLICY

VI.   ROLE SOURCES OF AMERICAN FOREIGN POLICY

VII.   INDIVIDUALS AS SOURCES OF AMERICAN FOREIGN POLICY

VIII. PATTERN AND PROCESS IN AMERICAN FOREIGN POLICY

AMERICAN FOREIGN POLICY
PATTERN AND PROCESS

THIRD EDITION

I

ANALYTICAL PERSPECTIVES ON AMERICAN FOREIGN POLICY

1

PERSISTENCE AND CHANGE IN AMERICAN FOREIGN POLICY: A THEMATIC INTRODUCTION

> I know of no change in policy, only of circumstances.
>
> *Secretary of State John Quincy Adams, 1823*

> It is quite true that the central themes of American foreign policy are more or less constant. They derive from the kind of people we are . . . and from the shape of the world situation.
>
> *Former Secretary of State Dean Rusk, 1983*

Throughout history, major wars have led to transformations of the international political system and to changes in the position of states within it. World War II, by far the most destructive and far-reaching global war in the twentieth century, was no exception. From it the United States emerged a superpower, acquiring capabilities unparalleled in history that made it unquestionably preponderant in world affairs. The British author Harold J. Laski described the circumstances that came into being thus:

> America bestrides the world like a colossus; neither Rome at the height of its power nor Great Britain in the period of its economic supremacy enjoyed an influence so direct, so profound, or so pervasive. It has half the wealth of the world today in its hands, it has rather more than half of the world's productive capacity, and it exports more than twice as much as it imports. Today literally hundreds of millions of Europeans and Asiatics know that both the quality and the rhythm of their lives depend upon decisions made in Washington. On the wisdom of those decisions hangs the fate of the next generation. (Laski, 1947: 641)

3

From this advantageous position the leaders of the United States forged a new vision of the role the U.S. was to play in world affairs, predicated on assumptions derived from the experience in world war which had catapulted the United States to the apex of the international hierarchy. A new foreign policy cloaked in internationalism was given shape and put into place, as the United States confidently approached the world with a clarity of vision and a consistency of purpose.

It has now been more than forty years since international involvement became the guidepost of American foreign policy. Over the course of those four decades, global circumstances have changed dramatically. The supremacy of the United States has been challenged. Its ability to influence others has eroded. Its position in and command over the international political economy have deteriorated. It faces unprecedented threats to its physical survival as its ability to prevent a military attack has been thrown into question. The world has changed.

The world has changed, but the basic tenets of American foreign policy have not. On the contrary, America's approach to the world has been governed by persistence, not by creativity. Indeed, perhaps the most distinctive feature of postwar American foreign behavior has been its remarkable continuity. Adaptations to changing international and domestic circumstances are discernible; but the same guiding principles and ultimate goals have persisted. The policy that was framed in the immediate aftermath of World War II has endured.

The theme of persistence and continuity which pervades this book derives from our definition of foreign policy: American foreign policy comprises the goals that the nation's officials[1] seek to attain abroad, the values that give rise to those objectives, and the means or instruments through which they are pursued. We maintain that continuity has tended to characterize American goals and values since World War II, while discontinuity, or, perhaps preferably, adaptation, has been largely confined to the use of various tactics in order to achieve these consistent goals. In other words, we posit that the goals or ends of American foreign policy have remained relatively constant in comparison with the more variable methods or means employed to realize them. Tactics have changed; objectives have not.

Clearly it would be misleading to exaggerate the contrast between an invariant foreign policy "vision" and a set of rapidly changing policy instruments. More often than not, the means to policy ends have evolved slowly in response to varying domestic and international developments. It would be equally misleading to characterize the making of foreign policy as occurring in the absence of debate about its ends. Questioning of the conventional vision is constant, and the prevailing consensus is always fragile and under challenge. Some would say that it is fragmented (Holsti and Rosenau, 1984), even "lost"

---

[1]Although important, the transnational contacts that U.S. nongovernmental actors (for example, businesspeople) maintain abroad do not constitute a primary focus of our inquiry.

(Quester, 1982). Thus, it would be mistaken to assume that the interpretation of American foreign policy elaborated in this book is the only possible one or that it is consistent with what American leaders themselves have perceived about the policies they engineered. Yet, whatever one's interpretation of these issues, we find it useful to think of American foreign policy in terms of persistent goals and somewhat more variable tactics. This task requires an analytical perspective which focuses on recurrent behaviors rather than transient events.

PATTERNS IN AMERICAN FOREIGN POLICY

To the extent that consistencies exist over time in foreign policy objectives, we may contend that *patterns* are characteristic of American foreign policy behavior. Patterns are historical generalizations that capture the overall thrust and direction of foreign policy. As generalizations, however, they do not necessarily describe accurately every foreign policy decision and the reasons behind it. Thus, when we make generalizations, we risk distorting history and committing occasional errors of interpretation. But what is gained by generalization is the ability to differentiate the common and perpetual from the infrequent and ephemeral.

To contend that American foreign policy has been patterned since 1945 does not suggest a historical determinism that denies the possibility of policy change nor an interpretation that sees policy as necessarily paralyzed by the past. Indeed, American foreign policy has shown a capacity for adaptation to changing conditions and, on occasion, for experimental innovation in pursuit of established objectives. Containment of the Soviet Union, for example, has been one of the most enduring themes in postwar American foreign policy. It first took the form of isolation of the Soviet Union under Truman, then emphasized threatening rhetoric with the associated tactic of ''brinkmanship'' (escalation to the brink of nuclear war) under Eisenhower. Competitive coexistence was emphasized under Kennedy and Johnson, with a shift from brinkmanship to deterrence based on the recognition of what policy makers called ''mutual assured destruction.'' Under Nixon, Ford, and Carter, détente became the watchword, with the containment strategy pursued by seduction and rewards for compliant behavior rather than coercion and force. Most recently, the Reagan administration's focus on strains in East-West relations and its choice of a confrontational posture toward the Soviet Union resurrected a militant orientation toward the long-standing goal of containing Soviet expansionism.

The containment theme, in short, has evolved rather dramatically in response to altered circumstances. Yet it has endured. Every time that containment has appeared to be fading or to be undergoing a metamorphosis, the illusion has been shattered as the premises of containment logic have reasserted their hold on American foreign policy thinking. Thus, containment has remained one of the guiding principles of American foreign policy for eight successive administrations, despite extraordinary changes in the foreign and domestic environment of the United States.

The hypothesis that the basic underlying objectives and values of postwar American foreign policy have remained fundamentally unaltered, despite some significant evolutionary challenges and adaptations, is thus an inviting one. A new occupant of the Oval Office often seems to perceive himself, at least initially, to be devising an innovative policy leading to a new era in American foreign relations. In fact, though, sharp departures or meaningful deviations from the established direction of policy have been rare. When they have occurred, they have seldom proved permanent. More typically, intermittent, sudden shifts have eventually given way to a resumption of prevailing assumptions with only modest deviations from ongoing courses of action. Why? Consider the view of Joseph A. Califano, formerly an adviser to Lyndon Johnson and a member of Jimmy Carter's cabinet:

> Presidents since Roosevelt have pursued essentially similar foreign policy objectives on the major issues that face this nation abroad. Where change has come . . . it has often been dramatically expressed. But it has invariably evolved through broad, bipartisan consensus. . . . The . . . international policies of most administrations are founded in a more substantial and nonpartisan ideological consensus than the rhetorical idiosyncrasies and disparate styles and means most presidents tend to reveal. . . . To some extent, a president is a prisoner of historical forces that will demand his attention whatever his preference in policy objectives. . . . Every president is a victim as well as molder of events. (Califano, 1975: 238; 245)

From this perspective the president's ability to change foreign policy is constrained by powerful circumstances that promote constancy and inhibit change. Furthermore, continuity is reinforced by the tendency of presidents to value consistency for its own sake, for there is both logic and reward to the stable pursuit of a continuous set of policy preferences: "Serious nations do not redefine their national interests every few years. . . . Foreign accomplishments generally come about because a nation has been able to sustain a course of action over a long period of time" (Destler, Gelb, and Lake, 1984). "A consistent and dependable national course must have a base broader than the particular beliefs of those who from time to time hold office," Secretary of State John Foster Dulles argued. This inclination to retain, not revise, existing national objectives is illustrated as well by Harry Truman's advice to his successor, Dwight D. Eisenhower: "What I've always had in mind was and is a continuing foreign policy."

Alternatively, continuity in American foreign policy may be characterized, not as the absence of change, but as movement forward that occurs only *incrementally*, that is by slow accommodation to emergent realities. Accordingly, although there is stability, there is also fluidity and evolution, with policy innovation constrained by the past but not prevented by it. This view of change is consistent with the characterization advanced by Roger Hilsman, a principal adviser in the Kennedy and Johnson administrations:

Rather than through grand decisions on grand alternatives, policy changes seem to come through a series of slight modifications of existing policy, with the new policy emerging slowly and haltingly by small and usually tentative steps, a process of trial and error in which policy zigs and zags, reverses itself, and then moves forward in a series of incremental steps. (Hilsman, 1967: 5)

Thus, because leaders must continually respond to new demands, changes in policy may occur; but because these modifications involve not so much reorientations as piecemeal readjustments, the basic pattern of American foreign policy is preserved.

By extending the logic implicit in these views, it can be argued that the decisions made in the immediate postwar period following the breakup of the American, British, and Soviet alliance against Nazi Germany largely presaged the next forty years of American foreign policy. American policy makers have possessed a consistent vision of the major characteristics of the international environment, a vision which has become institutionalized in the vast structure of federal bureaucracies that service American policies toward the outside world. As a result, precedent, habitual ways of thinking, and bureaucratic inertia have stifled consideration of radical policy alternatives. The problems of defining long-range goals have been avoided, and policy innovations have been rare. Consequently, the historical pattern of foreign behavior, while occasionally appearing on the surface to change, is marked by a preference for gradual adaptation rather than fundamental reorientation. Over the long run, disparate, ephemeral events have amounted to little more than slight fluctuations around a persistent trend.

INFERRING PATTERNED CONSISTENCY IN FOREIGN POLICY

To some the proposition that American foreign policy is best characterized by persistence and continuity may be disturbing. Moreover, the interpretation is certainly open to dispute.[2] To the casual observer of international events, change in American foreign policy appears endemic, almost constant. Headlines routinely proclaim that bold new initiatives in American foreign policy are being undertaken, that new approaches to world problems are being pursued, and that the current administration (whichever it might be) has rejected the tired policies of its predecessor for innovative new approaches and programs. The labels often attached to the policies of an administration (for example, Kennedy's "New Frontier," Johnson's "Great Society," and Nixon's

---

[2]Indeed, continuities in the external behavior of the United States will not be found unless the analyst searches for them, and different analysts almost invariably come to different conclusions about the common threads that most incisively define American action abroad. The title of a former policy maker's memoirs, *The Past Has Another Pattern* (Ball, 1982), illustrates the fact that different observers may discern different patterns that define American foreign policy. Crabb's *Policy Makers and Critics: Conflicting Theories of American Foreign Policy* (1976) is an excellent review of these divergent interpretations.

''Generation of Peace'') reinforce this image of imminent change. In fact, continuities in policy are often obscured by the requirements of presidential campaigns, in which every four years one or another presidential aspirant strikes a pose that emphasizes the need for policy change and his ability to produce it. Even incumbents seem to emphasize the changes and improvements they have made and will continue to make as reasons for reelecting them. The resulting political rhetoric gives the public the impression that change is automatically forthcoming. The appearance of major foreign policy change is made the more pervasive because the electoral process tends to focus voters' discussion of foreign policy on the new initiatives and policy pronouncements of different presidents and secretaries of state.

The record, however, suggests how mistaken exaggerated attention to high-sounding political rhetoric and transient departures in action can be. More often than not, when viewed from a long-term perspective, what initially looked like a turning point was instead another point at which the United States failed to turn. Existing policies were retained. Each administration failed (perhaps deliberately) to recognize the echo of previous policy statements in its own words. The grandiose slogans promising new courses of action often failed to fulfill those promises, and expectations excited by campaign rhetoric frequently have been unwarranted. The historically minded observer tends to experience a sensation of *déjà vu* when he or she compares current rhetoric and performance with those of the past, because what is sold as an innovation turns out to be at most a shift in emphasis from prior policies, clothed in new labels.

By looking only at current events, we risk failing to see the overall pattern and thus confuse temporary fluctuations with enduring change. An infatuation with current events diminishes our ability to see long-term and ultimately more significant trends and to identify turning points instituting new trends. Former Under Secretary of State George W. Ball, an occasional adviser to President Carter, has stated this thesis lucidly:

> Unhappily, the way we live, including dependence on television and visual impressions, reinforces the short attention span of most Americans. Our current foreign policy practices focus public concern on only one problem at a time, . . . *yet in the episodic and visual comprehension of our foreign policy, there is serious danger that the larger significance of developments will be lost in a kaleidoscope of unrelated events. Continuities will be obscured, causal factors unidentified.*
>
> . . .
>
> Because we do not have a sense of where things started or why they are leading where they are, we are surprised by events that should have been predictable. We are so often impressed by the symbols of policy—two political leaders shaking hands or drinking toasts together—that we fail to recognize those symbols as mere reflections that have meaning only as part of a process within a larger context. (Ball, 1976: 323–324; emphasis added)

An analogy with the stock market might clarify this idea. On any one day the stock market, as indexed, for example, by the Dow Jones Industrial Average, may go up or down, with exactly the opposite happening the next day. What is the meaning of such day-to-day fluctuations? The significance is difficult to determine unless we view the changes over a period of a week, a month, or even a year. Then we might begin to see a trend characteristic of a bull market (advancing stock values and prices) or a bear market (declining values and prices). In fact, we might even be able to go back to the daily stock market quotations and identify the point at which the old market trend was broken and a new pattern set into motion. In and of themselves, however, the daily quotations are quite meaningless—and in fact random for most of our purposes.

The stock market analogy also helps clarify how change may occur in American foreign policy. Just as the trends in the stock market may shift as a consequence of the daily activities of large numbers of investors, so new patterns in American foreign policy may emerge as the nation's policy makers devise new means to deal with old problems. Although we suspect that such adaptations will more often be incremental and marginal than comprehensive and revolutionary, over the long run gradual adaptations can accumulate so as to culminate in some basic shifts. It bears emphasizing, however, that we can only reach conclusions about change and continuity in American foreign policy if we view it as a dynamic, historical process, as a phenomenon which proceeds through the continued interaction of long-term and short-term forces. Thus in considering American foreign policy, it is necessary to take a long-term perspective in order to distinguish the overall trends often obscured by day-to-day variations and by the discordant details of current events. Viewed in this way, the postwar record reveals an overriding pattern of persistence and continuity.

FROM DESCRIPTION TO POLICY EVALUATION AND ANALYSIS

The thesis that the goals (and, to a lesser extent, the tools) of American foreign policy have been highly patterned needs to be documented and clarified. This is the purpose of chapters three, four, and five, which examine the ends and means of American foreign policy in order to define areas of persistence and areas of variation.

Those chapters identify the major assumptions that have guided American foreign policy since 1945 and explore the means used to achieve the objectives flowing from these assumptions. Additionally, the description given there of the pattern of American foreign policy invites evaluative questions: What are the *consequences* of the continuity that is revealed? What is the national interest? Has it been served, or harmed, by the maintenance of a single vision? Has the pattern remained stable because the assumptions on which it has been based have, on the whole, been warranted? Or, instead, have those assumptions been mistaken or rendered questionable by unfolding global developments? If so, does their continued maintenance in the face of global change spell eventual difficulties? Will the United States become a victim of its own orthodoxy? Is the decisional process that promotes that policy pattern deficient, making the United States, in the words of a recent book on the subject, "our own worst enemy" (Destler, Gelb, and Lake, 1984)?

Thus, in evaluating the themes in chapters three, four, and five, readers are encouraged to reflect on how a nation can best reconcile the conflicting needs for stability and for adaptive change. We will return to this question at the conclusion of the book, when the prospects for stability or change in American foreign policy will be considered.

But the purpose of this book is not merely to describe and evaluate the appropriateness of historical continuities in American foreign policy. Reasons for the posited persistence of American foreign policy goals must be sought in the social, political, and institutional milieu within which foreign policy decisions are made. For if continuity characterizes the *pattern* of American foreign policy, understanding the forces and factors from which it derives requires an analysis of the *process* of policy formulation and of the sources that coalesce to create those persisting patterns. What accounts for the consistency and continuity in American foreign policy goals, and what accounts for policy change? Why has American foreign policy been so immutable when the world itself appears so mutable? And, on those rare occasions when turning points in American policy are reached, what are the factors that contribute to them? The chapter which follows provides an analytic approach to this set of questions.

SUGGESTIONS FOR FURTHER READING

Brown, Seyom. *The Faces of Power: Constancy and Change in United States Foreign Policy From Truman to Reagan.* New York: Columbia University Press, 1983.

Destler, I. M., Leslie H. Gelb, and Anthony Lake. *Our Own Worst Enemy: The Unmaking of American Foreign Policy.* New York: Simon and Schuster, 1984.

Forsythe, David P., ed. *American Foreign Policy in an Uncertain World.* Lincoln: University of Nebraska Press, 1984.

Graebner, Norman A. *America As A World Power: A Realist Appraisal from Wilson to Reagan.* Wilmington, DE: Scholarly Resources, 1984.

Hoffmann, Stanley. *Primacy or World Order: American Foreign Policy Since the Cold War.* New York: McGraw-Hill, 1978.

Rainey, Gene E. *Patterns of American Foreign Policy.* Boston: Allyn and Bacon, 1975.

Schulzinger, Robert D. *American Diplomacy in the Twentieth Century.* New York: Oxford University Press, 1984.

Ungar, Sanford J., ed. *Estrangement: America and the World.* New York: Oxford University Press, 1985.

2

A FRAMEWORK FOR THE ANALYSIS OF AMERICAN FOREIGN POLICY: THE MANY FACES OF CAUSATION

> Foreign policy is the system of activities evolved by communities for changing the behavior of other states and for adjusting their own activities to the international environment. Within it, two types of activities may be singled out for special attention: the inputs flowing into it, and the output it produces.
>
> *George Modelski, 1962*

> Decisions and actions in the international arena can be understood, predicted, and manipulated only in so far as the factors influencing the decision can be identified and isolated.
>
> *Arnold Wolfers, 1962*

How can we organize our thinking and collect evidence to explain why the United States and other nations behave as they do in the international arena? To illuminate an understanding of the determinants of foreign policy, we employ an analytic framework first developed by the noted political scientist James N. Rosenau (1966, 1973, 1980, and 1984). Although originally designed to facilitate the comparative study of different nations' foreign policies, the framework is equally useful in comparing the *same* nation's policies over time and across a number of situations, and in tracing the factors that influence the direction of those policies' evolution.

Rosenau's seminal pre-theory contends that analytically *all* the factors capable of influencing a nation's foreign policy can be placed into five major categories: the *external* (global) environment, the *societal* environment of the nation, the *governmental* setting, the *roles* played by central decision makers, and the *individual* characteristics of foreign policy-making elites. Actually, each of these source categories encompasses a large cluster of variables which, collectively and simultaneously with clusters belonging to other source categories, operate to shape (in our case) the course of American conduct abroad. Thus, in order to construct explanations of *why* American foreign policy undergoes—or fails to undergo—changes over time, the factors affecting U.S. foreign policy must be identified. Furthermore, guidelines for assessing the relative potency of these factors must be provided that suggest possible hypotheses to account for the evolving performance of the United States in world affairs.

The logic contained in the framework of Rosenau's pre-theory performs these analytic services for us admirably.[1] That framework organizes our perceptions about American foreign policy. It slices reality into a set of analytical categories. It informs us about the sources of American foreign policy worthy of attention. It provides us with an intellectual "handle," a set of pigeon-holes, with which various ideas about the influences on American foreign policy might be classified for in-depth analysis. And it structures our observations about American external behavior in a theoretically meaningful way.

THE SOURCES OF AMERICAN FOREIGN POLICY

The premise underlying the Rosenau pre-theory is that each of the source categories it identifies is a causative agent and that those agents act in conjunction to determine how the United States behaves toward nations and other entities beyond its national borders. In other words, the framework stipulates a theoretical "funnel of causality" (Campbell et al., 1960), as illustrated in Figure 2.1

The figure depicts the "inputs" to the foreign policy-making process as the external, societal, governmental, role, and individual source categories of the pre-theoretical framework. Those inputs are policy "sources" because they give shape and direction to the kinds of behaviors the United States exhibits abroad, which can be thought of as the "outputs" of the policy-making process. In other words, the behavior of the United States abroad is the dependent variable—that which we wish to explain—and the source categories and the clusters of variables contained within them are the independent variables—the variables used to explain American behavior abroad. Thus the terms *source categories, inputs,* and *independent variables* all refer to the factors that exert a causal impact upon or determine the evolutionary path of American foreign policy. That policy, in turn, is captured in the terms *output(s)* and *depen-*

---

[1]Rosenau defines "pre-theory" as "both an early step toward explanation of specific empirical events and a general orientation toward all events, a point of view or philosophy about the way the world is" (1980: 127, no. 40). Thus a pre-theory helps to order facts and concepts into meaningful patterns, but is something less than a formal deductive theory, which links hypotheses deduced from axioms into a logical pattern so as to explain empirical generalizations.

FIGURE 2.1 The Sources of American Foreign Policy as a Funnel of Causality

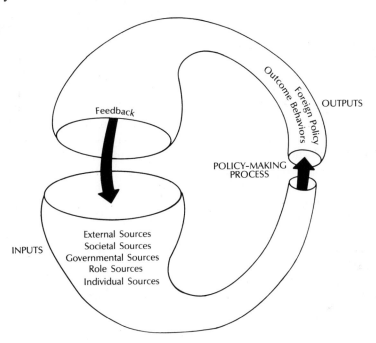

dent variable. In most instances, the dependent variable will be multifaceted, but we shall confine attention to those recurring patterns of behavior which define the continuous efforts of the United States to cope with external developments and problems.

Note, however, that whether one is attempting to explain a single foreign policy event or a whole sequence of related behaviors, no single source category fully determines output behavior. Rather, the source categories are interrelated and *collectively* determine foreign policy decisions, and hence foreign policy outputs. They do so in two ways: (1) by generating the necessity for foreign policy decisions and, ultimately, action abroad; and (2) by influencing the policy-making process (the procedures through which decisions are reached) that converts inputs into outputs.[2]

In the policy-making process, where decisions are made by those responsible for the formulation of American foreign policy, inputs (our independent

---

[2]Brady (1978) describes these ideas by observing that "in making foreign policy, decision makers continuously respond to situations created by stimuli. . . . Characteristics of these situations influence both the process by which foreign policy is made and the substance of foreign policy behavior." The "characteristics of . . . situations" referred to are those precipitating factors and preconditions that give rise to or cause specific foreign policy acts to be undertaken by policy makers.

variables, or sources) are transformed into foreign policy outputs (our dependent variables). The process is complex because of its many participants and because policy-making procedures cannot be divorced from all of the interdependent sources which shape decision makers' responses to situations demanding action. Conceptually, then, we can think of the foreign policy-making process as an intervening variable linking foreign policy inputs (the independent variables, or sources) to outputs (the dependent variables, or policy outcomes). In practice, however, we frequently will find it nearly impossible to separate inputs (sources) from the policy-making process which converts them into outputs. But once that conversion has been made (that is, once decisions are reached by those in authority), external action commences—in the form of policy pronouncements and declarations, for example, or in the sending of troops abroad and the granting of foreign aid. By monitoring these outcomes of the policy-making process, we can describe the pattern of American foreign policy.

It should be clear from this brief discussion that the model depicted in Figure 2.1 is explanatory. Each policy decision is viewed as the result of the multiple prior causal events taking place in the funnel. Thus the model stipulates the conditions which precede and promote policy decisions (bearing in mind that it is frequently difficult to distinguish decision making itself from its prior conditions, that is, the source categories). Policy outcomes depend on the prior conditions occurring in the funnel and are explained by the combined impact of the source categories on the dependent variable.

The diagram also implies a temporal sequence in the transition from inputs to outputs via the policy-making process. That is, changes in the sources of American foreign policy occurring at time t produce decisions at a later time $(t+1)$, which lead to policy outcomes in the external environment at a still later time $(t+2)$. Moreover, these policy outcomes have consequences for the source categories themselves at a later $(t+3)$ time (that is, they exert "feedback" on the independent variables), so that foreign policy actions alter the source conditions which influence subsequent $(t+4)$ policy making. For instance, a variety of internal and external factors at some point (t) led the United States to make decisions $(t+1)$ to send troops to Vietnam $(t+2)$; but this action exerted a "feedback" influence on American society, ultimately transforming $(t+3)$ internal conditions in such a way as to promote a revision $(t+4)$ of that original policy outcome. It could be argued, in the context of this illustration, that the original decision to draft large numbers of Americans into military service and send them into battle abroad produced demonstrations and riots at home, and that those conditions stimulated a reconsideration of the original policy—belatedly, to be sure.

Thus the model postulated here is dynamic. It can be used to account for past policy pronouncements and behaviors and for the effects of those outcomes on subsequent policy decisions. This feature of the model enables one to explain theoretically American foreign policy in historical perspective, since the model is not tied analytically to any one time period. Thus the entire record of American foreign conduct since 1945 can, in principle, be explained by the model. All policy outcomes affect the subsequent potency of the determinants, so that different outcomes may be better explained by different sets of source categories at different times since World War II.

The foregoing discussion implies something about the meaning of "explanation" and "cause" as they are used in this book. The terms require elaboration because their meaning is intimately linked to the analytical approach of this book, including its level of abstraction and generalization.

There are many types of explanations and many competing notions of what it means "to explain" phenomena. Because any one event or patterned series of events might be explained equally well by reference to different explanatory frameworks, no one explanation is necessarily "the best." Preferences, the purposes of inquiry, and the questions under investigation therefore largely determine which competing explanations are the most appealing and persuasive.

For the purposes of this book, we will employ the *nomological* mode of explanation.[3] Nomological explanations use lawlike statements (*nomos* is Greek for *law*) to explain a particular event or a class of events. Usually such statements explain events by reference to generalizations or covering laws, which attach cause to effect. "Civil unrest leads to foreign aggression" is an example of a generalized, lawlike statement relating cause to effect. Foreign aggression is, of course, the effect, and civil unrest is the cause, because our lawlike statement implies that civil unrest occurs prior to foreign aggression. In other words, *cause* implies a temporal sequence between event *A* and event *B*. Thus civil unrest is an antecedent, much as the source categories of American foreign policy depicted in Figure 2.1 are antecedent to foreign policy decisions.

Most lawlike statements in contemporary social science are hypotheses which link independent variables (causes) to dependent variables (effects) in terms of a tendency or probability.[4] Thus we cannot say with certainty that civil unrest will lead to foreign aggression, only that there is a tendency for this sequence to occur, or that the probability is high that it will happen. The following is a pertinent illustration of this mode of explanatory logic:

> An example of a general explanatory sentence, confirmed to some degree . . . might be that, of the national states that have a differentiated foreign affairs establishment [where decision-making power and authority are dispersed among several centers, not concentrated in any one], 90 percent also manifest continuity in their foreign policy behavior. This is a statistical law in the form, if A, the probability of B is [90 percent]. If someone asks why changes in administration from the Democratic to Republican parties and back again in the United States have not greatly affected the nature of American foreign policy, we could refer to our "law"

---

[3]For a discussion of this and other types of explanation, see Raymond (1975) and Isaak (1985).

[4]Since hypotheses are, in effect, only expectations, they must be confirmed through testing before they can be used with confidence as empirical generalizations to explain political reality. That is, confirming the validity of hypotheses requires that substantiating data be supplied.

for an explanation. Our generalization states that 90 percent of the states that belong to the class of states that have differentiated foreign policy bureaucracies also are members of the class of states that show continuity in foreign policy. Thus, because the United States has a differentiated foreign policy establishment, it is a member of the first class and very likely, but not certainly, a member of the second class; it is for this reason that changes in political leadership seem to have no effect. (McGowan, 1975: 64)

In this example the lack of radical change in the pattern of American foreign policy over more than forty years is explained by reference to a general law which posits that bureaucratic differentiation in foreign affairs establishments (in terms of the number of independent units which share responsibility for policy formulation and execution) is directly related to foreign policy continuity. The more differentiated the foreign affairs machinery, the more stable the foreign policy. This particular example of explanatory logic thus suggests how observable patterns of American foreign behavior can be explained by institutional features of the government that is responsible for the making and implementation of foreign policy decisions.

The example also illustrates the interdependence of description (what) and explanation (why) and the fact that explanation requires thinking in causal terms about classes of phenomena rather than about discrete events. In this book, the class of phenomena we seek to describe is the pattern of American foreign policy (our dependent variable), which we shall then seek to explain using the explanatory classes (the independent variables) labeled external, societal, governmental, role, and individual sources. Implicit in this notion is a rejection of the widespread tendency to search for a single cause of American foreign policy.

To reject out of hand single-factor explanations of American foreign policy is to reject what most of us wish for in seeking to understand complex social phenomena. Indeed, we know that humans instinctively seek to deal with the perplexities of a relentlessly ambiguous reality by resorting to concepts which artificially make order out of chaos. Similarly, efforts to understand the sources of American foreign policy are often reduced to psychologically satisfying single-factor explanations, wherein everything the United States does abroad is accounted for by reference to that single factor. For instance, some scholars have seen American foreign policy as essentially the product of a capitalist economic system. Others have viewed American action abroad as stemming exclusively from the conspiratorial efforts of invisible but all-powerful pressure groups. Both of these "explanations" of American foreign policy may contain kernels of truth and, under certain circumstances, may explain fairly adequately certain aspects of policy. However, because each relies so completely on a single-factor explanation in the face of a broad array of other equally plausible contributing factors whose explanatory impact cannot be dismissed, neither can be taken seriously as the sole explanation of American foreign policy. Foreign policy actions almost invariably result from multiple sources, and therefore we are well advised—if we want to capture the complexity of reality—to think in terms of multiple causes.[5]

Our rejection of single-factor explanations of American foreign policy is based in part on empirical observation and in part on the logic underlying the pre-theoretical framework that is employed. Let us turn, therefore, to a fuller explication of the sources of American foreign policy, derived from the pretheory, which organizes the subsequent explanatory analysis.

AN OVERVIEW OF THE SOURCES OF AMERICAN FOREIGN POLICY

Recall that the proposed analytic framework posits five source categories that explain and shape American foreign policy behavior: external, societal, governmental, role, and individual factors. Those categories are assumed to be exhaustive (including every source of American foreign policy) and to be mutually exclusive (nonoverlapping).[6] Let us now examine in more detail what each encompasses.

External Sources

The external category refers to the condition of the global environment beyond the borders of the United States and includes all variables related to the kind of international system in which the United States lives, on which it impacts, and to which it reacts. Rosenau (1980) defines this category as including the "aspects of a society's external environment or any actions occurring abroad that condition or otherwise influence the choices made by its officials." He notes that "geographical 'realities' and ideological challenges from potential aggressors" are obvious examples of external variables which can shape the decisions of foreign policy officials. Another way of defining this category is to say that external variables refer broadly to the impact of the state of the world on the United States. The cluster of external variables includes everything that happens outside the United States.[7] Thus it draws attention to the kinds of be-

[5]Hoffmann (1978) warns that scholars should not "peddle grand designs if the price paid for the sweep of vision is terrible oversimplification."

[6]Even though mutually exclusive, the five source categories are closely interrelated in the causative process, as noted above. This is especially true in the case of the governmental and role categories, where, as we shall show in later chapters, the two are so closely interwoven that it becomes difficult to analyze them as separate explanatory categories.

[7]In practice, most analysts using Rosenau's framework have found it useful to distinguish between "systemic" sources of foreign policy and "external" sources. The former are aggregate or general attributes of the international environment (for example, the amount of alliance or war) which are shared by all states—not just the United States. The latter are relationships between particular states (for example, interactions between the United States and the Soviet Union). In the context of this distinction, the subsequent elaboration of the external source category (chapters six and seven) will emphasize primarily external rather than systemic explanations of American foreign policy. Readers should be alert to the possibility that the external source category can be treated in alternative ways.

havior others direct toward the United States and explores how these foreign policy acts influence the response of the United States. Similarly, the external source category draws attention to the attributes of other societies and leads us to focus on how the kinds of nations with which the United States deals shape its foreign policy and behavior.

Because the external source category consists of so many variables (entailing *all* the characteristics common to the global arena), the questions derived from it are innumerable. How many sovereign nations are there in the system? What types of governments do they have? Are they richer or poorer than the United States? More populous or less? Are there many or few international organizations? Does the international legal system effectively prohibit certain kinds of behavior while encouraging other kinds? How many formal alliances and other military coalitions exist in the system? Do they have sufficient military might and internal cohesion to deter attack from outsiders? Do they possess nuclear arsenals capable of penetrating the United States, and against which no effective protection exists? What kinds of issues populate the global agenda, and what proportion of states assume a position toward them similar to the posture maintained by the United States? The answers to these questions and many others are assumed to influence significantly the kind of behavior the United States (or, for that matter, any nation) is likely to adopt. Thus the external environment is seen as one potentially powerful and multifaceted source of American foreign policy, and changes in it may be hypothesized to stimulate changes in American external conduct. By the same token, of course, changes in American behavior may affect the external environment.

Examples supporting the hypothesis that changes in the international environment stimulate changes in American foreign policy abound. For instance, could the Reagan administration's enthusiasm for massive increases in military spending in the early 1980s during a time of chronic domestic economic difficulties have received the support it did in the absence of substantial Soviet defense expenditures? Similarly, would the potential policy departure signaled in the 1980s by advocacy of trade protectionism and import restraints have been undertaken had American trade partners not mastered more efficient production techniques than their American counterparts? Or, likewise, would American policy toward the Arab oil exporting nations have shifted in the absence of the oil embargo and subsequent price hikes in 1973? Or could the Sino-American agreement on nuclear cooperation have been reached in 1985 without the continuing strain in relations between Moscow and Beijing (Peking)? Clearly, in these and many other examples, American foreign policy has responded to the initiatives of other states, and developments abroad have precipitated changes in it.

There is nothing new about the idea that a nation's foreign policy is conditioned by factors external to it. Indeed, the analytic tradition that emphasizes the causal relationship between the international system and American foreign policy making enjoys a wide following. "Political realists,"[8] for example, argue that the nature of the international system, more than anything else, influences how its nation-members act. Similarly, many historians have suggested that such developments as the advent and proliferation of nuclear weapons and the unprecedented level of American dependence on others for strategically vital resources have altered fundamentally the kinds of foreign policy options available to the United States. So, too, the growing incidence of international terrorism is often cited as a global development which has fundamentally altered the kind of external environment in which the United States resides and the kinds of policies it undertakes in response to this threat. To argue that American foreign policy is not shaped at least partially by external forces and foreign conditions would be to forget that a nation's actions abroad are necessarily affected by what others do and by shifts in what the international environment renders practicable.

As important as the external environment is, it would be wrong to think that it alone can dictate foreign policy. It is more accurate to argue that

> factors external to the actor can become determinants only as they affect the mind, the heart, and the will of the decision-maker. A human decision to act in a specific way . . . necessarily represents the last link in the chain of antecedents of any act of policy. A geographical set of conditions, for instance, can affect the behavior of a nation only as specific persons perceive and interpret these conditions. (Wolfers, 1962: 42)

Thus external factors do not alone determine how the United States acts. But they do influence how decision makers may choose to act, and to that degree they serve as a source of foreign policy.

External variables help define the limits of the possible; they preclude certain options and reduce the utility of others. In this way the international system imposes restrictions on American decision makers and limits their freedom to take policy initiatives. In other words, it promotes policy continuity by narrowing the range of workable choice. But the external environment can also operate as a stimulus to policy change. As chapters six and seven will make clear, the external source category may be a potent contributor to foreign policy consistency during eras of systemic calm, but it is likely to be an important source of foreign policy change when components of the global system undergo rapid change, thereby altering the place of a particular global actor, such as the United States, in the overall scheme of things.

---

[8]Political realism, a school of thought that focuses on the concepts of "national interest" and "power," argues that nations ought to pursue these rather than abstract moral or legal principles (see also chapter three). Because all states are assumed to be motivated by the same drives, the principal way to understand international politics and foreign policy is to follow the interactions of states in the international arena or, in other words, to focus on the external source category. A discussion of *realpolitik* reasoning as it applies to American foreign policy is provided in the chapter which follows.

Societal Sources

Societal sources of foreign policy may be defined as "those nongovernmental aspects of a society which influence its external behavior. The major value orientations of a society, its degree of national unity, and the extent of its industrialization are but a few of the societal variables which can contribute to the contents of a nation's external aspirations and policies" (Rosenau, 1980). In other words, nongovernmental national characteristics—those general features of American society which define the kind of nation it is and differentiate it from other nations—partially determine American foreign policy.

Like the preceding category, forces within the societal category traditionally have been stressed by those who see the domestic climate shaping American foreign policy more strongly than external conditions. That thesis, for instance, finds expression in the title of a recent book on the subject: *The American Style of Foreign Policy: Cultural Politics and Foreign Affairs* (Dallek, 1983). Similarly, societal sources have been used to explain . . . *How American Culture Led Us into Vietnam and Made Us Fight the Way We Did*, as another (sub)title of a book on that topic (Baritz, 1985) describes the explanatory focus it employs. The same source category has also been used by critics of American military policy in Vietnam who advance a neo-Marxist interpretation: America's capitalist system drove the United States to Vietnam to safeguard foreign markets for American economic penetration and exploitation. Or consider how American territorial expansion and imperialism in the nineteenth century have been rationalized by references to "manifest destiny" and the belief that Americans were a "chosen people" with a divine right to expand. Contemplate the thesis that the ideological premises of American leaders have at various times powerfully influenced American policies toward peoples outside the boundaries of American territorial jurisdiction. A focus on the "seeming incompatibilities between America's democratic ideals and its present world status" (Isaak, 1977) is exemplary of this mode of explication.

Currently, a number of theories purport to explain the diplomatic record of the United States since World War II in terms of the impact of its societal characteristics. Some, concentrating on the natural resources and size of the United States, contend that they drive the nation toward active internationalist policies in conformity with the superpower status geography has assigned to it. Others, focusing on the relationship between American public opinion and American foreign policy, posit that shifts in the former lead to changes in the latter. Included among these are explanations which emphasize the potential power of the mass media to shape public preferences on particular policy issues. And very prominent are societal-determinant theories which see American foreign policy as shaped by the activities of special-interest groups in American society. Included among them are various power elite explanations of American foreign policy, such as the one associated with former President Eisenhower's warning in 1961 about the "unwarranted influence" that the "military-industrial complex" could acquire. The reasoning behind theories which trace American foreign policy to different sets of societal variables is captured by the premise that "To change this country's foreign policy, its internal structure must change" (Isaak, 1977).

The prevalence of theories based on the belief that there are powerful domestic sources of foreign policy (see Rosenau, 1967) suggests the need to consider the potential power of societal variables in accounts of American foreign policy. This inquiry should consider how both constancy and change in societal variables influence American external conduct. For instance, what opportunities as well as constraints were presented to American decision makers by the consensus in American society about the appropriate role of the United States in world affairs between, say, 1949, with the "loss of China," and 1965, with the massive military buildup in Vietnam? What was the impact of the alleged erosion of that consensus on the willingness or unwillingness of the Carter administration to pursue a more active interventionist role in Third World conflicts? And if that bipartisan consensus has failed to be restored, as some argue, does this development explain why so few presidential foreign policy initiatives have gone unchallenged by segments of American society, and why even President Reagan, despite his overwhelming reelection margin in 1984, experienced repeated congressional resistance to his foreign policy programs? If so, the import of societal forces on American foreign policy would appear to be strong and multiple—a possibility that will be explored more fully in chapters eight and nine.

Governmental Sources

A third hypothesized source of American foreign policy is the governmental arrangement for the making of foreign policy decisions. Underlying the notion of governmental influences on foreign policy is the assumption of a relationship between the substance of policy and the process by which it is made. Rosenau (1980) describes this cluster of variables as referring "to those aspects of a government's structure that limit or enhance the foreign policy choices made by decision-makers. The impact of executive-legislative relations on American foreign policy exemplifies the operation of governmental variables."

The structure of the American government as it affects foreign policy making includes a large number of variables which influence, directly and indirectly, what the United States does—and does not do—abroad. For instance, it seems clear that American foreign policy is shaped by such institutional features as (1) the Constitution, which divides the making and implementation of foreign policy among the different branches of government;[9] (2) the growth

---

[9]The Constitution clearly was drafted by people familiar with the potential abuse of power in the hands of centralized authority and who therefore understood the necessity of dividing and diffusing power. The result—to the extent that the original philosophy has been retained—is a policy-making system encouraging deliberation and preferring delay to impulsive action in foreign affairs.

of bureaucracy, wherein a multitude of government agencies and organizations compete to enlarge their slice of the policy-making pie; (3) the rise of executive dominance in foreign policy making, culminating in what has been termed the "imperial presidencies" of Lyndon B. Johnson and Richard M. Nixon, followed in turn by a reassertion of congressional authority; and (4) the growth in the sheer size of governmental institutions, which may contribute to a fractionalized and inefficient[10] decision-making structure. To these might be added changes in the amount of interagency conflict, fluctuations in the distribution of power among the many government institutions having a hand in the foreign policy-making process, and changes in the extent to which the government is open to influences from American society. Nixon is reported to have noted in this context, "If we were to establish a new foreign policy for the era to come, we had to begin with a basic restructuring of the process by which policy is made." Jimmy Carter, echoing this theme in his 1976 presidential campaign, maintained that to change policy one must first change the machinery that produces it. Offering a variation on this same theme, Ronald Reagan argued in 1980 that the greatest policy failures in the past could be traced to the "excessive growth and unnecessary size of government" and pledged to implement more successful foreign policies by making government work more effectively (a promise he has had great difficulty fulfilling). Because each of these statements that now encapsulate the conventional wisdom on the subject underscores the extent to which American foreign policy is given definition by the institutions designed to create it, consideration of how governmental factors shape foreign policy would seem to be required.

Governmental variables undoubtedly constrain what the United States can do abroad and the speed with which it can do it. Size and bureaucratization, for example, militate against policy reversals. Those factors combine with the constitutional division of power between the executive and legislative branches of government to promote policy compromise and incrementalism over policy innovation and radical revision. Thus governmental factors in general and democratic institutions in particular certainly inhibit the nation's ability to change its course in world affairs, as the French sociologist Alexis de Tocqueville (1969) predicted when in 1835 he observed that "Foreign politics demand scarcely any of those qualities which a democracy possesses; and they require, on the contrary, the perfect use of almost all those faculties in which it is deficient."

In some instances, however, elements of the governmental machinery have facilitated, rather than diminished, rapid shifts in policy. State Department formulation in 1947 of the Marshall Plan for European economic recovery and White House initiatives in constructing the new international economic policies announced in August 1971 (which radically altered the nature of the inter-

---

[10]According to one of Parkinson's (1972–1973) laws, *"The useful results of diplomacy are usually in reverse proportion to the number of diplomatists"* (emphasis in original).

national economic order that had existed since the closing days of World War II) stand out as cases in point. Thus, whether in promoting change or inhibiting it, the structure of American government, which is subject to modest variation over time, becomes an important influence on the foreign policy of the nation.

Having said this, however, we must insert a word of caution. It would be dangerous to rely too heavily on the governmental source category as an explanation of American foreign policy, for this category fails to explain much about the kinds of foreign policy *goals* the nation's leaders select. The category tells more about why certain *means* are selected to satisfy particular objectives (and about the institutional environment in which those decisions are reached) than it does about why the objectives are selected in the first place.[11] Yet means become important reflections of ends. And they often reinforce the continued, almost habitual choice of the same ends, as will be shown in chapters ten, eleven, and twelve.

Role Sources

Governmental factors are closely associated with role factors as sources of and influences on American foreign policy. The concept of a "role" source category is perhaps the most difficult to grasp intuitively, but this set of variables is probably the most potent in accounting for the pattern of American foreign policy since World War II. The role source category refers to the impact of such things as the nature of the office on the behavior of its occupant. That is, we hypothesize that decision makers' actions in making foreign policy are influenced significantly by the roles they occupy, by the socially prescribed behaviors and legally sanctioned norms attached to a given position.[12]

The root notion here is that the positions policy makers hold substantially affect their behavior. Consequently, ultimate policy outcomes are influenced by the kinds of roles existing in the policy-making arena more than by the particular individuals who happen to be in authority at any given moment. Role

[11]If the governmental source category does less to determine than to reflect foreign policy objectives, then one might question whether it is regarded properly as an independent variable cluster comparable to the external, societal, role, and individual source categories. In fact, in his subsequent elaborations on his pre-theory, Rosenau has come to view the governmental source category as an intervening rather than independent variable. Given this formulation, the institutional setting would not be considered an explanation of foreign policy per se, but rather a set of structures that serve "as a filter through which the values that underlie individual, role, societal, and systemic variables must pass" (Rosenau, 1980).

For ease of exposition, we retain the conceptual notion that there are five *independent* sources of foreign policy, rather than treating four as independent sources and one as an intervening factor. As we shall have occasion to note again in chapter fifteen, however, our own conclusions about the relative potency of the five source categories in explaining American foreign policy are consistent with the proposition that the governmental source category is more properly viewed as an intervening than as an independent variable.

[12]All individuals occupy a variety of different roles by virtue of the demands and expectations that others place on them in given circumstances. The role an individual occupies is thus seen as a determinant of the kind of behavior he or she will exhibit.

theory goes far, its proponents claim, in explaining why, for example, each recent American president has acted, once in office, so much like his predecessors, and why each has come to view American interests and goals in terms so similar to the images maintained by previous presidents. The view that the office makes the man has been expressed thus:

> If we accept the proposition . . . that certain fundamentals stand at the core of American foreign policy, we could argue that any president is bound, even dictated to, by those basic beliefs and needs. In other words, he has little freedom to make choices wherein his distinctive style, personality, experience, and intellect shape America's role and position in international relations in a way that is uniquely his. It might be suggested that a person's behavior is a function not of his individual traits but rather of the office that he holds and that the office is circumscribed by the larger demands of the national interest, rendering individuality inconsequential. (Paterson, 1979: 93)

Correspondingly, so the reasoning goes, merely changing the person sitting behind the desk in the Oval Office will not bring about fundamental alterations in the nation's policies. Roles, it would seem, determine behavior more than do the qualities of individuals.

Role theory is also useful in explaining the kinds of policy decisions habitually made by and within the large bureaucratic organizations that bear responsibility for the implementation of foreign policy—that is, for explaining not individual behavior, but group behavior. Role pressures may lead, for instance, to attitudinal conformity within bureaucracies and to inertial respect for the orthodox views within an agency.[13] Such tendencies are clearly more conducive to policy continuity than to innovation or radical revision. In addition, role factors help account for the inability of presidents to get policies implemented by entrenched bureaucratic agencies acting (as role theory suggests they will) in terms of their own parochial needs and preferences rather than the needs of the nation. In addition, because bureaucratic agencies are inclined to compete with one another for influence over policy outcomes, decision making tends to be highly politicized; because decisions therefore emerge from a bargaining process, the ability of a president to pursue innovative policy goals is severely compromised, and the capacity of a nation managed by fragmented bureaucracies to change policy directions is limited. Roles, not preferences, explain the inability of American foreign policy to chart new directions, this reasoning maintains.

To be sure, not all the characteristics of the way the United States conducts itself in foreign affairs can be attributed directly to the effects of various roles

---

[13]Galbraith (1970–1971) argues that there is a "tendency for any bureaucracy, military or civilian, in the absence of the strongest leadership, to continue to do whatever it is doing. This is a matter of the highest importance, one that explains the most basic tendencies of our foreign policy."

in the foreign policy-making system. But it would be an error to minimize the extent to which American conduct abroad is influenced by role-induced behaviors. The "system" places a premium on behavioral consistency. The few who dare to escape their roles by rocking the boat and challenging conventional thinking are sometimes ignored or, perhaps more often, subjected to hostility and eventually ostracized. The result? The line of least resistance is usually taken, and established routines, norms, and standard operating procedures become the mechanisms for dealing with new situations as they arise. The lack of fundamental change in American foreign policy since World War II can be accounted for quite substantially by the existence of role-induced restraints on creativity and innovation.

Conversely, of course, adaptations in American policy can also be explained in part by changes in role definitions. Policy-making roles may be variously interpreted, and this is one of the ways in which role variables change. For example, occupants of the role of United States Ambassador to the United Nations (Adlai Stevenson, Arthur Goldberg, Daniel P. Moynihan, Andrew Young, Jeane J. Kirkpatrick, and Vernon Walters) have defined this role quite differently, with corresponding changes in the types of behavior exhibited. Thus changes in role definitions—rare though they generally are—may be sources of policy discontinuity, just as the maintenance of established definitions is a source of policy continuity.

The impact which role constraints exert on the processes through which foreign policy decisions are made will be examined more fully in chapter thirteen.

Individual Sources

Finally, our explanatory framework identifies a fifth set of variables presumed to influence the content and conduct of American foreign policy: the individual characteristics of decision makers responsible for policy formulation and execution. These include the skills, personalities, beliefs, and psychological predispositions which define the kind of people they are and the type of behavior they exhibit. Individual determinants have been defined as including "all those aspects of a decision-maker—his values, talents, and prior experiences—that distinguish his foreign policy choices or behavior from those of every other decision-maker" (Rosenau, 1980). Former Secretary of State John Foster Dulles's pious and moralistic religious values, stemming from his Presbyterian upbringing, exemplify the individual variable and the powerful impact it sometimes can exert on how American diplomacy is conducted (see Holsti, 1975).

The premise that attributes of individual decision makers may serve as a source of American foreign conduct rests on the assumption that decision makers possess unique personal qualities resistant to molding and modification by role variables. The thesis that every individual is unique is not difficult to accept, and the assumption that idiosyncratic qualities can make a difference in the kinds of decisions reached is plausible. Consider the following incidents:

1. Why did the United States persist in bombing North Vietnam for so long in the face of overwhelming evidence that the policy of "bombing the North Vietnamese into submission" was failing and, if anything, was hardening their resolve to continue fighting? Could the answer be that President Johnson was unable to admit failure, that he had a psychological need to preserve his positive self-image by "being right"?

2. Why did the United States act so forcefully toward the Soviet Union during the Cuban missile crisis? (President Kennedy estimated the odds of nuclear annihilation at 50–50.) Kennedy had been, by his own confession, humiliated and outbargained by Soviet Premier Khrushchev in their 1961 summit meeting in Vienna. Could it be that Kennedy's pride prompted him to teach Khrushchev a lesson, to show him his composure under pressure and his toughness? ("We stood eyeball to eyeball, and *he* was the first to blink.")

3. Why did Secretary of State Dulles publicly insult Chou En-Lai of Communist China by refusing at the 1954 Geneva Conference to shake Chou's extended hand? Could it be that he viewed the Chinese leader as a symbol of an atheistic doctrine so abhorrent to his own values that he chose not to associate with the symbol?

4. Would the United States have embarked on a vigorous campaign for human rights in the late 1970s, with moralistic overtones, had the country not been led by a president, Jimmy Carter, who was deeply committed to the moral and idealistic tenets of his Protestant (evangelical) faith?

Theories emphasizing the personal characteristics of political leaders often enjoy considerable popularity. This is partly because democratic theory leads us to expect that individuals elected to high public office will be able either to sustain or to change public policy in accordance with popular preferences. The habit of naming American policies after their presidential proponents (for example, Truman Doctrine, Kennedy Round, Reagan Doctrine) contributes to the image that individuals do, in fact, matter. It is an image further reinforced by the widespread tendency in American politics to think of presidents as "great men," or even heroes. However, for the same reason that other single-factor explanations of American foreign policy are suspect, we must be wary of ascribing too much importance to the impact of individuals. Individuals may matter, and in some instances they clearly do matter, but the mechanisms through which the individual influences foreign policy outcomes is likely to be much more subtle than popular impressions would have us believe.

As suggested above one way in which individual variables become important is through the interpretations different individuals attach to the roles they occupy. Roles are generally constraining forces that mold people's behavior regardless of their personal preferences or predispositions. But the boundaries of those constraints are neither fixed nor immutable. Instead, most roles, particularly those associated with the highest levels of the governmental structure, permit a range of interpretation. How the role is interpreted is thus a matter of idiosyncratic choice. One person may see his or her role as permitting considerable latitude in choosing among policy options; another occupant of the same role may see little room for maneuver. Then, too, the type of person holding office may affect the style if not the content of policy. This is especially obvious in the presidency. Truman and Eisenhower espoused very similar policies, but the manner in which the two men pursued those policies bears the imprint of their respective backgrounds and personalities. Likewise, the similarities in the policies of Kennedy and Johnson, and of Nixon and Ford, are contrasted sharply with the styles with which each pair of presidents pursued their respective foreign policy programs.

Hence, in explaining American foreign policy, we must include a consideration of the characteristics unique to those who make that policy (chapter fourteen), as well as the conditions, such as crisis situations (chapter fifteen), which make such variables especially important.

PUTTING THE PIECES TOGETHER: THE MULTIPLE SOURCES OF AMERICAN FOREIGN POLICY

What is especially inviting about the approach to explanation offered by a pre-theoretical framework incorporating five categories of influences on foreign policy is that it encourages adoption of an explicitly multicausal perspective. It begins with the premise that we must look in different places if we want to find the origins of American foreign policy. And it tells us where to look, thus providing a helpful guide to understanding that policy and how it is made. Rosenau provides an excellent illustration of the utility—and necessity—of explaining foreign policy decisions by reference to multiple factors.

Consider, for example, the U.S.-sponsored invasion of Cuba's Bay of Pigs in April 1961. To what extent was that external behavior a function of the individual characteristics of John F. Kennedy . . .? Were his youth, his commitments to action, his affiliations with the Democratic Party, his self-confidence, his close election victory—and so on through an endless list—relevant to the launching of the invasion and, if so, to what extent? Would any President have undertaken to oust the Castro regime upon assuming office in 1961? If so, how much potency should be attributed to such role-derived variables? Suppose everything else about the circumstances of April 1961 were unchanged except that Warren Harding or Richard Nixon occupied the White House; would the invasion have occurred? Or hold everything constant but the form of government. Stretch the imagination and conceive of the U.S. as having a cabinet system of government with Kennedy as prime minister; would the action toward Cuba have been any different? Did legislative pressure derived from a decentralized policymaking system generate an impulse to "do something" about Castro, and, if so, to what extent did these governmental variables contribute to the external behavior? Similarly, in order to pre-theorize about the potency of the societal variables, assume once more a presidential form of government. Place Kennedy in office a few months after a narrow election victory, and imagine the Cuban situation as arising in 1921, 1931, or 1951; would the America of the roaring twenties, the depression, or the McCarthy era have ''permitted,'' ''encouraged,'' or otherwise become involved in a refugee-mounted invasion? . . . Lastly, hold the individual, role, governmental, and societal variables constant in the imagination, and posit Cuba as 9,000 rather than 90 miles off the Florida coast; would the invasion have nevertheless been launched? If it is estimated that no effort would have been made to span such a distance, does this mean that systemic variables should always be treated as over-riding or is their potency diminished under certain conditions? (Rosenau, 1980: 130–131)

Regardless of how one might respond to these questions, the simple act of posing them facilitates appreciation of the numerous factors shaping foreign policy actions. Furthermore, it also helps to define the factors that presumably have contributed to the persistence of the view held by decision makers that Cuba is a ''problem'' and to explain variations in the way different administrations have responded to that problem. In the particular case of the Bay of Pigs episode, behavior clearly stemmed from more than one factor, and it can be explained only by reference to several variables. No single-factor explanation is adequate.

Similarly, long-term patterns in American foreign policy goals and instruments are amenable to, and require, explanation by reference to competing sources. Take, for instance, what is perhaps the dominant theme of American foreign policy since World War II: anticommunism and the focus on the Soviet Union that stems from that antagonism. As shall be seen in the next chapter, every administration in the postwar era has voiced opposition to communist ideology and pronounced its determination to contain the expansion of its influence. Why has this basic orientation of post–World War II American foreign policy remained so constant? Why has change, when it has occurred, been so gradual, so incremental?

To answer these questions, we must look in a variety of places. At the level of the international system, for instance, it can be argued that the advent of nuclear weapons and the subsequent fear of destruction from a Soviet nuclear attack promoted a status quo American policy designed primarily to deal with this paramount fear. Would the United States have acted differently over the past forty years had international circumstances been different? What if the Soviet Union had failed to achieve superpower status? Would that circumstance have removed the restraining fear that a war between the United States and the Soviet Union would devastate both? What if the United States and the Soviet Union had both been attacked by a Chinese-led coalition, or if World War II had been followed by another worldwide depression? Perhaps it was the international situation and prevailing circumstances that stimulated and perpetuated the anticommunist and anti-Soviet goals underlying American foreign policy.

But consider whether anticommunism would have been emphasized had nationalistic sentiments within American society eroded. Or if the American public had revolted against increased military expenditures. Or if the symbiotic relationship between military and industrial sectors had not developed to create a "complex" intent on preserving military spending. And ask as well whether American foreign policy might have shifted in the 1950s in the absence of the anticommunist, witch-hunting tactics that Senator Joseph McCarthy initiated shortly after the communist forces came to power in China in 1949, in what many Americans viewed as a Soviet gain at America's expense.

Or turn instead to the governmental sector. Would American foreign policy have been different had foreign policy making not become dominated by the office of the presidency—if instead the balance between the executive, legislative, and judicial branches of the government (encouraged by the Constitution) had been preserved throughout the 1960s? Indeed, would American foreign policy have been different and more flexible if the manner in which the United States government was organized for the implementation of foreign policy decisions had not entrenched the "cold warriors" within the foreign affairs bureaucracy or discouraged more vigorous challenge to their singular outlook by other civil servants? Or by the mass media?

And then consider whether American foreign policy might have escaped some of the rigidity of its anticommunist posture if roles had been defined to permit greater latitude and if ideological orthodoxy had been reduced by fewer role pressures for conformity. Would the decisions reached have been different had decision-making roles been less institutionalized, less formal, and more flexible, permitting more diversity of opinion? Might American foreign policy have shown a greater capacity for change had policy-making roles been defined so as to allow more long-range planning while correspondingly diminishing the tendency to let policy evolve through a series of small decisions and ad hoc responses to episodic crises?

And, finally, consider the hypothetical prospects for change in American policy had other individuals risen to positions of power. Would the cornerstone of American postwar policy have been so virulently anticommunist if Franklin Roosevelt had lived out his fourth term in office; if Adlai Stevenson, and not Eisenhower and Dulles, had been responsible for American policy throughout the 1950s; if Kennedy's attempt to experiment with tension-reduction initiatives toward the Soviets had not been terminated by an assassin's bullet; if Hubert Humphrey had managed to obtain the 400,000 votes in 1968 necessary to make him, and not Nixon, president; if George McGovern's challenge to the Nixon-Kissinger policy of massive bombing of Vietnam had been successful in 1972; if Henry "Scoop" Jackson, and not Jimmy Carter, had replaced Gerald Ford in 1976; or if Ronald Reagan's bid to turn Jimmy Carter out of office in 1980 had met with failure? What coloration would American foreign policy assume had either a psychological misfit's bullet taken the life of Ronald Reagan that rainy afternoon in March 1981, or a life-threatening cancer not been successfully removed by surgery in July 1985, placing the responsibilities of the presidency in the hands of George Bush? Indeed, would the presence of different officials with different kinds of personalities, psychological needs, and political preferences have made a difference in the ability of the United States to pursue imaginative new policies toward the Soviet Union? Or would other individuals have made little difference? Would the cross-pressures inherent in the multiple responsibilities of their respective offices have undermined any individual's ability to change the course of the nation's policy?

"What if" questions are interesting but nearly always impossible to answer. They do suggest, however, the nature of the problem of tracing causation, since they force consideration of the many possible factors influencing behavior. Thus, to answer even partially the question "Why has the United States acted the way it has in its external relations?" we need to examine each of the major sources of American foreign policy. Collectively, these identify the many constraints and stimuli facing foreign policy decision makers, thus providing insight into the factors that promote persistent patterns and also variation in American foreign policy.

Recognizing that each source category places some constraint on the latitude of foreign policy decision makers, the discussion will be presented in descending order of what might be thought of as the "spatial magnitude" of each explanatory category. Following description and interpretation of policy output patterns (chapters three, four, and five), the discussion will continue with the external environment (part three), which is clearly the most comprehensive of the categories influencing decision makers. We will then proceed to societal sources (part four), then turn to the way in which the American political system is organized for foreign policy making (part five), and from there shift focus again to role sources (part six), which partly flow from, and are closely associated with, the governmental setting. Finally, we will consider the importance of individual personalities, preferences, and predispositions in explaining foreign policy outcomes (part seven).

This organization provides readers with the opportunity to weigh the relative explanatory power of each of the source categories. By looking at external, societal, governmental, role, and individual sources of American policy independently, we can examine the causal impact *each* category exerts by itself on the external behavior of the United States. Completion of the survey should facilitate "putting the pieces together" and reaching some conclusions about the relative potencies of the five categories in accounting for the patterned consistencies and changes in American interactions with the rest of the world. This will enable us to probe better the dynamics of foreign policy continuity and change by looking (in chapter fifteen) at how the sources of American foreign policy are related, and finally at how those relationships affect the probable future of American foreign policy (chapter sixteen).

SUGGESTIONS FOR FURTHER READING

EAST, MAURICE A., STEPHEN A. SALMORE, AND CHARLES F. HERMANN, eds. *Why Nations Act: Theoretical Perspectives for Comparative Foreign Policy Studies.* Beverly Hills, CA: Sage, 1978.
ISAAK, ALAN C. *Scope and Methods of Political Science,* 4th ed. Chicago: Dorsey, 1985.

JENSEN, LLOYD. *Explaining Foreign Policy*. Englewood Cliffs, NJ: Prentice-Hall, 1982.

KEGLEY, CHARLES W., JR., AND EUGENE R. WITTKOPF, eds. *Perspectives on American Foreign Policy*. New York: St. Martin's, 1983.

McGOWAN, PATRICK J. "Meaningful Comparisons in the Study of Foreign Policy: A Methodological Discussion of Objectives, Techniques, and Research Designs," pp. 52–87 in Charles W. Kegley, Jr., et al., eds., *International Events and the Comparative Analysis of Foreign Policy*. Columbia: University of South Carolina Press, 1975.

ROSENAU, JAMES N. "Pre-theories and Theories of Foreign Policy," pp. 115–169 in *The Scientific Study of Foreign Policy*, rev. ed. New York: Nichols, 1980.

ROSENAU, JAMES N., ed. *Comparing Foreign Policies: Theories, Findings and Methods*. New York: Wiley, 1974.

SMITH, STEVEN M. *Foreign Policy Adaptation*. New York: Nichols, 1981.

WILKENFELD, JONATHAN, GERALD W. HOPPLE, PAUL J. ROSSA, AND STEPHEN J. ANDRIOLE. *Foreign Policy Behavior*. Beverly Hills, CA: Sage, 1980.

II

THE PATTERN OF AMERICAN FOREIGN POLICY

3

THE GOALS OF AMERICAN FOREIGN POLICY: THE POSTWAR DIPLOMATIC PATTERN

The period after World War II marks the first era of truly global foreign policy.
Henry A. Kissinger, 1969

A long-term consistency of behavior is bound to burden American democracy when the country rises to the stature of a great power.
Alexis de Tocqueville, 1835

On the surface the daily actions that collectively define American foreign policy appear to be fraught with inconsistencies and reversals. But behind the ostensible contradictions and vacillations, a pattern can be seen in the goals and underlying assumptions of postwar American foreign policy. Since World War II, American policy makers have maintained a coherent, enduring vision of the international environment, a consistent view based on certain fundamental assumptions about the world and the appropriate role of the nation in it. The purpose of this chapter is to describe American foreign policy goals and the postulates and perceptions upon which they have been based for almost five decades.

The guiding premises of American foreign policy thinking discussed here have rested on a consensual foundation, but that consensus has not been without its critics and detractors. Indeed, although agreement about the principles and priorities that ought to anchor foreign policy is discernible, policy makers who have subscribed to those principles would not necessarily use the same wording to describe their outlook or perceive the historical pattern in precisely the same way. In addition, not everyone has subscribed to those assumptions, and some have vociferously challenged the prevailing world view. Nevertheless, we contend that most of the time most of the leaders responsible for the formulation and implementation of American foreign policy since 1945 have adhered to a more or less consistent outlook.

What is that orthodox outlook? An examination of the major policy pronouncements and actions of the United States since World War II suggests that the following three tenets have been uppermost in the minds of American policy makers:

1. The United States must reject isolationism permanently and substitute for it an active responsibility for the direction of international affairs.
2. Communism comprises the principal danger in the world, and the United States must use its power to combat the spread of this menace.
3. Because the Soviet Union is the spearhead of the communist challenge, American foreign policy must be dedicated to the containment of Soviet expansionism and influence.

To be sure, this list is by no means exhaustive. Other operating assumptions, premises, and convictions about America's foreign priorities have been given expression as well. Nor is this incomplete summary meant to suggest that the world view outlined in the listing has necessarily been warranted. Nevertheless, the three tenets delineate essential beliefs that have given postwar American foreign policy its shape and direction, and promise to extend themselves even into the 1990s.

GLOBALISM

The history of American diplomacy from the birth of the Republic in 1776 until World War II can largely be written in terms of a debate between two opposing traditions in foreign affairs: isolationism versus internationalism.

Isolationism

On the one hand, an attitude of disinterest in and desire to withdraw from world affairs has periodically surfaced in American thinking about foreign policy. George Washington articulated this position when he cautioned the nation in his Farewell Address to "steer clear of permanent alliances with any portion of the foreign world." He probably spoke for most Americans at the time when he described European governments as untrustworthy and devious and warned that active global participation in balance-of-power politics could only result in danger, the violation of American ideals, and, probably, the erosion of democratic institutions and liberty. The nation that assumed responsibility for world problems would interact with corrupt governments and, he intimated, would become like them: lie down with dogs, get up with fleas.

When the nation was still in its infancy, Secretary of State John Quincy Adams extended this interpretation in an often quoted speech (given on July 4, 1821), wherein he explained why American interference in the concerns of others must be rejected and how isolationism might be practiced:

> Wherever the standard of freedom and independence has been or shall be unfurled, there will her [America's] heart, her benedictions, and her prayers be. But she goes not abroad in search of monsters to destroy. She is the well-wisher to the freedom and independence of all. She is the champion and vindicator of her own. She will recommend the general cause by the countenance of her voice, and by the benignant sympathy of her example. . . . [Otherwise] she might become the dictatress of the world. She would no longer be the ruler of her own spirit.

Thus, at the core of the isolationist heritage was the belief that any United States involvement in the world should be passive. The nation would act as an example, "a beacon of light on liberty," demonstrating to the world how a free society could run its affairs, and holding itself as a model for others to emulate if they chose. But the United States would *not* assume responsibility for the world, even in the name of freedom. It would *not* be an agent of international reform, seeking to impose its way of life on others. Moreover, it would *not* intervene in others' internal affairs (even if by word it might preach to them about the virtues of liberty). Instead of actively attempting to direct the course of world affairs, the United States would stop its reach at the water's edge; it would practice restraint, moderation, and withdrawal, and act only to defend itself against any predatory actions of others—by threat if possible, by force if necessary. But it would refrain from the kind of activist global involvement which, the founding fathers feared, would only subvert cherished ideals, the unique promise of the American vision, and ultimately, freedom at home.

Internationalism

On the other hand, American history has been marked by periods in which the penchant for active internationalism has been dominant. When the pendulum has swung in that direction, the United States has sought energetically to expand its influence by playing the game of international power politics. Like other great powers in history, in defining its actions it has behaved like an "ordinary" country (see Rosecrance, 1976), seeing the world's problems as its own and perceiving its interests to be always at stake in any international circumstance. During periods of internationalist endeavor, American foreign policy has accepted the opportunities and responsibilities of power with eagerness.

Actually, the internationalist tradition has taken several forms. It has entailed a willingness to exercise power, an impulse to intervene in others' affairs, a search for foreign markets, the economic penetration of other societies through foreign investment and free trade, maintenance of a high diplomatic profile, the quest for preponderant status, sensitivity to threats to the nation's honor, active promotion of American values abroad, and a corresponding willingness to transplant American institutions.

At the extreme, that tradition places the United States in the category of an imperial republic, or what George Washington termed a "nascent empire." A desire to spread American values internationally has found expression in expansionist diplomacy, as exemplified by the purchases of the Louisiana Territory, Florida, and Alaska; the annexation of Texas; the acquisition by military force of the Philippines, Puerto Rico, and Guam; and the assumption, with the Monroe Doctrine, of sphere-of-influence responsibilities throughout the Western Hemisphere. The treatment of Indians was reflective of yet another form of expansionism. Here "manifest destiny" was little more than a crude euphemism for, and rationalization of, a policy of expulsion and extermination of people who were, in contemporary terminology, members of "nonstate nations." The spirit of American expansionism that produced these episodes is reflected in the policy rhetoric of their proponents. For instance, in 1846 Secretary of State William H. Seward pledged, "I will engage to give you the possession of the American continent and the control of the world." Similarly, Senator Albert Beveridge, speaking in 1898, referred to Americans as "a conquering race." "We must obey our blood," he urged, "and occupy new markets and if necessary new lands."

In practice, those sentiments reflected less an American desire to acquire others' territory, resources, and possessions than an underlying attitude about the country's special place in the world of nations, its uniqueness, its innate virtue. From that view it has often been but a short step to a messianic, crusading approach to the world; self-righteously presuming its own virtuous innocence, the United States has on occasion operated almost from a moralistic sense of *mission* in its foreign policy. This moralistic outlook has pictured the world as a legitimate target for reform, and, during periods in which such thinking has been dominant, the urge to practice an outward-reaching, globalist foreign policy has proven irresistible. But these periods of global activism have not persisted continuously throughout American history.

Globalism Versus Retrenchment: Cyclical Patterns

Because American policy makers have been unable to agree historically on whether to withdraw from the world or attempt to reform it, the nation's posture toward the world has alternated between periods of "extroversion" and periods of "introversion." Prior to World War II there were both periods of global involvement and isolationist withdrawal. Throughout, debate was vociferous among policy makers as to which role best served the national interest, but the debate was never conclusively resolved. Instead, one conception dominated at one time only to be replaced later by the other (for example, an internationalist phase at the turn of the century and an isolationist one following World War I). More generally, it has been argued that historical cycles characterize America's vacillation between global involvement and isolationist withdrawal. One authoritative interpretation (Klingberg, 1952, 1979, and 1983) has suggested that rhythmic cycles, each taking twenty-five to thirty years to run their course, describe the introversion-extroversion pattern in the American diplomatic record, as follows:

Introversion	Extroversion
1776–1798	1798–1824
1824–1844	1844–1871
1871–1891	1891–1919
1919–1940	1940–1966
1967–1986	1986–2014

The importance of the legacy of the contest between internationalist and isolationist values cannot be overemphasized. Tradition (however ambivalent in the American case) can be a powerful determinant of any nation's foreign policy, serving as a frame of reference and a guide for future action. Thus the historical legacy of this dichotomized set of values, however contradictory, has provided decision makers with remarkably durable precedents for very dissimilar policies. The existence of competing traditions also has made for an American foreign policy capable of responding to changing international circumstances adaptively and with a measure of flexibility. In principle, the United States is able to accommodate itself to changing internal or external conditions and needs by emphasizing either tradition and the interests they seem to promote. It is not doomed by unseen historical forces to conform its policy to the direction dictated by the historical cycle's oscillating quarter-century swing. Instead, it has had the capacity to select either orientation in accordance with its perceived interests. Since World War II, however, internationalism has dominated the nation's isolationist impulse.

Globalist Internationalism in the Postwar Era

With hindsight, it is clear that World War II was a seminal event in American history. It was an episode that both crystallized a mood and acted as a catalyst for it; that resolved contradictions and helped clarify values; that set in motion a wave of events which eventually engulfed the nation and forced it to reach a consensus about its role. "Every war in American history," writes Arthur Schlesinger, Jr. (1967), "has been followed in due course by skeptical reassessments of supposedly sacred assumptions." World War II, more than any other, served such a purpose. Characteristically, American entry into the war was both reluctant and late, as the nation dealt with its isolationist instincts (symbolized by the Neutrality Acts of the 1930s). But with its entry into the war, the United States was transformed, perhaps irrevocably, as it grew to superpower status. The nation emerged from the war with extraordinary powers and a new sense of global responsibility. The isolationist heritage was pushed aside as subsequent events and circumstances were perceived to render it obsolete and as the nation's leaders plunged into the job of shaping the world to suit American security needs and other interests. The view that emerged as dominant was that the United States should not, and could not, retreat from active participation in world affairs as it had after World War I.

In 1947 President Truman set the tone of American postwar policy in the doctrine that bears his name: "The free peoples of the world look to us for support in maintaining their freedoms. . . . If we falter in our leadership, we may endanger the peace of the world—and we shall surely endanger the welfare of our own nation." Global responsibility became an accepted orientation of American foreign policy that few were reluctant to support. Using key words such as "involvement," "intervention," and "globalism," leaders' political rhetoric prescribed the United States' mission in world affairs as necessary for the "good of others"—to make the world a better place in which to live. "Other nations have interests," declared Secretary of State Dean Rusk in 1967; "the United States has responsibilities." "Our nation," John F. Kennedy asserted in 1962, was "commissioned by history to be either an observer of freedom's failure or the cause of its success." The kind of activism promoted by this self-image began a new epoch in American diplomacy as the nation jettisoned its historical ambivalence about internationalism. It became, by choice and not just by circumstance, a global actor. It made *A Covenant with Power* (Gardner, 1984).

Consistent with its new operational premise of global responsibility, the United States became actively involved in nearly every sphere of international relations. It was a primary sponsor and supporter of the United Nations. It pushed hard for a further expansion of foreign trade and the development of new markets for American business abroad. It engineered the creation of a vast complex of alliances, both formal and informal. It supported the activities of regional institutions, such as the Organization of American States, and the establishment of American hegemony in areas regarded as American spheres of influence. And it began in earnest to direct its vast resources toward the pursuit of its newly defined foreign policy objectives. The result of those efforts was a vast American "empire" circling the globe. The data summarized in Box 3.1 suggest the scope of America's postwar involvement in the world beyond its borders. The data clearly support Henry Kissinger's observation that "the period after World War II marks the first era of truly global foreign policy."

Not only does the postwar record demonstrate worldwide American involvement; equally conspicuous is the consistency with which the premises of globalism have been reiterated by every major policy maker since Truman. Consider the brief inventory of policy pronouncements presented in Box 3.2. These persistent assumptions stand out: (1) the United States has global responsibilities and obligations; (2) it stands as a guardian of freedom and morality on the international stage; (3) the future of the world depends on its

---

BOX 3.1   Military and Nonmilitary Involvements of the United States

---

Nonmilitary Involvements

In 1985, the United States maintained diplomatic relations with 153 governments and was a member of over 50 international organizations.

In 1984, U.S. direct investment abroad reached $233 billion. This represented a 2,000 percent increase from the 1950 level.

The value of U.S. exports (excluding services) nearly tripled since 1967, reaching $218 billion in 1984.

In 1983, the United States—the world's leading agricultural exporter— accounted for 18 percent of world agricultural exports.

In 1984, the U.S. Agency for International Development (AID) had permanent representation in 88 countries receiving bilateral U.S. economic assistance.

Between 1965 and 1983, the U.S. provided $59.5 billion in official development assistance, 23.5 percent of the total foreign economic assistance contributed toward development by the noncommunist nations.

In 1984, total foreign lending by the U.S. stood at $323.3 billion.

The United States government, through the U.S. broadcasting services, promotes its world view in 48 languages during 2,033 hours of broadcasting each week.

Military Involvements

The United States is committed through bilateral and multilateral treaties, executive agreements, and policy declarations to the defense of over 40 nations.

By the mid-1980s, military involvements resulting from treaties, executive agreements, arms sales, the stationing of troops, and various kinds of military assistance linked the U.S. to over 100 different countries. The estimated cost of maintaining these "commitments" between 1974 and 1984 exceeded $150 billion.

In 1984, U.S. military sales the world over amounted to $10 billion.

The U.S. policy of "global containment" as manifested in the Korean and Vietnam wars is estimated to have cost $190.6 billion.

In 1984, 511,000 U.S. military personnel were stationed overseas in more than a dozen different countries.

Of the 13,000 plus U.S. nuclear weapons capable of striking the Soviet Union, approximately 2,400 are "tactical" weapons based either in Europe, Asia, or on aircraft carriers; the other 11,000 are "strategic" nuclear weapons.

BOX 3.1   (continued)

In 1985, the U.S. spent $253.8 billion on military preparedness. This figure exceeds the Gross National Product of all but a handful of the 159 member states of the United Nations.

SOURCES: *The Defense Monitor* 8 (Vol. 13, No. 6, 1984), pp. 1, 6; *Statistical Abstract of the United States, 1986* (Washington, D.C.: U.S. Government Printing Office, 1985), pp. 331, 338, 342, 497; U.S. Arms Control and Disarmanent Agency, *World Military Expenditures and Arms Transfers, 1985* (Washington, D.C.: U.S. Arms Control and Disarmament Agency, 1985), p. 5; U.S. Department of State, *Atlas of U.S. Foreign Relations* (Washington, D.C.: U.S. Government Printing Office, 1985), pp. 8, 10, 14, 56, 60, 65, 66; *World Development Report 1985* (New York: Oxford University Press, 1985), pp. 208–209.

willingness and readiness to act abroad for the good of the world; and (4) the United States is to be the world's leader, a position it willingly accepts. The ethnocentric, paternalistic overtones of this missionary zeal notwithstanding, what emerges from the record is that the United States has persisted in its internationalist posture for almost five decades. Given the record of American foreign policy since World War II, the characterization of the United States offered by Zbigniew Brzezinski, President Carter's national security assistant, as "the first global society" seems fitting. President Reagan's contention that "our nation is the only nation on earth that can preserve the peace" suggests that globalism is deeply ingrained as a cornerstone of American foreign policy. There is not an aspirant to the White House who would risk challenging the appropriateness of the U.S. role as an active, global actor—for to do so would be to attack an image the country holds of itself that has become widely accepted, and that derives from the kinds of external involvements and ties it has accumulated since its entry into the second world war.

Clearly, therefore, globalism is one of the defining characteristics of American foreign policy, and it illuminates the kinds of missionary activities the nation has undertaken during the past four decades in what some call its self-conceived role of global policeman.

This is not to assume that, however entrenched, the globalist U.S. foreign policy orientation is necessarily permanent. According to the hypothesized twenty-five to thirty-year cycle in American foreign policy, the last phase of American extroversion should have concluded in about 1968, a date (coincidentally?) that marked the turning point in America's involvement in Vietnam and the beginning of popular pleas for a U.S. retreat from world affairs. President Nixon's statement in 1970 that "America cannot—and will not—conceive all the plans, design all the programs, execute all the decisions, and undertake all the defense of the free nations of the world" took cognizance of a resurgent isolationist mood. This confession, part and parcel of the Nixon Doctrine, signaled acceptance of the proposition that U.S. interests could be served by contracting the definition of what America's global involvement ought to entail. America's superpower status was questioned, and throughout the 1970s the

Box 3.2 Globalism Since 1945: Thirty-five Years of Missionary Policy Pronouncements

Policy Maker	*Statement*
Harry S Truman, 1945	"[The United States should] take the lead in running the world in the way that the world ought to be run."
Dwight D. Eisenhower, 1960	"My recent travels impressed upon me even more strongly the fact that free men everywhere look to us."
John F. Kennedy, 1961	"Let every nation know, whether it wishes us well or ill, that we shall pay any price, bear any burden, meet any hardship, support any friend, oppose any foe to assure the survival and success of liberty. This much we pledge—and more."
Richard M. Nixon, 1963	"I say that it is time for us proudly to declare that our ideas are for export. We need not apologize for taking this position."
Lyndon B. Johnson, 1965	"History and our own achievements have thrust upon us the principal responsibility for protecting freedom on earth. . . . No other people in no other time has had so great an opportunity to work and risk for the freedom of all mankind."
Gerald R. Ford, 1976	"America has had a unique role in the world . . . [a]nd ever since the end of World War II we have borne successfully a heavy responsibility for insuring a stable world order. . . . We have taken the role of leadership."
Jimmy Carter, 1977	"Because we are free we can never be indifferent to the fate of freedom elsewhere."
Ronald Reagan, 1980	"We in this country, in this generation, are, by destiny rather than choice, the watchmen on the walls of world freedom."

eagle appeared "entangled" (see Oye, Rothchild, and Lieber, 1979) in a web of constraints on its global power (see Hoffmann, 1968). The Carter administration acknowledged these growing limits while attempting to reduce them.

But America's continuing global activism and hegemonic strength (Russett, 1985), particularly as evidenced in the Reagan administration's rejection of the rhetoric of restraint, suggests that the suspension of globalist enthusiasm in the 1970s was temporary and that the internationalist thrust of American foreign policy since World War II has reasserted its hold. President Reagan's proclamations ("We hear it said that we live in an era of limits to our powers. Well, there are [also] limits to our patience") revealed his intention to restore global activism, to combat neoisolationism, and to make the eagle once again "defiant" (Oye, Lieber, and Rothchild, 1983). The world policeman role was reaffirmed and extended, along with the burdens it entailed. Reagan's policies and words come close to a formal repudiation of the Nixon Doctrine (Maynes, 1983), which stated that the cost of protecting international security would have to be shared with others. Secretary of State Shultz's characterization in 1985 summarized what is perhaps the dominant American preference for the role the U.S. should play in world affairs:

> . . . we are not just observers; we are participants, and we are engaged. America is again in a position to have a major influence over the trend of events—and America's traditional goals and values have not changed. Our duty must be to help shape the evolving trends in accordance with our ideals and interests; to help build a new structure of international stability that will ensure peace, prosperity, and freedom for coming generations. This is the real challenge of our foreign policy over the coming years.

Time will test the wisdom of this policy, and reveal whether America's interests are best served by it. "American foreign policy makers," it has been said (van den Haag, 1985), "appear to share a naive belief that American ideals and ideas can and should solve all the problems of the world and that it is their mission to actively apply these ideals abroad." Is this alleged belief warranted? In asking this question, we should consider former Secretary of State Dean Rusk's reminder, in 1983, that "No one named [the U.S.] to be the den mother of the entire world. . . . There are a lot of things which happen in the world which we cannot influence, which are none of our business." The view that America may "not have the expertise, the wisdom, the resources or the power to solve" global problems (van den Haag, 1985) is thus worthy of consideration. If so, and a readjustment in orientation is required, can a balance between globalism and isolationism, between moralistic crusading and escapist withdrawal, between overextension and paralysis, be found?

In probing these questions, the linkage of globalism to another pillar of postwar America foreign policy—anticommunism—must be illuminated. In assuming a globalist policy, has the United States—Secretary of State Adams's warning notwithstanding—gone abroad in search of monsters to destroy?

THE AMERICAN CHALLENGE TO INTERNATIONAL COMMUNISM

Fear of communism (and rejection of it) comprises another recurrent theme and defining attribute of postwar American foreign policy. That fear has played a major part in shaping the way the United States has perceived the world during the postwar period. American policy makers repeatedly have viewed communism as a structured, doctrinaire belief system diametrically opposed to the "American way of life" and intent upon converting the entire world to its vision. Combating this threatening, adversarial ideology has become almost an obsession—to the point, some would argue, that American foreign policy itself may have become ideological.[1]

Anticommunism has been premised on the conviction that ideas have consequences, and that Marxist-Leninist doctrine is composed of alien ideas that pose a threat to the United States and to the world at large. That conviction, in turn, has defined the kinds of goals the United States has pursued abroad. The United States has defined its mission in terms of what it opposes; it has said, in its words and deeds, that it is not necessarily *for* something (other than the classic goals of self-preservation and national enrichment) so much as it is *against* something: communist ideology.

The varied reasons for American preoccupation with and fear of communism as they were shaped in the decade following World War II rested on a set of corollary assumptions about "the nature of the beast." Included was the assumption that communism was an expansionist, crusading force which was intent on converting the entire world to its beliefs. There was also the assumption that communism was a cohesive monolith to which all adherents were bound in united solidarity. In addition, communism was necessarily assumed to be totalitarian, antidemocratic, and anticapitalistic, and, therefore, a real threat to freedom, liberty, and prosperity throughout the world.

Hindsight casts doubt on the validity of some of these assumptions. That communism is, for instance, monolithic is questionable. With the passage of time, communism has revealed itself to be increasingly polycentric; Communist Party leaders have been vocal about their own divisions and disagreements concerning communism's fundamental beliefs. Also, the greatest fear of some communist states today is of other communist states. The Sino-Soviet split, and warfare in the 1980s between Vietnamese, Chinese, Cambodian, and Laotian communists, are preeminent cases in point. These disputes are grounded fundamentally in nationalism, not ideology. The differences that divide communist Poland from communist Russia and the experimentation of

---

[1]For instance, with some hyperbole the sociologist S. M. Eisenstadt has asserted that "the United States is the most ideological society that has existed in the world" (Isaak, 1977). More cautiously, Parenti (1969) notes that "If America has an ideology, or a national purpose, it is anticommunism." For useful reviews which further explore this thesis, see Gamson and Modigliani (1971), Gardner (1970), and Commager (1983). For an analysis which contrasts America's foreign policy ideology with that of the Soviet Union, see Jönsson (1984).

the Chinese communists in the mid-1980s with free enterprise and capitalistic incentives demonstrate that the stereotypic image of communistic ideology is too simple. Thus nations of the same ideology may be in conflict with each other (just as nations with avowedly antagonistic ideologies—for example, the United States and China—may collaborate with one another for mutual benefits). Moreover, even if communism is expansionistic, its ideology has shown itself to be more flexible and elastic than initially assumed, setting no timetable for the conversion of nonbelievers. But regardless, the impact of the assumptions made about communism in the American policy-making community was enormous. Policy makers defined a world view which inevitably led to acceptance of the notion that successful opposition to communism was one of the most important interests of the United States. This world view persists today and contributes to the continuing anticommunist thrust of American foreign policy.

The premise of communism's challenge contributed in part to the rise of the Cold War and has continued to influence the ideological orientation of postwar international politics. From this perspective, international politics does not center on conflicts of interests between states but on contests between incompatible, inimical belief systems. Such ideological contests allow no room for compromise since they are perceived to pit right against wrong, good against evil itself. Diametrically opposed belief systems require victory. In such an atmosphere, where proponents feel righteous about their cause, the world tends to be seen as an arena for a religious war—a battle for the allegiance of people's minds. There is a tendency, moreover, to rationalize the use of any means to achieve that goal: the end justifies the means. Thus, on occasion, American policy rhetoric—like that employed to rationalize religious wars and religious persecutions in the past—advocated ''sleepless hostility to Communism—even preventive war'' (Commager, 1965). In short, the world came to be viewed by both adversaries in ''zero-sum'' terms: when one side won converts the other side necessarily lost them. Such an outlook almost guarantees pure conflict (see Schlesinger, 1983b; Commager, 1983) by recognizing no virtue in conciliation or cooperation with an ideological foe and by offering little tolerance of competing beliefs.

Official pronouncements about America's global objectives during this same period routinely stressed that communist doctrine represented a real menace to America. ''The actions resulting from the Communist philosophy,'' charged Harry Truman in 1949, ''are a threat.'' ''We face a hostile ideology— global in scope, atheistic in character, ruthless in purpose, and insidious in method. Unhappily the danger it poses promises to be of indefinite duration,'' warned President Eisenhower. Linked to those convictions was the associated assumption that communism was endowed with powers and appeals that made its continued spread likely, unless the United States resisted it. The so-called ''domino theory,'' which maintained that the fall to communism in one country would invite the fall of countries adjacent to it, so that like a stack of falling dominoes an endless and unstoppable chain reaction would unfold, was popularized in the 1960s to illustrate metaphorically the manner in which increasing proportions of the world's population might come under the domination of communist governments, and to heighten fears that this process would continue unabated unless checked by American resistance. "Communism is on the move. It is out to win. It is playing an offensive game," warned Richard Nixon in 1963, adding that American "policy for dealing with this great Communist offensive . . . shall [be to] hold the line against further Communist gains in the hope that Communism will eventually wither and die."

The goal of anticommunism became institutionalized after World War II. For nearly two decades thereafter, until the United States became mired in the Vietnam War, few who made American foreign policy challenged the assumption that communism was a conspiratorial movement, cohesive and powerful, that had to be opposed. Few challenged the belief that the Cold War was rooted in ideological causes. Policy debate was concerned largely with how the policy of anticommunism was to be implemented, not with its premises. Some of the ideological tone and fervor of American foreign policy rhetoric receded with the election of Richard Nixon, who embarked on a pragmatic program to limit communist influence through a strategy of détente. References in policy statements to communism itself as a force in world politics declined thereafter. President Carter went so far as to declare in May 1977 that "we are now free of that inordinate fear of communism which once led us to embrace any dictator who joined us in our fear."

But the anticommunist underpinnings of American foreign policy surely did not diminish. The theme of "communism as the principal danger" gained renewed currency as the United States moved into the 1980s. President Reagan's picture in 1980 of the world as a place where the forces of the noncommunist world, led by the United States, are arrayed in continuous battle against "godless Communism" indicated the enduring importance of that preoccupation among American policy makers. Reagan in 1983 summarized his view of the Soviet Union's ideology: "We've made it very plain: We don't like their system; they don't like ours." The extinction of communism's influence in the world remains a primary objective of the United States, and the premises on which that goal is based continue to exert their influence on policy planning.

THE CONTAINMENT OF SOVIET INFLUENCE

As the strongest physically and the most vocal rhetorically of the states embracing Marxism-Leninism, the Soviet Union was considered the cutting edge of the communist challenge. The development of a Russo-centric foreign policy followed from this perception. As a consequence, the American approach to the postwar international environment rested on the following corollary beliefs:

1. The Soviet Union is an expansionistic power intent on maximizing communist power through military conquest and "exported" revolutions.
2. The Soviet goal of dominating the world is permanent and irreversible; unless blocked by vigorous counteraction, it will succeed.
3. The United States is the leader of the "free world" and the only nation in a position to ward off Soviet aggression and restore the balance of power.
4. The United States must manage its affairs so as to increase its power relative to the Soviet Union, in order to better contain Soviet expansion.
5. Appeasement will not work; force must be met by force; and the United States is obligated to "fight for peace" in order to stop Soviet expansion.
6. The fate of the world is determined by superpower relations; relations with less powerful nations are secondary; a pyramid of tiered priorities in foreign policy should exist, focusing attention on the East-West confrontation above all else.

The factors that brought these assumptions and the containment strategy derived from them into play are difficult to trace. To understand how they came into being, why they became so prominent, and why they have remained so durable, it is necessary to review the circumstances which led to the Cold War.[2] Then, it is useful to chart the evolutionary course of American interactions with the Soviet Union from the inception of the containment policy to the present. This chronological survey of American policy toward, and relations with, the Soviet Union will permit detection of patterns in the relationship and will provide an opportunity to assess whether the containment strategy has proven consistent with American interests.

The Origins of the Cold War: Contending Hypotheses

One view of the causes of the Cold War maintains that the United States and the Soviet Union were destined by fate and circumstance to become rivals—that history had unfolded in a way that predestined the two countries to oppose each other. In 1835 Alexis de Tocqueville predicted that this confrontation would eventually ensue, arguing that "there are today two great peoples which, starting out from different points of departure, advance toward the same goal—the Americans and the Russians. . . . Each of them will one day hold in its hands the destinies of half of mankind."

[2]Emphasis must be placed on the fact that the roots of the Cold War are elusive and fraught with ambiguity and controversy. The abundance of authoritative but conflicting interpretations of the causes of the Cold War attests to the difficulties of resolving historical controversies which center on questions of motives. Relatively orthodox interpretations, which tend to absolve the United States of major responsibility for the start of the Cold War, include Dougherty and Pfaltzgraff (1986), Spanier (1985), Feis (1970), and Ulam (1983 and 1985). Revisionist treatments, which emphasize the contributions of the United States to the advent of the Cold War, include Kolko (1968), Horowitz (1971), Gati (1974), Yergin (1978), Crozier, Middleton, and Murray-Brown (1985), and May (1984). Works that critically compare contending assessments include Welch (1970), Schlesinger (1967), Crabb (1976), Melanson (1983), Nye (1984), and Kennan (1984). In considering rival theories, we must treat each as an hypothesis, not a statement of truth, and accept willingly the possibility that different versions of the origins of the Cold War all contain elements of truth even while they differ fundamentally from one another in the conclusions they reach.

The basis for this prophecy was Tocqueville's assessment of the territory and natural resources possessed by the two countries. He did not, or could not, foresee the emergence of Marxism or the possibility that ideological differences would contribute to the dispute he regarded as inevitable. Instead, he anticipated that the two countries, which he saw as so much alike, would become natural enemies. Why? Because they would become dominant powers in world politics. Preponderant status assured conflict, because rivalry and distrust among great powers have been constants in global politics throughout history (Morgenthau, 1985). Great powers have always found areas of vital interest over which to clash. They have always perceived actions by other powers as initial steps toward "aggrandizement" and have seen their interests served in preventing such expansion. Thus from this perspective, the ascent of the United States and the Soviet Union to top status in the international hierarchy, and the resultant global vision that such a position required each to assume, guaranteed that they would see their interests as divergent and that they would compete with one another.

According to a second interpretation, however, the Cold War is simply an extension of the animosity that the two powers maintained toward one another since the Russian Revolution, which brought a Marxist philosophy into practice in a society Marx himself felt would be unlikely to attempt a communist experiment. From the very birth of the Soviet state, relations between the two powers were strained. American troops intervened in Russia in 1918 in what became an effort to turn back the Bolshevik revolution; symptomatically, the United States did not even extend diplomatic recognition to the Soviets until 1933. When one takes the long-term view, therefore, the Cold War appears to be a product of the repugnance that the two states traditionally felt for each other's professed way of life. Burdened by ideologies that ruled out compromise or coexistence, American and Soviet leaders were destined to pursue a cold war. It is ironical that the ideology of each actor resembled in many ways the world view of the other (see Jönsson, 1982b).

A third view is the thesis that the Cold War originated in the experiences of the two countries during and immediately after World War II, when, ironically, they were allies. Recall that the common threat posed by Hitler's plan for world conquest threw the United States and the Soviet Union together in a united, antifascist coalition. Whether the Grand Alliance was simply a marriage of convenience or whether, instead, those joined in the common Allied cause were sincere in their expressions of mutual respect has been the subject of debate. Circumstances required their collaboration, for each needed the other to assure defeat of the Axis enemy. But could it be that, even while cooperating in the wartime alliance, the two countries simply reinforced latent suspicions and fears of each other's real intentions? Did the wartime experience breed mutual distrust?

The impression gleaned from perusal of the wartime foreign policy pronouncements of both American and Soviet leaders supports the view that the good will and trust of the two powers were neither illusory nor mere propaganda. Although to be sure differences between the Allies inevitably surfaced as they negotiated wartime strategy, the prevailing mood was not, on the whole, one of suspicion and distrust. In their official discourse, American and Soviet leaders envisioned cooperation. In fact, as World War II was drawing to a victorious conclusion, the goal of devising policies aimed at continued Soviet-American collaboration appeared well within reach. (Collaboration, in turn, revealed the capacity of the superpowers to subordinate their ideological beliefs to considerations of national interests). The resumption of their rivalry and the eruption of the Cold War looked neither preordained nor inevitable.

Indeed, the closer the Allies came to vanquishing the common enemy, the more the positive spirit of common endeavor prevailed, at least rhetorically. Negotiations among the allies about the shape of the postwar world commenced even before victory had been secured, and the atmosphere was conducive to the perpetuation of understanding and peace. It was Franklin Roosevelt's hope and expectation that wartime collaboration would persist in the aftermath of war. He believed that accommodation between the United States and the Soviet Union, based on mutual respect grounded in national interests, was possible. The thinking of the president at that time was captured by presidential adviser Harry Hopkins, who stated, ''The Russians had proved that they could be reasonable and farseeing and there wasn't any doubt in the minds of the President or any of us that we could live with them and get along with them peacefully for as far into the future as any of us could imagine'' (cited in Ekirch, 1966).

Part of the reason for Roosevelt's optimism was his conviction that the United States and the Soviet Union had succeeded in reaching understandings about a recipe for continued friendship. He envisioned that the agreements negotiated would permit both countries to enjoy the benefits of power, but each within its own *sphere of influence*. An informal agreement was reached that each power would enjoy dominant influence and freedom in specified areas of the globe (see Morgenthau, 1969; Schlesinger, 1967).[3] John Foster Dulles, adviser to the 1948 Republican presidential aspirant, Thomas E. Dewey, and later President Eisenhower's secretary of state, noted in January

[3]One indication of this agreement was provided during the waning days of the fight against Nazi Germany. General Eisenhower refused to let the American army penetrate to Berlin and the eastern portion of Germany; instead, the Soviet army was permitted to liberate those areas as a prize for the sacrifices the Soviet Union had made in the war against the Nazis. To some this decision reflected the naiveté of the American government about the postwar structure of international politics in Europe that was being built by the way the war against Germany was terminated. But to the Soviet Union it may have reinforced the view that the Western powers would accept legitimate Soviet security needs, particularly the need for a buffer zone in Eastern Europe, which had been a common invasion route into Russia for over three centuries. The United States stood by its promises and implemented its sphere-of-influence pledge in conformity with its own expectations that the agreement served American interests. Subsequently, of course, the United States began to reevaluate its position. Hence, when the American government began to challenge Soviet supremacy in East Germany and elsewhere in Eastern Europe, the Soviet Union felt threatened by what it perceived to be Western ''imperialist designs.''

1945, "The three great powers which at Moscow agreed upon the closest cooperation about European questions have shifted to a practice of separate, regional responsibility." Also implicit was the agreement not to oppose each other in areas not vital to national security, as reflected in the Yalta agreement (Ulam, 1983). Symbolic, too, of this implicit collaboration were the kinds of rules written into the United Nations charter, rules which obliged the United States and the Soviet Union to share, through the operation of the Security Council, responsibility for the preservation of world peace.

Why, given such ostensibly cordial relations and accommodative hopes, did this atmosphere disappear? What led to the failure of the aspirations expressed and to the emergence of the Cold War? Perhaps the hope for a postwar period of Soviet-American good will died with President Roosevelt; Truman, upon assuming power, jettisoned Roosevelt's policies aimed at maintaining postwar harmony with the Soviets and the flexible tactics that underpinned it, and substituted a belligerent, confrontational policy (Tugwell, 1971). Truman's statement that "if the Russians did not wish to join us they could go to hell" is said to have typified his attitude and approach (although Truman's reaction may, instead, have been an appropriate response to his perception of Soviet provocation). Still, the question remains whether the Cold War would have emerged had Roosevelt's flexible policies and sensitive approach to the Soviets survived the transition of authority to Truman. A different way of handling postwar problems might have produced a Soviet-American relationship markedly distinct from that which eventually resulted (see Theoharis, 1970).

A fourth and perhaps more convincing interpretation of the deterioration of the Soviet-American relationship is one which sees the Cold War as deriving from the fearful and suspicious way both antagonists interpreted the actions of the other. That is, the Cold War may have been precipitated by *misperceptions*—not conflicting interests but the inherent distrust each antagonist felt for the other and the consequent distortions of the other's behavior that each developed. The Cold War is thus explained in terms of the propensity of distrustful parties to see in their own actions only virtue and in those of the adversary only malice. Such *mirror images*, of course, breed conflict.[4]

To the extent that such mirror images existed, as they probably did in the final stages of World War II and shortly thereafter, cooperation was precluded and hostility made inevitable. As perceptions of the adversary's evil intentions became accepted as dogma, the prophecies that were made became self-fulfill-

---

[4]A number of observers have applied the concept of mirror images to the case of Soviet-American relations. Urie Bronfenbrenner (1975), for instance, has noted the proclivity of both Soviets and Americans to harbor the same perceptions of each other: *they* are the aggressors; *they* arm for war whereas *we* arm for peace; *they* intervene in others' territory to expand influence, whereas *we* do so to preserve the prospects for an acceptable way of life. Their *people* are good and peaceloving, but their *government* exploits its people; most of their people are really not sympathetic to the regime; it cannot be trusted; its policy verges on madness. Invariably, the product of such negative perceptual images is conflict between the parties maintaining them.

ing.[5] A month before Roosevelt died, he expressed to Stalin his desire, above all, to prevent "mutual distrust." Yet the events surrounding the origins of the Cold War indicate that mistrust, misperception, and consequent fear were the very foundations of the conflict. Stalin was as wary of the Americans as they were of him. Hostility and threats by one power were responded to in kind by the other, thus escalating the spiral of threat and distrust. The syndrome is illustrated in the opposing Soviet and American viewpoints of the events that unfolded during this epochal period which contributed so heavily to the Cold War.

To the Soviets, reasons for doubting American intentions were abundant. The Soviets lived with the memory of American participation in the 1918–1919 Allied military intervention in Russia, which turned from its initial mission of keeping arms from falling into the hands of Germany into an anti-Bolshevik undertaking. They were sensitive to the fact that the United States failed to recognize the Soviet Union diplomatically until 1933 in the midst of a depression, which was perceived to be a sign of capitalism's weakness and the beginning of its ultimate collapse. Moreover, the wartime experience had done little to remove Soviet suspicions of the United States. The Soviets recalled U.S. procrastination before entering the war against the fascists; the American refusal to inform the Soviets of the Manhattan project to develop the atomic bomb; the delay in sending the Soviets promised Lend Lease supplies; the failure to open up the second front (leading Stalin to suspect that American policy was to let the Russians and Germans destroy each other so that the United States could then pick up the pieces from among the rubble[6]); the American failure to inform the Soviets of wartime strategy to the extent that it informed Great Britain; and the use of the atomic bomb against Japan, perhaps perceived as a maneuver to prevent Russian involvement in the Pacific peace settlement (see, for discussions of this thesis, Alperovitz, 1965 and 1970; and Alsop and Joravsky, 1980). Those suspicions were later reinforced by the willingness of the United States to support previous Nazi collaborators in American-occupied countries, notably Italy, and by its pressure on the Soviet Union to abide by its promise to allow free elections in areas vital to Soviet national security, notably Poland. The Soviets were also resentful of the Amer-

---

[5]Prophecies are sometimes self-fulfilling because the future can be affected by the way it is anticipated. How predictions can make themselves come true in international relations is illustrated by the tendency of those who predict others' hostility to fearfully arm for defense and provocatively challenge those who they feel are threatening; they then discover themselves to be living in a world filled with enemies whom they have alarmed.

[6]Stalin's suspicions may not have been totally unfounded. While still a senator, for example, Harry Truman (*New York Times*, July 24, 1941) expressed the hope that following Hitler's invasion of Russia the Nazis and communists would destroy each other. He stated flatly, "If we see that Germany is winning we ought to help Russia and if Russia is winning we ought to help Germany, and in that way let them kill as many as possible, although I don't want to see Hitler victorious under any circumstances." Although Truman was not speaking for President Roosevelt or the U.S. government, such sentiments expressed publicly by a member of Congress are unlikely to be ignored by a foreign power. Those views resurfaced in the aftermath of World War II when, in a speech before the United Nations (April 26, 1945), Soviet Foreign Minister V. M. Molotov accused the Western powers of complicity with Hitler.

ican decision to cancel abruptly promised Lend Lease assistance which Stalin had counted on to facilitate the postwar recovery of the Soviet Union. (The United States later framed the European recovery program known as the Marshall Plan in such a way as virtually to guarantee Soviet nonparticipation.) Thus Soviet distrust of American intentions was presumed to stem, at least in part, from fears of American encirclement buttressed by a historical record of demonstrated hostility.[7]

To the United States, hostility toward the Soviet Union was considered more than justified. There seemed to be numerous indications of growing Soviet belligerence: Russian unwillingness to permit democratic elections in the territories they liberated from the Nazis; their refusal to assist in postwar reconstruction in regions outside Soviet control; their maintenance of an unnecessarily large postwar armed force; the stripping of supplies from Soviet areas of occupation; their selfish and often obstructive behavior in the fledgling new international organizations; their occasional opportunistic disregard for international law and violation of agreements and treaties; their infiltration of Western labor movements; and, perhaps most unacceptable, their anti-American propaganda and espousal of an alien ideology which promised to destroy the American type of economic and political system. The implied threats provoked more than an imaginary sense of fear on the part of Americans and were reinforced by the unwillingness of the Soviets to withdraw the Red Army from Eastern and Central Europe. The Soviet Union came to be perceived as a military rival straining at the leash to invade Western Europe and to acquire new satellites under Russian occupation. Thus, whereas Roosevelt had argued before the American people that postwar peace depended on Soviet-American collaboration, the actions and anti-American rhetoric of Soviet leaders led increasingly to the perception of the Soviet Union as the greatest threat to peace.

Even a cursory inspection of the Soviet and American images makes clear that the leaders of the two countries saw the world differently. They imposed on events different definitions of reality and became captives of those visions. Expectations shaped the way developments were interpreted: what they looked for was what they got. Hence, even though both countries saw the adversary in remarkably identical terms, the misperceptions involved became a source for conflict. George F. Kennan, the American ambassador to the Soviet Union in 1952, noted that misread signals were common to both sides:

> The Marshall Plan, the preparations for the setting up of a West German government, and the first moves toward the establishment of NATO were taken in Mos-

---

[7]Secretary of Commerce Henry A. Wallace, in a 1946 memorandum to the president, asked how American actions since V-J Day—especially American weapons production—looked to other nations. "These facts," Wallace concluded, "make it appear either (1) that we are preparing ourselves to win the war which we regard as inevitable or (2) that we are trying to build up a predominance of force to intimidate the rest of mankind. How would it look to us if Russia had the atomic bomb and we did not, if Russia had 10,000 mile bombers and air bases within 1,000 miles of our coastline, and we did not" (cited in Horowitz," 1971: 68).

cow as the beginnings of a campaign to deprive the Soviet Union of the fruits of its victory over Germany. The Soviet crackdown on Czechoslovakia (1948) and the mounting of the Berlin blockade, both essentially defensive . . . reactions to these Western moves, were then similarly misread on the Western side. Shortly thereafter there came the crisis of the Korean War, where the Soviet attempt to employ a satellite military force in civil combat to its own advantage, by way of reaction to the American decision to establish a permanent military presence in Japan, was read in Washington as the beginning of the final Soviet push for world conquest; whereas the active American military response, provoked by this move, appeared in Moscow . . . as a threat to the Soviet position in both Manchuria and in eastern Siberia. (Kennan, 1976: 683–684)

If we interpret the origins of the Cold War in terms of misperceptions, we can appreciate the role of mutual fear, oversensitivity about the motives of the other, and insensitivity about the impact of one's own actions. It is therefore plausible to view the Cold War as a missed opportunity for cooperation. It may also be inappropriate to ask who was to blame for deteriorating relations between the United States and the Soviet Union. Both were responsible because both were victims of their images and expectations. The Cold War was not simply an American response to communist aggression, which is the orthodox American view, nor was it simply a product of postwar American assertiveness, as many revisionist historians have argued (for a review of alternative interpretations, see Schlesinger, 1967). Each of the great powers felt threatened. And each had legitimate reasons to regard the other with suspicion. Thus the Cold War may be seen as a conflict over reciprocal anxieties bred by the way officials of both sides elected to interpret the actions of the other. Like a bad marriage that gets increasingly tense through constant bickering and mutual mistrust of motives, the Cold War may have arisen, according to this view, as a result of the unwillingness of both powers to take initiatives in order to reduce tensions.

Theories that explain the origins of the Cold War exclusively in terms of perceptual variables are only partially valid, however. They account for some aspects of Soviet-American rivalry, but not all. The origins of the Cold War are too complex for a single interpretation. Indeed, if an accurate picture of the sources of this conflict is ever to be constructed, it must include reference to a variety of interrelated factors which, together, produced the historic confrontation. Such other factors as the emergence of "power vacuums" which invited the clash, the pressures exerted on foreign policies by interest groups within each society,[8] the changes in the climate of American domestic opinion on international issues, the innovations in weapons technology and the shifts in strategic balances they introduced, and the role played by military planners

---

[8]For an informed account of *Russia's Road to the Cold War*, which attributes Soviet policy less to Stalin's master plan to rule the world than to his subordination of foreign policy objectives to the internal demands of the Soviet state, see Mastny (1979).

in each society in fomenting the conflict,[9] must also be considered in a comprehensive explanation.

Regardless of the reasons for the eruption, the Cold War ultimately became the central facet of postwar American foreign policy. Its shadow stretches across the entire spectrum of the postwar American response to its world environment.

To better understand the assumptions and actions that have given shape to America's policy toward the Soviet Union, we must go beyond inquiry into the origins of the Cold War and examine, first, the immediate circumstances that gave rise to the containment strategy, and, second, how the containment policy has evolved over time in response to changing circumstances and the way different administrations have sought to implement it. This can be accomplished by charting the course of containment from its birth in 1947 to the present.

The American Strategy of Containment: Evolutionary Phases

Whatever the origins of the Cold War, few could question that the containment doctrine that became a part of it also became the cornerstone of postwar American foreign policy. Indeed, the history of American foreign policy can largely be written in terms of how the containment doctrine has been interpreted and applied to the communist bloc in general and the Soviet Union in particular. Taking on different colorations in response to changing circumstances and situations, the policy of containing the influence of the Soviet Union has endured, largely intact, since 1947.[10]

As shown in the chronology in the Appendix, the record of major diplomatic events in the postwar period is dominated by American initiatives toward, and reactions to, the Soviet Union and its sometime allies in the context of the persistent foreign policy strategy of containment. Although the pattern remains constant, continual adaptation is also apparent.

Consider the quantitative evidence displayed in Figure 3.1. This chart shows at least three characteristics of Soviet-American interactions since 1948. First, a high level of conflict has existed between the superpowers. Second, short-term periods of intense conflict have been interspersed with short-term periods of relative cooperation, producing a discernible *cyclical* arrangement.

[9]See Sherry (1977) for an engaging analysis which attributes the origins of the Cold War to the planning of American strategists during World War II for the postwar era. According to his thesis, much of the reasoning and rhetoric of the Cold War derived from American military planning during World War II, which rationalized a global policeman role for the United States and identified the Soviet Union as the "next" enemy.

[10]It is difficult to date when the Cold War and its attendant containment strategy officially became recognized and operative, and to separate the precondition, formative stage from its active phase. Those "present at the creation" (Acheson, 1969) offer different accounts of when the containment strategy gained wide acceptance and began to exert a policy impact. Evidence from recently declassified documents suggests that within official circles, containment did not become fully operative until as late as the onset of the Korean War in 1950 (see May, 1984).

And third, a trend toward relaxed tensions and growing accommodation was evident in the decade between the mid-1960s and the mid-1970s—a trend reversed during the late 1970s, as the hostility that marked earlier periods returned. The resumption of antagonism has persisted into the mid-1980s, with evidence suggesting that superpower conciliation and détente rest, as ever, on foundations that are fragile at best.[11]

In accordance with the trends depicted in Figure 3.1, it is possible for analytical purposes to divide the history of the American foreign policy of containing the Soviet Union into five chronologically ordered phases. Although such a periodization is necessarily somewhat arbitrary, the diplomatic record seems to suggest that reading of the history of American policy.[12]

Belligerence, 1947–1952. The birth of the containment policy in 1947 was preceded (as already noted) by a brief period of wary friendship between the wartime allies, characterized by American apprehension about Soviet intentions and growing distrust of Soviet motives. This ambivalent interlude was punctuated by growing pessimism about the prospects for continued amity and growing reluctance to accept the Soviet Union as an ally. The years following this short period of rapidly deteriorating trust proved to be formative ones for American foreign policy. For it was in this period that the containment strategy was given birth and American policy toward the Soviets became decidedly *belligerent*. All pretense of collaboration with the Soviets ceased. The Cold War erupted and was in constant danger of becoming hot.

Let us review the sequence of events that led to the idea of containment and to the embittered relations with the Soviets that characterized this period.

In February 1946, Stalin gave a speech in which he spoke of "the inevitability of conflict with the capitalist powers. He urged the Soviet people not to be deluded that the end of the war meant that the nation could relax. Rather, intensified efforts were needed to strengthen and defend the homeland" (Lovell, 1970). Shortly thereafter, George F. Kennan, then the number two civilian diplomat in the American embassy in Moscow, sent to Washington his

---

[11]The reciprocal, action-reaction nature of Soviet-American interactions is also clearly evident in Figure 3.1. Periods when the United States directed friendly initiatives toward the Soviets have also been periods when the Soviets have acted with friendliness toward the United States; similarly, periods of American belligerence have been periods of Soviet belligerence. Harry Truman's expressed hope "that the Russians would return favor for favor" may not have been farfetched: American actions have tended to provoke similar reactions. Equally noteworthy is the tendency for each superpower to justify its behavior by employing the same rhetoric as its adversary, so that they verbally mimic one another (see Franck and Weisband, 1972). This "tit for tat," quid pro quo propensity suggests that it takes two to make a fight, two to prolong it, and two to reconcile it. "A long dispute," Voltaire observed, "means that both parties are wrong." The principle of reciprocity thus suggests that the United States and the Soviet Union share responsibility for the continuation of their conflicted relationship.

[12]See Gamson and Modigliani (1971), Quester (1971), Brzezinski (1972), Gaddis (1982 and 1983), George (1983a), Ulam (1983 and 1985), Kennan (1976 and 1984), Garthoff (1985), and the evaluations of four experts in Nye (1984) for similar but variant treatments of the evolutionary history and periodization of postwar Soviet-American interactions.

FIGURE 3.1   American-Soviet Relations, 1948–1985*

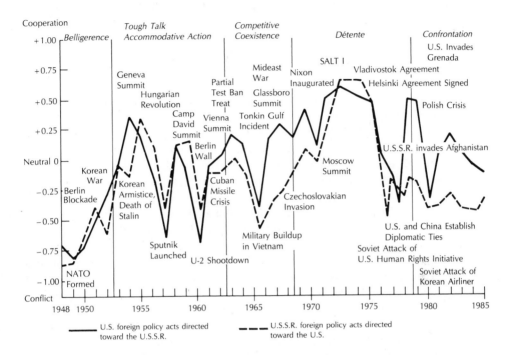

SOURCE: Adapted from Professor Edward E. Azar's Conflict and Peace Data Bank (COPDAB), with data based on Azar and Sloan (1973) as updated through 1978 with data supplied by Professor Azar. Data for 1979–1983 are derived from the World Event Interaction Survey (WEIS), as retrieved and compiled by Dr. Frederick A. Rothe. Data for 1984–1985 are provided by Llewellyn D. Howell of Third Point Systems, Inc., of Monterey, California.

*The net conflict index is obtained by summing the proportion of cooperative acts (+%) and conflictual acts (−%). For example, if in a given year, the United States sent 100 acts to the Soviet Union, with 75 being cooperative and 25 conflictual, then the index would be 0.75 −0.25 = +0.5. If no acts are initiated, or if the cooperative and conflictual acts balanced (that is, +50% and −50%), the index is zero, indicating a mixed, ambivalent relationship. Data for years prior to 1948 are not available. Data for 1984 through 1985 vary from the earlier WEIS data in the definition of "cooperation" by excluding "comments" and including "consult."

famous "long telegram" assessing the motivations of the Soviet leadership. The conclusions of Kennan's assessment were ominous: "In summary, we have here a political force committed fanatically to the belief that with [the] U.S. there can be no permanent modus vivendi, that it is desirable and necessary that the internal harmony of our society be disrupted, our traditional way of life be destroyed, the international authority of our state be broken, if Soviet power is to be secure."

Kennan's assessment was widely circulated in Washington and presumably had an important bearing on the crystallization of thinking about Soviet postwar intentions. Somewhat later (when he became head of the State Department's policy-planning staff), Kennan's ideas received even wider circulation through the publication of his famous article in the influential journal *Foreign Affairs* (1947), which he signed "X" instead of identifying himself as its author. In it, Kennan argued that Soviet leaders would forever feel insecure about their political ability to maintain power against forces both within Soviet society itself and in the outside world. Their insecurity would lead to an activist—and perhaps hostile—Soviet foreign policy. Yet it was in the power of the United States to increase the strains under which the Soviet leadership would have to operate, perhaps thus leading to a gradual mellowing or eventual end of Soviet power. Hence Kennan made what eventually became an often-repeated and accepted statement: "In these circumstances it is clear that the main element of any United States policy toward the Soviet Union must be that of a long-term, patient but firm and vigilant *containment* of Russian expansive tendencies" (Kennan, 1947, emphasis added). It was not long before this intellectual assessment received such wide publicity that Truman made it the cornerstone of American postwar policy. Provoked in part by domestic turmoil in Turkey and civil war within Greece (which he and some others believed to be communist inspired), Truman stated, "I believe that it must be the policy of the United States to support free peoples who are resisting attempted subjugation by armed minorities or by outside pressures."

Truman's declaration, eventually known as the Truman Doctrine, was based on a view of international politics as a contest for world domination, with the Soviet Union as an imperial power bent on world conquest. A crystallized American policy emerged, which placed as its point of departure a commitment to participate in this contest and to contain the Soviet Union's global designs:

> Whenever and wherever an anti-Communist government was threatened, by indigenous insurgents, foreign invasion, or even diplomatic pressure (as with Turkey), the United States would supply political, economic, and most of all military aid. The Truman Doctrine came close to shutting the door against any revolution, since the terms "free peoples" and "anti-Communist" were thought to be synonymous. All . . . any dictatorship had to do to get American aid was to claim that its opponents were Communist. (Ambrose, 1985: 86)

The crusade laid out by the Truman Doctrine was, of course, the Cold War with the Soviet Union. The war became a national obsession, demanding the commitment of many of the nation's resources. Containment became *the* foreign policy of the United States and colored everything else, including domestic politics.

Whether the policy of containment was appropriate, even at the time of its initial promulgation, remains controversial among historians. Kennan was surprised and eventually alarmed at the way his famous statement was misinterpreted, abused, and ultimately taken out of context. He has noted that, upon publication of his "X" article, containment soon became an "indestructible myth," a doctrine "which was then identified with the foreign policy of the Truman administration." But he has also noted the anguish he experienced with the way his assessment was interpreted:

> I . . . naturally went to great lengths to disclaim the view, imputed to me by implication . . . that containment was a matter of stationing military forces around the Soviet borders and preventing any outbreak of Soviet military aggressiveness. I protested . . . against the implication that the Russians were aspiring to invade other areas and that the task of American policy was to prevent them from doing so. "The Russians don't want," I insisted, "to invade anyone. It is not in their tradition. They tried it once in Finland and got their fingers burned. They don't want war of any kind. Above all, they don't want the open responsibility that official invasion brings with it." (Kennan, 1967: 361)

Ten years after his "containment" message had become American policy, Kennan reiterated that "the image of a Stalinist Russia poised and yearning to attack the West, and deterred only by our possession of atomic weapons, was largely a creation of the Western imagination." But Kennan's disclaimers[13] notwithstanding, the "containment myth," as Kennan called it in his memoirs, "never fully lost its spell." It became, and remains, one of the guiding premises of American foreign policy.

It was not until the Korean War, perhaps, that the containment strategy emerged as a clearly articulated approach toward coping with the Soviet threat (May, 1984). The policy prescriptions associated with it helped nonethe less to heighten the American tendency to view instability anywhere as Soviet conspiracy. It was not only the insurgency in Greece and the domestic strife in Turkey which were interpreted as part of a Soviet offensive. Nearly all other crises were explained by that model as well. The results were in part self-fulfilling, as a seemingly unending series of situations were defined as Cold War incidents, including the Soviet refusal to withdraw troops from Iran, the com-

---

[13]For a more recent statement of Kennan's position on American foreign policy toward the Soviet Union, see Kennan (1984); for a review of the evolution and interpretation of his thoughts on this subject, see Magastadt (1984).

munist coup d'état in Czechoslovakia, the Berlin blockade, the formation of NATO in 1949 and the Warsaw Pact in 1955, and, most importantly, the acquisition of power on the mainland by the Chinese communists and the Korean War and Taiwan Straits crises which followed. Hence the relationship between the two states was not simply "cold"; it was one of open belligerence. Relations became frozen in an embittered quarrel that continually threatened to erupt into open warfare. Revealingly, memoranda later released indicate that in 1952 President Truman twice considered all-out war against the Soviet Union and China (*New York Times*, August 3, 1980), and in 1954 Eisenhower and Dulles considered the use of the atomic bomb against the Chinese communists (*New York Times*, June 8, 1984).

To be sure, in the heat of confrontation there were moments of cooperation. In this period a few concessions, such as the lifting of the Berlin blockade, were interspersed with the hostile actions. But these were more "cooling" actions for the purpose of bargaining rather than true efforts at conciliation. Both the United States and the Soviet Union played the game of power politics with a vengeance, and both pursued the same goal: curtailing the influence of the other and stopping the adversary's presumed effort to conquer the world. The token acts of cooperation were little more than the kinds of communications between adversaries necessary to continue the contest. Each side saw the world in terms of pure conflict: what one side won, the other necessarily lost. Compromise within such "zero sum" thinking was impossible. Since each contestant projected a negative image onto its adversary, while maintaining a virtuous self-image, conflict was endemic. The strong kernel of truth in the perceptions of hostility by each reinforced and sustained the spiral of distrust and suspicion.

Tough Talk, Accommodative Action, 1953–1962. Although the phase of Soviet-American relations described as belligerence was marked by the expectation of general war between the two states, the United States enjoyed a clear military superiority over the Soviet Union, for it alone possessed "the winning weapon" and the means to deliver it.[14] But in 1949 the American atomic monopoly was successfully broken by the Soviet Union. Thereafter the relative strategic strengths of the two superpowers have had a noticeable effect on the entire range of their relations and evolving political postures toward each other.

The search by the Soviets for equality with American military capabilities led to a second phase in the evolution of the strategy of containment, a phase characterized by *tough talk but accommodative action.* The United States talked as if war were imminent, but in deeds (especially with the termination of the

---

[14]See Herken (1982) for an interpretation of the impact of the atomic bomb on the development of the Cold War.

Korean War) it acted with increasing caution and restraint.[15] President Eisenhower and his secretary of state, John Foster Dulles, promised a "roll-back" of the iron curtain and the "liberation" of the "captive nations" of Eastern Europe. They criticized the allegedly "soft" and "reactive" containment doctrine of Truman, and they claimed to reject containment in favor of an ambitious "winning" strategy that would end the confrontation with godless communism for good. But communism was not rolled back in Eastern Europe, and containment was not replaced by a bolder foreign policy strategy. In practice, Eisenhower and Dulles followed the same basic foreign policy as Truman and Acheson. " 'We can never rest [until communism is defeated],' Ike had said, but rest they did, except in their speeches" (Ambrose, 1985).

Thus, despite the threatening posture assumed by the United States toward the Soviet Union, more was promised than delivered. And significantly, in the midst of this verbal confrontation, behavior began to change. A first step toward détente, however halting and tentative, was taken with the Geneva Summit meetings (1955), when the two rivals established a precedent for mutual discussion of world problems. With hindsight it is clear that Geneva represented more a pause in hostilities than a fundamental change in policy, since throughout the 1950s the Cold War remained an ever-present threat to peace. More symptomatic of this period was Dulles's practice of brinkmanship and his threat of "massive retaliation," through which he hoped to force the Soviets into submission. But Geneva was a start.

Competitive Coexistence, 1963–1968. Beginning on the heels of Soviet missiles in Cuba and including the onset of the Vietnam conflict, a third discernible period in America's policy of containing the Soviet Union can be characterized as an era of *competitive coexistence*. Continuing, if restrained, hostility coincided with the emergence of an unrestrained arms race, which threw the ability of the superpowers to coexist without war into doubt and tested their ability to manage peacefully their recurrent crises.

But amidst these recurrences of Cold War politics were developments which may be interpreted as the origins of détente. All appear to have been tied to the growing parity of American and Soviet military capabilities and to the increasing awareness of the suicidal consequences of nuclear war. Given those incentives and the fact that the alternatives were coexistence or nonexistence, the superpowers searched for ways to coexist. Some of the major issues were resolved; for example, the United States tacitly accepted a divided Germany and Soviet hegemony in Eastern Europe. The precedent for communication established at Geneva and later at the 1959 Camp David meeting was

---

[15]That the period was punctuated by a series of Cold War crises and confrontations (notably Suez, Hungary, the U-2 affair, and Cuba) is undeniable. Noteworthy, however, was the fact that none of these threats to the peace culminated in war and that steps toward improved relations (for example, the Camp David meeting of 1959) were taken simultaneously.

followed by the installation of the "hot line" in 1963 linking the White House and the Kremlin with a direct communication system; the Glassboro summit meeting (1967); and negotiated agreements, such as the Antarctic Treaty (1959), the Partial Test Ban Treaty (1963), the Outer Space Treaty (1967), and the Nuclear Nonproliferation Treaty (1968).

At the American University commencement exercises in 1963, President Kennedy spoke about the necessity of reducing tensions:

> Among the many traits the people of [the United States and the Soviet Union] have in common, none is stronger than our mutual abhorrence of war. Almost unique among the major world powers, we have never been at war with each other. And no nation in the history of battle ever suffered more than the Soviet Union suffered in the course of the Second World War. At least twenty million lost their lives. . . .
>
> Today, should total war ever break out again—no matter how—our two countries would become the primary targets. It is an ironical but accurate fact that the two strongest powers are the two in the most danger of devastation. . . . We are both caught up in a vicious and dangerous cycle in which suspicion on one side breeds suspicion on the other and new weapons beget counterweapons.
>
> In short, both the United States and its allies, and the Soviet Union and its allies, have a mutually deep interest in a just and genuine peace and in halting the arms race. . . .
>
> So let us not be blind to our differences, but let us also direct attention to our common interests and to the means by which those differences can be resolved. And if we cannot end now our differences, at least we can help make the world safe for diversity.

Kennedy did not inaugurate a fundamental change in Soviet-American relations, but in tone and attitude he clearly signaled a shift in how the United States hoped to deal with a potentially hostile adversary. The Soviet Union by this time also had begun to change its political rhetoric. In particular, it began to emphasize (in a propagandistic fashion?) the necessity for the "peaceful coexistence" of capitalism and socialism, a view far different from the revolutionary thrust of traditional Marxist-Leninist principles. Admittedly those token moves were a far cry from sustained cooperation between the ideological antagonists—the Kennedy administration in many respects was as resolutely anti-Soviet as its predecessors—but they did signal a departure from the antagonism and threats that had typified Soviet-American relations. Cooperative behavior was evident, however intermittent and fleeting, amidst a pattern of continued competition for advantage and influence.

Détente: 1969–1978. A fourth stage in the evolution of America's containment strategy commenced with the inauguration of Nixon and the installation of

Henry Kissinger as his national security adviser.[16] A new and different American approach to the Soviets was initiated, an approach officially labeled, for the first time, *détente*: a policy and process designed to relax tensions between the superpowers.

As a strategy for peace, détente was meant to create "a vested interest in cooperation and restraint" (Kissinger, 1973), "an environment in which competitors can regulate and restrain their differences and ultimately move from competition to cooperation" (Kissinger, 1974b). The policy of relaxing tensions with the Soviets and of moving toward permanent accommodation and cooperation was based on a "linkage" theory: the development of economic, political, and strategic ties between the two nations, equally rewarding to both, would bind the two in a common fate, thereby removing the incentives for conflict and war. Soviet global aspirations would be mollified, according to proponents of the view, because Soviet peace and prosperity would depend on the continuation of peaceful links with the United States. The linkage strategy, in Kissinger's words, was "based on a balance between the carrot and the stick." It offered trade arrangements and technology exchanges to the Soviets in return for the exercise of restraint in their international conduct. Underlying the initiative was the belief that money could buy influence over the U.S.S.R.; enticed by the promise of economic subsidies and of Western pledges of non-aggression, the Soviets, it was reasoned, would behave according to American standards of international conduct and perhaps even relax their totalitarian grip and undergo domestic liberalization.

Did détente mark as fundamental a shift in American-Soviet relations as Nixon, Kissinger, and Ford were prone to claim? Did it signal the end of the containment policy that had guided American foreign policy since 1947? Did the enmity characteristic of Soviet-American relations cease with this new terminology and strategy? Probably not. The surface cordiality between the two countries was always tenuous and fragile, and the cooperative verbiage failed to terminate the consensus that American policy ought to place the containment of Soviet influence at the top of its agenda. Accordingly, détente can be seen as "part of the cold war, not an alternative to it" (Goodman, 1975). Détente thus entailed a departure in the *means* of containment, not a challenge to the *ends* of American policy (Litwak, 1984).

Détente was based on Kissinger's conviction that American power relative to that of the Soviet Union was rapidly diminishing, that the Soviet Union was no longer militarily inferior to the United States but was an ascendant power whose influence was growing. The central problem for the United States,

---

[16]Kennan (1976) suggests that what was to become known as "détente" actually could have commenced as early as 1965, had it not been victimized by (1) Soviet action in Czechoslovakia in 1968 and (2) American action in Vietnam: "It was not until the first could be forgotten, and the second brought into process of liquidation in the early 1970s, that prospects again opened up for further progress along the lines pioneered by Messrs. Johnson and Rusk some four to six years earlier."

given this predicament, was to create a situation in which American losses would be minimized and the status quo preserved. As cogently argued by Leslie Gelb (1976), the Nixon-Kissinger strategy for dealing with the challenging change in the geopolitical situation was "to evolve détente into a new form of containment of the Soviet Union—or, better still, self-containment on the part of the Russians." In Kissinger's conception, it was thus an attempt to devise "new means to the old ends of containment." Serfaty (1978) states the expectation behind the strategy this way: "Détente did not mean global reconciliation with the Soviet Union. . . . Instead, détente implied the selective continuation of containment by economic and political inducement and at the price of accommodation through concessions that were more or less balanced." When in a position of superiority, the United States had practiced containment by coercion and force; from a new position of parity, containment was now to be practiced by seduction and cooperation.

The reciprocated cooperation evident during the period of détente nevertheless represented an important shift in a critical global relationship. For the first time in several decades the expectation of war between the superpowers receded. As demonstrated in Figure 3.1, cooperative interaction became more commonplace than hostile relations. Visits, cultural exchanges, trade agreements, and collaborative technological ventures replaced threats, warnings, and confrontations as principal modes of interaction. Part of that change stemmed from the strategic necessity of avoiding suicidal war; part also presumably stemmed from awareness of the mutual advantages that could be derived from collaboration.

The change that transpired in this period can also be accounted for by each superpower's growing sensitivity to and empathy for the security needs of the other, by tacit revival of the sphere-of-influence concept and the advantages it could confer on the management of conflicts, and by shared concern for the aspirations of a potentially powerful China. The escalating costs of a continued arms race may also have contributed to the development of détente. And, without a doubt, the eroding position of the United States in the international hierarchy and growing awareness of the constraints that erosion placed on the ability of the United States to play the role of global policeman (as evidenced by the Nixon Doctrine) encouraged the creation of a new approach to the control of the Soviet menace.

Confrontation, 1979–The Present. The period of détente allowed the United States to attend to other foreign policy concerns. The Carter administration's "trilateral" approach, which emphasized an active pursuit of better economic and political relations with both industrialized and Third World[17] nations as a

[17]Third World refers to the (economically) developing or less developed countries (LDCs) of Asia, Africa, and Latin America. (A few European countries, such as Greece, Portugal, and Yugoslavia, are also sometimes included.) Although we shall use this term throughout the book, it is important to note that wide differences exist among developing nations. For example, the Third

way of averting the potential isolation of the United States in the global community, and its advocacy of human rights as the centerpiece of its foreign policy, underscored the reorientations that were envisioned. Thus in the period of détente American policy makers showed renewed concern for friendship with Japan and Western Europe and for alleviating the ills of the poor in hopes of eliciting good will toward the United States.

Despite such developments, and despite the careful nurturing of détente by the United States for nearly a decade, the policy did *not* become a permanent alternative to more militant forms of containment.[18] That fact was dramatically underscored in 1979, when a fifth stage in America's approach to the Soviet Union commenced with a return to confrontational posturing by the superpowers. Already in 1978, as events unfolded, strains of disharmony could be heard in the air of détente, and some observers began to ask if the two superpowers were moving into a postdétente phase best characterized as Cold War II.

Those subscribing to that view noted that confrontation rather than accommodation had once again become the dominant mode of interaction between the superpowers. The words and deeds that each directed toward the other became more bitter and hostile, reflecting the deterioration in their relationship. Others characterized the hardening of relations as confirmation of their belief that the Cold War had never disappeared, even during the period of normalized relations that was called détente. Indeed, the evidence summarized in Figure 3.1 suggests that the slide from détente to renewed conflict began during the Ford administration (1974–1976), perhaps dating from early 1975 with the failure to expand Soviet-American commercial ties anticipated by the Nixon administration (see chapter seven). The figure also suggests that the slide from détente gained speed steadily throughout the Carter years, propelled perhaps by the Carter administration's criticism of the Soviet Union's human rights record.

That trend reached its culmination following the Soviet intervention in Afghanistan. In the immediate aftermath of the invasion, President Carter announced that his opinion of the Soviet Union and its goals had changed more in a single week than throughout his existing term in office. Promptly thereafter, he enunciated a new "doctrine" when he warned in his State of the Union address that "an attempt by any outside force to gain control of the Persian Gulf region will be regarded as an assault on the vital interests of the United States of America and such an assault will be repelled by any means neces-

---

World includes the oil-rich nations of the Middle East, the handful of fast-growing developing nations known as the Newly Industrialized Countries, and the thirty-one nations considered by the United Nations to be the "least developed" (LLDCs) of the developing nations (Kegley and Wittkopf, 1985b: 81–86). Nations falling into the latter category are sometimes referred to as the Fourth World.

[18]For thoughtful interpretations of why détente failed, see Breslauer (1983) and Hoffmann (1984).

sary, including military force." The Soviet Union was clearly the intended target of the message, Afghanistan its prelude. Then, in May 1980, Carter described the perceived Soviet threat in even more dramatic terms: "Soviet aggression in Afghanistan—unless checked—confronts all the world with the most serious strategic challenge since the Cold War began." By that time the United States had already initiated a series of countermoves, including an effort to organize a worldwide boycott of the 1980 Moscow Olympics, suspension of American grain exports to the Soviet Union, and other limitations of the trade ties between the superpowers that had been nurtured during détente. Senate ratification of the SALT II treaty was doomed in the process.

With Ronald Reagan's assumption of power in 1981, the confrontational approach toward the Soviet Union that emerged in the wake of the Afghan intervention intensified to levels reminiscent of the atmosphere in Washington when the containment doctrine was first enunciated in the late 1940s. The rhetoric harkened back to the tough talk of Eisenhower, the competitiveness of Kennedy, and even the belligerence of Truman. President Reagan's statements revealed a belief system that viewed the Soviets as incorrigibly hostile (see Leng, 1984). He asserted that the Soviet Union "underlies all the unrest that is going on," and classified it as "the focus of evil in the modern world," governed by a regime willing "to commit any crime, to lie, to cheat" to attain world communism. This verbiage reinforced the expectation that tensions with the Soviets would not be relaxed. Again in Reagan's words: "It's time to stop pretending that détente with the Soviet Union is still alive." Richard Pipes's challenge in 1981 while a member of Reagan's National Security Council staff that the Soviets would have to choose either "peacefully changing their Communist system . . . or going to war," warned that escalation of the confrontation from talk to the actual use of force was not unthinkable.

The latest postwar phase found some of these tough words matched by equally tough diplomatic deeds. Economically, politically, and, most of all, militarily, the United States sought to challenge directly the Soviet Union in an effort to put it on the defensive. Included was not only a propaganda barrage but also the resumption of the arms race in which both participated energetically. The global reach of the East-West confrontation to new territory (for example, to Central America), efforts to sell the alleged virtues of their economic and political systems worldwide, and the willingness to put the contest with the adversary above all other goals, including economic growth, typified the superpowers' actions in the mid-1980s. A *Grave New World* (Ledeen, 1985) of superpower crisis prevailed that continued to provoke war fears, demonstrating that the superpowers are less capable of preventing crises from arising than of managing them after they erupt (George, 1983a). Crises symptomatic of the conflicted relationship included the destruction by the Soviets of a Korean Airlines 747 aircraft, the repeated threats by both sides to rupture arms control talks, the Soviet boycott of the 1984 Olympic Games in Los Angeles, and the American invasion of Grenada. President Mikhail Gorbachev summarized the alarming state of Soviet-American relations by observing (September 9, 1985) that "That situation is very complex, very tense. I would even go so far as to say it is explosive."[19] Absent was any pretense toward compromise or a willingness to mix cooperative maneuvers with conflictual ones. The East-West conflict thus veered toward patterns evident in the superpowers' relationship earlier in the postwar era, demonstrating once again their tendency to put the unilateral search for advantage ahead of the search for more collaborative and less antagonistic relations.

As the 1990s approach, the state of Soviet-American relations remains uncertain, the U.S. policy options unclear (Caldwell, 1985). Distrust lingers over a large number of issues, including the START talks (Strategic Arms Reduction Talks) on reducing long-range nuclear weapons, negotiations for an agreement to control intermediate-range nuclear weapons (INF), the testing of space weapons, superpower interventions in foreign conflicts, on-site inspections to ban the production of chemical weapons, the reduction of nonnuclear forces in Europe, stalemate on the long-running Stockholm Conference of Security and Cooperation in Europe, the debate over alleged human rights violations, and the continuing propaganda invectives which have exacerbated suspicions about both adversaries' professed desire to improve relations. These and other issues are destined to undermine the prospects for a relaxation of tensions. It is difficult to see how this wide chasm might be closed in the foreseeable future.

What *is* foreseeable is the likely continuation of the global containment strategy of the United States. It appears firmly entrenched. President Reagan's enthusiastic (and nostalgic) embrace of the anticommunist containment policy attests to the resilience of the postwar policy assumptions that gave containment its birth, and to the difficulty of framing an alternative conception on which to base American foreign policy and which wide segments of the American public can understand and support. As explained by a recent assistant for national security affairs, Robert C. McFarlane, ". . . The rivalry between the United States and the Soviet Union is close to immutable," with the result that "Anyone who works on the concrete issues dividing these countries knows that practical policy decisions are never made on the assumption that a fundamental change in Soviet-American relations is anywhere in sight. To the contrary, we have to take competition as a given and do the best we can."

Although a militant, confrontational approach toward containing the Soviet Union enjoyed wide currency in the Reagan administration, it is important to recall that the postwar record suggests that the premises underlying the containment policy will likely be questioned intermittently in the future. As Secretary of State George Shultz reminded his countrymen in late 1984:

> Historically, American policy has swung from one extreme to another. We have gone through periods of implacable opposition—forgoing negotiations, building up our defenses, and confronting Soviet aggression. Then, concerned about confrontation, we have entered periods of seeming détente, during which some were

---

[19]For an analysis of Soviet leaders' perceptions of Reagan's foreign policy, see Talbott (1984b).

tempted to neglect our defenses and ignore Soviet threats to our interests around the world—only once again to be disillusioned by some Soviet action that sent us swinging back to a more implacable posture.

If this characterization is accurate (that is, if the past cyclical pattern is a guide to the future), then American policy might at some point in the future once again experience a period in which the level of tension with the Soviets is reduced and efforts are made to reach lasting accommodations. But the historical pattern does *not* predict the eventual abandonment of containment as the cornerstone of American foreign policy.

If an oscillation between the extremes of militancy and moderation toward the Soviet Union is characteristic of American foreign policy over the long term, the conclusion is invited that what Zbigniew Brzezinski (President Carter's assistant for national security affairs) termed ''contestation'' is likely to prove fundamental to the Soviet-American relationship. The term seems relevant because a *contest* involves elements of both conflict and cooperation, and both the United States and the Soviet Union seem compelled simultaneously to oppose one another throughout the globe and to cooperate because their common need to avoid nuclear devastation necessitates it. Former Under Secretary of State Lawrence Eagleburger summarized well the policy predicament: ''Our policy toward the U.S.S.R. starts with the fact that both of us have weapons of almost unimaginable destructive force. Each of us can do mortal damage to the other in an afternoon. We have radically different political values, visions of the proper social order and aspirations for the future of the international system. We must steer a middle course between the friendship we cannot have and the war we must not have.''

THE POSTWAR PATTERN OF AMERICAN FOREIGN POLICY: ALTERNATIVE CHARACTERIZATIONS OF GUIDING PREMISES

It would be misleading to suggest that the foregoing three assumptions—that the United States should pursue an internationalist, indeed, globalist, foreign policy; that communism constitutes the primary threat to the nation; that the Soviet Union, as the leader of the communist challenge, must be contained—adequately capture all the objectives and values on which postwar American foreign policy has been founded. To a considerable extent, nevertheless, they have substantially shaped American behavior abroad for over forty years. Although simplifications, the assumptions describe the central premises underlying American foreign policy, and they depict what is most continuous and most characteristic about the policy.

Still, they have not operated in isolation. Other assumptions have also characterized the pattern of postwar American foreign policy. Some of these, to various degrees, have also helped to shape the three premises which have been highlighted and have contributed to their postwar persistence. Here we focus attention on four of these secondary characterizations,[20] the theses that American foreign policy is (1) antirevolutionary; (2) imperialistic; (3) moralistic; and (4) "realistic." All of these have been linked, in one way or another, to the themes of globalism, anticommunism, and containment. All have helped to preserve these patterns.

The United States: An Antirevolutionary, Status Quo Power in a Revolutionary Age?

Critics of contemporary American foreign policy (for example, Lens, 1964; Gurtov, 1974; Heilbroner, 1968) allege that in the process of playing the role of great power on a global scale, the United States has shown a marked preference for the prevention of social revolutions in other countries: America has sought preservation of the status quo and has taken repeated actions to guard against potentially disruptive revolutions elsewhere, most notably in the Third World countries of Asia, Africa, and Latin America. The United States, in short, has become a counterrevolutionary nation in a revolutionary age. In the process, it has prostituted its own democratic ideals, thereby raising the question of whether "a democratic superpower [is] a contradiction in terms" (Isaak, 1977).

Given the United States' own revolutionary heritage, a fear of the overthrow of repressive regimes is ironic. Senator J. William Fulbright, in a speech before his colleagues in the United States Senate in 1965, summarized this view by asserting, "We are not, as we like to claim in Fourth of July speeches, the most truly revolutionary nation on earth; we are, on the contrary, much closer to being the most unrevolutionary nation on earth."

Why? The American fear of communism, it is argued, has led the United States to equate revolution with communism and therefore to oppose the forces of change within other societies. That posture denies the possibility that some upheavals are merely local reactions to oppression and to the totalitarian governments (left or right) which deny freedom to their own people. Neal Houghton (1968) summarizes this interpretation: "The convenient 'Communism' label, carrying a connotation of incarnate evil, has facilitated Washington's . . . efforts to prevent or destroy all unwelcome basic social revolutions, everywhere on earth." The consequences of this assumption have been summarized by the observation that "In the contest between the colonial powers of Europe and their colonies, the United States took the side of the former, not because it was in favor of colonialism, but because it was afraid that Communism might be the alternative to colonialism. The champion of freedom became the defender and restorer of the colonial status quo" (Morgenthau, 1985).

---

[20]For still other descriptions of the beliefs that give definition to the American approach to world affairs, see Crabb (1976); Stupak (1976); Kegley and Wittkopf (1982b); and McCormick (1985).

The symptoms of this counterrevolutionary penchant are numerous. Consider the following:

1. For a time during the Truman administration, the Declaration of Independence (defending the right of peoples everywhere to rebel against an unjust government) was removed from American overseas libraries. The principles expressed in the Declaration were apparently considered too inflammatory for other people—it might give them ideas!

2. On more than one occasion, the United States has suppressed democratic elections. A case in point occurred in Germany following World War II when the Russians, against their self-interest, proposed the holding of elections which they could not possibly win. Surprisingly, the United States objected to them for the ostensible reason that the communists might gain control through the ballot (Tullock, 1974).

   A better known case occurred in 1956, when the United States refused to permit United Nations-supervised elections to be held in Vietnam, as called for by the 1954 Geneva Accords on Indochina. The reason? The democratic electoral process was to be encouraged as long as the election of communists was not risked. Eisenhower (1963) reported in his memoirs: "I have never talked or corresponded with a person knowledgeable in Indo-Chinese affairs who did not agree that had elections been held . . . possibly 80 percent of the populace would have voted for the Communist Ho Chi Minh as their leader."

3. American support for countries ruled at one time or another by dictators is indisputable. Spain, Portugal, Paraguay, Argentina, the Dominican Republic, Guatemala, Brazil, Haiti, Greece, Cuba, South Korea, Taiwan, Vietnam, the Philippines, and Iran are among them. In these and many other cases, the United States has armed and otherwise supported some of the most ruthless tyrannies in the modern world (while referring to their governments as members of "the Free World"!). Such dictatorships shared a common characteristic, however: they were anticommunist.

The record indicates, in other words, that the United States has generally (though there are exceptions) chosen to play it safe by siding with the existing governing elite, no matter how antidemocratic, rather than side with the forces of social change. That led the U.S. to support "governments throughout the world whose political philosophy and practice were completely at odds with what goes by the name of American principles of government" (Morgenthau, 1985). President Kennedy perhaps as well as anyone helped to explain this antirevolutionary instinct when he commented on the situation faced by the United States in the Dominican Republic following the assassination of Dominican dictator Rafael Trujillo:

There are three possibilities in descending order of preference: a decent democratic regime, a continuation of the Trujillo regime [a dictatorship] or a Castro regime [a communist government]. We ought to aim at the first, but we really can't renounce the second until we are sure that we can avoid the third. (cited in Schlesinger, 1965: 769)

It was that perceived dilemma which led the United States in Cuba to support Fulgencio Batista and create Fidel Castro; in Vietnam to support Ngo Dinh Diem and Nguyen Van Thieu and end up with Ho Chi Minh and his successors; in Iran to support the Shah and find itself opposed by Ayatollah Khomeini. By taking a militant antirevolutionary position, the United States has repeatedly found itself on the side of the oppressors and against the people, or, in other words, against local nationalism.

Paradoxically, by supporting the opponents of social change, the United States has helped create the conditions most conducive to success by its communist adversaries, who play on popular aspirations (see Box 3.3). It seems that the more strenuous are America's efforts to restrain insurrection abroad, the less likely are democratic institutions to flourish, and, perhaps, the more inevitable become further revolutions (LaFeber, 1983). Could it be that this policy pattern has produced for the United States the very outcomes it has sought to avoid, namely, repression, communism, and regimes relentlessly anti-American in allegiance? Indeed, could it be that a globalist policy aimed at preserving the status quo runs counter to the nation's long-term interests? "Once America stands for opposition to change," warned Henry Wallace in 1947, "we are lost. America will become the most hated nation in the world."

BOX 3.3 Frank Church, Former Chairman of the Senate Foreign Relations Committee, Reflects on the Fallacies of Postwar American Foreign Policy

---

". . . The stupidity of it! . . . [W]e seem unable to learn from the failure of our Vietnam policy, or the equally evident failure of our hard-line policy toward Castro in Cuba. It is this idea that the communist threat is everywhere that has made our government its captive and its victim.

"Somehow, some day, this country has got to learn to live with revolution in the Third World. It's endemic. It's relatively easy to suppress revolution in Grenada, so we congratulate ourselves. It's more difficult to suppress it in Nicaragua or Central America, so we fret about that. But it will be impossible when it comes to Brazil or Argentina.

"This country has become so conservative—so fearful—that we have come to see revolution anywhere in the world as a threat to the United States. It's nonsense. And yet that policy we have followed has cost us so many lives, so much treasure, such setbacks to our vital interests, as a great power ought not to endure.

"Until we learn to live with revolution, we will continue to blunder, and it will work to the Soviets' advantage. It will put them on the winning side, while we put ourselves on the side of rotten, corrupt regimes that end up losing.

"And each time one of those regimes is overthrown, it feeds the paranoia in this country about the spread of communism. It furthers the premises of the national security state, which means more militarism, more censorship, more spending, more deficits—and more casualties.

"The thing that is so discouraging is that no one seems to challenge the premise of our policy. . . ."

SOURCE: David A. Broder, "Frank Church's Challenge," The *Washington Post National Weekly Edition*, February 6, 1984, p. 4.

Is American Foreign Policy Imperialistic?

Historians known as revisionists (see Melanson, 1983) have advanced a set of propositions pointing to another possible wellspring of postwar American diplomatic practice: economic imperialism.[21] According to the revisionists, profits, not peace, have been the nation's top priority; preserving economic prosperity at home through foreign trade and investment is the primary objective of American foreign policy. The beliefs that American foreign policy accordingly seeks to serve the interests of investment bankers, that political and military actions are taken for the purpose of addressing economic problems, and that special economic interest groups seek to promote a globalist foreign policy for their own financial benefit are also part of their thesis. American foreign policy is thus seen as responding to the needs of capitalism more so than to any other factor. Foreign policy is seen, therefore, as an extension of the predominant domestic policy. It is axiomatic, from this perspective, that American foreign policy must necessarily be virulently anticommunist as well.

It is difficult either to substantiate or to refute interpretations of American foreign policy that focus on motives. Intentions cannot be inferred easily from behavior patterns. Yet, as evidence, advocates of the imperialism interpretation point to instances where American foreign policy clearly can be traced to commercial goals. The flag *has* followed trade on occasion. American policy makers *have* taken actions to protect foreign investments (not to enhance strategic interests); they *have* sought to sustain and expand the global reach of American enterprises. "Dollar diplomacy" has been a recurrent motif (see

[21]Economic revisionism, which is referred to here, is not to be confused with other revisionist accounts which address the expansionist tendencies of the United States (recall the discussion on the origins of the Cold War above). Economic revisionism is a school of history that sees the United States expanding in search of world markets for the surpluses of capitalism, whereas the diplomatic revisionist school sees the creation of an American imperium as the product of the American pursuit of national power or of its desire to project and to impose its political system on those living abroad. For discussions of empire as a component of America's efforts to achieve political, not economic, preeminence, see Hoffmann (1978) and Liska (1978). It should be noted that both schools share certain assumptions about the sources of American foreign policy that are also held by Marxists in general and the Soviets in particular. But there are important differences. For a review of the multiple determinants the Soviets perceive of American foreign policy, and an assessment of the policy implications of these perceptions, see Griffiths (1984).

Munro, 1964). American foreign aid, trade, tax, and loan policies *have* been affected significantly by the desire to serve American overseas business interests or, on occasion but less frequently, to safeguard domestic markets from foreign penetration.[22] The title of a book-length treatment of the subject, *Empire as a Way of Life* (Williams, 1980), thus summarizes this alleged American approach to its external environment.

Moral Idealism

Two divergent ways of thinking about international affairs are believed to compete for dominance in the value systems of American policy makers. On the one hand, there exists the intellectual tradition of *idealism*, with roots going back to the origins of the Republic. On the other hand (as described below) there resides the so-called *realist* tradition. The history of American diplomacy may be written in terms of the influence of these divergent schools of thought (see Osgood, 1953). When Henry Kissinger spoke while secretary of state of the major problem in American foreign policy being how to avoid "these oscillations between excessive moralism and excessive pragmatism, with excessive concern with power and total rejection of power," he was giving attention to the pronounced impact these incompatible outlooks have periodically exerted on the course of American foreign policy. They have shaped the cyclical movement of American policy between its isolationist and internationalist instincts. Let us examine idealism first.

As a world view, idealism assumes that politics is affected by the fact that human beings are essentially "good" and capable of altruism and cooperation. From this follows a belief that progress is possible, as does the assumption that bad or wicked behavior is the result not of bad people, but of bad institutions which breed such behavior. Consequently, undesirable but recurrent events in international politics such as war can be diminished in frequency and, with appropriate reforms of domestic and international institutions, possibly eliminated.

In order to realize humanitarian objectives and moral values in world affairs, American political idealists have advanced a number of foreign policy proposals that the United States should pursue to universalize those ideals to which the country has traditionally aspired. Support for international organizations, advocacy of an effective global legal order that could bring war under legal controls, search for arms control and disarmament, support for free trade believed to produce good will among nations as well as prosperity

---

[22]The validity of this interpretation of the pattern of American foreign policy is questionable. But the substantial scholarly literature advancing the thesis requires that it be given serious consideration. Exemplary of treatments which emphasize the economic sources of American foreign policy goals, and their imperial consequences, are Williams (1972 and 1980), Magdoff (1969), Julien (1973), Kolko (1969), Oglesby and Shaull (1967), and Gardner (1976). For discussions and critiques of these views, see Taubman (1973), Swomley (1970), Stillman and Pfaff (1966), Tucker (1968 and 1971), and Crabb (1976).

within them, respect for human rights, and, above all perhaps, encouragement of the growth of democratic governments worldwide—these are among the most salient recommendations idealists have made historically for creating a more secure, just, and orderly world environment.

Idealism is often equated with America's preoccupation with what *ought* to prevail in international affairs. Moral idealism finds expression in a self-righteous belief in the inherent ethical virtue and morality of American actions abroad; an ethnocentric disposition to assume that American values and institutions are superior to those of others and that they should be universal; a consequent proclivity to study other people for their own good and to lecture them on how they ought to behave; and a vision of the globe as an arena in which the forces of good and evil continuously combat each other for dominance. Secretary of State George Shultz expressed the tradition of this moralistic sentiment with the claim that "America has a moral responsibility. The lesson of the postwar era is that America must be the leader of the free world; there is no one else to take our place."

Moral idealism tends to extremes of either isolationism or internationalism, for such thinking invites either a withdrawal from an immoral world or a quest to reform it. "An absolute national morality," contends Louis Hartz (1955), "is inspired either to withdraw from 'alien' things or to transform them: it cannot live in comfort constantly by their side." This penchant may thus contribute to the cyclical swings between globalism and disengagement noted above and so evident in the pattern of American diplomatic history.

The years between World War I and World War II are often said to have been the "heyday" of idealist logic, and Woodrow Wilson's ideas about foreign policy usually are regarded as the expression *par excellence* of moral idealism. Fighting "a war to end all wars," pursuing a diplomacy of "open convenants, openly arrived at," "making the world safe for democracy," and advocating the substitution of collective security for interlocking alliance systems and the balance of power system which they lubricate were among the most significant foreign policy initiatives indicative of Wilson's idealism.

Policy pronouncements routinely reveal the grip that this world view continues to exert on American foreign policy thinking even today. The human rights initiative of the Carter administration—captured in the former president's statement that "human rights is the soul of our foreign policy"—is but one of the recent manifestations. So, too, is "Project Democracy," a 1983 initiative of the Reagan administration designed to "foster the infrastructure of democracy" and to preach and spread the gospel of democracy's benefits throughout the world.

The assumption underlying the moral element in American foreign policy is that the United States is somehow unique and special, and that it is morally right for it to engage in a global *missionary* activity to inculcate its values worldwide. From there it is a short step to a messianic, crusading approach to the world; self-righteously presuming its own innocence, the United States on occasion has operated almost from a sense of evangelical crusading in its foreign policy. "The assumption is that we are the anointed custodians of the rules of international behavior," Arthur Schlesinger (1984) has written, "and that the function of United States policy is to mark other states up or down, according to their obedience to our rules." The idea seems predicated on the belief that the nation's mission in the world was ordained not by circumstance, but by God.

Not surprisingly, the kind of activist involvement that can be traced to such messianic assumptions about America's uniqueness and destiny has had its critics. "The hardest thing for the American people to understand," lamented Jimmy Carter in 1978, "is that we are not better than other people." Similarly, John F. Kennedy admonished in 1962 that "we must reject over-simplified theories of international life—the theory . . . that the American mission is to remake the world in the American image."

A foreign policy rooted in moral idealism, critics point out, is dangerous. Such an approach to international problems, George Kennan (1951) has warned, may lead the nation, in its quest for moral absolutes, to pursue punishment of international sinners absolutely, without limit or restraint, to the potential detriment of American interests. Arthur Schlesinger, Jr., a Kennedy adviser, observed worriedly, "All nations succumb to fantasies of innate superiority. When they act on those fantasies . . . they tend to become international menaces" (Schlesinger, 1977). The possibility that the United States has fallen into this category has not been lost on those living abroad, including America's allies. For instance, the *Times of London* characterized America's self-image in 1981 by noting that "The United States was born out of the violence of conquest, rebellion and civil war. Its myths are those of the frontier where the fastest gun was king and every man had his fate in his own hands. The U.S. has risen to become a major industrial and military power claiming universality for its values while seeming unable to shake off the darker elements in its tradition."

These concerns underscore the need to critically evaluate the consequences which may result from a moralistic approach to world affairs and to recognize that not everyone sees American motives and actions as favorably as Americans themselves are inclined to.[23]

---

[23]In addition to the charge that moral idealism is a characteristic of the world view of the United States, some allege that the nation has a penchant to think and act legalistically. For example, the tendency to justify foreign policy actions by citing legal precedents and to operate on the assumption that disputes necessarily involve legal principles and can be resolved by legal remedy are manifestations of such a tendency. Some proponents of this view trace the reverence for law to the fact that many of those who make American foreign policy have legal backgrounds and related professional experiences which presumably encourage political and military controversies to be seen in terms of their legal and contractual implications. Thus, when confronted with a policy predicament, American policy makers are not necessarily likely to ask "What alternative best serves the national interest?" but instead, "What is the legal thing to do?" Other proponents argue that the United States is driven by its traditions and cultural assumptions to transpose its domestic legal institutions to the international arena and thereby to use legal reasoning to define the limits of permissible behavior for states.

Political Realism

Juxtaposed with moral idealism is the heritage of *political realism* (or *realpolitik*), a legacy which has asserted its prominence among policy makers especially since World War II. At the risk of oversimplifying their message, it can be said that adherents to the logic of *realpolitik* base their views on the following assumptions about world politics and America's role in it:

1. A reading of history indicates that humanity is by nature sinful and wicked.
2. Of all human beings' evil ways, no sin is more prevalent or more dangerous than their instinctive lust for power, their desire to dominate others.
3. If this inexorable and inevitable human characteristic is acknowledged, realism forces dismissal of the possibility of progress in the sense of ever hoping to eradicate the instinct for power.
4. Under such conditions, international politics is a struggle for power, a war of all against all.
5. The primary obligation of every state in this environment—the goal to which all other national objectives should be subordinate—is to promote the national self-interest, defined in terms of the acquisition of power.
6. National self-interest is best served by doing whatever is necessary to ensure self-preservation.
7. The fundamental characteristic of international politics requires each state to trust no other, but above all never to entrust self-protection to international organizations or to international law.
8. The national interest necessitates self-promotion, especially through the acquisition of military capabilities sufficient to deter attack by potential enemies (read as "all others").
9. The capacity for self-defense might also be augmented by acquiring allies, providing they are not relied upon for protection.
10. If all states search for power, peace and stability will result through the operation of a balance of power propelled by self-interest and lubricated by fluid alliance systems.

It is often said that most postwar American foreign policy makers have inherently thought about international politics in terms of the assumptions elaborated above. Many presidents have even called or labeled themselves at one time or another "realists," and nearly all have rationalized their decisions in the vocabulary of realism. As a world view and theory,[24] realism has retained its popularity in part because its assumptions seemed to receive confirmation by the events occurring throughout the postwar international system. Its view has fit the needs of a pessimistic era in which the Cold War, the balance of terror, an arms race unprecedented in scale, terrorist activities, and militant,

---

[24]The classic statements of realism as an explicit theory can be found in Carr (1939), Morgenthau (1952, 1983a, and 1985), Thompson (1958 and 1960), Niebuhr (1947), Kennan (1954, 1967, and 1985), and Kissinger (1957 and 1964). For more recent discussions and critiques, see Cohen (1975), Crabb (1976), Stupak (1976), Keohane and Nye (1977), Kegley and Wittkopf (1985b), Mansbach and Vasquez (1981), Vasquez (1983), Graebner (1984), Gilpin (1984), and Ashley (1984).

confrontational diplomacy have appeared to be the salient characteristics of world politics. Nations *have* seemed to pursue only their own self-interest, to the exclusion of other values and at others' expense; the world *has* often appeared to be an arena characterized more by struggle and the search for national self-advantage than by collaborative pursuits for mutual gain.

Under such conditions, those urging the United States to "act realistically" by seeking power and by pursuing, like other nations, only its own self-interest have attracted a large following. The American preoccupation with the East-West conflict, with the balance of power, with the sphere-of-influence logic of geopolitics, and with strategic calculus as opposed to the pursuit of ideals can be traced to that outlook. The equation of military might with national power also stems from realist assumptions. It is instructive to note that debates about military preparedness, alliance networks, the containment of Soviet influence, and the like routinely have been cloaked in the language of realism. President Nixon's contention in 1972 that "we deal with individual nations on the basis of their foreign, and not their domestic policy," reflects but one instance of this orientation. A self-professed realist (see Anderson and Kernek, 1985), President Reagan's foreign policy statements similarly read like the litany of the assumptions of *realpolitik*, including, for example, his belief that "The lesson of history is that among the great nations only those with the strength to protect their interests survive." From this perspective, his administration's goal of making the United States first in military strength, its acceptance of the pursuit of national advantage through global activism, its distrust of Soviet intentions, and its search for power with which to deter the Soviets and contain their quest for power all derive directly from an American *realpolitik* outlook which assumes that all states are, and should be, motivated by national interests and power considerations. That intellectual tradition rejects as mistaken considerations of morality in foreign policy, and instead assumes that the promotion of American interests above all else is the only acceptable moral obligation the U.S. must consider. In Reagan's words, "I will be firm in my intentions to preserve the interests of the United States and, as President, I will choose the methods by which this shall be accomplished."

This orientation has served to promote and perpetuate the globalist containment strategy of postwar American foreign policy. To assume that international conflict is the norm in international politics (that collaboration and peace are not be expected) is to rationalize vigilant and constant attention to the global dangers perceived. Likewise, to assume that an adversary like the Soviet Union is motivated exclusively by its desire to expand its power at others' expense is to rationalize a strategy of containment to prevent that objective from being realized.

Paradoxically, therefore, realism and idealism *both* have contributed to the postwar pattern of U.S. foreign policy, even though they operate from fundamentally different premises about reality and recommend different means to accomplish the goal that both approaches seek, the preservation of peace.

And, to repeat, realism and idealism are *both* continuous traditions in

American diplomatic history. They compete with each other as conceptions of how the United States ought to define its foreign policy objectives, even while they coexist with one another. While one tradition may predominate over the other at any single point in time, much as internationalism periodically dominates isolationism, neither has managed to obliterate the influence of the other.

Thus the tradition of American foreign policy encompasses both moral idealism and raw self-interest. Both survive, Osgood (1953) suggests, because they recognize two needs: to stand for ideals worthy of emulation, and to adaptively protect the nation from threats to its self-preservation in a hostile world. The duality they engender accounts for the willingness of the United States at times to sacrifice its cherished ideals for an expedient action, even while reaffirming its ideals and promoting their maintenance.

Other Characteristics and Underpinnings of the American Approach to World Affairs

"The United States," the late French President Charles de Gaulle once observed, "brings to great affairs elementary feelings and a complicated policy" (cited in Bloomfield, 1974b). As the foregoing discussion of American foreign policy objectives and values has suggested, it is easy to find adjectives to characterize those feelings but not easy to reach a consensus about their ultimate consequences for the nation's interests. What we look for in the policy record in part determines what we find.

If we searched for them, other characterizations would be found that further define the postwar pattern of American foreign policy and give it its distinctive quality. Exemplary is the hypothesis that American foreign policy thinking and behavior manifest not just a latent imperialistic and antirevolutionary flavor, but also an underlying *racist* element (see Weston, 1972; Irish and Frank, 1975; and Coplin, McGowan, and O'Leary, 1974). Another is the view that the United States pursues a global policy from a decidedly *regional*, sphere-of-influence outlook (see Paterson, 1979; Gregg and Kegley, 1971). A third contention is that what makes for the marked stability in America's foreign policy pattern is its affinity for diplomatic "doctrines," a penchant to "seek universal formulae or doctrines in which to clothe and justify particular actions" (Kennan, 1967). This *doctrinal* approach has been labeled "a distinctly American phenomenon" which has been "greatly accelerated in the postwar era" (Crabb, 1982). Still a fourth position maintains that, doctrinal rigidities notwithstanding, what is most conspicuous about postwar American foreign policy is its absence of a true positive purpose: the United States has pursued a policy that is merely *reactive*, and policy making in the United States, in the words of W. W. Rostow, an adviser to President Johnson, "consists in a series of reactions to major crises." This alleged improvisational, ad hoc approach is perhaps the price associated with a globalist, even imperial, outreach, for no nation, no matter how powerful, can police the entire world at once.

Or perhaps some can, given sufficient power. This possibility suggests a final thesis: that America's global foreign policy is driven substantially by its means, by its military capabilities. If your most powerful tool is a hammer, it may be tempting to treat everyone in your environment like a nail. Given its awesome capabilities, has the United States developed a *martial* foreign policy that makes foreign policy subordinate to defense policy? (For discussions, see Leckie, 1968; Weigley, 1973; Small, 1980; and Millett and Maslowski, 1984.) Has the acquisition of those capabilities contributed to the globalist, anticommunist, containment strategy and its persistence since 1945?

In contemplating these and other questions about the values that give rise to American foreign policy goals, we must ask how each of the continuities inferred comes into play under different international circumstances. Do the ends of American foreign policy retain their force and continuity as various means are employed? Does each tactical maneuver serve to preserve and reinforce the prevailing consensus about fundamental assumptions? Or, instead, does the use of various foreign policy instruments and tactics affect the kinds of goals sought abroad, thereby exerting pressure for goal change? It is to these questions that attention now turns.

SUGGESTIONS FOR FURTHER READING

AMBROSE, STEPHEN E. *Rise to Globalism: American Foreign Policy Since 1938*, 4th rev. ed. New York: Penguin, 1985.

GADDIS, JOHN LEWIS. *Strategies of Containment: A Critical Appraisal of Postwar American National Security Policy*. New York: Oxford University Press, 1982.

GARTHOFF, RAYMOND L. *Détente and Confrontation: American-Soviet Relations from Nixon to Reagan*. Washington, D.C.: Brookings Institution, 1985.

GEORGE, ALEXANDER L., ed. *Managing U.S.-Soviet Rivalry: Problems of Crisis Prevention*. Boulder, CO: Westview, 1983.

HOFFMANN, STANLEY. *Dead Ends: American Foreign Policy in the New Cold War*. Cambridge, MA: Ballinger, 1983.

JÖNSSON, CHRISTER. *Superpower: Comparing American and Soviet Foreign Policy*. London: Francis Pinter, 1984.

MCCORMICK, JAMES M. *American Foreign Policy and American Values*. Itasca, IL: Peacock, 1985.

NYE, JOSEPH S., JR., ed. *The Making of America's Soviet Policy*. New Haven: Yale University Press, 1984.

SPANIER, JOHN. *American Foreign Policy Since World War II*, 10th ed. New York: Holt, Rinehart and Winston, 1985.

4

THE INSTRUMENTS OF AMERICAN FOREIGN POLICY: ARMS AND NATIONAL SECURITY

We will maintain sufficient [military] strength to prevail if need be, knowing that if we do so we have the best chance of never having to use that strength.
President Ronald Reagan, 1981

[T]he paradox of peace [is] that to preserve it, the peacemaker must be prepared to use force and use it successfully. Only if we can convince any potential adversary that the cost of aggression would be far greater than any possible benefit, can we be certain that aggression will be deterred and peace preserved.
Secretary of Defense Caspar W. Weinberger, 1985

America's globalist, anticommunist, and containment foreign policy goals have relied on a variety of military, diplomatic, and economic instruments for their pursuit. Understandably, therefore, patterns in the postwar U.S. reliance on military might and interventionist means are detectable—as are changes in the uses to which these policy instruments have been put. It is the purpose of this and the subsequent chapter to examine these patterns.

Conventionally, the term foreign policy "instruments" refers to the various *means* necessary to achieve fundamental objectives (see Hermann, 1982). They include the threat or actual use of force, military intervention, economic and military assistance, arms sales, propaganda, diplomatic bargaining, and clandestine operations. In this chapter we will examine the evolution of strategic doctrines governing the U.S. goal of defending itself (and its allies) from external attack. Then, in chapter five, we will examine America's use of military capabilities for political purposes, its use of covert intelligence operations, its conduct of public diplomacy, and its reliance on economic and military assistance programs in pursuit of its dominant foreign policy objectives. In much of this we will be concerned with that subset of foreign policy known as national security policy. *National security policy* refers to those objectives and programs whereby the government seeks to ensure the nation's security and survival in a potentially hostile international environment. It is a somewhat narrower concept than *foreign policy*, which refers to the totality of objectives and programs whereby the government seeks to cope with the external environment.

THE EVOLUTION OF STRATEGIC DOCTRINE: "COMPELLENCE," DETERRENCE, AND MILITARY PREPAREDNESS

The dropping of the atomic bomb on two Japanese cities in the waning days of World War II is the single most important event distinguishing prewar from postwar international politics. The stopped clocks of Hiroshima record the beginning of the new age at 8:15 in the morning of August 6, 1945, when, in the blinding flash of a single weapon and the shadow of its mushroom cloud, the international arena was transformed from a "balance of power" system to a "balance of terror" system. Ever since, two central questions facing the United States have been what to do with atomic (and later thermonuclear) weapons and what to do about them. Should they be used, and if so, how? Also, how can the United States prevent their use by others against itself? Indeed, no administration from 1945 to the present has failed to appreciate the dangers (or, to some, the opportunities) such weapons of mass destruction have posed to the United States and the world at large.

But some important trends in thinking about that central fact of international life can be perceived in American strategic doctrine. While the existence of incredible weapons of mass destruction has been a constant throughout the postwar period, the United States has assumed varying postures toward their use. For analytic convenience, American policy can be broken into three periods: first, the period of America's atomic monopoly (1945–1949); second, the period of American superiority in strategic weapons (1949 until roughly 1960); and third, the subsequent period of rough nuclear parity, during which the United States has no longer stood alone in its capacity to annihilate another nation.

Weapons and War During the Period of America's Atomic Monopoly

The seed of the atomic age was planted in 1939, when the United States began to lay the basis for the Manhattan Project, whose purpose was construction of a superweapon with which a successful war could be waged. As atomic physicist J. Robert Oppenheimer of the Manhattan Project noted about atomic bombs, "We always assumed if they were needed they would be used." Thus the precedent was established for a strategy based on, and backed up by, the desire to possess weapons of extraordinary means of destruction with which to deal with enemies. President Truman's decision to drop the A-bomb on Japan was the culmination of that thinking.

Why did the United States use the bomb to demolish two Japanese cities—an action that took over 100,000 lives? (For a description of the human and physical damage, see Schell, 1982.) The official reason for the momentous action was that the bomb was dropped "[i]n order to end the war in the shortest possible time and to avoid the enormous losses of human life which otherwise confronted us" (Stimson and Bundy, 1947). However compelling (and compassionate) this justification, the notion that the bomb was necessary for ending the war remains in dispute.[1] Some revisionist historians (see especially Alperovitz, 1970 and 1985) contend that the use of the bomb was motivated by a desire not to save American lives but rather to keep the Soviet Union out of any settlement of the war in the Far East. A parallel interpretation contends that the intention in using the bomb was to impress the Soviets with its power and with the willingness of American officials to use it.

Whatever the purposes behind the decision to drop the bomb, it is clear that the atomic age ushered in a departure from the traditional American approach toward military weapons. Prior to the availability of such means of mass destruction, weapons had been seen largely as the means to short-range military ends. Now, however, they were also recognized as instruments for diplomatic bargaining and for preserving peace. The shift was profound; it marked the beginning of an era in which weapons of mass destruction could be employed for the psychological purpose of molding others' behavior (including allies of the moment—in this instance the Soviet Union). During the period of America's atomic monopoly, the concept *compellence* (Schelling, 1966) describes the new American view of nuclear weapons as instruments of influence, used not for fighting but to get others to do what they might not otherwise do.

In practice, despite the nation's atomic monopoly, the Truman administration subsequently approached the use of nuclear weapons cautiously. But at the level of rhetoric, there is evidence that the awesome destructive power unleashed on Hiroshima and Nagasaki influenced official American thinking about postwar policy instruments and goals. As Gar Alperovitz (1970) has noted, President Truman and Secretary of War Henry L. Stimson counted on

---

[1]For a review of opinion on this controversy, see Alsop and Joravsky (1980). In retrospect, it is clear that Japan desperately wanted to surrender to the United States on acceptable terms. Tokyo was already in ruins; Japan's fate was certain. As the U.S. Strategic Bombing Survey (cited in Alperovitz, 1970) concluded, "certainly prior to 31 December 1945 Japan would have surrendered even if the atomic bonds had not been dropped. . . ." The United States knew through diplomatic channels a month before the bomb was actually dropped that the Japanese government wished to sue for peace. Also see Rufus E. Miles, Jr., "Hiroshima: The Strange Myth of Half a Million American Lives Saved" (1985) for a revisionist view of the use of the bomb.

the new power to help in forcing the Soviet Union to accept American terms for settling outstanding war issues, particularly in Eastern and Central Europe. Stimson was momentarily persuaded, Walter LaFeber (1976) reports, that the United States should "use the bomb to pry the Soviets out of Eastern Europe." He reversed his position shortly thereafter. But his advice points to American thinking during that formative period. The bomb was to be a tool that could be used.

American Strategic Doctrine During the Period of Superiority

The same contrast between action and rhetoric manifested by the Truman administration was evident in Eisenhower's. Although the United States has never used atomic weapons since those two fateful days in August 1945, it has sought to gain bargaining leverage by conveying the impression it was willing to use them against others. Truman felt it was possible to "win through intimidation" because the United States alone possessed the greatest intimidator of them all, the bomb. Even though monopoly gave way to superiority in 1949 when the Soviet Union also acquired an atomic weapons capability, the assumption that America's adversaries, especially the Soviet Union, could be made to bend to American wishes through atomic blackmail became a cornerstone of the Eisenhower containment strategy, particularly as it was acted upon by the chief architect of that policy, Secretary of State John Foster Dulles.

By virtue of U.S. possession of the bomb, Dulles and Eisenhower were able to operate in the opening era of the Cold War from an almost exaggerated sense of overconfidence. Truman's position had been that it was mandatory to "face Russia with an iron fist and strong language." Eisenhower and Dulles parroted that theme (and accepted the assumptions on which it was based) by devising a strategy founded on three concepts: *rollback, brinkmanship*, and *massive retaliation*. Those three terms defined the strategic policy of the United States during the 1950s and made clear how salient nuclear weapons had become in America's foreign policy. The first concept, *rollback*, stated the goal the United States was to pursue: reject merely containing the spread of communist influence and instead "roll back" the iron curtain by liberating communist-dominated areas. "We can never rest," Eisenhower vociferously argued in the 1952 campaign, "until the enslaved nations of the world have in the fullness of freedom the right to choose their own path." And Dulles clarified that policy goal when he promised that the United States would practice rollback— and not merely promise it—by employing "all means necessary to secure the liberation of Eastern Europe." Implicit in his pledge was the assumption that no one would freely choose communism over another system of government, that citizens of communist countries were "captives."

American strategic superiority was assumed to make *brinkmanship* practicable. Dulles explained how nuclear power could be harnessed for bargaining purposes in his explication of brinkmanship:

You have to take chances for peace, just as you must take chances in war. Some say that we were brought to the verge of war. Of course we were brought to the verge of war. The ability to get to the verge without getting into the war is the necessary art. . . . If you try to run away from it, if you are scared to go to the brink, you are lost. We've had to look at it square in the face. . . . We walked to the brink and we looked it in the face. We took strong action. (Dulles, 1952: 146)

Brinkmanship, in short, was a strategy for dealing with the Soviets by backing them into the corner with the threat of nuclear annihilation. The Soviets could be compelled to conform to American wishes, Dulles believed, because the United States was dealing from a position of strength.

To be effective, brinkmanship had to be backed by a credible threat. Hence the doctrine of *massive retaliation* was announced as an innovative nuclear weapons strategy (labeled the "New Look" because, allegedly, it was a departure from Truman's strategy). Massive retaliation was a *countervalue* nuclear weapons strategy that sought to achieve (with an affordable weapon system) American foreign policy objectives by threatening mass destruction of the things the Soviet leaders were perceived to value most—their population and industrial centers. Massive retaliation grew out of the simultaneous impulses of the Eisenhower administration to save money and to regain control of a foreign policy that was perceived to have become largely a reflexive reaction to communist initiatives. The administration's goal was to enhance American flexibility by reserving the right to decide which communist initiatives would result in retaliation by the United States. No longer was containment to be directed toward localized communist initiatives; instead, it was to be directed at the very centers of communist power. Hence massive retaliation meant a pledge to use nuclear weapons if they were considered necessary to accomplish foreign policy objectives. As Dulles explained, "[In a confrontation, atomic] weapons would come into use because, as I say, they are becoming more and more conventional and replacing what used to be called conventional weapons."

Despite the hostility and boldness implied by such rhetorical posturing, the record indicates that Eisenhower and Dulles actually practiced a fairly cautious foreign policy. Few of the threats enunciated in the tough talk by Eisenhower and especially Dulles were actually carried out (see chapter three). But the doctrines of rollback, brinkmanship, and massive retaliation suggested an American policy built around atomic and thermonuclear weapons and the threat of force for diplomatic purposes. In a position of strategic superiority, the United States practiced a form of compellence, essentially the continuation of a strategy Truman had initiated.

From Superiority to Parity: Doctrinal Adaptations in Strategy

A shift away from the compellence strategy began in the late 1950s and became readily discernible with the Kennedy administration in 1961. One reason for the shift was the changed strategic situation relative to the Soviet Union; another was the new way American policy makers began to think about the uses to which weapons of mass destruction could be put. As the strategic advantage possessed by the United States during the 1940s and 1950s gradually eroded and the United States itself became vulnerable to nuclear attack (especially with the development of intercontinental ballistic missiles), the assumption that weapons of mass destruction could actually be used as an instrument of war began to be challenged. "On the day the Soviets acquired [the bomb as] an instrument and the means to deliver it," George Ball (1984b) observes, "the bomb lost its military utility and became merely a means of mutual suicide . . . [for] there are no political objectives commensurate with the costs of an all-out nuclear exchange." President Kennedy expressed this view before the United Nations General Assembly (September 25, 1961):

> Today, every inhabitant of this planet must contemplate the day when this planet may no longer be habitable. Every man, woman and child lives under a nuclear sword of Damocles, hanging by the slenderest of threads, capable of being cut at any moment by accident or miscalculation or by madness. The weapons of war must be abolished before they abolish us.
> Men no longer debate whether armaments are a symptom or cause of tension. The mere existence of modern weapons—ten million times more powerful than any that the world has ever seen, and only minutes away from any target on earth—is a source of horror, and discord and distrust.

And later, in the aftermath of his willingness to go to the brink of a nuclear war with the Soviets following Soviet introduction of offensive missiles into Cuba in 1962, Kennedy expressed a viewpoint different from his predecessors' when he spoke of "the living envying the dead" in the event of a nuclear exchange and he cautioned that we should "never fear to negotiate." The decline of American strategic superiority commanded a new perspective, one which took cognizance of the suicidal and inhumane perils of nuclear weapons. Weapons of mass destruction ceased to be thought of as instruments for compellence in diplomatic bargaining; hereafter, they were seen as performing primarily a deterrent function.[2] They would be relied on to prevent wars from happening (particularly, but not exclusively, those directed at the United States). Indeed, every president since Kennedy has acknowledged that the bomb is not merely another weapon that can be used offensively to combat aggression. "Our best hope of persuading [adversaries] to live in peace," argued Ronald Reagan, "is to convince them that they cannot win a war."

[2]Nuclear threats still intermittently appear, either implicitly or explicitly, as means of superpower bargaining, as during the 1973 Middle East War and again during the 1979–1980 Iranian hostage episode and the Soviet intervention into Afghanistan. There are some, moreover, who continue to advocate nuclear blackmail for political goals and even advance the view that it might be possible to fight, survive, and even win a nuclear war (see Gray and Payne, 1980; for a critique, see Howard, 1981). The prevailing American view since 1962, however, has been that nuclear weapons cannot successfully be used to compel an adversary into doing something it would not otherwise do. Instead, their primary purpose is defensive.

Deterrence means discouraging an adversary from taking military action by convincing him that the cost and risk of such action would outweigh the potential gain. *Strategic deterrence* has, as a practical matter, come to mean that weapons of mass destruction will be used to impose unacceptably high costs directly on the homeland of an aggressive adversary. To ensure that such costs can be imposed, a second-strike capacity is necessary. The term *second-strike* is based on the notion that American offensive strategic forces must be able to withstand an initial strike by an adversary so as to be able to respond with a devastating second blow. In this way the adversary will be assured of destruction, thus deterring the initial preemptive attack. Hence strategic deterrence requires means for ensuring the survivability of American strategic forces.

Assured destruction[3] is the principle on which the Kennedy administration's doctrine of strategic deterrence rested. It differs from massive retaliation in that the latter presupposed strategic superiority on the part of the United States. Thus the United States could choose the time and place where nuclear weapons might be used, which implied that the provocation might be something less than an overt act of aggression. The principle of assured destruction, on the other hand, emphasized that a direct Soviet attack against the United States would result in an American retaliatory nuclear strike. Therefore the initiative would be given to the Soviet Union, under the assumption that it would not undertake the first strike if convinced that a first strike against the United States (or perhaps its NATO allies) would assure its own destruction.

Because the shift from massive retaliation to strategic deterrence based on the principle of assured destruction rests on changing perceptions of Soviet military capabilities, it has also come to mean that what holds for American deterrence of Soviet moves holds for Soviet deterrence of American moves. Hence *mutual deterrence* based on the principle of mutual assured destruction has come to characterize superpower relations in the present (note the common acronym for mutual assured destruction: MAD). The term "balance of terror" accurately describes the essential military stalemate between the superpowers, for mutual deterrence is based on the military potential for, and psychological expectations of, widespread death and destruction for both combatants in the event of a nuclear exchange.[4]

---

[3]Assured destruction means that enough strategic forces would survive the worst possible attack an aggressor can mount to still be able to inflict unacceptable damage on the aggressor in retaliation. Unacceptable damage is frequently defined in terms of destruction of some percentage of the attacker's population and industry (Ackley, 1976). Kennedy's Secretary of Defense Robert McNamara once defined unacceptable damage as "say, one-fifth to one-fourth of the [Soviet] population, and one half of [Soviet] industrial capacity" (quoted in Congressional Research Service, 1976).

[4]As Robert Oppenheimer pointed out in a now-famous analogy, the superpowers were like two scorpions in a bottle—if one attacked the other, it would do so at the price of its own destruction. Thus nuclear deterrence "is like a gun with two barrels, of which one points ahead and the other points back at the gun's holder," writes Jonathan Schell (1984). "If a burglar should enter your house, it might make sense to threaten him with this gun, but it could never make sense to fire it."

During the Nixon administration, national security strategy shifted from one which sought military superiority against the Soviets to one which rested on the principles of sufficiency and parity. It came to be called by its proponents *realistic deterrence* and was a key part of Nixon's overall foreign policy strategy avowed to be based on the principles of strength, sharing of the burden of defense, and a willingness to negotiate with adversaries.

The shift in strategy that occurred during the 1960s was based in part on the continued growth in Soviet military capabilities as compared to the United States. Whereas assured destruction as conceptualized by the Kennedy and Johnson administrations presupposed a strategic edge over the Soviet Union (although not the same superiority required by massive retaliation), by the time Nixon was elected it had become apparent that Soviet destructive power was comparable to that of the United States. This "disappearing capability gap" was paralleled by gnawing questions about the utility of acquiring ever more destructive power. Henry Kissinger cogently summarized these trends:

> The paradox of contemporary military strength is that a gargantuan increase in power has eroded its relationship to policy. . . . The capacity to destroy is difficult to translate into a plausible threat even against countries with no capacity for retaliation. The margin of superiority of the superpowers over the other states is widening; yet other nations have an unprecedented scope for autonomous action. . . . [P]ower no longer translates automatically into influence. This does not mean that impotence increases influence, only that power does not automatically confer it. (Kissinger, 1974a: 59–60)

Cognizance of the new realities set the stage for the pursuit of national security through a "dual track" approach, wherein efforts were made to obtain an acceptable deterrent capacity and strategic balance with the Soviet Union not only through weapons acquisitions but also through arms control negotiations with the Soviets. As Secretary of State George Shultz explained, "the arms control process has always had as a main goal to ensure deterrence by enhancing stability and balance in the strategic relationship." As awareness of vulnerabilities and the diminishing utility of military power grew, arms control took on new significance. This set the stage for the Strategic Arms Limitation Talks (SALT) between the United States and the Soviet Union.

Maintaining the Military Balance: SALT as an Approach to Deterrence

Given that the superpowers' awesome strategic capabilities had reached rough equivalence, or parity, it became an American goal to keep the Soviet Union from attaining superiority over the United States. This emergent balance in the two superpowers' strategic arsenals laid the basis for the Strategic Arms Limitation Talks (SALT) agreements of 1972, which can be interpreted as efforts by both sides to prevent the collapse of the fragile balance of terror that supports mutual assured destruction.[5] The SALT negotiations attempted to guarantee each superpower's second-strike capacity and thereby to preserve the fear of retaliation on which stable deterrence presumably rests.

Agreement was not easy. Principal among the difficulties was how to compare the superpowers' strategic forces. The problem was compounded by the fact that the United States enjoyed a substantial lead in MIRV technology (multiple independently targetable reentry vehicles—in other words, more than one independently targetable warhead on a single missile). This enabled it to opt for a force posture built on a large number of comparatively small weapons, whereas the Soviet Union relied on fewer but larger weapons. As a result, by 1974 the Soviet Union had more than a two-to-one advantage over the United States in "raw megatons." However, when account was taken of the fact that much of the explosive energy of very large weapons is wasted, and hence its destructive area reduced, the apparent disparity between the two sides appeared much less. Measured in "equivalent megatonnage," which accounts for destructive effectiveness, the United States had about 4,100 megatons in its strategic forces in the mid-1970s compared to about 4,300 megatons in the Soviet strategic forces (*The Defense Monitor*, May 1974: 3).[6] In this sense there was "parity" in the two sides' strategic forces, recognition of which enabled the superpowers to move, however modestly, to place a limit on what threatened to become an unlimited arms race.

SALT I consisted of (1) a treaty that restricted the deployment of antiballistic missile defense systems by the United States and the Soviet Union to equal and very low levels, and (2) a five-year interim accord on strategic offensive arms, which restricted the number of ICBM (intercontinental ballistic missile) and SLBM (submarine-launched ballistic missile) launchers that each side was permitted to have. The SALT I agreement was essentially a confidence-building, "stopgap" step toward a longer term, more comprehensive treaty. The SALT II agreement of 1979 sought to realize that objective in that it substantially revised the quantitative restrictions of SALT I and began as well to place certain qualitative constraints on the superpowers' strategic arsenals.

The essentials of SALT II, although perhaps the most extensive and complicated arms control agreement ever negotiated, were nevertheless quite simple. First, the agreement called for placing an eventual overall ceiling of 2,250 on the number of ICBM launchers, SLBM launchers, heavy bombers, and ASBMs (air-to-surface ballistic missiles with ranges over 600 kilometers) that each side was permitted to maintain. Within this overall ceiling, several subceilings specified additional restrictions on particular types of nuclear sys-

---

[5]The roots of SALT can also be traced to other political and diplomatic factors that predated the Nixon administration, as noted in the preceding chapter.

[6]The importance of calibrating different elements of strategic forces is suggested by the Carter administration's principle of "essential equivalence," which meant that "any advantages in force characteristics enjoyed by the Soviets are offset by other United States advantages" (*Department of Defense, Annual Report, Fiscal Year 1979*, Harold Brown, Secretary of Defense, February 2, 1978).

tems, most notably the numbers of missiles that could be equipped with MIRVs.

Taken together, these limitations were estimated at the time that SALT II was signed to have reduced by as many as 8,500 the total number of strategic nuclear weapons that the United States and the Soviet Union would have possessed by 1985 without SALT II. The number of strategic nuclear delivery vehicles that SALT II permitted the Soviet Union to deploy was also substantially less than the number American defense planners believed it otherwise would have deployed.

But the difficulty of agreeing to control arms is illustrated by the problems that the SALT II agreement encountered. The United States Senate deferred ratification of the SALT II treaty "indefinitely" following the Soviet invasion of Afghanistan. Although both superpowers continued to abide by the basic terms of SALT II, despite their renewed confrontation in the postdétente era and notwithstanding threats to cease to be governed by its provisions, the "final result as embodied in SALT II was a clear disappointment to the hopes generated in the early 1970s. In essence, SALT II failed to achieve actual arms reductions. Its basic fault was that it would have permitted substantial growth in the strategic forces of both sides" (U.S. Department of State, 1983c).

Alongside these developments still other adjustments were made in an effort to keep thinking about the design and potential use of the U.S. nuclear arsenal abreast of changes in weapons technologies and force ratios. Recall that a countervalue posture was the nuclear weapons strategy decided upon in 1954, when Secretary of State Dulles announced the doctrine of massive retaliation. As noted earlier, a countervalue strategy means that the population and industrial centers of each side are held hostage by the other. However, as early as 1962 Secretary of Defense McNamara suggested that the United States might adopt a *counterforce* option, targeting its destructive capacity on the enemy's military forces and weapons rather than population centers. In 1974 Secretary of Defense James Schlesinger publicly declared the United States would pursue a counterforce capability which would enable U.S. strategic forces to attack heavily protected Soviet military targets. Such a nuclear option requires a weapons technology providing improved accuracy in nuclear delivery systems and increased "hard-target kill"[7] warhead yield capacity. It also presumably requires a multitude of types of nuclear weapons so as to make a limited nuclear strike feasible. In his pronouncement, Schlesinger criticized assured destruction, the principle of strategic deterrence opted for under Kennedy and carried forward into the Ford years under the guise of realistic deterrence, as "insufficiently flexible and selective to allow the President to order a less than all-out nuclear attack" (Barnaby and Huisken, 1975).

[7]Hard-target kill capacity refers to the destructive capacity of weapons directed against an opponent's land-based intercontinental ballistic missile (ICBM) forces. For both the United States and the Soviet Union, those ICBM forces are vital to the second-strike capability which, in turn, is widely assumed to be necessary for effective deterrence.

The counterforce option became the official strategic posture of the United States in 1980, when President Carter signed Presidential Directive (PD) 59. Known in official circles as the *countervailing* and "war fighting" strategy, the new posture, which in fact was little more than an extension of ideas advanced earlier by the Ford administration, was designed to enhance deterrence by targeting *both* military forces and weapons *and* industrial centers in the Soviet Union. The strategy thus permitted the controlled use of nuclear weapons by increasing the range of available options so as to ensure that unacceptable damage could be inflicted on the Soviets.[8] Secretary of Defense Harold Brown described the new strategic posture thus:

> Our countervailing strategy . . . makes clear that no course of aggression by [the Soviet Union] that led to use of nuclear weapons, on any scale of attack and at any stage of conflict, could lead to victory, however they may define victory. Besides our power to devastate the full target system of the USSR, the United States would have the option for more selective, lesser retaliatory attacks that would exact a prohibitively high price from the things the Soviet leadership prizes most—political and military control, nuclear and conventional military force, and the economic base needed to sustain a war. . . . The essence of the countervailing strategy is to convince the Soviets that they will be successfully opposed at any level of aggression they choose, and that no plausible outcome at any level of conflict could represent "success" for them by any reasonable definition of success. (*Report of Secretary of Defense Harold Brown to the Congress*, 1981: 39–40)

Critics of PD 59 and the countervailing strategy questioned whether an enhanced counterforce capability and an expressed willingness to use nuclear weapons would increase deterrence and lessen the possibility of all-out nuclear war with the Soviets. Because an effective countervailing strategy could eliminate the Soviets' ability to mount an effective second strike, might it be interpreted as a move by the United States to achieve overwhelming offensive strategic superiority and a corresponding first-strike capability? Did it offer, as Richard Barnet (1981) wondered, "an illusion of victory that makes nuclear war seem less unthinkable and thus more likely"? If so, the strategy would undermine the fragile structure of the balance of terror, thereby hastening rather than preventing the nuclear holocaust three generations of Americans had been spared.

Or was the United States now signaling that it believed it possible to control the use of nuclear weapons in an actual conflict situation, that is, to fight a limited nuclear war? President Reagan—to the alarm of European leaders—implied as much by his comment in October 1981 that he "could see where you could have an exchange of tactical weapons against troops in the field without it bringing either one of the major powers to pushing the buttons." If so,

---

[8]The top-secret American master plan for waging nuclear war, called SIOP (Single Integrated Operational Plan), identifies for devastation both military and nonmilitary targets. For a description and critique of the SIOP, see Ford (1985) and Pringle and Arkin (1983).

would not decision makers be more inclined to push the nuclear button? And if escalation of conflict proved impossible to prevent, as many believe it would (including, incidentally, former Defense Secretary Brown), Armageddon would be hastened. Again, in Brown's words, the security of the United States would seem, as a result of strategic developments during the postwar era, to have been seriously compromised. He noted in 1983 that "If one takes as a measure of national security the ability of the people of the United States to determine their own future without being influenced by what happens outside their own borders, the threat of nuclear destruction means that U.S. national security has deteriorated markedly and probably irreversibly since the early 1950s."

Conclusive responses to such questions and concerns—which have reappeared in debates concerning American strategic doctrine for over two decades—cannot be found. What is certain is that the countervailing strategy was only a recent round in the effort of American policy makers to cope with the continuing growth of Soviet military capabilities. Defense Secretary Brown gave voice to that fact in saying:

> As the strategic balance has shifted from overwhelming U.S. superiority to essential equivalence, and as ICBM accuracies have steadily improved to the point that hard target kill probabilities are quite high, our doctrine must adapt itself to these new realities. . . . The unquestioned Soviet attainment of strategic parity has put the final nail in the coffin of what we long knew was dead—the notion that we could adequately deter the Soviets solely by threatening massive retaliation against their cities. (*Report of Secretary of Defense Harold Brown to the Congress*, 1981: 39)

CHALLENGES TO SALT AND MUTUAL ASSURED DESTRUCTION

The perception of improved Soviet capabilities provided the foundation for the program that the Reagan administration made the centerpiece of its foreign policy. "Our ability to deter war and protect our security declined dangerously during the 1970s," Reagan claimed. Accordingly, he promised the United States would do whatever was necessary "to prevail." Thereafter, and in conformity with his belief that "if you want peace, prepare for war," increases in defense spending unprecedented in scale were authorized. The United States committed itself to race for strategic advantage.

This is not to imply that the U.S. and Soviet strategic arsenals did not already contain destructive capabilities of unimaginable magnitude. The two superpowers' current nuclear arsenals make clear the lethal characteristics of the present strategic atmosphere. The warheads on one American Trident submarine are capable of destroying 192 cities in the Soviet Union with eight times the explosive power of all the bombs used during World War II. The first generation of atomic bombs (like the single device that reduced Hiroshima to rubble, which is now classified as a "tactical" weapon) had a destructive area of three square miles, and the delivery systems then available limited the destruction to a single target. The U.S. MX missile, if deployed, could destroy an area seventy-eight times as extensive as the area leveled in Japan and devastate ten targets at once. Moreover, refinements in military technology enable the superpowers to deliver these weapons within a few hundred feet of their targets, as far away as nine thousand miles in less than thirty minutes, and intermediate-range missiles can travel between Western Europe and Moscow in six minutes.

In addition, the superpowers' nuclear arsenals continue to grow, as Figure 4.1 amply demonstrates. When World War II ended, there was but one atomic bomb still in existence. By 1985, the United States had stockpiled about 11,500 strategic nuclear weapons, the Soviets about 8,500. In addition, the United States is estimated to possess 13,000 tactical nuclear weapons, and the Soviet Union 11,000. (Tactical nuclear weapons are designed for the direct support of combat operations.) The current rate of growth in nuclear weaponry is an average of three additional bombs a day (Sivard, 1982). It is commonplace to note that the number of warheads in existence globally represents an explosive force of roughly 3.5 tons of TNT for every person on earth. Stated differently, on the basis of the number of weapons stockpiled in 1983, it has been estimated that the warheads carried aboard U.S. submarines contained enough force for nearly 18,000 "Hiroshima-equivalent" explosions; those on U.S. ICBMs another 27,000 Hiroshimas; and those on U.S. bombers still another 33,400 Hiroshimas. And as unimaginable as it may seem, Soviet strategic nuclear forces were capable of even greater destruction, with the megatonnage necessary for some 115,600 Hiroshima-equivalent explosions (Harris and Markusen, 1986: 25–26). It is obvious that the use of such weapons in large numbers would threaten the destruction, not only of entire cities and countries, but possibly, when radiation effects and the potential of a "nuclear winter" are considered, of the entire world population (see Ehrlich et al., 1983 and 1985; Sagan, 1983–1984). The threat is vividly captured in Albert Einstein's famous remark that he did not know what the weapons of a third world war would be but that in a fourth they would be "sticks and stones."

Despite the obvious "sufficiency" of each superpower's arsenal to wreak devastation on the other, each has continued research and development on new weapons systems out of fear the other side might achieve an innovative, technological "break out." Each also has continued to make the kinds of quantitative and qualitative improvements permitted by the few arms agreements they have been able to forge.

By the time of Reagan's election in 1980, it was widely feared that the decades-long buildup of Soviet strategic forces had achieved superiority over the United States. The trend data in Figure 4.1, which are summarized in Table 4.1, do show certain Soviet advantages. The Soviets have gained numeric superiority in terms of missiles and missile warheads (but not bomber-delivered weapons). They also enjoy an advantage in missile throw-weight, one measure of the destructive power that a ballistic missile is able to push into the at-

FIGURE 4.1   Trends in American and Soviet Strategic Offensive Delivery Vehicles and Warheads, 1969–1985.

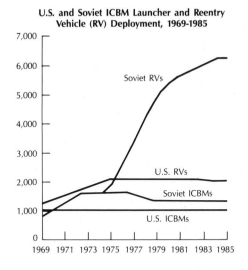

U.S. and Soviet ICBM Launcher and Reentry Vehicle (RV) Deployment, 1969-1985

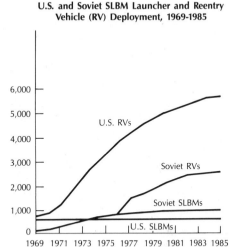

U.S. and Soviet SLBM Launcher and Reentry Vehicle (RV) Deployment, 1969-1985

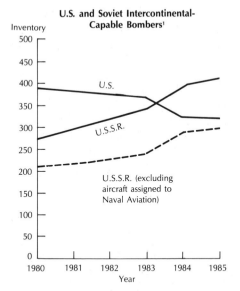

U.S. and Soviet Intercontinental-Capable Bombers[1]

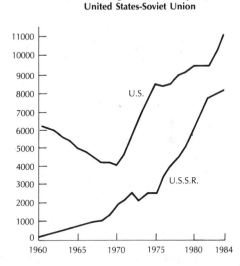

Total Strategic Nuclear Weapons, United States-Soviet Union

[1]U.S. data include B-52, FB-111; Soviet data include BEAR, BISON, and BACKFIRE.

SOURCE: *Soviet Military Power 1985* (U.S. Government Printing Office, April 1985), pp. 30, 33, 34, 56; *The Defense Monitor* (Vol. 13, No. 6, 1984), p. 3.

mosphere. Together these factors opened what the Reagan administration called a "window of vulnerability" to a Soviet attack on the U.S. land-based missile leg of the nation's strategic triad. What the data fail to show—and the "window of vulnerability" concept failed to acknowledge—is the widely held conviction that the weapons in the American arsenal are more sophisticated technologically than are those in the Soviet arsenal. They also ignore the fact that Soviet strategic systems, being heavily concentrated in land-based missiles (over 70 percent of Soviet warheads are on ICBMs), are far more vulnerable to destruction than American systems, where reliance on submarine-launched ballistic missiles gives the United States a comparatively invulnerable force. Finally, quantitative data on the strategic balance between the superpowers ignore the critical question of the intentions of the adversaries, and on this question there is wide disagreement.

Despite these uncertainties, the Reagan administration committed itself to upgrading U.S. strategic capabilities, and thus continued the evolutionary drift of American strategic doctrine toward counterforce targeting and thinking. Fearing in particular Soviet technological developments that appeared to render the U.S. Minuteman land-based missile force vulnerable to a devastating first strike (which would undermine the U.S. second-strike capability, but not eliminate it due to the SLBM forces), the administration appeared to accept the view that the Soviet Union could no longer be deterred simply with the threat of assured destruction. Instead, it found it necessary to develop a war-fighting deterrent posture which emphasizes not merely the survivability of U.S. strategic forces in the event of a first strike, so that a devastating second strike can be launched, but also the endurance of strategic nuclear forces—the ability to deter a second strike by threatening a third.

To some, this emphasis merely presaged and revealed a hidden purpose: to consider moving U.S. strategy toward a preemptive capacity. Talk of striking the Soviet Union with a devastating first blow (so destructive that it could not mount a retaliatory strike) fed the speculation. So, too, did talk of the "winability" of a nuclear exchange and, in the event deterrence should fail, of "damage limitation," a strategic concept that seeks to minimize destruction of the United States and its allies by destroying a portion of the Soviet strategic forces before they are launched. (Civil defense and other defensive measures also fall under the rubric of damage limitation.) Thus the administration effectively moved to embrace the ideas of nuclear utilization theory as part of the nation's strategic thinking, even while it continued to embrace some elements of traditional deterrence incorporated in a MAD world.[9]

---

[9]It nevertheless is no longer part of United States strategic planning to target civilian populations per se; instead, the focus has shifted to Soviet war-supporting industries and economic recovery capabilities (Ball, 1983). In practice, however, the distinction may be largely meaningless, since military and industrial sites are often co-located with population centers. "Simply by virtue of associated industrial and military targets, all of the 200 largest Soviet cities and 80% of the 866 Soviet cities with populations above 25,000 are included in US war plans" (Ball, 1983: 33). "Collateral damage" is the concept war planners use to talk about damage inflicted on the nontargeted surrounding human and nonhuman resources as a result of military strikes on enemy forces or military resources.

The nuclear weapons policy of the United States, as delineated in the current single integrated operational plan, SIOP-6, prepared by the Reagan administration, is intended to "create a capacity to fight and 'prevail' in a nuclear war." The current policy emphasizes the need to be able to fight a protracted nuclear war and to have enough resilience and flexibility of response so that even after a major first exchange the United States would have power to bargain. (Craig and Jungerman, 1986: 83)

Even while the administration moved in the direction of explicitly incorporating a war-fighting capacity into American strategic doctrine, the debate between nuclear utilization theorists (NUTs) and the advocates of MAD continued to rage (see Kegley and Wittkopf, 1985a). Nuclear utilization advocates believed it possible to fight a protracted nuclear war, implying a conviction that any use of nuclear weapons would not necessarily escalate to an unmanageable, all-out nuclear exchange. Furthermore, they believed that by making nuclear weapons more usable, they would enhance deterrence rather than detract from it by making the nuclear threat more credible.

The proponents of MAD, on the other hand, held that deterrence remained the only sane role to assign nuclear weapons, because the outbreak of nuclear war would surely end in nuclear catastrophe. According to this view, the technical requirements and human capacity to wage protracted nuclear war undoubtedly would be strained beyond the breaking point. They often pointed in particular to the vulnerability of the nation's command, control, communications, and intelligence (C^3I) capability. A Soviet attack by a comparatively small number of weapons would effectively "decapitate" the nation by killing its political leaders and destroying the communication links necessary to ensure a coordinated and coherent U.S. retaliation, they argued (see Schneider, 1985, and Ball, 1985). Furthermore, because it would lower the nuclear threshold, many believed that a nuclear strategy premised on the usability of nuclear weapons in war would in fact make war more likely, not less, and thereby diminish the weapons' deterrent capability. From this viewpoint, both superpowers are destined to live in a MAD world, even if, ironically, this means that they will remain in the "mutual hostage relationship" in which their earlier weapons decisions have imprisoned them (see Keeny and Panofsky, 1981).

Even as the strategic debate waged, both superpowers continued research, development, and deployment of the kinds of weapons that nuclear utilization theory requires. Then, abruptly, the United States shifted the focus from offense to defense when, in 1983, President Reagan called for a high tech "Star Wars" ballistic missile defense (BMD) system that foreshadowed a distant future in which the United States might be able to neutralize Soviet offensive weapons launched in fear or anger. Officially known as the Strategic Defense Initiative (SDI), the proposal suggested a profound shift in U.S. nuclear strategy away from reliance on offensive missiles to deter an attack—that is, from dependence on mutual assured destruction, which President Reagan deemed "morally unacceptable."

TABLE 4.1   A Balance Sheet on Strategic Arms and Arms Proposals, 1985

	Current Balance		Soviet Proposal, Oct. 1985		U.S. Proposal, Nov. 1985	
	U.S.	SOVIET UNION	U.S.	SOVIET UNION	U.S.	SOVIET UNION
STRATEGIC FORCES						
intercontinental ballistic missiles (ICBMs) and submarine-launched ballistic missiles (SLBMs)	1,630 (1,030 ICBMs) (600 SLBMs)	2,352 (1,398 ICBMs) (954 SLBMs)	815 Applies 50 percent cut across the board using U.S. figures. Soviet Union counts all U.S. strategic and medium-range systems at 3,360 and Soviet ones at 2,500 (not including SS-20s). Using Soviet figures, 50 percent cut would result in 1,680 systems for U.S. and 1,250 for Soviet Union.	1,176	1,250–1,450 Freedom to mix between ICBM and SLBM launchers.	1,250–1,450
ICBM and SLBM warheads	7,506 (2,130 ICBMs) (5,376 SLBMs)	8,830 (6,420 ICBMs) (2,410 SLBMs)	6,000 Only 3,600 of any one type; 6,000 limit also applies to gravity bombs and short-range attack missiles (U.S. rejects this inclusion).	6,000	4,500 No more than 3,000 on ICBMs.	4,500
Heavy bombers	263	480 Includes 300 Backfires. Soviet Union says this is not a strategic bomber.	131	90 Backfires not included.	350	350 Includes 300 Backfires.
Air-launched cruise missiles	1,176	200	0 Part of larger total ban on long-range cruise missiles.	0	1,500	1,500

Missile throw-weight*	4.4 million pounds	11.9 million pounds	Not included	Not included	Not to exceed 6 million pounds.	Not to exceed 6 million pounds.
New systems				Ban on new types of ICBMs, SLBMs, and heavy bombers. Soviet Union has not defined what it considers to be new types.		Ban on all new heavy ICBMs and mobile missiles, including Soviet SS-18 modernization and replacement plans, Soviet SS-24 and SS-25 mobile missiles, and U.S. Midgetman mobile missiles.
MEDIUM-RANGE FORCES						
Medium-range launchers	134 Pershing 2s and ground-launched cruise missiles (one warhead each)	270 SS-20s in Europe plus 171 in Asia for total of 441 (3 warheads each)	No Pershing 2s; 100 ground-launched cruise missiles.	243 SS-20s in Europe plus a freeze on SS-20s in Asia, currently at 171.	140 ceiling on Pershing 2s and ground-launched cruise missiles.	140 SS-20s in Europe and 89 in Asia, totaling 229.
Medium-range bombers	254 (198 F-111s and 56 FB-111s)	553 (includes Backfires)	127	276	Willingness to discuss restraints.	
			Derived from applying 50 percent cut to U.S. figures.			

SOURCE: *New York Times*, November 13, 1985: A10. Based on data compiled by the House Committee on Foreign Affairs.

*Weight that can be lifted off and carried onto target.

Considerable uncertainty surrounds Star Wars. Official statements about the program raise expectations that doubtless will not be met until well into the next century, if ever. Conceptually, SDI envisions a "layered" defensive system in which threatening Soviet missiles and warheads would be destroyed at some point between launch and impact. Figure 4.2 displays an artist's simplified rendering of the required tasks. Even this sketch suggests how complicated they will be: the curvature of the earth, the short time span for decision, the inherent advantages of the offense, including deliberate deceptions during attack, all render a defensive posture unimaginably complex.[10] The billions of virtually instantaneous computer calculations such a system would require will not be met until the next generation of computers come online in the 1990s or thereafter, for example. Furthermore, many observers believe the Soviets will increase their nuclear arsenal to ensure that they will possess sufficient force to overwhelm U.S. defenses, while at the same time proceeding with development of their own defensive system. A new lap of the arms race would doubtless ensue, one that promises to be the most expensive one yet. The Reagan administration projected the expenditure of $27 billion by 1990 on SDI research and development alone. Even this fact is a potential source of friction in Soviet-American relations. As Ambassador Marshall D. Shulman observed:

> From the Soviet point of view, the SDI will force the pace of military competition on grounds where the United States has the advantage of technological superiority. Whether or not the systems are ultimately deployed, or whether they work as promised, the Soviets must anticipate that the great intensification of research proposed is likely to yield spinoffs that will add to U.S. offensive capabilities.

What would be the likely impact of SDI on the decades-long commitment of the United States and the Soviet Union to reach negotiated arms control agreements? Again, the answer is unclear. The 1972 ABM treaty, part of the package known as SALT I, remains the only "enduring accomplishment of fifteen years of Soviet-U.S. strategic arms control negotiations" (Carnesale, 1985). Some interpretations of the ABM treaty suggest a prohibition on SDI, except, perhaps, research and development. Others believe even deployment may be permitted. The differences suggest profoundly different views of the effects of SDI on the prospects for the United States and the Soviet Union to moderate their differences through negotiated arms agreements.[11]

---

[10]The tragedy that befell the space shuttle Challenger and its brave crew of seven in early 1986 reinforced the uncertainty surrounding SDI by raising serious questions about the ability of extraordinarily complex machines to perform flawlessly and of humans to devise the technology necessary to command and control such machines.

[11]It is important to distinguish between arms control and disarmament, and to remember that arms control "accepts conflict among nations as an inevitable part of contemporary international politics and views military force as a necessary (and legitimate) instrument of national policy" (Blechman, 1984). Accordingly, it seeks more modest objectives than does disarmament:

Proponents of the SDI maintain that strategic defense is just what is needed to pave the way to meaningful reductions. Effective defenses, they argue, would reduce the military utility of ballistic missiles and therefore weaken the resistance to eliminating some, or perhaps even all, of them. Others disagree, maintaining that the more likely Soviet response to a U.S. defense against ballistic missiles would include expansion of and improvements in offensive forces to counter the U.S. defense and probably also further deployments of Soviet defenses. They see the SDI as paving the way not to arms control but to an accelerated arms race. (Carnesale, 1985: 200)

Simultaneously with the Strategic Defense Initiative, the Reagan administration pursued a dual track approach to the Soviet-American strategic competition by pursuing arms limitation talks and a military buildup at the same time. Early in the first Reagan term there was little willingness to discuss arms limitations, but a combination of domestic and international pressure gave impetus to two sets of negotiations, the START, or Strategic Arms Reduction Talks, aimed at reducing the superpowers' strategic forces, and the INF, or intermediate-range nuclear force talks, directed toward limiting the deployment of theater nuclear force weapons in Europe. The principal weapons of concern were the so-called Euromissiles, consisting of the Soviet SS–20 missiles and U.S. ground-launched cruise missiles and Pershing II intermediate-range ballistic missiles, both of which the NATO alliance decided to build in 1979 as part of a force modernization program designed to counter Soviet weapons advances. The Soviet objective in the INF negotiations was to prevent NATO deployment of its new weapons. When that failed, the Soviets abruptly ended the INF talks in November 1983 and the START negotiations shortly thereafter. It was as frigid a point in Soviet-American relations as at any time since the height of the Cold War in the 1950s and 1960s.

The debates surrounding the NATO force modernization decision of the late 1970s and the later INF negotiations suggested a continuing concern for the credibility of the American commitment to defend Europe from a Soviet attack. At issue was the concept of *extended deterrence*, namely, how best to make credible the nuclear threat to prevent an attack not only on the United States but also on its Western European allies (see Weede, 1983). Similarly, there was discussion of *horizontal escalation*, suggesting that deterrence could be extended to the enemy's remote and vulnerable outposts in retaliation for its adventures elsewhere. Thus, deterrence was seen as necessary not just to guard the nation's homeland but also to prevent the enemy from attacking al-

---

The theory of ''arms control'' is based on the rather modest notion that decisions to acquire certain types or quantities of weapons can aggravate political conflicts and thereby *in themselves contribute to the risk of war.* This is not to say that such decisions are a primary or even secondary cause of conflict, only that such decisions are one factor which influence the relative probabilities that political conflicts are resolved peacefully, remain unsettled, or result in war.'' (Blechman, 1984: 125)

FIGURE 4.2 Star Wars: Scenario for Space Defense

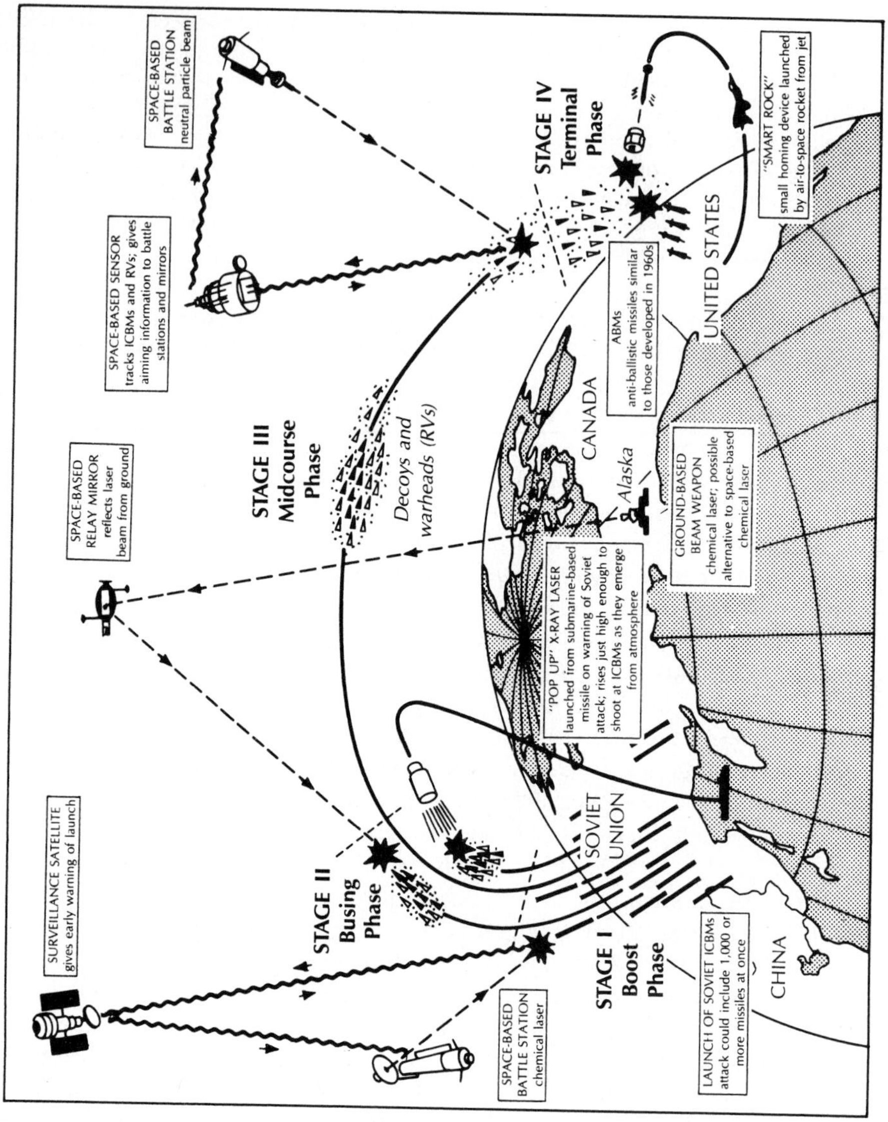

SPACE-BASED BATTLE STATION
neutral particle beam

SPACE-BASED SENSOR tracks ICBMs and RVs; gives aiming information to battle stations and mirrors

STAGE IV
Terminal
Phase

"SMART ROCK"
small homing device launched by air-to-space rocket from jet

SPACE-BASED RELAY MIRROR reflects laser beam from ground

STAGE III
Midcourse
Phase

Decoys and
warheads (RVs)

UNITED STATES

ABMs
anti-ballistic missiles similar to those developed in 1960s

CANADA

Alaska

GROUND-BASED BEAM WEAPON
chemical laser; possible alternative to space-based chemical laser

"POP UP" X-RAY LASER launched from submarine-based missile on warning of Soviet attack; rises just high enough to shoot at ICBMs as they emerge from atmosphere

SURVEILLANCE SATELLITE
gives early warning of launch

SOVIET
UNION

STAGE II
Busing
Phase

STAGE I
Boost
Phase

SPACE-BASED BATTLE STATION
chemical laser

LAUNCH OF SOVIET ICBMs
attack could include 1,000 or more missiles at once

CHINA

How Star Wars Would Protect the United States from a Missile Attack

President Reagan's Strategic Defense Initiative has been described as an "astrodome defense," but it would actually consist of a vast network of hundreds—perhaps thousands—of machines in space, in the air and on the ground. All must work together with unprecedented precision.

Where the antiballistic missile systems of the 1960s dealt only with the "terminal phase" of a ballistic missile's flight, SDI plans call for additional layers of defense directed at one or more of the earlier phases of an ICBM attack. Warheads that escaped one layer would be attacked by the next.

This diagram shows a tiny, simplified composite of events and objects that might be involved. SDI researchers are studying various weapons, only some of which are indicated here. The exact combination, should planners and policy-makers choose to develop the entire system, will not be selected for years.

Stage I: Boost Phase

When Soviet ICBMs blast off, exhaust heat is sensed by surveillance satellites. Computers assign targets to nearest space-based battle stations or to X-ray laser "popped up" from sub or to ground-based beam weapon. Boost-phase weapons are the most important because each "kill" eliminates the need to deal with many warheads and decoys later.

Stage II: Bus Deployment Phase

After rocket engines burn out, ICBM's nose cone disgorges "bus" that coasts onward and "MIRV's," releasing 10 real warheads and 100 decoys. Space-based sensors must discriminate between the warheads and decoys so that battle stations don't waste fuel and time on harmless decoys.

Stage III: Midcourse Phase

Once the reentry vehicles (RVs) containing warheads are released, they coast in ballistic trajectory to the United States. Beam weapons may still shoot but, if 10 percent of RVs get this far, weapons may have to cope with a "threat cloud" of 1,000 bombs and 10,000 decoys. If discrimination fails, weapons must destroy 12 targets every second to protect the United States. Still, sensors must distinguish live RVs from destroyed RVs and debris.

Stage IV: Terminal Phase

As threat cloud reenters atmosphere, friction slows light decoys, leaving RVs easy to spot. Radars take over tracking and give guidance to surface-to-air ABMs or to "smart rocks" launched from rockets carried aloft on fighter jets. Interception must be several miles up because RVs may be set to explode if anything comes too near. Hydrogen bombs detonating at lower altitudes could destroy cities.

SOURCE: *Washington Post National Weekly Edition*, March 18, 1985: 6.

lies and targets outside the country's own defensive perimeter and alliance network. Because horizontal escalation globalizes deterrence by spreading it worldwide, it has also been called *geographical escalation* and a *war-widening strategy* (see Epstein, 1983).

Eventually a basis was laid for renewal of arms control talks between the superpowers. At the Geneva summit in November 1985 the two sides laid out proposals containing an area of potentially wide agreement: both agreed that deep cuts in their strategic forces were in order. They differed substantially in how those cuts should be accomplished, however, as shown earlier in Table 4.1. Again, the issue turned essentially on how to deal with the differences in the two sides' force composition. As a traditional land power, the Soviet Union has placed heavy reliance on land-based missiles, as noted before. The United States sought to reduce their number, fearing these as the gravest threat to U.S. land-based forces. Conversely, the Soviets, facing an American strategic force more widely dispersed among the three legs of the strategic triad, sought cutbacks that would directly offset areas of United States superiority, adding U.S. weapons in Europe that are able to strike the Soviet Union but excepting Soviet weapons able to strike Western Europe. The Soviets also expressed deep apprehension about SDI, but the Reagan administration gave little evidence it was willing to yield on its determination to forge ahead on the plan.

In the months that followed the Geneva summit, both sides offered a number of proposals and counterproposals designed to advance their particular interests. Although wide differences remained, the dialogue between the United States and the Soviet Union, much of it occurring through media sources, suggested that room for bargaining was once more being made.

ARMS AND (IN)SECURITY

The Reagan administration's approach to the twin questions that have haunted American foreign policy makers for over four decades—what to do with nuclear weapons, and what to do about them—has been a blend of that same curious mixture of approach-avoidance that has characterized the policies of its predecessors. Its policies have rested on the twin pillars of an arms buildup alongside efforts to stabilize those levels through negotiated arms control agreements. The United States would continue to *rearm* while seeking to convince the Soviets to *disarm*. Not unlike the approach of its predecessors, the administration insisted that it was necessary to cement an agreement to control arms only *after* the U.S. advantage was secured. Only then could the United States negotiate from a position of strength. Therefore, it was argued, the American approach would be to build up U.S. weapons *before* seeking to dismantle them through an arms agreement. The ultimate product sought was protection of American national security. ''The American eagle holds arrows in one hand and the olive branch in the other,'' George Shultz observed in the spring of 1985, ''and his eyes look toward the olive branch. Our goal is peace, and, therefore, we are always ready for serious dialogue with our adversaries on ways to control and reduce weapons.''

If there was a new wrinkle, it was the Strategic Defense Initiative, a conviction that somehow a defense from the heavens could neutralize, and hence eliminate the need for, the offense. The continuities in the nation's quest for national security are striking nonetheless. The United States has repeatedly placed its confidence in the acquisition of military might to ''prepare for the common defense.'' That reliance has been unwavering since World War II. American policy makers have assumed that weapons of mass destruction could both preserve the peace and, under some circumstances, provide leverage in the exercise of influence over adversaries. Thus, while strategies and doctrines regarding the uses to which military might could be put have changed over time as changes in the strategic balance have occurred, dependence on weapons of mass destruction has remained a cornerstone of postwar American national security policy. A global outlook and containment strategy have helped to perpetuate this patterned reliance. And American strategy has sought to modify the global environment in which the United States resides— through defense spending, the development of new weapons systems, and, on occasion, arms control—while never seriously questioning the premise that peace is best preserved by preparing for war.

However, as had been noted, the ability to use weapons as instruments of influence has eroded as their destructive capability has increased. Their suicidal nature has deterred their use. Many believe they no longer have a policy function for any purpose other than to prevent their use by others. Thus, the military might that America has acquired in such awesome proportions has not given it a corresponding power to influence the direction of world affairs.

Does this circumstance leave the United States, a military giant, powerless in its political dealings with other states? Perhaps, but that ignores the variety of alternate policy instruments—some military, some not—on which the United States has come to rely in its efforts to achieve its foreign policy objective captured in the themes of globalism, anticommunism, and containment. Let us now turn to consider those other instruments.

SUGGESTIONS FOR FURTHER READING

BARNET, RICHARD J. *Real Security: Restoring American Power in a Dangerous Decade.* New York: Simon and Schuster, 1981.

BROWN, HAROLD. *Thinking About National Security: Defense and Foreign Policy in a Dangerous World.* Boulder, CO: Westview, 1983.

COLLINS, JOHN M. *U.S.-Soviet Military Balance 1980–1985.* Washington, D.C.: Pergamon-Brassey's, 1985.

FREEMAN, LAWRENCE. *The Evolution of Nuclear Strategy.* New York: St. Martin's, 1981.

JERVIS, ROBERT. *The Illogic of American Nuclear Strategy.* Ithaca, NY: Cornell University Press, 1984.

KEGLEY, CHARLES W., JR., AND EUGENE R. WITTKOPF, eds. *The Nuclear Reader: Strategy, Weapons, War.* New York: St. Martin's, 1985.

MILLETT, ALLAN R., AND PETER MASLOWSKI. *For the Common Defense: A Military History of the United States of America.* New York: Free Press, 1984.

SMOKE, RICHARD. *National Security and the Nuclear Dilemma: An Introduction to the American Experience.* New York: Random House, 1984.

WEIGLEY, RUSSELL F. *The American Way of War: A History of United States Military Strategy and Policy.* New York: Macmillan, 1973.

5

THE INSTRUMENTS OF GLOBAL INFLUENCE: MILITARY MIGHT AND INTERVENTIONIST MEANS

> The United States is, and always should be, a global power, with global concerns and responsibilities that are an integral part of our national security.
> *Secretary of Defense Caspar W. Weinberger, 1981*

> I don't see why we need to stand by and watch a country go Communist due to the irresponsibility of its own people.
> *Special Assistant for National Security Affairs Henry Kissinger, 1970*

America's postwar push for a global presence and power, guided by its quest to contain communism and Soviet influence, has demanded the development of resources and techniques by which those goals could be effectively pursued. That demand has been fed by the need to deal with the threat of the growing strategic capability of the Soviet Union, a threat which has necessitated the creation of a retaliatory nuclear force sufficient to deter any aggressive Soviet designs. That threat, understandably, has become a fixation. With it, and with America's own global goals, has emerged a foreign policy highly dependent on the possession of powerful military, paramilitary, and related instruments through which its fundamental objectives can be pursued. As Under Secretary of State Lawrence S. Eagleburger stressed in March 1984, the first principle shaping American foreign policy "is that military power is an essential part of diplomacy."

The preceding chapter focused on the *strategic* instruments of American foreign policy, that is, on the strategies and armaments used by the United

States to defend itself from military attack. Here we broaden that focus to accommodate other important policy instruments. Attention will be given to the political use of military force, military intervention, covert and other intelligence activities, public diplomacy, and military and economic assistance programs. Each has played a prominent role in the foreign policy of the United States since 1945; all derive from the *realpolitik* assumption American foreign policy makers have made that security needs be at the top of the nation's agenda and that a number of decidedly militaristic and interventionist courses of action are required to meet those needs. For that reason we begin by examining the thesis that the goals of American foreign policy have over the course of the postwar years become "militarized."

MILITARY GLOBALISM

The logic of *realpolitik* is said to encourage the practice of coercive behavior abroad. Dependence on nuclear weapons for purposes of both compelling and deterring others is one symptom of that instinct. Another concerns how foreign policy planning in general may have become dominated by military thinking. Some maintain that American foreign policy has been "militarized" in the sense that the nation's policy makers have routinely defined international political problems in terms of military solutions. Former Assistant Secretary of Defense Adam Yarmolinsky (1970–1971) argues, for instance, that for at least a quarter of a century following World War II, American foreign policy was based on a battleground conception in which communist forces were pitted against those of the United States and the "Free World." It was assumed that any success experienced by the communists or their sympathizers contributed to Soviet strength and correspondingly diminished that of the United States. One consequence of such military thinking was to avoid estimating the adversary's intentions and instead to emphasize his capabilities, assuming that he would do "whatever mischief he can." The second consequence was "to emphasize readiness for the worst contingency that might arise," particularly as the Soviet Union began to develop a nuclear strike potential. In the European context the result was a preoccupation with the idea that the Soviet Union would launch a massive surprise attack against Western Europe. The preoccupation prevented any realistic test of Soviet willingness to arrive at a European diplomatic settlement. And in other areas bordering the communist world outside Europe, American diplomacy concentrated on building up a ready military force to the exclusion of almost all other political or economic considerations.

If the consequences are potentially so counterproductive, why has that style of thinking come to prevail? As will be explored in detail in chapter eleven, a primary reason may be found not in the policy-making role played by professional military leaders, but in the tendency of civilians to adopt military ways of considering political problems.[1] It was not until the painful Vietnam experience was digested that many Americans began to suspect that military firepower and political influence are not synonymous.

The rhetoric of American leaders has consistently emphasized the martial[2] outlook derived from *realist* assumptions. The premise that security and influence are functions of military might has been parroted by American's decision makers over the entire postwar period (see Box 5.1). Indeed, the premise has been reiterated so often that it has become dogma.

To evaluate the record, let us first inspect the worldwide network of forward bases (military bases on the periphery of the communist world) and the otherwise enormous peacetime military establishment the nation has maintained, and the actual instances where military forces have been employed for essentially political purposes.

Force Projection: Forward Bases and Conventional Weapons

The network of over 300 overseas military bases and the stationing of more than half a million soldiers, sailors, airmen, and Marines abroad are two visible manifestations of the nation's perception of its responsibilities and of its commitment to the containment of communism. European and Asian bases were especially important in the 1950s in enhancing the credibility of the nuclear weapons strategy of massive retaliation, for they provided the forward bases from which American strategic bombers could strike at the heartland of the communist monolith. With the advent of the intercontinental missile, the strictly strategic importance of such bases waned, but they continued to play a role in the nation's overall national security strategy, particularly as a way of demonstrating commitments to allies. In Europe, for example, American troops serve a trip-wire function. In the event of an attack by Warsaw Pact

---

[1]The observation that civilian policy makers came to adopt military ways of thinking is, as Richard J. Walton (cited in Donovan, 1974) astutely observed, important, for "Civilian control versus military control is a distinction without a difference if the civilians think the same way the military does." For additional comments on this point, see Feis (1966), Donovan (1974), Alperovitz (1965 and 1970), Parenti (1971), Ambrose (1985), Sherwin (1973), LaFeber (1976), and Horowitz (1965).

[2]The diplomatic heritage of American foreign policy is shot through with inconsistent ideas regarding the American use of military instruments and force. Americans are said to display "a peculiar ambivalence toward war. They have traditionally perceived themselves as a peaceful, unmilitarized people, and yet have hardly ever been unwarlike" (Millett and Maslowski, 1984). Legend maintains that the United States is both peace loving and unbeatable in war; that it opposes the maintenance of standing armies but concurrently keeps an effective and sizable militia; that it enters wars only reluctantly, and always for moral purposes, but then wages them enthusiastically and concludes them victoriously; that it stands opposed to the use of force to get its way internationally, but that it is prone to intervene militarily in the affairs of others "if necessary" to protect its global interests; and that it stands in awe of military power, seeks to acquire it, but fears to use it. Those often incompatible images reveal a kind of love-hate attitude in America's approach to war and preparations for it. The nation is believed to be at once proud of both its nonmilitaristic ideals and a martial tradition that commands respect worldwide and includes an enviable record of performance on the battlefield as well as innovation in military tactics and technology.

BOX 5.1 The Militarization of American Foreign Policy: Forty Years of Policy Pronouncements

---

Policy Maker	Statement
Harry S. Truman, 1945	"We must continue to be a military nation if we are to maintain leadership among other nations."
Dwight D. Eisenhower, 1953	"Regardless of the consequences, the nation's military security will take first priority in my calculations."
John F. Kennedy, 1961	"[O]nly when our arms are sufficient beyond doubt can we be certain beyond doubt that they shall never be employed."
Lyndon B. Johnson, 1964	"United States military strength now exceeds the combined military might of all nations in history, stronger than any adversary or combination of adversaries. . . . Against such force the combined destructive power of every battle ever fought by man is like a firecracker thrown against the sun."
Richard M. Nixon, 1970	"Peace requires strength. So long as there are those who would threaten our vital interests and those of our allies with military force, we must be strong. American weakness could tempt would-be aggressors to make dangerous miscalculations."
Gerald R. Ford, 1976	"Our military forces are capable and ready. Our military power is without equal. And I intend to keep it that way."
Jimmy Carter, 1979	"In the dangerous and uncertain world of today, the keystone of our national security is still military strength—strength that is clearly recognized by Americans, by our Allies, and by any potential adversary."
Ronald Reagan, 1984	"Peace through strength is not a slogan; it's a fact of life—and we will not return to the days of hand wringing, defeatism, decline and despair."

forces against Western Europe, there is a high probability that some Americans will be killed. In this way the "wire" assuring an American retaliation would have "no choice" but to respond. The trip wire was an integral element of the Eisenhower–Dulles national security strategy. Today American troops in Europe continue to serve this function, but the purposes of deploying mili- in Europe continue to serve this function, but the purposes of deploying military troops and hardware overseas, and maintaining a large military establishment generally, have since become more varied. "Major war deterrence" were the key words used by the Nixon and Ford administrations to describe concern for conventional military threats to the United States and its allies. The strategy of "flexible response," devised during the Kennedy and Johnson years and adopted as the official NATO defense posture in 1967, became the means for coping with conventional war threats. Flexible response remains the official strategy for deterring nonnuclear war, particularly in the European theater.

Preventing all-out nuclear war is the purpose of strategic deterrence. Deterring war at something less than the global level, such as in Europe or Asia, and using something less than strategic nuclear weapons, such as tactical nuclear weapons or conventional means, is called *major* or *general war deterrence.* U.S. General Purpose Forces, which constitute the largest program expenditure in the defense budget, are the instruments of general war deterrence. Those forces link the United States to its allies by providing the primarily conventional military capabilities necessary to fulfill the many foreign commitments the nation has accumulated since World War II. The United States also maintains what are sometimes called Theater Nuclear Forces (forward-based systems, primarily in Europe but also in Asia), but the label is misleading because their purpose is to provide a link between American conventional and strategic nuclear forces, thus tying American nuclear capabilities to the defense of its allies. The term itself suggests the possibility of theaterwide (for example, on the order of World War II) conflict involving tactical nuclear weapons without an escalation to global conflagration involving strategic weapons.

The capabilities the United States currently maintains at the less-than-strategic level to ensure its own national security and to contribute to that of its allies are formidable. Included are nearly 15,000 tactical nuclear weapons as well as a vast arsenal of conventional weapons. Also included are some 2.2 million men and women in the armed forces in 19 divisions, about 350,000 of whom are in Europe with another 146,000 in Asia and the western Pacific. To this picture can be added a naval force of nearly 600 ships that includes deployable battle forces of diverse types and awesome capabilities.

Flexible response is the concept under which President Kennedy and his secretary of defense, Robert McNamara, sought to increase conventional war capabilities as a substitute for reliance on massive (nuclear) retaliation. In 1962 the capacity to wage "2½ wars" at once was embraced as the official strategy. Apart from a nuclear war, the 2½ wars were to include simultaneously a conventional war in Europe with the Soviet Union, a Southeast Asian war, and a lesser engagement (half a war?) elsewhere. With the hindsight of Vietnam, which shook the notion of American military invincibility to its very foundations, the 2½ war strategy appears preposterous. At the time, however, it was not so perceived, a fact which led one observer to view the strategy as a "military expression of the U.S. national policy goals that reached out for Pax Americana [worldwide peace imposed by the United States] and 'world hegemony'" (Melman, 1974).

President Nixon reduced the 2½ war strategy to 1½ wars, with general purpose forces maintained for simultaneously meeting a major communist attack in either Europe or Asia and contending with a lesser contingency elsewhere. That move was part of the reordering of the nation's role in world affairs envisioned in the Nixon Doctrine, which called for a "low profile" for the United States in the post-Vietnam era and for increased pressure on American allies to provide for their own defense.

The Carter administration pursued essentially the same strategy. President Carter observed, for example, that "however wealthy and powerful the United States may be—however capable of leadership—this power is increasingly in need of being shared." But events in Afghanistan and the Persian Gulf area in 1979 and 1980 spurred plans already in the works to develop a Rapid Deployment Force (RDF) capable of intervening militarily in world trouble spots to defend American interests. The Carter Doctrine, enunciated in the president's 1980 State of the Union address, affirmed that the ability to rapidly intervene militarily to safeguard American security interests would be preserved. The emphasis on conventional capabilities during the era of nuclear parity with the Soviet Union itself derived from the conviction that neither the United States nor the Soviet Union could conceivably win a nuclear war. The parallel with both the thinking and the rhetoric of the Kennedy years is striking.

With respect to the European theater, the nation's long-standing drive to get the NATO allies to pay a greater share of the costs of North Atlantic defense was intensified.[3] In response, some European allies pledged themselves to increase defense spending, and the United States simultaneously committed itself to the force modernization necessary to enable NATO, as described by Defense Secretary Brown, "to respond appropriately to any level of potential attack and to pose the risk of escalation to higher levels of conflict." Included in that commitment was the controversial decision to deploy several hundred theater nuclear force weapons in Europe (both ground-launched cruise missiles and Pershing II medium-range ballistic missiles). As noted in chapter four, the decision was a direct response to the Soviet Union's growing

---

[3]"Burdensharing" refers to the principle that each member of the NATO alliance must do its part to assume a fair share of the cost of the common defense of the North Atlantic area. It is a controversial principle since there is no single formula that measures each country's contribution. If defense expenditures as a percent of Gross National Product is used as the measure, it is clear there are wide differences among the NATO allies, ranging (in 1982) from 1 percent of GNP for Luxembourg to 6.4 percent for the United States and 6.9 percent for Greece (U.S. Department of State, 1985a: 5).

medium-range capability (specifically the SS-20 missile and the Backfire bomber), which was beyond the strategic weapons framework of the SALT negotiations. It was also tied to a pledge to seek negotiations with the Soviet Union on limiting theater nuclear forces—an issue of particular salience to many Western European countries. The Carter administration thus reaffirmed the principle of flexible response. Tactical nuclear weapons multiply the options available to decision makers in the event that conventional forces are unable to contain aggression. Indeed, the NATO alliance reserves the right of "first use" of nuclear weapons, a policy that became the object of controversy in the "peace movement" that emerged on both sides of the Atlantic in the late 1970s and early 1980s (see Kegley and Wittkopf, 1985a).

The Reagan administration's early military planning accepted some of the assumptions of its predecessor while rejecting others. The Carter Doctrine was reaffirmed and extended, with plans for the direct introduction of American troops into the Persian Gulf area if necessary to protect access to its vital supplies. It was also given much broader application: "the United States would henceforth use force anywhere on the earth where vital U.S. interests are in jeopardy" (Klare, 1985). "The United States," Defense Secretary Weinberger explained in 1981, "is, and always should be, a global power, with global concerns and responsibilities that are an integral part of our national security."

To protect that security, the administration continued to rely on strategic and tactical nuclear weapons for deterrence,[4] but the assumption that any conventional war with the Soviet Union would be of short duration and either settled by negotiation or escalated into a nuclear confrontation was jettisoned. Instead, the Reagan administration assumed that any conventional war with the Soviet Union would be protracted, with fighting occurring in numerous locations around the globe and without any necessary escalation to nuclear confrontation. Thus American forces were to be readied to protect the nation's interests as far from home as their resources would permit. Moreover, plans were made to augment those resources with more weapons, supplies, equipment, and transport capabilities. Domestic defense industries were also to be readied to support the possibility of a prolonged, global conventional war. Eventually greater attention was also given to preparations for "low intensity" conflicts, such as guerrilla wars and terrorist attacks, with counterinsurgency capabilities given priority in a manner similar to the Kennedy administration's emphasis two decades earlier. The assumption was that Third World instability provided the Soviet Union "targets of opportunity" and thus posed a threat that might be dealt with militarily.

---

[4]In the words of Secretary of State Alexander M. Haig in 1981: "Our deterrence achieves its credibility by the perception of our willingness to do whatever is necessary to protect our vital interests if they are challenged. And that must include the arsenal of nuclear weapons." Later (as discussed in detail in chapter four), the administration sought to shift the discussion from defense to offense with its Strategic Defense Initiative, even while it continued to rely on traditional forms of deterrence.

Retrospectively, it is unclear whether the administration was able to accomplish its ambitious goals. Internal Defense Department documents reportedly showed in 1984 that, after three years of the Reagan military buildup, only the Navy had more combat-ready units than previously; the number of combat-ready Army and Air Force units had actually declined (Hiatt, 1984a). Furthermore, at the same time that the president and secretary of defense boasted that increased military readiness enabled the nation to respond quickly in a crisis and to sustain operations to support the expanding list of United States commitments, Admiral Wesley L. McDonald, commander in chief of the Atlantic fleet, testified before Congress that "our forces continue to be very heavily committed around the world, and stretched so thin that very little surge capability exists for rapid response to additional crises." General John W. Vessey, Jr., chairman of the joint chiefs of staff, also conceded that the military would be unable to respond to Soviet threats on as many fronts simultaneously as official Defense Department documents claimed (Hiatt, 1984a). To many critics, the reasons were to be found in the emphasis given to the procurement of complex high-tech conventional weapons as well as nuclear weapons at the expense of maintenance and sustainability—and ultimately the soldier in the field and the sailor aboard ship.[5] Moreover, bureaucratic foul-ups caused by interservice rivalries (discussed in chapter eleven) remained a persistent problem, as witnessed during the military operation in Grenada, and the specter of faulty intelligence and bungled military capability with which Reagan had charged Carter three years earlier (when eight American servicemen died in an abortive attempt at a military rescue of U.S. diplomatic personnel held hostage in Teheran) was raised with the truck-bombing of Marine headquarters in Beirut in late October 1983, which left nearly 250 American servicemen dead. To some it seemed as though expanding military budgets had purchased few improvements.

The Reagan administration's commitment to force modernization in the European theater culminated in its decision to proceed with the deployment of the intermediate-range nuclear weapons. The decision was controversial because the political climate in Western Europe had changed since NATO agreed to the plan in 1979 with the rise of a "peace movement"—fueled in part by the administration's hawkish rhetoric and Reagan's own prediction that a nuclear war centered on Europe, with the United States standing aside, might be possible—which challenged both the Atlantic alliance and the domestic base of the governments comprising it. The result was a Soviet boycott of the INF and START (Strategic Arms Reduction Talks) negotiations with the United States.

On another front, the superpowers have since 1973 sought in a forum

---

[5]As Mandelbaum (1986) observes, "Over the next decade, limits on available resources may yield a military establishment rich in powerful, complicated, expensive weapons but poor in spare parts for them, short of the funds to exercise and maintain these armaments, and, because of insufficient pay scales, without skilled personnel to operate them."

known as the Mutual and Balanced Force Reduction (MBFR) negotiations to agree on a reduction of their European conventional forces to equal and significantly lower levels. That effort was supplemented by the Conference on Disarmament in Europe (CDE), which was convened in January 1984 in Stockholm. Composed of the 35 states participating in the 1975 Helsinki Accords, the conference suceeded in September 1986 in adopting the first East-West security agreement in a decade. That historic pact provides participating states the mandatory right to send military observers to watch large military maneuvers and exercises in any state in Europe, and allows aerial inspections of suspicious military activities that have not been announced. The "confidence building" measures was interpreted as a significant step toward improved US-Soviet relations.

Unlike the CDE, the MBFR talks have not gone well, and progress in the MBFR talks has been slow. Here the principal point of contention is not the goal of force reduction; instead, it is the base from which one begins to count.

As the principle of "flexible response" implies, with its concomitant threat to use nuclear weapons, the United States and its NATO allies believe themselves to be at a disadvantage vis-à-vis the Soviet Union and its Warsaw Pact allies. In part this is simply a matter of their differing geostrategic situations—the Soviet Union, an essentially European power, would be able to strike with its allies against Western Europe more quickly and potentially more decisively than the United States and its allies would be able to respond. Beyond such obvious geostrategic asymmetries, the two sides differ fundamentally about how to interpret data regarding estimates of relative strength and capabilities, including especially the questionable reliability of some national units.

The NATO allies believe the current balance of conventional forces heavily favors the Warsaw Pact. It estimates that in the mid-1970s the NATO alliance had but 2.6 million troops in place and rapidly deployable, compared to 4 million for the Warsaw Pact. The asymmetry continues across other force comparisons: 88 NATO divisions compared to 112 Warsaw Pact divisions; 13,415 tanks compared to 26,875; 10,920 artillery and mortars compared to 18,905; 1,960 fighter bombers compared to 2,250 (U.S. Department of State, 1985a: 8).

The basic dispute between the two alliances turns on the size of the Warsaw Pact forces. Warsaw Pact figures for its ground and air forces are about 200,000 less than Western estimates. The difference is critical, since the end goal is parity between the two alliances. The Warsaw Pact believes parity already exists, which implies that both sides should make equal force reductions. To agree to the West's figures, which show a margin of Warsaw Pact superiority of about 20 percent, would, the Warsaw Pact nations argue, be tantamount to handing NATO an unfair military advantage. NATO disagrees, alleging the Eastern bloc already enjoys superiority. Equal reductions would therefore violate the agreed upon objective of a common ceiling on each side's military manpower. There is little prospect this fundamental dispute will be quickly or easily resolved.

Military Force and Political Purposes

The discussion here and in chapter four of both major war and strategic doctrinal shifts suggests that the purpose of American military might has been primarily preventive: to deter politically the use of military force by someone else, notably the Soviet Union.

In addition to prevention, American military forces have been used for the purpose of changing the behavior of foreign actors. As shown in Figure 5.1, there has been a total of 286 instances, traceable across the entire period from 1946 to 1984, in which the United States has threatened to unleash some of its military might to influence, indirectly, the decisions of other states; that is, force has been used to cause the target either not to do something or to do something that it would not otherwise do.[6]

Figure 5.1 suggests two peaks in postwar American "gunboat diplomacy," the period from 1957 to 1965, and from 1981 to 1984. In the first, the average annual frequency of events where American force was used as a political instrument was 12.6, compared with the average frequency of 7.3 incidents per year across the entire thirty-nine-year period. In the second, which coincides with President Reagan's first term in office, the average was 11.5 incidents. It is also clear that reliance on military forces for the achievement of political ends has been a preferred instrument of influence of virtually every administration since World War II.

Several examples of U.S. reliance on this instrument of influence illustrate the modern tactic of "gunboat diplomacy." One is the joint air exercises the United States undertook with Egypt and the augmenting of its Indian Ocean naval patrols as a signal to the Soviet Union not to extend its invasion of Afghanistan westward; another the sending in 1980 of sophisticated electronic surveillance planes to Saudi Arabia during the 1980 Iran-Iraq war as a signal to the combatants not to widen the war; a third the decision in 1981 to send helicopters to monitor the cease-fire ending the border dispute between Ecuador and Peru. Others include the stationing of a carrier task force in the Mediterranean in 1983 to dissuade Libyan dictator Muammar Qaddafi from launching an attack on Sudan, and the staging of naval maneuvers on both sides of the Honduran isthmus in 1983 in an effort to intimidate leftist guerrillas active in Central America and to deter support of them by Cuba, Nicaragua, and the Soviet Union. Clearly, on these and many other occasions, the practice of gun boat diplomacy was designed for purposes other than protecting the immediate physical security of the nation.

The Reagan administration used force without war more frequently than any administration except Kennedy's. The contrast between it and the Carter

---

[6]Military forces can also be used to attain desired ends directly. Blechman and Kaplan's (1978) and Zelikow's (1984 and 1986) surveys are instead concerned only with those instances where the force itself does not obtain the objective, but rather affects the perceptions of others, thereby influencing their decision(s).

FIGURE 5.1   The Frequency of the Use of Military Force for Political Purposes, 1946–1984

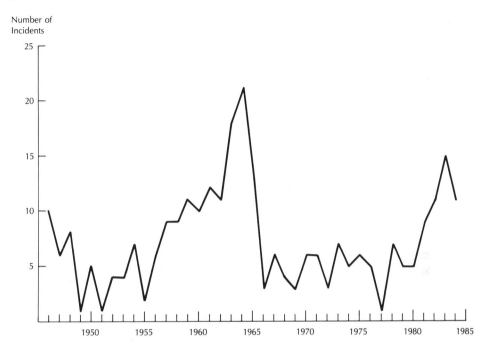

SOURCE: Adapted from Blechman and Kaplan, 1978: 547–553, and Zelikow, 1986: forthcoming.

administration (during which the average number of incidents per year was only 4.5) is especially striking and is consistent with the resurgence of public support for an assertive America many believe to have occurred in the 1980s. For perhaps a decade following the peak of American involvement in Vietnam, the attitudes of many Americans, both inside and outside of government, suggested that there would be considerable restraint on the use of military force abroad in the future. Already by the early 1980s, however, matters appeared to have returned to their "normal" state. As national security adviser Zbigniew Brzezinski observed in 1979, "The nation has finally thrown off aversion to military spending and possible intervention that was the legacy of Vietnam." Although restraints on the use of force remain formidable (Cohen, 1984), the dispatch of several dozen American military advisers to El Salvador in 1981 and of a peace-keeping force of 800 Marines (with more to follow) to Lebanon in 1982 was consistent with the view that military force once more occupied a central role propelling active American involvement in world affairs. Overt military intervention in Grenada reaffirmed it, as did the military attack on Libya in 1986.

Military Intervention

The maintenance of a high military profile abroad and displays of force comprise two elements of the interventionist thrust of America's globalist foreign policy posture. Outright military intervention is another. Here, too, there has been a striking consistency in the willingness of postwar administrations to intervene in the affairs of others. On five conspicuous occasions—in Korea (1950), Lebanon (1958), Vietnam (1955, 1961, or 1965, depending on one's definition), the Dominican Republic (1965), and Grenada (1983)—the United States openly and directly used its military power in another country in order to accomplish its foreign policy objectives. Although other instances might be cited (such as the U.S. attacks on Cambodia in 1970 and 1975 and the hostage rescue operation in Iran in 1980), those five cases, perhaps more than anything else, have pinned the interventionist label on postwar American foreign policy and created seemingly *endless enemies* (Kwitny, 1985) in an increasingly unfriendly world.

Measured in terms of size, Grenada was the smallest operation, involving only 1,900 American assault troops (joined by 300 soldiers from the Caribbean nations making up the Organization of Eastern Caribbean States) in an operation that met opposition from a local military force of only 1,200 troops plus roughly 700 armed Cuban construction workers. Lebanon was next in size, involving 14,000 American troops in what was essentially a bloodless intervention. The Dominican intervention ranks third in size, with 22,000 troops and some combat activity on the part of American forces. Korea and Vietnam were, of course, much larger. In casualties alone, the Korean War outstripped the number of troops involved in the Dominican affair by 11,000. And in Vietnam, where at one point over 550,000 troops were engaged, the Vietnam Veterans Memorial in Arlington Cemetery commemorates the 58,000 Americans who lost their lives in an intervention that spanned two Republican and two Democratic administrations.

Despite the recurrent nature of American interventionism, the interventionist label may be questioned. How does one explain the far larger number of instances in which the United States did not intervene when its interests were threatened, as in the decision not to bail the French out of Indochina when they faced defeat at Dienbienphu in 1954? That case and the unwillingness of the United States, with the single exception of Lebanon in 1958, to become directly involved militarily in the Middle East's turmoil, stand out as glaring examples of nonintervention. How do we reconcile those facts with the interventionist stigma? Herbert K. Tillema's *Appeal to Force* (1973) is concerned with precisely that question. His answers are instructive.

Tillema identifies nearly 150 postwar conflict situations in which the United States might have become involved. In fact, however, it became overtly involved militarily in only four during his period of observation (1945–1970). These situations indicate that American intervention was resisted whenever one or more of several different inhibiting factors were present. Among those factors are the perceived need to use nuclear weapons, the prior presence of Soviet troops, the willingness of the president to let some other component of the decision-making structure (such as Congress) veto an intervention decision, the absence of armed conflict, or the absence of a specific request for intervention. But, Tillema concludes, "On those occasions when a Communist threat was thought to exist and when none of the other restraints was operative, intervention has followed." His view of overt military intervention thus holds that American intervention occurs if, and only if, a communist takeover appears likely in another country, and none of the above-mentioned types of restraints to an armed intervention is present.

Tillema's perspective on the pattern of American action during the 1950s and 1960s is informative. Despite changes in the policy-making personnel involved in the decisions to intervene militarily in the four situations mentioned, and despite some obvious differences in the situations they faced, each new case was treated in the same manner as previous ones. "Whatever differences there may have been in the purposes that different policymakers have seen in the use of force," writes Tillema, "all have used it in the same way. The continuing restraints upon intervention have shaped its use to the same mold." This pattern presumably continued to apply in the 1970s (see Tillema and Van Wingen, 1982).

Interestingly, the Reagan administration's decision to intervene in Grenada followed very much the pattern of American action in the 1950s, 1960s, and 1970s. The event which precipitated the invasion was the overthrow of the Marxist-oriented government of Prime Minister Maurice Bishop and his subsequent execution by what President Reagan called "a brutal gang of leftist thugs." The administration provided three primary reasons for choosing military action. The first was to rescue Americans on the island—primarily students at the local medical school—whose safety was threatened. Fear of "another Iran," referring to the incarceration of American diplomats in Teheran for 444 days beginning in late 1979, reportedly weighed heavily on the president's mind. The second was the invitation of Grenada's neighbors in the Organization of Eastern Caribbean States (OECS). The argument was that the action was based on article 8 of the OECS Treaty (of which Grenada was a signatory), which relates to the organization's collective defense against external aggression. The final argument, and doubtless the strongest one, was fear that Grenada might become another Cuba. For some time the administration had worried about the purpose of a 10,000-foot airport runway in Grenada, alleging it could be used by Soviet military aircraft and thus become a vehicle for spreading communist influence throughout the region and threatening U.S. security. In testimony before the House Foreign Affairs Committee, Deputy Secretary of State Kenneth Dam argued that "Grenada could be used as a staging area for subversion of nearby countries, for interdiction of shipping lanes, and for transit of troops and supplies from Cuba to Africa, and from Eastern Europe and Libya to Central America." The intervention was thus a means to rid the Caribbean of a potential Cuban and Soviet outpost and to divert what the administration believed to be the drift toward radical regimes in the Caribbean. The logic was strikingly similar to that used by the Johnson administration to intervene in the Dominican Republic nearly twenty years earlier. That intervention was first rationalized by the need to protect American lives in a chaotic civil circumstance that threatened to bring a leftist regime to power, but President Johnson later admitted that fear of "another Cuba" was a greater concern.

COVERT ACTIVITY AND INTELLIGENCE OPERATIONS

Yet another pattern has contributed to the interventionist label so frequently attached to postwar American foreign policy. It derives from the persistent covert involvement of the United States in the affairs of other nations.

American defense policy and its related interventionist posture over the past four decades developed in an atmosphere in which decision makers held widely shared perceptions shaped by fear of communism generally and of Soviet expansionism in particular. In April 1950, the National Security Council (NSC), a top-level interagency body that advises the president on foreign policy matters, issued its now famous National Security Council paper number 68, in which the connection between the containment of communism and military preparedness was spelled out. A decisive sentence in NSC 68 asserted, "Without superior aggregate military strength, in being and readily mobilizable, a policy of 'containment'—which is in effect a policy of calculated and gradual coercion—is no more than a policy of bluff." NSC 68 also called for a nonmilitary counteroffensive against the Soviet Union, which included covert economic, political, and psychological warfare designed to foment unrest and revolt in Soviet bloc countries. By as early as November 1951, at least some in Washington recognized that such broad and comprehensive undertakings as delineated by the National Security Council could be accomplished only by the establishment of a worldwide structure for covert operations (*Final Report of the Select Committee to Study Governmental Operations with Respect to Intelligence Activities*, Vol. IV, 1976; hereafter cited as *Final Report*, I-VI, 1976).

In the ensuing years, the Central Intelligence Agency (CIA) became infamous worldwide as the arm of the American government that was responsible for perhaps otherwise inexplicable political events in other countries. As a Senate select committee investigating American intelligence activities put it:

> The CIA has been accused of interfering in the internal political affairs of nations ranging from Iran to Chile, from Tibet to Guatemala, from Libya to Laos, from Greece to Indonesia. Assassinations, coups d'état, vote buying, economic warfare—all have been laid at the doorstep of the CIA. Few political crises take place in the world today in which CIA involvement is not alleged. (*Final Report*, I, 1976: 141)

The accuracy of that picture of CIA covert operations is open to debate. But sufficient information about intelligence activities overseas is available to indicate that covert political actions may have been as integral a part of national security as military programs. Such activities further illustrate the country's interventionist strategy and its role as global policeman.

Intelligence collection per se provokes little concern or criticism. Since foreign policy decision makers are expected to protect the physical security and general welfare of the population, they require detailed information necessary for understanding the varied military, economic, political, scientific, domestic, and foreign issues and events requisite to sound policy making. Providing such information is the task of the intelligence community (the institutional features of which are described in detail in chapter eleven). More specifically, its task is to produce "finished intelligence," defined as "data collected from all sources—secret, official, and open—which has been carefully collated and analyzed by substantive experts specifically to meet the needs of the national leadership" (Marchetti and Marks, 1974). Much of what constitutes raw intelligence (the uncollated and unanalyzed data) is not acquired through mysterious cloak-and-dagger escapades but rather comes from readily available public sources, such as the reports of journalists, professional diplomats, and information and cultural officers, and the publications of governmental agencies, private businesses, and scholars. Data from such public sources are supplemented by so-called hard intelligence derived from code breaking and reconnaissance satellites.

Covert operations, on the other hand, are secret activities undertaken abroad (usually) against foreign governments, installations, or individuals with the expressed purpose of directly influencing the outcome of political events. The term *"covert operation"* is itself often used interchangeably with the terms *"covert action"* and *"clandestine political operation."* Covert operations are conceptually distinct from the clandestine collection of intelligence, or espionage (the illegal collection of intelligence through agent networks), in that the former attempt to influence events directly, while the latter does not.[7]

Many have argued that certain clandestine intelligence activities are necessary, particularly since access is universally denied to important information relevant to sound policy making, such as that relating to the military capabilities and intentions of potential adversaries. Informed and responsible decisions about the appropriate American position in the SALT talks, for example, would not have been possible without information gained from satellite reconnaissance and other technical sources. Yet efforts to obtain information on the capabilities and intentions of other nations have themselves often resulted in significant foreign policy ramifications. Perhaps the most celebrated example occurred in 1960, when the CIA U-2 spy plane piloted by Francis Gary Powers

[7]The Department of the Army in *Special Forces Operation: U.S. Army Doctrine* defines these terms thus: "unconventional warfare operations may be covert, clandestine, or overt in nature. Covert operations are conducted in such a manner as to conceal the identity of the sponsor, while clandestine operations place emphasis on concealment of the operation rather than the identity of the sponsor. Overt operations do not try to conceal either the operation or the identity of the sponsor" (U.S. Department of the Army, 1969).

was shot down deep within Soviet territory on the very eve of the Paris Summit between President Eisenhower and Soviet Premier Khrushchev. The summit was never held, and American-Soviet relations became as frigid as at any point during the Cold War. Another example occurred in 1968 when the North Koreans captured the ELINT (electronic intelligence) spy ship *Pueblo*, operated by the navy and the National Security Agency, near the coast of North Korea. The immediate foreign policy problem created by the incident was the return of the captured crewman and the ship. The former was eventually accomplished; the latter was not, a fact which, presumably, contributed to Soviet knowledge of American electronic intelligence capabilities.

Both of those incidents illustrate the kinds of embarrassments and complications which can arise out of an otherwise legitimate need for policy-making information. More questionable in the eyes of critics are the many instances of covert actions undertaken by intelligence agencies, particularly the CIA (for example, assassination plots against foreign leaders), in an effort not simply to gather information but actually to carry out plans and programs designed to accomplish specific political ends. Among the more notorious cases that have come to public light are the CIA-engineered coups in Iran and Guatemala in the 1950s and Vietnam in the 1960s; the CIA-trained, financed, and directed armies which sought to overthrow Cuba's Castro and which conducted a "secret" war in Laos in the 1960s; the CIA-supported political action programs designed to prevent Marxist-oriented President Salvador Allende from winning and then exercising political power in Chile in the 1970s; and "Operation Feature" designed to recruit mercenaries to fight in Angola with arms costing $32 million in the mid-1970s.[8]

If the initial impetus toward covert operations was provided by the increasingly hostile international political environment of the late 1940s and early 1950s, the perceived success attributed to the CIA in carrying them out contributed to its status as an instrument of policy implementation. By as early as 1953, the CIA had gained a reputation for its political action and paramilitary warfare, a reputation reinforced by what were widely regarded as two of its boldest and most spectacular operations—the overthrow of Premier Mohammed Mossadegh in Iran in 1953 and the coup which ousted President Jacobo Arbenz of Guatemala in 1954 (see Immerman, 1982; and Schlesinger and Kinzer, 1983). By those quick and virtually bloodless operations two allegedly procommunist leaders were replaced with pro-Western officials. Out of such early acclaimed achievements both the agency and Washington policy makers acquired a sense of confidence in the CIA's capacity for operational success.

---

[8]Other, less famous CIA operations disclosed in Senate subcommittee investigations strain the imagination. For instance, it was revealed that in 1959 CIA agents tested LSD on a houseful of unwitting people in San Francisco who thought they had been invited to a party. Those same hearings revealed that the CIA tried once to humiliate Fidel Castro by dusting the Cuban leader's shoes with a substance that would make his hair fall out; less humorously, the investigation reported that Castro had survived at least eight CIA-sponsored assassination plots.

Throughout the 1950s the CIA was directed by Allen Dulles. Master spy of OSS (Office of Strategic Services—forerunner of the CIA) operations in Switzerland during World War II and brother of Secretary of State John Foster Dulles, Allen Dulles was personally interested in the intrigue of clandestine operations. Under his tutelage the CIA moved from being the servant of other government agencies, such as the State and Defense departments, to being the initiator in defining the ways in which covert operations could enhance foreign policy goals and in determining how specific operations could enhance particular policy objectives. Thus it achieved the enviable bureaucratic position of not only defining foreign policy programs for top-level decision makers, but also of providing the information on which policy makers would base their decisions and then implementing them once they were made. The invasion of Cuba at the Bay of Pigs in 1961 by a band of CIA-trained and financed Cuban exiles, which combined in one agency the roles of information collection, policy formulation, and program implementation, stands out as a classic case of CIA prominence in policy making.

The Bay of Pigs operation was to be the CIA's method of eliminating the problem posed by Castro. Although it was engineered along the lines of the successful 1954 Guatemalan operation, the defeat suffered by the Cuban exiles tarnished the agency's reputation—and cost Allen Dulles his job. But covert operations nevertheless continued to be seen as an acceptable policy option. Operation Mongoose was one manifestation of that perspective. Mongoose consisted of paramilitary, sabotage, and political propaganda activities directed against Castro's Cuba between October 1961 and 1962. Paramilitary operations were also initiated in Laos, where over 30,000 tribesmen were organized into a kind of private CIA army. However, as the 1960s wore on, the Vietnam issue came to dominate the CIA, as it did other government agencies. In one CIA operation there, known as Phoenix, an estimated 20,000 to 40,000 suspected Vietcong were killed over a period of less than three years (Marchetti and Marks, 1974).

The catalog of both proven and alleged CIA involvement in the internal affairs of other nations could be broadened. Indeed, the Senate select committee on intelligence (*Final Report*, I, 1976) used the phrase "several thousand" to describe the number of covert action projects undertaken since 1961 alone. Not unlike the preference for military solutions to political problems, covert operations have been common because the assets have been available to foreign policy decision makers. "To these officials, including the President, covert intervention may seem to be an easier solution to a particular problem than to allow events to follow their natural course or to seek a tortuous diplomatic settlement," write Victor Marchetti and John Marks (1974). "The temptation to interfere in another country's internal affairs can be almost irresistible, when the means are at hand."

One cannot understand the reliance on either covert or military forms of intervention without recognizing the extent to which fear of communism and the drive to contain it have motivated postwar American foreign policy. The war might have been cold, but it was war nevertheless. Hence, it was deemed appropriate to use the same tools as the other side, no matter how repugnant they might be. Questions of morality and legality were seen as irrelevant; a higher purpose—the "national security"—was being served.

As we have seen in chapter three, the more virulent forms of the anticommunist drive receded somewhat during the 1970s as domestic criticism of known intelligence abuses led both the president and Congress to impose restraints on the foreign and domestic activities of the intelligence community. Indeed, the justification for covert operations changed sharply from the early 1950s, when their purpose was framed in terms of opposition to international communism, to the 1970s, when covert actions were described simply as those secret activities designed to further American policies and programs abroad.[9] American involvement in Chile illustrates the point.

The facts[10] of the "Chilean connection" include efforts going back as far as 1958 to prevent the Marxist-oriented Salvador Allende from gaining political power in Chile. In the next dozen years perhaps a billion dollars in funds were committed, directly or indirectly, to the "battle to preserve democracy in Chile," a battle designed essentially to prevent the political left from assuming power (Fagen, 1975). The efforts, supervised by the National Security Council's 40 Committee, included covert actions directed against Allende in the 1964 presidential election as well as overt financial support to the Christian Democratic government, which governed Chile throughout the 1960s. Thus, by 1970, when Allende appeared likely to win popular election to the Chilean presidency, the outlines of American involvement in Chilean affairs were already well established. The highest levels of the government—including President Nixon and Henry Kissinger (national security adviser at the time)—subsequently approved several efforts designed to prevent, and later subvert, the legitimate acquisition and exercise of power by Allende's Popular Unity government. The means approved (not all were employed) included $400,000 in covert expenditures to oppose the Allende candidacy; $350,000 to bribe Chilean congressmen to vote not for Allende but for his opponent (congressional approval was necessitated by Allende's plurality rather than majority victory in the popular election); and $8 million in expenditures designed to

---

[9]Perhaps it is also not surprising, therefore, that concern for domestic "dissidents" and unrest at the time of the Vietnam War led the Nixon administration to create a special intelligence group within the White House known as the Plumbers, whose ostensible purpose was to fix news "leaks" and "flush" dissident opinion out of the American political system. Creation of the Plumbers was prompted by Dr. Daniel Ellsberg's release of the Pentagon Papers, which contained national-security-related classified information. The group was responsible—in the name of national security—for the burglary of the office of Dr. Ellsberg's psychiatrist. It was also responsible somewhat later for the surreptitious entry of Democratic National Headquarters in the Watergate Hotel complex in the summer of 1972.

[10]The meanings and motivations underlying some of the facts surrounding the events in Chile between 1970 and 1973 are perhaps more controversial than the actual events themselves. For relevant discussions see Fagan (1975), Petras and LaPorte (1972), Farnsworth (1974), and Sigmund (1974a and 1974b).

destabilize the Allende government in the period 1971–1973 (Fagen, 1975: 298).

Pressures were also brought to bear by the restriction of American credit against which the Chilean government might purchase American goods. Similar restrictions were imposed by multilateral lending institutions (multination international organizations, such as the World Bank) and private banks. (In the eyes of many commentators, those actions, too, were the result of influence exerted by the U.S. government.) A close working relationship developed between the U.S. government and giant U.S.-based multinational corporations doing business in Chile, whose corporate interests were being threatened by the Allende nationalization program. Ultimately the combination of international pressures from without Chile and domestic pressures from within was too great. The Allende government was overthrown in a bloody coup in September 1973. With that coup, a military dictatorship, ruthlessly brutal, replaced a democracy.

What are the lessons? Although there is evidence that the traditional concern for communism and the "domino effect"[11] in Latin America and elsewhere motivated anti-Allende thinking, more instructive was the apparent willingness of Washington officials to use all means available to achieve ends only tangentially related to the containment of communism. It wasn't just the CIA. And it wasn't clearly communism. It was a concerted governmentwide effort, which enlisted the support of non-American agencies, against a popularly elected government which could claim a commitment to social reform rather than a commitment to Soviet communism. Thus Chile illustrates how the American fear of "almost any Third World experiment in socioeconomic transformation not directly under [American] control" inevitably invites covert activities (Fagen, 1975).

While Chile illustrated the willingness of the government to use a range of instruments to oppose those who experiment in leftist domestic political programs, events in Iran and Afghanistan in late 1979 seemed to rekindle support for opposition to more traditionally defined communist threats and led to cries within both the executive branch and Congress to "unleash" the CIA by lifting some of the restraints that earlier had been imposed on the agency.[12] William Casey, CIA director in the Reagan administration, pledged in response to "minimize" the restrictions placed on the CIA by Congress in the 1970s, while Congress itself expressed a willingness to ease some of those restrictions, as we shall see in chapters eleven and twelve. Revelations about United States involvement in "secret wars" in Afghanistan and Nicaragua

---

[11]As described in chapter three, the so-called domino theory holds that any communist ascendancy abroad will breed other communist victories, so that (inevitably) the entire world will fall to communism like a row of dominoes collapsing in chain reaction. Hence the need, according to proponents of the theory, for strong American resistance to any communist initiative appearing to comprise the first thrust toward this outcome.

[12]Efforts by the Reagan administration and its supporters begun in 1981 to repeal the Clark Amendment prohibiting CIA support of various factions opposing the Marxist government of Angola, which were finally successful in 1985, were indicative of the shifting sentiment.

dramatized how much the pendulum had swung since the 1970s; the CIA was back in business.

The intention of the United States to support anticommunist movements worldwide was underscored by President Reagan when he declared in his 1985 State of the Union address (in what became known as the "Reagan Doctrine") that "We must not break faith with those who are risking their lives on every continent from Afghanistan to Nicaragua to defy Soviet supported aggression and secure rights which have been ours from birth. . . . Support for freedom fighters is self-defense."

The implications for the CIA were clear, and while much of its activity remained shrouded in secrecy, press reports suggested its capacity for covert actions in terms of staff and budget were greatly reenergized under Casey. Among the missions the media purported to have uncovered were covert support for Iranian exile groups seeking to overthrow the Ayatollah Khomeini, and the provision of arms and financial assistance to military forces in Chad and the Sudan, with Ethiopia, Angola, Liberia, and Cambodia also sometimes cited (see Tyler and Ottaway, 1986). Afghanistan and Nicaragua became the most celebrated cases. In Afghanistan the CIA provided guns, ammunition, and other support at a cost exceeding in 1986 $500 million annually for the Moslem insurgents challenging Soviet troops and the pro-Soviet regime; in Nicaragua its support was extended to the contra (counterrevolutionary) commando forces challenging the leftist Sandinista regime.

When the CIA's activities became visible, they were not always supported publicly. Critics of administration policies toward Nicaragua in particular questioned whether the anticommunist crusade there was so clear-cut. Furthermore, CIA involvement in planning and executing naval blockades, air strikes, espionage, and propaganda operations was of such magnitude as to spark charges that the agency had once more gotten out of hand. The agency's role in producing a manual that called for "neutralization" (read assassination) of Nicaraguan officials and in mining Nicaraguan harbors led some to challenge the legality of its acts under domestic law and those of the United States under the law of nations.[13]

Clearly the activities of the United States in Nicaragua, Afghanistan, and elsewhere indicated that it was once more willing to engage in the same kinds of actions as its adversaries if that was what was required to defeat them. As Fred C. Iklé, under secretary of defense for policy, put it in reference to covert

[13]Harvard Law Professor Abram Chayes, who earlier in his career laid the legal foundations for the Kennedy administration's naval quarantine of Cuba during the 1962 missile crisis with the Soviet Union, elected to represent Nicaragua in its suit against the United States in the World Court, in which it challenged the legality of U.S. operations, overt and covert, designed to undermine the Nicaraguan government. Believing that the Nicaraguan leaders were acting "to uphold the rule of law in international affairs," Chayes stated that he thought it appropriate for the United States, which "purports to be bound by the rule of law," to be judged under "appropriate international procedures." He stated that "there is nothing wrong with holding the United States to its own best standards and best principles" (*New York Times*, April 11, 1983). In the summer of 1986 the World Court ruled that U.S. actions in support of the contras were indeed a violation of international law.

war, "The [Reagan] administration has tried to reduce the asymmetry, the extent to which the Soviet Union can use all means—terrorist, covert, arms shipments, what have you—to topple governments or support governments that are opposed by the people, while the United States would be left with the choice between vacating the field, abandoning the friends of democracy, or getting into an all-out conflict." In this sense the strategies and tactics of the United States and the Soviet Union often resemble one another (see Jönsson, 1984), for the Reagan Doctrine mirrors the Soviet doctrine unveiled in 1960 that the U.S.S.R. would support "wars of national liberation" in the Third World. The result was a resurgence of the "traditional" kinds of covert activities abroad which gave the CIA its notoriety in an earlier stage of the East-West conflict. The conclusions drawn several years ago by two critics of the CIA thus remain relevant to the late 1980s:

> The feeling remains strong among the nation's top officials, in the CIA and elsewhere, that America is responsible for what happens in other countries and that it has an inherent right—a sort of modern Manifest Destiny—to intervene in other countries' internal affairs. Changes may have occurred at the negotiating table, but not in the planning arena; intervention—either military or covert—is still the rule. (Marchetti and Marks, 1974: 251)

INFORMAL PENETRATION

The overt and covert interventions the United States has embarked on through its military and intelligence apparatus in the postwar era are, on the surface, qualitatively different from the extensive "public diplomacy" initiatives it has also undertaken in the same period. Yet they derive from the same globalist and anticommunist orientations, and they have become persistent and prominent instruments defining the American approach to the external world. Moreover, they form part of a nexus of informal penetrations of other societies that may contribute to the kinds of covert and overt interventions discussed previously. In the sense that a fine line distinguishes involvement from intervention, therefore, they are also part of that interventionist strategy.

Public Diplomacy

"Public diplomacy" is a polite term for what many would regard as straightforward propaganda (the methodical spreading of information to influence public opinion). The United States Information Agency (USIA) is in charge of American public diplomacy efforts aimed at winning support around the world for America and its foreign policy. Its instruments are cultural and informational activities directed overseas at both masses and elites which have essentially two functions: (1) the projection, interpretation, and advocacy of current U.S. foreign policy; and (2) the portrayal of American society as a "complex, pluralistic, tolerant and democratic community" (*Commission on the Organization of the Government for the Conduct of Foreign Policy*, 1975).

The USIA carries out its tasks through a worldwide network of overseas offices using a variety of media tools, including radio, television, films, libraries, and exhibitions. Among the most well known are the Voice of America, which broadcasts news, political journalism, music, and cultural programs in 48 languages to many parts of the globe, and Radio Free Europe and Radio Liberty, which broadcast respectively to Eastern Europe and to the Soviet Union. The Reagan administration added Radio Marti, which broadcasts to Cuba, to USIA's broadcasting network. The agency's 29,300 staff members (in 1985) also administer a variety of cultural exchange programs. Under those programs, American athletes, artists, dramatists, musicians, and scholars travel abroad, and foreign political leaders, students, and educators are brought to the United States for study tours or other educational purposes.

The assumption underlying information and cultural programs is that specialized communications can be used to make world opinion toward the United States more favorable. Within that framework, however, opinion varies widely regarding the appropriateness of public diplomacy as an instrument of policy. Should such efforts be designed only to provide information? Should public diplomacy aggressively promote American culture and its values, as was the explicit purpose behind the Reagan administration's "Project Democracy" initiative in the early 1980s? Or should it be linked intimately to the political contests in which the United States becomes engaged, notably the struggle against communism?

In practice, each role has been dominant at one time or another. During the 1950s, for example, the USIA was heavily involved in supporting the anticommunist containment policy, and during the Vietnam conflict emphasis was placed on justifying American intervention. The emphasis during the Carter administration shifted to cultural exchange programs, which "evoke more cooperative sentiments" when compared to information activities that have "the image of a more confrontational posture" (Adelman, 1981). Reflecting the tilt toward cooperative public diplomacy, the Carter administration removed the motto "Telling America's story abroad" from USIA's headquarters and renamed the unit the International Communication Agency (ICA) (Reagan subsequently restored the previous name). Under the Reagan administration the shift was clearly toward the policy-oriented information activities of USIA, through which it vigorously sought to promote U.S. policies abroad and to engage in the "war of ideas" with the nation's adversaries. Public diplomacy thus once more became an active instrument of the containment foreign policy strategy (its budget was increased accordingly). Indeed, in its efforts to sell U.S. policies abroad, critics (see, for example, Nichols, 1984) suggested that there was a tendency to view these propaganda efforts in essentially *military* terms. In the words of President Reagan's USIA Director Charles Z. Wick, "The only war the United States has fought in the past four years has been the propaganda war." Still others, including members of Congress, wondered whether such a bold approach to "telling America's story to the world" would politicize USIA's exchange programs, suggesting an inherent tension between the agency's policy-oriented and non-policy-oriented activities (Malone, 1985).

Even if it were possible to agree on the nature and role of public diplomacy, evaluating its impact is difficult and elusive. During the Polish labor turmoil of 1980, the Soviet Union criticized American broadcasts beamed at Poland as being "provocative and instigatory" and as "aimed at generating among the Polish population unfriendly sentiments with regard to the Soviet Union" (cited in Adelman, 1981.)[14] Should one conclude that American interests were being served in Poland by such broadcasts, because authorities in Poland complained of them? Or instead, were American interests, defined as preventing the deterioration of relations with the Soviet Union, damaged by them? If that situation seems ambiguous, an earlier, analogous one does not. In 1956 Hungarian freedom fighters revolting against Soviet domination received messages from Radio Free Europe implying that American assistance was on its way. It never came.

Even the exchange programs of public diplomacy seem to yield ambiguous results. Although more than 45,000 American scholars and 85,000 foreign students, teachers, and scholars have participated in the well-known Fulbright Program (Adelman, 1981: 926), some of the most vociferous foreign critics of the United States have been able to visit the country under the sponsorship of the American government. It would seem, then, that advocates of public diplomacy must necessarily view it "as a long-term foreign policy asset, one designed to present foreigners with a mosaic impression of America's mosaic society and to incline them favorably toward American values" (Adelman, 1981). But in the short run, public diplomacy can also be expected to encounter criticism, particularly when it offers to other societies ideas and values that may not always be welcome and in a manner that may sometimes breed resentment.

Military Assistance

Giving aid and lending money are other ways the United States has sought to influence other nations. Of the two forms of foreign aid, military and economic, the former has been more clearly related to the military orientation of postwar American policy. Indeed, it has been a favored foreign policy instrument ever since the Korean War. Coming out of that conflict was the Mutual Security Act, which provided the legislative umbrella under which all foreign aid was distributed until it was replaced by the Foreign Assistance Act of 1961.[15] The view that military aid is an essential element of defense and secu-

---

[14]Some of these verged on the ludicrous, including production of "a worldwide television extravaganza called *Let Poland Be Poland*, which featured Frank Sinatra crooning *Ever Homeward* in pidgin Polish. The show drew howls of ridicule" (*Time*, September 9, 1985, p. 33).

[15]Foreign military sales (discussed below) are now governed by the Arms Export Control Act, first passed in 1968. The Foreign Assistance Act continues to govern other military aid programs; economic assistance is authorized by both statutes.

rity planning has been reaffirmed many times. In his report to Congress Secretary of Defense Caspar Weinberger explained why security assistance has been and would remain ''an essential foreign policy tool''; he noted that

> Security assistance programs contribute directly to the national security of the United States by helping friendly and allied countries defend themselves. Through the sale of equipment and services, some of which are supported by financial assistance, our programs enable recipient countries to make better use of their own resources, assist in fostering self-reliance, and advance the shared goal of collective security and regional stability around the world.
>
> At the same time, these programs promote closer military working relationships between U.S. forces and the armed forces of other countries, help strengthen our alliance relationships, and improve our power projection and forward defense capabilities through access to overseas facilities and retention of base rights abroad. . . . (Secretary of Defense Caspar W. Weinberger, *Annual Report to the Congress*, 1985: 271).

As shown in Table 5.1, the total dollar amount of American military aid to other nations since the onset of the Korean War (including commercial sales), stood at nearly $257 billion by 1985. Even that is likely to be a conservative estimate, since it is based on unclassified information and does not include the value of ''outdated'' military hardware the United States routinely gives away.[16]

Historically, the Military Assistance Program (MAP) served as the principal mechanism through which recipient countries were provided articles, defense services, and training. All assistance was grant aid, requiring no repayment on the part of recipients.[17] Beginning in fiscal 1976 training of foreign military personnel has been provided under the International Military Education and Training Program. Between 1950 and 1985, over 530,000 were trained either under MAP or its successor.

Today foreign military sales (FMS) are the most important component of U.S. military assistance links with other nations. They accounted for three quarters of the $133 billion in military assistance and sales provided other nations during the Carter and (first) Reagan administrations.[18] Although most

---

[16]By 1985 the accumulated acquisition cost (fiscal years 1950 through 1985) of outdated military equipment distributed under the Excess Defense Articles Program stood in excess of $6.5 billion (*Foreign Military Sales, Foreign Military Construction Sales and Military Assistance Facts*, 1985: 67).

[17]Between 1965 and 1975, some military aid was also provided out of funds appropriated to the military organizations in the Defense Department (known technically as Military Assistance-Service Funded—MASF). These monies were expended primarily in connection with the Vietnam War, when, for example, in fiscal 1973 Vietnam alone received $3.7 billion in such assistance.

[18]For purposes of this calculation, military assistance is defined as MAP grants, credit financing, International Military Education and Training Program expenditures, transfers from excess stocks, other military grants, and foreign military sales. In Figure 5.2 later in this chapter, security supporting assistance is added to the above to define military assistance. Semmel (1983) provides a useful description of the various military assistance programs, the purposes they are designed to serve, and trends in their use and disbursements.

TABLE 5.1 American Military Assistance and Foreign Military Sales in the Postwar Era (millions of dollars)

Military Assistance Program (MAP)	$ 56,442
International Military Education and Training Program	2,200
Foreign Military Sales (FMS) and FMS Construction Agreements	173,631
Commercial Exports	24,526
	$256,799

SOURCE: Adapted from *Foreign Military Sales, Foreign Military Construction Sales and Military Assistance Facts*, 1985: 3ff.

NOTE: Data are for fiscal years 1950 through 1985.

government-to-government sales are on a straight cash basis, the Defense Department provided more than $37 billion in credits toward foreign military purchases between 1976 and 1985. A large proportion of the sales have been to Saudi Arabia and, prior to the 1979 revolution that toppled the Shah, to Iran, both of whom were major suppliers of oil to the United States in the 1970s, and for whom the United States became a major arms supplier. Between fiscal 1973 and 1978, for example, they accounted for almost four-fifths of all American foreign military sales agreements[19] (Israel accounted for another 15 percent). Thereafter, Saudi Arabia alone accounted for 29 percent (fiscal years 1979 through 1985).

As suggested by the title Mutual Security, United States military assistance programs were conceived historically in terms of the Cold War competition with the Soviet Union. The rationale underlying the distribution of aid was therefore linked closely to the policy of containment. Military assistance was justified on grounds that it augmented the capabilities of American allies to resist Soviet and Soviet-backed expansionism. Special attention was therefore given to the members of the NATO and SEATO (South-East Asian Treaty Organization) alliances, plus other nations bordering on the communist world, some of which were covered by bilateral defensive arrangements with the United States. In the period between 1950 and 1965, for example, those nations accounted for well over three-fourths of MAP aid, which in turn accounted for approximately 77 percent of the $4.1 billion in American military assistance allocated during this period. Another manifestation of the Cold War motivation was the use of military aid for "rental" of base rights in countries such as Spain and the Philippines and for landing rights for ships and planes elsewhere.

In the period between 1966 and 1975, when the dollar value of U.S. military aid and sales totaled $61.6 billion, the emphasis shifted, reflecting the changing international circumstances surrounding that policy instrument. One

[19]Military sales to Iran were curtailed sharply following the Iranian revolution in 1979. Sales dropped to $36 million in fiscal 1979 compared to an average of $2.1 billion for the five prior years. No sales were recorded in fiscal 1980.

of the most obvious changes was in the substantially greater emphasis given to developing nations, which in turn reflected the more self-reliant economic capabilities of Western European nations. Whereas NATO nations received 53 percent of the American military aid pie between 1950 and 1965, their share dropped to only 20 percent in the 1966–1975 period. Also apparent is the substantial cost of the Vietnam involvement. The four nations bordering on the communist world which were extended the protection of SEATO (Pakistan, South Vietnam, Cambodia, and Laos) alone accounted for 27 percent of total aid and sales between 1966 and 1975 compared with only 7.6 percent in the earlier period. Non-SEATO nations bordering on the communist world (which includes South Korea and Taiwan) also showed a substantial increase, moving from 15 percent in 1950–1965 to 24 percent in 1966–1975.[20] Thus the persistent anticommunist security motivation of U.S. military assistance programs is apparent across the two time periods, but the shift from developed to developing nations generally, and from Europe to Asia in particular, is also clear.

The most dramatic reflection of the changing international situation has shown up in the tremendous increase in arms purchases by Middle Eastern nations, particularly since the early years of the first Nixon administration. The flow of arms to those nations grew in part out of the persistence of the Arab–Israeli conflict and in part because of the tremendous surge in world oil prices which first occurred in 1973–1974, thus giving the oil exporting countries substantial financial resources with which to purchase arms.

From the American viewpoint the shift in arms assistance policy from grants to sales during the Nixon administration was a direct consequence of the Nixon Doctrine—the pledge that the United States would provide military and economic assistance to its friends and allies, but that those nations would be responsible for protecting their own security. The foreign military sales program itself, however, goes back to the early days of the Kennedy administration, which began to experiment with foreign military sales as an alternative to grant assistance.[21] The reasons for doing so were opposition to outright grants emanating from Congress, the continuing adverse balance of payments the nation suffered, and a growing concern for the lack of an integrated logistical system among the NATO nations (Louscher, 1977). The same forces served to sustain the program once it was started. Over time FMS became a multipurpose instrument of policy designed to symbolize American resolve, to project American credibility, and to strengthen American allies generally and, in the case of Europe, to encourage greater logistical cooperation, upgrade European defense systems, and spread the financial burdens of the collective defense. Among developing nations, FMS was viewed as a vehicle for

[20]Data used in making the preceding calculations were drawn from *Foreign Military Sales and Military Assistance Facts*, 1975.

[21]As David Louscher (1977) notes in his excellent survey of the development of FMS, the search for an alternative to outright grant assistance actually goes back to the Eisenhower years. At that time American economic aid programs shifted in emphasis from grants to loans and sales of foreign agricultural surpluses as forms of aid.

generating regional power balances, controlling arms races, maintaining American influence, and selectively modifying recipients' policies regarding human rights.

Thus the shift from gifts to arms sales, which reached massive proportions during the Nixon and Ford years reflects a change from the earlier emphasis on anticommunism and the benefits assumed to accrue to the United States from stable, anticommunist regimes overseas. The overriding motivation remains an overtly political one—to enhance the ability of the United States to influence others so as to realize its own foreign policy objectives. But some of the presumed benefits from FMS are of a more subtle nature, reflecting the supplementary economic motivations behind the program. Thus proponents of increased arms sales cite the following as rationales: (1) to generate high employment levels in defense industries; (2) to produce a more favorable U.S. balance of payments; (3) to maintain a "warm base" for U.S. armaments production, in other words, an industry already geared up for production; and (4) to lower the cost of each item by increasing production. Proponents also argue that arms sales remove incentives others might otherwise have to acquire nuclear weapons. And they contend that the United States cannot control the desire of other nations in an intensely nationalistic world to acquire arms. Furthermore, they point out that other Western nations, as well as the Soviet Union and its allies, are both able and willing to provide military hardware to other nations.[22] To these advantages, advocates also add the beliefs that this policy tool enables the United States to gain political leverage over recipients, to build and maintain alliances, to demonstrate a commitment to friendly states, to maintain the balance of power, and to prevent the Soviet Union from cultivating allies (see Hammond et al., 1983). Hence the reasons for the United States to avoid the arms business do not appear compelling.

Despite the arguments in favor of arms sales, some critics ask if American grants of advanced military technology to countries and regions where the incidence of conflict is high, as in the Middle East, might not actually contribute to the likelihood of local aggression. They note the frequency with which the United States has armed both (or all) parties in Third World regional conflicts, as in the conflicts between India and Pakistan (which erupted into war in 1971), between Greece and Turkey over Cyprus (1974), and between Israel and Jordan (1973). It is also true, they observe, that the neighbors of those armed by the United States have often turned to the Soviet Union for assistance. Moreover, the possibility that today's allies may be tomorrow's enemies is strong, especially in Third World nations where the incidence of political instability is high. Time and again, those designated as in need of American arms to protect themselves from Soviet penetration later became new clients of the Russians. Ethiopia and Yemen were examples in the late 1970s, Nicaragua in the early 1980s.

---

[22]One of the consequences of competition among arms suppliers is the widespread use of agents' fees and bribery of foreign officials to obtain arms sales contracts.

To many critics of American policy on arms sales, the fact that today's friends may become tomorrow's enemies is precisely the message of the Iranian revolution in 1979. For despite pumping billions of dollars worth of arms into Iran, the United States was unable to stem the collapse of the Pahlavi regime. The Shah's demise also discredited the Nixon Doctrine, for it appeared to destroy the doctrine's underlying assumption that peace could be preserved by stocking a developing nation with sophisticated armaments. In the wake of the Shah's departure and the Ayatollah Khomeini's rise to power, not only did the United States find itself without the regional power it had sought for purposes of maintaining stability in the critical Persian Gulf region, but it also faced a population bitter with resentment toward the United States.

The more general question critics ask is whether massive arms sales are consistent with the nation's avowed goal of seeking world peace. President Carter raised that issue in a speech before the Foreign Policy Association while campaigning for the presidency in 1976 when he asked: "Can we be both the world's leading champion of peace and the world's leading supplier of the weapons of war?"

Consistent with his campaign position, Carter in 1977 announced in Presidential Directive No. 13 (PD 13) that henceforth arms transfers would be viewed as "an exceptional foreign policy implement, to be used only in instances where it can be clearly demonstrated that the transfer contributes to our national security." A policy of "restraint" was announced that included negotiations with the Soviet Union on limiting arms transfers, a pledge not to develop new weapon systems solely for export, and, subsequently, a ceiling on sales to nonaligned countries designed to reduce foreign military sales. As the world's leading exporter of arms, Carter believed that the United States should bear "special responsibilities" by taking the lead in restraining its sale of weapons.

Carter's policy of restraint was plagued with difficulties from the beginning. The arms transfer ceiling specifically exempted military sales to Western European allies, Japan, Australia, and New Zealand. It also was confined to "weapons-related equipment," which meant that billions in military construction projects were excluded from the ceiling. The result, as administration officials conceded, would actually be an increase rather than reduction in total arms sales. Yet Carter argued that further reductions in sales "would violate commitments already made, including our historic interests in the Middle East, and would ignore the continuing realities of world politics."

Apparently those "commitments," "interests," and "realities" led Carter increasingly to treat arms sales as an acceptable, rather than exceptional, policy instrument. Congress was asked to approve sales of sophisticated airborne radar planes (AWACS) to Iran and, later, F-15 fighter planes, the most advanced in the U.S. arsenal, to Saudi Arabia as part of a massive arms package involving Egypt and Israel as well. And in 1980 Carter approved development of a new fighter aircraft solely for the export market (Congressional Quarterly, 1980b). Meanwhile, conventional arms transfer talks initiated with the Soviet

Union ended in stalemate while, at the same time, Soviet, French, and British trade in arms captured an increased share of the overseas market. Collectively, those factors sounded the death knell for the policy of restraint: in March 1980 Secretary of State Cyrus Vance announced that the United States would discontinue efforts to reduce arms sales. Thus the only serious attempt to curb what became during the 1970s the growing trade in sophisticated American weapons of war ended in failure.

The Reagan administration, for its part, cast all pretense of restraint aside as it embarked on a program designed to *increase* substantially the transfer of American military hardware to the nations of Europe, Africa, Asia, Latin America, and especially the Middle East. In his presidential directive of July 8, 1981, PD 13 was "formally rescinded" and the "export oriented policies of the Nixon and Ford administrations" were "restored" (Klare, 1984). The use of military assistance to achieve diplomatic aims was thus reasserted as a key instrument in American foreign policy. As national security adviser Richard V. Allen noted in late 1981, "the U.S. views the transfer of conventional arms and other defense articles as an indispensable component of its foreign policy." Subsequently, the number of countries receiving U.S. arms increased substantially (see U.S. Arms Control and Disarmament Agency, 1985), while the resumption of shipments to Pakistan and the agreement to transfer arms to the People's Republic of China signaled an important expansion of the program. As Defense Secretary Weinberger noted in 1985, "we have established the United States as a reliable partner [in agreements to transfer U.S. arms] with more countries than ever before."

Military sales and military assistance have contributed greatly to the globalism of American foreign policy. The linkages forged by foreign aid and sales often combine to entail quasi commitments by the donor nation to support the recipient nation—if for no reason other than to "protect" the donor's "investment." Transfers of high-technology weapon systems, for example, often require the influx of large numbers of technicians and military advisers into recipient countries. The result: American military obligations arising out of arms aid and sales, the stationing of troops or advisers abroad, and treaties and executive agreements had involved the United States between 1979 and 1983 in commitments to some seventy-six different nations (U.S. Arms Control Disarmament Agency, 1985: 131–134).

What is especially interesting about those commitments is that many of the recipient governments could clearly be classified as dictatorships. In the mid-1970s it was estimated that 56 percent of the recipients of U.S. arms were dictatorships (*The Defense Monitor*, August, 1975). Using somewhat different terminology, a large proportion of the recipients cannot be classified as "free" (see Gastil, 1984). Specifically, nearly 18 percent of U.S. arms recipients, cumulative for the period of 1979 through 1983, were "non-free" countries, and 20 percent of the total U.S. arms sales during that period were to "non-free" countries (U.S. Arms Control and Disarmament Agency, 1985; Gastil, 1984). One wonders whether American military ties with recipient countries might also have retarded the growth of democratic governments throughout the world. One study of this question (E. Rowe, 1974) has suggested that regardless of the intentions of American military aid programs, the consequences include an increased probability that military groups within recipient countries will intervene in the politics of those societies. Although most developing nations in the postwar era have not been under the control of their military, arms transfers have contributed to the militarization of foreign governments (see Luckham, 1984), and, when these governments become recipients of military aid in the form of money, equipment, and training, the probability also increases that they will experience political instability in the form of successful and abortive military coups (see Weede, 1978). Similarly, when the military is already in control, the evidence suggests that the receipt of military aid has increased even further the military's entrenched hold. "In short, U.S. military assistance appears to be a contributing factor in undermining civilian elements and increasing the incidence of praetorianism in the less developed areas of the world" (E. Rowe, 1974).

Military control of Third World governments remains pervasive (see Manning, 1983). This bodes ill for the ability of arms transfers to contribute to one of the alleged goals of American foreign policy—the expansion of democratic forms of government worldwide. Indeed, "many recipients of U.S. security systems have used them to terrorize the public at large," and have practiced "state terrorism" against their own citizens; the use of U.S. supplied arms for this purpose by the governments of El Salvador, Haiti, and Guatemala in the mid-1980s attests to the potential dangers (see Klare, 1984). In the long run, warns one observer, foreign-supplied arms can imbue "dissidents and insurgent forces with an abiding resentment of the suppliers of such hardware. This was clearly the case in Iran and Nicaragua. . . . Furthermore, . . . these exports help to ensure that such dissent will ultimately take violent forms—often to the detriment of U.S. interests" (Klare, 1984).

Economic Assistance

Questions about the political character of the regimes being assisted with American aid have plagued economic assistance programs much as they have military assistance programs. That should not be surprising, of course. The same international circumstances and corresponding rationales gave rise to both programs. The importance of economic aid as an instrument of policy is demonstrated in Table 5.2, which shows the aggregate distribution of economic aid over the four major periods of the American aid-giving effort.

Although the amount of economic aid the United States has sent abroad is clearly substantial, a comparison with Table 5.1 indicates that military assistance (including military sales) is comparatively more important. Indeed, it became increasingly so in recent years, as illustrated in Figure 5.2, a point to which we will return below.

TABLE 5.2   Commitments of Economic and Technical Assistance Distributed by the United States in the Postwar Era (millions of dollars by fiscal year)

Postwar Relief Period (1946–1948)	$ 12,482
Marshall Plan Period (1949–1952)	18,634
Mutual Security Act Period (1953–1961)	24,053
Foreign Assistance Act Period (1962–1984)	123,019
Gross total	$174,138
Less repayments and interest	− 28,797
Net total	$145,341

SOURCE: Adapted from *U.S. Overseas Loans and Grants and Assistance from International Organizations*, 1985: 4.

NOTE: Numbers do not add due to different reporting concepts in the pre- and post-1955 periods. Data include security supporting assistance totaling $38.7 billion between 1949 and 1985.

Currently the major American economic assistance programs are carried on under the aegis of the Agency for International Development (AID), the Food for Peace Program, the Peace Corps, subscriptions to international lending organizations, and refugee assistance. Of the two largest programs, AID commitments refer to loans and grants, including technical assistance grants and "security supporting assistance" or "economic support funds" (these are grants designed to help the recipient cope with immediate security problems—such as insurgency, as in Vietnam—or, more recently, to assist economies with heavy military expenditures, such as Israel); Food for Peace commitments refer to sales of agricultural commodities on credit terms which are repayable in dollars[23] and to grants for emergency relief, for promoting economic development, or for assisting voluntary relief agencies.[24]

Historically, the first major peacetime effort to utilize foreign aid as an instrument of foreign policy was the remarkably successful Marshall Plan—or European Recovery Program, as it was formally known. Directed toward Western European countries ravaged by world war, the Marshall Plan was designed to use American capital to rebuild the economic, social, and political infrastructures (basic facilities and systems) of European societies in the hopes of rebuilding a market for American products and enhancing Europe's ability

[23]Prior to fiscal year 1977 some sales were also made payable in local currencies (the currency of the purchasing country), which were then used for local purposes such as maintenance of U.S. government facilities in the purchasing country.

[24]Food for Peace expenditures, perhaps more widely known as PL 480 expenditures in reference to the Agricultural Trade Development and Assistance Act of 1954 which created the program, account for $35.2 billion of the $174.1 billion in American economic assistance. Of this amount, 61 percent has been in the form of sales for American dollars or local currencies, 15 percent in emergency relief or economic development grants, and 24 percent in donations to voluntary relief agencies. Interestingly, PL 480 contributed to the legitimacy of the idea, in Congress in particular, that commodity sales constitute a form of aid, making possible the subsequent emphasis on military arms sales as a way of assisting other nations (Louscher, 1977).

FIGURE 5.2 U.S. Economic and Military Assistance, 1977–1984 (billions of dollars by fiscal year)

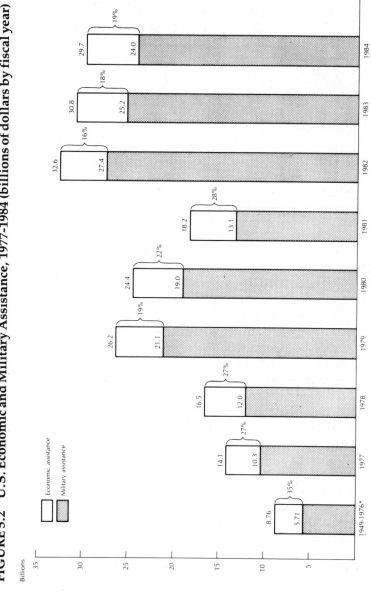

SOURCE: Adapted from *U.S. Overseas Loans and Grants and Assistance from International Organizations*, 1980: 4; *U.S. Overseas Loans and Grants and Assistance from International Organizations*, 1985: 4; and *Foreign Military Sales, Foreign Military Construction Sales and Military Assistance Facts*, 1985: 2ff.

NOTE: Military assistance is defined as security supporting assistance, MAP grants, credit financing, International Military Education and Training Program expenditures, transfers from excess stocks, other military grants, and foreign military sales. Economic assistance makes up the balance, consisting primarily of AID loans and grants, Food for Peace grants and loans, and contributions to international financial institutions.

* Annual average.

to resist communist subversion. During the Korean War, the emphasis shifted from recovery to containment, and from Europe to Asia. As shown in Figure 5.3, Europe received 78 percent of the U.S. aid dollar in 1950; by 1960 two-thirds was going to the Middle (Near) East and the Far East (Asia). The overwhelming concern of the United States during the post-Marshall Plan period was reflected in the title of the governing legislation—Mutual Security Act.

By the 1960s it had become apparent that economic and social progress was the dominant concern of many of the newly emerging Third World nations, not the Cold War which had been the primary motivating force behind aid to that point. Castro's rise to power in Cuba demonstrated that security and economic and social progress were not necessarily incompatible concerns, but the degree of emphasis and the appropriate means became problematic.

The American response to the rising challenge presented by developing nations was the Foreign Assistance Act of 1961, which replaced the Mutual Security Act as the legislation governing economic and military aid programs. AID was created as the administering agency for economic assistance; greater emphasis was placed on development capital and technical assistance[25] relative to defense support aid. The Alliance for Progress was launched in an attack on incipient revolution and communism in the Western Hemisphere.

Specific factors related to the allocation of economic aid under the Foreign Assistance Act can be categorized roughly into clusters reflecting (1) the political importance of aid recipients to the United States, (2) Cold War considerations, (3) recipients' need and performance, and (4) the availability of alternative sources of assistance. Those allocation criteria are in turn related to four underlying motivations which appeared predominant not only in the United States but in the programs of other Western aid donors as well:

> (1) achievement of greater national security, (2) fulfillment of humanitarian obligations to provide assistance to less fortunate nations and peoples, (3) economic gains brought about either through opening and maintaining access to less developed country markets on favorable terms or through ensuring access to raw material supplies in less developed countries at favorable prices, and (4) diplomatic gains achieved through the expansion of national prestige and power. (Frank and Baird, 1975: 140–141)

Although those motivations and their related allocation criteria are multifaceted, it is noteworthy that in both the Mutual Security (1953–1961) period and the Foreign Assistance Act period through 1975, nations formally aligned with the United States received roughly 60 percent of the total bilateral-aid pie. Similarly, Third World nations formally aligned with the United States received 41 and 45 percent of the share in the two periods, respectively, and nonaligned nations bordering on the communist world received roughly 20

---

[25]Although some technical assistance existed prior to 1949, most can be dated from that time, when President Truman, in "Point Four" of his inaugural address, called for a bold new program to transfer American technical knowhow to less developed nations.

FIGURE 5.3   Regional Distribution of U.S. Overseas Loans and Grants

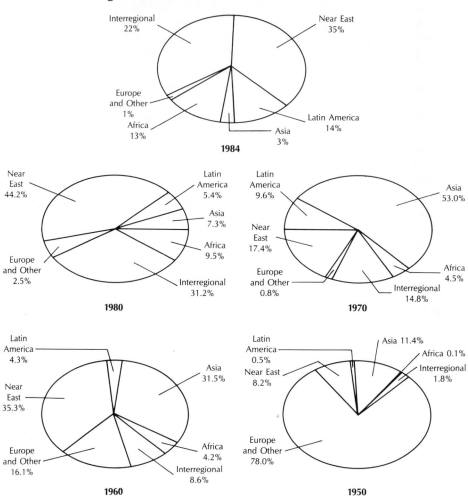

SOURCE: 1950–1980 from U.S. Department of State, 1983b: 14; 1984 adapted from *U.S. Overseas Loans and Grants and Assistance from International Organizations*, 1985: 7ff.

NOTE: Interregional includes Food for Peace emergency relief and economic development contributions to international financial institutions.

percent in each period. The security concern is reflected in the overwhelming attention given Asia during the Vietnam War era (see Figure 5.3). Indeed, the only significant changes between the two periods are a decline in developed nations' share of the aid pie (from 16 percent to 1.5 percent), and an increase in the proportion received by the least developed Third World nations (from 25 percent to 38 percent).[26] This might be taken as evidence supporting a growing humanitarian strain, but we must be cautious about making such an inference, since the greatest increase in the number of the world's poorest nations occurred during the Foreign Assistance Act period, particularly in Africa.

The humanitarian strain became more apparent after 1975—not so much because of the total dollars allocated to different types of countries as the relative importance of humanitarian thinking in justifying the dollars spent. In 1973 Congress sought to shift the emphasis of development assistance (primarily funds administered by AID) from social infrastructure projects to projects directly helping the poorest in developing societies. In part that decision was related to growing congressional concern with linking aid allocations to the human rights practices of Third World countries. After the "new directions" legislation of 1973, meeting "basic human needs" became a dominant goal of aid-granting countries and international institutions. The underlying belief is that it is just as important to improve the distribution of income and basic services to the very poorest people as it is to promote capital intensive projects designed to stimulate economic "takeoff."

The basic needs perspective is closely identified with the efforts of Robert McNamara, the former Defense Department secretary who served as president of the World Bank during the 1970s. McNamara sought to focus attention on the plight of the poorest of the poor in what amounted to a critique of previous theories of economic development, particularly those which argued that the benefits of economic growth would "trickle down" to the needy. Because that seldom happened—more typical was "dualism" in developing societies, with one modern, growing sector, and one traditional, stagnant sector—meeting basic human needs came to be perceived as necessary. The new approach also enjoyed the political advantage of linking the plight of the world's poor directly to Third World countries themselves. Leaders of Third World countries often prefer to lay the blame elsewhere; in the context of the North-South debate (see chapter six) many have asserted that their problems are the result of the inherent inequality between the world's rich and poor nations, which the structure of the international system reinforces and perpetuates. The human needs perspective often places blame at home.

National security considerations, as we might expect, remain a predominant justification for foreign economic assistance. But even here the overlapping concerns at the base of the aid program are apparent. During the 1960s in particular, the argument advanced was not that aid would result in direct po-

[26]Data used in making the preceding calculations were drawn from *U.S. Overseas Loans and Grants and Assistance from International Organizations,* 1976.

litical benefits to the United States but rather that aid would contribute to recipients' economic development. Economic development would be accompanied in turn by the emergence of stable democratic governments, the existence of which would ensure peaceful and cooperative relations among countries. This complicated reasoning was used not only to rationalize the aid program but also to guide the actual allocation of aid dollars, with emphasis placed on economic efficiency criteria (for example, the ability of recipients to generate savings out of current income or to increase Gross National Product growth rates) rather than overt political considerations.

In practice, aid has often been allocated on the basis of short-run political considerations. As part of the Egyptian-Israeli peace treaty signed in 1979, for example, the United States committed itself to substantial sums of assistance to the two historic antagonists: $1.5 billion in arms loans to Egypt; $2.2 billion in arms loans to Israel plus $800 million to cover the cost of relocating two Sinai air bases. In the years that followed the two received billions more, accounting for half to three quarters of AID's security supporting assistance, as part of the glue designed to cement the Middle East peace process. Strategic considerations also motivated the ambitious Caribbean Basin Initiative, a Reagan administration program of tariff reductions and tax incentives designed to promote the growth of industry and trade in Central America and the Caribbean in hopes of thwarting the economic conditions on which Marxist revolutionaries thrive.

The Reagan administration sought in other ways to reemphasize the underlying security motivations of U.S. economic aid and thus to underscore its role as an instrument of foreign policy. It promoted a congressional mandate that states' voting behavior in the United Nations be taken into account in aid decisions: hereafter, no aid was to be granted to a country that the president found to be "engaged in a consistent pattern of opposition to the foreign policy of the United States."[27] At the same time, the administration systematically allocated a greater proportion of its aid package to what are largely security purposes. Figure 5.2 captures part of that reorientation. It illustrates the shrinkage of the economic proportion of the nation's total aid budget. In part this is due to the greater proportion of resources devoted to security supporting assistance (which, for purposes of Figure 5.2, are categorized as military assistance). The pattern reflects the administration's orientation toward Third World conflict situations and the role of the United States in them. Aid to El Salvador, for example, grew to three quarters of a billion dollars during Reagan's first term, more than half of which was in security supporting funds. The total was three times the American largesse the tiny, poverty stricken Central American country had received in the prior three-and-a-half decades

---

[27]See Wittkopf (1973) and Rai (1980) for detailed examinations of the relationship between foreign aid allocations and United Nations voting, wherein moderate relationships between American aid allocations and voting agreements with the United States are demonstrated. Moon (1985) provides a useful critique of the conceptual orientation underlying such approaches to understanding the foreign policy behavior of Third World countries.

(*U.S. Overseas Loans and Grants and Assistance from International Organizations,* 1985: 47).[28]

Although foreign aid has been made to serve American political purposes, there is little evidence that the relatively modest inflows of external capital have contributed significantly to economic growth. Part of the reason is that economic policies pursued by some developing nations have led to inefficient use of external capital. It is also a consequence of the enormous needs of developing nations. A gap between expectation and performance is perhaps inevitable, therefore, but it is a gap that has opened the aid program to much criticism. Among other things, the lack of a clear and strong connection between foreign aid and economic growth has undermined the national security justification for aid. For reasons not unlike those discussed earlier regarding foreign military assistance, critics, such as former Senator William Fulbright, have argued that aid in fact is detrimental to security, for it involves the United States in countries in which it initially has little real interest. According to this reasoning, "[f]oreign aid is the 'slippery slope' that leads eventually to an over-extension of commitments and to a greater likelihood of military involvement" (Frank and Baird, 1975).

Concern for the "slippery slope" leading to military involvement has been especially vocal in Congress, which traditionally has used the foreign aid program as a vehicle for scrutinizing the executive's conduct of foreign policy. The scrutiny was sharpened in the wake of Vietnam, on which Congress felt it had been misled. It was also increased by congressional sensitivity to critical domestic needs that appeared to go unanswered at the same time the United States was involved in a massive "giveaway" program overseas.[29]

Whether American commitments to Egypt and Israel designed to solidify their 1979 peace accord and efforts by the Reagan administration to bend foreign aid programs to serve its ideological prescriptions in Central America and elsewhere risk wider American involvement in overseas conflict situations might be asked. In the Central American case, for example, critics drew parallels with the incremental decision-making process in Vietnam that ultimately led to the direct use of over 500,000 combat and support personnel in a major Asian land war. Also reminiscent of Vietnam according to critics were the supposedly domestic roots of El Salvador's turmoil; Reagan administration officials countered by emphasizing Soviet (and Cuban) expansionism. Although the president denied the Vietnam parallel by noting that El Salvador is located in "our front yard," Acting Assistant Secretary of State John Bushnell in-

[28]As shown by the regional distributions in Figure 5.3, it is only recently that Latin America has figured prominently in U.S. aid programs. The Central American focus of the Reagan administration is a principal reason.

[29]The "giveway" conception is inaccurate for two reasons. First, as noted below, most foreign aid is in the form of credits that enable the recipient to purchase goods and services in the United States. In some sense, therefore, it can be interpreted as a subsidy to American producers. Second, most capital aid is provided on a repayable basis. As shown in Table 5.2, repayments and interest on past loans are 16.5 percent of the total aid allocated since World War II and offset new loans to that extent.

voked an Hispanic version of the domino theory once prevalent in justifying American involvement in Southeast Asia: "I know these guerrillas are committed to fight tomorrow in Guatemala and the next day in Honduras." U.N. ambassador Jeane Kirkpatrick sounded a similar theme in arguing that the cause of the Salvadorian turmoil was not social injustice but the introduction of arms by outsiders in an attempt to transform Central America into a vast military base—from which, presumably, the United States itself might some day be threatened.

The continuing controversy over foreign aid has placed the very existence of the program in annual jeopardy.[30] At different times the result has been different emphases. Shifting from "government-assisting" toward "people-oriented" programs, as implied by the basic human needs approach, is one example. For a time aid advocates also preferred greater emphasis on multilateral aid, accomplished by making donations to international organizations, which then administer the funds. More recently, the Reagan administration, skeptical about multilateral assistance, has argued that the United States is better able to control the use of its funds if they are allocated on a bilateral basis. Accordingly, it proceeded to reduce U.S. contributions to international financial institutions in an effort to make foreign aid a more immediate and malleable instrument of American foreign policy. As noted earlier, the emphasis is reflected in the enhanced role the administration accorded security supporting assistance and the diminished emphasis it placed on economic development aid. Its corresponding enthusiasm for free-market approaches to domestic economic problems and for capitalist principles of free trade internationally blended well with the pattern.

Regardless of shifting preferences, the aid program has survived—and it is likely to persist in one form or another as an instrument of policy. Presidents find it useful to pursue their objectives, whatever they may be, and "members of [Congress] are unwilling to lose an opportunity to serve the cause of peace—or to face the charge of weakening the nation's position in the world" (Esterline and Black, 1975). Such a charge would be serious in a world where the components of power and prestige are often intangible. The domestic economy is the hidden beneficiary. In the words of Secretary of State George P. Shultz:

> About 70% of our bilateral foreign assistance funds is spent in the United States. Virtually all of our military financing, both grant and loan, is spent in the United States on U.S.-produced equipment. Our PL 480 program supports U.S. agricultural exports. Thus, our assistance programs, essential instruments of U.S. foreign policy, help to generate increased economic activity in the United States, which, in turn, helps boost trade and economic prospects in developing countries.

---

[30]Only rarely in recent years has Congress been able to agree on a foreign aid appropriations bill, thus requiring temporary appropriations measures to permit continuation of the controversial aid program.

Against this backdrop it nevertheless remains unlikely that the volume of American resources channeled abroad will increase substantially in the future. The annual volume of foreign economic aid has grown only modestly over time, moving from an average of about $4 billion throughout the 1960s to only $8.2 billion by the early 1980s. The conservative ideology of the Reagan administration, reinforced by the nation's mounting debt burden, persistent federal government budget deficits, and a trade imbalance with the rest of the world of enormous proportions are among the many factors (to which "donor fatigue" might be added) that promise to inhibit any substantial expansion of the level of U.S. economic aid. From the viewpoint of recipient nations, which have experienced tremendous population increases in the postwar period, per capita aid receipts have actually declined. From the viewpoint of donors, whose economies have grown enormously in both real and inflated dollars, the volume and value of aid given also have actually declined. Measured in comparable dollars, American foreign aid in the decade ending in 1955 was nearly double the amount allocated in the decade ending in 1985. Put differently, the $40 billion spent on postwar relief and reconstruction between 1946 and 1952 would today amount to $150 billion (U.S. Department of State, 1983b: 12–13). Thus the "burden" is comparatively small. When measured against Gross National Product (GNP), the aid effort of the United States is among the least burdensome of all Western industrialized nations, as indicated by the fact that its official development aid in 1985 stood at two-thirds of 1 percent of its GNP. The United States ranked *lowest* of seventeen Western foreign aid donors in the percentage of GNP given in aid to other nations (*New York Times*, May 18, 1986: EI), and far below the internationally agreed upon target of .7 percent.[31]

POWER AND PURPOSE: IN PURSUIT OF THE NATIONAL INTEREST

Are the ends of American foreign policy always served by the means used to pursue them? Or do they from time to time inadvertently undermine the nation's security and welfare? The persistent uneasiness in Congress about supporting a foreign aid program because of questions about its ability to accomplish desired ends might be applied to a broader spectrum of policy instruments and issues. It is true that the expenditure of $174 billion in economic aid and an even vastly greater sum in military assistance has made the world neither more democratic nor more sympathetic and friendly toward the United States. Does it follow, then, that the nation ought to withdraw programs that have had the effect of deeply involving it through a process of in-

---

[31]Keep in mind that public (that is, official) foreign aid differs from private assistance, in which the American people have been extraordinarily generous historically in their efforts to alleviate human suffering abroad.

formal penetration in the internal affairs of others? Or is it perhaps only motivations and expectations that need rethinking, with a shift toward the view
that developing nations' need for external assistance will continue for years to
come and that fulfilling those needs is right regardless of specific benefits to
the United States? Such a shift undoubtedly would reorient the way the U.S.
government chooses to assist others, particularly when it comes to military
hardware, but would it not also have the effect of removing the moral stigma
that some critics now attach to government actions?

Even more questions arise out of the nation's penchant for covert operations, particularly when the CIA's activities are monitored:

> [The CIA] engages in espionage and counterespionage, in propaganda and disin-
> formation (the deliberate circulation of false information), in psychological warfare
> and paramilitary activities. It penetrates and manipulates private institutions, and
> creates its own organizations (called ''proprietaries'') when necessary. It recruits
> agents and mercenaries; it bribes and blackmails foreign officials to carry out its
> most unsavory tasks. It does whatever is required to achieve its goals, without any
> consideration of the ethics involved or the moral consequences of its actions. As the
> secret-action arm of American foreign policy, the CIA's most potent weapon is its
> covert intervention in the internal affairs of countries the U.S. government wishes
> to control or influence. (Marchetti and Marks, 1974:5)

To this could be added involvement in assassination plots, kidnapping, and
blackmail against foreign leaders. And all of those activities have had the effect of damaging the ability of the United States to exercise moral leadership in
the world. The climate supporting such activities eroded in the 1970s but
seems to have been resurrected in the 1980s, with a return of the practices circumscribed a decade earlier.

National security policy making often occurs behind closed doors, and the
issue of morality essentially raises the question of what might be seen if we
peer behind the doors. At issue is democratic control of covert operations. If
we do not know what is going on behind the doors—and that often means
elected officials as well as the public—how is it possible to pass judgment? The
dilemma is heightened by the fact that the secrecy which shrouds covert activities is often justified as the handmaiden of national security. But security is
a phenomenon prized by all. Indeed, it is what ultimately becomes the yard-
stick against which decision makers are measured when it comes to matters of
foreign policy. Are the American people more secure because their government pursued for over four decades a foreign policy strategy dedicated to the
exertion of influence whenever feasible and by all expedient means? Or, perhaps more to the point, has reliance on military might for foreign policy purposes accomplished the intended task? Why, then, was an armada of missiles
and bombers capable of inflicting horrendous destruction on the nation's adversaries unable to prevent the emergence of a communist government only
ninety miles from Florida's shores? Why have even more powerful weapons

been unable to restrain that same government from doing what the United States clearly opposes, not only on its own island home but in Africa and Central America as well? And what did Vietnam accomplish? After $122 billion, 58,000 American lives, and countless Vietnamese casualties, Vietnam stands out as the first country on a periphery of the "Sino-Soviet bloc" to come under indisputable communist domination since Czechoslovakia in 1948.

Perhaps national security (or more correctly a definition of national security which equates security with military force) can become, as Kenneth Boulding once put it, "a mental disease." There is no question of the reality of nuclear holocaust. President Carter's observation that "the truth of the nuclear ages is that the United States and the Soviet Union must live in peace or we may not live at all" dramatizes the security dilemma and illuminates the grim fact that modern weapons have become so destructive that they cannot, dare not, be used as instruments of national policy. They have lost their power to provide more than a deterrent function to their possessors. Could it be that the irrelevance of nuclear weapons to foreign policy objectives applies to a wider range of instruments?

The conventional military power the United States has acquired at astronomical expense has also failed to give it the degree of control over the course of international events that is perhaps sought. The use of military force at the conventional level is relatively rare, in part because its use risks escalation to unthinkable dimensions. In this environment, threats and shows of force act as substitutes for actual warfare as an instrument of foreign policy. Similarly, the temptation to mold outcomes through covert operations becomes irresistible, and reliance on public diplomacy and military and economic assistance as instruments of influence continues.

The contributions these instruments make to the nation's security and welfare are often debated. But they will continue to mark the pattern of American foreign policy, for a global actor cannot operate in the contemporary world without reliance on some combination of them as it pursues its national interests.

SUGGESTIONS FOR FURTHER READING

BLECHMAN, BARRY M., AND STEPHEN S. KAPLAN WITH DAVID K. HALL, WILLIAM B. QUANDT, JEROME N. SLATER, ROBERT M. SLUSSER, AND PHILIP WINDSOR. *Force Without War*. Washington, DC: Brookings Institution, 1978.

COHEN, ELIOT A. "Constraints on America's Conduct of Small Wars." *International Security* 9 (Fall 1984): 151–181.

FARLEY, PHILIP J., STEPHEN S. KAPLAN, AND WILLIAM H. LEWIS. *Arms Across the Sea*. Washington, DC: Brookings Institution, 1978.

FRANK, CHARLES R., JR. AND MARY BAIRD. "Foreign Aid: Its Speckled Past and Future Prospects," *International Organization* 29 (Winter 1975): 133–167.

HAMMOND, PAUL Y., DAVID J. LOUSCHER, MICHAEL D. SALOMONE, AND NORMAN A. GRAHAM. *The Reluctant Supplier: U.S. Decisionmaking for Arms Sales*. Cambridge, MA: Oelgeschlager, Gunn and Hain, 1983.

KLARE, MICHAEL T. *American Arms Supermarket*. Austin: University of Texas Press, 1984.

MARCHETTI, VICTOR, AND JOHN D. MARKS. *The CIA and the Cult of Intelligence*. New York: Knopf, 1974.

RAVENAL, EARL C. *Never Again: Learning from America's Foreign Policy Failures*. Philadelphia: Temple University Press, 1978.

YARMOLINSKY, ADAM, AND GREGORY D. FOSTER. *Paradoxes of Power: The Military Establishment in the Eighties*. Bloomington: Indiana University Press, 1983.

III

EXTERNAL SOURCES OF AMERICAN FOREIGN POLICY

6

THE INTERNATIONAL POLITICAL SYSTEM IN TRANSITION

Our well-being as a country depends not on this or that episode or agreement. It depends rather on the structural conditions of the international system that help determine whether we are fundamentally secure, whether the world economy is sound, and whether the forces of freedom and democracy are gaining ground.

Secretary of State George Shultz, 1984

At no time in our peacetime history has the state of the Nation depended more heavily on the state of the world; and seldom, if ever, has the state of the world depended more heavily on the state of our Nation.

President Gerald R. Ford, 1975

The state of the nation and the state of the world are so inextricably linked that what happens—economically, politically, or socially—beyond the nation's borders today undeniably makes a difference in the kind of society the United States is and the kind of posture it assumes toward international issues. The price of gasoline at American service stations is now determined by people meeting in foreign capitals. The availability of color televisions to the American consumer is governed not simply by internal market forces but also by agreements between Washington, on one hand, and Tokyo, Tai-pei, and Seoul, on the other. And decisions reached in the Kremlin influence the level at which Americans are taxed and how the revenues generated will be spent. In short, developments abroad and the conditions at home are perhaps more

149

closely linked now than at any time in American history. It is little wonder, then, that much of American foreign policy so often appears to be shaped by international events.

In chapters six and seven we will explore how the external environment serves as a source of American foreign policy. In what fundamental ways has the international system changed? How have those changes produced shifts in American external policy since 1945? The questions under consideration are based on the assumption that the external environment serves simultaneously as a stimulus to and constraint on change in foreign policy, thereby promoting variations in the nation's external behavior while contributing to persistence and continuity in it as well. This is not to suggest, however, that the external environment determines or causes American behavior directly. Rather, changes in the external environment provide the nation with opportunities, subject to the perception of decision makers, for the realization of foreign policy objectives. How, or even whether, an opportunity is perceived is as important as the actual events that precede the action finally taken. Hence, we can think of the external environment as a cluster of variables which at any time may create opportunities for achieving foreign policy goals, or, alternatively, for accommodating new realities. Yet care must be exercised lest we assume that such opportunities will necessarily be seized or such accommodations will occur automatically.

In order to simplify the difficult task of assessing the impact of the international environment on American foreign policy, we will begin in chapter six by focusing on some of the dominant political dimensions of the world system in transition. Three aspects of the changing international political system will be given particular attention: shifts in the world distribution of power; the postwar emancipation of former colonies and the consequent emergence of the Third World; and the rise of nongovernmental actors. Those developments identify primary political forces in the system which have both fostered and hindered change in foreign policy.

In chapter seven we will continue this line of investigation by focusing attention on the economic dimensions of the world system in transition. There we will delve more directly into the topic of interdependence as we explore the important intersection of international politics and international economics. Specifically, we will focus attention on the role of the United States in the changing international monetary and trade systems and the relationship between those shifts and continuity and change in American foreign policy.

SHIFTS IN THE DISTRIBUTION OF POWER

There are two distinguishing features of the international political system, both of which have been operative since the founding of the United States more than 200 years ago. The first is its *decentralized* nature. The actors (countries, in this case) which make up the system continue to monopolize power in the absence of a central institution, such as a world government. No authority above the nation-state exists to enforce order among them. Consequently, nations continue to rely primarily on bargaining and self-help (including the threat and actual use of force) in their quest for national security in a politically insecure, competitive environment. A decentralized system places a premium on the quest for power as a means of defense and influence. In such a primitive system, is it any wonder that so many states have been inclined to arm for defense out of fear, or that violent conflict has erupted so routinely?

Decentralization is related to a second feature: the highly *stratified* character of the international political system. The equality of nations is a (legal) myth. Power is distributed very unevenly and hierarchically. A few hegemonic nations near the apex (the United States and the Soviet Union) possess a vast proportion of power, whereas the other nations near the bottom of this metaphorical pyramid are relatively powerless. The perceived and ascribed status of states, as well as the distribution of resources, are also very unevenly distributed within this system structure.

But the nature of that decentralized, stratified political system has changed since 1945. Those changes have affected the kinds of policies open to the United States, calling for adjustments to shifting circumstances. Let us briefly examine some of the changes and the response of the United States to them.

Hegemonic Dominance: A Unipolar World

The postwar period began with the United States emerging as the only major industrial power unscathed by the ravages of World War II. In fact, that war spurred the transformation of the American economy. The Gross National Product (GNP) rose from $239.2 billion in 1941 to $329.3 billion in 1944; agricultural production increased by 25 percent; and civilian consumption of goods and services rose by 20 percent (Lovell, 1970: 93). In contrast, the Soviet economy had suffered enormous devastation. Its industrial, agricultural, and transportation systems had either been destroyed or severely damaged. The death of an estimated 20 million Soviet soldiers and citizens is an index of the enormous costs of the war to the Soviets. Although the United States had suffered some 300,000 casualties, the ratio of Soviet to American war deaths was about seventy to one.

The Soviet Union had, of course, secured control over vast areas of Eastern Europe following the war, and it was over this issue that much of the mutual antagonism characterizing American-Soviet interactions in the period from 1947 to 1953 centered. On balance, however, the United States was clearly in the superior position. In 1947, for example, the United States alone accounted for 50 percent of the world's total GNP. (The size of a nation's GNP relative to that of other countries is a commonly used index of that nation's potential power.) And the nation's monopoly of the atomic bomb gave it military superiority.

It is against this background that we can begin to see how fundamental the shifts in the international distribution of power have been during the past forty years. The postwar era began with the United States possessing the capability—if not the will—to dominate international politics as perhaps no other nation before. It alone possessed the military and economic might to unilaterally defend its security and sovereignty; its position of strength relative to other states was unchallenged, as Sir Harold Laski's (1947) depiction (recall chapter one) vividly captures. The unparalleled supremacy of the United States may, without risk of exaggeration, permit the system during this interlude to be termed a *unipolar* one, for the power within it was concentrated within the hands of a single state. So unchallenged was American dominance at the time that some observers, such as Henry Luce, spoke hopefully of ''the American century,'' of a prolonged period in which American power would enable it to shape the world to its interests.

However, that situation began to change almost as soon as it received recognition for what it was when the atomic monopoly was cracked with the successful Soviet atomic test in 1949. Then, in 1953, the Soviets exploded a thermonuclear device less than a year after the United States. And in 1957 the Soviet Union shocked the Western world by being the first nation to orbit a space satellite—a feat which proved as well its capability to deliver a nuclear warhead. Thereafter the competition to build ever more sophisticated delivery systems for increasingly destructive weapons continued without restraints.

The Bipolar System

The term *bipolarity* describes the way the global distribution of power came to be concentrated in the hands of the United States and the Soviet Union during the period from roughly the late 1940s until the Cuban missile crisis of 1962. The dual concentration of power was reflected in the creation of alliance systems, which were manifestations of the tendency of less powerful nations to look to one or the other of the superpowers for protection in a hostile international environment. The North Atlantic Treaty Organization (NATO), linking the United States to the defense of Western Europe, and the Warsaw Pact, linking the Soviet Union in a formal alliance to its Eastern European satellites, are the two major examples. Correspondingly, each superpower's allies gave it forward bases from which to carry on the competition with the other. The competition was punctuated by recurrent confrontations that marked the superpowers' concern for power and security in an atmosphere of mutual suspicion.

The bipolar distribution of power contributed to a crisis-ridden postwar atmosphere.[1] As John Spanier (1975) has observed, by grouping the nations of

---

[1]The bipolar system was crisis-prone in the sense that the threat of war was ever present. However, one of the ironic features of such a fearful environment was that, amidst endemic threats, major war did *not* occur. Some (for example, Waltz, 1964) have argued that the bipolar world was actually a stable world because relatively little violence between states actually occurred. We might thus ask if perhaps the perpetual competition and overwhelming destructive power of the era paradoxically might have produced caution and restraint rather than boldness and recklessness.

the system into two blocs, each led by a superpower, the bipolar structure bred insecurity among all actors. The balance was constantly at stake. What one side gained was seen as a loss for the other. Utmost importance was therefore attached to recruiting new friends and allies, while fear that an old ally might desert the fold was ever present. Little room was left for compromise in the bipolar world. Every maneuver appeared to be a new initiative toward world conquest; hence every act of hostility was to be met by a retaliatory act of hostility. Endemic to the struggle was the notion that conciliation was impossible, that the most that could be hoped for was a momentary pause in overt hostilities based on mutual fears and consequent hesitations to challenge the territorial status quo.

The Bipolycentric System

Over time, the rigid structure of the bipolar distribution of power began to weaken. The gradual loosening of the major Cold War ties associated with bipolarity was symptomatic. As bipolarity eroded, what has been described as a *bipolycentric* system (Spanier, 1975) began to replace it. Bipolycentrism recognizes the continued military superiority of the United States and the Soviet Union and the continued reliance, at least ultimately, of the weaker alliance partners on their respective superpower patrons for security. At the same time, the new system allows considerable room to maneuver on the part of weaker members; hence the term *polycentrism*, connoting the possibility of many centers of power and diverse relationships among the nations subordinate to the superpowers. In a bipolycentric system, each superpower is assumed to seek links with the secondary powers formally aligned with its adversary, such as those that were once nurtured between the United States and Romania, on the one hand, and those between France and the Soviet Union, on the other. At the same time, the secondary powers are assumed to use those ties, as well as others established across alliance boundaries by the secondary powers themselves (for example, between Poland and West Germany), to enhance their bargaining position within their own alliance. While the superpowers remain dominant militarily, alliance members have greater fluidity in their diplomacy than is true in a strictly bipolar system. And new foreign policy roles (other than simply "aligned" or "nonaligned" status) are created for actors in this less-rigid system.

Rapid technological innovation in the major weapon systems of the superpowers was one of the principal catalysts of change in the polarity structure of the international system. In particular, the advent of technologically sophisticated intercontinental ballistic missiles (ICBMs) decreased the need for forward base areas to strike at the heart of the adversary,[2] thereby diminishing

---

[2]That consideration applied more at that time to the United States than the Soviet Union, since the latter did not enjoy forward bases of the sort maintained in Europe and Asia by the United States. Soviet forward bases on its border in Eastern Europe were better conceptualized as "buffers" separating the Soviet Union from possible Western European aggression. Soviet efforts

the usefulness of cohesive alliance systems composed of reliable defense partners. In addition, the deterioration of alliance groupings was accelerated by the narrowing of the difference between Soviet and American military capabilities. As the "balance of power" became a "balance of terror," European members of NATO in particular began to question whether the United States would indeed trade New York City for Paris or Bonn. The credibility of the U.S. threat of massive retaliation was especially open to question, but even the concept of "flexible response" as advocated by Kennedy, and adopted as official NATO strategy during the Johnson administration, did not dramatically improve credibility. Since the president of the United States would still be faced with the decision to escalate a local conflict into a global one, the question "At what point?" remained unanswered. Also unanswered was how the Soviet leadership would know the conditions under which Washington would be willing to risk a nuclear holocaust. Such uncertainty raised for many Europeans the question of whether flexible response did not in fact signal more reluctance than ever on the part of the United States to expose itself to destruction for the sake of ensuring the security of its European allies. It was a growing sense of uncertainty that led to France's decision in the late 1950s to develop its own nuclear *force de frappe* and to its later decision, in the mid-1960s, to evict NATO headquarters from French soil and to withdraw from the integrated NATO command. Despite Washington's assurances to the contrary, the uncertainty has persisted to the present. At the same time, many Europeans have expressed a growing fear (see Puchala, 1985) that as the superpowers develop the capacity and perhaps the will to pursue a limited nuclear engagement, Europe may be devastated in a "limited response" nuclear exchange between the superpowers, that is, by a nuclear attack confined to the European theater without escalation to general war between the superpowers themselves.

Just as apprehension over the willingness of the United States to defend Europe has continued, the polycentrism that first emerged in the 1960s has remained. Indicators of the changes since the passing of bipolarity included verbal acceptance by the United States and the Soviet Union that conditions of nuclear parity ought, in the interests of stability, to be preserved (as signaled by the SALT agreements); the superpowers' intermittent pledges to avert nuclear war between them and their tentative approach toward acceptance of a

---

to convert Cuba into a forward base comparable to American forward areas in Europe were largely unsuccessful, as witnessed by the abortive attempt to place strategic missiles in Cuba in 1962. (To support Cuba's economy and maintain its allegiance, the Soviets subsidize it at considerable expense; it has been estimated that the subsidy is on the order of $5 billion per day, Fossedal [1985a] reports.) More recently, however, Soviet efforts to establish forward bases have been pursued with vigor, but these have often met with determined local resistance (as the Soviet push to convert Afghanistan into a satellite state illustrates). More typical has been the pursuit of these efforts through proxy states; the presence of Soviet-bloc combat troops in Angola, Ethiopia, Laos, and Cambodia in the early 1980s is symptomatic of this approach.

"no first use" principle (see Bundy et al., 1982); the growing skepticism among members of both blocs about the willingness of their own superpower protector to come to their defense in the event of an attack by the other; the resultant efforts of several countries to shift from reliance on others to self-defense (mostly notably by joining the nuclear club or retaining the technical option of doing so); and the growing feeling that the old alliance structures were becoming obsolete as fears of territorial expansion through conventional warfare abated and the destructiveness ofd the modern weapons seemed to render defensive alliances irrelevant. What purposes were served by an alliance which could not insure the security of its members against a nuclear strike, it was asked. Did membership in an alliance diminish rather than increase national security by making the member a certain target in a superpower nuclear exchange? If so, should the value of membership—and the cost—be reconsidered? The posing of these questions by many leaders led to a decline in the cohesion of the alliance systems.

The unwillingness of some members of NATO to participate in American-initiated sanctions against the Soviet Union for its invasion of Afghanistan in 1979 or to support the American attack on Libya in 1986 illustrated the tensions and differing perceptions inherent in the Western alliance. So, too, did the decision of several Western European states to facilitate construction of the Yamberg pipeline to transport Soviet natural gas from Siberia to Western European markets. A rise in the importance of nonmilitary issues coincided with those specific events. Questions relating to such issues as trade, agricultural policy, unemployment, the international monetary system, debt servicing and rescheduling, and access to energy (issues to which we shall give attention in the next chapter) became paramount.

It can be argued, in fact, that the present international system is in many respects dominated by concerns and fears unrelated to the military and strategic considerations of the bipolar world. This is reflected in the criticism which many of America's closest allies directed at the Reagan administration. Although Reagan emphasized the threat of Soviet communism using the rhetoric and images of earlier periods in postwar American diplomacy, many other nations, particularly in the industrial world, did not share his concerns and did not accept his inclination to interpret every issue from a narrow East-West perspective. Instead, they saw a broad range of nonsecurity issues which had come to the fore with what they perceived to have been a receding of external security threats. Such differences are the essence of polycentrism.

The heightened salience of nonmilitary issues may also be attributed to the growing capabilities of America's alliance partners—to the point that the United States has suffered a decline in its ability to impose its own chosen solutions to nonmilitary questions. If in 1947 the United States accounted for half of the world's total GNP, that proportion had declined to 34 percent in 1960 and 24 percent in 1983. The phenomenal growth of the Japanese and Western European economies in the postwar period largely accounted for the relative decline of America's economic dominance. In 1983 the combined output of the thirteen European Community (EC) countries[3] and Japan was over $1,137 billion greater than U.S. output; only thirty years earlier it had been less than three-quarters of that output.

This erosion in the economic position of the United States in the international hierarchy suggests that America was no longer singularly predominant at the apex of power. The "century" of American hegemony predicted by Henry Luce lasted less than twenty-five years. The U.S. now had rivals. The decline of American hegemony, it should be noted, was *not* due to a decline in the capacity of the American economy to expand, for, indeed, the economy had nearly quadrupled its product since the second world war. The decline was *relative*. The rates of growth of other countries' economies steadily exceeded that of the United States over the course of nearly four decades, with the result that the United States was no longer economically able to command the *proportion* of the world's economic product that it once did. Other states now could claim a bigger share of that pie. Militarily, of course, the United States remained without rival in the Western world, and economically its production was in 1983 79 percent greater than that of its Soviet superpower rival (U.S. Arms Control and Disarmament Agency, 1985: 81, 88).

We know, of course, that Europe is not united, and that Japan, for decades restrained in its willingness to utilize its industrial capacity to build military strength, has yet to acquire the weapons necessary to allow it to play an independent military role in the global arena (see Burgess, 1985). By themselves, therefore, trends in relative national economic growth rates do not fully capture the ability of other states to rival the military power of either the United States or the Soviet Union, even though they rival the superpowers economically. Neither the Soviet Union nor China approach Western Europe economically, and in the mid-1980s Japan's economy exceeded that of the Soviet for the first time, while the gap between Japan and China has widened even further. Yet the Soviet Union retains superpower status by virtue of its military strength, derived from its conscious decision to allocate relatively scarce economic resources for military development, while China's membership in the nuclear club is, no doubt largely responsible for its emergence as a significant regional, if not global, actor. A rough indication of the relative equality of

---

[3]The European Community (EC) comprises the European Economic Community (EEC—a customs union created by the 1958 Treaty of Rome), the European Coal and Steel Community (ECSC—a sectoral common market created in 1952), and the European Atomic Energy Community (EURATOM—created in 1958). The EEC, ECSC, and EURATOM are served by certain common institutions, including a council of ministers, a commission (with secretariat), a court of justice, and a parliament. The EC initially comprised Belgium, France, Italy, Luxembourg, the Netherlands, and West Germany. It was expanded in 1973 to include Denmark, Ireland, and the United Kingdom. Greece became the tenth member of the organization in 1981, and Spain and Portugal joined in 1986; Turkey retains associate status and may become a full member of the EC in the future if it can obtain the support of Greece for its membership.

American and Soviet military strength as well as their dominance with regard to the rest of the world is provided by the facts that each accounted for roughly a quarter of total world military expenditures in each year from 1963 to 1983 and that collectively the two never accounted for less than 55 percent of all military expenditures in the world during those years (U.S. Arms Control and Disarmament Agency, 1975, 1976, 1978, 1980b, and 1985).

Nevertheless, the growing economic strength of Western Europe and Japan relative to the United States and the resultant lessening of their dependency on the United States has facilitated the ability of each to steer a course independent of the United States. Militarily, that potential can only be realized sometime in the future. However, when coupled with intense nationalism, particularly in Western Europe, the potential is already a reality insofar as economic issues are concerned. The continued diffusion of wealth and productivity are destined to exacerbate efforts by the U.S. to resolve major international economic issues by the assertion of a U.S. position and the compliance of three or four other powers. With the diffusion of economic power has come the end of the American ability to dominate its allies in the Western community.

The fragmentation and factionalization of global alliance systems has been an Eastern as well as Western phenomenon—and for many of the same reasons, with internecine ideological quarrels an added source of factionalism. The Sino-Soviet split, dating back to the 1950s, is the most visible and well-known manifestation of the breakup of what was once seen as a communist monolith. Growing out of ideological differences as well as security concerns befitting two giant neighbors, the dispute was elevated in the 1960s to a clear rivalry for leadership of the world communist movement. It has opened the possibility of a new era of triangular politics involving Washington, Moscow, and Beijing, as discussed below. In Europe, diminishing alliance solidarity has contributed to fissures within the Warsaw Pact, offering the United States opportunities to quietly cultivate new relationships with members of that formerly cohesive bloc (see Oberdorfer, 1984).

In some respects, polycentrism within the Soviet bloc is not new. Periodic assertions of Eastern European independence, despite the shadow of the Red Army, marked the behavior of the East Germans, the Poles, and the Hungarians during the 1950s. During the 1960s, one of the most visible examples of polycentric tendencies within the Warsaw Pact occurred in Czechoslovakia, whose experiment in domestic liberalism was abruptly terminated by the intervention of other members of the Warsaw Pact in 1968. The primacy of domestic concerns was also illustrated by the labor unrest in Poland in the early 1980s, which proceeded despite the threat of Soviet military intervention.

Less striking, but perhaps more durable, are the assertions of independence from ''Moscow's line'' manifested by other Eastern European nations, of which Romania's polycentric deviation is notable. Romania has remained staunchly authoritarian at home, thus side-stepping the fate suffered by

Prague's Spring (as the 1968 Czech experiment in democratization is sometimes called), but it has successfully deviated from the wishes of its bloc leader (the Soviet Union) on some foreign policy issues. Romania has joined several international organizations in which other communist nations have refused to take part (for example, the World Bank and the International Monetary Fund); it received Presidents Nixon and Ford, and Communist Party chairman Hua Kuo-feng of China in major state visits; and it agreed to the provisions of the 1974 U.S. Trade Act, thereby becoming the first communist nation to receive most-favored-nation treatment under its terms.[4]

As in the case of NATO, the polycentric fragmentation of the Warsaw Pact is both part of and a reflection of the evolving structural characteristics of the international system at large. The Helsinki agreement (signed by the United States, the Soviet Union, and leaders of thirty-two other states in 1975 as the culmination of the European Security Conference the Soviets had sought for so long) symbolized the diminished perception of threat relative to the bipolar period perhaps more than any other document. By its signing the postwar division of Europe was given a degree of legitimacy as never before, thereby laying to rest, in principle at least, many of the sources of East-West antagonism; and it laid the foundation for the substantial expansion of NATO-Warsaw Pact trade that was later experienced. Thus the necessity of maintaining a well-armed military alliance, directed from the top and poised in readiness for attack, seemed less relevant to the states of Europe (even if the two superpowers continued to emphasize that need).

A barometer of the perceived level of tension in Europe is the variation in the extent to which leaders of NATO and the Warsaw Pact countries have expressed the belief that conflict will occur. As gleaned from public statements by heads of state, government members, or their representatives, these reports demonstrate that the climate of opinion on the European continent has changed dramatically over time. Based on that measure, it is clear that perceived East-West tension in Europe was relatively high until the early 1950s, when the death of Stalin (1953) and the de-Stalinization program announced by Nikita Khrushchev (1956) appear to have abated the expectation of conflict. Tension then increased subsequently in response to the downing of an American U-2 spy plane over Russia (1960) and the ill-fated Paris summit of that year, the Berlin crisis (1961), and the Cuban missile crisis (1962). But perceived tension decreased markedly following the 1963 Nuclear Test Ban Treaty. The only notable rise thereafter occurred with the Soviet invasion of Czechoslovakia in 1968, but even that proved to be an interlude of relatively short duration. Indeed, the general pattern provided by European leaders' statements

---

[4]Hungary was granted most-favored-nation (MFN) status in 1978, and Poland applied for membership in the International Monetary Fund in 1981. Hungary has been in the 1980s the most daring advocate of East-West détente of the Soviet Union's satellites (see Drozdiak, 1984). At the same time, Romania's MFN status has been threatened by congressional and Reagan administration dissatisfaction with its human rights practices, as noted in chapter seven.

points unmistakably to a clear trend away from the expectation of conflict and invites the conclusion that as a process détente was well under way in the European context by the time it became the official policy of Soviet and American leaders in the late 1960s and early 1970s (for supporting trend data and interpretations, see Goldmann, 1973, and Goldmann and Lagerkranz, 1977).

With the stalling of Soviet-American détente in the late 1970s, and with the efforts of the Reagan administration to reassert the centrality of the East-West conflict in American foreign policy, pressure was exerted for NATO and Warsaw Pact leaders to fall in line with the thinking of their superpower patrons and conform their policy positions accordingly. However, the superpower confrontation of the 1980s did not bring an end to intraalliance differences, especially within the Western camp. Détente became more important to Europe than to the United States, in part because Europe is a likely battleground for a conventional war, and perhaps a nuclear war, between the United States and the Soviet Union.[5] Furthermore, on security issues outside Europe, the United States and its Western European allies often have differing perceptions of the issues because the interests at stake vary. For example, many European governments openly disapproved of American policy in Vietnam during the 1960s; they refused landing rights to American planes resupplying Israel during the 1973 Yom Kippur War; they gave only lukewarm support in 1979 to American efforts to squeeze Iran economically in an effort to secure release of American hostages there; they have differed with Washington's policies for dealing with Soviet troops in Afghanistan, with domestic turmoil in Central America, and with "state-sponsored terrorism" in Libya and elsewhere; and they resisted the U.S. effort to block the construction of the Siberian natural gas pipeline to Western Europe.

In the mid-1980s, opinion in Western Europe swung further toward neutralism, pacifism, and a challenge to the underpinnings of the "Atlanticist" orientation that bound the U.S. and Western Europe together between 1955 and 1975. Tensions in European-American relations became more pronounced, as signaled by "the unprecedented booing of an American President at the European Parliament and the coming of age of a "successor generation" unschooled in traditional Atlanticism" (Puchala, 1985). Evidence from leadership opinion surveys in the 1980s underscores the conclusion that:

> . . . the community of Western Europeans and Americans, if measured in terms of amity, mutuality, confidence and responsiveness is less integrated than it was twenty years ago. The disintegration is largely the result of changes in Western European sentiments concerning the United States. These changes have been caused

---

[5]Observes Winik (1985): "When NATO was founded in 1949, it was basically a unilateral American nuclear guarantee of European security in the guise of an alliance. This situation has remained largely unchanged. But with the advent of at least strategic parity, the U.S. nuclear commitment to defend Europe has been reduced to a pact of mutual suicide. It has lost much of its credibility, if not sense."

by altered perceptions and interpretations of United States international behavior, particularly U.S. behavior in the context of superpower rivalry. (Puchala, 1985: 42)

Much the same is true of Japan, whose delicate domestic political situation has inhibited its willingness to contribute to the mutual defense effort to the extent that Washington would prefer. And for both Europe and Japan, differences with Washington over a range of nonmilitary issues are often deep and likely to remain so.

The Soviet Union's task in inducing its allies to toe the line is perhaps less difficult than the job of the United States (given its domination of them), but the periodic assertions of independence by Eastern European countries make clear that concern for maintaining alliance cohesion is not confined to the West. Hence polycentrism within the major Cold War alliances remains a continuing feature of the international political system.

Where does China fit in this evolving structural trend? China does not fall neatly into the bipolycentric description, which includes the notion that the secondary powers of the major alliances built at the height of the Cold War will be inclined to look to their respective superpower patrons for military protection. Although for years the United States rigidly maintained the view that the Chinese perceived Moscow solely as their loyal protector, that was not the Chinese view. Nor does a multipolar power system similar to the classical European balance of power system describe the situation. Such a system would include, say, five actors of relatively equal power, consistent with President Nixon's declaration in 1971 that the bipolar world had given way to a five-power world. Although one might envision a multipolar system in which the United States, the Soviet Union, Japan, China, and a united Europe were the major actors, the equilibrating mechanisms of the classical balance of power, predicated on *realpolitik* assumptions, are of doubtful relevance to the contemporary world. The classical system was maintained by the willingness of the major actors to enter into alliances with anyone (ideology notwithstanding) and to use war as an instrument of policy.[6] Even if one could plausibly envision a relative equilibrium of military capabilities involving the United States, the Soviet Union, China, Japan, and a united Europe by, say, the year 2000, the destructiveness of modern weapons makes it difficult to imagine a reemergent balance-of-power system with operating characteristics analogous to the classical nineteenth-century European state system. The ongoing[7] ideological

[6]But war was typically limited in duration, extensiveness (in terms of population and industrial centers), and devastation—limitations imposed by the lack of technologically sophisticated weapons, as compared to today's weapons.

[7]The seventh round of normalization talks in Beijing in October 1985, aimed at mending the twenty-five-year rift in relations between the feuding Chinese and Soviet communist parties, was concluded with China's statement that the Soviet threat to its borders ruled out any immediate restoration of ties. The Chinese Communist Party severed all links with its Soviet counterpart in 1966 after a series of ideological disputes in which both parties claimed to be standard bearers of world socialism. Of course, China's experimentation with capitalistic principles to stimulate economic growth (see Rowen, 1985b) dramatized the extent of the rift between the two societies with a 4,000 mile common border.

conflict between the Soviet Union and China further undermines the relevance of a multipolar vision of the future.[8] Some model of "triangular politics" seems a more appropriate way to account for the role of China in the world power equation and the evolving structure of the international system.

The Tripolar System

Tripolarity[9] describes a system comprising three nations with relatively equal potential as defined by their economic and military capabilities, especially in the area of nuclear weapons. Tripolarity is a useful way to think of the role of a powerful China in the future. However, the term does not apply fully to present realities. Objectively, China cannot be defined as the power rival of either the United States or the Soviet Union. Nor is it likely to achieve such status quickly. But as the Chinese continue development of nuclear weapons and a capacity to deliver them within at least the Asian theater, they may achieve a limited second-strike capability which minimally will complicate the delicate strategy of deterrence on which the Americans and Soviets have come to rely. Deterrence would have to be directed not simply at one actor, but two, and in particular toward preventing a military attack by two against one.

Indeed, preventing "two against one" would appear to be the key element defining foreign policy behavior in a tripolar system. Considerable attention and resources are likely to be spent by each nuclear power on its relations with its rivals so as not to be left outside the structure of triangular relations. That, in turn, implies bargaining situations involving collusion and bluffs between and among the participants as each seeks to maximize its interests. Even cooperative initiatives by two actors not intentionally directed against the third are likely to be interpreted ominously by the third. One's primary interest in this context is axiomatic: avoid permanent diplomatic isolation. Foreign policy behavior under conditions of tripolarity would thus be based on a rational calculation of interest (and power) in which ideology is a peripheral consideration.

It is important to emphasize that tripolarity does not currently exist. In the present system possession of a second-strike nuclear capacity and the means to deliver it are preconditions for a power to be considered a "pole." China, which does not possess such capabilities, cannot be said therefore to comprise a third pole. But tripolarity may come into existence as China further develops its nuclear arsenal and further develops its industrial base. China has already successfully tested a long-range missile capable of striking Moscow or the

---

[8]The difficulties inherent in conceptualizing the current and emergent configuration of the international system are illustrated by the many terms that have been used to describe the system's structure: bimodal, bipolar, loose bipolar, very loose bipolar, tight bipolar, bimultipolar, bipolycentric, complex conglomerate, détente system, diffuse bloc, discontinuity model, heterosymmetrical bipolarity, multipolar, multihierarchical, multi-bloc, pentapolar, polycentric, oligopolistic, tripolar, and three-tiered multidimensional system within a bipolar setting (Nogee, 1975).

[9]The following brief discussion of tripolarity is based on Yalem (1972), Spanier (1975 and 1981), and Starr (1982).

west coast of the United States. Eventually, therefore, China may develop sufficient weaponry to be considered a pole in a tripolar arrangement. As for most other military and economic capabilities, however, China is likely to remain far less powerful than either United States or the Soviet Union for several decades.

The tripolar concept is nevertheless useful in drawing attention to the way in which the external environment serves both as a source of and a constraint on foreign policy, for it captures many of the important elements that have characterized American, Soviet, and Chinese behavior toward one another during the past decade or more. The concept helps explain Chinese apprehensiveness about Soviet-American détente; it provides insight into Soviet concern for Sino-American rapprochement; and it renders understandable American support of polycentric tendencies in the communist camp generally, and fear of Soviet-Chinese fence mending in particular. Reagan's bid to China in the spring of 1984 to "lay aside disputes and cooperate in trade and space" and the December 1984 Sino-Soviet agreement to develop trade and science together over the next twenty-five years indicate that triangular maneuvering will likely continue. Each rival may be expected to seek diplomatic leverage by discouraging rapprochement between the others while encouraging self-serving linkages with each of them.

A vivid symbol of the triangular politics associated with tripolarity was provided by Richard Nixon's historic visit to China in the winter of 1972. The visit was preceded by Henry Kissinger's announcement in February 1970 that the U.S. "would no longer treat conflict with the U.S.S.R. as automatically involving the People's Republic." The visit by Nixon, a long-time anticommunist ideologue, thus was made possible by the Nixon-Kissinger efforts of the previous year to end the isolation of China, which had been the cornerstone of American containment policy in Asia since 1949. Formal diplomatic ties between the United States and China were established by the Carter administration, whose officials openly spoke of playing the "China card" in an effort to moderate Soviet behavior around the globe. The Reagan administration continued along the same path. Even though President Reagan threatened during his 1980 campaign for office to slow and perhaps reverse the process of normalizing relations with China, the parade of Washington officials visiting Beijing has continued without interruption. Secretary of Defense Caspar Weinberger also made classic use of the "China card" in the spring of 1981 when he threatened that the United States might sell arms to China if the Soviet Union intervened militarily in Poland.[10] Later in the year, without any specific reference to Poland or other events, the Reagan administration lifted restrictions on the sale of arms to China. The subsequent decision in April 1984 to permit the People's Republic of China to buy civilian nuclear reactors from the United States added a new dimension to the strategic equation, al-

---

[10]As befits the tripolar concept, one could, of course, easily interpret Chinese receptivity to American overtures as the playing of their "American card."

though the Chinese pledged not to use the resultant spent nuclear fuel to facilitate the efforts of countries trying to acquire nuclear weapons.

Each of those steps in triangular politics is more consistent with the model of tripolarity than bipolarity. As John Spanier notes, in contrast to a bipolar system, nations in a tripolar system

> need not be quite so sensitive to slight increments of power by any pole as the emphasis shifts from continual crises toward maneuver and from rigid confrontation to flexibility. Whereas in a bipolar system each state thinks that it must match the other, in a tripolar system some gain in power can be permitted because, if the increase should become too threatening to the other two poles, they are likely to combine their power. (Spanier, 1981: 126)

The picture emerging from the foregoing historical survey of changes in the global distribution of power shows that that distribution has undergone substantial alteration since Hiroshima. A unipolar system gave way to a bipolar system, followed by the emergence of a bipolycentric world, which may subsequently be replaced by a tripolar or a multipolar configuration of four, five, or more centers of power atop a multitude of weak states on their periphery. Still other possibilities could also arise. For instance, one view forsees the future crystallization of a Washington-Tokyo-Beijing axis balancing another composed of Bonn-Paris-Moscow (Brucan, 1984).

The overall postwar trend in the power distribution has been toward the dispersion of power globally. Part of that dispersion has been due to the general erosion of American power with respect to other nations in the world political system. The era of American hegemony has ended. The erosion of American power has required policy adjustments as the United States has had to accommodate itself to the disintegration of the bipolar world and the emergence of the new, more complex external circumstances that replaced it.

The decline of American power in world affairs and the deterioration of the U.S. position internationally has placed limits on the country's options and also has stimulated the birth of different foreign policy orientations toward these external realities. The Nixon, Ford, and Carter administrations sought to accommodate the nation to the growing limits of American military and economic power, while also, in the pessimistic view of Henry Kissinger, seeking to retard the pace of America's future decline. The Reagan administration, on the other hand, has denied the existence of these deteriorating circumstances and has attempted to alter perceptions through military spending and militaristic diplomacy; its policies have sought to reassert American influence over the course of international events. The pursuit of regained stature was designed to restore a world in which power was once again concentrated in the hands of a single superpower, thus reversing the trend toward the global dispersion of power that had accelerated since Hiroshima.

The efficacy of the Reagan administration's orientation toward the dilemmas posed by the diffusion of global power and the erosion of America's position will be tested by subsequent events. In wrestling with those fundamental changes, the United States must also contend with the challenge posed by the burgeoning number of less powerful nations. It is to them we now turn.

AN INTERNATIONAL SYSTEM WITH NEW MEMBERS: THE THIRD WORLD

Another conspicuous feature of the international political system is the dramatic growth in the size of its membership. Since World War II there has been an enormous increase in the number of independent nation-states. By 1985 the United Nations had grown to 159 members, a more than threefold increase over the original 51 members. For the most part this expansion has been accomplished by the postwar breakup of the vast British, French, Spanish, Dutch, and Portuguese empires, most of which were created little more than a century ago. Because from today's perspective we tend to think of the international system as populated by sovereign, independent states spread the world over, perhaps we forget both the magnitude and speed of the decolonization process. In the postwar ebbing of the tidal wave of imperialism that swept the world a century ago, nearly a hundred territories today containing over two billion people have been freed from colonial rule. Such a spectacular move toward political emancipation is unparalleled in history.

The consequence of the proliferation of new states is the rise of the Third World, whose numbers comprise five-sixths of the United Nations' membership. Those nations at the periphery lack the capabilities shared by the superpowers and the industrialized nations of Eastern and Western Europe clustered in formal alliance around them. Indeed, some would even question the appropriateness of the term nation-state to describe Third World countries, for many lack the most basic attributes of nationhood. In terms of the global distribution of power, those nations for the most part are particularly lacking in that combination of large population and economic capacity traditionally associated with the "powerful." In 1983, for example, 38 countries in Asia and Africa had an annual per capita Gross National Product of less than $400; of these, roughly two-thirds had a population of less than 10 million (Sewell, Feinberg, and Kallab, 1985: 215–216, 218).

The division between the world's rich and poor generally follows the equator, with the rich to the North and the poor in the South. The nations of the Third World are generally found in Latin America, Africa, and Asia, and the North-South division has come to overlay the East-West cleavage as one of the dominant features of contemporary world politics.

The sharp reality of the gap between North and South is captured by the fact that the roughly three-quarters of the world's people who live in the South account for less than one-fifth of its aggregate Gross National Product, whereas those in the North, making up only one-quarter of the world's population, account for more than 80 percent of its production (see Figure 6.1). On a per person basis, this means that the average annual income for each person

FIGURE 6.1   The Distribution of Global Gross Domestic Product, 1960, 1970, and 1980 (billions of dollars)

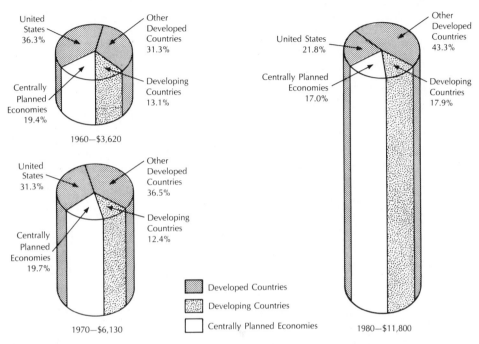

SOURCE: Reprinted with permission from *U.S. Foreign Policy and the Third World: Agenda 1985–86*, edited by John W. Sewell, Richard E. Feinberg, and Valeriana Kallab, U.S.-Third World Policy Perspective, No. 3 (New Brunswick, NJ: Transaction Books for the Overseas Development Council, 1985), p. 231. © Overseas Development Council, 1985.

in the 141 countries making up the Third World was less than $790 in 1982, whereas the average income in the thirty countries making up the First (Western industrialized) and Second (socialist) Worlds was nearly $9,500, or twelve times as much (see Figure 6.2) (Sewell, Feinberg, and Kallab, 1985: 214). Translated into human terms, the disparity between North and South reflected in such statistics indicates that nearly three-quarters of the earth's inhabitants have a bleak present and future virtually unknown—and incomprehensible—to Americans:

> In effect, our world today is in reality two worlds, one rich, one poor; one literate, one largely illiterate; one industrial and urban, one agrarian and rural; one overfed and overweight, one hungry and malnourished; one affluent and consumption-oriented, one poverty-stricken and survival-oriented. North of this line, life expectancy at birth closely approaches the Biblical threescore and ten; south of it, many do not survive infancy. In the North, economic opportunities are plentiful and social mobility is high. In the South, economic opportunities are scarce and societies are rigidly stratified. (Brown, 1972: 41)

FIGURE 6.2   **Per Capita Gross National Product in Developed and Developing Countries, 1975–1981 (based on constant 1980 dollars)**

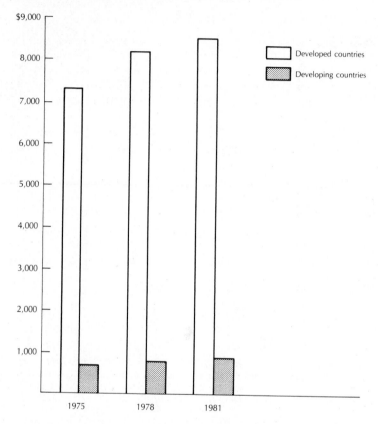

SOURCE: Reprinted with permission from *U.S. Foreign Policy and the Third World: Agenda 1985–86,* edited by John W. Sewell, Richard E. Feinberg, and Valeriana Kallab, U.S.-Third World Policy Perspective, No. 3 (New Brunswick, NJ: Transaction Books for the Overseas Development Council, 1985), p. 228. © Overseas Development Council, 1985.

A comparison of the trend data in Figures 6.1 and 6.2 reveals two interesting facts: developing nations have increased their share of the global product during the past two decades; but the per capita income gap separating them from the world's rich nations has widened, not narrowed. Indeed, the gap between the world's rich and poor has grown markedly since World War II and is projected to widen even further by the end of the century. There are exceptions to this pattern, of course, especially among a small group known as the *Newly Industrializing Countries* (NICs)[11] which, at least until the mid-1980s, had

[11]Brazil, Mexico, South Korea, Taiwan, Singapore, and Hong Kong are generally regarded as NICs. Others sometimes included in the group include Argentina, Spain, Portugal, Yugoslavia, and Greece.

experienced such spectacular economic growth as to actually close the gap with the North. In general, however, global trends reveal a clear pattern: the rich get richer, and the poor get poorer (for evidence, see Brown, 1972; *The Global 2000 Report to the President*, 1980; Sewell, Feinberg, and Kallab, 1985; and Sivard, 1985). That conclusion holds despite projections that developing nations will in the long run realize higher rates of economic growth than developed countries (see, for example, *World Development Report, 1985*, 1985: 138–139). Against this background, the stark differences between North and South reflect their enormous population differentials. Despite the fact that the economic output of developing countries grew more rapidly than that of developed countries between 1960 and 1980, the per capita differential between the two continued to widen as a consequence of the much higher population growth rates of developing countries.

Worldwide, the rate of population growth is believed to have peaked at about 2 percent in the mid-1960s and to have declined to about 1.7 percent in the mid-1980s. Vast differences characterize different world regions, however. The greatest population increases have occurred in the developing countries, where the medical and agricultural revolutions have most dramatically affected the incidence of death; population has increased least in the developed countries, where births and deaths have nearly stabilized. Among the developed nations of the North, for example, the rate of natural population increase ranges from as little as .1 percent in Western Europe to .7 percent in the United States and .8 percent in Canada. In Latin America, on the other hand, the population growth rate is 2.3 percent, and in Africa it is an astounding 2.9 percent (Population Reference Bureau, *1985 World Population Data Sheet*, 1985). This means Africa's 551 million people will double in only 24 years, growing to 1.4 billion by the year 2020. Figure 6.3 illustrates the differences among the regions of the world today and projects them into the future. As the figure indicates, by the year 2000 the nations making up the First World will comprise but 13 percent of the world's population; the Third World will account for nearly 80 percent.

Although a large population traditionally has been associated with being powerful, for many developing nations today it would appear that their rapidly expanding populations are contributing more to persistent poverty than to the achievement of international prestige and power.[12] To the extent that population growth inhibits economic development, it deprives others in an interdependent world of expanding markets for their economic output. The social and political stresses associated with population pressures promise to be shared nonetheless. Among them are strains on the earth's delicate life-support systems, on the global food regime and the goal of ensuring global food security, and on the ability of developing nations to provide jobs and social

---

[12]See Kegley and Wittkopf (1985: esp. 259–298) for an examination of the causes and consequences of a rapidly expanding world population and of the variations in the population profiles of developed and developing nations.

FIGURE 6.3 Regional Distribution of World Population in 1981 and 2000 (in billions and as a percent of total)

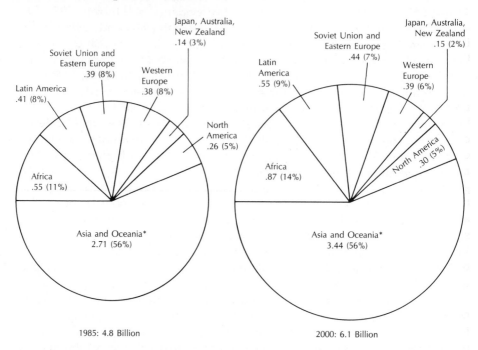

SOURCE: Adapted from Population Reference Bureau, *1985 World Population Data Sheet*, 1985.

*Excluding Japan, Australia, and New Zealand.

NOTE: Percentages do not add to totals because of rounding.

services in rapidly expanding urban agglomerations. In these and other ways rapid population growth is a prescription for political instability, which frequently spills into the wider international arena (McNamara, 1984). Political turmoil in turn has been a major contributor to what in the second half of the twentieth century has been "an unprecedented explosion in the number and impact of refugees" whose "numbers since 1945 are estimated to be as high as 60 million" (Smyser, 1985: 155). Already, and without the refugee problem associated with political strife, the United States has become a haven for many illegal immigrants fleeing their labor-rich job-poor homes in search of opportunities elsewhere. To cope, Third World countries may be expected to turn to authoritarian regimes. Many, perhaps most, of them can be expected to adopt anti-American foreign policies, especially so as the widening income gap between rich and poor countries becomes more pronounced in a world in which the United States and its allies make up only a tiny fraction of the world's over 5 billion inhabitants.

Although rapid population growth and poor average standards of living characterize the Third World as a whole, there are wide variations in the applicability of these descriptions to particular countries, for the Third World is characterized by diversity as well as uniformity. At the risk of oversimplifying, it is useful nonetheless to describe other circumstances common to much of the Third World. They include (1) a heritage of colonialism; (2) a highly uneven distribution of wealth, with most concentrated in the hands of a few; (3) high rates of illiteracy and infant mortality, and low levels of public expenditures for public education and health; (4) economic "dualism" characterized by the existence of a rural, impoverished, neglected sector alongside an urban, developing, and modernizing sector; (5) adverse terms of trade due to export concentration on primary products, such as foodstuffs and other basic commodities, and import reliance on relatively more expensive manufactured goods; (6) massive indebtedness, both public and private, often accompanied by runaway inflation; (7) domestic instability and high levels of civil strife; (7) a condition of *dependence* on the economic assistance, trade, loans, technology, security protection, and arms supplied by states from the First and Second Worlds;[13] alongside (8) the *penetration* of the Third World by alien cultures and by the omnipresent influence of First World multinational corporations and international financial institutions controlled by First World nations.

These are, understandably, national circumstances Third World leaders do not accept willingly. No country's leaders would. Not surprisingly, therefore, the Third World comprises nations whose interests and objectives are often dissimilar from those of the older, more established nations. Those foreign policy orientations may be interpreted as symptoms of a basic dissatisfaction with the existing international system. The emergent nations had little to say about the rules and privileges which govern the international system, rules embedded in international law which, those nations collectively contend, deprive them of the ability to achieve power and status equal to those of their material superiors. Such resentment stems from the perception that "the system" insures that the rich countries will continue to get richer at the expense of the poor.

From this perspective it is not difficult to imagine the posture Third World states assume toward the system they feel imprisons them in their position at the bottom of the international political hierarchy. They don't like it. They wish to overturn it, or to escape from it. They would like to see the world's income and resources redistributed. Or, at a minimum, they would like to see the rules of the game of international politics changed so that they can begin to compete for development and self-respect, playing by rules that do not doom them permanently to compete from a disadvantaged position.

---

[13]For a sampling of some of the extensive dependency-theory literature, see Amin (1974), Baran (1968), Emmanuel (1972), Frank (1969), and the special issue of *International Organization* on dependence and dependency in the global system edited by James A. Caporaso (1978).

Various foreign policy postures of Third World states reflect these aspirations. A foreign policy strategy of nonalignment as it relates to the Cold War competition between the United States and the Soviet Union is one manifestation of differences in the politico-security area. That strategy had the effect historically of stimulating keen interest and activity on the part of the United States and the Soviet Union as each superpower sought to woo the noncommitted to its own side while preventing their alignment with the other. Demands for a New International Economic Order (NIEO) underscore them in the politico-economic sphere. The net effect of restructuring the existing economic order along the lines once envisaged by the NIEO would be to direct substantial amounts of the world's wealth away from those who now have it to those who do not. Intense "anti-Americanism" (see Rubinstein and Smith, 1985) takes on meaning in this context, for, as the world's wealthiest and most privileged state, the United States is a convenient target. Third World countries resent and challenge the "global liberalism" philosophy of the United States that they perceive to have contributed to the poverty that plagues them (see Krasner, 1985). Third World nations, like people generally, are in favor of equality if equalization will bring about an improvement of their relative condition (we all want to be equal to our superiors; but no one wants to be equal to one's inferiors). The politics of resentment, of challenge, of attack on the status quo by the Third World is an outgrowth of the emergence of a political system of gross disparities between the rich and the poor. *Structural Conflict* (Krasner, 1985) between North and South is the consequence.

The United States and others have responded to the Third World in a variety of ways. Recognizing that their self-interest, and their ability to compete for allies, are served in part by alleviating the adverse economic conditions Third World nations face, economic aid, as discussed in detail in chapter five, has been a favored instrument of policy. Other approaches of the United States include reliance on military aid and sales; a willingness to interfere covertly in the affairs of others in order to shape the course of political events in conformity with U.S. preferences; and a proclivity toward overt military intervention. All of those means of American foreign policy flow from a common wellspring, the foundations of which are globalism, fear of communism, and the drive to contain it.

The approach of the United States to developing nations in the context of its competition with the Soviets has not always been without concern for the welfare of developing nations, however. Despite the fact that aid programs historically have been motivated more by security considerations related to a foreign policy strategy of containment than by humanitarian impulses, for example, the net result has been a substantial bilateral (United States to specific other nations) effort to alleviate the conditions of poverty in which so many of the world's billions are mired. Moreover, the United States has been instrumental in encouraging other nations within the Western world to assist in the development aid effort (which is not to say, however, that its motivation for the encouragement was purely a concern for the poor). It has also been a key supporter of multilateral assistance agencies,[14] which have joined the process of providing development aid to the world's less fortunate. The result is that the volume of resources transferred from rich to poor in the postwar period has been considerable. The developing countries of the West are estimated to have averaged $21.7 billion annually in contributions in the early to mid-1970s, and to have provided $319.7 billion between 1980 and 1983 (Sewell, Feinberg, and Kallab, 1985: 203). A considerable portion of this has been channeled through multilateral institutions and private voluntary agencies. Similarly, the communist countries and, more recently, OPEC (Organization of Petroleum Exporting Countries) members have made substantial aid commitments, although precise amounts are difficult to determine. Economic aid from the U.S.S.R. and Eastern Europe[15] has fluctuated between 8.1 and 12.2 percent of total aid between 1970 and 1983, and OPEC bilateral and multilateral aid ranged from a low of 4.9 percent in 1970 to a high of 28.9 percent in 1975; its contribution in 1983 represented 15.2 percent of the total (Sewell, Feinberg, and Kallab, 1985: 204).

For whatever reasons, therefore, several hundreds of billions of dollars have been channeled from rich to poor during the past four decades. Yet few significant strides have been made in alleviating the plight of developing nations. In fact, the effort pales to insignificance when compared to the tremendous needs of developing nations, or alternatively, to the consumption patterns of many developed nations. In the United States, for example, Americans spent more than three times as much on toys and sports supplies in 1983 as their government spent on official development assistance ($18.1 billion compared to $8 billion) and more than eight times as much on alcoholic beverages (Sewell, Feinberg, and Kallab, 1985: 211). But even while the resources are insufficient to the task at hand, for the many reasons discussed in chapter five there is virtually no prospect that the amount of resources will increase in the future.

The use of foreign aid, military as well as economic as an instrument of Cold War competition becomes understandable in view of the foreign policy strategy of nonalignment adopted by most developing nations toward the Cold War antagonists. In effect, nonalignment enabled developing nations to play one superpower off against the other in order to gain advantage for themselves, while the superpowers, in keeping with the sensitivity each manifested toward the other in the context of the bipolar distribution of power,

---

[14]Included in this category are such institutions as the World Bank (International Bank for Reconstruction and Development—IBRD); International Finance Corporation (IFC); International Development Association (IDA); Inter-American Development Bank (IDB); Asian Development Bank (ADB); African Development Bank and African Development Fund (AFDB); United Nations Development Program (UNDP); U.N. Children's Fund and Regular Program of Technical Assistance, plus the U.N. Specialized Agencies; and the European Economic Community (EEC).

[15]Typically there are vast differences between the amount of communist aid commitments to developing nations and their actual disbursements. One source (Sewell, 1977: 241), for example, estimated communist aid commitments between 1971 and 1975 as $8.7 billion, while the OECD reports that communist disbursements during this period were only $4.7 billion.

were willing players in the game. But with the passing of bipolarity, some have asked why the superpowers continue to engage in what is perceived to be (but objectively is not) such a costly game of trying to buy friends?

If the traditional reasons for aiding the world's poor have dissipated, those leading to interference in their internal affairs have not. As the case of American intervention into Chile briefly discussed in the previous chapter suggests, Third World nations that experiment without American direction in socioeconomic reform are likely to be viewed with suspicion. Yet the temptations for experimentation are nearly irresistible, for they grow out of the desire to correct the combination of enormous population pressures, grinding poverty, and the associated ills most Third World nations face. Internal political instability and a high incidence of violent conflict involving others are products of the adverse conditions many developing nations face.

An indication of the relationship between poverty, instability, and foreign involvement can be gleaned from the high incidence in which "local" wars have broken out during the postwar era in Third World countries. Between 1945 and 1976 there were 120, making the internal antiregime war within the Third World the world's most prevalent form of contemporary conflict (Kende, 1978: 232). Equally striking is the extent of foreign participation in these civil wars; some form of it occurred in fully 77 percent of seventy-three antiregime wars that occurred in the Third World (Kende, 1978: 232). It is precisely that kind of involvement that has made internal instability spill over frequently into international conflict.[16]

Although developing nations generally lack the capabilities with which to sustain foreign wars for prolonged periods, the probability that conflict will occur in the developing world nevertheless remains high. That probability has provoked the Third World states to join the rest of the world in its quest to acquire the weapons of war. The increasing commitment to the armaments game worldwide is illustrated by the fact that global armament expenditures increased from above $10 billion at the turn of the century to roughly $950 billion annually by the mid-1980s. The United States and Soviet Union together with their NATO and Warsaw partners continue to account for the bulk of the world's military expenditures. But efforts by developing nations to enhance their military capabilities have become one of the most striking manifestations of their intense nationalism and their often equally intense determination not to be mere pawns in the East-West struggle. As shown in Table 6.1, the proportion of the resources that otherwise poverty-stricken nations have devoted to military expenditures is substantial. Indeed, the data demonstrate that "some of the poorest countries in the world were spending a large percent of GNP on their military establishments while some of the richest were spending relatively little. . . . Some [Third World] countries . . . spent over thirty per-

---

[16]The decreased participation of metropolitan powers (former European colonial powers) in wars in their former colonies, and the increased presence of foreign forces from Third World countries in wars in other Third World countries, represent two recent trends in this postwar pattern.

TABLE 6.1   Relative Burden of Military Expenditures, 1983

Military Expenditures as % of GNP	GNP Per Capita (1982 dollars)					
	UNDER $200	$200–499	$500–999	$1,000–2,999	$3,000–9,999	$10,000 AND OVER
10% and over	Laos Vietnam Kampuchea	Yemen (Aden) Cape Verde	Angola Yemen (Sanaa) Zambia Nicaragua	Iraq North Korea Jordan Syria Mongolia	Israel Oman Libya Soviet Union	Saudi Arabia Qatar
5–9.99%	Somalia Ethiopia	China Guyana Mauritania Guinea Pakistan Afghanistan	Egypt Morocco Zimbabwe Peru Honduras	Lebanon Taiwan Albania South Korea Cuba Malaysia Iran	Bulgaria East Germany Greece Czechoslovakia Singapore Poland United Kingdom	United Arab Emirates United States
2–4.99%	Burma Burkina Faso Mali Benin Chad Bangladesh	Guinea-Bissau Lesotho Mozambique India Burundi Equatorial Guinea Liberia Tanzania Togo Senegal Madagascar Kenya	El Salvador Thailand Swaziland Botswana Indonesia Nigeria Cameroon	Turkey Chile South Africa Yugoslavia Congo Portugal Uruguay Tunisia Algeria Argentina Guatemala	Romania Hungary France Cyprus Belgium Netherlands Trinidad and Tobago Italy Gabon Suriname New Zealand Spain	Kuwait Bahrain West Germany Sweden Norway Australia Denmark Canada
1–1.99%	Zaire Nepal	Central African Republic Sao Tome & Principe Malawi Sri Lanka Haiti Rwanda Uganda	Bolivia Philippines Sudan Ivory Coast Papua New Guinea	Panama Paraguay Ecuador Dominican Republic Jamaica Fiji Colombia	Ireland Austria Venezuela Malta Japan	Switzerland Finland Luxembourg
Under 1%		Sierra Leone Niger The Gambia	Costa Rica	Brazil Mexico Ghana Mauritius	Barbados	Iceland

SOURCE: U.S. Arms Control and Disarmament Agency, 1985: 7.

NOTE: Within each category, countries are ranked in descending order according to military expenditures as percent of GNP.

cent of their GNP on their military establishments'' (U.S. Arms Control and Disarmament Agency, 1985: 5). Often, these expenditures far outstripped public expenditures on education and health.

But Third World militarization is not simply a product of military expenditure. The world has been transformed by the *transfer* of weapons—through sales, gifts, and loans—by the First and Second Worlds to the Third,[17] as shown in Figure 6.4. Between 1979 and 1983, fully 88 percent of all arms exported came from the NATO and Warsaw Pact countries. Especially noteworthy in Figure 6.4 is the proportion of Third World arms transfers shown to find their way to the politically volatile Middle East—a manifestation of the way the United States and the Soviet Union (and others) compete for allies and influence among the nonaligned countries. Since that competition carries with it important economic as well as political motivations on the part of arms suppliers worldwide (as noted in chapter five), the chances that this type of international interaction will be altered substantially are minimal at best.

The rise of a new class of impoverished state actors has presented new problems for American diplomacy and has led, almost inevitably, to adaptations in the kinds of policies the United States has pursued abroad. Indeed, many of the doctrinal and behavioral shifts in postwar American foreign policy, described not only in this chapter but also in previous ones, have been linked closely to the alteration of the composition of the international *political* system. And it is highly probable that future shifts in American foreign policy will continue to be linked closely to the changed and changing international *economic* system, as we will show in the next chapter.

THE RISE OF NONSTATE ACTORS

The growth in the number of nation-states and the dispersion of economic and military capabilities among them are twin features of the external environment that have certainly altered the options open to American foreign policy makers. Another noteworthy characteristic of the postwar period is the growth in the number of international institutions and other types of nonstate actors, of which international intergovernmental organizations (IGOs), international nongovernmental organizations (INGOs), and multinational corporations (MNCs) are the most obvious and powerful types.[18] To these must be

[17]A significant development in the 1980s is the decision of many Third World countries to produce their own weapons for *export* (see Peleg, 1980). In 1973, the developing countries accounted for only 2 percent of the world market share in arms exports; by 1983, it had risen to 11 percent, and the rate of its growth in the 1980–1983 period accelerated to 32 percent (U.S. Arms Control and Disarmament Agency, 1985: 9). Thus while the superpowers continue to dominate the arms trade market, they are receiving competition from the Third World itself, which perceives trade in arms to be a lucrative basis for generating income.

[18]IGOs are international organizations, such as NATO, whose members are nation-states; INGOs comprise people representing subnational groups, such as the International Red Cross; and MNCs are business enterprises organized in one society with activities abroad growing out of direct investment (as opposed to portfolio investment through shareholding), such as the International Telephone and Telegraph Company, an American-based international corporation involved in activities in over seventy countries.

FIGURE 6.4   Value of Arms Transfers, Cumulative 1979–1983, by Major Supplier and Recipient Region (billions of current dollars)

Area of circles (suppliers) and squares (recipients) is proportional to cost of arms transferred or received.

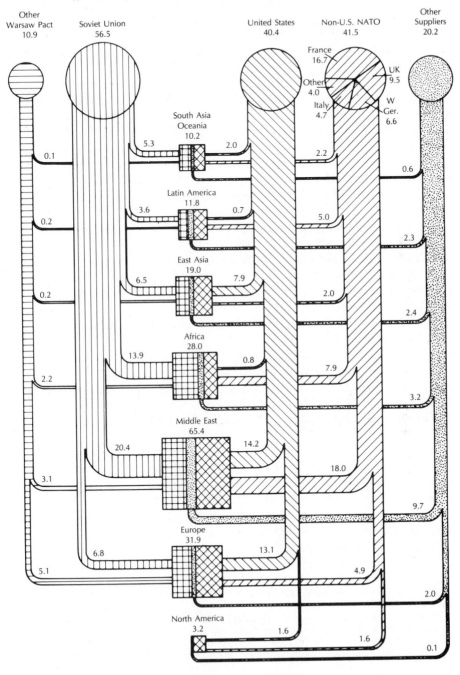

added the increasing prominence of another, less benign type: international terrorist groups.

Nonstate actors have provided both forums for international contact and the glue of interdependence. Their exponential growth in numbers and membership, and their rising prominence, have also made the international environment considerably more complex by proliferating the number of political actors actively engaged in efforts to resolve international policy issues to their own satisfaction.

By 1980, 347 intergovernmental organizations and 4,265 nongovernmental organizations were involved actively in a panoply of transnational political, economic, and social arenas (Jacobson, 1984: 81).[19] This represents, as a conservative estimate, at least a doubling of both types since the 1950s.[20]

Somewhat more difficult to identify are trends in the growth of multinational corporations (MNCs), although there is reason to believe their increase has been even more dramatic. It has been estimated that in the early 1980s, worldwide, about 18,000 MNCs controlled assets in two or more countries and that these were responsible for marketing roughly four-fifths of the world's trade (excluding that of the centrally planned economies) (Clairmonte and Cavanagh, 1982: 149, 152). Regardless of the magnitude of growth trends, however, the vastness of the network of multinationals is clear. In 1977, nearly 10,400 business firms based in nineteen Western industralized nations had at least one foreign affiliate in one or more host countries (Commission on Transnational Corporations, 1979: 8).

Two facts stand out about the distribution of multinational companies and their affiliates. One is that MNCs prefer to operate in other First World nations, where investment opportunities and returns on investments are apparently perceived to be greater. Three-quarters of some 98,000 MNC affiliates identified by the United Nations (Centre on Transnational Corporations, 1983: 327–335) are located in developed market economies, and only a quarter are located in the developing world (Centre on Transnational Corporations, 1983: 34).

American dominance of the network of multinationals is the second. Although several analysts have observed that the American-based MNC is declining as a proportion of the world total, the United States was in 1980 the headquarters for almost half of the top 200 MNCs (defined in terms of sales), and these accounted for over 50 percent of the sales attributed to MNCs (Clairmonte and Cavanagh, 1982: 155).

What import does the growth of nonstate actors have for American foreign policy? Many of the institutions described above can be thought of as interna-

---

[19]Jacobson (1984) provides a useful overview of the activities and functions of international organizations.

[20]There may be perhaps several thousand additional transnational entities whose organizational characteristics do not fit precisely the traditional definition of a nongovernmental organization. If a more inclusive set of definitional criteria is used, in 1980 there were in existence as many as 1,039 IGOs and 9,398 INGOs (Jacobson, 1984: 51). Eighty percent of these are limited membership/specific purpose organizations focused on a regional or issue-area basis, rather than multiple-purpose *universal* organizations such as the United Nations (Jacobson, 1984: 48).

tional actors in their own right, that is, as institutions that carry out their own "private foreign policies" largely unfettered by nation-states. As such, they may be more powerful than some sovereign states, particularly those transnational entities that are economically well endowed. But we can also think of those actors as helping to build and broaden the foreign policy agendas of national decision makers by serving as "transmission belts of policy sensitivities across national boundaries" (Keohane and Nye, 1975). From that perspective, it has been hypothesized that the existence of transnational interactions may influence the international system by (1) *changing attitudes* of elites and nonelites alike by altering their opinions and perceptions of reality through face-to-face contacts with citizens of different states; (2) increasing *international pluralism* by linking national interest groups in transnational structures, usually for the purposes of transnational cooperation; (3) increasing the constraints on states through *dependence and interdependence*, particularly in the areas of international transportation and finance; (4) creating *new instruments of influence* whereby some governments, as a result of the unequal distribution of transnational linkages, may be able to carry out more effectively their wishes regarding other governments; and (5) as already noted, creating new *autonomous international actors* capable of pursuing their interests largely outside the direct control of nation-states while at the same time frequently involving governments in particular problems as a result of their activities (Nye and Keohane, 1971).

Assessing each of those hypotheses would carry us far beyond our principal task here,[21] which is to determine how such features of the external environment influence American foreign policy behavior, and in what ways. A few general observations are in order, however. Traditional international relations theory, consistent with its *realpolitik* emphasis, sees nation-states as the primary actors. Hence the term *state-centric* is used to describe most views of international politics. But in fact the term *state* is merely a shorthand way of referring to a set of institutions and processes through which authoritative decisions are made for territorially defined portions of world society. The globe may be divided into territorial units called nation-states, but governments do not manage all intercourse that crosses these national boundaries. In that context it is appropriate to view transnational institutions and their interactions as factors and actors which influence governments. These actors contribute to the agenda-building process within governments (the process through which issues of public policy are created), and they help governments to define the issues that will receive their attention and demand their time. Those functions seem to flow naturally from the growing numbers of IGOs and INGOs, in particular, for both are outward manifestations of increasing cooperation across

---

[21]For an assessment of the "traditional relations" approach to the study of international relations, see the collection of essays in the special issue of *International Organization* edited by Keohane and Nye (1971); the full-length study of *Power and Interdependence* by Keohane and Nye (1977); the analyses of nongovernmental forces in world politics by Feld (1972 and 1979) and of nonstate actors by Mansbach et al. (1976) and Taylor (1984); and the study of transnational participation by Angell (1969).

national boundaries, which, in turn, is likely to place constraints on the ability of states to "go it alone." For example, governmental decisions in the area of human rights insofar as they affect international politics are unlikely to be made without cognizance of the policies and programs of the United Nations in this area, and the International Federation of Air Line Pilots Associations is likely to influence international efforts to control aircraft hijackings. Another way of saying this is to note that the activities and influence of nonstate transnational actors help to blur the distinction between domestic and foreign policy issues.

It is also worth noting that the greatest growth of INGOs has been among those involved in activities of direct concern to governments—namely, the economy, industry, commerce, finance, and technology—and not among those concerned with essentially noneconomic matters, such as sports and religious affairs (Feld, 1972). And INGOs, we may hypothesize, exert their greatest impact in advanced industrial societies with pluralistic orientations, such as the United States, since those societies are most likely to involve interest groups in the policy-making process.

The growth in the number of IGOs has followed an analogous pattern, with the largest increase occurring among regional organizations concerned with socioeconomic matters. In a sense, then, the greatest growth in IGOs has occurred among those that can be thought of as collective problem-solving institutions, that is, organizations designed to cope with common problems confronting their national members as opposed to organizations wherein the behavior of some other national actor is seen as the problem. The latter group consists, of course, of organizations such as NATO, concerned primarily with national security issues.

The enormous financial resources at the disposal of multinational enterprises necessarily give them a particularly strong voice in determining states' goals. By 1980, the combined revenues of the top 200 multinationals had climbed to account for 29 percent of the gross world product (Clairmonte and Cavanagh, 1982: 154), and it has been estimated that by the year 2000 half or more of all industrial production will be accounted for by a relative handful of MNCs (Heilbroner, 1977). Additional perspective on what that possibility may mean for the state-centric view of world politics can be gained by comparing the size of various nations' GNPs with gross annual sales of the largest multinational firms. The results of such a comparison show that in 1981, Exxon and Royal Dutch Shell outranked all but twenty-two nation-states. Among the top fifty entries, multinationals account for only eight, but in the next fifty, thirty-four entries are multinationals (Kegley and Wittkopf, 1985b: 152–153).

The economic power and reach of American multinational firms to some extent have enabled them to become a global extension of American society, serving as an engine of transfer for investment, technology, and managerial skill across national boundaries. Although such transfers may prove to be beneficial to developing nations in particular, Third World countries are especially sensitive to the costs which the economic giants can also impose on host countries. From the perspective of an underdeveloped country, therefore, both debits and credits accrue to the impact which MNCs exert on their welfare (see Box 6.1). Critics argue, for example, that the Third World has become dependent on technology imported via MNCs from the industrial world, even though that technology may be inappropriate to the local setting. A variant of

---

Box 6.1 The Multinational Corporation in World Politics: A Balance Sheet of Claims and Criticisms

There are many views of the MNC. Its contributions seen as ''positive'' are listed below on the left side, and those considered ''negative'' are listed on the right. Whether one classifies a contribution as positive or negative will depend largely on one's ideological perspective. Although the arguments for and against MNCs are not as simple as the characterization and classification given here suggest, they may be classified and summarized by noting that proponents and opponents have asserted, in one fashion or another, that multinational corporations . . .

Credit

- increase the volume of world trade.

- assist the aggregation of investment capital that can fund development.

- finance loans and service international debt.

- lobby for free trade and the removal of barriers to trade, such as tariffs.

- underwrite research and development that allows technological innovation.

- introduce and dispense advanced technology to less developed countries.

Debit

- give rise to oligopolistic conglomerations that reduce competition and free enterprise.

- raise capital in host countries (thereby depriving local industries of investment capital) but export profits to home countries.

- breed debtors and make the poor dependent on those providing loans.

- limit the availability of commodities by monopolizing their production and controlling their distribution in the world marketplace.

- export technology ill-suited to underdeveloped economies.

- inhibit the growth of infant industries and local technological expertise in less developed countries while making Third World countries dependent on First World technology.

Box 6.1   (Continued)

Credit

- reduce the costs of goods by encouraging their production according to the principle of comparative advantage.

- generate employment.

- encourage the training of workers.

- produce new goods and expand opportunities for their purchase through the internationalization of production.

- disseminate marketing expertise and mass-advertising methods worldwide.

- promote national revenue and economic growth; facilitate modernization of the less-developed countries.

- generate income and wealth.

- advocate peaceful relations between and among states in order to preserve an orderly environment conducive to trade and profits.

- break down national barriers, accelerate the globalization of the international economy and culture and the rules that govern international commerce.

Debit

- collude to create cartels that contribute to inflation.

- curtail employment by driving labor competition from the market.

- limit wages offered to workers.

- limit the supply of raw materials available on international markets.

- erode traditional cultures and national differences, leaving in their place a homogenized world culture dominated by consumer-oriented values.

- widen the gap between the rich and poor nations.

- increase the wealth of local elites at the expense of the poor.

- support and rationalize repressive regimes in the name of stability and order.

- challenge national sovereignty and jeopardize the autonomy of the nation-state.

that theme sees the MNC as a vehicle for the export of western materialistic values and hence an agent of "cultural imperialism." In addition, since MNCs seek to maximize profits, which are then repatriated to shareholders in the industrial world, they may retard rather than promote the economic growth of Third World countries by depriving them of much needed capital. Finally, the allegation that multinational firms sometimes engage in unsavory political practices in host countries can be added to the list of negative effects.

Ultimately, the challenge posed by multinational corporations is whether they are beyond the control of national governments. Prior to and immediately following the election of Salvador Allende to the Chilean presidency in 1970, for instance, International Telephone and Telegraph (ITT) sought to subvert the Chilean political process, first by preventing Allende from winning the presidency, and then by seeking his overthrow. In the process ITT sought to forge an alliance with the CIA to ensure that "its" (the reference is internationally ambiguous) interests would not be adversely affected. And in 1973 American-based oil companies operating in the Middle East participated in the oil embargo initiated by the Arab members of OPEC and directed at the United States and the Netherlands following the outbreak of the Yom Kippur War. The ITT case illustrates simultaneously the ability of MNCs to initiate their own "private foreign policies" and the lengths a government may be willing to go in order to protect the interests of its corporate citizens. The oil embargo case suggests that those same citizens may pursue policies and programs at variance with the interests of their home governments. More generally, multinational firms lobby their governments for policies and programs favorable to their own private interests; their motives are primarily global profits, not the alleviation of poverty or the interests of a particular state (see Barnet and Müller, 1974).

Transnational terrorist organizations are another type of nonstate actor that pose vexing challenges to the nation-state. Although terrorism is not peculiar to the contemporary world, its ubiquity and growing activity have commanded attention in recent years. International terrorism has become a phenomenon of epidemic proportions (see Figure 6.5). As President Reagan warned in 1985, "In recent years, there has been a steady and escalating pattern of terrorist acts against the United States and our allies and Third World nations friendly toward our interests. . . . The number of bombings alone [in 1984 averaged] almost one a day."

Terrorism as a form of violence arises so frequently because it is a strategy that even the weak can employ. Modern technology may have contributed inadvertently to its apparent increasing incidence, for a crucial part of the terrorists' strength derives from the access that television provides as a medium of communication in which to publicize their grievances. Indeed, international communication has made any terrorist act against prominent figures an instant international media event. The ability to bring the terrorist act into the global spotlight by securing publicity is a catalyst to the fear that the act is intended to generate (which is why international terrorism has so often been

FIGURE 6.5 International Terrorist Incidents, 1968–1985*

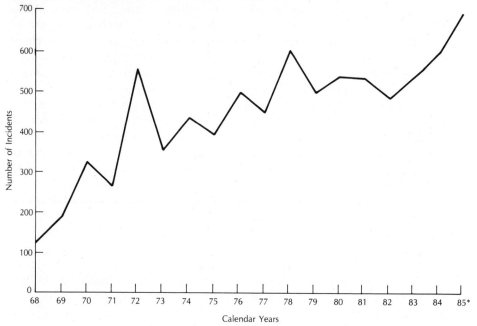

SOURCE: Caspar W. Weinberger, *Report of the Secretary of Defense Caspar W. Weinberger to the Congress* (Washington, DC: Government Printing Office, February 5, 1986, p. 70).

*Preliminary estimate as of November 30, 1985.

NOTE: Total incidents = approximately 8,200.

likened to theater). And part of what makes terrorism so terrifying is the message that anyone can become its victim.

The conspicuous attributes of international terrorism include the variety of methods that terrorists employ in pursuit of their goals. Included are traditional techniques for inflicting terror (for example, kidnappings, assassinations, hijackings, the taking of hostages, and sabotage). But governments have strengthened their capabilities to deter these methods, through greater security at airports, the guarding of likely kidnap victims, specially trained commandos to deal with hostage situations, and the like. Therefore, terrorists have adjusted their mode of operation, moving to hit-and-run tactics, especially through the increased use of bombings and tactics that require more violence. Sniping and direct armed attacks are examples. One consequence is that greater violence may be necessary to gain attention. As one expert on terrorism has observed, "if terrorism stops terrorizing—if it ceases to have an explosive impact on public opinion—then terrorists have an innate tendency to escalate [the violence] in order to recapture the headlines" (in Kempe, 1983).

Terrorism is a tactic of the powerless against the powerful. Thus it is not surprising that many acts of terrorism are perpetrated by minorities or other ethnic movements. Those seeking independence and sovereign statehood, like the Palestinians in the Middle East, the Basques in Spain, and nationalists in Puerto Rico, typify the kinds of aspirations in which international terrorism is often grounded. In the industrialized world, terrorism often occurs where discrepancies in income are severe and where minority groups are sometimes deprived of the political rights and freedoms enjoyed by the majority. Here guerrilla warfare normally associated with rural uprisings is not a viable route to self-assertion, but terrorist tactics are.

Attention to the motives of terrorists underscores the fact that terrorism is not perceived by all to be a disease. One person's terrorist may, to another, be a liberator. In fact, both governments and countergovernment movements claim to seek liberty, and both are labeled terrorists by those they oppose. The difference between a freedom fighter and a protector of freedom often lies in the eye of the beholder—a problem that makes the identity of a terrorist group not altogether obvious (see O'Brien, 1977).

Put into a historical context, terrorism can be seen as something more than the effort of relatively powerless movements to upset by threat of violence the established order within and among nations. Although many terrorist groups today are undeniably groups without sovereignty that seek it, a broader definition of terrorism would acknowledge that some terrorist acts are state supported (see Stohl and Lopez, 1984). Indeed, some states condone and support the terrorist activities of movements espousing philosophies that they embrace (or challenging the security of states they see as enemies). This *state terrorism* is part of the claim that the United States has leveled at the behaviors of the Soviet Union, Syria, and Libya, among others. In an analogous way, the United States has been accused of sponsoring terrorist activities in Vietnam, Chile, Nicaragua, and elsewhere.

Whatever terrorists groups' origins and composition, the alarming rate with which international terrorist activity has continued to spread has unquestionably altered the global environment in which American foreign policy must operate. Terrorism poses new challenges and constraints because Americans are increasingly the victims and targets of this lethal tactic: it is estimated that "U.S. citizens and U.S. interests have been consistently the target of 30%–35% of worldwide terrorist attacks" (Oakley, 1985: 1). Global terrorism thus is an American problem: "the problem for the United States is likely to continue to be external to the United States, not internal; and the threat against U.S. interests abroad is likely to increase proportionately to the increase of total incidents" (Oakley, 1985). "We are in the midst of an undeclared war," is the way CIA Director William Casey characterized the nature of the problem, which is highly resistant to control; it is a contagious disease whose spread is facilitated by an anarchic international political system that legitimizes the use of violence (see Kegley, Sturgeon, and Wittkopf, 1986).

While counterterrorist action begs for a concerted international response, the United States, whose citizens and interests are primary targets of terrorist tactics, has taken largely a unilateral approach toward the deterrence of terrorist activity. But disagreement over strategies has materialized among American policy makers because alternative approaches promise to entail substantial costs and risks while appearing limited in their efficacy. For instance, Secretary of State Shultz's preference for fighting terrorism with violence—by conducting retaliatory or even preemptive military actions against international terrorism—risks innocent lives, attacking wrong targets, and further legitimizing violence and terror by removing the blurred distinction between terror by states and terror by nonstate actors. In its practice of counterterror by force,[22] would the United States become like the perpetrators of the very behavior it sought to extirpate, critics asked (see Stohl and Lopez, 1984)? And, in the course of its pursuit of this end, would American ideals be compromised, perhaps even prostituted?

THE AMERICAN FOREIGN POLICY REACTION TO A TRANSFORMED POSTWAR GLOBAL ENVIRONMENT

The trends toward systemic diffusion of economic and military capabilities among the great powers, the emergence of an impoverished set of new states, and the increase in the number of nonstate international actors identified in this chapter are among the most salient changes that have occurred in the postwar international system. Those developments have converged simultaneously to provoke the necessity for the United States to make foreign policy adjustments, and to diminish its capacity to exercise control over the course of events abroad. The constraints in particular are revealed by the gradual deterioration of American power in the world, as compared to the dominant position it enjoyed in the immediate postwar years.

Taken separately as indicators of what is happening in the global environment, however, these trends may be moving in divergent directions. Renewed nationalism and Third World participation, on the one hand, suggest continuation of the nation-state as the dominant form of political organization in the world, whereas the rise of collaborative efforts across national boundaries as manifested in the rise of nonstate actors, on the other, suggests greater interdependence and, therefore, reduced American autonomy. The general erosion of American power and position relative to other global actors reduces the nation's ability to deal effectively with either of these developments.

---

[22]It was this dimension of the problem that resulted in National Security Decision Directive 138 (April 3, 1984), which authorized twenty-six agencies to "go to the source" and hold states accountable for the terrorism they allegedly sponsor, and to employ "every legal means" of counterterror "pre-emptive and pro-active" methods to deter them. The strike against Libya in 1986 signaled that the threat would be carried out. The Directive implied that the U.S. would continue to turn a blind eye to the use of terror by governments with which it is allied (see Kinsley, 1985).

American foreign policy thus is to some extent molded by both the structures and processes of an evolving international political system. Changes in that system have precipitated pressures for policy adaptation. Over the past forty years, the United States has struggled, with some reluctance perhaps, to accommodate its foreign policies to monumental transformations of the international political system in an effort to keep pace with the tempo of global change, and, most importantly, to encourage the development of a world receptive to American national interests. Increasingly, however, it has met with frustration and failure as the external environment has become less hospitable to those interests.

That was not the case in the immediate post-World War II years. At that time the global system was fraught with opportunity for the United States. From a position of strength, the United States embraced global responsibilities and pursued an assertive posture that shaped a world compatible with the American vision.

It was in accordance with that privileged position that the United States energetically took the lead in forming a variety of new global institutions, including especially the United Nations, an institution shaped by American values and molded after its own political institutions. It sponsored formation of the North Atlantic Treaty Organization and followed it with involvement in a complex network of peacetime military alliances. It pushed friendly nations to augment their defensive capabilities and assisted them by providing increasingly sophisticated weapons systems. It ushered in the nuclear age with its own technological innovations. It embraced the fight against colonialism and pushed the creation of international financial institutions that eventually sought to promote the economic development of the newly emergent nations. It also promoted development of a multilateral trade regime designed to encourage free exchange between countries in an effort to avert repetition of the disaster of the Great Depression. And U.S.-based multinational corporations assumed a high profile in the world system. To a large degree, therefore, the nature of the postwar international political system was a product of American foreign policy. Its salient attributes are traceable in many important respects to the programs and policies the United States itself advocated and supported in the late 1940s, the 1950s, and beyond.

Paradoxically, the United States today finds itself burdened by its responsibilities and attacked by other countries and in the institutions created through its own initiatives. These institutions have become the unwelcome symbols of a contemporary international political system that has proven intractable and inhospitable to American interests. The system is no longer amenable to American control and management, it seems. It is, instead, one that openly challenges the United States and often asserts influence over it.

The American foreign policy response to this fundamentally changed environment is multifaceted. The nature of that response has already been addressed in part in previous chapters and will be the subject of subsequent commentary. Here we can only suggest briefly some aspects of it that are especially germane to the previous discussion in this chapter.

One response to the changed and changing global system reflects hostility toward, and retrenchment from, involvement in some of the most important multilateral institutions that simultaneously symbolize the external environment and pose a challenge to American interests within it. No longer able to exercise its will freely, the United States has recently attacked the very international organizations it once helped to create. The United Nations is one. The United States has curtailed its financial commitments to the world organization and its family of affiliated organizations and agencies. Simultaneously, high ranking officials have disparaged its utility. Jeane Kirkpatrick, United States Ambassador to the United Nations during the first Reagan administration, publicly decried the General Assembly as ''a theater of the absurd'' and attacked the Security Council as a ''Turkish bath: a place to let off steam rather than to resolve conflict.''

Unilateralism is a second approach recently embraced. If multilateral solutions to global problems prove ineffective or resist American direction, then the prescription is to disassociate from the institutions that bind the United States unwillingly in cooperative linkages with others. The decision of the Carter administration to withdraw from the International Labor Organization (ILO) and of the Reagan administration to withdraw from the United Nations Educational, Scientific, and Cultural Organization (UNESCO) reflect disenchantment with multilateralism and a preference for going it alone, as does the Reagan administration's indifference to and attack of the World Court.

A third response to recent challenges has been reassertion of American control by confronting those simultaneously challenging America's hegemonic influence and symbolizing it. The approach has been especially evident in the Reagan administration's combative posture toward the Soviet Union and others believed to be supported by and sympathetic toward the nation's historic adversary.

Debate exists in the United States about the wisdom of these approaches and about how the nation can best assert its interests and protect its security, welfare, and values in a turbulent world. The United States finds itself significantly affected by the multiple changes which have swept the international political system since Hiroshima. Taken together, shifts in the distribution of world power, in the composition of the world community, and in the kinds of actors populating it have created an external environment radically different from that existing in 1945. We clearly live in a transitional period, an era, according to former national security adviser Zbigniew Brzezinski, in which ''an old world order is coming to an end and the shape of a new world order is yet to be defined.'' That transformation will stimulate—indeed, it may well necessitate—changes in American conduct abroad, just as past global changes have promoted important adaptations in American foreign policy as the United States continually has sought realization of its persistent foreign policy objectives.

In contemplating the future of American foreign policy, therefore, we should give consideration to the impact which trends in the international political system make on the position and policies of the United States. "The idea that the United States, acting alone in an interdependent world, can somehow renew the mythical golden era of the immediate postwar years when we seemed invulnerable to international political and economic developments," warned former Secretary of State Alexander Haig in 1985, "is a dangerous illusion." In advancing that warning, he reminded us of the extent to which the shape of the world can give shape to and constrain American foreign policy. The admonition is especially pertinent at this critical juncture in the nation's historic development. As Kenneth Oye (1983) has observed, "The Reagan administration entered office committed to enlarging the capacity of the United States to control the international environment. Ironically, the evolution of Reagan administration foreign policy may appear, in retrospect, as a textbook example of how the international environment shapes foreign policy."

SUGGESTIONS FOR FURTHER READING

FRANCK, THOMAS M. *Nation Against Nation: What Happened to the U.N. Dream and What the U.S. Can Do About It.* New York: Oxford University Press, 1985.

KEGLEY, CHARLES W., JR., AND EUGENE R. WITTKOPF, eds. *The Global Agenda: Issues and Perspectives.* New York: Random House, 1984.

KEOHANE, ROBERT O., AND JOSEPH S. NYE, JR. *Power and Interdependence: World Politics in Transition.* Boston: Little, Brown, 1977.

KRASNER, STEPHEN D. *Structural Conflict: The Third World Against Global Liberalism.* Berkeley: University of California Press, 1985.

MCNAMARA, ROBERT S. "Time Bomb or Myth: The Population Problem," *Foreign Affairs* 62 (Summer 1984): 1107–1131.

SABROSKY, ALAN NED, ed. *Polarity and War: The Changing Structure of International Conflict.* Boulder, CO and London: Westview, 1985.

SEWELL, JOHN W., RICHARD E. FEINBERG, AND VALERIANA KALLAB, eds. *U.S. Foreign Policy and the Third World: Agenda 1985–86.* U.S.-Third World Policy Perspectives, No. 3. New Brunswick, NJ: Transaction Books for the Overseas Development Council, 1985.

STOHL, MICHAEL, AND GEORGE A. LOPEZ, eds. *The State as Terrorist: The Dynamics of Governmental Violence and Repression.* Westport, CT: Greenwood Press, 1984.

TAYLOR, PHILLIP. *Nonstate Actors in International Politics: From Transregional to Substate Organizations.* Boulder, CO: Westview, 1984.

7

THE INTERNATIONAL POLITICAL ECONOMY IN TRANSITION

Protectionism is not the remedy to an illness. It is itself an illness. It is a hidden tax on the consumer, often an extremely regressive tax. Hold onto your pocketbooks when politicians start trying to "protect" you against buying what you want to buy. . . . Protectionism keeps prices up, reduces living standards, and stifles growth.

Secretary of State George Shultz, 1985

If [poor countries] have economic disorder, it translates into political disorder, and political disorder in various parts of the world overflows and affects us strategically. . . . Our economy is much more dependent today than it was ten or fifteen years ago on the strength of the economies of the world, including the developing world.

*Former Secretary of Defense
and World Bank President
Robert S. McNamara, 1981*

"Interdependence" captures the essence of the increasingly interlocked national economies of the world and the corresponding intersection between domestic and international politics. The predominate role the United States plays in this global scene is illustrated by comparing the nation's GNP, which now stands in excess of $4.1 trillion, with that of other nations. American output is roughly 25 percent of the total produced in the world, about five times its proportion of the world's population. The consequence of the overwhelming size of the nation's economy is that little can be done in the United States without repercussions abroad. Recession in the United States becomes recession abroad; domestic inflation is shared elsewhere; the general health of the U.S. economy becomes a worldwide concern.

Part of the reason for the worldwide importance of the U.S. economy stems from the international position of the dollar, which throughout the postwar period has been a reserve currency for other nations. That means that the dollar has been used as a medium of exchange to settle international accounts. The dollar also has become a "parallel currency" that central banks in other countries either buy or sell in currency exchange markets in order to maintain the value of their own currencies. Mammoth American investments abroad, which in 1984 stood at $233.4 billion, and the dominant position of the United States (whose 1983 share was 22 percent of world merchandise exports) in the world network of trade relationships are two more factors.

Normally we think of economic activities in a pluralized democratic society as being the concern of private entrepreneurs, largely unencumbered by governmental interference. But the domestic economy is actually a mix of private ownership and government regulation, as is international economic activity. Hence international economic relations have become part of, and subject to, the way the United States seeks to cope with its external environment. For interdependence implies not only a world sensitive to the United States but also an American economic and political system intertwined with developments abroad over which the United States often has neither influence nor control.

The purpose of this chapter is to explore the changing nature of the link between politics and economics through an examination of selected aspects of U.S. monetary and trade ties with Western industrialized societies, Third World countries, and communist countries.[1] Throughout we shall be concerned with America's place within the evolving international political economy. As we study those developments, keep in mind our operating assumption: both change and continuity in American foreign policy are influenced by an international economic order that has been undergoing change of often revolutionary proportions during the past four decades.

THE FIRST WORLD: INDUSTRIALIZED NATIONS

As envisioned in the Bretton Woods agreements of 1944, the wartime allies sought to create a postwar international monetary system characterized by stability, predictability, and orderly growth. The International Monetary Fund (IMF) was created at that time to assist states in dealing with such matters as maintaining balance-of-payments equilibria (that is, stability in the balance between their financial inflows and outflows) and exchange-rate stability (that

---

[1]In the idiom of international diplomacy, these countries are known, respectively, as developed-market economies, developing economies, and centrally planned economies. Collectively, developed-market economies are also often referred to as the First World, the communist nations of Eastern Europe and the Soviet Union as the Second World, and developing nations as the Third World.

is, the rate at which one nation's currency is exchanged for another's) and, more generally, to ensure international monetary cooperation and the expansion of trade (see Box. 7.1). Over time, the IMF evolved to serve as the most useful and influential of the many new international organizations created during and immediately after World War II. During the period known as the

---

BOX 7.1   The Bretton Woods Conference and Its Twin Institutions

The International Monetary and Financial Conference of the United and Associated Nations was convened in Bretton Woods, New Hampshire, on July 1, 1944. By the time the conference ended on July 22, 1944, based on substantial preparatory work, it had defined the outlines of the postwar international economic system. The conference also resulted in the creation of the International Monetary Fund (IMF) and the International Bank for Reconstruction and Development (IBRD, or the World Bank)—the Bretton Woods twins.

The World Bank was to assist in reconstruction and development by facilitating the flow and investment of capital for productive purposes. The International Monetary Fund was to facilitate the expansion and balanced growth of international trade and to contribute thereby to the promotion and maintenance of high levels of employment and real income. Also discussed at Bretton Woods were plans for an International Trade Organization (ITO). This institution did not materialize, but some of its proposed functions are performed by the General Agreement on Tariffs and Trade (GATT), which was established in 1947.

The discussions at Bretton Woods took place with the experience of the interwar period as background. In the 1930s every major country sought ways to defend itself against deflationary pressures from abroad—some by exchange depreciation, some by introducing flexible exchange rates or multiple rates, some by direct controls over imports and other international transactions. The disastrous consequences of such policies—economic depression with very high unemployment—are well known. The participants in the Bretton Woods conference were determined to design an international economic system where "beggar thy neighbor" policies, which characterized the international economic community when World War II began, did not recur. There was also a widespread fear that the end of World War II would be followed by a slump, as had the end of World War I.

Thus the central elements of the system outlined at Bretton Woods were the establishment of convertibility of currencies and of fixed but adjustable exchange rates, and the encouragement of international flows of capital for productive purpose. The IMF and the World Bank were to assist in the attainment of these objectives. The economic accomplishments of the postwar period are in part the result of the effectiveness of these institutions.

SOURCE: *World Development Report, 1985,* 1985: 15.

Bretton Woods system (1946–1971), the IMF helped member states to maintain fixed rates of exchange for their currencies (as required by the Bretton Woods agreements). This gave the IMF considerable influence in getting member states (especially the economically less powerful ones) to undertake the often difficult domestic tasks of coping with the causes of balance-of-payments disequilibria. More recently, it has played a role in assisting nations' adjustment to the two surges in worldwide oil prices (1973–1974 and 1979–1980) induced by the Organization of Petroleum Exporting Countries (OPEC) cartel in the recent past and to the crushing external debt burden that many nations experienced in the wake of the OPEC oil price squeezes. More generally, the IMF has served as both a catalyst to, and forum for, negotiations among the world's monetary powers on how to organize the international monetary system.

In the immediate postwar years, however, the IMF and the World Bank (the International Bank for Reconstruction and Development, IBRD, also created at Bretton Woods) proved insufficient for the task of managing postwar economic recovery. Those institutions were simply given too little authority and too few resources to cope with the enormous economic devastation suffered by Western European nations during the war. The United States stepped into the breach.

The Role of the United States in Managing the International Monetary System

The Early Years. The dollar became the key to the American managerial role.[2] Backed by a vigorous and healthy economy, a fixed relationship between gold and the dollar ($35 per ounce of gold), and a commitment by the U.S. government to exchange gold for dollars (known as *dollar convertibility*), the dollar in effect became as good as gold. Indeed, it was preferable to gold. Dollars earned interest, which gold did not; they did not entail storage and insurance costs; and they were needed to buy imports necessary for survival and postwar reconstruction.

The problem in the immediate postwar years was how to get American dollars into the hands of those who needed them. One mechanism was the Marshall Plan, which provided Western European nations with resources to buy the American goods necessary to rebuild their war-torn economies. Eventually $17 billion in Marshall Plan assistance was channeled to Western Europe. International liquidity (reserve assets used to settle international accounts) in the form of dollars was also provided by the deliberate American encouragement of deficits in its own balance of payments, partially accomplished through massive outflows of foreign aid and expenditures to maintain the burgeoning American overseas military commitments. In addition to providing international liquidity, the United States supported European and Japanese

---

[2]The subsequent discussion of the role of the United States in the management of the international monetary system draws on Blake and Walters (1983) and especially on Spero (1985).

trade competitiveness, as well as protectionism (for example, Japanese restrictions on American exports) and discrimination against the dollar (for example, the European Payments Union, a multilateral European group which promoted intra-European trade at the expense of trade with the United States). Those short-run costs were incurred on the basis of the long-run assumption that a rejuvenated Europe and Japan would provide widening markets for American exports. The perceived political benefits of strengthening the Western world against the threat of world communism were also considerable.

"The system worked well. Europe and Japan recovered and then expanded. The American economy prospered in spite of, or partly because of, the dollar outflow, which led to the purchase of American goods and services" (Spero, 1985). Furthermore, the "top currency" role of the dollar facilitated the globalist foreign policy posture the United States assumed in the postwar years (Strange, 1971). Other nations were more than happy to hold dollars as a reserve currency, even without convertibility into gold. The foreign economic and military aid programs as well as the massive military presence of the United States overseas were made possible by acceptance of the dollar as the means of paying for them. Business interests could readily expand abroad because American foreign investments were often considered desirable, and American tourist dollars could be spent with few restrictions. In effect, the United States operated as the world's banker. Others were required to balance their financial inflows and outflows. In contrast, the United States enjoyed the advantages of operating internationally without the constraints of limited finances. The political and economic importance of the United States also meant that developments within the nation had significant implications for the monetary affairs of other nations. Through the global ubiquity of the dollar, the United States came to exert influence on the political and economic affairs of most other nations.

Yet costs were associated with this condition: just as the United States was able to exert influence over others, it became sensitive to what was happening elsewhere. Massive private investments overseas perceived to be linked to domestic prosperity created new fears of potential nationalization. The vast number of dollars held by others also made the American domestic economy vulnerable to financial shocks abroad. Decision makers therefore sought to insulate the American economy from these shocks, but the task was made more difficult because some tools available to others were proscribed by the status of the dollar as a reserve currency.

For most countries an imbalance between financial inflows and outflows could be corrected most readily by changing the rate of exchange of its currency, that is, the value of one nation's currency in relation to that of other nations. A country with an adverse balance of trade (one that imports more from other nations than it exports to them) could devalue its currency. That would have the effect of making its exports more attractive to foreign buyers, since the exports would become less costly in relation to the goods of other countries. At the same time, imports from other countries would become relatively less attractive to domestic consumers. The consequent improvement in the balance of trade—caused by promoting exports and curtailing imports by redirecting domestic demand from foreign to domestically produced products—would contribute ultimately to a favorable balance-of-payments position by increasing financial inflows and reducing outflows. Reducing domestic unemployment by promoting exports would be an additional benefit realized, in principle, by devaluing one's currency. But this simple mechanism—devaluation (and revaluation) of currency exchange rates, which lies at the heart of international financial adjustments—was made more difficult for the United States because of the pivotal role of the dollar. Devaluation, for example, would affect adversely political friends and military allies who had chosen to hold large amounts of dollars and was an action therefore unlikely to be taken in an environment of hostility toward and competition with Soviet communism. Furthermore, because of the importance of the dollar in other countries' reserve assets, a devaluation of the dollar by the United States could easily be offset by a subsequent devaluation of the currency of the country adversely affected by American action—which effectively would restore the status quo before the U.S. action.

Toward Interdependence and the Demise of Bretton Woods. By as early as 1960 it was apparent that the "top currency" status of the dollar was on the wane. Thereafter, the dollar-based international monetary system unilaterally managed by the United States became a multilaterally managed system under American leadership. Several factors explain the dollar's declining position.

If a dollar shortage was the problem in the immediate postwar years, by the 1960s the problem had become a glut, which eroded the willingness of others to hold the dollar as a reserve currency. Indeed, the costs of overseas military activities, foreign economic and military aid, and massive private investments produced increasing balance-of-payments deficits, which earlier had been encouraged but were now out of control. Furthermore, American gold holdings in relation to the growing number of foreign-held dollars declined precipitantly. Given those circumstances, the possibility that the United States might devalue the dollar led to a loss of confidence by others and hence an unwillingness to continue to hold dollars as reserve currency. The French under the leadership of Charles de Gaulle even went so far as to insist on exchanging dollars for gold.

At the same time that a dollar glut came to characterize the international liquidity situation during the 1960s, massive transnational movements of capital accelerated monetary interdependence. The internationalization of banking, the internationalization of production (via multinational corporations), and the development of a Eurocurrency market (Eurocurrencies are dollars and other currencies held in Europe as bank deposits and lent and borrowed abroad, primarily in Europe) outside direct state control were all catalysts to interdependence. The result was an increasingly complex relationship between economic policies engineered in one country and their effects on another. This in turn spawned a variety of less formal groupings of the central bankers and finance ministers of the leading economic powers who devised various ad hoc solutions to their common problems.[3] Among them was the need to protect the value of states' currencies from attack by speculators. A mechanism for swapping the currency of one nation for claims held by another, known as the Basel Agreement, soon evolved to cope with the various foreign exchange crises that punctuated the 1960s, particularly those affecting the British pound. Various mechanisms to ease the strain of a run on American gold stocks were also devised, since such a run could undermine confidence in the dollar and hence the system as a whole. Finally, a form of "paper gold" known as Special Drawing Rights (SDRs) was created in the IMF to facilitate the growth of international liquidity by means other than increasing the outflow of dollars.

Although the United States typically gave the most support to the various remedial efforts devised in the 1960s to assure monetary stability, it found them of little help when crises affected the dollar in the late 1960s and early 1970s—crises which were products of the changing international political system as well as the changing economic system. By the 1960s European and Japanese economic recovery from the war was complete, which meant that American monetary dominance and the privileged position of the dollar were no longer palatable. The Europeans and Japanese came especially to resent the prerogatives the United States derived from its position as the world's banker and from its ability to determine the level of international liquidity through its balance-of-payments deficits. Not only did those prerogatives affect the economies of Europe and Japan, they also gave the United States the ability to make foreign expenditures for political purposes that came to be less and less acceptable to others.

Among the U.S. political pursuits with which many European nations disagreed was the Vietnam War. And among the economic conditions which they came to share was inflation, which in the United States was stimulated by the Johnson administration's unwillingness to raise taxes to finance either the Great Society or the Southeast Asian war. In a sense, Europe was "forced" to pay for American foreign policy adventures about which they had fundamental reservations.

Soviet-American détente also eventually entered the picture. The decline in fear of and hostility toward the Soviet Union as an external threat carried with it a decline in the willingness of allies to accede deferentially to American leadership. In short, the changing international political as well as economic environment militated against continued American hegemony in international monetary matters (see Kindleberger, 1977).

---

[3]One, established in 1962 to discuss monetary issues, is known as the Group of Ten, which still operates today. Its members are the finance ministers and central bank governors of the United States, Belgium, Canada, France, Great Britain, Italy, Japan, the Netherlands, Sweden, and West Germany. The agenda of the Group of Ten is set by the Group of Five, consisting of the finance ministers of the United States, France, Great Britain, Japan, and West Germany.

America's leadership position also began to erode, particularly as domestic inflation contributed to a relative loss in competitiveness of American goods and services overseas. Historically, the United States had enjoyed a favorable balance of trade. That was important, since the favorable trade balances were used to offset the unfavorable payments balances—which by the end of the 1960s had become chronic. The favorable trade situation itself began to deteriorate by 1971, however, when for the first time in the twentieth century the United States suffered a trade deficit (of $2 billion). The situation worsened in 1972, when the deficit reached $6.2 billion. Cries by industrial, labor, and agricultural interests, which already had begun to adopt protectionist positions regarding trade policy (designed to insulate the American economy from foreign competition), became even more shrill.

The reasons for the inability of the United States to control its balance-of-payments deficits were many and varied. Included among them were an unwillingness to pull back from the costly, globalist foreign policy the nation had pursued since World War II and a lag in modernization of its industrial facilities growing out of the decision of American-based multinational firms to build branch plants abroad rather than new facilities at home (Block, 1977).

Whatever the fundamental causes of its payments deficits, part of the blame for the newly emergent trade deficit was laid at the doorstep of the major trading partners of the United States. Japan and West Germany in particular were criticized for their undervalued currencies, which made their goods attractive internationally (and to American consumers), and which in turn enabled them to generate balance-of-payments surpluses. Regardless of the reasons, there was little question the position of the United States in international trade was deteriorating. Although the value of American exports had increased tremendously during the postwar years, the nation's share of total world exports declined from 16.7 percent in 1955 to 11.7 percent in 1971.[4]

Faced with those factors, President Nixon in August 1971 imposed wage and price controls at home, suspended the convertibility of dollars into gold, and levied a surcharge of 10 percent on all imports as a way of forcing the nation's trading partners into a revaluation of their currencies. Eventually the dollar was devalued by some 18 percent (effected by increasing the price of an ounce of gold) and the currencies of other nations adjusted to better reflect their real values. There emerged finally a system of free-floating currency values, in which exchange rates were determined by market forces rather than governmental regulations and intervention,[5] as had been required under the Bretton Woods system. Together, these actions had the effect of suspending the 1944 Bretton Woods agreements under which the international monetary system had operated for nearly three decades.

---

[4]By way of contrast, the European Common Market increased its share from just over 30 percent in 1955 to 41 percent in 1971; and Japan increased its share from 2.1 percent in 1955 to 6.4 percent in 1971.

[5]In fact, even the system of free-floating exchange rates has not operated entirely without government intervention and hence is sometimes called a "dirty float."

Nixon's actions in 1971 came as a shock (not even the State Department was consulted, much less other members of the international monetary system) and represented a new stridency in the nation's approach to international economic matters that perhaps reflected the growing realization that the United States was increasingly, perhaps irreversibly dependent on the rest of the world and could no longer determine the course of international monetary affairs alone. Yet the willingness of the United States to play a leadership role was one of the important political foundations on which the successful operation of the Bretton Woods system had rested. Thus the political bases on which the system had been built lay in ruins. American leadership was no longer willingly accepted by others nor exercised willingly by the United States. Power, once concentrated in the hands of a small number of Western nations, had come to be more widely dispersed; and the interests that once bound them together, including a commitment to the precepts of liberal economic thought and antipathy toward and fear of communism, had dissipated. The fragility of once firm political foundations likewise impeded efforts to find an acceptable replacement for the Bretton Woods system.

The "OPEC Decade." Formal negotiations on reform of the international monetary system were begun in the summer of 1972. Before anything could be decided, however, the world economic system suffered yet another shock—a fourfold increase in the price of oil effected by the Organization of Petroleum Exporting Countries in the immediate aftermath of the 1973 Yom Kippur War in the Middle East. The ensuing "OPEC decade" proved extraordinarily disruptive as the global political economy was tested as never before. The system survived, but many of the global and national economic problems of the 1980s were rooted here.

The OPEC decade ended in March 1983 when, in response to a worldwide oil glut, OPEC for the first time in its history agreed to cut its official price of oil and to set a ceiling on its aggregate production levels. It had begun ten years earlier when, in the period between October 1973 and November 1974, the price of a barrel of Saudi Arabian crude oil went from $2.10 to $10.24. The oil-import costs of the United States and the other Western industrialized nations skyrocketed from $30 billion in 1973 to nearly $90 billion a year later. Similarly, the oil bill of the non-oil-producing, developing nations moved from $6 billion in 1973 to $16 billion in 1974 and $17 billion in 1975—or from 9 percent of their export earnings to 20 in those two years (*International Economic Report of the President*, 1976: 5).

Energy prices remained fairly constant for about five years following the 1973–1974 "oil shock." Then, in 1979–1980, following the Iranian revolution that ousted the Shah of Iran, an American protégé whose country had become one of the world's leading suppliers of oil, the global political economy suffered a second oil shock as oil prices jumped even more dramatically than they had a half decade earlier. For the United States, whose dependence on foreign sources of oil had grown appreciably since the first oil shock, the cost of imported oil became staggering. Over $40 billion was spent for imported petroleum and petroleum products in 1977. Then, in 1980, a record $74 billion was spent. Coincidentally, the value of the dollar in the international marketplace—where it was now permitted to fluctuate in response to market forces—declined precipitantly, as America's seemingly insatiable energy appetite eroded the willingness of others to hold dollars. Persistent inflation—itself fed by rising fuel costs, the cumulative costs of past wars and present defense expenditures, and growing federal government budget deficits—was also a factor. Ironically, the decline of the dollar may itself have been a contributing factor to domestic inflation as both the dollar cost of foreign-produced goods and their proportion of the U.S. GNP increased. In the decade ending in 1979, American imports as a percentage of GNP more than doubled, moving from 4.2 percent in 1970 to 8.7 percent in 1979.[6]

The impact of the surging cost of energy following the first oil shock was reflected in worldwide recession. Paradoxically, worldwide inflation also persisted. *Stagflation*—the term coined to describe a stagnant economy accompanied by rising unemployment and high rates of inflation—entered the economic lexicon. Inflation persisted despite the return to economic growth in 1976 and contributed to OPEC's desire to continue to increase the price of oil so as to maximize the return on its resources, behavior that in turn fueled the inflationary flames. It was not until the "oil glut" of 1980–1981 that oil prices began to soften, thereby undermining OPEC's monopolistic pricing policies and the inflationary spiral they helped to produce.

In a related development, the sharply increased price of energy caused substantial dislocations in many nations' balance-of-payments positions, as billions of "petrodollars" flowed to the oil-producing states. The impact on the balance of payments of oil-producing and oil-consuming nations is shown in Table 7.1. It shows clearly how closely the fortunes of the influential Middle Eastern oil producers (the most important members of OPEC) and those of the industrialized nations were intertwined, with increases in the oil-producing countries' balance-of-payments surpluses offset by declines in the industrialized nations', and vice versa; it also shows the persistent and devastating impact of the two oil shocks on the Third World.

The initial problem posed by the massive energy-induced shift in wealth was how to recycle the petrodollars from the oil producers to the oil consumers. Although some observers had predicted that the magnitude of the recycling problem would lead to the collapse of the international economic or-

---

[6]The inflationary impact of more costly foreign goods may be compounded by domestic producers, who, when faced with reduced competition, may increase their own prices in order to maximize their profits. Similarly, workers may seek to boost their wages to maintain their real incomes in the face of rising costs of foreign-produced goods. But domestic price and wage inflation eat up the positive effects of American trade and payments balances that derive from the greater competitiveness abroad of American goods made possible by the devaluation of the dollar. Appreciation of the dollar also reduces its competitiveness and increases the attractiveness of foreign imports. This is what happened when the dollar's decline reversed itself in the 1980s, thereby encouraging an even greater increase in imports as a proportion of GNP.

TABLE 7.1 Current Account Balances of Industrial and Developing Countries, 1970–84 (billions of dollars)

Country group	1970–72[a]	1973	1974	1975–78[a]	1979	1980	1981	1982	1983	1984
Industrial countries	7.0	10.3	−14.6	12.1	− 5.6	−38.8	3.1	1.2	2.2	−34.2
United States	0.4	9.1	7.6	1.2	2.6	6.6	10.7	− 3.8	−35.5	−93.4
Other six large industrial countries	9.3	0.6	−10.4	19.0	4.6	−18.7	8.8	17.7	39.0	53.2
Middle Eastern oil exporters	2.0	6.5	55.9	33.8	61.9	99.6	56.3	3.3	−11.1	− 6.0
Developing countries[b]	−12.8	−9.1	−21.0	−39.5	−51.7	−68.0	−105.1	−99.2	−56.7	−35.6

SOURCE: *World Development Report, 1985*, 1985: 33.

NOTE: World total does not equal zero because of measurement errors and incomplete coverage.
[a]Annual average.
[b]Based on a sample of ninety developing countries.

der, recycling did occur despite obstacles, even after the oil price increases imposed by OPEC in 1979 and 1980. In addition to the IMF, the World Bank, and individual nations, private banks in the United States and Europe proved particularly effective in managing the flow of funds. In the process, however, the debt burden of many nations, particularly in the Third World, assumed ominous proportions. By the end of 1983, the total debt of the developing nations amounted to roughly $810 billion (Clausen, 1984), and the communist countries owed tens of billions more. The threat of massive defaults by countries unable to service their debts pushed the international monetary system to the brink of crisis in the early 1980s, thereby challenging in yet another way the viability of the established global political economy. We shall return to the debt crisis later, when we focus on the Third World.

Toward Reform: The International Monetary System in the 1980s. Following the second oil shock, the world plunged into what became the longest and most severe economic recession since the Great Depression of the 1930s. After the first oil-induced recession, the leading industrial powers (which are also the largest importers of oil) concentrated on conventional economic and fiscal policies in an effort to reflate their economies. Following the second, they chose instead to shift their priority to controlling inflation. Their strict monetarist policies were accompanied by large fiscal deficits and sharply higher interest rates, both especially apparent in the United States. The pivotal role of the United States in the global political economy combined with the growing interdependence of the Western industrialized nations to ensure that none could escape the consequences of these developments.

During the 1970s, when the United States was consuming between 25 and 30 percent of all the oil produced in the world, the massive influx of U.S. dollars into the international monetary system depended on others' willingness to hold dollars. By the latter part of the decade it appeared as though the dollar had lost its attractiveness as its value relative to other currencies declined precipitantly. Then, following the second oil shock and the Reagan administration's shift toward monetarist policies designed to curb inflation, the dollar reversed its decline and rose to record heights on foreign exchange markets, as shown in Figure 7.1. Renewed economic growth and a sharp reduction in inflation helped restore faith in the dollar. More importantly, interest rates in the United States remained high relative to interest rates in other countries, and the United States was seen as a safe haven for financial investments in a world otherwise marked by political instability and violence. Foreigners therefore rushed to acquire the dollars necessary to take advantage of profitable investment opportunities in the United States.

For the United States, the appreciation of the dollar was a mixed blessing. On the one hand, it reduced the cost of imported oil.[7] On the other hand, it

[7]Because oil is not only priced in dollars but also typically paid for with dollars, appreciation of the dollar reduces the cost of oil to the United States but increases it for others, since it requires more foreign currency (such as yen, marks, or francs) to acquire the dollars necessary for an

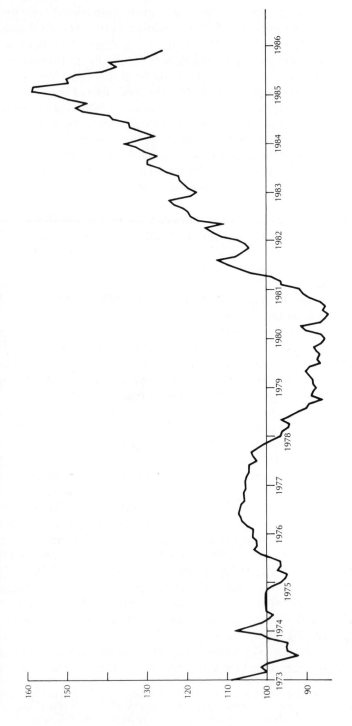

FIGURE 7.1 The Value of the United States Dollar, 1973–1985 (March 1973 = 100)

SOURCE: *Federal Reserve Bulletin*, various issues.

NOTE: The index is the weighted average value of the U.S. dollar against the currencies of the other nine major industrialized nations plus Switzerland.

increased the cost of American exports to foreign buyers, thereby reducing the competitiveness of American products in overseas markets. This meant a loss of tens of thousands of jobs in American industries that produced for export.

In a normally functioning market, this situation should set in motion self-corrective processes that would return the dollar to its equilibrium value. Growing American imports, for example, though beneficial to United States' trade partners in generating jobs and thus stimulating their return to economic growth, should create upward pressure on the value of others' currencies. Conversely, a drop in American exports should ease the demand for dollars, thereby reducing the dollar's value in exchange markets. Most analysts agree that in the early to mid-1980s these mechanisms did not work as they should have because of the persistently high interest rates in the United States. These were believed to be sustained by the federal government's huge budget deficits, themselves sustained by unparalleled military spending. Until Congress passed mandatory deficit-reduction legislation in late 1985, military spending was expected to continue to increase throughout Reagan's tenure in office, and the budget deficits were expected to continue much longer.

Historically, the United States had been loath to intervene in the international marketplace to affect the value of the dollar. In 1978, the Carter administration, in response to yet another dollar crisis, instituted a new restrictive monetary policy as one of several moves designed to shore up the sagging dollar. The move was significant in that it was the first time in the postwar era that domestic economic policy had been altered significantly for international monetary reasons. Previously the United States had sought to keep domestic and international monetary policy concerns on separate tracks.

The Reagan administration reverted to the historic pattern—at least for a time. Despite the obvious and ubiquitous interconnectedness of the national and world economies, it pursued policies at home that largely ignored their impact abroad (Garten, 1985). Erosion of American trade competitiveness in overseas markets due to the overvalued dollar had especially pernicious domestic consequences, however. They appear to have induced the administration to abandon its market-oriented approach in favor of a more realistic assessment of the costs and benefits of United States involvement in an interdependent global political economy.

The first clear indication of the administration's about-face occurred in the fall of 1985, when the Group of Five (the United States, Britain, France, Japan, and West Germany) decided to coordinate efforts to bring down the overvalued dollar. Change of heart did not motivate the administration; politics did. The America-first approach pursued during Reagan's first term, during which

---

equivalent amount of oil than when the dollar was "worth less." The reverse, of course, is also true. Thus, when the dollar declined relative to other currencies between 1978 and 1980, this reduced the cost of oil to much of Europe and Japan, which depend heavily on imported oil. The cost increased following the reversal of the decline of the dollar in 1980 and may have contributed to the lag in the other industrial countries' economic recovery, compared with that of the United States.

multilateral efforts to cope with transnational political economy issues were spurned, proved ineffective in coping with the adverse consequences associated with the high-flying dollar. On the up side, the dollar helped finance the U.S. government budget deficit as high interest rates sucked in investment dollars from abroad, reduced the cost of imported goods, and helped to reduce and keep domestic inflation rates low (Feldstein, 1985). On the down side, the nation's trade deficit soared, reaching a record $148.5 billion in 1985 as the competitiveness of U.S.-produced goods overseas plummeted. One politically troublesome result, as Treasury Secretary James Baker put it in the spring of 1985, was that ''we're coming to the point where the trade deficit is so large that we're beginning to export jobs.'' Many critics of the administration's policies had reached the same conclusion much earlier.

At roughly the same time, the United States became for the first time in more than half a century a debtor nation, meaning it owed more money abroad than others owed the United States—another potentially ominous symbol of the nation's inability to set its financial house in order without involving, or affecting, others (see Box 7.2).

The second and perhaps decisive signal that the administration had abandoned its America-first orientation was contained in Reagan's 1986 State of the Union message, in which he declared ''the constant expansion of our economy and exports requires a sound and stable dollar at home at reliable exchange rates around the world. We must never again permit wild currency swings to cripple farmers and other exporters.'' In acknowledging United States efforts to begin ''coordinating economic and monetary policy among our major trading partners,'' the president seemed to share the sentiments of French President François Mitterand, who earlier had called for a formal alternative to the defunct Bretton Woods system, noting that ''monetary disorders fuel economic wars between friends.'' Both sentiments reflected widespread dissatisfaction with the free-floating exchange-rate system (see Spero, 1985).

Agreement on alternatives to the system of free-floating rates is seldom easy. The European Community has already moved toward creation of its own monetary system, which may be a precursor of a system of regionalized monetary and trading schemes that finds Europe, the United States, and Japan as core states in a compartmentalized political economy from which other powers are effectively excluded.

As the dominant economic power in the 1980s, as in previous decades, the United States is likely to seek to thwart regionalization. A global approach that seeks a mid-course between the Bretton Woods system of fixed exchange rates and the post-Bretton Woods system of floating exchange rates, which would legitimize government intervention to affect exchange rates so as to achieve other desired policy objectives, is a likely prescription. Whether the United States will be able to realize its preferences as it once did is less clear. Even if the United States is willing once more to assume a leadership role in the management of international monetary affairs, it is uncertain whether others will follow.

BOX 7.2   The United States as a Debtor Nation

. . . U.S. public and private investments abroad no longer [exceed] the value of foreign holdings of this country's public and private assets. In that sense the U.S. has become a debtor nation.

Joining the ranks of the world's Micawbers has no immediate consequence for people in this country. There is no debtor's prison for nations. The change in status should not cause this country to hold its head less high in the councils of nations even if, as is widely expected, the United States displaces Brazil as the world's largest debtor. Nor will foreign investors suddenly liquidate their U.S. holdings, leaving this country scrambling to pay off its foreign debts.

The significance of the debt measure is that it takes broad account of this country's economic position vis-à-vis the rest of the world. . . . [T]he merchandise trade deficit, the focal point of recent concern, doesn't tell the whole story. The United States could afford to go on importing far more goods than it is able to export as long as that merchandise imbalance was offset by surpluses in service exports or returns from U.S. investments abroad. The trouble . . . is that the huge merchandise deficits the country has been running have overwhelmed surpluses in the service accounts. As a result, the country has been amassing foreign debt. The cost of paying interest and other returns to the foreign holders of that debt further aggravates the balance-of-payments problem, since the United States can no longer depend on net returns from its foreign investments to help offset trade deficits. And in the long term, that means this country may have to sacrifice some of its own standard of living to finance its foreign obligations.

. . . [T]he United States grew and prospered as a debtor nation during the 19th century. In those years it imported huge amounts of foreign capital and labor to exploit its enormous resource base—an investment that paid off handsomely both here and abroad. The difference now is that capital formation in this country has not, at least so far, been commensurate with the inflow of foreign capital. Instead, much of our recent foreign borrowing has gone to finance private consumption through tax cuts and public consumption through government spending. In a very real sense, the country is borrowing from its future.

SOURCE: *Washington Post National Weekly Edition*, October 7, 1985: 26.

The Role of the United States in Managing International Trade

The restructuring of America's place in the international monetary system since World War II has been matched by its changing position in the network of international trade relations. The preeminent position of the United States has not been replaced, though in neither the international monetary system nor the network of international trade relations is it what it once was.

Returning to the postwar economic system as envisaged during World War II, management responsibilities were to be entrusted in addition to the IMF and IBRD to an International Trade Organization (ITO), whose purpose was to lower restrictions on trade and set rules of commerce. The hope was that these three organizations could assist in avoiding repetition of the international economic catastrophe that followed World War I. But ITO was stillborn.

The United States was the prime mover behind all three specialized international agencies. ITO failed when the liberal trading system envisioned in the Havana Charter was so watered down by demands from other countries for exemptions from the generalized rules that the U.S. government deemed the document worthless. In its place, the United States sponsored the General Agreement on Tariffs and Trade (GATT). In a sense, GATT, which is now an established international agency, became the cornerstone of the liberalized trading scheme originally embodied in the ITO. The mechanism of free and unfettered international trade, of which the United States has been a strong advocate throughout most of the postwar period, was the most-favored-nation (MFN) principle. According to this principle the tariff preferences granted to one nation must be granted to all other nations exporting the same product. Under the aegis of GATT and the most-favored-nation principle, a series of multilateral trade negotiations aimed at reducing tariffs (and resolving related issues) was conducted. The seventh and most recent session, the Tokyo Round of Multilateral Trade Negotiations (MTN), so named since the basis for the negotiations was established in Tokyo in 1973, was brought to a successful conclusion in Geneva in 1979 after nearly five years of bargaining. Prior to the Tokyo Round, the last major international effort to reduce tariff rates was the Kennedy Round of negotiations, which actually took place during the Johnson administration (1964–1967).

Domestically, three major statutes (as amended) have governed the American approach to international trade issues: the Reciprocal Trade Agreements Act of 1934; the Trade Expansion Act of 1962; and the Trade Act of 1974. Under each, Congress has granted the president authority to engage in international negotiations on trade issues, often with specific grants of authority to lower American tariff barriers if other nations will do the same. (Congress has also restricted presidential prerogatives in some important areas, as we shall note later in this chapter.) The Trade Expansion Act of 1962 and the Trade Act of 1974 set the stage for the Kennedy and Tokyo rounds of negotiations, respectively. A fourth statute, the Trade Agreements Act of 1979, implemented rules agreed upon during the Tokyo Round.[8]

---

[8]The Trade Agreements Act of 1979 sailed through Congress with unusual speed and support due to the unique procedures that were used to consider the bill. The 1979 Trade Act, which prohibited amendments to the MTN-implementing legislation, was written jointly by members of Congress and officials in the Carter administration. Political support for the legislation was assured by involving major industry groups in determining American negotiating strategy.

The fact that both the Trade Expansion Act and the Trade Act presaged major new international efforts at tariff reductions attests to the importance of the United States in the postwar international trade regime. Its importance derives from the size of the American economy, the proportion of international trade for which the nation accounts, and the fact that it is the principal supplier of many products traded in the world marketplace. More importantly, the United States was the principal mover behind the postwar negotiating sessions and, throughout the 1940s and 1950s, it was willing to accept fewer immediate benefits than its trading partners in anticipation of the longer term benefits of freer international trade. In effect, the United States was the locomotive of expanding production and trade worldwide. By stimulating its own growth, the United States was an attractive market for the exports of others, and the outflow of U.S. dollars stimulated the economic growth of other nations in the "American train." Evidence supporting the link between trade liberalization and export growth is found in the fact that as the average duty levied on imports to the United States was reduced by more than half between the late 1940s and the early 1960s, world exports nearly tripled.

The high point of the movement toward liberalized trading was reached with the Kennedy Round in the mid-1960s, which grew out of the 1962 Trade Expansion Act. It was motivated in part by concern for maintaining American export markets in the face of the growing economic competition from the European Economic Community (EEC),[9] and the act itself granted the president broad power to negotiate tariff rates with EEC countries in particular. The EEC (otherwise known as the European Community) today rivals Canada as the country's principal trading partner (based on trade turnover, that is, exports plus imports), as shown in Figure 7.2. Similar ties are apparent in American overseas investments. Seventy-five percent of the nation's direct investment abroad is in developed nations, with Western Europe accounting for nearly three-fifths of that proportion (see Figure 7.3).

Progress was made during the Kennedy Round of negotiations on tariffs on industrial goods, to the point that by the time of the Tokyo MTN, the United States and the European Community had reduced tariff rates on industrial products to an average of about 9 percent. But little headway was made on the important question of agricultural commodities, which were of growing importance to the United States. The lack of progress on this issue, and subsequent disagreements over it, began to raise doubts among American policy makers about the wisdom of expansionist economic policies. The immediate challenge was posed in 1966 by the EEC's Common Agricultural Policy (CAP). Toward others, CAP was a protectionist tariff wall designed to maintain politically acceptable but artificially high prices for farm products pro-

---

[9]The rhetoric surrounding passage of the act cloaked trade liberalization in the mantle of national security, and the act itself was described as an essential weapon in the Cold War struggle with the Soviet Union. See Berkowitz, Bock, and Fuccillo (1977) for an account of the foreign and domestic forces giving rise to the Trade Expansion Act.

FIGURE 7.2   Trading Partners of the United States, 1985

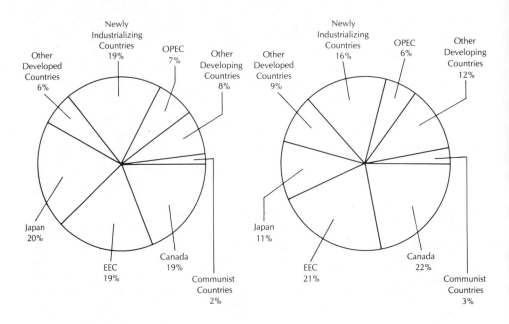

SOURCE: Adapted from U.S. Bureau of the Census, 1985: Tables 5 and 8.

duced within the EEC. The effect was to curtail American agricultural exports to the EEC.

Concern in the United States about the challenge of an economically revitalized and politically united Europe was among the factors that marked a change in the postwar multilateral trade system. Other factors that began to erode the foundations of the liberalized trading system included the extension by the European Community of preferential trade treatment to nations in Africa, the Mediterranean, and the Caribbean; the expansion of the Community from six members to nine in 1973; the extension of associate status to others; and the feeling by many Western nations that Japan continued to pursue highly protectionist trade policies in contrast to the liberalized trading scheme the others were seeking to create. Generally, the forces undermining the trade structure were much the same as those which undermined the international monetary system. The collapse of that system itself contributed to the lack of forward movement on trade matters. Thus, no new trade negotiations were held in the six years between the end of the Kennedy Round and the Tokyo Round.

The lack of international progress on trade matters also was related to developments in the United States. The president's authority to negotiate trade

FIGURE 7.3   United States Cumulative Direct Investment Abroad (billions of dollars)

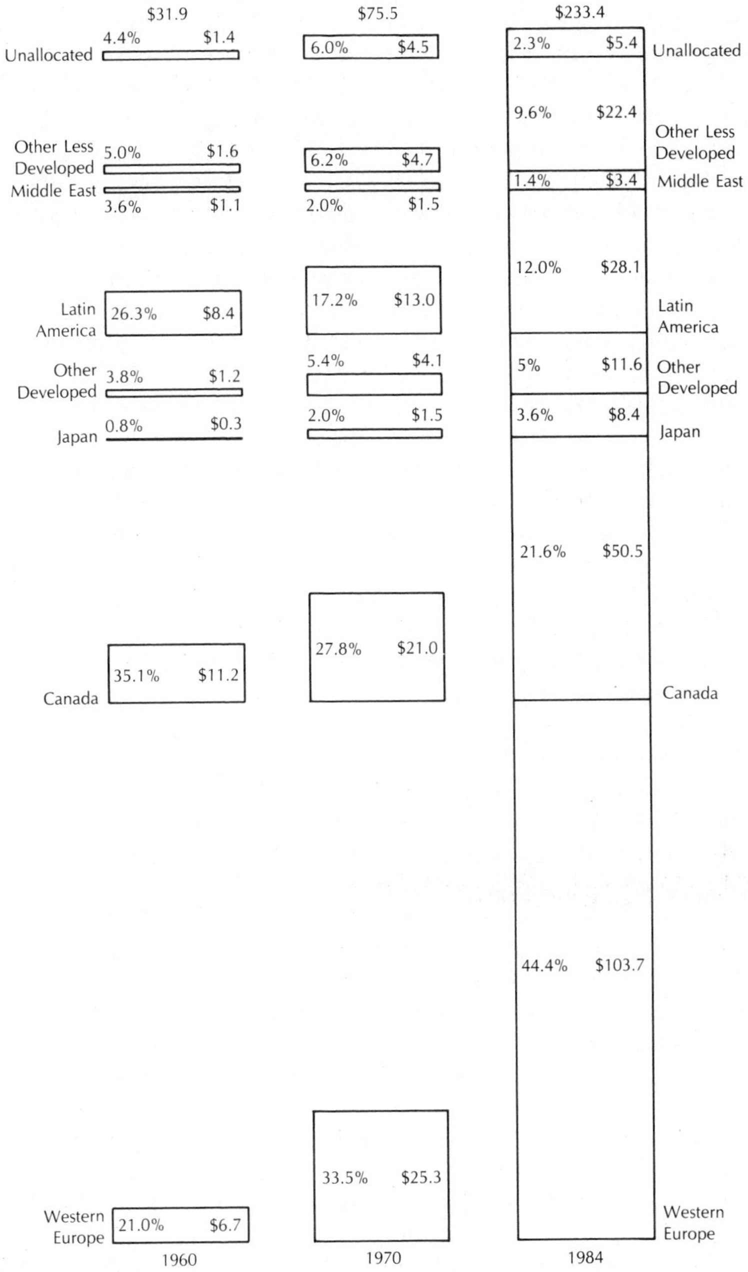

	$31.9		$75.5		$233.4	
Unallocated	4.4% $1.4		6.0% $4.5		2.3% $5.4	Unallocated
					9.6% $22.4	Other Less Developed
Other Less Developed	5.0% $1.6		6.2% $4.7			
Middle East	3.6% $1.1		2.0% $1.5		1.4% $3.4	Middle East
					12.0% $28.1	Latin America
Latin America	26.3% $8.4		17.2% $13.0			
Other Developed	3.8% $1.2		5.4% $4.1		5% $11.6	Other Developed
Japan	0.8% $0.3		2.0% $1.5		3.6% $8.4	Japan
					21.6% $50.5	
Canada	35.1% $11.2		27.8% $21.0		44.4% $103.7	Canada
Western Europe	21.0% $6.7		33.5% $25.3			Western Europe
	1960		1970		1984	

SOURCE: 1960 figures from *International Economic Report of the President, 1977*: 24; 1970 figures adapted from *Statistical Abstract of the United States, 1980*, 1980: 865; 1984 figure adapted from *Survey of Current Business*, August 1984: 36.

matters under the Trade Expansion Act expired with the end of the Kennedy Round. Thereafter, Presidents Johnson and Nixon fought a rearguard action against increasingly strong domestic protectionist forces that demanded trade restrictions from Congress. The reasons for the waning of support for a multilateral free-trade system were related to the many factors we have already discussed: "specific threats to particular industries, general and increasing weakness of the American economy, the worsening of the U.S. balance of trade, and the feeling that the protectionist policies of the EEC and Japan were a source of U.S. problems" (Spero, 1981). The shifting political forces within the Western world and between it and the communist world were also important. The consequence was a loss of American leadership within the system.

As noted previously, Nixon's economic policies announced in August 1971 had the effect of suspending the Bretton Woods agreements under which the international monetary system had operated for a quarter of a century. Nixon's almost bellicose approach to monetary and trade matters was a serious blow to the multilateral free-trade scheme. However, the world was spared a spiral of retaliatory, protectionist trade measures such as the 1930s had witnessed. Instead, once the immediate crisis had receded, the major industrial powers committed themselves to a new round of multilateral trade negotiations. But new obstacles had yet to be surmounted. High inflation was one, for it, too, encouraged protectionist practices in order to ensure adequate domestic supplies. It was in this context that Nixon dealt Japan another of his famous "shocks"; in 1973 he placed soybeans, which the Japanese imported in large quantities, under export control.[10] Worldwide recession induced by the 1973–1974 oil price increases also had to be overcome. And in the United States the Congress was not only attempting to deal with a trade proposal that sought to increase the president's power to negotiate trade matters beyond what previous statutes had accorded him; it was also grappling with an issue that made presidential power appear excessive already—Watergate.

By the time the Tokyo Round commenced, trade negotiators found themselves in a radically different environment from that of the previous GATT sessions. Trade volume had grown enormously worldwide, economic interdependence among the world's leading industrial powers had reached unparalleled levels, tariffs were no longer the principal barriers to trade, and the United States was no longer an unfaltering economic giant. In such an environment, increased emphasis was placed during the MTN on reducing barriers to the free flow of agricultural products and on coping with nontariff barriers to trade.

Nontariff barriers refers to a wide range of government regulations that have the effect of reducing or distorting international trade, including health and safety regulations, restrictions on the quality of goods that may be imported,

---

[10]The earlier shock had been dealt in 1971, when Nixon announced—without any prior consultation with Japan, the United States' most important East Asian ally—that he was going to visit Mainland China.

antidumping regulations (designed to prevent foreign producers from selling their goods for less abroad than they cost domestically), and domestic subsidies. Import and export quotas also have been used to place quantitative restrictions on certain goods traded internationally. The United States, for example, has used types of export quotas known as *orderly market arrangements* and *voluntary export restrictions*, which are negotiated with exporting countries to limit the flow of such products as autos, steel, textiles, and footwear into the United States.[11] Nontariff barriers comprise one of several *neomercantilist*[12] challenges to the principle of free trade, which have assumed paramouncy in American foreign economic policy as its economic preeminence relative to others has declined. The allegation is that the gulf between *free trade* and *fair trade* is often very wide.

The principle of *free trade*, based on the theory of comparative advantage, promises that all countries will benefit from international trade when each specializes in the production of those goods in which it enjoys advantages and trades them for goods in which others enjoy advantages. *Fair trade*, on the other hand, draws attention to the role that governments play in creating comparative advantages.

Historically, the United States has espoused a laissez-faire attitude toward trade issues, believing that market forces are best able to stimulate entrepreneurial initiatives, investment choices, and the like. Increasingly, it has come to believe that "the playing field is tilted"—that American businesspeople are unable to compete on the same basis as others, notably the continental European states, Japan, and less developed countries, where governments routinely intervene actively in their economies and play entrepreneurial and developmental roles directly. Senator Lloyd M. Bentsen, a long-time advocate of free trade, captured the shifting sentiment when he said of free trade, "I think in theory, it's a great theory. But it's not being practiced, and for us to practice free trade in a world where there's much government-directed trade makes as much sense as unilateral disarmament with the Russians."

An urge to "level the playing field" motivated the Reagan administration to seek a new round of multilateral trade negotiations designed to cope with a world rife with trade subsidies, invisible import restraints, and other unfair trade practices (see also Anjaria, 1986). The hope was that reductions of barriers to trade in services (for example, insurance) and high technology, where the United States enjoys competitive advantages, would also follow.

---

[11]Not all nontariff barriers are designed specifically to limit trade. Health and safety standards, for example, have come to be regarded as necessary and legitimate forms of government regulation. They have no necessary bearing on international trade, though they are sometimes used to limit external competition rather than to safeguard domestic welfare. It is often difficult, however, to distinguish legitimate nontariff barriers from regulations designed primarily to limit foreign competition and to protect domestic industries.

[12]Neomercantilism refers to "a policy whereby a state seeks to maintain a balance-of-trade surplus and to promote domestic production and employment by reducing imports, stimulating home production, and promoting exports" (Blake and Walters, 1983).

Other nations were not quick to agree to the analogy of an uneven playing field skewed in their favor. They were sensitive nonetheless to the need to keep protectionist sentiments in the United States at bay. Because U.S. imports stimulated the economic growth of its trade partners, thus enabling the United States to act as the engine of Western economic growth generally, as it had in the 1960s, America's trade partners could not be unresponsive to the argument that new trade talks were necessary to cope with issues of special concern to the United States. Conversely, the Reagan administration used the proposed trade talks to stem the rising tide of protectionist sentiments at home, where, at one time during 1985, some 300 bills were pending before Congress that offered protection to one industrial sector or another, ranging from steel, copper, lumber, and automobiles to shoes, textiles, neckties, and waterbeds.

As noted in our discussion of the role of the United States in the management of the international monetary system, the rising value of the dollar between 1981 and 1985 stimulated protectionist demands as the competitiveness of American goods overseas eroded and the attractiveness of foreign-produced goods to the American consumer increased. Thus, while free trade, based on the liberal economic principle of comparative advantage, may promise benefits to all, the costs to particular groups confronting adverse economic circumstances as a result of free trade are often substantial. To workers standing in an unemployment line because the factory in which they worked could no longer compete with foreign producers and was forced to close, the fact that other consumers are able to buy a cheaper product is little consolation. Business and labor alike are therefore prone to argue for protection. Because they are politically powerful, they frequently get protection. Foreign economic policy in such circumstances is motivated by domestic political considerations. The American steel industry, for example, historically one of the giants of American industrial power, has sought protection from more efficiently produced, and hence cheaper, foreign imports. The case of steel underscores the fact that recent protectionist cries in the United States stem from the simple fact that industries affected by foreign competition have been unable to sustain demand for their products adequate ''to maintain price, profit, and employment at politically acceptable levels'' (Spero, 1981).

Japan has come to symbolize many of the trade challenges facing the United States in the 1980s and beyond. Japan is often viewed in the United States as the preeminent neomercantilist power, based on the belief that its spectacular export growth during the past two decades resulted from an intimate government-business alliance. The enormous trade imbalance the United States experienced with Japan in recent years reinforces the belief that Japanese neomercantilist policies are inherently disadvantageous to American business. In 1985, for example, United States imports from Japan topped $72 billion, but its exports to that island nation were less than $24 billion (see Figure 7.4).

FIGURE 7.4   U.S. Trade Balances with Various Countries, 1985 (billions of dollars)

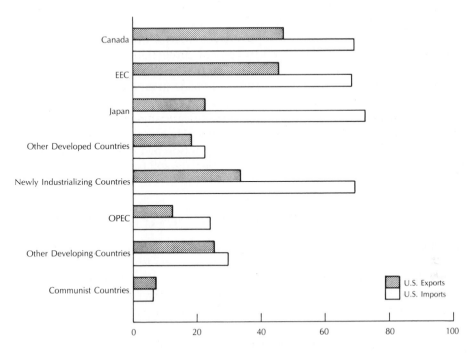

SOURCE: Adapted from U.S. Bureau of the Census, 1985: Tables 5 and 8.

Beyond the demonstrable preference of millions of Americans for products made in Japan, a broad array of trade restrictions doubtless constrain the ability of American producers to penetrate the Japanese market. Included in addition to traditional tariff barriers are such nontariff restraints as restrictions on license transfers on medical devices and pharmaceuticals, limits on the acceptance of foreign clinical data for medical items and drugs, and product testing of telecommunications equipment. Penetration of the Japanese market is hampered further by a cultural tradition that views foreign products as ill-suited to the Japanese consumer. Furthermore, the domestic savings rate in Japan is considerably higher than the average savings rate among the other Western industrialized nations. This implies that domestic consumption in Japan is low, which also means Japanese industry must look overseas for growth. In other words, the excess of savings over investment, and of production over consumption, finds its way abroad (Feldstein, 1985). Until policies are designed to offset the impact of Japan's high savings rate, Japan will continue to have an important impact on the global political economy generally—and on the American economy in particular, for it has become Japan's most important overseas market. It should be recognized, moreover, that just as the drive to erect protectionist barriers in the United States is a potent political issue, dismantling those barriers is an equally emotional issue on the other side of the Pacific basin.

The foregoing will likely shape Japanese-American trade ties well into the future despite multilateral efforts to contain protectionist pressures. Meanwhile, Japanese exporters will not willingly give up the market shares they acquired as the value of the dollar rose to unprecedented heights during the first half of the 1980s. Even as the dollar fell and the yen appreciated in 1986, Japanese products continued to command a significant share of the dollars spent by American consumers, suggesting that the process of adjusting to the underlying political and economic forces set in motion by the shifting fortunes of the dollar during and following the OPEC decade will be neither swift nor assured.

THE THIRD WORLD: THE NORTH-SOUTH DIALOGUE

The international monetary and multilateral trading systems that evolved during the postwar decades did so primarily under the aegis of the Western industrialized nations whose interests and objectives they served. Developing nations on the periphery largely were outside the privileged circle. Many of these nations came to view the existing international economic structure as a cause of their underdog status.

Already in the 1950s the nonaligned nations began efforts to promote their common interests. The strategy was to develop a unified posture toward the superpowers in the context of the Cold War and to press for consideration of their special problems and needs in the context of the economic structure. Not until the 1960s, however, did the developing nations begin to realize their objectives. Taking advantage of their growing numbers in the United Nations, developing countries were able to utilize that forum to make repeated demands for a restructuring of the existing international economic order. They were successful in having convened, in 1964, a United Nations Conference on Trade and Development (UNCTAD). In that conference, the Group of 77 (sometimes referred to simply as G-77) was formed as a coalition of the world's poor to press for concessions from the world's rich.

UNCTAD conferences have been held at periodic intervals since 1964. UNCTAD itself has become an autonomous structure within the family of United Nations organizations; as a practical matter the organization has come to be a voice for the interests of the poor. And the Group of 77 (which still goes by that label but now numbers well over 100 states) continues to operate as an economic negotiating caucus of the world's less fortunate nations.

The G-77 effectively joined the nonaligned movement during the 1973 Algiers summit of nonaligned nations, when issues relating to economic as well as political "liberation" came to the fore. Algeria, then the chair of the nonaligned countries, led the call for what became the Sixth Special Session of the

United Nations General Assembly, held in the spring of 1974. Using their superior numbers, the Group of 77 secured passage of the Declaration on the Establishment of a New International Economic Order (NIEO). It is significant that both the special session and the declaration coincided with the worldwide food and energy crises the world experienced in the mid-1970s, for not until the OPEC cartel successfully raised petroleum prices were the demands of the Third World from the South given serious consideration by the Western industrial nations of the North. OPEC's success also augmented the stridency of developing nations' demands, for whom the phrase ''New International Economic Order'' became the rallying cry for their drive for a basic restructuring of the existing international political economy.

Third World demands for a NIEO effectively challenged the Liberal International Economic Order (LIEO) of the 1950s and 1960s, in which the United States played a hegemonic role. Some moderate concessions to Third World countries were made during this period, for ''a hegemon is a stability-seeking power that recognizes that its dominant ideology and the attendant institutional structure cannot endure for long unless the nonhegemonic members of that structure accept its legitimacy. This legitimacy is secured through incrementalist, gradualist, marginalist accommodation of nonhegemonic discontent'' (Bhagwati, 1984). The NIEO effectively challenged that legitimacy and the processes that sustained it. Egged on by the belief that ''commodity power'' endowed Third World nations with the political strength necessary to challenge the advanced industrial nations of the North, they felt their superior numbers could yield influence in the United Nations, UNCTAD, the IMF, the World Bank, the Third United Nations Law of the Sea Conference, and various other global and regional forums. In these institutions the Third World called for more rapid economic development, increased transfers of resources from industrialized to developing nations, and a more favorable distribution of global economic benefits. Other issues were raised having to do with aid, trade, foreign investment, foreign ownership of property, activities of multinational corporations, debt relief for developing nations through cancellation or rescheduling, commodity price stabilization, compensatory financing mechanisms to stabilize export earnings, and price indexation (which would tie the prices developing nations receive for the goods they export to the capital goods they import from the North). If implemented as envisioned by developing nations, the net effect of Third World demands for a New International Economic Order would have been a redistribution of income and wealth from rich nations to poor. As importantly, the effect would have been a relocation of the locus of decision making and political influence internationally by a substantial alteration of the rules and institutional structures governing the international flow of goods, services, capital, and technology. What the Third World sought, in short, was *regime change*, a modification in the system's rules and procedural norms (Krasner, 1985).

The Third World drive for regime change was (is) based on the belief that the international political economy is structured so as to perpetuate developing nations' underdog status. The feeling is widespread among Third World nations that present international economic institutions, such as the IMF and GATT "and the political/economic process governed by them are deeply biased against developing countries in their global distribution of income and influence" (Hansen, 1980). The perception is buttressed by a legacy of colonial exploitation and the continued existence of levels of poverty and deprivation unheard of in the North. "Equity" is therefore a driving force behind Third World demands for institutional reform.

The North rejects the view that the economic woes of developing nations are a product of the current international order; instead, it locates the cause of those problems in the domestic systems of Third World countries themselves.[13] That view helps explain the halting, incremental steps the North took to accommodate Third World demands. It also helps explain Northern rejection of Southern efforts to radically alter existing international economic institutions. Beginning in 1979, for example, the Third World sought a new round of North-South negotiations known as Global Negotiations, in which the South hoped to move the decision-making process from functionally specific forums, such as the specialized agencies of the U.N., in which the North controls outcomes, to universal membership organizations, like the United Nations, where the Third World could use its superior numbers to advantage. Neither the Carter nor the Reagan administration endorsed the Global Negotiations, however, and the incentives for the North to do so were rapidly disappearing. By the time of the UNCTAD VI meeting in 1983, it was apparent that the "commodity power" with which the South had hoped to force the North to come to terms was a transient phenomenon.[14]

Between UNCTAD V in 1979 and UNCTAD VI in 1983, there was a general and prolonged economic slump which hit Third World countries particularly hard. Economic growth rates were down in many Third World countries, and some, particularly in Africa, had negative growth rates. The prices of many of the commodities exported by Third World nations fell sharply compared with the prices they had to pay for their imports. Faced with reduced export earnings and high interest rates, the debt burdens of many Third World nations

[13]For a statement of the Third World perspective which locates the solution of developing countries' difficulties in the reform of their own political and economic institutions, see Addo (1981).

[14]The clearest signals of the decline of commodity power were provided by the softening of oil prices worldwide and the erosion of OPEC's ability to control the oil regime through its pricing and production policies. It was also clear by 1983 that, for a number of both economic and political reasons, efforts to cartelize other commodity markets would be unsuccessful (Kegley and Wittkopf, 1982a and 1985b).

Even in the absence of effective producers' cartels, the Reagan administration frequently invoked the specter of a coming resource war when it first arrived in Washington, pointing in particular to potential threats to secure access to strategic minerals in the southern part of Africa. The war did not materialize, of course, and detailed analyses of U.S. mineral dependence suggest that, while the minerals in question are doubtless important and irreplaceable, few realistic threats are on the horizon (see Russett, 1984; Shafer, 1982; and *The Defense Monitor*, Vol. 14, No. 9, 1985).

and the costs of servicing them assumed ominous proportions. Thus, by the time of UNCTAD VI, their acute economic problems meant, for many, austerity at home, which caused them to focus more on immediate and practical issues than on the longer term drive for structural reform of the international political economy that had been launched a decade earlier.

If "commodity power" proves to be but a historical footnote to the decades-long dialogue between North and South, as seems likely, the political bases from which the Third World mounts renewed efforts to realize its objectives with respect to the structures and processes of the global political economy are by no means clear. With the exception of a handful of Third World nations of special interest to the United States for security purposes (such as Saudi Arabia, the Philippines, and various Central American countries), for example, most are relatively powerless. Portions of the Third World, however, are not so easily dimissed. In 1985, twelve Third World nations were among the dozen most important trade partners of the United States (based on trade turnover), and the Third World as a whole accounted for 46 percent of the nation's $231.3 billion in trade with the rest of the world (see Figure 7.2). Concomitantly, the Third World has become increasingly sensitive and vulnerable to United States' fiscal and monetary policies, as well as its trade and security policies. *Interdependence* thus increasingly applies to U.S.-Third World linkages, much as it applies to those among the advanced industrial societies of the West.

We will briefly examine the consequences of U.S.-Third World interdependence and the context of the contention that divides North and South by examining three areas in which the interests of the United States and the developing nations intersect: trade in manufactures and commodities other than fuel and food; trade in agricultural products; and the debt crises of the 1980s.

Trade in Commodities, Manufactures, and U.S. Trade Policy

Trade-related issues are at the core of the contention between North and South. The structure of trade relationships between developed and developing nations evolved during the age of imperialism, when colonies existed for the presumed benefit of the colonizers. Frequently that arrangement meant that the colonies were sources of primary products, such as agricultural commodities and mineral resources, and markets for the finished manufactured goods produced in the mother country. That pattern persists today as a general description of the structure of trade ties between developed and developing nations. As shown in Figure 7.5, in 1980 developing nations as a whole relied on primary products (including fuels and related materials) for 79 percent of their export earnings (the money necessary to buy goods from abroad), while more than 60 percent of their imports were in the form of manufactures. That pattern is virtually the reverse of developed nations', for whom primary products are comparatively insignificant (although for the United States in particular, farm exports are quite important, as discussed in more detail be-

FIGURE 7.5 The Composition of World Exports and Imports, by Groups of Countries, 1980

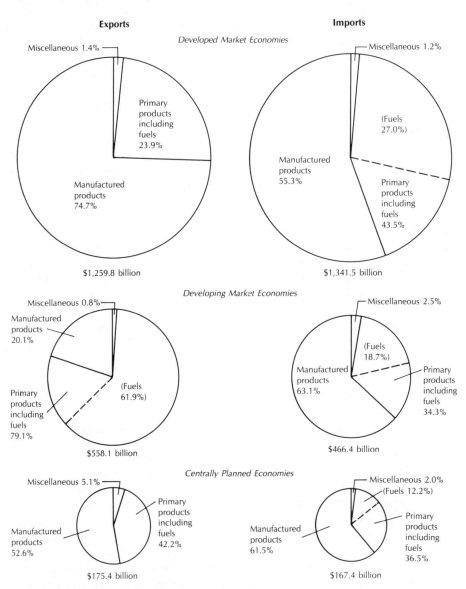

SOURCE: Adapted from Lewis and Kallab, 1983: 248.

*World import figures include certain imports that, because their regions of destination could not be determined, are not otherwise included in the import figures in this table.

NOTE: Data do not include trade among the centrally planned economies of Asia, the exports of Zimbabwe, or the trade between the Federal Republic of Germany and the German Democratic Republic.

low). At the same time, the developed market economies of the First World are the principal source and destination of the manufactured goods that enter the international marketplace.

Developing nations argue that their dependence on a narrow range of primary product exports underlies their terms of trade problems. They believe that the prices they receive for their exports vary erratically in the short run and deteriorate steadily in the long run, whereas the prices of the manufactured goods that they import increase steadily.

The structural characteristics of the international economic order are among the alleged causes of the deteriorating terms of trade (Pirages, 1978). The South remains critically dependent on the North not only for manufactured goods but also for technology. The greater technological sophistication of the North causes natural resources to flow into markets where they can be transformed into finished goods most efficiently. Powerful labor unions and giant corporations institutionalize, through wage and fringe benefit programs, the comparatively high cost of the technologically sophisticated products produced in the North, the demand for which is sustained by worldwide advertising compaigns. Developing nations are unable to compete on similar terms with the North. The South cannot bid up the prices for the materials produced in developing nations. In a system where those with the most money determine prices, Third World nations find themselves unable to determine the terms of trade for their products.

There is no question that developing nations' primary product exports are subject to sharp price fluctuations. As noted earlier, for example, non-oil commodity prices dropped sharply during the recession induced by the second oil shock. According to the World Bank, by 1982 commodity prices had reached a lower level in real terms (after adjusting for the rise in prices of manufactures imported by developing nations) than at any time since World War II. "Food prices fell most—by 30 percent (in nominal terms) between 1980 and 1982—and nonfood agricultural commodities by 24 percent, while metal and mineral prices declined by 17 percent" (*World Development Report, 1983*, 1983: 11). Whether such fluctuations are a result of a long-term structural deterioration of the terms of trade developing nations face or of short-term perturbations related to changes in the business cycle remains a matter of controversy among analysts. Regardless, the policies pursued by the Third World leaders are influenced by such perceptions.

Faced with the circumstances described above, diversification of export industries, rather than continued dependence on a few primary products, is a preferred goal of many developing nations. At the same time, they have sought new means of ensuring stable and remunerative prices for the commodities they already export. Such was the goal of the Integrated Programme for Commodities pushed by the G-77 and the UNCTAD secretariat as a central element of the drive for a New International Economic Order. As originally conceived, the Integrated Programme was an ambitious buffer-stock arrangement that sought commodity price stabilization through a common fund supported by producing and consuming nations and administered by an international agency. In terms of its managerial requirements, the proposal was in many ways unprecedented (see Rothstein, 1979).

The Common Fund that finally emerged in 1979 after two years of negotiation was a far cry from the ambitious one once sought, and its budget of only $750 million severely limited its operation. By mid-1985, the Common Fund still remained short of the ninety ratifications necessary to bring it into existence. The United States was among those who refused to ratify the agreement, even though the Carter administration had earlier signed it. The agreement was restricted further by the fact that only individual international commodity organizations could be parties to it. Few of these organizations based on agreements between commodity producers and consumers currently exist, and the process of creating them is exceedingly complex and difficult (Puchala, 1983a).

The refusal of the Reagan administration to ratify the Common Fund agreement was consistent with its market-oriented approach to commodity prices. In response to the resistant environment within which the G-77 now pursued its global political economy objectives, developing nations, in the UNCTAD VI meeting in 1983, sought an immediate action program for commodities that was decidedly less radical than the integrated program endorsed nearly a decade earlier. Developed countries stiffened their opposition further by rebuffing the suggestion implicit in the latest Third World proposals, namely, that structural inadequacies remained the cause of its plight. They argued, instead, that

> Even though the world was suffering from a severe recession . . . it was not undergoing a fundamental crisis caused by structural rigidities. The recession was largely a cyclical downturn caused mainly by deliberate national policies designed to bring inflation under control. With inflation falling and recovery underway in several countries, especially the United States, no special measures were needed to counter the recession. Recovery alone would end the cycle, and this recovery would benefit both the developed and the developing countries. The greatest threat to recovery was protectionism, and thus the principal measures to be taken by the international community were those that would preserve the liberal international trading and financial system. (Spero, 1985: 261)

The belief that U.S. economic growth would ultimately benefit Third World nations echoed the "locomotive" analogy so often applied to trade relations between the United States and other First World nations. The protectionist charge leveled against developing nations likewise echoed an increasingly familiar note.

As described earlier, the rise of protectionist sentiment in the United States can be traced to the early 1970s, when domestic inflation began to erode the trade competitiveness of United States' products overseas. It was spurred by the "stagflation" that followed the first oil shock and by subsequent developments at home and abroad that inhibited the process of structural adjustment to the changing world economy (see *World Development Report, 1985*, 1985: 37–40). Among those changes was increasing competition from a small group of exporters of manufactured goods (such as consumer electronics) known as the Newly Industrializing Countries (NICs), of which Brazil, Hong Kong, Mexico, Singapore, South Korea, and Taiwan are the most important. All six were among the dozen Third World trade partners most important to the U.S. in 1985. Spurred on at that time by the high-flying dollar, the favorable trade balance the NICs amassed with the United States during that year was surpassed only by Japan's (see Figure 7.4), thus contributing to the view that they, too, have stimulated the export of American jobs and the deindustrialization of the United States economy.

Exploiting advantages in the cost of labor in particular, the NICs have achieved spectacular economic growth rates in recent years compared to other Third World nations by pursuing export-led rather than import-substitution industrialization policies. A successful export-led scenario requires access to First World markets. But the more successful it is, the more it stimulates domestic protectionist sentiments in the importing countries.

As described in chapter five, foreign aid has been a preferred mechanism whereby the United States has sought to augment Third World efforts to realize economic growth and development. But "trade, not aid" has been a persistent plea of many developing nations, which feel they have been denied access to markets in developed countries through tariff and nontariff barriers alike. The Multifiber Arrangement (MFA) is a classic case in point. Designed in the 1950s as a mechanism to protect textile producers in the United States from imports from the Far East, the scheme today is an elaborate market-sharing arrangement among more than three dozen textile-producing countries that effectively denies access to others. Because textiles are among the simplest semimanufactures that Third World nations aspiring to export-led growth might hope to ship abroad, the MFA is a blatantly discriminatory barrier to free trade.

To overcome the obstacles Third World nations face in their drive to gain access to First World markets, developing nations have sought preferential, as opposed to most-favored-nation, trade treatment. Such preferential treatment would enable them to build diversified export industries capable of competing on equal terms with those in the North.

In partial response to that plea, the United States established (by the Trade Act of 1974) a Generalized System of Preferences (GSP), thereby joining most other industrialized nations in establishing a system of nonreciprocal and nondiscriminatory tariff preferences for developing nations. The principle of nonreciprocity was extended by the Tokyo Round of Multilateral Trade Negotiations, thereby enabling developed nations to grant trade preferences to developing nations without violating GATT's rules regarding most-favored-nation trade treatment. The extension of preferential treatment is a significant departure from the nondiscrimination principle dominant throughout the Bretton Woods period.

Despite these apparent Northern concessions, their effects have been disputed. The U.S. GSP as initially designed covered only a limited number of products (Hansen, 1976), for example, and the Tokyo MTN failed to grapple with the protectionist sentiments in the North that were often directed at products, such as textiles and steel, in which some developing nations, notably the NICs, already enjoyed competitive advantages. The MTN not only failed to devise a code to limit the effect of protectionist measures in the North on those nations; following the insistence of the United States, it also included a "graduation clause" stipulating

> that as Southern countries reach higher levels of development, or "graduate," they should be given less special treatment and should trade on a more equal footing with the industrialized states.
>
> The developing countries, especially the NICs, objected strenuously to this principle, which they saw as a device that the North could use to withdraw preferential treatment whenever the developing countries began to threaten the Northern economies. (Spero, 1985: 253)

Concern for that threat surfaced during the congressional debate on renewal of the GSP, which was due to expire in 1985. Opponents of the trade preferences argued that the vast majority of GSP benefits went to the NICs who, they argued, "don't need special treatment anymore." In fact, the value of duty-free GSP imports in 1982 from more than one hundred developing nations totaled only $8.4 billion, or 3 percent of all U.S. imports, but nearly two-thirds came from only five nations: Brazil, Hong Kong, Mexico, South Korea, and Taiwan. Electronic products, primarily from the Asian NICs, alone accounted for more than a billion dollars in duty-free imports (Congressional Quarterly, 1986b: 131). As various labor groups and business interests mobilized to exempt their products from duty-free status, Congressman Bill Frenzel remarked that "It has often been said facetiously that if Congress had known what GSP was in 1974, it never would have included it in the Trade Act."

Eventually, in October 1984, Congress passed an omnibus trade bill that extended the GSP until 1993. But for the first time Congress tied the preferences to steps by the beneficiaries to open their markets to U.S. exports and to other issues of importance to the United States, such as the protection of intellectual property rights (patents and copyrights).[15] It also denied GSP benefits to countries with per capita incomes over $8,500.

Interdependence, it bears repeating, implies *mutual* sensitivity and *mutual* vulnerability. At the same time that the United States reacts to barriers against its exports, the barriers it has erected against foreign imports are formidable and growing. The World Bank concludes, for example, that the proportion of

---

[15]Textbooks and Apple computers are among the products and technologies some NICs have pirated in violation of international standards and copyright laws designed to protect intellectual property rights.

imports subject to restriction via nontariff barriers in the United States more than doubled between 1980 and 1983, with some 8 percent of its imports from developed countries and 13 percent of its imports from developing countries subject (in 1983) to nontariff barriers (*World Development Report, 1985*, 1985: 40).[16]

The theory of free trade projects benefits to all who specialize in the production of those goods in which they enjoy comparative advantages, trading them for the goods produced by others pursuing their own comparative advantages. That theory's conclusion is irrefutable, and was recognized as such by policy makers who, contemplating the global economic disaster of the 1930s, determined that the institutional arrangements that were to govern the post-World War II world should encourage the free flow of capital and goods across national boundaries. The political task today is to balance promised benefits against the immediate costs imposed by the structural adjustments that free trade inevitably demands. The task is more difficult when one or more of the partners believes the game is biased. The political economy of North-South trade relations, and of the role of the United States within it, promises to continue to be colored by contention over what *is*, and over what is *believed* to be, true, and by the inevitable contest between parochial, short-term national interests, on the one hand, and collective, long-term interests on the other.

Population Growth, Global Food Security, and U.S. Foreign Agricultural Policy

Agricultural products comprise a class of commodities of special interest to the United States, for the economic well-being of American agriculture depends more heavily on exports than do other sectors of the U.S. economy. Two out of every five acres of farmland are harvested for export. Agricultural exports accounted for about 20 percent of total U.S. exports and earned $38 billion in fiscal year 1984. Each billion dollars in agricultural export sales is estimated to create 26,000 jobs (Congressional Quarterly, 1986b: 158). Furthermore, the United States is the source of about 55 percent of world trade in coarse grains (for example, corn), about 35 percent in wheat, and more than 75 percent in soybeans and soybean products. In all cases, however, the dominance of the United States has been severely challenged, and the value of U.S. agricultural exports has declined sharply from the historic peak of $43.8 billion in 1981. Several factors explain the erosion of American agricultural export supremacy, including the strong dollar, worldwide recession, and increased production by and competition from others. The result is the advent in

---

[16]The World Bank also reports that the trade restrictions of the European Community increased by 38 percent between 1980 and 1983, with 10.2 percent of its imports from developed countries and 21.8 percent of its imports from developing countries subject to nontariff barriers in 1983 (*World Development Report, 1985*, 1985: 40).

the mid-1980s of an enormous global surplus food stock in which, for the first time in generations, supply exceeds demand.

United States policy remains committed to a liberal trading system that enhances the export opportunities for U.S. agriculture. Importantly, however, and in contrast to others among the growing number of exporters of agricultural products (particularly the new, developing country exporters), U.S. agricultural policy has been "driven more by the need to protect a major domestic economic, social and political interest than by the need for foreign exchange produced by these exports, no matter how significant those trade earnings may be" (Insel, 1985).

As competition has grown among exporters, each seeking to realize its particular policy objectives, international trade in agricultural products (particularly grain) has been affected by aggressive national strategies designed to increase the competitive advantage of one exporter over another, including "a variety of export incentives and subsidies, such as differential export taxes, tax rebates, direct support payments to allow lower export prices, subsidized domestic credits, subsidized export credits and 'food aid'" (Insel, 1985). The widespread use of such tactics—which, incidentally, the United States itself employs in varying degrees—has led to growing political pressure in the United States to fight what are believed to be unfair trade practices in this area.

The impact of the increased export competition (and the increased productivity that makes it possible) on different countries and regions, and ultimately on the goal of realizing both global and individual food security, has varied widely. It is useful to place the problem in historical perspective in order to appreciate its implications.

Food security is usefully defined as *"access by all people at all times to enough food for an active, healthy life"* (Reutlinger, 1985).

> Its essential elements are the availability of food and the ability to acquire it. Conversely, food insecurity is the lack of access to sufficient food and can be either chronic or transitory. Chronic food insecurity is a continuously inadequate diet resulting from the lack of resources to produce or acquire food. Transitory food insecurity, on the other hand, is a temporary decline in a household's access to enough food. It results from instability in food production and prices, or in household incomes. The worst form of transitory food insecurity is famine. (Reutlinger. 1985: 7)

Achieving food security became an item on the North-South agenda during the 1970s when, at about the same time as the first OPEC-induced oil shock, the ability of the multitude of nationally based agricultural systems to produce sufficient food for the world's growing billions was severely challenged. The food crisis of the early 1970s renewed interest in the specter raised by the Reverend Thomas Malthus who, over a century and a half ago, argued that the world's population growth would ultimately outstrip its ability to sustain its exponentially growing numbers. That argument became especially pertinent to the Third World, where the increase in the number of new mouths to feed each year grew nearly as rapidly as indigenous sources of food supplies. In the decade and a half ending in 1979, for example, the food production of developed nations increased by more than 40 percent, resulting in an increase in per capita food consumption of roughly 23 percent. In the developing world, by way of contrast, the average amount of food consumed per person increased by only 6 percent during this same period, despite the fact that total food production grew by 58 percent (Sewell, 1980: 177). The reason for the striking differences, of course, is population growth, and in particular the much higher growth rates of developing nations.

The particulars surrounding the food crisis of the 1970s, which saw world grain reserves, defined in terms of days of worldwide grain consumption, drop from over a hundred days in 1968 to only forty days in 1974 (Sewell, 1980: 178), included a series of weather-induced crop failures in China, the Soviet Union, and Africa; the boost in oil prices that added to the cost of fuel and fertilizer used in agricultural production; and the decision of the Soviet Union to enter world grain markets in an unprecedented way to make up for shortfalls previously absorbed by the Soviet economy. That decision set the stage for the purchase of huge amounts of American grain in 1972. The Soviets quietly set up contracts to purchase 28 million tons of grain—most from the United States—in the largest commercial transaction in history (Brown, 1974). Total Soviet purchases in 1972 and 1973 increased nearly fourfold over the previous two years, a fact which contributed significantly to the rise in demand for food supplies elsewhere in the world. Japan and Western Europe also added to the rising demand by substantially increasing their import requirements over previous years. The combined impact of all of these factors was a 300 percent increase in the price of grain in the face of what worldwide was only a 3 percent shortfall in grain production (Sewell, 1979: 60-61). The result was that "rising food prices added as much to . . . global inflation as did rising petroleum costs" (Sewell, 1979).

As food prices soared worldwide, famine struck in Africa, where starvation and death became daily occurrences in broad stretches of the Sahel, ranging from Ethiopia in the East to Mauritania in the West. The situation was repeated a decade later, when, in Ethiopia in particular, world consciousness was awakened by the tragic specter of tens of thousands suffering from malnutrition and dying of starvation at a time of unprecedented food surpluses worldwide.[17] Indeed, Africa is the one world region where Malthus's grim prediction that population growth would outstrip food production has proven accurate. During the 1970s African food production increased by only 1.8 percent annually, while population grew at the rate of 2.8 percent. Per capita food

---

[17]One observer concludes that "[t]he entire shortfall in Sahelian grain this year [1985] has been estimated at three to four million tons, while the world holds grain surplus stocks of nearly 190 million tons. . . . Financing the whole shortfall would cost perhaps $500 million, barely a footnote to U.S. export credits and food aid totaling $7 billion, and to comparable European programs now approaching $1 billion yearly" (Insel, 1985: 905).

production actually declined in thirty-five African countries during the decade and increased in only six ("Food 1983," 1983: 72).

In addition to those suffering transitory food insecurity, the Food and Agriculture Organization of the United Nations estimated in 1974, at the time of the World Food Conference in Rome, that 460 million people in the developing world suffered from malnutrition, a number that grew by 1980 to perhaps 730 million (Reutlinger, 1985: 7). These—about two-thirds of whom live in South Asia and another fifth in sub-Saharan Africa—are among the victims of chronic food insecurity, those who cannot buy food, even if it is available, because they do not have incomes sufficient to enable them to register effective demand for food. Interestingly, the victims of chronic food insecurity have probably declined as a proportion of the total population in developing countries, but their *numbers* have increased due to population growth (Reutlinger, 1985). Given the causes of widespread chronic food insecurity, addressing its deleterious effects requires more than simply increasing food production or imports.

The pattern of world trade in grain that evolved during the 1970s demonstrated the extent to which food consumption depends on wealth. North America became both the "breadbasket" and "feedbag" for virtually the entire world. By 1980 Latin America, Western Europe, Eastern Europe and the Soviet Union, Africa, and Asia had all become net importers of grain (Brown et al. 1985). Australia and New Zealand were alone among the non-North American world regions in being net exporters. The Soviet Union and several of the newly industrializing countries registered sharp increases in both wheat imports and coarse grains, while most First World countries increased only their imports of feed grains (Food and Agriculture Organization, 1982; Hathaway, 1983). In all cases, however, food imports permitted enhancement of both the quality and variety of the importing nations' dietary intake.

As the world came to depend on Canada and the United States to meet its food needs, American farmers enjoyed an unprecedented level of export-led prosperity. Furthermore, their future looked bright, as present and projected economic growth trends forecast vastly increased world demand for food between 1980 and the year 2000 as well as sharply higher real food prices. *The Global 2000 Report to the President* (1980), based on the best projections of the United States government, included such forecasts. *Global 2000* also warned that projected demand for food would require substantial increases in Third World agricultural productivity. And while ecologists worried that the projected demand would result in environmentally hazardous soil erosion and deforestation and outstrip the ability of improved farm technology to meet the increase in demand, for the American farmer the future was bright, not gloomy.

This situation changed radically in only a half decade. As described by an agricultural analyst in the U.S. Department of State, "the world of the American farmer lies in disarray, with mounting surpluses, heavy farm debt, and massive farm subsidy costs. Demand for U.S. farm products is weak, land values are down, and farm policy seems to be at a dead end'' (Avery, 1985). The reasons underlying ''the bad news for the American farmer,'' he continues, ''is that the global bad news is wrong. The world is not on the brink of famine or ecological disaster brought on by desperate food needs.'' The ecological and other ''constraints that were expected to limit food production during the 1980s and 1990s have been far less severe than almost anyone foresaw,'' while the productivity of farmers in developing nations has grown rapidly in response to ''improved technology and stronger incentives to use it'' (Avery, 1985). As noted earlier, additional near-term constraints that eroded the export competitiveness of American agricultural products included the rise in the value of the dollar, global economic recession, and increased competition from others.

Viewed from a long-term perspective, revised projections that forecast somewhat less growth in demand due to population and income growth, and somewhat greater world grain production than earlier thought possible due to advances in agricultural technology, suggest that the Malthusian pessimism of the recent past is no longer warranted. Debate persists among analysts about the shape of the economic and ecological demands that can be expected to exert pressure on the global food regime as the world moves toward the twenty-first century and what now appears to be the realistic goal of producing enough food for the generations who will live in that century.[18] But from the viewpoint of ensuring global food security,

> [t]he main issue is not the worldwide availability of food, but the capacity of nations, groups within nations, and individuals to obtain enough food for a healthy diet. . . . Ultimately it is not countries but individuals who suffer from a shortage of food—not because of fluctuations in national production but because of higher food prices, which they cannot afford, or because of inadequate arrangements for marketing food. Their diet will improve only when their general economic state does. (*World Development Report, 1984*, 1984)

The United States will continue to play an active role in efforts to realize global food security through its food aid and agricultural development assistance programs and through its domestically managed system of grain reserves that can be used to cushion year-to-year fluctuations in grain production. It will doubtless also play a critical role in meeting the increased demand for food that rising population and income will inevitably generate. From a near-term perspective, however, the important issue of foreign agricultural policy will be coping with increased foreign competition.[19]

---

[18]Avery (1985), Brown et al. (1985), and Insel (1985) provide a useful sample of some of the issues and ideas.

[19]Reutlinger (1985) reminds us that ''it is important to distinguish between foods that are internationally traded, whose prices and level of supply are largely determined by world prices and the exchange rate, and nontraded foods, whose prices are determined by domestic demand and production. The domestic supply of traded foods can be increased only by deliberate measures to

At the beginning of the 1980s, the United States, Canada, Australia, Argentina, and France were the only significant food exporters, and most of the rest of the world was a potential market. By mid-decade dramatic increases in productivity in the European Community, China, India, Brazil, Thailand, Pakistan, Indonesia, and elsewhere focused attention in these countries, not on local needs, but on export markets (Insel, 1985). Furthermore, technological advances and their diffusion have eroded, perhaps irrevocably, the comparative advantages in production once enjoyed by the U.S. agricultural industry. Some also wonder whether the proclivity of the United States to use the food as an instrument of foreign policy may not have contributed to lost markets.

The most celebrated effort of the United States to brandish the "food weapon" occurred in 1980, when the Carter administration sought—unsuccessfully—to punish the Soviet Union for its 1979 invasion of Afghanistan by embargoing grain sales to the Soviet Union (above the amounts agreed to in the 1975 grain agreement). Although the United States had used its position as a primary food supplier to realize foreign policy objectives in the past, the Soviet grain embargo was the first American attempt to use its food power on such a massive scale and for so blatantly political an objective.

The failure of the American experiment can be attributed to many factors (Paarlberg, 1980). Domestic political considerations in the United States and the inappropriateness of the change in Soviet behavior sought by the United States were among them. The critical factor, however, was "leakage" in the embargo caused by the willingness and ability of others to make up the difference in Soviet food imports caused by the American action. Argentina in particular greatly expanded its exports to the Soviet Union, thus largely negating the intended effects of the American embargo. The result should have been anticipated; the grain embargo predictably failed because others were willing and able to divert production of a supply-elastic resource to the highest bidder. In the meantime, critics argued, the image of the United States as a reliable trade partner had been tarnished, causing buyers to go elsewhere in search of reliable grain suppliers.[20]

Public Law 480, the "Food for Peace" program, is a more ubiquitous and time-worn mechanism whereby the United States brings agri-power to bear

---

increase imports or restrict exports. The supply of nontraded foods can be increased only by increasing domestic production." Public policies relating to traded and nontraded foods and their effects on different groups within society therefore differ.

[20]This issue was raised again in 1985 when the Reagan administration embargoed trade with Nicaragua. Some farm spokesmen expressed fear that economic sanctions directed against the Sandinista government would again cause distrust among U.S. trade partners in Europe and Asia, and particularly the Soviet Union. Agriculture Secretary John R. Block responded, saying "This action will not make the United States an unreliable supplier of farm products, but it will tell the world that our sanctions will be effective, and that means they will be across the board." The phrase "across the board" referred to President Reagan's pledge when he lifted the Soviet grain embargo not to single out agriculture for any future embargo action. The pledge was based on the belief that farmers and agricultural commodities bore the brunt of United States efforts to retaliate against the Soviet Union.

on its foreign policy objectives while simultaneously meeting domestic needs. As noted in chapter five, PL 480 is the procedure used by the United States to channel credit sales of U.S.-government owned agricultural surpluses to other countries. The political character of the program is underscored by the fact that priority is given to nations considered friendly to the United States,[21] even while its primary objective is to generate overseas markets for U.S. grain (Insel, 1985). Analysts dispute whether, in creating dependence on imported grain, Food for Peace shipments may not in the long-run be detrimental to developing countries by eroding the incentives to develop their own agricultural capabilities. Beyond question is that the surplus-disposal program ensures American farmers of a "market" for their products and it operates as a subsidy to the American agribusiness. In this way PL 480 serves the interests of the domestic agricultural industry as well as the nation's foreign economic and security policy.

Like the United States, the European Community uses "food aid" to dispose of surplus commodities produced under the protective umbrella of its Common Agricultural Policy; and both have used export subsidies to capture overseas markets and to protect domestic producers. As noted earlier, many of the newcomers to the agricultural export business are motivated less by domestic interests and more by foreign economic objectives. Among those objectives is export growth so as to expand foreign exchange earnings and debt-servicing capacity. Ironically, the economic well-being of the United States and other First World nations has become tied to Third World nations' success in realizing that objective, even while Third World exports increasingly challenge First World preeminence in the global political economy.

World Debt and the Challenge of Interdependence

OPEC's success in cartelizing the global oil regime during the 1970s was important in galvanizing the non-oil-producing developing nations into the belief that "commodity power" would enable them to "force" the North into replacing the Liberal International Economic Order with a new order more amenable to their interests and objectives. Ironically, however, the two oil shocks of the 1970s created an environment in which many Third World nations deemed it prudent to borrow heavily from abroad, while they simultaneously eroded the economic bases on which repayment of those loans depended. The result was a "debt crisis" that first erupted in 1982 and that continued to bubble thereafter, surfacing from time to time to engage the attention of top-level policy makers. The United States pursued an arm's-length, if not always hands-off, strategy toward the debt problem when it first assumed crisis proportions; later, in apparent recognition of its own intimate stake in the issues

---

[21]The political character of the Food for Peace program is underscored by the fact that of the sub-Saharan African nations most vulnerable to the drought and famine of 1984–1985, only the Sudan and Zaire were included on the list of congressionally approved PL 480 beneficiaries (Insel, 1985).

and outcomes, it pursued a more active role in devising strategies aimed at a long-term resolution of the problem.

As it first emerged in the early 1980s, the debt crisis extended to a broad group of countries, ranging from Poland in Eastern Europe to Brazil in Latin America, from the Philippines in the Far East to Nigeria in West Africa. It grew out of a combination of heavy private and public borrowing from private and public sources during the 1970s that led to an accumulated debt estimated to have been $700 billion by 1982 and more than $800 billion two years later. Many debtor nations found that they needed to borrow more money not to finance new projects but simply to stay even. That is, they needed new loans to meet their debt service obligations (interest and principal payments) on previous loans. Some with the largest debts—including Poland and especially the newly industrializing countries of Mexico, Argentina, and Brazil—required special treatment to keep them from going into default when they announced they did not have the cash necessary to pay their creditors. Eventually attention focused principally on Third World debtor nations, especially those in Latin America. Although the debt obligations of many Eastern European nations remained perilously high, their improved trade status with the West eased concern about their ability to meet their debt obligations.[22]

The foreign debt accumulation of the 1970s was part of a process that saw private loans and investments and official nonconcessional loans become more important than public foreign aid for all but the poorest countries. During the 1960s official development assistance represented about 60 percent of the total capital flows to developing nations, but by 1982 this proportion had been cut to 28 percent (Burki, 1983: 17; also Lewis and Kallab, 1983: 275, 282). Among the many results was a greater sensitivity to the interdependence of the North and the South as "the financial solvency of a great number of developing and some developed countries became a major preoccupation of the commercial banks and other developed country investors" (Burki, 1983). Governments in turn became concerned since many of the world's major private banks had significant exposure in these countries.

> Default by the debtor nations thus could have had several serious consequences for the international monetary system: a collapse of confidence in the international banking system, possible illiquidity or insolvency of the banks, dangerous disruption of the financial markets and—in a worst-case scenario—world recession or depression. Central bankers, finance ministries, and heads of government were determined to prevent any such threat to the international financial system and so came to the aid of the debtor nations and the banks. The United States played an important leadership role in mobilizing international management, and in the process, the central banks and the IMF assumed a significant role in debt management. (Spero, 1985: 79)

[22]The hard currency debt of Eastern Europe and the Soviet Union to Western banks stood at $86.3 billion in 1980 and was projected to range between $148 billion and $168 billion by 1985 (Congressional Quarterly, 1984: 121).

The first oil shock gave impetus to the "privatization" of Third World capital flows. As dollars flowed from oil consumers in the West to oil producers in the Middle East and elsewhere, the latter, unable to invest all of their newfound wealth at home, "recycled" their petrodollars by making investments in the West. In the process the funds available to private banks for lending to others increased substantially, enabling them to expand their lending outlets worldwide.

Many of the non-oil-exporting developing nations became the willing consumers of the private banks' investment funds. The fourfold rise in oil prices effected by the OPEC cartel hit these nations particularly hard. Thus to pay for the greater cost of imported oil along with their other imports, they could either tighten their belts at home so as to curb their economic growth or borrow from abroad so as to sustain that growth and to pay for needed imports simultaneously. Many chose the latter.[23] Private banks for their part were willing lenders, since "sovereign risk"—the risk that governments might default—was believed to be virtually nonexistent (see Box. 7.3).

Whether developing nations always spent their borrowed money wisely can be questioned. Argentina, for example, is reported to have spent between 1978 and 1982 an estimated $6 billion on sophisticated military equipment, which it used against Britain during the Malvinas, or Falkland Islands, war (*Washington Post*, September 13, 1982: A18). Others have alleged that the capital flight from debtor nations was in many instances as great or greater than the amount of new loans made to them, with much of the money flowing from unscrupulous political leaders into private accounts in the very banks extending the loans to the governments in the first place (Henry, 1986; Ayittey, 1986). Whether caused by corrupt officials (the Marcoses' wealth when they left the Philippines in 1986 for refuge in the United States was estimated to be $10 billion) or middle class entrepreneurs seeking a safe haven for their profits, the outflow of money reduces that available for the investments that create new jobs and new wealth.

At the same time that developing nations' debt grew substantially during the 1970s, however, so did the resources needed to service it. Consequently, the burden of the growing debt—whether measured by the ratio of the debt to exports or by the ratio of debt service payments to export earnings—was essentially the same in 1980 as it was in 1970 (*World Development Report, 1983*, 1983).

But the picture changed sharply after 1980. The drop in commodity prices associated with the worldwide recession caused the ratio of Third World debts to exports to rise markedly between 1980 and 1982. Economic growth slowed as the prices of the commodities needed to pay for the debt dropped and the money needed to pay off the loans simply failed to materialize. The apprecia-

---

[23]Many actually preferred to borrow from private banks rather than other governments or multilateral agencies, because the banks generally placed fewer restrictions on the use of the borrowed money than did the public sources.

BOX 7.3 Sovereign Risk and Its Implications for International Lending

---

When a government borrows from abroad or guarantees a loan, the legal status of the contract is unlike that between two private companies. It is much harder to enforce, since a sovereign borrower may reject a claim against it within its own territory. The problems arising from this limited enforceability are complicated by the fact that governments have considerable discretion over policy choices that affect their own ability to fulfill a contract. Many of these policies—shifts in monetary policy, limits on exchange remittances, changes in competition policy, changes in taxes—could not be deemed a breach of contract, even though their effect might be to negate the substance of the loan.

The ability of governments to influence economic outcomes, coupled with a lender's limited scope for imposing legal sanctions, means that contracts between developing countries and the private market have little economic value unless both parties feel it is in their long-term interest to honor their obligations. This means that the (present discounted) economic value to a borrower of meeting its obligations must be equal to or greater than the present value of not meeting them. In short, the countries that are most likely to service their debts are those that would suffer most if they did not do so.

To a borrower, the cost of possible sanctions depends on the importance of its future trade and finance with the lender (and its sponsoring government). Countries that are heavily involved in international trade depend on a continual flow of finance, the use of transport facilities, smooth customs clearance, and so on. They are therefore very open to sequestration orders and to a cutoff of trade credits. Their past success has been made possible by the network of trade and finance. They are unlikely to choose to jeopardize the chances of future success by excluding themselves from that network.

The major international banks have a comparative advantage in dealing with sovereign risk because they are closely involved in a number of facets of a developing country's international business. This helps explain the growth in importance of banking intermediation during the 1970s.

SOURCE: *World Development Report, 1985*, 1985: 92.

tion of the dollar in foreign exchange markets added to the debt burden, since many of the loans held by developing nations were denominated in dollars. The ratio of debt service obligations to export earnings also rose sharply, moving from 13.6 percent in 1980 to 20.7 percent in 1982, as a consequence of rising interest rates (*World Development Report, 1983*, 1983: 21). The magnitude of the debt also grew to staggering proportions, increasing from $474 billion, or 113 percent of exports in 1980, to $664 billion, or 144 percent of exports in 1983 (for non-oil-producing countries). For countries in the Western Hemisphere, the ratio of debt to exports jumped from 178 percent in 1980 to 243 percent in 1983 (International Monetary Fund, 1983: 201).

The linkage between interest rates and Third World debts illustrates clearly how interdependent the North and South had become. The banks lending to developing nations began to make variable-rate loans (that is, loans whose interest rates rise and fall with market conditions) so as to ensure their own profitability in a period of uncertainty. The Western industrialized nations at the same time adopted strict monetarist policies as a way of coping with their persistent inflation. Thus, as interest rates climbed in the West, the developing nations found that their external debt obligations mounted accordingly. In Brazil, for example, each percentage point increase in interest rates is estimated to have cost the country an additional $700 million annually (*New York Times,* April 12, 1984: A27).

Not all of the debtor nations were hit equally hard by the difficulties described above, but many found themselves severely strained, as indicated by the fact that in 1983 more than twenty debtor nations negotiated to *reschedule* more than $51 billion in debts, that is, to stretch out the original repayment schedules so as to ease the immediate debt burden. Both the number of debtors and the dollars involved far surpassed anything witnessed in the previous decade. Yet in 1985, over $116 billion in debt held by some two dozen debtor nations had to be rescheduled (*World Development Report, 1985,* 1985: 28).

The specific event that triggered the debt crisis was the threat in August 1982 that Mexico would default on its loans. The United States was instrumental in averting the disaster, and it urged at that time that the International Monetary Fund (IMF) assume a leadership role in securing debt relief for many Third World countries. It has done so not only by providing access to IMF resources but also by inducing private lenders to make even more credit available to their debtors. But the IMF's aid comes with strict conditions that the organization monitors to ensure the recipient countries' compliance. When the IMF makes a loan to a country it imposes programs designed to curb inflation, limit imports, restrict public spending, expose protected industries, and the like. At the same time the loan recipient is urged to increase its exports. The fact that the "conditionality" of the IMF's aid adds so clearly to the strains on debtor nations' political and social fabric has led some commentators to ask whether the IMF's policies might not be self-defeating. As one caustically remarked, "The I.M.F. is probably the most effective neocolonialist instrument the modern world has yet devised" (Krauthammer, 1983).

Economic austerity caused by demands for drastic economic reforms were blamed for the overthrow of the U.S.-supported Sudanese government of President Jaafar Nimeri in 1985. "The aid from Western donors was not flowing," lamented Sudan's ambassador to Washington shortly before the military coup that ousted Nimeri. "The Sudan was down to rationing gasoline to two liters a week trying to meet IMF demands," he continued. "Do you pay the IMF back or buy gas for your country? Where do we get the money from unless we suspend all imports into the country?"

The prospect of domestic turmoil existed elsewhere, as the debt and related financial issues inflamed domestic political conflict in many of the most heavily indebted nations, including Brazil, Argentina, Mexico, Chile, and Nigeria, among others. Fidel Castro sought to capitalize on the situation and to assume a leadership role among the nations of the crisis-ridden Western hemisphere in their confrontation with U.S. banks over their $360 billion debt. Espousing a view widely shared in Latin America—that the huge debt is "unpayable" anyway—Castro repeatedly urged that the debt simply be "erased." He also warned in a June 1985 speech that the alternative to a political solution that would somehow cancel the debt was "revolutionary social explosions." In a similar vein, Peru's new president, Alan Garcia, announced during his inauguration speech in the summer of 1985 that he would limit debt repayments to 10 percent of Peru's export earnings, thereby serving notice of his intention to keep from diverting all of Peru's resources to debt servicing. Later in the year he declared in a dramatic speech before the United Nations General Assembly that "It is either debt or democracy. . . . We believe the objective must be the unity of debtor countries and a radical change of the current situation." Brazilian President José Sarney joined the growing chorus of radical voices in announcing before the General Assembly that "Brazil won't pay its debt with unemployment or hunger."

It was in this emotionally charged atmosphere that the United States assumed a leadership role in seeking to devise a long-term solution to the debt issue. In the fall of 1985 Secretary of the Treasury James A. Baker unveiled a $29 billion plan that would use resources from both the World Bank and the private sector in a new effort to stimulate Third World economic growth. According to the Baker plan, new loans would still be made only if debtor nations undertook domestic economic reforms. The initiative was significant nonetheless. "For the first time the [Reagan] Administration officially recognized that the debt crisis is here to stay, and that austerity has to give way to growth" (Bogdanowicz-Bindert, 1985/1986).

The Baker initiative also signaled that leadership in dealing with the debt crisis would shift toward the World Bank and away from the IMF. Implicit, perhaps, was a recognition that the export-led adjustment scenario to resolution of the debt problem that previously motivated the Reagan administration was no longer viable. According to this view, the revival of economic growth in the industrialized nations, with the United States as the locomotive pulling the rest of the Northern train forward, will revive the demand (and hence the price) for the South's commodities and other exports, thus enabling Third World nations to service their debts and return to economic growth.

Because of the importance of Third World markets to many Northern producers, some economists questioned whether it is possible to sustain economic growth in the long run by using a "North first, South later" strategy. In 1985, for example, 39 percent of the United States' exports went to developing nations. Reduced economic growth in Third World nations combined with IMF-led efforts to reduce imports thus adversely affect Northern producers and may brake further economic output. The persistence of a strong dollar in international exchange markets also inhibited the export of American products by reducing their competitiveness. The paradox of reduced competitiveness is that it is the recipe for neomercantilist protectionism, as American workers seek to protect their jobs from the threat posed by less expensive foreign products. Because the revival of sustained growth among the developing nations presupposes improved access to Northern markets made possible by a reduction in tariff and nontariff barriers to Southern exports, the strength of the dollar may, ironically, contribute to a choking off of Third World economic revival that the American locomotive is supposed to promote.

In the months following the Baker initiative the decline of the dollar in foreign exchange markets and of interest rates in the United States eased the burden on some debtor nations. For the oil-producing nations, however, of which Mexico, Venezuela, and Nigeria were among the most heavily in debt, it sharply reduced the revenues necessary to repay previous loans.[24] Elsewhere cheap oil removed the incentive to explore for more oil or to develop alternative energy technologies. By stimulating economic growth, it also encouraged the use of more oil which, in the case of the United States, led to an increase in the volume of oil imported from abroad, thereby threatening renewed dependence on foreign sources of energy. Some wondered whether the stage was not being set for the onset of another OPEC decade in the 1990s, one which, like the first, might stimulate another debt crisis. As James R. Schlesinger, secretary of energy in the Carter administration, mused in early 1986, ''We have OPEC just where they want us.''[25]

THE SECOND WORLD: THE SOVIET UNION AND EASTERN EUROPE

During World War II Western planners anticipated the participation of the Soviet Union in the postwar international economic system, just as they originally anticipated Soviet cooperation in maintaining the postwar political order. Trade between Eastern and Western Europe had been extensive before the war, and even though economic ties between the Soviet Union and the West had not been extensive, the war itself, through American Lend Lease assistance, contributed to closer links. Furthermore, the Soviet Union had participated in the Bretton Woods negotiations, which ultimately led to creation of the IMF and the World Bank.

---

[24]At $20 per barrel, OPEC's revenues would slip to only $100 billion, compared to the $130 billion generated in 1985 and $280 billion in 1980 (Morse, 1986). At $10 per barrel, roughly the price of oil on the spot market in the spring of 1986, OPEC's revenues would dip to only $50 billion. Venezuela and Nigeria are both members of OPEC, and while Mexico is not, the price of its oil, and hence the impact on its revenues, generally tracks OPEC's experience.

[25]Growing United States dependence on foreign sources of oil was one of the stimulants to the OPEC decade, just as reduction of that dependence through conservation and other measures contributed to its demise. See Kegley and Wittkopf (1985b) for a discussion of forces surrounding the rise and demise of the OPEC decade, and Morse (1986) for a discussion of the politics of oil resulting from the rapid fall in world oil prices in the mid-1980s.

Shortly after the war, however, the expectation of establishing close economic ties between East and West began to wane. The critical year was 1947, when President Truman effectively committed the United States to an anticommunist foreign policy strategy. In June 1947 Secretary of State George Marshall outlined an American commitment to aid in the economic recovery of Europe. In devising the European Recovery Program, popularly known as the Marshall Plan, which was put in place the following year, American policy makers considered the possibility that the Soviet Union itself might participate in the recovery program (see Jones, 1964). Whether the Soviets were ever serious contenders for Marshall Plan assistance can be doubted, however, for the program was formulated in such a way that the Soviet Union would have had to divulge information about its internal conditions and to permit Western involvement in its reconstruction efforts. Moreover, much of the debate in Congress over the plan was framed in terms of "stopping the onslaught of communism" (Berkowitz, Bock, and Fuccillo, 1977). That was certainly not the kind of rhetoric which would endear the recovery program to Soviet policy makers. In any event, the Soviet Union rejected the offer of American aid and also refused to permit Poland and Czechoslovakia, both of which had been offered Marshall Plan assistance, to accept it (Spero, 1985). Thereafter East and West developed essentially their own "regional" economic systems from which the other was excluded. Bipolarity contributed to the mutually perceived necessity of isolation, and economic warfare joined political hostility to create the Cold War.

The economic isolation of East from West continued for a decade or more. Some trade between the United States and the Soviet Union did occur during the mid-1960s, but not until the late 1960s and early 1970s did the Soviets and the Americans begin to shift their views about commercial ties with "the other side." (Communist countries still remain largely outside the international monetary system described above.) As shown earlier in Figure 7.2, American trade with communist countries is still insignificant compared to trade with other parts of the world. Yet it grew appreciably during the 1970s, as shown in Figure 7.6, with American agricultural exports accounting for a significant share of this growth.

The shift in American-communist trade relations was both a symptom of and a spur to détente. Trade became part of a series of concrete agreements on a range of issues that would contribute to what Kissinger described as a "vested interest in mutual restraint" on the part of the superpowers. The contrast with peak years of the Cold War is striking. Going back even before 1951, when Congress stripped communist countries of most-favored-nation tariff treatment, the United States evolved over the Cold War period numerous legislative and administrative regulations designed to restrict communist nations' access to American exports, aid, and commercial credits. The United States was particularly sensitive about trade in so-called strategic goods, items that might bolster Soviet military capabilities and thus threaten Western security. Accordingly, the United States sought to embargo the sale of strategic

FIGURE 7.6   United States Trade with the Soviet Union and Eastern Europe, 1971–1985 (billions of dollars)

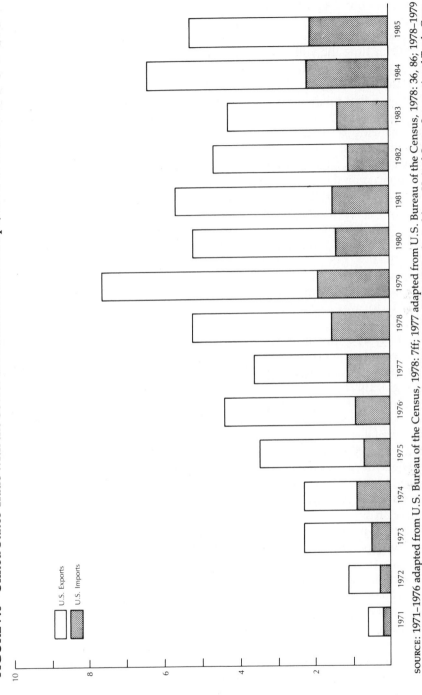

SOURCE: 1971–1976 adapted from U.S. Bureau of the Census, 1978: 7ff; 1977 adapted from U.S. Bureau of the Census, 1978: 36, 86; 1978–1979 adapted from United States International Trade Commission, 1981: 11, 21; 1980–1982 adapted from United States International Trade Commission, 1983: 8, 20; 1983–1984 adapted from United States International Trade Commission, 1985: 15, 25; 1985 adapted from U.S. Bureau of the Census, 1985: Tables 5 and 8.

goods to the Soviet Union and its allies, and it sponsored the Coordinating Committee (Cocom) as a mechanism for inducing its own allies to join in the development of a common policy on limiting exports to communist countries.

Over time the willingness of other industrialized nations to restrict trade with communist countries waned, with the result that they captured the major share of communist trade with the West.[26] Therefore the commercial advantages that might accrue from greater trade between the United States and the Soviet Union and its allies were added to the overtly political reasons for normalizing relations. But the principal motive, from the viewpoint of the United States, remained political. The "vested interest in mutual restraint" envisioned by Kissinger would be accomplished by giving the Soviets "a stake in international equilibrium." Expanded commercial intercourse with the Soviet Union would thus become a key element in Kissinger's *linkage strategy* for the containment of Soviet influence and expansionism.

From the Soviets' point of view, two interrelated political factors and a third, principally economic one contributed to their desire for increased commercial ties. The first was the growing tension between the Soviet Union and China. That conflict placed a premium on the Soviets establishing relatively stable relations with the West, a stability that trade might facilitate. The second factor was a growing Soviet perception, even without Soviet rivalry with China, of the desirability of reducing tensions with the United States, presumably as a way of decreasing the threat of war and the cost of armaments. The economic motive was based on the Soviet desire "as a superpower . . . to fly its flag in the entire world's economy, not merely that of its own bloc" (Yergin, 1977).

To fly its flag the Soviet Union had to move from the "extensive" mode of economic development ("growth based upon increases in the labor force and the capital stock") to an "intensive" mode ("growth resulting from improved technology leading to higher productivity") (Yergin, 1977). Accordingly, the Soviets' desire for increased commercial ties between East and West was motivated by a third concern, one primarily economic. Access to Western technology and the credits necessary to buy it were sought as means to rejuvenate the sluggish Soviet economy, and grain imports were necessary to supplement shortfalls in Soviet agricultural production.

Perhaps the high point of détente was achieved at the 1972 Moscow summit when the two Cold War antagonists initialed the first Strategic Arms Limitation Talks (SALT) agreement. SALT was certainly the cornerstone of détente, but expanded East-West trade was part of the mortar. A joint commercial commission was established at the summit, whose purpose was to pave the way for the granting of most-favored-nation status to the Soviet Union and the extension of U.S. government-backed credits to the Soviet regime.

The Nixon administration also expressed interest in selling greater quantities of American grain to the Soviet Union. During the Moscow summit over-

---

[26]In 1976, for example, other Western industrialized nations captured 29 percent of communist trade, while the U.S. share was only 2.5 percent (U.S. Department of Commerce, 1978: v).

tures were made to a seemingly unresponsive Soviet leadership suggesting that grain sales to the Soviet Union would have a beneficial impact on American public opinion, symbolizing to the American public the tangible rewards of the waning of the Cold War and the advent of détente (Kissinger, 1979). Shortly thereafter the American government negotiated an agreement providing the Soviet Union with $750 million in credits with which to buy American agricultural products.

Unknown to the administration at the time, the Soviet Union was facing a catastrophic crop failure. The Soviets desperately needed American grain. Hence they quietly set about putting together a series of contracts to purchase American grain, which ultimately contributed to a surge in world grain prices. The United States learned firsthand the difference between the market economies of the First World, where prices play an important role in encouraging production and regulating the distribution of goods and services, and the command economies of the Second World, where economic decisions regarding production and distribution are made by the government. As Kissinger notes in his memoirs:

> Each of our grain companies, trying to steal a march on its competitors, sold the largest amount possible and kept its sale utterly secret, even from the US government. Not for several weeks did we realize that the Soviets had, by a series of separate transactions, bought up nearly one billion dollar's worth of grain in one year—nearly our entire stored surplus. And we had subsidized the deals at a time when the Soviet Union quite literally had no other choice than to buy our grain at market prices or face mass starvation. . . . (Kissinger, 1979: 1270)

Thus, what was to have produced a positive impact on American public opinion turned into a blunder, casting a shadow over the entire question of expanded East-West trade. "At first the sale was hailed as a political masterstroke," recalls Kissinger. "It led to the usual maneuvering as to who should get credit. . . . Soon, however, no one wanted any credit; the grain sale rapidly became a political scandal; Nixon was accused of selling at bargain rates to our adversaries and driving up the price to American consumers" (Kissinger, 1979). Eventually, in 1975, an agreement providing for more orderly entry of the Soviet Union into the American grain market was negotiated, but the political damage wrought by "The Great American Grain Robbery" was substantial.

Even more damaging was the fate of most-favored-nation status and increased credits for the Soviet Union. Most-favored-nation treatment was to have been granted by the Trade Act of 1974, which provides most-favored-nation status for the Soviet Union and other communist countries in fulfillment of the 1972 Trade Agreement between the United States and the Soviet Union. But a congressional amendment (known as the Jackson-Vanik amendment) made that status contingent upon liberalization of communist policies toward Jewish emigration. Evidence suggests that the Soviet Union did tacitly agree to permit freer emigration of Soviet Jews, but in January 1975 it rejected those conditions, labeling them a violation of the 1972 Trade Agreement, which had called for an unconditional elimination of discriminatory trade restrictions and the principle of noninterference in domestic affairs. Hungary and Romania were eventually granted most-favored-nation status, subject to annual review by Congress of each's human rights policies.[27] Relations with Romania in particular were often strained. Under pressure from Congress, the Reagan administration in 1985 threatened that Romania might lose its special status unless its treatment of various religious and ethnic groups improved.

Denial of most-favored-nation status was a slap in the Soviet face, for it "symbolized [the Soviet Union's] exclusion from the international economic system, whereas the restoration of most favored nation status symbolized the end of Western discrimination" (Spero, 1985). The insult was aggravated when the United States played the "China card" and granted the People's Republic of China, the Soviet Union's principal communist rival, most-favored-nation status in early 1980.

More significant than symbolic was the issue of American-backed credits. Because Soviet and Eastern European currencies are not convertible (that is, they are subject to government controls and therefore are not easily exchanged for Western currencies), and because the exports from which they earn hard (Western) currencies have been relatively limited, the command economies of the Second World generally have lacked the foreign exchange necessary to buy the goods from the West that they desire. During the 1970s that situation changed as a consequence of heavy borrowing from the West. Year by year, the debt mounted; by 1983 it exceeded $64 billion (Spero, 1985: 366), up from only a few billion dollars a decade or so earlier. The debt itself created the need for greatly increased export earnings by the Eastern nations or the extension of government-backed credits by the West, particularly the United States.

The issue of American credits to the Soviet Union evolved in a manner similar to that of MFN status. In late 1974 Congress passed the Stevenson amendment to the U.S. Export-Import Bank authorization bill, effectively placing a ceiling on credits authorized over the next four years that was less than the Soviets had received in the previous two. Congressional action appears to have been motivated by a desire to assert legislative control over the activities of the Export-Import Bank as well as concern growing out of the 1972 grain deal and the abuses unveiled by the Watergate scandal. But in retrospect "it . . . appears that the Stevenson Amendment was the decisive reason that the Soviets refused to put the trade agreement into effect." Credits were necessary if trade was to expand substantially. Instead, "[i]t looked very much as

---

[27]The United States also granted Poland and Yugoslavia most-favored-nation status. In these cases, however, the grants were made before passage of the 1974 Trade Act and are therefore not subject to annual review by Congress before the annual extension of the status by the president. In the case of Hungary and Poland, the congressional review procedures under the Jackson-Vanik amendment embodied a "one-house veto" provision which may fall under the legislative veto provisions (discussed in chapter twelve) ruled unconstitutional by the Supreme Court in 1983.

though the Congress were putting a ceiling over trade rather than a floor under it" (Yergin, 1977).

Upon assuming office the Carter administration committed itself to the policy of détente and apparently to the principle of normalizing East-West commercial relations. But partly because of congressional constraints, United States trade with the Soviet Union and Eastern Europe failed during the latter half of the 1970s to keep pace with earlier expectations.

Furthermore, the Carter administration's worldwide campaign on behalf of human rights often led to sharp attacks on the Soviet Union. Eventually trade ties were used as leverage in support of that campaign. In 1978, as a reprisal for the trials of Soviet human rights dissidents, Carter imposed new controls on the sale of oil technology to the Soviet Union, and he canceled the sale of a computer to the Soviet news agency *Tass* that was to have been used at the 1980 Summer Olympics in Moscow. Additional punitive measures were instituted following the Soviet military intervention in Afghanistan in late 1979, including a partial grain embargo and further restrictions on other American exports.

As noted earlier, the grain embargo did not impose the kinds of burdens on the Soviet Union that the Carter administration had envisioned when it announced its intention to punish the Soviet Union for its military occupation of Afghanistan. Nevertheless, the effect on trade between the United States and the Soviet Union was devastating. American exports to the Soviet Union in 1980 were less than half the 1979 level of $3.6 billion and far short of what earlier had been anticipated for the year. The commercial ties that a decade earlier had been both a spur to détente and a reflection of it thus became the victim as well as the instrument of sharply increased Soviet-American rivalry. Détente had given way to renewed superpower hostility.

The Reagan administration's deep-seated hostility toward the Soviet Union reinforced the rupture of East-West commercial ties caused by Afghanistan. "Reagan reversed a policy—begun in 1963 with President Kennedy's grain deal with the Soviet Union and fully realized in the era of détente—that used trade as an inducement to moderate Soviet behavior, encourage domestic reform, and thereby improve overall East-West relations. The new U.S. policy was to use trade not as a carrot but as a stick . . . " (Spero, 1985). The restrictions that the United States had earlier placed on the export of energy technology to the Soviet Union were stiffened in the early Reagan presidency as the United States sought, first, to punish the Soviets for their presumed complicity in the imposition of martial law in Poland, and, second, to win cancellation of the planned Soviet-Western European pipeline that would eventually bring natural gas from Soviet Siberia to markets in Western Europe.[28]

---

[28]Elsewhere, the Reagan administration's policies toward Nicaragua illustrated the lengths to which it was willing to go to bring economic pressure on a pro-Marxist regime.

In January 1981, the United States terminated its bilateral aid program, including "Food for Peace" shipments and suspended a $10 million wheat sale. Later that year, the United States blocked a $30 million credit from the Interamerican Development Bank for a fish-

In the important case of grain exports, however, domestic political considerations outweighed the administration's ideological predispositions. Making
good on an earlier campaign promise, one of Reagan's first foreign policy decisions was to lift Carter's ban on grain sales to the Soviet Union. Eventually,
in 1983, Washington and Moscow concluded a new long-term grain sales
agreement. Interestingly, the accord—the first major bilateral pact negotiated
since the Soviet invasion of Afghanistan—contained language that effectively
pledged the United States not to interrupt future grain shipments in pursuit
of its self-defined foreign or national security goals. A week after the agreement was signed, the Soviet Union shot down a Korean civilian airliner, killing all of its 269 passengers. Despite clamors by some members of Congress to
abrogate the new grain agreement in retaliation, it was permitted to stand.
Domestic politics again reigned supreme.

As in earlier periods, the Reagan administration found that U.S. allies did
not always share its views on how to deal with the Soviet Union in the economic sphere. The pipeline issue in particular created a serious split in the Atlantic Alliance.

Serious intra-NATO fissures appeared when the United States tried not
only to persuade other Western nations to embargo the sale of energy technology to the Soviet Union but also to require foreign subsidiaries of United
States-based multinational corporations to conform to the dictates of American policy. Supporters of a hardline stance cited Lenin's prophecy that the
capitalists would gladly sell the rope with which they would be hung—and
contended that the Siberian pipeline was just such a rope, for it provided
high-technology equipment to the Soviet "military machine." Many European allies of the United States simply did not share that view. Nor did they
share with the United States the belief that completion of the trans-Siberian
pipeline would make Western Europe unduly dependent on Soviet sources of
energy. What they did was to point to the inconsistency in American policy
that attempted to pressure the Western Europeans into not selling the Soviets
energy technology at the same time that the United States sold them grain.

Eventually a face-saving measure was devised that enabled the United
States to back away from an unwinnable issue without conceding it had lost.
The fracas illustrated once more, however, that the United States and its allies
approach the issue of commercial ties with the Second World quite differently.
The Reagan administration now faced the resistance the Carter administration
encountered when it sought to resuscitate economic leverage against the So-

---

eries project. In May 1983, the U.S. import quota for Nicaraguan sugar was cut 90 percent
and subsequently terminated in May 1985 when a total bilateral trade embargo was imposed. (Hufbauer and Schott, 1985: 732)

The sanctions were not successful in their dual attempt to stem support for guerrilla forces in El
Salvador and to destabilize the Sandinista government for two reasons. First, they were not applied quickly and forcefully enough; second, "the United States again discovered that international support for sanctions is hard to come by—the world has many white knights willing and
able to perform economic and political rescues" (Hufbauer and Schott, 1985).

viet Union following its invasion of Afghanistan. Even during the height of the Cold War, the United States, while able to achieve a measure of agreement with its allies on limiting trade with the East, was never able to elicit from them comparable enthusiasm for the use of economic instruments to prosecute the Cold War. Allied differences with Washington stem from European domestic political considerations, from the geographic proximity of Western Europe to the Soviet Union and its Eastern European allies, and from the fact that to Western Europe (and Japan) communist countries are generally more important trade partners than they are to the United States (see Spero, 1985, for an elaboration). Those facts alone ensure that East-West commercial interactions face an uncertain future.

From the point of view of the superpowers themselves, the record of the past demonstrates how each is driven by the complex demands of domestic politics, the requirements of intraalliance cohesion, and the dual compulsion of competition and cooperation with the other. As each seeks to balance and manage these demands, any one may appear predominant at any particular time. In the long run, however, neither the dictates of consumerism in Kiev nor the perquisites of politics in Peoria will be permitted to determine the course of superpower relations. Instead, as the deterioration of superpower relations during the Reagan years illustrates, East-West economic collaboration and political-military confrontation are incompatible—the latter must recede before the former can advance. Unless the United States and the Soviet Union are able to resolve the political and military issues that divide them, commercial relations between them will remain relatively inconsequential.

At the same time that the momentum of expanding trade between the United States and the Second World stalled following Afghanistan, U.S. trade with the People's Republic of China increased sharply, as illustrated in Figure 7.7. The Reagan administration for essentially political purposes actively sought to promote the increase as a counterpoint to the Soviet Union and as part of the process of normalizing Sino-American relations. In each year from 1980 through 1985, trade turnover with China approximated or surpassed trade turnover with the Soviet Union and Eastern Europe combined. If agreements concluded in the early 1980s are carried forward, China is destined to remain perhaps the most important U.S. trade partner among the communist countries.

A STATUS QUO POWER IN A WORLD OF CHANGE

The changing nature of the international political economy combines with the evolving structural characteristics of the international political system described in chapter six to underscore how radically different the world of the 1980s is from the world in which the United States first emerged a superpower. Throughout those decades of evolutionary change, the United States has shown itself capable of adapting to new situations and new circumstances, although often the adaptations have come neither rapidly nor with

FIGURE 7.7   United States Trade with the People's Republic of China, 1978–1985 (billions of dollars)

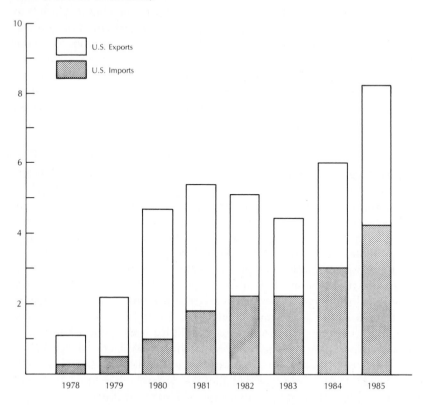

SOURCE: 1978–1979 adapted from United States International Trade Commission, 1981: 11, 21; 1980–1982 adapted from United States International Trade Commission, 1983: 8, 20; 1983–1984 adapted from United States International Trade Commission, 1985: 15, 25; 1985 adapted from U.S. Bureau of the Census, 1985: Tables 5 and 8.

enthusiasm. Yet in the process of adaptation it is difficult to find evidence that the nation's fundamental goals and objectives have also changed. On the contrary, in both economic and political matters, the same goals have persisted, with the United States seeking in different ways preferred position, if not dominance, in the world order.

The United States remains the single most important actor in the global political economy, much as it remains preeminent, if not unchallenged, in the military sphere. In the latter case the United States continues to share with few other nations the ultimate decision on the fate of the world. It is less easy to draw a caricature of how United States preponderance plays out in political economy matters, however. What is clear is that the leveling effect that has brought the Soviet Union into rough military parity with the United States has been even more pronounced in reducing the economic disparity between the

United States and other First World nations. Less distance in "power potential" now separates the United States from its allies than at any other time in the postwar era. Resurgent nationalism and an associated degree of polycentrism within the major postwar alliance systems have combined with leveling to make the international system less hierarchically organized than in the past. The stratification between rich and poor is more apparent, however, and the United States continues to appear ill equipped to understand the forces of change operating in many of the world's less advantaged societies, suggesting that its own revolutionary heritage is largely irrelevant to the underlying social and economic injustices that plague so many nations in the contemporary world.

The neomercantilist challenge to the Liberal International Economic Order (LIEO) embodied in the rise of protectionist sentiment in the United States is in part a response to the nation's loss of control over its own well-being. It reflects a penchant to deal aggressively and unilaterally with the costs of complex interdependence, which, ironically, is the product of the success the United States realized in promoting a LIEO. The complexity of the system is itself a principal reason for the United States' loss of control over its environment. "There are more issues and more actors; and the weak assert themselves more. The dominant state still has leverage over others, but it has far less leverage over the whole system" (Keohane and Nye, 1977). Thus the era of American domination of the international arena has ended. What looked four decades ago like the beginning of the American century, an era of *Pax Americana* in which U.S. dominance of world politics, like that of the British in the nineteenth century, would be the defining feature of the international system, now appears to have been a short, transitory period. The global system has changed, and many of the changes brought about by recent global developments have not been beneficial to American interests. As a consequence, the external environment is henceforth likely to provide even more pronounced stimulants to and constraints on what the United States does abroad.

SUGGESTIONS FOR FURTHER READING

BHAGWATI, JAGDISH N., AND JOHN GERARD RUGGIE, eds. *Power, Passions, and Purpose: Prospects for North-South Negotiations*. Cambridge, MA: MIT Press, 1984.

COHEN, BENJAMIN J. "International Debt and Linkage Strategies: Some Foreign-Policy Implications for the United States," *International Organization* 39 (Autumn 1985): 699–727.

CONGRESSIONAL QUARTERLY. *Trade: U.S. Policy Since 1945*. Washington, DC: Congressional Quarterly, 1984.

DRUCKER, PETER, F. "The Changed World Economy," *Foreign Affairs* 64 (Spring 1986): 768–791.

LENWAY, STEFANIE ANN. *The Politics of U.S. International Trade*. Boston: Pitman Publishing, 1985.

MORSE, EDWARD L. "After the Fall: The Politics of Oil," *Foreign Affairs* 64 (Spring 1986): 792–811.

SEWELL, JOHN W., RICHARD E. FEINBERG, AND VALERIANA KALLAB, eds. *U.S. Foreign Policy and the Third World: Agenda 1985–86*. New Brunswick, NJ: Transaction Books, 1985.

SOROOS, MARVIN S. *Beyond Sovereignty: The Challenge of Global Policy*. Columbia, SC: University of South Carolina Press, 1986.

SPERO, JOAN EDELMAN. *The Politics of International Economic Relations*, 3rd ed. New York: St. Martin's, 1985.

IV

SOCIETAL SOURCES OF AMERICAN FOREIGN POLICY

8

THE IMPACT OF NATIONAL VALUES: POLITICAL CULTURE, ELITISM, AND PLURALISM

Democracies forgo certain [foreign policy] options by the nature of their societies and the whole set of ideals they represent.

Former Secretary of Defense James Schlesinger, 1985

Representative government on Capitol Hill is in the worst shape I have seen in my sixteen years in the senate. The heart of the problem is that the Senate and the House are awash in a sea of special interest lobbying and special interest campaign contributions.

Senator Edward M. Kennedy, 1978

The process of foreign policy making is often seen as somehow "above politics." According to this view, national interests are put ahead of group and personal interests. The international strategic situation, not domestic considerations, is what matters. People lay aside their partisan differences and support their government's policies toward world affairs. Politics, in short, stops at the water's edge.

How realistic is such a view? Are foreign policy decisions made without regard to domestic interests and consequences? Do leaders really choose among foreign policy options solely in terms of their expected effect on international circumstances? Or are foreign policy actions derived from a combination of domestic and international considerations?

Picture for a moment the following hypothetical scenario: The president begins his morning routine in the Oval Office at 6:45 A.M. with briefings from his principal advisers. His chief domestic adviser begins with economic reports of growing budget deficits, rising unemployment, and a worsening balance-of-trade picture. The latest polls indicate that the president's popularity among the American electorate has plummeted to a record low. The domestic adviser ends with the observation that the president's opponent in the forthcoming election has accused him of pursuing a "wishy-washy" policy toward the nation's allies in the Middle East. The national security adviser is next. The president is told that CIA reports indicate the Middle East is about to erupt in armed conflict again. The president is advised to take immediate action to protect American interests and investments in the area. A strategy session is quickly crammed into the day's agenda, which includes separate consultations with representatives from the American Petroleum Institute and from groups calling themselves "Friends of Israel" and "Citizens for Arab Justice."

What factors will influence the president's behavior when he is confronted with the opportunity or necessity of making a foreign policy decision in circumstances such as those described above? Although an observer cannot get into the mind of a president, the relative influence of determining factors can be inferred from past behavior and from the nature of the situation. Forced to reach a decision, a leader probably will ask himself, "What is the likely domestic consequence of action X or Y? Will it enhance my public standing or erode my support among influential segments of American society? Will it undermine the strength of the political party I lead? And might it convert, perhaps overnight, my political supporters into antagonists?" The urge to give priority attention to the domestic repercussions of a foreign policy decision may be irresistible. Consider one eminent former policy maker's description of decision logic, wherein it was concluded that American leaders have had:

> the tendency to make statements and take actions with regard not to their effect on the international scene to which they are ostensibly addressed but rather to their effect on those echelons of American opinion . . . to which the respective [statesmen] are anxious to appeal. The questions, in these circumstances, became not: how effective is what I am doing in terms of the impact it makes on our world environment? but rather: how do I look, in the mirror of domestic American opinion, as I do it? Do I look shrewd, determined, defiantly patriotic, imbued with the necessary vigilance before the wiles of foreign governments? If so, this is what I do, even though it may prove meaningless, or even counterproductive, when applied to the realities of the external situation. (Kennan, 1967: 53)

That observation suggests that foreign policy decisions are often made by implicit reference to the kinds of reactions they will provoke at home. The necessity of maintaining one's power base, the pragmatic desire to preserve one's future freedom to maneuver, the psychological desire to be respected and loved—all contribute to the tendency to formulate foreign policy in ways designed to elicit favorable domestic responses. At the extreme, theater appears to operate as a substitute for policy—the management of images takes on more importance than the formulation of coherent strategies for dealing with international problems.

The purpose of this and the next chapter is to explore the proposition that attributes of the domestic society operate as an important source of American foreign policy. From among the complex array of interlocked domestic factors that could be examined, we will focus attention in this chapter on the political culture—the beliefs that Americans hold about their political system and the way it operates—as it relates to foreign policy. We also examine the role that "elites" and special-interest groups play in transmitting the political culture to foreign policy makers, as well as in advocating policies compatible with the interests of more specialized groups. Then, in chapter nine, we will examine the functions that public opinion, presidential elections, and the mass media perform in the policy-making process.

The societal factors that conceivably can influence the direction of American foreign policy are almost infinite in number, limited only by the analyst's imagination. We focus on those conventionally regarded as the most prominent. But readers are encouraged to speculate about the extent to which the nation's capacity to act, and its course of action abroad, may be influenced by other societal characteristics and changes in them, such as the economic growth rate, chronically expanding deficits in the federal budget and national debt, resource scarcities, racial divisions and the degree of civil unrest, demographic changes, the gap between advantaged and disadvantaged, and the like. Some of the characteristics defining the domestic setting of American foreign policy outlined in chapter three, such as the country's intellectual and historical traditions, deserve examination in this context, and readers are encouraged to derive propositions about their impact on foreign conduct. We are all accustomed to theories which link America's conduct abroad to internal characteristics at home. For instance, American foreign policy is sometimes said to be shaped by a legalistic mind set. Is this because two-thirds of the world's lawyers ply their trade in the United States (*Wall Street Journal*, October 3, 1983: 30)? Does the presence of so many lawyers contribute to the prevalence of a legal mentality in the way foreign policy issues are defined in the United States? Similarly, the United States suffers from an unusually high level of violent crime compared to other nations. A 1985 study by the government's Bureau of Justice Statistics estimated that Americans have one chance in 133 of being murdered in an entire lifetime, and that each year about 6 million Americans (3 percent of the population older than twelve) are victimized by robberies, rapes, or other assaults (*The State*, May 6, 1985: 4, 13). What are the consequences of this constant exposure to the threat of violence, to the experience of living in a society where violence is common? Could it be that the Americans who make the country's foreign policy are inclined to think of violence as normal, and to transfer this expectation to the international environment, and to assume subconsciously that human interaction is destined to be governed by continually high levels of violence? If so, is a militant foreign policy focusing on this expectation the consequent product?

To extend this kind of inquiry about the potential domestic sources of American foreign policy, let us consider how American's national attributes and internal conditions may make the U.S. different from other countries.

AMERICAN SOCIETY IN THE COMMUNITY OF NATIONS: A DEVIANT CASE?

It is useful to review some of the attributes which make the United States the kind of nation it is, since ultimately such characteristics influence how Americans are inclined to think about themselves and the proper role of their nation in international affairs. Table 8.1 presents some of the more salient national at-

TABLE 8.1 American Society Among the 41 Wealthiest Market Economies: Comparative Rankings

National Attribute and Its Indicator	Date of Observation	U.S. Rank Among Other Countries
ECONOMIC STATUS		
Gross National Product	1985	1
GNP per capita	1983	4
Average Annual Growth Rate of Gross Domestic Product, 1973–1983	1983	25[a]
Average Annual Growth Rate of GNP per capita, 1965–1983	1983	29[b]
Average Annual Rate of Inflation, 1973–1983	1983	9
Gross Domestic Savings (as percentage of GNP)	1983	35
Gross Domestic Investment (as percentage of GNP)	1983	29[f]
Public Consumption (as percentage of GNP)	1983	12[f]
MILITARY STATUS		
Military Expenditures	1983	1
Military Expenditures (as percentage of GNP)	1983	7
Military Expenditures per capita	1983	6
Military Expenditures per soldier	1982	7
Armed Forces	1983	1
Armed Forces per 1,000 people	1983	15
RESOURCES		
Energy Consumption per capita	1983	4
Average Annual Growth Rate of Energy Production, 1973–1983	1983	30
Crude Oil Reserves (proved)	1983	8
Natural Gas Reserves (proved)	1983	3
Crude Oil Consumption	1983	1

TABLE 8.1   (continued)

National Attribute and Its Indicator	Date of Observation	U.S. Rank Among Other Countries
EDUCATION		
Public Expenditures per capita	1982	11[f]
School Age Population per Teacher	1982	12[a]
Literacy Rate	1982	3[a]
Percent of School Age Population in Secondary School	1982	4
Percent of School Age Population in Higher Education	1982	1
HEALTH		
Public Expenditure per capita	1982	10
Public Expenditure (as percentage of total government expenditure)	1982	9
Population per Physician	1982	21[e]
Population per Hospital Bed	1982	31[f]
Infant Mortality per 1,000 Live Births	1983	12[c]
Life Expectancy at Birth	1983	10[f]
Calorie Supply per capita	1982	5
Percent of Nutritional Requirements Met	1982	15
Percent of Population With Safe Water	1982	7[f]
SOCIAL		
Index of Economic/Social Standing	1982	4
Average Annual Growth of Population, 1973–1983	1983	23[d]
Percentage of Population of Working Age	1983	7[f]
Urban Population (as percentage of total population)	1983	21
GOVERNMENTAL		
Central Government Expenditures (as percentage of GNP)	1982	26

SOURCE: Sewell, Feinberg and Kallab, 1985; U.S. Arms Control and Disarmament Agency, 1985; *World Development Report, 1985*, 1985; Sivard, *World Military and Social Expenditures 1985*, 1985; *Facts & Figures 1983* (Dharan, Saudi Arabia: Aramco).

NOTE: Comparisons are with those states which in 1983 had Gross National Products per capita of $2,000 or more. Included are only industrial market economies, high-income oil exporters, and upper middle income countries (newly industrialized states) as defined by the World Bank (1985: 175). The rankings therefore are among 41 of the world's wealthiest countries, excluding the nonmarket countries of the Second World (see the *World Development Report, 1985*, p. 175, for a listing).

a. Tied with Canada.
b. Tied with Australia and the United Kingdom.
c. Tied with Ireland and Singapore.
d. Tied with Spain.
e. Tied with Uruguay.
f. Tied with more than two countries.

tributes together with a comparison of the United States with its peers—with the other relatively rich countries of the First World with whom the United States shares company at the apex of power in the international system. These indicators suggest, collectively, that the United States is far from the typical society in the international community of nations. It is the world's fourth largest country in both geographical size and population, and it is extraordinarily endowed with vast natural resources, technological sophistication, and mobilized power, a country with nearly all the prerequisites of a superpower among the advanced industrial states. Relatively speaking, Americans are urbanized, highly educated, and militarily prepared and mobilized. The adult citizenry is literate and informed by a sophisticated communications system and a free and active media. Moreover, American society is well off materially (even though its rate of economic growth is relatively low); although Americans comprise less than 6 percent of the world's population, in any given year they produce (and consume) over a fifth of the world's total economic output. The distribution of that wealth among all sectors of American society is far from equal, but the ''average'' American is better off than his or her counterpart living in all but three other countries in the world.[1] American society, in short, is in many respects quite unlike that of other nations.

Although the foregoing attributes describe the nation's enormous capabilities and resources, we must resist the temptation to accept the kind of simplistic, single-factor explanations of foreign policy which posit a direct causal linkage between such structural characteristics of a society on the one hand and the kinds of foreign policy it pursues on the other. Propositions of the sort asserting that ''large, populous countries inevitably are imperialistic,'' that ''educated societies pursue peaceful foreign polices,''[2] or that ''militarized

---

[1]Among countries with a population of a million or more, Kuwait, Switzerland, and the United Arab Emirates had a higher Gross National Product per capita in 1983 than did the United States (*World Development Report, 1985*, 1985: 175).

Readers will note that even though the United States is among the wealthiest nations in the world, its performance on various social indicators relating to such things as health and education is often far less impressive. The failure of the United States to provide more adequate social services (when compared to other prosperous countries) more likely reflects a philosophical predisposition than an inability to provide such benefits. The United States could, for example, reduce its infant mortality rate if it chose to; it has the means but lacks the willingness to pay the costs. It is also important to remember that averages can be very misleading, especially in a heterogeneous society like the United States where wealth is not equally shared. ''About one-fifth of one percent of the population, the 'super rich,' own almost 60 percent of the corporate wealth . . . approximately 1.6 percent of the population own 80 percent of all stock. . . . There are about seventy billionaire families in the United States and over 200,000 millionaires'' (Parenti, 1980: 8). In addition to wealth, income is not distributed evenly; in 1982, the top fifth were the recipients of 42.7 percent of income received, whereas the share of the bottom fifth was 4.7 percent (Stone and Barke, 1985: 9). In addition, many Americans are not strangers to poverty, hunger, and desperation. In 1985, 14 percent of Americans lived below the government's official poverty line (LeLoup, 1986: 569), and it has been estimated that millions suffer from conditions of hunger and malnutrition—a poverty syndrome that is self-perpetuating because children born to poor families tend to be born mentally retarded because of prenatal malnourishment (Parenti, 1980).

[2]Evidence does not support the notion that educated people are necessarily more peaceful or hold more conciliatory attitudes with respect to foreign affairs. A highly educated populace sup-

countries are necessarily expansionistic,"[3] for instance, are much too crude and lack empirical support. Too many counterexamples exist to make such speculations credible. Moreover, since most societal characteristics remain stable over extended periods, they are not powerful precipitants of changes in foreign policy content. They are conditions that promote policy continuity more than policy change. Thus, when viewing the foreign policy functions of such relatively objective national attributes as size, population, and resources, it is preferable to consider their influence as indirect, as factors which make some foreign policy options possible while limiting the feasibility of others.

Another way to think of the impact on foreign policy of the relatively stable features of American society is as data (or cognitions) which form part of decision makers' perceptual maps of the world and their nation's place in it. Policy makers perceive society in a particular way, and these subjective perceptions and beliefs may shape foreign policy more strongly than do more objective conditions (see Dallek, 1983). Changes in American society—in the form of stable rates of population growth, increased economic dependence on imported raw materials, life style changes, preferences as reflected in low rates on savings and investments alongside high rates of consumer consumption, elevated levels of public and private indebtedness, or the declining quality of the environment—may also shape decision makers' thinking about the country's proper role in the world and ultimately influence the kinds of policies and programs proposed.

When we understand the role that perceptions play in translating the effects of relatively stable, objective, societal characteristics to policy makers, it is easy to understand the dominant role played by even less tangible and more subjective aspects of American society rooted in the minds of both the citizenry and its leaders, such as ideology, belief systems, and historical traditions—in short, the *political culture* of the nation.

POLITICAL CULTURE AND FOREIGN POLICY

It is inviting to postulate that the set of values, cognitions, ideas, and ideals held by the majority of the American people affects substantially American foreign policy. Political attitudes forming American society's political culture may be assumed to influence the American response to international events.

As plausible as this proposition may be, however, it is difficult to verify. The concept of political culture is very broad and elastic (see Rosenbaum, 1975, for elaboration). Like its related concept, national character (which has

---

ported the imperialism of Nazi Germany, for instance. Educational level is a poor predictor of foreign policy attitudes because the crucial determinant of such attitudes is not the level of information possessed but the kind of information about war and peace that is propagated in the educational system.

[3]The difficulty with this proposition is that it is dangerous to infer intentions from capabilities. That is, countries which allocate large proportions of national income to armaments do not necessarily plan to use them for aggressive purposes.

been largely discredited because of its many deficiencies), political culture must be defined carefully so as to differentiate between the traits of subcultures or of individuals in American society and the composite behavioral patterns of the nation as a whole. Aggregated characteristics of the whole nation cannot be safely generalized to all parts of the population, for example, since we do not necessarily know the characteristics of an individual simply by knowing the characteristics of the groups of which he or she is a part. If a nation acts belligerently in its foreign policy, for instance, that does not make each citizen or policy maker a warmonger.

But used judiciously, the concept of political culture can provide insight into the domestic sources of American foreign policy. To the extent that deepseated values, beliefs, and self-images are shared by Americans—on the assumption that most Americans were socialized by the same cultural values—those orientations and national values may be linked to the kinds of policies pursued abroad by the United States. To the extent that "the United States was founded upon values that were different from the rest of the world" (McCormick, 1985), American foreign policy may be uniquely different from the policies of other states.

What are the core values of American society? On this question opinions certainly vary, not only because the existence of political subcultures and alienated groups makes it difficult to generalize safely about the degree to which some values are universally shared, but also because the American political tradition strives for consensus but simultaneously tolerates disagreement, parochial loyalties, and counterallegiances. The American political culture is often torn between competing values and impulses (production and consumption, saving and spending, work and leisure, individualism and community, moralism and realism, and the like). The United States is said to possess a "loosely bounded culture" (see Merelman, 1984) because American society is fluid, egalitarian, highly personal, and open, which leaves the individual citizen free to embrace his or her own philosophy.

Despite the diversity (and respect for it), though, certain dominant norms can be said to prevail in a pluralistic American political culture. There *are* values and principles to which *all* American politicians appeal in their campaigns for office, irrespective of the particular political philosophy they espouse, and to which the general populace largely responds.

Although no single definition adequately captures its essence, the complementary assumptions that comprise "mainstream" American political beliefs may be labeled *liberalism*. That is, the dominant political culture of the United States traces its roots to the seventeenth-century liberal philosophy of the English thinker John Locke.[4] More generally, the nation's ideology contains the premises of both classical democratic theory and classical capitalism, a syn-

---

[4]For a summary of the competing ideas extant within Lockean liberalism, which demonstrates its hold on almost all political thought in America (including "individualist conservatism," which is related to nineteenth-century liberalism), see Dolbeare and Dolbeare (1971).

ergy that combines to form a deeply entrenched ideology of "democratic capitalism" (Greenberg, 1985). "Capitalism and liberalism," write Dolbeare and Dolbeare (1971), "represent the mainstream because they are the established, enduring, 'orthodox' ideologies that have dominated the thinking of American political and other leaders."

Different versions of liberalism place varying emphases on particular premises, just as the American self-image is kinetic and variant. Over time, successive reformulations of the American ethos have occurred in response to the demands imposed by changes in America's national and international circumstances. But the convictions basic to the Lockean liberal tradition find expression in the rhetoric of American leaders and in the documents Americans celebrate on national holidays. Lincoln's espousal of government of, by, and for the people is fundamental to the liberal heritage. The Declaration of Independence likewise incorporates liberal values and boldly asserts them in the proposition that legitimate political power arises only from the consent of the governed, that the only justification of government is the protection of individuals' civil and political rights. Many other interdependent principles and values embellish the liberal tradition: limited government, individual liberty, due process of law, self-determination, capitalism, free enterprise, inalienable (natural) rights, the equality of citizens before the law and with respect to their opportunity to participate in public affairs, majority rule, minority rights, the division of power between national and local governments through federalism, the separation of powers within government, and legalism ("a government of laws, not of men"). All are consistent with Locke's liberal contentions that government's role should be a limited one, designed to protect the individual's life, liberty, and property through popular consent, established laws, impartial judges, and limited but effective executives. It is upon these central values that the dominant political culture of the United States rests,[5] and it is because they are subscribed to as part of the American ethos that Americans think of themselves as a "free people."

The interpretation forwarded here has been argued persuasively by others.[6] For instance, in *The Liberal Tradition in America*, Louis Hartz (1955) contends that Lockean liberalism has become so embedded in American life that Americans may be blind to what it really is, namely, ideology. The basis for that ideology, so the reasoning holds, is the "exceptional American experi-

---

[5]See Devine (1972), McClosky and Zaller (1984), and Greenberg (1985) for extensive evidence, drawn from scores of public opinion polls and supplementary historical data, supporting the contention that the Lockean liberal tradition is indeed dominant in the American political culture and that the values embedded within it are widely shared by the mass of the American people.

[6]The interpretation also has been trenchantly challenged. For an example of a Marxist critique in the context of American foreign policy, see Parenti's "We Hold These Myths to Be Self-Evident" (1981). Because characterizations of the dominant American values stem partly from ideology, readers should be alert to the dangers of putting the American political culture into any all-encompassing mold. For discussions of alternate ways of conceiving the American political culture, and assessments of the implications for public policy that derive from them, see Elazar (1972), Dolbeare and Edelman (1985), and Rodgers and Harrington (1981).

ence,'' which includes the absence of pronounced class and religious strife at the time of the nation's founding, complemented by the fortuitous blessing of geographic isolation from most of the political and military conflicts of Europe (see Box 8.1).

Strands of the linkage between ideological traditions and foreign policy behavior may be detected in American diplomatic history from the Monroe Doctrine to today. As integral parts of our ideological tradition, such themes as

---

BOX 8.1 Does American "Exceptionalism" Influence American Foreign Policy? Three Views

''American exceptionalism expresses the conviction that the U.S. has a moral mission which flows out of its identity and which should guide its policies. Our exceptional character, which was originally used to justify disdaining alliances and quarrels of the so-called old world, has often been cited as the grounds to improve the world.''

U.S. Ambassador to the United Nations
Jeane J. Kirkpatrick, 1984

''Our confidence in democracy . . . in our approach to the rest of the world is, of course, a projection of our own national experience. Beyond that, however, it has proven to be an effective force—perhaps the most effective force—in our foreign policy. We emphasize our support for democracy not only because our own experience gives us great sympathy for the democratic aspirations of other people; we have also become convinced through hard experience that our own national interests are best served through the creation and strengthening of functioning pluralistic democracies in other countries.''

U.S. Ambassador to the Philippines
Stephen W. Bosworth, 1984

''America began free; its struggles were never to become free, but to stay free. Moreover, it never, for a single moment, lost its freedom. History, in other words, has made America naive. It has made Americans the luckiest and the least understanding people in the world. Indeed, the happy American experience with freedom may be at the root of the time-honored American inability to find its proper global place. The appeal of American isolationism and the awkwardness of American interventionism—both may be owed to the American unfamiliarity with the political oppression and social injustice that is the common experience of most of the rest of the world. Our natural consciousness of freedom has equipped us badly for the spreading of it. That may be history's bad joke on the American century.''

The New Republic, April 30, 1984, p.1

self-determination, self-identification, and self-preservation have appeared continually as justifications for policy action. As Edward Weisband observes:

> American foreign policy has been alternately criticized for being too economically driven and imperialist, too moralistic and interventionist, too utilitarian and isolationist. All, paradoxically, are equally correct. For the concern with wealth, power, status, moral virtue, and the freedom of mankind were successfully transformed into a single set of mutually reinforcing values by the paradigm of Lockian liberalism. (Weisband, 1973: 62)

Although decision maker's references to the themes of the political culture were undoubtedly mere window dressing at times, argues Weisband, this lip service has been used as a way of mobilizing public opinion in support of U.S. actions and endowing those actions with moral value as well as functional utility. This was clearly the motive, for example, behind President Reagan's "Saving Freedom in Central America" speech on July 18, 1983, in which he linked American policy in Central America to American ideological principles by stating,

> Our democracy encompasses many freedoms—freedom of speech, of religion, of assembly, and of so many other liberties that we often take for granted. These are rights that should be shared by all mankind. . . . Central America . . . is now being exploited by the enemies of freedom. . . . We have an obligation to help [freedom-loving Central Americans]—for our own sake as well as theirs.

The way in which political-development doctrines derived from the liberal traditions came to be played out in the postwar American foreign aid program illustrates the relationship between political culture and foreign policy. Four logical assumptions may be derived from the exceptional American experience: (1) change and development are easy; (2) all good things go together; (3) radicalism and revolution are bad; and (4) distributing political power is more important than accumulating it (Packenham, 1973). The diverse meanings associated with those liberal assumptions lend coherence to apparently disparate and inconsistent American actions. Robert A. Packenham finds a counterpart to the first two assumptions in the economic approach of U.S. aid programs. That approach assumed that fantastic results would flow from what in fact was a rather meager effort and that economic development would beget political development and a host of "other good political things." Cold War anticommunist doctrines are rooted in the third assumption. And the fourth is manifested in a democratic mentality that has rationalized the export of American political institutions, especially to Latin America, or as evidenced by "Project Democracy" or by the National Endowment for Democracy (NED) initiatives in the Reagan administration. Each of those manifestations of the liberal tradition by itself provides important insight into the reasoning underlying U.S. aid efforts. At the same time, however, the liberal tradition, derived from a unique historical experience, also lends a coherence to efforts that otherwise might not be apparent. As Packenham observes:

> Though ostensibly separate and conflicting, the three approaches [to foreign aid— the economic, Cold War, and explicitly democratic approaches] are actually integrated and consistent. . . . Deviations from the patterns of economic and political development as they occurred in the United States—especially radicalism and revolution—are due to "unnatural growths," which the United States then tries to remove "by diplomacy or war." In this fashion the "right" hand of the liberal tradition (as manifested in the Cold War approach) counters what the "left" hand (the economic and explicit democratic approaches) has helped to create. (Packenham, 1973: 163)

Clearly more evidence is required before precise conclusions about the relationship between political culture and foreign policy processes can be made. The logic underlying such a relationship seem unassailable, however.

The capitalistic premises of American culture certainly help to explain the repulsion American foreign policy expresses toward communism and the placement of containment as the centerpiece of America's postwar policy. The country's ascent to world power after World War II also helps to explain how a nation committed to "limited government" could nonetheless justify the growth of government size and power in order for the nation, as the world's leading economic and military power, to practice a globalist policy employing interventionist methods. The frequent criticism that American foreign policy has sought to remake the world in the nation's own image assumes that this compulsion springs from the nation's cultural traditions. Many plausible other propositions relating foreign policy predispositions to the influence of American values also can be speculated. The appropriate question seems not *if* there is a relationship, but *how* it operates.

A probable link can be posited here. Although decision makers are not drawn at random from American society (as we shall see in a moment), there is every reason to believe they embrace the basic value assumptions of American society. A "law of anticipated reactions" may therefore be hypothesized as one mechanism whereby the political culture affects foreign policy: decision makers screen out certain alternatives because of their anticipation that the options would be adversely received, an anticipation born of the American value tradition in which they share. In other words, we can hypothesize that the political culture helps to define *in the minds of decision makers* the range of permissible foreign policy goals, alternatives, and actions.[7] Robert Kennedy's

---

[7] In fact, decision makers may not even be conscious of the way in which the political culture helps to define in their minds the range of permissible policy. As Daniel J. Elazar argues: "Political culture, as such, determines behavior in relatively few situations or in response to relatively few particular issues. Its influence lies in its power to set reasonably fixed limits to political behavior and provide subliminal direction for political action . . .; limits and direction all the more effective because of their antiquity and subtlety whereby those limited are unaware of the limitations placed upon them" (Elazar, 1970: 257).

argument against[8] using an air strike to destroy the Soviet missiles surreptitiously placed in Cuba in 1962 illustrates the hypothesized screening process:

> Whatever validity the military and political arguments were for an attack in preference to a blockade, America's traditions and history would not permit such a course of action. Whatever military reasons [former Secretary of State Dean Acheson] and others could marshal, they were nevertheless, in the last analysis, advocating a surprise attack by a very large nation against a very small one. This, I said, could not be undertaken by the U.S. if we were to maintain our moral position at home and around the globe. Our struggle against Communism throughout the world was far more than physical survival—it had as its essence our heritage and our ideals, and these we must not destroy. (Kennedy, 1971: 16–17)

It must quickly be added parenthetically that this screening process has at times been rendered inoperative by the sacrifice of ideological ideals to *realpolitik* calculations of self-interest. Where principles have clashed with pragmatic needs, the former have not always predominated over the latter. Two examples in the 1980s stand out: U.S. immigration policy and U.S. trade policy. President Reagan labeled the United States an "island of freedom," a land placed here by "divine Providence" as a "refuge for all those people in the world who yearn to breathe free," and the Statue of Liberty was refurbished as a symbol of America as a "melting pot" society of immigrants from other countries. The 1980 census revealed that 14 million people listed their birthplaces in 155 countries other than the United States. And yet, American policy has officially sought to stem the tide of refugees seeking to flee to the United States, a growing proportion of whom enter illegally. The "open door" has been closed because, presumably, the domestic social and economic environment cannot sustain the costs that adherence to American ideals would entail (see Fallows, 1983; Segal, 1984). And with respect to the tenet of American capitalistic democracy that places respect for principles of free trade practices high within the nation's hierarchy of values, we find that here, too, pressing economic exigencies have generated strong pressure for a compromise of this cornerstone of America's political culture; calls for protectionism and neomercantilist programs became intense in the mid-1980s as the trade balance worsened to historically high levels and the federal deficit reached unprecedented proportions (see chapter seven). Thus the precepts of American political culture may give way on occasion to their violation. When they do, political culture ceases to act as a powerful influence on American foreign policy.

Still another potential link between American political culture and foreign policy can be noted. Although durable, it can sometimes change gradually in

---

[8]Although this is the orthodox interpretation of Robert Kennedy's role during the deliberations over the Cuban missiles, recently released transcripts of taped conversations during those meetings suggest that Kennedy was actually a proponent of the invasion option, of which air strikes would obviously be a part. See "White House Tapes and Minutes of the Cuban Missile Crisis" (1985).

fundamental ways, as developments coalesce over time to stimulate new values and beliefs. Consider what happened to a whole generation of Americans in the 1960s. Raised to believe that the United States was a splendidly virtuous country, young Americans found—through the Bay of Pigs invasion; racial discrimination in Selma, Alabama, and elsewhere; the assassinations of President Kennedy, his brother Robert, and Martin Luther King Jr.; and then Vietnam—that ideals were prostituted in practice. Outraged, numbers of alienated Americans protested the abuses which undermined seemingly sacred assumptions. The result was that the American culture underwent a substantial shift in emphasis as the nation wrestled with its commitment to emphasize the idealistic values within its tradition.

Although it cannot be demonstrated that this cultural transformation caused American policy to change, its association with major political events in the late 1960s and early 1970s is hard to deny. A war ended ignominiously. Two American presidents were toppled, one in the face of enormous political pressure from domestic as well as international forces, the other in disgrace. Legal barriers to racial discrimination were dismantled. New constraints were placed on the use—both overt and covert—of American force abroad, and the range of permissible action was given a reduced definition whose import is still felt today. Thus it appears that changes in the political culture—whether they stem from public disillusionment, impatience, failure, or whatever—may indeed affect the kinds of policies that are subsequently proposed and the ways in which they are carried out.

The period just described is not unique. Every age reevaluates the past in light of the needs of the present, and the American political culture is therefore constantly undergoing modification. Indeed, the cultural realignment since the late 1970s toward pragmatic *realpolitik* thinking illustrates the propensity for different values within the American tradition to receive varying degrees of emphasis in different periods and circumstances.

Because American foreign policy inevitably is colored by the current interpretation of the political culture (just as that culture finds expression in the policy pronouncements of American decision makers), changes in the prevailing climate of opinion about the nation's self-image and its place in the world exert a potentially powerful influence on American foreign policy: they impose new constraints on what decision makers may regard as viable policy options.

But whether cultural change in fact precipitates policy change depends ultimately on how those in power perceive the American political culture. For although we might argue for a link between cultural and policy changes, cultural changes themselves do not bring about policy changes. Political culture, to repeat, expresses itself in a variety of ways, which are amenable to different interpretations. It restricts the range of policy choice, but does not determine it or confine it to operate along a narrow, inflexible course. Indeed, American political culture prescribes often incompatible traditions in foreign policy on which policy makers may draw, as the twin impulses for isolationism and in-

terventionism exemplify (recall chapter three). So there is not a direct correspondence between a set of ideological principles and the American practice
of diplomacy. Rather, cultural changes help to create an atmosphere that
makes new policies acceptable and old policies unacceptable. As the law of
anticipated reactions implies, the critical variable linking an altered cultural atmosphere with policy change still resides with those in positions of authority.
Thus we can hypothesize that changes in the political culture will not affect
foreign policy making unless those who make policy both appreciate the
changes and are willing to accommodate their policies to them. To understand
more fully the domestic sources of American foreign policy, therefore, we
must look beyond the opportunities and constraints provided by American
political culture. We must also examine the way in which decision makers and
others who influence policy making serve as links between national values
and external policy and how, indeed, foreign policy makers may concurrently—by virtue of the things they say and do—change those values.

DEMOCRATIC LIBERALISM IN THEORY AND PRACTICE

How do policy-making elites employ the values and traditions of American
society at large in the policy-making process? According to liberal democratic
theory, the answer is simple: leaders are chosen to represent and reflect societal preferences.[9] The values of society at large are thus converted into public
policy by a leadership sharing those views. By extension, American foreign
policy is ultimately an expression of the prevailing political values of the
American people; the national interest can be equated with the majority's
opinion.

How realistic is that theory? Do elected leaders indeed devise policies
which correspond to the general preferences of the public? Or do they, instead, devise policies that appeal to the specialized interests of that portion of
the American public from which the leaders themselves are drawn? How, in
short, does liberal democratic theory operate in practice?

Does a Power Elite Control the Making of American Foreign Policy?

The United States is undeniably a democratic society. The complication with
the accuracy of that description is that the United States is also a special-interest society (as well as a bureaucratic society, an information society, a welfare
society, a scientific-technological society—many other characterizations also
apply). In particular, when we examine the characteristics of those chosen to
make American foreign policy and ask whether those leaders share the convictions and attributes of Americans in general, perplexing and, perhaps,
troublesome findings emerge.

---

[9]The meaning of democracy, and the democratic premise, is captured by its Greek root: de-
mokratia = *demos* (people) + *kratia* (power).

Who is chosen to lead? Not many, in terms of numbers: "Great power is concentrated in a tiny handful of people. A few thousand individuals out of 238 million Americans decide about war and peace . . . (Dye, 1986: 1). It is also quite clear that only certain types of people have for years been *recruited* into positions that enable them to direct the nation's foreign policy. Not everyone is eligible for public office; the process by which individuals are recruited is selective; it encourages certain types of "acceptable" people into office, and the system denies entrance to those who do not fit the general pattern. Deviations from the pattern are rare and short lived; those who fail to conform to the conventional way of thinking and behaving are usually rejected or eliminated from leadership roles. The proposition holds especially for those who seek to occupy nonelected decision-making roles (see chapters thirteen and fourteen). Furthermore, because some—by virtue of family connections, income, and education—hold advantages in the competition for positions of power, opportunities are not in fact equal, and top officials are not drawn equally from all segments of society. The result is an "elite"—not only in the sense that a small minority occupies positions of authority, but also in the sense that those in authority are seldom recruited from among the mass of "average" Americans.

The elitist character[10] of those responsible for foreign policy making becomes apparent when we ask, "What are the social attributes of those making up the foreign policy-making community?" Because of the remarkable similarity in background and experience of those who have comprised what has been termed "the foreign policy establishment," their composition is not difficult to characterize. Consistent with what is usually meant by the term "elite," the group is (1) rather small and (2) very enduring, having changed little for almost forty years. The postwar pattern has been one in which for nearly four decades (3) the top positions have been filled by people from the upper class who were (4) highly educated at the best schools. They are, as the title of a prize-winning book put it, *The Best and the Brightest* (Halberstam, 1972).[11] Furthermore, (5) they have tended to come from predominantly white, Anglo-Saxon, Protestant (WASP) backgrounds; (6) a disproportionate number have been trained in law; and (7) many have had extensive experience

---

[10]Lasswell and Lerner (1952) summarize the core idea behind elitism in policy making thus: "The discovery that in all large-scale societies the decisions are typically in the hands of a small number of people confirms a basic fact: Government is always by the few, whether in the name of the few, the one, or the many." Even if one accepts the elitist perspective, determining the size and composition of the elite is difficult. Dye and Pickering (1974) estimate that only 5,500 people control key industrial, banking, communications, and cultural organizations in the United States or hold key federal government jobs. An empirical profile of those who make it to the top, and further elaboration of the elitist perspective, can be found in Bachrach (1971), Burch (1980), Brownstein and Easton (1983), Destler, Gelb, and Lake (1984), Domhoff (1971, 1980 and 1984), Dye (1979, 1983, and 1986), Dye and Zeigler (1981), Froman (1984), and Prewitt and Stone (1973).

[11]The perceptive reader will note that although American policy makers as a group are highly educated and trained, erudition is not necessarily a guarantee against foolish policy decisions. Indeed, one of the main points of Halberstam's book is that intelligent people are capable of making wicked and stupid decisions.

in big businesss. Indeed, (8) foreign policy decision makers typically occupy official positions of power in government for short periods; most of their careers are spent as managers or owners of major corporations and financial institutions[12] or on the faculty of the nation's elite universities, and more often than not the government positions occupied by members of "the establishment" are appointive rather than elective.

In effect, those who make American foreign policy tend to glide between government and the private sector or educational institutions and the mass media through a kind of revolving door, in front of which the line is never very long. The names of Robert McNamara, Henry L. Stimson, James F. Byrnes, Arthur Goldberg, Charles Hitch, the Dulles brothers (Allen of the CIA and John Foster of the Department of State), George F. Kennan, Dean Acheson, Clark Clifford, Nelson Rockefeller, Paul Warnke, the Bundy brothers (William and McGeorge), Dean Rusk, Elliot Richardson, John Mitchell, George W. Ball, Walt Rostow, Henry Kissinger, Zbigniew Brzezinski, James R. Schlesinger, George Bush, Cyrus R. Vance, George Shultz, Alexander M. Haig, and Caspar W. Weinberger come readily to mind. Many more fit the pattern. The overwhelming evidence is that the same people, with the same set of attitudes, have assumed major responsibility for the determination of U.S. foreign policy. Richard J. Barnet has summarized the homogeneous social and occupational attributes of the people who have made American foreign policy during the postwar period:

> Between 1940 and 1967, when I stopped counting, all the first- and second-level posts in the huge national security bureaucracy were held by fewer than four hundred individuals who rotate through a variety of key posts. The temporary civilian managers who come to Washington . . . , the national security managers, were so alike one another in occupation, religion, style, and social status that, apart from a few Washington lawyers, Texans, and mavericks, it was possible to locate the offices of all of them within fifteen city blocks in New York, Boston, and Detroit. Most of their biographies in *Who's Who* read like minor variations on a single theme—wealthy parents, Ivy-League education, leading law firm or bank (or entrepreneur in a war industry), introduction to government in World War II. . . . Seventy of the ninety-one people who have held the very top jobs . . . have all been businessmen, lawyers for businessmen, and investment bankers. (Barnet, 1972: 48–49)

Since the people largely responsible for American foreign policy for decades have resembled each other in terms of backgrounds, experiences, and attitudes, they may be expected to propose and carry out the same sorts of foreign policies (akin to Karl Marx's famous observation that "the ideas of the

---

[12]In an extensive investigation of the careers of 234 major foreign policy decision makers, Kolko (1969) found that in the period 1944–1960 over 60 percent of those leaders began their careers in the areas of investment banking, law, or business. For further analyses of the characteristics of American foreign policy officials, see Brownstein and Easton (1983), Burch (1980), and Mennis (1971).

ruling class are in every epoch the ruling ideas"). Hence, if we wish to find a convincing explanation for the persistence and continuity which have marked postwar American foreign policy, we can certainly find one in the durability of the shared characteristics of the people who have been in charge of that policy. That conclusion is reinforced by the observation that the elite is a self-selecting, self-recruiting, and self-perpetuating governing body, a group of individuals who "guard" American foreign policy by advising incumbent administrations and ensure that those who enter into policy making roles share the views and attitudes of their predecessors (Domhoff, 1971, 1980, and 1984). Every postwar president has found himself dependent on this elite and their advice. Perhaps it was recognition of this fact which led John F. Kennedy to respond, when urged in his 1960 campaign to hit his critics harder: "That is not a very good idea. I'll need them all to run this country."

Important insight into the mechanism just described is provided by Thomas R. Dye (1978 and 1986). His analysis of the recruitment and advisory role of the Council on Foreign Relations and the Brookings Institution illuminates the process whereby the values of corporate and financial elites have often been funneled into the foreign policy-making process.

Take, for example, the Council on Foreign Relations, which Dye (1978) describes as "[t]he most influential private policy-planning organization in foreign affairs." The council's limited membership is drawn from among the most prestigious and best connected of the nation's financial and corporate institutions, universities, foundations, media, and government bodies. Its members (limited by by-laws to 1,900 individuals), past and present, include most of those previously named as moving through the revolving door between private enterprise or education and government service. "Every person of influence in foreign affairs" has been a member (Dye, 1986), including presidents of the United States; among them was Jimmy Carter, who as governor of Georgia was appointed to the council's multinational wing known as the Trilateral Commission.[13] Its purpose is the coordination of economic policy among the United States, Western Europe, and Japan. The Trilateral Commission was headed at the time of Carter's appointment by political science professor Zbigniew Brzezinski of Columbia University. Brzezinski subsequently became Carter's national security adviser.[14]

---

[13]The Trilateral Commission officially disavows any "formal ties" with either the Council on Foreign Relations or the Brookings Institution, although the organization acknowledges that "a considerable number of Commission members are involved in one or more other organizations of this sort," and its coordinator, George S. Franklin, served formerly as executive director of the Council on Foreign Relations.

[14]In addition to Brzezinski, other Trilateral Commission members who found their way to top positions in the Carter administration included W. Michael Blumenthal (secretary of the treasury), Harold Brown (secretary of defense), Walter Mondale (vice president), Cyrus Vance (secretary of state), Paul Warnke (director of the Arms Control and Disarmament Agency), and Leonard Woodcock (U.S. representative to the People's Republic of China) (Dye, 1978). In fact, by one count (*Washington Post*, January 16, 1977: A1, A4) nineteen of those who had been among the Trilateral Commission's sixty-five members were appointed to top positions or served as official advisers in the first month of the Carter administration. Those findings stood in sharp contrast to Carter's

Apart from the interlocking connections among elites both within and out-side of government, Dye argues that the role of such policy-planning organi-zations as the Council on Foreign Relations in the policy-making process is played out through the research and other efforts they undertake to achieve a consensus on action that ought to be taken on problems:

> Their goal is to develop *action recommendations*—explicit policies or programs de-signed to resolve national problems. These recommendations of the key policy-planning groups are distributed to the mass media, federal executive agencies, and the Congress. The White House staff, Congressional Committee staffs, and top ex-ecutive administrators are contacted with increasing frequency by representatives of policy-planning organizations, when it is felt that the time has come for govern-ment action. The purpose is to lay the groundwork for making policy into law. Soon the results of elite decision-making and consensus-building will be reflected in the actions of elected officials—the ''proximate policy-makers.'' (Dye, 1978: 312)

The history of Council recommendations and U.S. foreign policy pro-posals and actions have shown remarkable consistency. Included in the record of consistency has been the origination of such policies as containment, the NATO agreement, the Marshall Plan, the challenge of ''flexible response'' to the doctrine of ''massive retaliation,'' the initial impetus toward military in-volvement in Vietnam, and the subsequent policy of withdrawal. The Council was also responsible for the formulation of the Carter administration's ''hu-man rights'' campaign and the temporary curtailment by it of arms sales. The consistency between the Council's ''1980s Project'' and the presumed vision of the Carter administration is striking:

> The [1980s] project began in 1975, and it includes (1) an international campaign on behalf of ''human rights''; (2) a series of alternative approaches to nuclear stability, including a new strict policy toward nuclear proliferation; (3) an effort to restrict in-ternational arms sales; and (4) a study of ''North-South global relations''—rela-tions between richer and poorer countries. (Dye, 1978: 318)

Dye concluded his analysis[15] of the Council on Foreign Relations with: ''It should come as no surprise to [Council] watchers that each of these concerns [was] reflected in the administration of President Jimmy Carter.''

---

campaign pledge to move beyond ''the establishment'' in choosing individuals to serve in his ad-ministration. Clearly the revolving door principle remained in operation under Carter.

[15]The influence ascribed to the Council on Foreign Relations by critics on the left who attack it as an ''imperial brain trust'' and those on the right who preceive it as an organized global con-spiracy has been challenged by others. John Kenneth Galbraith has argued (in Ungar, 1985b) that ''Most of the proceedings [of the Council on Foreign Relations] involve a level of banality so deep that the only question they raise is whether one should sit through them.'' Another scornful inter-pretation (Schulzinger, 1985) alleges that the Council has a myopic, centrist orientation which has made it modestly effective in some policy areas but overall mostly irrelevant.

It is also instructive that it was the Council on Foreign Relations which called for a fundamental reevaluation of the Soviet-American relationship in response to the Soviet military buildup, even before Ronald Reagan took office. Reagan subsequently made a U.S. military buildup the centerpiece of his foreign policy. The Reagan administration also relied heavily on Council advice in its management of the relationship, as the Council's intimate involvement in the initiation of the INF and START arms control talks with the Soviet Union and its advocacy of the "No First Use" principle regarding nuclear weapons indicate (see Dye, 1986). The continuing influence of the Council is also suggested by the fact that Vice President George Bush, Secretary of Defense Caspar Weinberger, Secretary of State George P. Shultz, Secretary of State Alexander Haig, Secretary of the Treasury Donald Regan, and CIA Director William Casey were all Council on Foreign Relations members.

The obtrusive role that this governing elite has played in the formulation of American foreign policy has survived over a prolonged period. That role continues, although its cohesion and power may have begun to wane in the 1980s as the composition of the country's foreign policy elite has been challenged by new centers of power and wealth, and by the ascendance to influence of a "neoconservative" movement which questions the liberal assumptions of those who maintained faith in the ability of government to address all problems. These neoconservatives nonetheless are deeply committed to the realist faith in military power and the necessity of pursuing a global policy of containment by interventionist means. Other factions within the elite have begun to surface as a division has emerged between "the new-rich, southern, and western *cowboys* and the established eastern, liberal *yankees*" (Dye, 1986). And "the establishment" has been challenged by the ascendance of a new class of foreign policy "professionals" whose managerial, technocrat outlook differs from the perspective of the traditionally defined "establishment" (Destler, Gelb, and Lake, 1984). The effects of these changes in the composition of the foreign policy elite are difficult to predict. But the appearance of fissures within it may not produce any major policy changes if emerging factions continue to operate from the same assumptions about foreign policy as those maintained by the "old guard."

The consistency between government policy and the recommendations of those who seek to influence policy from outside of government as well as those who join the government does not necessarily pose a problem for liberal democratic theory, because a democracy encourages the participation of people and the expression of their preferences. But what if we ask the related question, "Are foreign policy-making elites and others with influence different in values and outlooks from the Americans they represent?" We have already suggested they continue to be in terms of the special social, economic, and political experiences of the "sunbelt cowboys" and the "established yankees" as well as the neoconservative and the professional elite. If those in power and those who influence them are atypical Americans in those terms, might they also have values different from the people they lead? Do these values make a difference, if they are the only ones which receive serious consideration in the councils of government? Does a small minority therefore actually control the majority?

Available evidence on these issues is mixed. On one hand, it is noteworthy that elites generally have been "public regarding" and have supported domestic policies associated with the welfare state and foreign policies consistent with the precepts of active internationalism. In both policy arenas most Americans have generally registered approval of those overall thrusts. On the other hand Thomas Dye and L. Harmon Zeigler have argued that elites and masses do differ, ironically, in their attitudes regarding the democratic process itself:

> Democratic values have survived because elites, not masses, govern. Elites in America—leaders in government, industry, education, and civic affairs; the well-educated, prestigiously employed, and politically active—give greater support to basic democratic values and "rules of the game" than do the masses. And it is because masses in America respond to the ideas of democratically minded elites that liberal values are preserved. (Dye and Zeigler, 1981: 17)

Dye and Zeigler also observe, however, that the commitment of elites to liberal democratic values is only *relatively* greater than that of the masses. That commitment may turn out to be especially fragile during a crisis period; when war threatens, fearful elites tend to

> . . . respond by curtailing freedom and strengthening security. Dissent is no longer tolerated, the news media are censored, free speech is curtailed, potential counterelites are jailed, and police and security forces are strengthened, usually in the name of "national security," or "law and order." Elites convince themselves that these steps are necessary to preserve liberal democratic values. The irony is that in trying to preserve democracy, the elites make society less democratic. (Dye and Zeigler, 1981: 21)

Less apocalyptically, elites cannot be expected to formulate policies that threaten their power and privileges. Therefore, even in routine circumstances, elites may be expected to protect their advantaged positions.[16] The result? "Changes and innovations in public policy," argue Dye and Zeigler (1981), "come about when elites redefine their own values. The general conservatism of elites however—that is, their interest in preserving the system—means that changes in public policies will be incremental rather than revolutionary. Public policies are often modified but seldom replaced."

[16]Interestingly, the majority of Americans also see government leaders as driven primarily by their desire to promote their own power. Public opinion surveys reveal that from 1970 to 1985 between 55 and 80 percent of the American public agreed with the statement that the United States government is run by a few big interests looking out for themselves, whereas between 20 and 40 percent believed that it is run for the benefit of all (*Public Opinion*, September 1985: 21).

The democratic theory that American foreign policy makers necessarily reflect and represent the views of the public is thus undermined by the perpetuation of a community whose members are quite unlike average Americans. Indeed, the picture is that of a "power elite" (Mills, 1956) consisting of a select few who govern America[17] without direction from the general public. The American political system gives the public participation (for example, elections) without power, involvement without influence, while a small set of elite participants, acting both openly and behind closed doors, makes all the important decisions. (There are thus elites operating in the domestic as well as the foreign policy arena.) Even elected officials, from this perspective, might properly be thought of more as "proximate policy makers" whose actions give official sanction "knowingly or unknowingly" to the values of the power elite (Dye, 1978; 1979) than as simple conduits through which the preferences of the American mass public are translated into policy. As a consequence, not only are the social backgrounds and values of elites and the mass of the American people different, but their interests may diverge as well. The public cannot be safely equated with the government, for the actual authority for government does not reside—the doctrine of popular sovereignty notwithstanding—in majority opinion. It resides instead in a select minority's power, especially in the area of foreign policy.

This alleged discrepancy is often believed to make itself most visible with respect to the "military-industrial complex," which we might think of as a variant of the elitist model described above.

Does a Military-Industrial Complex Determine American Foreign Policy?

It was President Eisenhower, a highly decorated World War II general, who first brought national attention to the "military-industrial complex" when he warned, in an often quoted passage from his farewell address (January 17, 1961):

> This conjunction of an immense Military Establishment and a large arms industry is new in the American experience. The total influence—economic, political, even spiritual—is felt in every city, every statehouse, every office of the Federal Govern-

[17] The term "power elite" as used in the context of foreign policy making is essentially synonymous with "the establishment" described above, which includes those who have access to persons occupying foreign policy decision-making roles and who themselves from time to time assume positions of authority. Note, however, that the "power elite" or "the establishment" is not necessarily synonymous with the "governing elite," a term which refers exclusively to those who occupy positions of authority in the government. Particularly at the top levels of government, of course, there is an overlap between "the establishment" and "the governing elite"—an overlap which provides an important channel between those inside government and those on the outside. Although the existence of various interlocks and overlaps among different elites makes it difficult to segment them into discrete, empirically identifiable groups, those same connections among variously defined minorities are among the empirical proof of the veracity of the elitist perspective on public policy making.

ment. We recognize the imperative need for this development. Yet we must not fail to comprehend its grave implications. Our toil, resources, and livelihood are all involved; so is the very structure of our society.

In the councils of government we must guard against the acquisition of unwarranted influence, whether sought or unsought, by the military-industrial complex. The potential for the disastrous rise of misplaced power exists and will persist.

We must never let the weight of this combination endanger our liberties or democratic processes . . . .

Eisenhower's warning to the American people has been interpreted in a variety of ways. Perhaps the most careful early statement is contained in the popular writings of C. Wright Mills (1956), which theorized that a power elite exists in the United States, acting in implicit and explicit collusion to promote policies designed to serve its own, rather than the nation's, interests. This is akin to Harold D. Lasswell's (1962) prophecy that a "garrison state" governed by "specialists in violence" will eventually emerge and dominate policy making. According to the military-industrial complex thesis, the American foreign policy-making community acts from an elitist position to undermine the countervailing forces of a potentially pluralist society that would otherwise keep in check the abuse of power. Specifically, the partnership is seen as one consisting of "(1) the professional soldiers, (2) managers and . . . owners of industries heavily engaged in military supply, (3) top government officials whose careers and interests are tied to military expenditure, and (4) legislators whose districts benefit from defense procurement" (Rosen, 1973). In Mills's own words:

> What is called the "Washington military clique" is not composed merely of military men, and it does not prevail merely in Washington. Its members exist all over the country, and it is a coalition of generals in the roles of corporation executives, of politicians masquerading as admirals, of corporation executives acting like politicians, of civil servants who become majors, of vice-admirals who are also the assistants to a cabinet officer, who is himself, by the way, really a member of the managerial elite. (Mills, 1956: 278)

According to Mills, the partnership among these interests is more a natural coalition than a conspiracy. The interests do occasionally join forces to strive for the same self-serving ends, but not necessarily by design, and not frequently in a cohesive, coordinated fashion. "The power elite," wrote Mills, "is composed of political, economic, and military men, but this institutionalized elite is frequently in some tension: it comes together only on certain coinciding points and only on certain occasions of 'crisis'." Members of this elite speak in a cacophony of voices over key issues. Nonetheless, the power of the elite is highly institutionalized (if disorganized), and is believed to derive as a natural outgrowth from an American capitalistic system which depends on foreign investment and international arms shipments for the maintenance of economic health.

Flowing from such assumptions are a number of propositions clearly tied to the politics of policy making. Included are the contentions that the contemporary arms race and the high level of American military spending are due to the self-aggrandizing activities of the military and industrial sectors of American society. The military-industrial community, so the reasoning goes, systematically propagates policies favorable to its interests through lobbying and mass advertising, which emphasize fear of foreign foes, the existence of capability gaps, and the need for vigilance. It is a "peddler of crisis" (Sanders, 1983), a business which benefits from trouble (see Sampson, 1977). Underlying the proposition is the possibility that a military-industrial complex in the Soviet Union, which requires an American threat to justify the benefits it receives from Cold War tension, may also contribute to the power of the American military-industrial complex. By extension, a kind of uncoordinated collusion between the superpower's two complexes may be operative. As Arthur Schlesinger (1983b) observes: "The irony is that the Pentagon and the Soviet Defense Ministry prosper symbiotically. There is no greater racket in the world today than generals claiming the other side is ahead in order to get bigger budgets for themselves." In a related vein, the military-industrial complex is said to perpetuate an ideology of international conflict by deliberately creating international tension and artificially contriving foreign threats for the purpose of rationalizing continued military spending. Corollary arguments hold that the government purposely exaggerates external dangers for the purpose of justifying unnecessary expenditures and weapons programs, and that it is the dissemination of war scares by the complex which partly perpetuates American hostility toward the Soviet Union and preserves the containment strategy as the backbone of American foreign policy. James N. Rosenau summarizes the linkages between the power-elite thesis and the activities presumed to flow from the related assumption of a military-industrial complex:

> [The power-elite thesis] posits a master internal variable, a coordinated leadership that thrives on and is supportive of a Cold War strategy and capable of generating and sustaining public support for such a strategy. It also posits this variable as linked to the external world in the sense that any conciliatory tendencies in the Communist world are seen as evolving a suspicious response on the part of the controlling elites, while any aggressive tendencies abroad are seen as reinforcing their commitment to the prevailing strategy. . . . [N]othing can happen within the United States that will conduce to alterations in the orientations of the elites. They are seen to be too entrenched and too dependent on the continuation of the Cold War for their power to accommodate to a shifting world scene. . . . It amounts to a closed system of thought in which basic transformations are neither empirically nor conceptually possible. (Rosenau, 1973: 424)

Overall, then, the influence of the all-powerful military-industrial complex can be hypothesized to have contributed to the militarization of both American society and American foreign policy. In the latter case military solutions often have been sought for political problems and military might has been retained as a cornerstone of American tactics for managing its international affairs.

The key to the military-industrial complex variant of the power-elite thesis is the assumption that the efforts of its various military and industrial components outweigh any countervailing forces in American society. The complex is assumed to be all-powerful, capable of "calling the shots" in American foreign policy. It operates as the single most influential interest group in American society, dominating the rest. Again, in Eisenhower's words:

> The Congressman who seeks a new defense establishment in his district; the company in Los Angeles, Denver, or Baltimore that wants an order for more airplanes; the services which want them, the armies of scientists who want so terribly to test their newest views; put all of these together and you have a lobby.

Like many special-interest groups, the complex promotes parochial interests and the maintenance of foreign policies that may be beneficial to itself but detrimental to the nation as a whole. But what makes the complex so special is the extraordinary influence it exercises on the whole of American society as well as the disproportionate expenditures it consumes.

How accurate is that theory? The available evidence fails to support all of the propositions implied. Conclusively demonstrating the presumed interlock between defense contractors and top-level decision makers in government has proven especially difficult. Nevertheless, sufficient evidence is available to lend substantial credibility to the general military-industrial complex thesis. Consider some commonly observed symptoms:[18]

1. The domestic work force in America is highly dependent on continued military spending: "The jobs of one out of ten Americans depend directly or indirectly on defense spending" (Tempest, 1983: B1) Moreover, "according to Defense Secretary Weinberger, every $1 billion in defense spending creates 35,000 jobs" (Tempest, 1983: B9) and the same amount of expenditures in arms exports "directly supports about 50,000 jobs" (*Time*, October 26, 1981: 36).
2. During the 1950s and 1960s, Congress, instead of checking defense spending, often appropriated more federal money for military spending than originally requested by the president. Since then, it often has funded particular programs or weapons systems not supported in the president's budget request.[19] Congress is said to contribute to the problem rather than to serve as a solution to the abuses in waste and mismanagement within the Pentagon's weapons procurement pro-

---

[18]Supporting data and additional information for each of these observations can be found in Atkinson and Hiatt (1985), Dolbeare and Edelman (1974 and 1985), Domhoff (1971), Donovan (1974), Etzioni (1984), Fossedal (1985), Goodwin (1985), Hiatt and Atkinson (1985), Horowitz (1969), Kolko (1969), Parenti (1974 and 1980), Pincus (1985a), Proxmire (1970), and Rosen (1973). For contrasting views of some of the relevant data, see Carey (1969), Clotfelter (1973), Dye (1983), Lens (1970), and Schiller and Phillips (1972).

[19]Senator Warren Rudman underscored the symbiotic relationship between Congress and the military-industrial complex with the observation that "There is not a member of this Senate, or a member of the House, who does not have some defense facility in their state, some of which are

cess that surfaced so conspicuously in the 1980s. The tendency exists for some congressmen to treat the military budget as a source of patronage (to protect contractors in their districts) and to saddle the Pentagon with extra expenditures which escalate their costs (see Mossberg, 1983). Congressional pressure is said to have jumped the costs of each MX missile from $150 million in 1978 to $600 million—and rising—in 1985, or escalated the costs of the B-1 bomber from $1 million in 1970 to $220 million in 1984. One observer of the weapons procurement process and of congressional entanglement and responsibility in it notes that "to survive the scrutiny of the complex, a missile must of course be able to hit its target. But not too well—if so, it might threaten some continuing project, as the stealth bomber threatened the B-1 throughout the 1970s and 1980s. It must be built in the right congressional districts . . . " (Fossedal, 1985b).

3. The profits of defense contractors greatly exceed those in other industries. Why? Perhaps because the Pentagon practices a form of corporate welfare for its suppliers, in which the regular rules of free, competitive trade are nonexistent. "Somebody said that the Pentagon runs the world's second-largest planned economy after the Kremlin," asserted defense analyst Wolfgang Demisch. "I think that's a little harsh, but there's something to it" (cited in Atkinson and Hiatt, 1985). The Pentagon's 20,000 prime contractors and 150,000 subcontractors and vendors labor under "a funny form of capitalism" which practically assures corporate profits: "The arms bazaar remains a business like no other, part regulated utility, part national asset, part reaper of subsized profit. . . . [W]hen the Pentagon orchestrates the competition, the loser often wins." (Atkinson and Hiatt, 1985).

A number of procedures insure that a defense contractor will profit from doing work with the Pentagon. Procurement dollars are seldom awarded through competitive bidding. Contractors are "cushioned from the impact of their inefficiency" by a process known as "contract nourishment." According to the Extraordinary Contractual Relief Act (Public Law 85–104), the government has since 1958 given grants on more than 6,000 occasions to bail out defense contractors in trouble; the cost of these grants has totaled $1.4 billion. The Pentagon, moreover, picks up the costs for "even unsolicited and unsuccessful proposals," and awards hundreds of millions of dollars in interest-free loans. The government also allows its contractors to defer taxes on their huge profits, sometimes for many years, through a practice known as "The Method"[20] (Hiatt

---

necessary and some of which are not." Examples of the alleged influence of the military-industrial complex in Congress are abundant. For instance:

In early 1961 some of the White House people were trying to slow down the arms race. . . . At that point the United States had 450 missiles; McNamara was asking for 950, and the Joint Chiefs of Staff were asking for 3,000. The White House people had quietly checked around and found that in effectiveness . . . the 450 were the same as McNamara's 950. . . .
"What about it, Bob," Kennedy asked.
"Well, they're right," McNamara answered.
"Well, then, why the nine hundred and fifty, Bob?" Kennedy asked.
"Because that's the smallest number we can take up on the Hill without getting murdered," he answered. (Halberstam, 1972: 72)

[20]General Dynamics Corporation, the nation's largest defense contractor, has paid no federal taxes since 1972; Lockheed has paid no taxes since 1979, Boeing since 1980, and "General Electric,

and Atkinson, 1985). The picture painted by these practices is one in which the "fix" appears to be deeply ingrained. Military industries profit well from their business with the military, and the military assures that its quest for new weapons will be supplied by happy contractors. It appears to be a marriage in which the two partners actively collaborate to sustain.

4. Military contracts routinely involve costs far in excess of original cost estimates. Fraud, waste, and corruption have been chronic (Roth, 1984), as abuses such as the government's payment of $640 to Lockheed corporation for airplane toilet seats reveal (Gergen, 1985). Extravagantly expensive military gadgetry has added immeasurably to contractors' corporate profits, and yet "in 77 cases of shoddy construction work reviewed by Pentagon auditors in 1982, only once was the contractor forced to pay for his mistakes" (Atkinson and Hiatt, 1985).[21]

5. Universities now do a substantial amount of the Pentagon's basic research. In 1985, for example, universities accounted for more than $200 million in contracts for the Strategic Defense Initiative (*The Defense Monitor*, vol. 15, no. 3, 1986: 5) Because universities have been seduced into partnership they no longer serve as a countervailing balance to the military-industrial community.[22]

6. The complex is said to have become since the 1960s even more complex and powerful with the creation of numerous private "consulting firms" and "nonprofit" think tanks designed to assist the government with its defense needs (and charge it handsomely for that assistance). Although they often compete with themselves over a share of the growing "research monies" that have become readily available, participation in this competition has proven lucrative for most. It is instructive that "few civilian analysts are to be found" in the employment of these firms; the "beltway bandits," as they are known, are populated with former Pentagon personnel and retired officers (Brewer and Bracken, 1984; see also Pincus, 1985a). The parade of officers into the firms they supervise is unlikely to dwindle; 2,240 senior military and civilian Defense Department officials took jobs with major defense contractors over a three-year period in the 1980s (*U.S. News and World Report*, April 29, 1985: 27). And the advice emanating from them has a remarkable tendency to advocate policies that serve the Defense Department's interests; "studies that challenge higher authority, that deviate much in either tone or color from the represented service's pitch or uniform hue" are few and far between (Brewer and Bracken, 1984).

7. Defense spending has been steadily increasing in absolute terms and continues to account for a high percentage of federal outlays. Even under conditions of massive budget deficits and accelerating federal debt, military expenditures consumed in 1985 29.4 percent of the federal budget, and were projected to rise to 34.6 percent by 1989 (Committee on the Budget, U.S. House of Representatives, 1984: 66B). Under the Reagan administration, the military-industrial com-

---

ranked fourth in the defense industry, earned $6.5 billion in profits from 1981 to 1983. Yet it paid no federal income tax and claimed a refund of $283 million" (Atkinson and Hiatt, 1985).

[21]The consequences of poorly built equipment has been the expansion of the Pentagon's staff and subsequent budget to manage its operations. In the wake of disclosures in 1984 that the Defense Department was paying $400 each for $8 claw hammers, Reich (1985: 36) reports that "the military is said to have added 7,000 additional staffers to solve its spare-parts problems."

[22]The absorption of both academic and governmental sectors into the military-industrial complex has enhanced its collective power and correspondingly called for a broadened definition captured by the acronym MAGIC (military-academic-governmental-industrial complex).

plex has prospered. "At the mid-point of President Reagan's eight-year, $2.3 trillion defense buildup, the Pentagon is spending an average $28 million every hour—24 hours a day, seven days a week. In the time it will take you to read [these two sentences] aloud, the United States will spend $160,000 for defense" (Atkinson and Hiatt, 1985: 6). The priority assigned to defense spending is a partial (albeit imperfect) indicator of influence, for the money that goes for the interests of the military-industrial complex can only come at the expense of the ability of federal tax revenue to service the needs of other segments of American society.[23]

These insights provide empirical support for the alleged existence of a complex of military-industrial interests in the United States. They also lend credence to Richard Barnet's (1972) telling observation that United States foreign policy is "an elite preserve . . . made for the benefit of that elite."

But it would be irresponsible to posit that the military-industrial complex is the exclusive determinant of American foreign policy. The complex undoubtedly colors much of what the United States does abroad and at home to prepare for external action. But we cannot assume that all recent American initiatives abroad, including the repeated incidence of foreign military intervention, derive solely from pressures emanating from the faceless complex. The evidence is too contradictory (see Leiberson, 1971).

And some components of the theory are either unconvincing or illogical. While it may be true that pressures for increased defense spending are brought to bear by some lobbyists and defense contractors, the conclusion that the military-industrial complex single-mindedly pursues this objective above all others does not follow. Nor does the conspiratorial version of the theory, which sees conniving generals and industrialists collaborating to corruptly enrich themselves; instead, "the problem is not conspiracy or corruption, but unchecked rule" (Galbraith, 1969b). Furthermore, the profits of American industry are not contingent exclusively on military sales.[24] And to argue that the complex benefits directly from war or that it actively promotes

---

[23]One estimate (Russett, 1970: 137–146) notes that for each dollar spent by the government for military purposes, forty-two fewer cents are available to U.S. citizens for personal consumption. Stated somewhat differently, since every tax dollar spent on defense must come from some other sector of the economy, those results show that 42 percent of the costs are borne by a reduction in personal consumption. Russett (1970: 140–141) also shows that for every dollar increase in defense spending, twenty-nine cents comes from fixed capital formation, ten cents from exports, and eighteen cents from federal, state, and local government expenditures. To a considerable extent, therefore, the American public subsidizes what may be unnecessary military spending from its own pocket; defense spending in the Reagan administration has reduced expenditures for health and education to a particularly pronounced extent (Russett, 1982).

[24]"The one hundred largest industrial corporations," report Dye and Zeigler (1981: 127–128), "depend on military contracts for less than 10 percent of their sales," and "the price-earnings ratios for military-oriented companies are substantially lower than for civilian-oriented companies." On the other hand, Barnet (1981: 137) notes that "of the fifty largest American industrial companies, thirty-two make or export arms." For an in-depth study of one of America's largest defense contractors and its relationship to the U.S. government, see Goodwin's (1985) *Brotherhood of Arms: General Dynamics and the Business of Defending America.*

foreign adventure and derives pleasure from international instability is patently ridiculous. Both war and foreign adventure directly threaten the financial interests of corporate America and the lives (though not the prospects of promotion) of military officers.

Clearly some segments of American society realize benefits from a militant foreign policy posture, but where there is interest, there is not necessarily influence. The conclusion of one analysis of the theory of the military-industrial complex remains relevant today:

> Demonstrating that some segment of the military-industrial complex will benefit from a given policy is not tantamount to a proof that the policy was in fact initiated for this purpose. Inevitably, private interests will be served by a [multi-billion dollar] annual procurement, but it does not follow that these interests determine policy. . . . Overall, we may say that C. Wright Mills has been sustained in the essential propositions of his theory, though some of the more simplified conspiratorial versions developed by his most ardent followers must be rejected. (Rosen, 1973: 4, 25)

The Military-Industrial Complex and the Continuity of American Foreign Policy

The hypothesized existence of powerful military-industrial interests combined with the homogeneous social characteristics of decision makers create an environment that operates in favor of continuity in foreign policy. The influence on foreign policy exerted by that amalgamated force may be a factor that promotes the continuation of existing policy, for, presumably, the interests of that interlocking set of actors have not changed over time. Reason and evidence suggest that the pressure on policy makers exerted by the self-aggrandizing activities of the military-industrial complex has been fairly constant since World War II. It follows, then, that that pressure constrains policy innovation by creating obstacles to alterations in the kinds of foreign policies the United States pursues. The ever-present dependence of governmental officials on the military-industrial complex creates powerful incentives for leaders to choose policies that resemble those of their predecessors. To change the policy would be to challenge the entrenched and vested interests of the military-industrial complex which supports it. Although informed insiders have called for reforms (see Fallows, 1982; Luttwak, 1985) in order to make for a stronger, more efficient defense, without waste and fraud, the foundations of the military-industrial complex are strongly supported and are unlikely to undergo serious revision. Because an influential portion of Americans benefit from military spending, American foreign policy has been frozen in the perpetual pursuit of national objectives through military preparedness and by military means. And because of the nation's superpower status and its pursuit of a global role, it has been driven to maintain an inordinately large military-industrial establishment that may be beyond the government's capacity to control (Yarmolinsky and Foster, 1983).

THE IMPACT OF SPECIAL-INTEREST GROUPS ON AMERICAN FOREIGN POLICY

Support for the power-elite thesis and the related concept of the military-industrial complex does much to challenge the theory of liberal democracy. If in practice an elite indeed rules, and if its behavior is supported by a gargantuan military-industrial complex, then democratic policy-formation practice itself may be eroded. Foreign policy making under such conditions probably becomes less an expression of the values and interests of the American people at large and more a reflection of the values and interests of a privileged minority.

But there is an alternative view—individual Americans seeking to influence policy by organizing themselves into groups whose purpose is to petition the government on behalf of their shared interests and values. That is the pluralist model of public policy making. Indeed, the mere existence of large numbers of competing groups leads to the description of American society as a *pluralized* one. The United States has been labeled an "interest group society" (Berry, 1984) because Americans are so active in voluntary associations.

Pluralism purports to explain how liberal values and democratic institutions might be preserved even while democracy in its purest (direct) form is precluded. Pluralist theorists acknowledge that the demands of a modern, complex government with global interests necessarily concentrates power in the hands of the few. Citizens cannot participate directly in the making of public policy. Nonetheless, so pluralism contends, the potential tyranny of elites is prevented, and democracy preserved, because multiple public interests are represented by leaders who themselves are in competition with one another. Public preferences therefore find expression through bargaining among interest-group elites, who take the public into account not simply because they are sincerely concerned about the public welfare but also because the public exerts pressure upon them through voluntary interest-group membership (as well as through political parties and elections). Thus people do, after all, have the means of influencing policy, and ultimately society's preferences are translated into public policy. The mechanism is competition of interest groups, each pursuing its own particularistic interests; the public good is served much as Adam Smith theorized it is served in the economic sphere, where the invisible hand of the marketplace supposedly translates the pursuit of private interests into the general welfare. The potential abuse of power is controlled by competition among countervailing centers of power. The product is government for the people, but not necessarily by them.[25]

However reassuring to democratic theory such an interpretation may be, in the foreign policy arena, where the questions at issue are often technical and remote from the daily lives of Americans, the presence of numerous and presumably powerful groups gives American foreign policy making the image of

---

[25]For an influential treatment contending that pluralism has become irrelevant because the immense growth of government has placed control of public policy in the hands of special interests, see Lowi's *The End of Liberalism* (1979).

being dominated by narrowly vested interests. Because interest-group activities are not always visible or attended by the press, interest groups often are assumed to be secretly working behind the scenes, dictating American action abroad. Indeed, the proposition that foreign policy is somehow mechanically determined by the activities of pressure groups has many adherents. They are illustrated by those who attribute particular decisions to the influence of special groups (for example, Jewish groups are often assumed to exert pro-Israeli influence on American policy, and were, for instance, given credit for America's recognition of Israel only eleven minutes after it declared its independence; for a discussion of the ''myth'' of this influence, see Spiegel, 1985). The more absurd conspiracy theories of groups like the John Birch Society also illustrate this kind of thinking.[26]

How accurate is the proposition that influential special-interest groups operate both openly and behind the scenes to pressure the government for certain policy positions toward others in the external environment—in essence controlling the content of American foreign policy? If the theory is accurate, are private interests, but not the public welfare, being served?

Interest-Group Activity and Foreign Policy Making

Clearly many different voluntary associations of national scope can be found operating in American society, each seeking in its own way to influence governmental policy abroad in a way beneficial to itself. The more than 17,500 organizations which Americans join and support to further their political causes (Dolbeare and Edelman, 1985: 445), range in size from the large, powerful groups representing heterogeneous constituencies (such as the AFL-CIO or the National Chamber of Commerce), to smaller, more homogeneous groups organized around rather specific issues (such as the China Lobby, which for over two decades advocated that the United States refuse to recognize the communist regime on Mainland China). More generally, the major types of interests within American society organized for purposes of affecting policies abroad include religious, scientific, professional, labor, arts, ethnic, sports, cultural, business, and education groups.

In an even broader sense, foreign governments should be regarded as interest groups (by law, nondiplomatic representatives of other nations are required to register as lobbyists), because foreign representatives seek to influ-

---

[26]Ethnic groups comprise a special category of interest-group influence on American foreign policy (see Said, 1981). The John Birch Society, on the other hand, is representative of an ideological group with a narrow point of view. It claims that a self-recruiting and self-perpetuating elite of world leaders has conspired to make all major decisions, including the outbreak of wars, over the last 400 years. Members of this alleged conspiracy have included not only Lenin, Stalin, and Hitler, the Birchers claim, but Earl Warren, Henry Kissinger, Henry Ford II, Dwight Eisenhower, and Nelson Rockefeller, among others. The Birchers claim that such elites and New York's investment bankers finance communist revolutions and left-wing activities throughout the world to divert attention from the real threat to freedom in the Western democracies—de facto world government by the capitalist elite headquartered in New York City.

ence the decisions of American foreign policy makers. The presence of foreign powers' lobbyists should not be underestimated; in 1985 there were 850 registered agents of foreign countries and firms whose $150 million outlays in lobbying efforts greatly exceeded "the $42 million reportedly spent [in 1984] by the 7,200 domestic lobbyists registered by Congress" (*U.S. News and World Report*, June 17, 1985: 35). Similarly, agencies of the U.S. government act much like interest groups, since they have their own conceptions of the appropriate policy of the United States and take steps to ensure their conceptions are represented in decision-making circles.[27] The Pentagon, for example, historically has employed (using taxpayers' dollars, of course) hundreds of "congressional liaisons," whose purpose is to secure legislation favorable to itself. The size and complexity of American government has expanded the lobbying role of bureaucratic agencies, whose activities occur largely outside the public eye. The formation of "iron triangles" consisting of the interlocking expertise, specialization, and coordinated activities of lobbies pushing for their own interests, bureaucrats in charge of the administration of policy with respect to those special interests, and the congressional subcommittees dealing with them, are a noteworthy phenomenon. These triangles comprise an invisible, powerful layer of governance that dominates the making of public policy in some areas.

The major types of conventionally defined public interest groups (sometimes known as PIGs) serve as substitutes for perhaps more conventional means of seeking to influence government policy (such as writing letters to congressional representatives). They provide a means of acting politically, because organized groups often have administrative personnel and substantial sums of money behind them. Thus they become important vehicles for the expression of values and interests on a wide range of policy issues.

How effective are their efforts, particularly in the area of foreign policy? Conclusions of scholars who have studied the linkage between domestic pressure groups and foreign policy decisions in the United States (primarily Cohen, 1959; and Milbrath, 1967) may be summarized as follows:

1. As a general rule, interest groups exert a far greater impact on domestic than on foreign policy issues because the requirements of national security give the government elite relative immunity from domestic pressures.
2. Interest-group activity operates as an ever present, if limited, constraint on policy making. But the impact *varies with the issue*; in particular, "the less the importance of the issue, the greater the likelihood of group influence" (Milbrath, 1967).

---

[27]Although the behavioral characteristics of these two types of groups bear similarities to nongovernmental, domestic interest groups, representatives of foreign governments are preferably conceptualized as conduits for transmitting external stimuli to policy makers, while the descriptive characteristics of bureaucratic organizations are better conceptualized in terms of their governmental function (chapter eleven), and their behavior patterns properly fall within the role source category (chapter thirteen).

3. Similarly, the occasions when interest groups are most influential are rare. Interest-group influences are greatest when the issue is not in the public spotlight, attended by the mass media, and when only a small segment of the populace is affected.
4. Crises tend to stimulate interest; as the crisis level increases, the interests of
   more groups are likely to be at stake, and groups are likely to try to exert more
   influence. But "as the crisis level increases further, and especially as decision
   time shortens, there is relatively little opportunity for group interests to be
   taken into account [and] the President has enormous power to shape public
   opinion and receives little effective challenge from interest groups" (Milbrath,
   1967).
5. Influence between the government and interest groups is reciprocal, but it is
   more probable that government officials manipulate pressure groups than that
   pressure groups exercise influence over government policy.
6. The capacity of interest groups to mold opinion on foreign affairs is very limited; mass attitudes are not amenable to persuasion by interest-group efforts
   (even though most groups concentrate their efforts on attempts to influence
   public opinion rather than policy itself).
7. Special-interest groups have more influence than large, national, general-pur-
   pose organizations.[28]
8. Interest groups sometimes seek inaction from government and maintenance of
   the status quo; such efforts are generally more successful than efforts to bring
   about policy change. For this reason interest groups are generally regarded as
   agents of policy stability.
9. The influence of interest groups tends to expand during election years, when
   candidates for office are most prone to open channels of communication and to
   give interest groups access.
10. Pressure groups exercise power over policy most effectively through Congress;
    correspondingly, when congressional interest in a foreign policy issue mounts,
    interest-group activity and influence increase.
11. The ability of a special-interest group to exert influence on foreign policy in-
    creases in those situations—such as national security—where "symbols" can
    be created which are unlikely to be opposed by other groups with material in-
    terests in that symbol.[29]
12. Pressure groups will tend to exert their greatest influence on nonsecurity is-
    sues that entail economic considerations commanding attention over a long pe-
    riod of time (Cohen, 1983).

Those characteristics of pressure-group efforts to mold and guide foreign
policy suggest that the mere presence of such groups, and the mere fact they

[28]The influence of specific (single-issue) groups is limited largely to their special policy interest. For instance, "commodity groups have no effect on foreign policy beyond whatever arrangements they are able to make respecting the treatment of their particular commodities in international trade or a foreign aid program. Ethnic groups have no influence on policy with respect to
areas of the world other than those to which they have a direct connection" (Cohen, 1959).

[29]America's postwar African policy provides some examples in which "groups with interest
in symbols were influential where there were no groups with material interests opposing them or
where they could supplement their case by arguments showing that tangible resources could be
secured or fostered by their policy preferences" (Ogene, 1983).

are organized with the intent of persuasion, does not guarantee that they are penetrating the policy formation process. Interest groups may be effective on certain special issues. More often, however, it would appear that the foreign policy-making process is relatively immune from direct pressure by interest groups.

Special-Interest Groups, Pluralism, and the Continuity of American Foreign Policy

Several reasons can be offered for failure of interest groups to determine the policies of the nation abroad, except in the most episodic circumstances relating to discrete policy decisions and specific issues. In the first place, the ability of any one interest group to exert influence is offset by the tendency for *countervailing powers* to materialize over the disposition of any one issue. As one group emerges and begins to be powerful, other groups tend to spring up to balance it. The efforts of one group to pursue its parochial interests are countered by the efforts of other opposing groups; when an interest group seeks vigorously to push policy in one direction, other groups or coalitions of groups—aroused that their interests are being threatened—are stimulated to push policy in the opposite direction. A classic illustration of the process was the threat during the Industrial Revolution that Big Business would gain control of American society. But Big Business was balanced by the emergence of Big Labor, which, once it grew in disproportionate influence, was balanced in turn by Big Government. Contemporary illustrations might include the resistance to the nuclear energy lobby mounted by those concerned with threats posed by nuclear power, the opposition to abortion posed by the "right-to-life" movement, or the manner in which the advocacy of the Equal Rights Amendment generated a countermovement dedicated to the defeat of that proposal. With respect to foreign policy, the rise to disproportionate influence by a special-interest group may well be met by other groups challenging that influence. Arthur Cox's (1976) accounting of the nongovernmental domestic political proponents and opponents of détente during the period when that process first rose to the status of an enunciated policy (recall chapter three) suggests something about the manner in which countervailing forces tend to arise when an issue of foreign policy becomes salient; the controversies that surrounded the détente strategy provoked the emergence of the following groups:

PROPONENTS OF DÉTENTE	OPPONENTS OF DÉTENTE
Arms Control Association	American Legion
Federation of American Scientists	Veterans of Foreign Wars
Center for Defense Information	AFL-CIO (leadership)
Center for National Security Studies	Various Zionist organizations
Center for the Study of Democratic	Various organizations representing
Institutions	Americans with ancestry in Eastern

SANE (Committee for a Sane Nuclear
  Policy)
Council for a Liveable World
United Nations Association
World Federalists USA
World Peace Through World Law
Women's Strike for Peace
Friends Committee on National
  Legislation
League of Women Voters

Europe or the Baltic states
John Birch Society
American Enterprise Institute for Public
  Policy Research
Coalition for a Democratic Majority

To this accounting, of course, must be added influential members of the business community, representatives of some consumer groups, members of Congress and otherwise important segments of the Republican and Democratic parties, and various executive department agencies, such as the Arms Control and Disarmament Agency and the Department of Defense. Little wonder that the wisdom of relaxing tensions with the Soviet Union resulted in protracted debate in which during this period neither pro- nor antidétente forces appeared to gain the decisive voice.

Because détente is controversial as a policy and encompasses such broad philosophical issues, it was (and remains) destined to provoke a variety of interest groups to line up against each other. Issues such as those raised by détente are seldom settled. No side can ever claim permanent victory, for each decision that takes policy in one direction merely sets the stage for the next round of the contest, with the possibility that the losers of the moment will be winners tomorrow. The result with respect to fundamental foreign policy issues is usually a kind of unstable equilibrium, with no permanent resolution of the struggle. Even in the icy period of the Reagan administration's confrontational stance toward the Soviet Union, the debate about the merits of differing approaches toward the containment of Soviet global influence continued, and within this debate advocates of varients of a revived linkage strategy that was once the underpinning of détente could still be heard.

More discrete foreign policy issues, such as those entailing single decisions, also have the capacity to arouse interest groups counterpoised against each other. President Carter's decision in June 1977 not to deploy the B-1 bomber, for instance, was influenced by pressure from a coalition of three dozen opponents that included Clergy and Laity Concerned, the American Friends Service Committee, the National Taxpayers Union, the Federation of American Scientists, the Women's International League of Peace and Freedom, and Common Cause (Ornstein and Elder, 1978). Of course the pressure exerted by proponents of the B-1 (which included the Department of the Air Force), was enormous, too. Perhaps the intensity of the debate helps to explain why President Carter characterized his choice as "one of the most difficult decisions that I have made since I have been in office."

The presence of countervailing forces on all fronts suggests another reason for the relative impotence of interest-group influence on American foreign policy: interest groups maintain crisscrossing relationships with one another and have overlapping memberships. This tendency creates *cross-pressures* within and among the multiplicity of groups operating within the domestic political setting. Because of the number and diversity of groups striving for influence, the predominance of any one is precluded. Bargaining and competition between and among the various groups prevent any one group from gaining advantage over others and establishing preeminent power over foreign policy. Cross-pressures pull individuals in opposing directions, thereby reducing their capacity to concentrate on any single set of interests as social and political divisions within interest groups prevent any one group from monopolizing power and influence. Thus it is the fragmentation of power within a pluralistic domestic environment that keeps the foreign policy process from being penetrated and dominated by any one interest group.

Counterbalancing pressure groups comprise a constant in the otherwise turbulent game of foreign policy making. The nature of the game has been modified, however, by the emergence of single-issue-group politics and of ideologically committed *political action committees* (PACs).

The two developments are symbiotically related. Committed to but one cause (to the exclusion of others), single-issue groups strive to pursue their single objective with singular dedication. The number of such groups has risen spectacularly, as have their financial resources and the intensity of their supporters' beliefs. As a result the freedom of action of policy makers has been reduced. Because a zealously committed interest group is intolerant of compromise, it will accept no decision as satisfactory that promises anything less than complete agreement with its cause. In a policymaking arena shaped by the activities of such groups, the bargaining that in a pluralist system is supposed to produce an equitable definition of the public interest is precluded, and agreement or compromise solutions are nearly impossible to obtain. It is that feature of special-interest lobbying that led Senator Edward Kennedy to lament in 1978 that "Representative government is in the worst shape I have seen in my sixteen years in the Senate. The heart of the problem is that the Senate and the House are awash in a sea of interest lobbying and special interest campaign contributions."

In an effort to rectify some of the problems posed by the growing influence of single-issue groups, Congress passed a number of election reform laws designed to limit individual financial contributions to candidates for political office. Inadvertently, Congress thereby compounded the problem, rather than solving it, by creating the conditions conducive to the development of *political action committees*. The number (as well as the following and the financial resources) of PACs has increased substantially—rising from about 600 in 1974 to nearly 3,400 by 1983 (*Congressional Quarterly Weekly Report*, November 3, 1979: 2455; the *New York Times*, January 11, 1983: 7). Their numbers have expanded since then, but their rate of growth began to level off in the mid-1980s even while their financial resources continued to rise (Twentieth Century Fund, 1984; Sabato, 1984). Evidence indicates that PAC contributions comprise an increasing proportion of total candidate funds, and are approaching a level that equals that contributed by political parties themselves (Sabato, 1984).[30]

PACs exert their political muscle on behalf of the ideological beliefs of both the political left and what in the 1980s has been termed the "New Right."[31] Consider, for example, the ways in which PACs lined up during their ascendance in influence in the late 1970s and early 1980s in support of the massive increases in military spending contemplated by the Reagan administration: the Committee on the Present Danger, the American Security Council, the Coalition for Peace Through Strength, the Emergency Coalition Against Unilateral Disarmament, the American Conservative Union, the National Conservative Political Action Committee (NCPAC), the Conservative Caucus, and the Committee for Survival of a Free Congress. The proponents were opposed by a countercoalition of other groups, which fought its case largely with published research,[32] thus suggesting that the countervailing power critical to effective operation of pluralism may remain intact. (Although the opponents of increased military spending lost the initial skirmishes to the more lavishly funded New Right PACs, the drama has been replayed throughout the Reagan presidency.) Still problematic, however, is the question of whether the overlapping memberships typical of a pluralist situation will be able to bring the ideological left and right together.

Assuming that even with the rise of single-issue politics and PACs countervailing power persists, the foregoing interpretations lead to the conclusion that, although no particular interest group dominates American foreign policy making, the plurality of interest-group activity nevertheless exerts a collective impact on the style and content of external policy. In the aggregate, the interacting behavior of interest groups makes foreign policy formulation a product of bargaining among different groups with different interests, which fre-

---

[30]Data on PAC spending provided by the Federal Election Commission showed that, in 1982, total PAC spending was $83.1 million—$27.4 million from corporate PACs, $20.2 million from labor, $21.7 million from associations, and $13.9 million from other PACs (Stone and Barke, 1985: 163).

[31]PACs may be differentiated from the "think tanks" and "idea factories" which service them. Examples of the New Right's idea factories include the Hoover Institution at Stanford University, the Institute for Contemporary Studies, the Heritage Foundation, and the Center for Strategic and International Studies of Georgetown University (see Easterbrook 1986, for a discussion). Examples of think tanks on the left include the Center for Defense Information, the Institute for Policy Studies, the World Policy Institute, and the Center for National Security Studies.

[32]For a description of the position and activities of one such group—the Center for Defense Information, headed by retired Admiral Gene LaRocque—see Baber (1981).

The financial resources of the "peace through strength" coalition far exceeded those of the coalition seeking to countervail it (which suggests that money can buy influence). "In 1979," according to Barnet (1981: 103), "the combined budgets of the American Security Council and the American Security Council Foundation—both working to defeat SALT II—came to three million dollars, and the American Conservative Union spent about a million three hundred thousand to oppose the treaty." The American Security Council had enough funds behind it to film the alarmist and widely broadcast *The SALT Syndrome*, which was shown an average of sixteen times a day in South Dakota during the campaign to defeat George McGovern's bid for reelection to his Senate seat (Baber, 1981).

quently renders policy making little more than a process of negotiated compromise among contending special interests. More aptly, it makes foreign policy making resemble a taffy pull: every group attempts to pull policy in its own direction while resisting the pulls of others, with the result that policy fails to move in any discernible direction. The process encourages solutions tending toward the middle of the road and maintenance of the status quo. Thus we can hypothesize that American foreign policy has been so resistant to change over the past four decades at least partly because of the effects of a plurality of competing interest groups petitioning the government for favors. As Karl W. Deutsch concludes:

> When almost everybody is organized, society reaches a point where almost nothing can be done. Groups with limited power usually find it easier to veto someone else's proposal than to push through any positive policy of their own. When this happens, politics becomes negative, and interest groups turn into veto groups. Even where positive policies are possible, any substantial proposal has to be cleared with every relevant interest group. And the larger the number of organized groups, the more of them that must be consulted, the longer are the resulting delays, and the harder it becomes to turn any idea into action. (Deutsch, 1974: 61)

Is it any wonder why, given that reasoning, the foreign policy of the United States has manifested such continuity in the midst of often rapidly changing international circumstances? One of the reasons, it seems, is that this society is pluralistic, comprising a diversity of competing interest groups struggling for power. Policy innovation in such a domestic environment is unlikely.

SOCIETAL SOURCES OF FOREIGN POLICY CONTINUITY

We purposely have avoided judging the veracity of the elitist and pluralist models in relation to one another. The balance of evidence tends to be weighted in favor of the elitist model (in the context of foreign, if not domestic, policy making), but it is by no means conclusive. More important, however, neither model depicts the translation of widely shared precepts about liberal democracy into foreign policy outcomes in a manner consistent with the principles of one-man-one-vote participatory democracy. On the contrary, both depict a process in which the ordinary citizen matters very little when it comes to foreign policy making. As we shall see in the next chapter, when we examine the possible impact exerted by public opinion, presidential elections, and the mass media, there is little available evidence that would lead us to reject that conclusion.

At the same time, however, the evidence discussed here clearly indicates that societal factors have an impact on the substance, direction, and tone of American foreign policy. Overall, societal changes may stimulate adaptations in foreign policy (for example, the effects of a transformed political culture in the aftermath of Vietnam and Watergate), but they also act as constraints on policy innovation (as seen, for example, in the pull of interest-group competition, in the perpetuation of an elitist decision-making structure, and in the continued influence of the military-industrial complex). Such constraints help explain why policy change, when it does occur, usually comes in small, tentative, incremental steps rather than as grand designs for radical innovations. But to understand more fully how societal forces influence foreign policy, other factors must yet be worked into the equation. It is to these we now turn.

SUGGESTIONS FOR FURTHER READING

BELLAH, ROBERT N., RICHARD MADSEN, ANN SWIDLER, WILLIAM M. SULLIVAN, AND STEVEN M. TIPTON. *Habits of the Heart: Individualism and Commitment in American Life.* Berkeley, CA: University of California Press, 1985.

DALLEK, ROBERT. *The American Style of Foreign Policy: Cultural Politics and Foreign Affairs.* New York: Knopf, 1983.

GERSHMAN, CARL. "The Rise and Fall of the New Foreign-Policy Establishment," *Commentary* 70 (July 1980): 13–24.

McCLOSKY, HERBERT, AND JOHN ZALLER. *The American Ethos: Public Attitudes Toward Capitalism and Democracy.* Cambridge, MA: Harvard University Press, 1984.

McCORMICK, JAMES M. *American Foreign Policy and American Values.* Itasca, IL: Peacock, 1985.

MILBRATH, LESTER W. "Interest Groups and Foreign Policy," pp. 231–252 in James N. Rosenau, ed., *Domestic Sources of Foreign Policy.* New York: Free Press, 1967.

ROSEN, STEVEN, ed. *Testing the Theory of the Military-Industrial Complex.* Lexington, MA: Heath, 1973.

SCHLESINGER, ARTHUR M., JR. "Foreign Policy and the American Character," *Foreign Affairs* 62 (Fall 1983): 1–16.

WEISBAND, EDWARD. *The Ideology of American Foreign Policy.* Beverly Hills, CA: Sage, 1973.

9

THE IMPACT OF PUBLIC OPINION, PRESIDENTIAL ELECTIONS, AND THE MASS MEDIA

Nobody can know what it means for a President to be sitting in that White House working late at night and to have hundreds of thousands of demonstrators charging through the streets. Not even earplugs could block the noise.

President Richard M. Nixon, 1977

The biggest advantage a modern president has is the six o'clock news. Presidents can be on the news every night if they want to—and usually they want to. They can easily make themselves the focus of every major news report, because the president of the United States is the most powerful individual in the world.

President Ronald Reagan, 1984

Is American foreign policy influenced by characteristics of and changes in American society in general? Are foreign policy decisions in part a response to domestic stimuli? The foregoing chapter has suggested several ways in which American foreign policy making is colored by domestic considerations and that attributes of American society tend to define the bounds of permissible policy choice.

Continuing our investigation of this idea, we will now consider other societal variables which demarcate American foreign policy objectives, and the means employed to pursue those objectives. The nature of American public opinion as it affects the nation's conduct beyond its national borders is certainly one variable. The role that presidential elections play in the translation of public preferences into policy is another. Finally, the impact of the mass me-

286

dia—radio, television, and the press—on the process of policy determination is a third. Let us probe each of these additional components of the societal source category in succession.

PUBLIC OPINION AS A SOCIETAL SOURCE

Americans expect their attitudes and opinions to be considered when policies are promulgated by their leaders because those leaders have been elected to represent and serve the interests of their constituents.[1] After all, the Constitution speaks of "we the people" in an active sense, an affirmation reinforced by the popularity of campaign slogans promising "power to the people."

The theory that public policy is conditioned by mass opinion is attractive, but it raises troublesome questions. Does American public opinion direct and lead American foreign policy, as democratic theory would have us believe, or is the relationship more subtle and complicated? Is there evidence to support the thesis that foreign policy is a function of shifts in American public attitudes? Or is the relationship one of policy first and opinion second?

The Nature of American Public Opinion

Before probing the linkage between public opinion and foreign policy, we must identify the major properties of public sentiments. What follows is a brief inventory of the salient characteristics of American opinions as they relate to foreign policy issues. After perusing them, we will be in a better position to assess the public's potential impact on foreign policy.

American Public Opinion Is Uninformed About Politics and International Affairs. What Americans are thinking and doing has been probed extensively by surveys and opinion polls. Repeatedly, those studies have concluded "that the 'people' are neither thinking nor doing" (Rosenau, 1963). That most Americans fail to possess even the most elementary knowledge about their own political system, much less international affairs is an inescapable fact. Moreover, often the "information" held is so inaccurate that it might better be

---

[1]The presumed importance of public opinion is almost axiomatic in today's world. As Childs (1965) put it, "Politicians court it; statesmen appeal to it; philosophers extol or condemn it; merchants cater to it; military leaders fear it; sociologists analyze it; statisticians measure it; and constitution-makers try to make it soverign."

Despite the importance of public opinion, politicians' views of it are often uncomplimentary. John F. Kennedy's view, as described by his aide, Theodore C. Sorensen, is perhaps representative of leaders' images:

> Public opinion is often erratic, inconsistent, arbitrary, and unreasonable—with a compulsion to make mistakes. . . . It rarely considers the needs of the next generation or the history of the last. . . . It is frequently hampered by myths and misinformation, by stereotypes and shibboleths, and by an innate resistance to innovation. (Sorensen, 1963: 45–46)

labeled "misinformation." The following reveal the often startling level of ignorance and misinformation:

- In 1985, 28 percent of those surveyed thought that the Soviet Union and the United States had fought each other in World War II; 44 percent did not know the two were allies at that time (Clymer, 1985b: 48).
- In 1955, and again in 1970, almost 40 percent of the population was unaware that presidents are limited to two terms in office (Weissberg, 1986: 33).
- In 1979, only 23 percent of the adult population knew the two countries involved in the SALT negotiations (Erikson, Luttbeg, and Tedin, 1980: 19).
- In 1964, only 58 percent of the American public thought that the United States was a member of NATO; almost two-fifths believed the Soviet Union to be a member despite the fact that NATO's explicit purpose is to protect Western Europe and North America from Soviet attack (Free and Cantril, 1968: 60).
- In 1985, only 63 percent of the public knew that the United States supported South Vietnam in the Vietnam War, which cost 58,000 Americans their lives (Clymer, 1985a: 1).
- In 1950, and again in 1966, only two-thirds of the American people were able to identify the name of the U.S. secretary of state (Smith, 1972: 271); by 1978, the proportion had fallen to 34 percent (Erikson, Luttbeg, and Tedin, 1980: 19).
- In 1983, 47 percent of the American people did not know whether the United States supported or opposed the Sandinista government in Nicaragua; only 45 percent knew that the United States backed the government in El Salvador (*Public Opinion*, August–September, 1983: 21).

Evidence demonstrating the extent of political misunderstanding and ignorance about basic issues could be greatly expanded, but it would only reinforce the picture of an American citizenry ill informed about major issues of public policy and ill equipped to follow the ins and outs of government policy making. The issues about which the public is persistently ignorant are not "flash-in-the-pan" current events but typically are issues that have figured prominently on the national political agenda for a number of years. Strike a blow against democratic theory!

The American Public Is Uninterested in Public Affairs. The absence of basic knowledge about foreign affairs does not stem from deficiencies in U.S. educational institutions. It stems from lack of interest. Public awareness is a function of public inattention, for people are knowledgeable about what is important to them. And more Americans can identify the winner of the Super Bowl than can identify the most elementary facts about the political system which governs their lives. Correspondingly, the "Americans interested in foreign affairs constitute a dedicated few" (Elder, 1960). Data corroborating that judgment, as inferred from a wider array of information about public involvement in public affairs, are clear:

- *Apathy and inattention to public issues.* In 1982, barely half of the American public indicated they were "very interested" in reading articles dealing with "national news," and only 45 percent indicated they were "very interested" in "news about the relations of the United States with other countries." The proportion of those closely following specific foreign policy issues is even lower (Rielly, 1983: 8).

- *Voter turnout*. In comparison with voter behavior in other societies, the American electorate is highly inactive. (Many other democratic countries have higher turn-out rates.) The percentage of eligible voters who voted in presidential elections has ranged from 51 percent (1948) to 63 percent (1960) in the ten presidential con-tests since World War II. If, in 1980 and again in 1984, the number of "no shows" is added to those who voted against the president, Ronald Reagan was twice elected by only about a quarter of the American voting-age population.

- *Other forms of political participation*. The proportion of Americans who profess to have worked for a political party or candidate never exceeded 7 percent between 1952 and 1984 (Conway, 1985: 7). In 1978, only 23 percent of the public indicated they had written or spoken to a public official about some political issue in the preceding three or four years; of these, only 18 percent—4 percent of the entire population—had written or spoken to a public official about an issue concerning foreign affairs (Rielly, 1979: 30).

Available data suggest that even though the United States purports to have a mass democratic system of government, few are deeply involved in politics and most lack the interest and motivation to become involved. Moreover, most Americans seem more interested in domestic than in foreign policy (although concern is low in both categories). The conclusion, as Gabriel A. Almond (1960) describes it, is that "the characteristic response to questions of foreign policy is one of indifference."

Or is it? There is no question that most Americans are touched more fre-quently by events at home than by events abroad, but we must be careful not to jump to the conclusion that the public is incapable of holding opinions about foreign policy issues. The mass public may be uninformed about and seemingly indifferent to the details of policy of the sort that is reported by, say, the mass media. But it is able to identify issues salient to it, and foreign and national security policy issues repeatedly rank near the top. Evidence supporting that conclusion is found in the pattern of response given to opin-ion pollsters' question "What do you think is the most important problem fac-ing the country today?" In twenty-six polls using that (or a similar) question between 1949 and 1963, foreign policy concerns headed the list nineteen times. During (roughly) the next decade, Vietnam was frequently the most sa-lient issue, topping the list ten times (of twenty-two polls taken between 1964 and 1972) with more general foreign policy concerns preeminent three times (Nie, Verba, and Petrocik, 1976: 100–103).

Thereafter a prolonged period unfolded in which economic needs and is-sues headed the list of most important problems. Not until early 1980, appar-ently in response to events in Iran, did foreign policy emerge as the single most important concern of the American people (see *Public Opinion*, Febru-ary–March, 1980: 21). Unemployment and, occasionally, other economic prob-lems remained paramount for some time thereafter, but in late 1983, the fear or threat of war and international tensions emerged as the most salient issue(s). During the ensuing presidential election year the same item was found to be most important in two of the four Gallup polls that asked the question, and was tied with unemployment in a third (Gallup, 1984, and Gallup, 1985). It was also the most salient issue in a mid-1985 poll (the *New York Times*, June 24, 1985). Thus the overall record suggests that, more often than not, foreign policy issues are more important to the American people than are domestic concerns, and their views and beliefs about who will best handle the issues salient to them historically have been important predictors of the outcome of presidential elections (Gallup, 1985). Strike a blow in favor of democratic theory!

American Opinion of Foreign Affairs: Inflexible, Erratic, or Amenable to Long-term Change? Shifts in public attitudes are one of the reasons why public opinion is conventionally regarded as such a potent determinant of foreign policy. However, despite sophisticated polling and research techniques, studies of shifts in public opinion have failed to yield consistent and conclusive findings. The question "How stable is public opinion?" can be answered in different ways.

First, we may talk about basic *beliefs* about or general *images* of foreign relations. Here the evidence indicates that beliefs are remarkably stable. Most images concerning foreign affairs, it seems, are formed at a fairly early age (adolescence) and remain relatively fixed unless disturbed by a dramatic traumatizing event. In fact, it has been argued (Deutsch and Merritt, 1965) that while peer group influences and authority figures may exert a modifying impact on images, only the most dramatic of international events (war, for example) have the capacity to completely alter foreign images. Thus core beliefs, formed through an early learning experience, structure how an individual will approach and interpret future international events. For many Americans, World War II, the Cuban missile crisis, the Vietnam conflict, or the threat of nuclear annihilation have structured images of international affairs ("competitive," "dangerous," "intractable"). Such images, once formed, serve as perceptual filters through which subsequent events are interpreted. They usually become fixed features of most people's perceptions and cognitions; when images do change as a result of a traumatic event, they are usually replaced by a new, equally simplified image. Recall William James's adage that "most people think they are thinking when they replace one set of prejudices for another," and Charles Sanders Peirce's instructive comment on the dynamics of image change: "Surprise is your only teacher."

Attitudes[2] about particular foreign issues and policy choices (as opposed to stable images), however, are highly volatile. The character of the issue, the acquisition of new information, or the impact of the opinion of a friend may pro-

---

[2]The terms "attitude" and "opinion" are often used interchangeably in this book. See Wittkopf (1986) and Kegley (1986a) for discussions of the distinctions that are drawn between the two concepts in the professional literature.

voke such attitude shifts. So may "herd instincts," wherein attitude change is stimulated by what others (especially opinion leaders) appear to be thinking. Thus in the short run, the attitudes of Americans toward specific issues (economic aid to El Salvador, intermediate-range nuclear weapons in Europe, and so on) are amenable to quick changes.

A third way of looking at change in public opinion is by observing long-term fluctuations in what Gabriel Almond termed *moods*.[3] The term refers to aggregate transformations over time in the way Americans think about international affairs.

Using that concept, it can be argued that, until recently, perhaps, internationalism has been the foreign policy mood dominant among the American people throughout the period following World War II. Internationalism effectively describes the "majority opinion" of Americans regarding the appropriate role of the United Sates in world affairs, but fluctuations have also occurred in the level of support for such a globalist foreign policy posture. During the 1960s and early 1970s in particular, support for internationalism appeared to decline, reaching a low point during the final phase of American involvement in Vietnam. More recently, however, internationalism appeared to reassert itself, with roughly 60 percent of the American people espousing internationalist attitudes in the early 1980s and again in the mid-1980s, compared to only 44 percent at the time of Carter's election in 1976 (see Figure 9.1). But whether the internationalist sentiments of the 1980s are the same as those evident in previous periods is problematic. Indeed, at the same time that internationalism appeared to enjoy a resurgence, the proportion of Americans supporting active involvement in world affairs declined in 1982 to a bare majority (53 percent), the lowest point at any time since the question was first asked in the immediate aftermath of World War II. The trend may point toward "the twilight of internationalism" (Hughes, 1985–86) as the nation moves toward the 1990s. The causes are found in the recent past.

Several analysts have concluded that the internationalist mood of the American people underwent a transformation during the early to mid-1970s, precipitated largely by differing perceptions of the meaning of the Vietnam experience (recall the discussion in chapter three). Antipathy toward communism and a belief in the need to contain Soviet expansionism were core elements in the pre-Vietnam internationalist sentiment. Corollary elements included not only a willingness to use force if necessary to realize American objectives but also a cognizance of the need for the United States to cooperate with others to realize a more peaceful and prosperous world order. In short, internationalism implied a mixture of antagonistic and conciliatory strategies toward other nations (see also Holsti and Rosenau, 1983 and 1984).

Evidence from public opinion polls indicates that by the mid-1970s *cooperative internationalism* and *militant internationalism* had become identifiably distinct elements of public attitudes toward foreign policy. (Maggiotto and Witt-

---

[3]Almond's (1960) concept of mood actually describes the "plastic or formless" manner in which attitudes seem to undergo alterations in reaction to changing circumstances.

FIGURE 9.1   Internationalist/Isolationist Trends in American Public Opinion, 1964–1985*

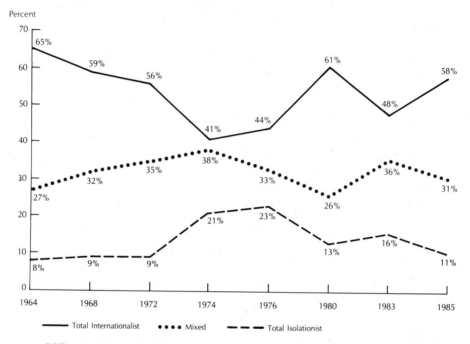

SOURCE: William Watts. Reprinted by permission of William Watts, President, Potomac Associates. The authors gratefully acknowledge the Potomac Associates, the Institute for International Social Research, and the Gallup Organization who are responsible for collecting the survey data on which these figures rest.

*Trends based on questions asked of national cross-sections of the public in years shown. The figures for 1964 and 1968 are derived from responses to five statements concerning the general posture that the United States should assume in world affairs. The figures for subsequent years reflect responses to the same set of five statements, as well as two new statements regarding possible U.S. military intervention in defense of allies.

†The term "mixed" refers to the proportion of respondents who could not be clearly classified as either internationalists or isolationists.

kopf, 1981), and that the distinction persisted into the 1980s (Wittkopf, 1984 and 1985).[4] Communism's threat, the policy of détente with the Soviet Union, willingness to use American troops abroad, and the wisdom of assuming an activist, global responsibility are among the issues that separated those holding militant and cooperative internationalist predispositions. *Hard liners*

---

[4]See also Wittkopf (1981) and Wittkopf and Maggiotto (1983a and 1983b). Other analysts who have reached analogous conclusions include Mandelbaum and Schneider (1979) and Holsti and Rosenau (1984). Mandelbaum and Schneider use the terms "liberal" and "conservative internationalists" to delineate those alternative postures toward the external environment; Holsti and Rosenau use the terms "Cold War" and "post-Cold War internationalists."

tended to view communism as a threat to the United States, to oppose détente with the Soviet Union, and generally to espouse an interventionist predisposition. In contrast, *accommodationists* emphasized cooperative ties with other nations, particularly détente with the Soviet Union, and rejected the view that the United States could assume a go-it-alone posture in the world. *Internationalists* continued to support elements of both cooperative and militant internationalism; *isolationists* continued to oppose American involvement in the affairs of others.

Many of the policies pursued by the Nixon, Ford, and Carter administrations tended more toward accommodationist than hard-line predispositions. President Carter's assertion in 1977 that the inordinate fear of communism had been lifted epitomized the shift to a conciliatory internationalism that tolerated diversity, and détente was its manifestation. Underlying the shift in emphasis was a belief that containing communism should no longer be the guiding principle of American foreign policy. As one analyst argued, "That the containment of Communism by the United States was neither possible, nor necessary, nor even desirable . . . was the 'lesson of Vietnam' [drawn by the Carter administration]" (Gershman, 1980). Other elements associated with that basic thrust included the beliefs that military power was no longer a viable instrument of policy, that the Soviet Union had become a status quo power, that the United States should assist the "forces of change" in the Third World, and that "trilateralism," implying a deepening of cooperation, should come to characterize U.S. relations with Europe and Japan (Gershman, 1980).

By the end of Carter's term in office, however, the emphasis had shifted from accommodation back to a hard-line posture. A critical factor underlying the shift was the behavior of the Soviet Union, particularly its intervention in Afghanistan in December 1979. Carter's assertion that "Soviet aggression in Afghanistan . . . confronts all the world with the most serious strategic challenge since the Cold War began" was indeed a far cry from his earlier statements concerning communism. His decision to withdraw from Senate consideration the SALT II treaty, which had been the cornerstone of the policy of détente, underscored the reorientation in policy emphasis.

Public opinion also changed, precipitated at least in part by the shift in the administration's orientation and emphasis and by its seeming inability to secure the release of American diplomats held hostage in Iran. Thus, according to Daniel Yankelovich and Larry Kaagan (1981), "By the time of the 1980 presidential election . . . voters were more than ready to exorcise the ghost of Vietnam and replace it with a new posture of American assertiveness." With President Reagan's election in 1980 and his reelection in 1984, the American public found a leader attuned to its hard-line assertive mood.

But it cannot be safely assumed either that accommodationist values are permanently in retreat or that the pre-Vietnam internationalist consensus can be rebuilt. Holsti and Rosenau (1984, 1979a, and 1979b) argue persuasively that for many potential foreign policy leaders, in particular, the Vietnam experience may have been one of those catalytic events that fundamentally alters foreign policy belief systems. Some have adopted a "present danger" perspective that emphasizes the centrality of the Soviet threat to American interests and the need to counter perceived Soviet expansionism; others emphasize a "world order" perspective in which East-West relations constitute only one among many global problems toward which American attention should be directed; and still others have adopted a "semi-isolationist" orientation, in which domestic problems become the first order of business. That trichotomy of beliefs suggests that while one stratum of opinion may be dominant at one time, the others may be in relative retreat only but not be eliminated.[5]

It is also important to recall the global challenges posed by economic trends in the external environment (see chapter seven). Many that now confront the United States, and that will continue to confront it in the 1990s, require cooperative endeavors with other nations. Militant internationalism rooted in an innate anti-Sovietism may prove inappropriate to the tasks ahead (Chace, 1978). Indeed, the changing character of the global political environment itself must be recognized, for, unlike the situation in an earlier period, American economic and military dominance is now challenged, making it difficult to take bold, simple initiatives for the purpose of vindicating American pride (see Yankelovich and Kaagan, 1981).

We should neither ignore nor minimize the direction of present trends, however. The vision of multilateralism that undergirded the active involvement of the United States in world affairs for nearly four decades is much in retreat. Global challenges may require transnational cooperation, but the United States has done little in the recent past to seize opportunities to build international regimes capable of promoting national as well as global interests (Keohane and Nye, 1985). On the contrary, many of the basic tenets of the internationalist paradigm—including the rule of (international) law, support for international institutions, and economic internationalism—have been abused verbally and flaunted in practice by those at the pinnacle of power in Washington (Hughes, 1985–86).

How, then, should we characterize the foreign policy mood of the American people? Internationalism still seems an apt description of public attitudes toward the role of the United States in world affairs, but its precise character and content have shifted over time in response to emerging world developments and domestic interpretations of them.

Frank L. Klingberg (1952, 1979, 1983) has, in fact, argued that public attitudes regarding the appropriate world role of the United States undergo cyclical swings between isolationist and internationalist moods (see chapter three).

---

[5]As Senator George McGovern put it in advising his colleague, Edmund Muskie, when the latter left the Senate to become secretary of state:

> The division in America over how we interpret the lessons of Vietnam and integrate them into future policy still remains the central unresolved question of American foreign policy. Yet since the end of the Vietnam war, those who correctly warned against the dangers of that futile and senseless intervention have not put forward a coherent new perspective on American security or on America's global role. (McGovern, 1980: 5)

According to Klingberg, such mood swings typically occur every twenty-five to thirty years, implying that public attitudes toward foreign policy change every generation quite independent of dissatisfaction with particular experiments (such as military intervention in Vietnam).[6]

The cyclical character of public attitudes is especially notable in the way Americans regard the acceptability of war as an instrument of national policy. Public approval of war appears to occur prior to and just after the inception of a foreign war, followed, predictably, by a gradual but steady decline in bellicose attitudes and a concomitant rise in pacifist attitudes. The Korean and Vietnam conflicts reveal the capacity of public opinion to reverse itself on life and death issues. John Mueller's (1971) comparative study of public attitudes during those foreign involvements, for example, shows that over time enthusiasm for war was closely related to casualty rates: as the casualty rates went up, support for the wars declined. The findings suggest that American attitudes toward war are episodic rather than steady; in the context of actual war involvement, public attitudes range from initial acceptance to ultimate disfavor (Campbell and Cain, 1965).

Another cyclical swing may be seen in the issue of military spending. American opinion was relatively stable—and silent—until the late 1960s, when a "revolt of the masses" (Russett, 1972) erupted and a majority of Americans began advocating, for the first time since World War II, reductions in military spending. As shown in Figure 9.2, however, the "revolt" turned out to be of relatively short duration. By 1977 more Americans supported increased defense spending than reductions, with the level of support for more spending approaching a two-decade high point. According to Louis Kriesberg and Ross Klein (1980), "Three interconnected changes between 1973 and 1978 appear to have produced the trend toward increased popular support for greater arms spending: (1) the decline in the impact of the Vietnam war, (2) a rise in particular elements of conservative ideology, and (3) an increase in anti-Soviet and anticommunist sentiment" (see also Kriesberg, Murray, and Klein, 1982).

By 1980, both President Carter and his presidential challenger, Ronald Reagan, were calling for greater defense spending. Policy-maker support thus combined with other factors associated with shifting public mood regarding the appropriate role of the United States in world affairs to produce support of defense spending at a level unsurpassed since the onset of the Ko-

[6]See Holsti and Rosenau (1980) for an examination of the impact of generations on the post-Vietnam beliefs of American leaders and Holmes (1985) for an exploration of Klingberg's cyclical thesis. Note that the emergence of an assertive public mood in the early 1980s, to the extent that it may be regarded as a manifestation of a return to support for global involvement characteristic of the pre-Vietnam foreign policy paradigm, suggests that the country's turn toward introversion in the 1960s and 1970s will have run its course more quickly than the twenty-five to thirty-year cycle posited by Klingberg. That would suggest, in turn, that the memory of Vietnam may be receding more rapidly than might otherwise have been expected (for which there is some evidence, as noted in note 17 below). On the other hand, the retreat from multilateralism described above, associated in particular with the policy and rhetoric of the Reagan presidency, closely parallels a two- to three-decade wave in which introversion remains the dominant pattern.

FIGURE 9.2   Trends in American Public Opinion About Defense Spending, 1957–1985

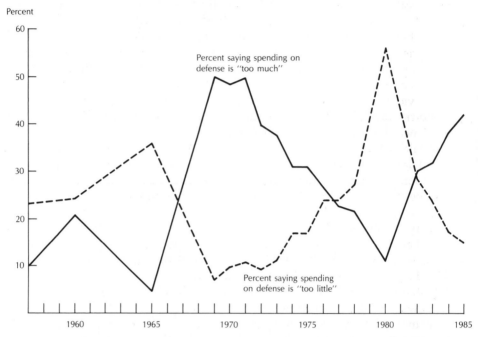

SOURCE: Adapted from Kriesberg and Klein, 1980: 81; Russett and DeLuca, 1981: 383; and *Public Opinion*, June–July 1985: 35.

rean War in 1950. Support subsided thereafter, as Figure 9.2 illustrates. In part this shift appears to have been a result of concern for the traditional "guns versus butter" trade-off, which was augmented by mounting federal government deficits fueled by massive defense spending for expensive military technology. But it also reflected in part satisfaction with the Reagan administration's rearmament program as an approach to projecting American strength and resolve abroad, alongside reduced public fears that the U.S. military was lagging (see Schmidt, 1983).

The foregoing conclusions indicate that while *images* of foreign affairs held by Americans are resistant to change, *attitudes* toward specific issues can be unstable in the short run, and *moods* regarding general policy preferences can manage over long spans of time to undergo substantial change (often in a cyclical pattern). The implications of those characteristics of American public opinions will be explored subsequently.

The Public "Temperament": Nationalistic and Permissive. Like the citizens of most nations, Americans tend to be nationalistic, that is, to value loyalty and devotion to their own nation and promotion of its culture and interests as opposed to those of other nations. Nationalism entails seeing other nations as rivals in a competitive game for power and prestige (Deutsch, 1953). It includes the belief that the United States is (or should be recognized as) superior to other nations and should therefore serve as a model for others to emulate.

Although no one would argue that all Americans think nationalistically all the time across all foreign issues, there is nevertheless a general predisposition to perceive international problems in terms of in-group loyalty and out-group competition (Rosenberg, 1965). In the extreme, nationalism results in a world view that accepts the doctrine "my country, right or wrong."[7]

Nationalistic attitudes tend to color the way Americans view the world and influence the way they interpret foreign actions. War and "buy American" campaigns are obvious ways in which nationalistic sentiments find expression. Nationalistic attitudes also affect the way Americans respond to the foreign policy initiatives of their leaders. In general, that response most typically may be characterized as a "permissive" one, a concept Gabriel Almond (1960; see also Caspary, 1970) used to describe public acceptance of foreign policy leaders' internationalist initiatives in the immediate post-World War II period. The characterization continues to hold: to a remarkable degree American public opinion tends to acquiesce to decisions made by leaders. Americans are inclined to equate loyalty to the nation with loyalty to the prevailing leadership. It is that equation which confuses love for the representatives of the government with love for country and its symbols.

A major consequence of such unquestioning loyalty is that it gives decision makers extraordinary freedom to alter drastically American foreign policy. Under all but the most extreme situations the president can assume that the American people will stand behind him, regardless of his policy. Consider the evidence summarized in Figure 9.3. Although there are wide fluctuations in the level of popular support presidents receive, the opinion data indicate that every postwar administration has enjoyed periods of near majority support,[8]

---

[7]Moreover, nationalism historically has been a major source of antagonisms between nations. Deutsch (1974) underscores the sobering reality of this fact: "Nationalism has not only increased the number of countries on the face of the earth, it has helped to diminish the number of its inhabitants. All major wars in the twentieth century have been fought in its name." Kenneth Boulding is reported (Nelson, 1974) to have emphasized this point in even more forceful terms by noting that "the only religion that still demands human sacrifice is nationalism."

[8]Based on Gallup poll ratings (*The Gallup Poll Index*, December 1980: 57, and *The Gallup Report*, September 1985: 4), the average level of popular support for each president from Truman to Reagan is as follows:

PRESIDENT	AVERAGE APPROVAL RATING (AS A PERCENT) WHILE IN OFFICE
Truman	41
Eisenhower	64
Kennedy	70
Johnson	55
Nixon	49
Ford	46
Carter	47
Reagan (first term)	50

FIGURE 9.3   Fluctuations in Public Approval of Presidential Performance, 1945–1985

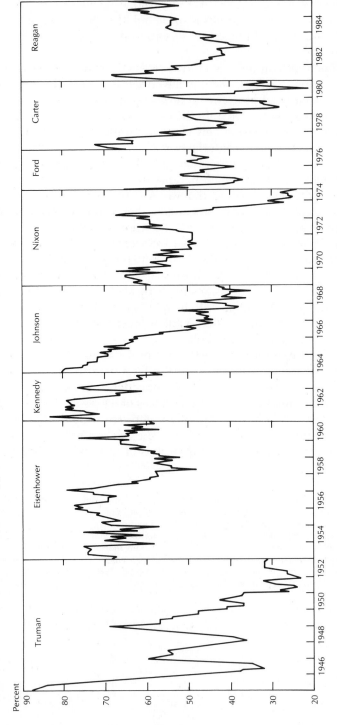

SOURCE: Adapted from *The Gallup Opinion Index*, October–November 1980; and *The Gallup Report*, September 1985, pp. 3–4. Data appear in monthly intervals beginning in June 1945 and ending in August 1985. In months with multiple polls, the last poll was used, in months where no poll was taken, the data were extrapolated using preceding and/or succeeding monthly data. For an explanation of the sampling procedures, see Gallup (1985).

despite divergent presidential styles, personalities, programs, and circumstances. Americans, it seems, fail to distinguish the man from the office he holds. Few presidents have had to govern under conditions of overwhelming and persistent unpopularity.

Several inferences may be drawn from that characteristic of American public opinion. The fact that most administrations have enjoyed high levels of popular support has made for flexibility in pursuing various policy options. As an offsetting factor, however, presidential support tends to decline over time. Every administration has suffered a gradual erosion of popularity, perhaps because of growing public dissatisfaction and lost patience with unfulfilled campaign promises, or perhaps because familiarity has a way of breeding contempt. The so-called honeymoon period of any new president—the crucial first few months following an election in which the president is relatively free of harsh public criticism—is short-lived. With every presidential decision (including "nondecisions"), opposition forms or becomes more vocal, Congress looks increasingly to its own parochial concerns, and the president's support seems to ooze away imperceptibly but methodically.

The tendency is symptomatic of the difficulties of running a government and managing a nation's foreign policy in a manner satisfactory to the majority. Dwight D. Eisenhower—the only chief executive to serve two full terms in the postwar era (Reagan's record at the time of writing was incomplete) and the only president whose percentage of public disapproval was never greater than his percentage of approval—came the closet to escaping the syndrome. But even he was not immune, having left office with less support than when he entered.

Ronald Reagan enjoyed approval ratings during his first term in office rivaling those of Eisenhower and Kennedy, the two most popular postwar presidents. And things that affected other presidents adversely—ranging from factual errors in public statements to the extraordinary number of peacetime casualties suffered by American servicemen—seemed not to "stick" to Reagan, leading some to describe Reagan's as a "Teflon presidency," implying an immunity from the forces that eroded his predecessors' popular base. The metaphor was reinforced by the paradox that Reagan's personal popularity outstripped public approval of many of his policies and programs by a wide margin, with the implication that Reagan "is so charming that people do not blame him for any problems they have with his policies" (Sussman, 1985).

Close inspection reveals, however, that Reagan is not that different. True, his enormous personal appeal sustained itself well into his second term, surpassing Truman's, Nixon's, and even Eisenhower's popularity ratings at comparable periods in their second terms.[9] But the record of his first term shows

---

[9]In August 1985, 65 percent of the American people approved Reagan's job performance, and 26 percent disapproved. Nixon's ratings in August 1973 were 36 percent approve, 54 percent disapprove; Eisenhower's in August/September 1957 were 50 percent approve, 23 percent disapprove; and Truman's in September 1949 were 51 percent approve, 31 percent disapprove (*Washington Post National Weekly Edition*, September 16, 1985, p. 38).

his popularity declined in a manner analogous to others, closely tracking the nation's unemployment rate in particular. Fifteen months into office his level of public support was little different from Ford's and Carter's at comparable periods, and considerably less than Kennedy's, Johnson's, and Nixon's. By month thirty his position relative to the same list of predecessors, all of whom had suffered an erosion of popularity, remained much the same. Only Carter's popularity dipped more precipitously (*Public Opinion*, February–March, 1984: 34). But Reagan's personal second-term popularity underwent a resurgence, even while questioning of the wisdom of his policies increased. This suggested that at least with respect to this president the public separated their image of the president from their image of the administration he led (see Ferguson with Rogers, 1986).

Apart from the general downward trend in popular support suffered by every administration, short-term variations in presidential popularity stem from a variety of circumstances, both international and domestic.[10] Interestingly, international events often have "rally 'round the flag" effects which boost a president's popularity with the public. One study (Lee, 1977) of changes in presidential popularity associated with some forty-eight different events spanning presidencies from Franklin Roosevelt's to Gerald Ford's indicates an increase in presidential popularity in thirty-six of the cases, and a decline in only eleven cases. If those cases defined as international setbacks are excluded (ten in all), and attention is focused on events involving wars, crises, American peace efforts, summit conferences, and American policy initiatives, the average increase in presidential Gallup ratings is a substantial 5.6 percent. The fact that President Carter's popularity rating jumped 13 percent following the Camp David Middle East accords in September 1978 is a dramatic illustration of this persistent tendency. In general, the more active a president looks (for example, the frequency of his new pronouncements, trips abroad), the greater will be the support he will tend to receive at home. Apparently, presidents projecting images of decisive, energetic leadership receive rewards for these images, just as crises afford opportunities for presidents to show the public their courage (if not always their wisdom).[11]

Exceptions to those tendencies are discernible, of course. Every president has not enjoyed unconditional support. But in those cases where presidential

---

[10]There is a sizable literature that seeks to explain fluctuations in presidential popularity, much of it focused on the impact of economic variables. Ostrom and Simon's (1985) effort to incorporate foreign policy variables in their model, which seeks to explain variations in presidential popularity from Eisenhower to Reagan, is exemplary.

[11]Indeed, the nature of a crisis may not influence significantly the extent to which a president's popularity will soar. A case in point is John Kennedy's public approval rating, which rose to its high point (83 percent) in the aftermath of the Bay of Pigs disaster. President Carter's popular approval shot from 38 to 61 percent following the Iranian hostage incident in late 1979, and President Reagan's popularity increased following the Soviet attack on the Korean airline flight 007 in September 1983 and again following the truck-bombing of Marine headquarters in Beirut the following month. The lesson seems to be that nothing succeeds like a crisis, even one that may be managed poorly, at least in its immediate impact.

popularity suffered a prolonged erosion, the reasons were compelling: for Truman, the Korean War; for Johnson, the Vietnam War and riots in the cities; for Nixon, the continuation of the Vietnam War (despite the 1968 campaign pledge of a "secret plan" to end the war), the massive bombing of North Vietnam during Christmas of 1972, and finally Watergate; for Carter, the inability to secure release of Americans held hostage in Iran. We thus cannot ignore the fate experienced by Truman, Johnson, Nixon, and Carter. But neither should we dismiss the fact that most administrations enjoy a high level of popular support, with images of international activity often adding important short-term boosts.[12]

If a nationalistic public temperament has led to permissive compliance on many issues and policy twists, part of the reason stems from the tendency of nationalistic thinking to encourage the public to view "things foreign" with hostility and fear. Research indicates that international politics is often viewed as esoteric, secret, complicated, and unfamiliar—the type of problem better left to "experts" who allegedly "know better" (and who, in turn, are quite willing to perpetuate the notion)—rendering public attitudes in the realm of foreign policy especially vulnerable to manipulation. People who feel threatened seek strong leadership to deal with the perceived threatening agent, a tendency long recognized by policy makers.[13] The proposition appears to have particular validity at times of real or imagined threats from abroad, when, in response, a president tends to realize the widest freedom of action (Waltz, 1971). Public apprehensiveness of foreign affairs during crises in conjunction

---

[12]Although most crises produce "rally 'round the flag" effects, the exceptions are puzzling. One explanation may be found in the responses of a president's critics and the way the media report them.

> If opposition leaders are silent or supportive of presidential action . . ., press and television accounts of the "politics" surrounding crises will be unusually full of bipartisan support for the president's actions. The public responds accordingly. When opinion leadership does not rally or run for cover, the media must and do report this fact. At such times, the public receives countervailing elite evaluations of presidential performance and appears to look to the events themselves for information with which to update its judgment of how well the president is handling his job. (Brody, 1984: 42)

A comparative evaluation of media coverage of the *Pueblo* and *Mayaguez* affairs supports this argument. At no time during the ten days that the *Mayaguez* rescue operation was a major news story did negative comment by a recognized opposition leader make front-page news, and President Ford's approval rating jumped a healthy 11 percentage points (despite the fact that thirty-eight marines and airmen were killed and another fifty wounded). In the *Pueblo* case, however, Republican senators criticized the president's policies only four days after the story broke, and Johnson's approval rating dropped 7 percentage points between the two polls that bracketed the event (Brody, 1984: 41–42).

[13]It was the Nazi Hermann Goering who expressed the idea by contending, "Voice or no voice, the people can always be brought to do the bidding of the leaders. That is easy. All you have to do is to tell them they are being attacked and denounce the pacifists for lack of patriotism." And a former American secretary of state, John Foster Dulles, expressed the same opinion when he noted: "The easiest and quickest cure of internal dissension is to portray danger from abroad. Thus group authorities find it convenient always to keep alive among the group members a feeling that their nation is in danger from one or another of the nation-villains with which it is surrounded."

with nationalistic fears thus serve both to reduce the constraining effects of public opinion on foreign policy and to enhance the ability of the government to mold and manipulate public attitudes. The implications of such a linkage are sobering:

> To put it cynically, one could say that nothing helps a leader like a good war. It gives him his only chance of being a tyrant and being loved for it at the same time. He can introduce the most ruthless forms of control and send thousands of his followers to their deaths and still be hailed as a great protector. Nothing ties tighter the in-group bonds than an out-group threat. (Morris, 1969: 31)[14]

Numerous additional characteristics of American public opinion could be added to the brief list above.[15] Among them, the confidence that Americans repose in the nation's political, economic, and social institutions deserves mention, for it has undergone important changes over time and has been affected by the Vietnam War, Watergate, and the challenges of the OPEC decade to the nation's economic independence and well-being, with potentially important implications for the conduct of the nation's foreign policy.

Jimmy Carter captured the trends symptomatic of the changing "public voice" when, in a 1979 nationwide speech, he spoke of "a fundamental threat to American democracy." The threat, he said, was a "crisis of confidence" reflected in "a growing disrespect for government and for churches and for schools, the news media and other institutions." Carter thus drew attention to the sharp downturn in public confidence, which began in the mid-1960s, in government and a wide variety of other institutions, (Lipset and Schneider, 1983). Among the trends was a declining sense of political efficacy—the feeling that the individual citizen matters and can influence government policy—and a general feeling of despair, alienation, and powerlessness regarding the future. An American public that once appeared to be naive, simplistic, and jingoistic (ultrapatriotic) now seemed more aware of and cynical about foreign policy issues. Public disclosure of the lies Americans were told by their own government presumably accounts for many of those characteristics and changes. Included in the disclosures were the half-truths regarding U.S. involvement in Vietnam, and the revelations about what was undertaken in the name of national security by presidential staffers, military organizations, and

---

[14]An interesting variant of this proposition is examined by Ostrom and Job (1986), who show that both the absolute and relative level of a president's popularity are important in explaining the political use of force short of war (recall chapter five) in the post-World War II era.

[15]An unfortunate conceptual consequence of the foregoing discussion of public attitudes is that it invites a negative estimate of the intelligence of the American people and their importance in the political system. The fallacious implication that might be drawn is that Friedrich Nietzsche was right when he said "the masses are asses." This conclusion is certainly not supported by our data; to be unconcerned and uninformed about foreign policy issues is not to be incapable of holding opinions or understanding those issues. Another possible error that the profile might invite is the notion that the leaders should ignore the uninformed opinions of the masses, along the lines akin to Oscar Wilde's famous adage that "those who try to lead the people can only do so by following the mob."

intelligence agencies—including assassination plots, wiretapping, mail rifling, mind-control experiments on unsuspecting Americans, and burglary, to name but a few. A decade of excessive inflationary pressure challenged the proposition that the American economy was as "sound as the dollar," and the OPEC oil squeeze of 1973–1974 (repeated in 1979–1980) demonstrated the limits of America's abundance. Disclosures about fraud by public officials and governmental waste and corruption fed further the alienation many Americans felt from their government.

Evidence from polls taken between 1981 and 1985 contained mixed signals, suggesting a possible attenuation of the decades-long slide in Americans' confidence in their institutional leadership. A 1983 Harris poll concluded that "a record high 62 percent of Americans have expressed sad and bitter alienation toward those running society and feel powerless to do anything about it" (cited in Lipset and Schneider, 1983). A 1982 survey by the University of Michigan's Institute for Social Research, on the other hand, led to the conclusion that, while "the American public remains predominantly negative toward government and public officials," the trends suggested that "confidence is turning up" (Miller, 1983).[16] A 1985 Gallup poll reinforced that view with the finding that public confidence in the Supreme Court, Congress, public schools, and the military had increased sharply since 1983 (*The Gallup Report*, July 1985).

Whether these findings portend a reversal of otherwise long-term, adverse trends remains to be seen. Indeed, these and related polls invite conflicting interpretations (see Lipset, 1985). Past findings nevertheless contain an important message for the nation's political leaders:

> Public criticism appears to be directed at the performance of these [social and political] institutions and their leaders: their competence, trustworthiness, and integrity. . . . Americans have not turned against the political system itself. They still see it as fundamentally good. The problem in their eyes lies in inadequate, inept, and even corrupt leadership. Such sentiments suggest that any effort to change the low level of confidence in government must focus not on changing public attitudes, as President Carter proposed in his July 1979 speech, but on making government more responsive and effective in dealing with the key problems of society. (Lipset and Schneider, 1983: 401; see also Lipset, 1985)

Political and Sociodemographic Correlates of Foreign Policy Attitudes. Examining the general characteristics of American public opinion in the manner presented here can be somewhat misleading. Public attitudes are significantly influenced by, and vary with, many factors such as age, educational level, gender, political philosophy, party identification, income, occupation, racial background, religious identification, and region of the country. For example,

---

[16]Interestingly, the data do not support the otherwise simple conclusion that President Reagan's popularity explains the rebound of confidence shown in the Michigan survey. Instead, the positive signs were linked to the positive performance of the economy (Miller, 1983).

higher-income groups and those with more education generally are better in-formed about international affairs than lower-income groups and those with less education. Similarly, the better educated and more wealthy, those in pro-fessional occupations and those residing in the eastern part of the country, and self-described liberals are generally more supportive of an internationalist role for the nation than other sectors of society. They are the same societal groups which, when the internationalist consensus split between cooperative and militant internationalism during the 1970s, were most likely to support the policy of détente and to disagree with the proposition that a communist takeover virtually anywhere in the world was necessarily a threat to the vital interests of the United States (Wittkopf and Maggiotto, 1983b; Hughes, 1978).

One of the sharpest distinctions in public attitudes occurs between "elites," on the one hand, and the mass public, on the other. There are no clear guidelines to determine who comprises the "elite," but one series of polls of some 300 Americans in leadership positions both inside and outside of government (Rielly, 1975, 1979, 1983) depicts that subset of Americans clas-sified as elites as far more supportive of the traditional tenets of international-ism than the mass public. In 1982, for example, 98 percent thought it best if the country took an active part in world affairs, compared to only 54 percent of the public at large (Rielly, 1983: 37). The leaders were also substantially more likely to oppose economic protectionism and to support free trade principles, basic pillars of postwar internationalism, and to adopt a generally more inter-ventionist orientation toward world affairs than the mass of the American people. At the same time, when elites and masses are partitioned among the more abstract attitude clusters described above, elites consistently subscribe to internationalist and accommodationist values in greater proportions than the mass public, which is more likely to hold hard-line values (Wittkopf, 1985).

Elites are not of one mind, however. In a pioneering study of the foreign policy beliefs of nearly 3,000 American leaders, Holsti and Rosenau (1983, 1984) demonstrate, as noted earlier, that the legacy of Vietnam continues to color significantly the world views of those surveyed, leading to divisions that carry important policy implications for United States's, relations with the So-viet Union, with developing nations, and for the use of force abroad, among others. As in studies of the mass public, the occupation and political ideology (liberal versus conservative) of American leaders were also found to distin-guish among those subscribing to the trichotomy of foreign policy beliefs de-scribed above as "present danger," "world order," and "semi-isolationist" in nature. Importantly, however, the "lessons of Vietnam" (about which, how-ever, there is no consensus) have had an enduring impact on leaders' belief systems across diverse circumstances from the mid-1970s into the 1980s.[17] For

---

[17]The lingering effects of Vietnam on mass political beliefs are suggested in a 1985 *Washington Post*-ABC News poll (*Washington Post National Weekly Edition*, April 29, 1985, p. 37), in which a ma-jority responded that the cause for which American troops fought was not worthwhile and that they did not have a clear idea what the war was all about and what the nation was fighting for.

many who will move into key foreign policy roles in the decades ahead, the "Vietnam analogy" may well replace the "Munich analogy" as a decision-making guidepost.[18]

A PUBLIC IMPACT ON AMERICAN FOREIGN POLICY?

The foregoing description of the attributes of American public opinion suggests a partial answer to the opinion-policy question: the proposition from democratic theory that foreign policy is merely a reflection of public preferences and beliefs is too crude and simplistic. Policy formation does not derive from the simple preferences of an uninformed, uninterested, unstable, acquiescent, and manipulable "public voice." Consequently, public opinion provides neither a clear nor a meaningful guide to policy making. "To be sure, the results of public opinion polls are usually sufficiently clear that public officials might *claim* that their behavior is consistent with the public will, but such a claim assumes qualities in this opinion not completely borne out empirically . . ." (Weissberg, 1976).

Rather than formulating policy by drawing on public opinions for guidance, policy-making elites are likely to make choices on the basis of other considerations. As a consequence, it may be asked if most elites do not define their appropriate role as one of leading rather than following. A former Kennedy adviser put it thus: "No president is obliged to abide by the dictates of public opinion. . . . He has a responsibility to lead public opinion as well as respect it—to shape it, to inform it, to woo it, and win it. It can be his sword as well as his compass" (Sorensen, 1963).[19]

Those conclusions presumably contributed to the view, expressed by 60 percent of the respondents, that the United States' handling of the war had made them personally distrustful of the nation's leaders.

At the same time, however, there is evidence that the memory of Vietnam may be fading. A ten-year retrospective look at Vietnam in a 1985 *New York Times* poll suggested a weakening of the 1970s view "that whatever the United States did in foreign affairs, it should avoid doing anything that seemed repetitive of Vietnam" and a strengthening of "the trust in government which Vietnam helped to shatter," especially among young people (Clymer, 1985a). The often woeful lack of knowledge about Vietnam unearthed by the poll also suggested that the changing conclusions about the restraining effects of the Vietnam experience "may be less the result of anyone's changing his or her mind as it is of an unspoken national attempt to forget Vietnam altogether" (Clymer, 1985a).

[18]The Munich analogy draws on the experience of the late 1930s, when Britain and France agreed to the annexation of a portion of Czechoslovakia by Nazi Germany in the mistaken belief that it would avert war in Europe. For many who came to occupy leadership positions in the American foreign policy-making establishment in the decades following World War II, the "lesson" drawn from that experience was that expansionism by totalitarian states cannot be appeased. Contrariwise, the "lesson" of Vietnam may be that there are limits to American power requiring a more cautious and selective approach to global involvement. A radically different interpretation, on the other hand, suggests that war, once entered, should not be prosecuted "with one arm tied behind the our back." See May (1977) and Neustadt and May (1986) for examinations of the role that "lessons of the past" play in current policy making, and Gershman (1980) for a critical appraisal of the "Vietnam syndrome."

[19]A similar position was espoused by Theodore Roosevelt, who stated bluntly, "I did not 'divine' what the people were going to think. I simply made up my mind what they ought to think

The notion that policy makers see public opinion as something to be shaped, not followed, is understandable when we recall the tendency of the public to acquiesce to government decisions. The propensity of the public to accede to leaders' choices minimizes the impact on foreign policy that the public could exert. The responsiveness of government to public preferences is further reduced by the unwillingness of a passive public to make a meaningful contribution. The conclusion that follows from such a line of reasoning is that the American public participates (through elections, for example) without exercising power. It is involved but does not have influence.

Such a conclusion certainly requires qualification. Rather than asking if there is a direct causal connection between public beliefs and the content of foreign policy, it may be more appropriate to inquire into the functions of the public in the process itself.

Public Opinion as a Constraint on Foreign Policy Innovation

One of the reasons American foreign policy has been so resistant to change since World War II is that public images of international relations have themselves been resistant to change. Fundamental beliefs regarding foreign relations are often inflexible:

> Almost nothing in the world seems to be able to shift the images of 40 percent of the population in most countries, even within one or two decades. Combinations of events that shift the images and attitudes even of the remaining 50 or 60 percent of the population are extremely rare, and these rare occasions require the combination and mutual reinforcement of cumulative events with spectacular events and substantial governmental efforts as well as the absence of sizable cross-pressures. (Deutsch and Merritt, 1965: 183)

Public opinion thus acts as a brake on policy change, not by stopping innovations, but by restricting "foreign policy modifications because of the perceptions which decisionmakers have as to the inflexibility of public opinion and its unpredictability" (Peterson, 1971). If decision makers *think* the public voice will not permit certain initiatives and fear that the public may become mobilized against new innovations, that in itself may restrict the kinds of alternatives considered. It is perhaps for that psychological reason that American foreign policy is perceived by so many analysts and statesmen to be constrained by public attitudes: "Mass opinion may set general limits, themselves subject to change over time, within which government may act" because "[t]he opinion context . . . fixes the limitations within which action may be taken" (Key, 1961). "Fear of electoral punishment," even if unrealistic, serves

---

and then did my best to get them to think it." Similarly, former adviser to President Truman, George Elsey, confided, "The president's job is to *lead* public opinion, not to be a blind follower. You can't sit around and wait for public opinion to tell you what to do. . . . You must decide what you're going to do and do it, and attempt to educate the public to the reasons for your action."

to limit what decision makers are likely to do, if for no other reason than their (often erroneous) assumption that "the public will never stand for it" (Waltz, 1971).

Although public opinion may serve as a constraint on foreign policy, it would be a mistake to ascribe too much importance to the limits it imposes. The ability of public opinion to constrain foreign policy (by defining a range of permissible policies) is undermined by the acquiescent attitudes of most Americans toward most foreign policy initiatives. If the public sets the outer limits of policy actions, those limits are very broad. Indeed, recall that one of the characteristics of public opinion is the extent to which it is "blindly obedient" to almost any policy change proposed by the government. Consider the following regarding public acceptance of policy reversals pronounced by the government. Before Johnson announced his Vietnam policy in 1965, only 42 percent of the public favored such a policy. After the announcement, 72 percent favored it. While 7 percent favored an invasion of Cambodia before, after Nixon announced the 1970 "incursion," 50 percent were then in favor. And in 1977, following the signing of the Panama Canal treaties, there was an 18 percent increase in public support for turning the canal over to Panama (from 8 percent to 26 percent) (Brewer, 1980: 80). Many more examples are available.[20]

What emerges from those data is additional evidence supporting the proposition that public opinion is inclined to approve of the decisions that leaders make. Moreover, because of the historical tendency of the public to go along with most government actions, decision makers can assume they have mass support. The passivity and acquiescence of the public would seem to invite presidents to act first and then wait for public approval afterward. Indeed, most of the time officials are encouraged to create a climate of opinion favorable to contemplated policies. Rather than reflecting on and responding to public opinion, policy makers may turn to public opinion to obtain support for policy actions already chosen.

Public Opinion as a Stimulus to Foreign Policy Innovation

Exceptions to the general rule of public apathy and powerlessness are rare, but on some very specific issues changes in American public opinion can precede rather than follow policy changes. Consider the issue of American policy toward the admission of Mainland China to the United Nations. A growing

[20]A January 1983 *Washington Post*-ABC News poll showed that only 30 percent of the respondents approved President Reagan's handling of the situation in Lebanon, and a majority of 59 percent concluded the government had no clear goals for the Marines who had been sent there. After the Marines were killed by a terrorist attack on October 23, and following the United States invasion of Grenada two days later, Reagan made an emotional nationwide television address in which he defended his policies in those countries. Another *Washington Post*-ABC News poll the next day revealed that a majority of Americans then supported Reagan's Lebanon policies (*Washington Post National Weekly Edition*, February 6, 1984, p. 37).

See Weissberg (1976) and Brewer (1980) for additional examples, and Sigelman (1979) for a critique of the practice of inferring the impact of governmental action on public attitudes from before and after opinion polls.

proportion of the public favored admission at the same time that most segments of the policy-making community remained in rigid opposition to it. In 1950 less than 15 percent of the American public favored admission, but by 1969 over half supported it (Mueller, 1973: 15–17), a level of support which may have made the eventual U.S. decision not to block admission possible. In other words, with respect to the China issue, shifts in public preferences preceded foreign policy change.

Another instance where changes in public attitudes were ahead of policy shifts was the Vietnam imbroglio, where public dissatisfaction with continued intervention was often deeper and more vocal than among government leaders. Similarly, public demonstrations of outrage toward South Africa's racial policy, *apartheid*, in 1985 by a small group of activists appeared to rally public opinion and to be critical in bringing congressional pressure to bear on the administration to abandon its South Africa policy known as ''constructive engagement.''[21]

Such instances suggest that the public may, on occasion, serve as a stimulus to policy change, especially when the issue is specific and the public is mobilized. But it would be unsafe to suggest that changes in public attitudes *cause* policy innovation. It is probably more accurate to argue that a mobilized public can influence the course of policy only indirectly, by changing ''the image of public opinion held by persons capable of affecting policy decisions'' or by altering ''the image of public opinion held by the public itself'' (Rosenberg, 1965). That is, public attitudes may serve as a source of foreign policy by affecting how policy makers think about the international environment, the choices in it, the climate of domestic opinion, and the latitude available for their decisions.

Public Opinion as a Resource in International Bargaining

There are advantages to foreign policy making that derive from a quasidemocratic process. Public attitudes may not only reduce the inclination toward risk and foreign adventure; they may also give policy makers important bargaining advantages when dealing with foreign diplomats. The more unified public opinion, and the more supportive it is of official government policy, the stronger is the leadership's bargaining power with other nations. Here public preferences are seen as a resource to be used by policy makers in the execution of foreign policy. American officials, for instance, may enhance their ability to get their way at the bargaining table by claiming that the American pub-

---

[21]Shortly after the 1984 presidential election, anti-apartheid protestors began demonstrating in Washington and some two dozen other cities or on college campuses. In January 1985, a *Washington Post*-ABC News poll found that about half of the respondents had heard of the protests, among whom 46 percent approved. A second poll taken six months later found that 62 percent had heard of the protests. Once more 46 percent of them approved, but by this time the number who had heard of the picketing in Washington and elsewhere were much larger (*Washington Post National Weekly Edition*, July 29, 1985: 37).

lic would never tolerate a proposed concession. Such claims sometimes work because American leaders can describe national opinion to foreigners as they wish and because those leaders may understate their capacity to manipulate public opinion. By describing themselves as victims of popular preferences, American statesmen may indeed gain considerable bargaining leverage.

The above observations about the functions of public opinion illuminate the fact that the links between mass attitudes and foreign policy behavior are complex. Simple conclusions are misleading, for the relationship between opinion and policy is affected by a cluster of intervening factors (for example, the nature of the issue, of the leadership, of the perception of policy makers, and of the international and domestic circumstances prevailing at the time of decision).[22] Rather than viewing decision makers as acting in conformity with the pressures of public opinion, is it not more accurate to say that they formulate their policies independently and then mold public opinion to support them? Indeed, may not the notion "that the people are inherently wise and just, and that they are the real rulers of the republic" be appropriately termed "a democratic myth" (Almond, 1960)? But is it also not true that, when mobilized, public opinion can have a direct and immediate impact? More characteristic is the quiescence of public opinion, the impact of which is subjective and latent, entering into the calculations that are made by decision makers.[23] But as Richard R. Fagen (1960) warns, "the fact that this decisional process may

[22]Page and Shapiro (1983) conclude from an examination of some "357 instances of significant change in Americans' policy preferences between 1935 and 1979" that opinion and policy are congruent roughly two-fifths of the time. They also argue that in about half of these cases "it is reasonable . . . to infer that opinion change was a *cause* of policy change, or at least a proximate or intervening factor leading to government action, if not the ultimate cause." See also Monroe (1979), wherein the congruence between opinion and policy is shown to be higher with respect to foreign than to domestic policy issues.

[23]A possible example—which also illustrates the fact that while the public is usually pliant and able to be manipulated by policy makers, this is not always the case—may be found in public attitudes toward U.S. Central American policies. Despite prolonged efforts to depict Nicaragua's Sandinista government as inimical to United States interests and the security of the Americas (which included efforts to equate the contras [counterrevolutionaries] supported by the United States as the equivalent of the Lexington and Concord freedom fighters), public opinion consistently lagged behind administration preferences. In March 1982, for example, 62 percent of the American people disapproved of U.S. attempts to overthrow the Nicaraguan government. On a related issue, nearly the same proportion disapproved of the sending of military advisers to El Salvador (*Washington Post National Weekly Edition*, May 14, 1984, p. 37). In April 1984, only 39 percent supported supplying military assistance to Central American governments friendly to the United States, while 49 percent said the United States should not get involved in the affairs of these governments (Gallup, 1985: 86). Several polls also showed that the overwhelming proportion of the American people believed the situation in Central America would be likely to end in another Vietnam. Furthermore, a series of Gallup polls taken between April 1983 and April 1984 showed that, on the average, only 27 percent of the American people approved of Reagan's handling of the Central American situation. "The fact is," observed Barry Sussman (1984), director of polling for the *Washington Post*, "27 percent approval is almost as low as presidents ever record for their handling of specific issues. It is worse than Jimmy Carter got for his handling of inflation, worse than Gerald Ford got for pardoning Richard Nixon, and almost as unfavorable as sentiment toward Nixon for his involvement in the Watergate scandal." Although there can be no conclusive proof, it is reasonable to believe that the Reagan administration's Central American policies would have been more actively belligerent had public support for such a posture been forthcoming.

not in reality originate in the will of the people does not diminish the significance or usefulness of symbolically casting the threshold of national tolerance in terms of public opinion.''

Finally, we should note that over an extended period there is a strong correspondence between public preferences and foreign policy goals and means. That relationship may seem paradoxical, since there is considerable evidence supporting the existence of short-run discrepancies between public attitudes and foreign policy behavior. Yet the paradox itself points to the indirect nexus between public opinion and foreign policy. Hence, Bernard Cohen's conclusion in his effort to wrestle with the problem of the public's impact on foreign policy asks how

> to deal with the paradox that a policy making system which has mastered all the modes of resistance to outside opinion nevertheless seems, from a long-run perspective, to accommodate to it. The troublesome question, which has bedeviled an accurate assessment of the role of public opinion in foreign policy making, may be put as follows: given all the psychological and institutional mechanisms for cushioning, deflecting, and absorbing external opinion so that its day-to-day impact on foreign policy is minimal, and given the apparent immunity of the foreign policy establishment to electoral accountability, how can we account for the occasional but important shifts in the ethos and ideology of foreign policy that seem to follow upon comparable shifts within the larger population? How, in other words, can we reconcile the lack of governmental responsiveness in the short run with an apparent responsiveness in the long run? (Cohen, 1973: 205–206)

We have already suggested some answers to Cohen's closing question, particularly in the ability of decision makers to mold public opinion to fit their preferred policy choices. But that also means that in the long run decision makers may become prisoners of their own past efforts to shape public preferences. Public opinion thus becomes a source of mass-induced inertia serving to restrain policy innovation. Or, as Alan Monroe (1979) concludes a comparative study of consistency between public preferences and public policy, the policy-making system makes it ''more difficult to pass publicly approved changes than to maintain the status quo.'' J. David Singer's observations thus serve as a fitting summary of the general proposition that this particular societal factor intrudes into the policy-making process only indirectly: ''public attitudes and beliefs play a relatively minor and essentially indirect role in determining the behavior of nations and their consequent interaction. . . . At the very most, public opinion is a limiting, conservative factor and has seldom been a force for diplomatic innovation, in either its genuine or perceived state'' (Singer, 1963: 14).

In a subsequent section of this chapter we will focus attention on the role played by the mass media in the process whereby public preferences (indirectly) influence the policy process. Before adding that complication, however, let us briefly consider another aspect of the opinion-policy linkage more directly related to democratic theory—the role of elections.

PRESIDENTIAL ELECTIONS AND FOREIGN POLICY CHANGE

Elections are conventionally viewed by the press and public alike as opportunities for policy change, if for no other reason than the prospects they raise for bringing about new leadership. The commonly held assumption is that new leadership will mean new policies and programs. A corollary assumption deserving attention here is that elections enable voters' preferences on foreign policy issues to be translated into policies which reflect those preferences. The question is, "Are citizens' votes viable means of expressing policy preferences, thereby rendering electoral processes critical in translating public preferences into policy making?"

On the one hand, it would seem plausible that decision makers' fear of electoral punishment would lead them to propose policies that would maintain their popularity and thereby enhance their prospects for gaining and retaining office. On the other hand, what Bernard Cohen (1973) referred to as the "apparent immunity of the foreign policy establishment to electoral accountability" is notable. Research on the two alternative propositions has been extensive. The results have "not, on the whole, been kind to democratic theory," showing "that policy voting is quite rare" and that citizens, for a variety of reasons, fail to vote for candidates on the basis of policy preferences. "In short, voters are incapable of policy rationality" (Page and Brody, 1972).

Although sometimes conflicting and in flux, data supporting the "issue-less politics" hypothesis—that voter choice is determined neither by the nature of the issues nor candidate's positions on them—are abundant (see Asher, 1984). Foreign policy is not an exception to the pattern. Although Americans clearly do hold opinions about foreign policy matters, their opinions are not transmitted by elections into the policy-formation process. How do we account for such a failure? One inviting explanation is that although many Americans may regard foreign policy issues as among the most important facing the nation, those issues nevertheless fail to arouse the depth of personal concern raised by issues closer to the daily lives of the population. In addition, foreign policy issues are not the ones that "divide the populace into contending groups. . . . In general foreign issues, involving as they do the United States *versus* others, tend to blur or reduce differences domestically" (Nie, Verba, and Petrocik, 1976).

That does not mean that *party* outcomes are unaffected by foreign policy issues during presidential elections, however. How the public views foreign policy has been shown to be related to the partisan votes cast in each election between 1952 and 1980 (Asher, 1984). Republicans benefited from those perceptions in seven of the eight elections. The 1964 election was the only instance in which voter preferences on foreign policy issues favored the Democrats. The common belief that Republicans produce different policy outcomes (for example, "peace with poverty") than Democrats (for example, "war with wealth") may have something to do with the results.[24]

Or consider President Carter's electoral fate. The public generally gave Carter high marks on personal attributes (for example, integrity) but low marks on performance. Public evaluations of his foreign policy performance were especially critical and generally paralleled his overall decline in popularity.[25] Following Carter's surge in popularity after the seizure of American embassy personnel in Teheran, the president's inability to secure their release seemed to have fueled public dissatisfaction with the president's overall performance. His challenger, Ronald Reagan, criticized the policy of détente Carter and his predecessors had promoted, called for substantially increased defense spending, and hammered away at the theme of alleged American impotence in international affairs. In this context, "the continuing crisis in Iran came to be seen as a living symbol and constant reminder of all that Reagan had been saying" (Hess and Nelson, 1985).

Four years later, Reagan's reputation for leadership proved a strong force motivating voters to choose the incumbent president over his challenger, Walter Mondale. Certainly there were elements in Reagan's foreign policy record that could be criticized, but four years of relative peace had overcome the fear that "a reckless Reagan would provoke a war" (Keeter, 1985). In fact, among voters who cited military spending and foreign affairs as critical issues in their choice of candidates, Reagan was the overwhelming favorite. Of other potential foreign policy issues, only among those for whom nuclear arms control was the most important issue was Mondale clearly the preferred choice (Keeter, 1985; see also Kemble, 1985). On too many other issues, apparently, his stance smacked of "me-tooism." Thus, as one observer put it, "No longer

---

[24]These perceptions may be changing. Gallup poll data (*Public Opinion*, December–January 1985: 38) show that, since 1981, more Americans perceive the Democratic party as better for peace than the Republican party, a reflection, perhaps, of uneasiness with the hawkish rhetoric of the Reagan administration and its seeming quickness to approach political problems with military solutions. Conversely, the Republicans have often been perceived as better for prosperity than the Democrats. The data on this item are less clearcut than for the peace issue, but again they suggest that popular perceptions linking the Reagan administration to the economic upturn of the 1980s explain the shifting fortunes of the two major political parties.

[25]Compared to his predecessors, Jimmy Carter ranked poorly in the public's view of his foreign policy performance. A Louis Harris poll taken in January 1981 found that only 5 percent of the public rated Carter best in foreign affairs among the eight presidents holding office between 1933 and 1980. Richard Nixon ranked highest (chosen as best by 30 percent of the respondents), followed by John Kennedy (20 percent), Franklin D. Roosevelt (11 percent), Harry Truman (11 percent), and Dwight Eisenhower (10 percent). Only Lyndon Johnson and Gerald Ford ranked lower than Carter (The Harris Survey for the *Chicago Tribune*, January 19, 1981). *New York Times/CBS News* polls in 1984 and 1985, however, showed that 24 percent of the public thought that Carter had done more for world peace than any other recent president, compared to 21 percent for Reagan, and that the 1978 Camp David accord, engineered by Carter, was the most successful foreign policy venture in recent years. Nixon ranked highest among all presidents, chosen by 32 percent, as the president who had done most for world peace.

fearful that the President's policies might lead to war, the public had no compelling reason to abandon him" (Keeter, 1985).

It nevertheless remains difficult to determine the separate effects of particular foreign policy questions on citizens' behavior at the polls. Because most elections involve a variety of different and often overlapping issues, "no one can really tell whether the majority who voted for the winning candidate did so because of his policy stand on one particular issue or *in spite of* his policy stand on that particular issue" (Hilsman, 1971). Moreover, voter behavior is more likely an aggregate judgment about past performance than a guide to future action. And history points to the conclusions that "parties do not offer clear policy alternatives in election campaigns; voters do not have their choice as to the policy positions of the candidates; and candidates are not bound by their campaign pledges anyway" (Dye and Zeigler, 1981). Nevertheless, because policy makers act—evidence to the contrary—*as though* voters make choices on the basis of their policy preferences, they pay attention to the anticipated responses of voters in shaping their policy choices.

The Vietnam episode illustrates many of these conclusions. In 1964, 1968, and again in 1972 the American electorate had the opportunity to pass judgment on past performance in a way that might have had clear implications for future behavior on the part of their government leadership. Did they vote their preferences on the issue? What was the relationship between those preferences and policy?

Vietnam became a major foreign policy issue in 1964, when President Johnson's overwhelming electoral victory was widely interpreted as a mandate for restraint in the prosecution of the growing U.S. involvement in the Southeast Asian conflict. His Republican opponent, Barry Goldwater, had campaigned on the pledge of pursuing "victory" against communism in all quarters of the globe, but especially in Vietnam by "any means necessary." Johnson's subsequent escalation of the conflict was therefore viewed by some as a violation of his mandate, indeed, as implementation of Goldwater's program. In fact, however, as national surveys indicated:

> There was relatively little relationship between candidate and policy preference, with Johnson winning the support of both "doves" and "hawks." While 63 percent of those favoring withdrawal from Vietnam voted for the President, so did 52 percent of those who favored "a stronger stand even if it means invading North Vietnam" as did 82 per cent of those who preferred to "keep our soldiers in Vietnam, but try to end the fighting." (Pomper, 1968: 251)

In fact, the results of that election as it related to Vietnam were so ambiguous as to lead one scholar to conclude: "What could the 1964 vote have told [Johnson] about popular support for various war options? In brief, it could have told him anything he cared to believe" (Boyd, 1972).

By 1968 the war had reached enormous proportions by any measure. The predictable consequence—as we noted above—was growing unpopularity and dissatisfaction with the war. Support declined as the length of the war in-creased and its casualty lists grew longer. Campus unrest, mass demonstra-tions against the war, increasingly vocal minority opposition, including chal-lenges from within the president's own party by Eugene McCarthy and Robert Kennedy—all were indicative of the changing climate of opinion. The widespread popular impression was that Johnson's decision not to run for a second full presidential term was a direct result of this popular opposition. We would expect, therefore, that in 1968 the voters would have made a clear judg-ment on past performance and would have provided a clear mandate for the future. They didn't.

In terms of Vietnam, the 1968 vote was as "issueless" as the Eisenhower-Stevenson encounter of 1956. Although "hawks" tended to vote for Nixon in somewhat greater proportion than "doves," overall Vietnam opinions ac-counted for only between 1 and 2 percent of the variation in voting behavior (Page and Brody, 1972: 982). In short, "[v]oters did not treat the 1968 election as a referendum on Vietnam policy" (Page and Brody, 1972). This was largely because the electorate (correctly) perceived little difference between the posi-tions of the candidates (Nixon and Humphrey) on Vietnam policy. The voters were in fact deprived of a meaningful foreign policy choice, and the electoral mechanism thus failed to serve as a vehicle for the expression of growing pub-lic dissatisfaction with the war, because both candidates adopted essentially a middle-of-the-road stance on the issue.[26]

Hence again in 1968 no clear foreign policy mandate for one course of action over another was provided by the electoral process. Nixon's subsequent shift to what was called "peace with honor" did not emanate from the elec-tion. Nor was the promise to end the war promptly fulfilled. An agonizingly slow process ensued. The "Vietnamization" strategy, announced phased troop withdrawals, and the beginning of peace talks in Paris all came belatedly. It was not until October 1972, shortly (coincidentally?) before the next presiden-tial election, that Secretary of State Kissinger declared to the public that "peace is at hand."

But peace was not *in* hand. So November 7, 1972, became the first election since the Korean War election of 1952 in which foreign policy was the major is-sue. The available survey data indicate clearly that the American electorate cast their votes this time with Vietnam an issue uppermost in their minds (Miller et al., 1976). Somewhat less clear-cut, however, was the meaning for Vietnam policy of Nixon's landslide victory. Interpreting the victory as elec-toral approval for what was perceived, rightly or wrongly, as Nixon's policy of deescalation of the war (Steeper and Teeter, 1976) may be the most compelling way to view the results. But the question of whether the voters voted the way

---

[26]Page and Brody (1972: 990–993) strike a blow in favor of democratic theory by showing that not only did the electorate perceive there was little difference between Nixon and Humphrey on the Vietnam issue, but also that they did perceive differences on the issue among the primary can-didates, namely Eugene McCarthy, Robert Kennedy, George Wallace, and Ronald Reagan.

they did because they wanted a negotiated peace or because they desired a military victory remains unanswered.

Given the foregoing discussion of the major characteristics and functions of public opinion, the conclusion that in major electoral contests most Americans tend to support existing government actions should come as no surprise. What is perhaps surprising, however—particularly in light of the nationalistic sentiments of the public and the relative unimportance of foreign policy to most Americans—is that a foreign policy issue became a major item on the electoral agenda at all. The explanation appears to lie in the perceived cost of the war. When foreign policy issues begin to affect significantly the resources and relationships that touch the daily lives of Americans, they are likely to be looked upon much more as domestic political issues. Vietnam was precisely such an issue. Mothers and wives, fathers and sons, taxpayers and draftees—all were intimately touched by Vietnam, a fact which distinguished this war, like others, from most foreign policy questions. Yet the striking fact remains that even in that case, the relationship between public preferences and policy outcomes was essentially an indirect one that does little violence to the general proposition that decision makers lead and the public follows. Little wonder that the characterization holds for the less costly and less disruptive (but infinitely more numerous) issues that comprise the bulk of U.S. foreign policy. Public preferences in general, and during elections in particular, serve as a "source" of American foreign policy, it seems. But they do so more by coloring the vocabulary of decision making than by determining the policy outcomes. Elections are not mechanisms through which the public exercises control over American foreign policy. They are instruments for the selection of personnel, not policy.

THE MASS MEDIA AS A SOCIETAL SOURCE

A potentially important component in the public opinion-foreign policy linkage is the role played by the mass media—television, the press, and radio. The mass communications industry may be hypothesized to play a central role in the process of policy formulation because (1) public moods related to policies are influenced (some would say created) by the information disseminated to the public through the communications network, and (2) the behavior of policy makers themselves is affected by the image of the world conveyed by the mass media. From either perspective, the mass media appear to affect the kinds of foreign policies the United States carries out.

In terms of both popular images and policy makers' images, the mass media have been attributed almost dictatorial powers. Many Americans are apparently taken with the theory that their attitudes about international politics are shaped by the mass media from which they receive most of their information. Many see the media and the information they disseminate as a cause of public opinion. Indeed, some might even say that the media are public opinion.

Policy makers have likewise attributed wide powers to the media. Most recent policy makers' views of the media have ranged from awe and fear to downright hatred. Nixon's claim in 1962 that the press wouldn't have him to "kick around" anymore, followed by his subsequent efforts, once in the White House, to get revenge on his alleged enemies in journalism, is a case in point. More generally, presidential attitudes perhaps have been captured best in Oscar Wilde's famous remark that "the President reigns for four years, but Journalism reigns forever." Accordingly, presidents actively court the favor of the press, and they ascribe to it the power to make or break government policy. It is no accident, therefore, that many consider the mass media a fourth branch of the government.

Although it is hard to deny that the mass media have an effect both on public opinion and on the kinds of policies decision makers choose to pursue, the notion that the media are instrumental in determining foreign policy is questionable. The relationships are much more complex. In general, we might ask if the mass media perform more of a mediating than a determining role. Let us examine that question by looking first at the relationship between the mass media and the public and second at the relationship between the mass media and policy makers.

The Mass Media and the Public

With respect to mass public opinion, the proposition that the mass media exercise overwhelming influence is tempting if for no other reason than that they comprise the primary vehicle for the transmission of knowledge—and "knowledge is power." The industries from which most Americans get their primary information are highly developed. Ninety-eight percent of all American households own at least one television set (which is viewed an average of seven hours a day), and there are nearly 1,700 daily newspapers in the United States, with total daily circulations exceeding 63 million. This news establishment has the ability to determine "what the news is," to define behaviors as important actions, and thereby to make them into events.

But the mere existence of the media establishment fails to document its influence. We cannot simply assume that what the mass media report directly determines mass political attitudes. The relationship is more subtle than that. Consider the following five hypotheses, which add important qualifiers to the notion that public attitudes are structured by what the mass media say about foreign affairs.

The Mass Media Do Not Determine Public Attitudes Because Most People Are Inattentive to Foreign Affairs. The American public does not closely follow coverage of, and is largely uninterested in, politics generally, and foreign affairs in particular.[27] Public indifference to foreign affairs means that the

---

[27]Cohen (1963) notes that the average amount of newspaper coverage of foreign policy issues read by adults is less than half a column. V. O. Key (1961) estimated that the proportion of Ameri-

mass public removes itself from the alleged influence of the mass media; public attitudes cannot be influenced by the press and television if an apathetic public consciously or unconsciously tunes out information reported by the mass media. Repeated studies of mass reactions suggest that most Americans are more interested in weekly television series than in a news commentator's observations on the state of the world. If the mass public does not listen to news disseminated by the mass media, obviously those media cannot influence opinion.

Although that conclusion is unassailable, it fails to acknowledge the important role that the mass media play in setting national agendas. Most people may be inattentive to foreign policy matters most of the time. But in the (rare) event that they do show interest, however inadvertently, the mass media tell them what to care about. Therefore the media may create new issues simply as a consequence of the attention they give them, and items may become added to the agenda because of the symbolic significance the media accord them. Would Reagan's decision in 1985 to visit the cemetery with Nazi war dead at Bitburg, West Germany, have become so controversial had it not been for the attention the media gave it? Did that attention tarnish the president's journey to the annual economic summit of Western leaders to the point that it undermined his efforts to forge a consensus on how best to cope with the Western community's common economic problems?

The importance and meaning the public may have ascribed to the presence of Cuban troops in Angola in late 1975 and 1976 and to alleged Cuban arms shipments to Nicaragua in 1981 may also have been determined in part by media attention. Put succinctly, the media may not tell us what to think, but they do tell us what to think *about* (see McCombs and Shaw, 1972). Thus, the capacity to define what is significant, what comprises a problem, what constitutes an issue, what poses a crisis, and what alternatives are available resides with the media.

Furthermore, once the agenda of issues has been set, the media function as "gatekeepers" by filtering the news and shaping the way it is reported. Research suggests that over the long run "the media tend to reinforce mainstream social values." By serving as "gatekeepers," the media transmit " 'normal' or legitimate issues and ideas to the public and [filter] out new, radical, or threatening perspectives" (Bennett, 1980).

The Mass Media, By and Large, Are Themselves Relatively Inattentive to Foreign Affairs. If the mass media reflect the values and interests of their audience, then that explains, perhaps, why the mass media are more concerned with domestic than foreign news. Foreign affairs may receive comparatively less treatment in part because of the absence of a mass market for foreign policy news. It has been estimated that foreign affairs news coverage constitutes

cans who are careful readers of political news that is construed as entailing more than just foreign affairs news is probably less than 10 percent. Although now dated, there is no more recent evidence available to refute these data.

on the average only 11 percent of all stories in American newspapers in periods when there are no major crises (Graber, 1985: 308). For perhaps similar reasons, few reporters are paid to cover international affairs. Television programing, furthermore, is overwhelmingly oriented toward local news, not national or international news. The consequence of the relative inattention of America's mass media to foreign policy (compared to domestic issues) is obvious: media neglect of foreign events minimizes their potential impact on public attitudes regarding foreign policy.

An exception to the foregoing is the foreign affairs coverage by the so-called prestige press, of which the New York Times is the most notable,[28] and the ABC, CBS, and NBC network broadcasts. A 1972 sample of the New York Times news coverage, for example, showed that the Times allocated nearly 44 percent of its total national and international coverage to foreign news. Network coverage ranged from just under 31 percent for ABC to about 36 percent for NBC (Frank, 1973: 58)[29] How many American people consume that coverage and even how much there is to consume remain problematic, however. The circulation of the Times constitutes but a fraction of the nation's newspaper subscribers, and it has frequently been noted that a full transcript of the nightly television network news—foreign and domestic—would not fill half of the front page of an average daily newspaper.[30] Yet it is on this source that 74 percent of the American people depend for most of their foreign affairs information (Schneider, 1984: 18).[31] We will have more to say about television in a moment.

The Influence of the Mass Media on Mass Foreign Policy Attitudes Is Undermined by the Diversity and Heterogeneity of the Media Establishment. The mass media are not monolithic, cohesive in their approach to foreign affairs, and consistent in their interpretation of international events. "Pack journalism"—a troublesome phenomenon which refers to the tendency of most re-

---

[28]See Semmel (1977) for an analysis of the global distribution of press coverage of four U.S. "quality" dailies: the New York Times, the Miami Herald, the Chicago Tribune, and the Los Angeles Times. Kelly and Mitchell's (1984) analysis of press coverage of transnational terrorism also gives insight into variations in press treatment of international affairs.

[29]The three national news magazines, Time, Newsweek, and U.S. News and World Report, also give substantial attention to foreign affairs. Frank's data do not extend to the news magazines, but Gans (1979) usefully compares these national media to the television networks.

[30]The facts cited here are not meant to minimize the importance of the prestige press or the television networks in providing foreign affairs coverage. As Doris Graber (1985) notes, virtually all foreign affairs coverage is provided by only seven newspapers (the New York Times, Washington Post, Los Angeles Times, Baltimore Sun, Chicago Tribune, Wall Street Journal, and Christian Science Monitor), the two wire services (the Associated Press and United Press International), and the three national television networks. Furthermore, newspapers such as the New York Times provide news to other newspapers, which often follow the lead of the prestige press in the way news stories are presented to local audiences. For a discussion of the influential prestige press, see Halberstam (1979).

[31]The growing importance of television is suggested by the fact that "most American children begin watching television at the age of three months and, by the time they finish high school, have spent less than 12,000 hours in front of a teacher and more than 22,000 hours in front of a

porters to follow the lead of one or a few others in deciding what is (or is not) news—often leads to remarkably similar news accounts, particularly among the national print and electronic media. Across the range of news sources, however, it is clear that the American media offer a varying amount of foreign affairs coverage (but generally ranging from nil to little) from a diversity of standpoints.[32] Since a variety of opinions are disseminated by the mass media, and the media themselves transmit inconsistent information and thereby do not speak with a single voice, the ability to inculcate a particular set of values is reduced.

Public Attitudes Are Relatively Impervious to New Information Provided by News Sources. The agenda-setting function of the mass media draws attention to the important role of the media in shaping citizens' perceptions. Because the mass public often has no prior information on which to rely in forming attitudes about new developments abroad, the media play a potentially critical role in shaping perceptions about events simply because the information they supply is new—and the information is often proffered in such a way as to suggest, and thus to shape, "appropriate" preferences. In the absence of preconceptions—of Libya's Colonel Muammar Qaddafi, of racial strife in South Africa, of Thatcherism in Britain—"media-created" preferences become accepted wisdom.

It is important to examine the role of television at this point. This incredible medium of intrusion into the homes and daily lives of millions of Americans

---

television set . . . '' (Ranney, 1983: 4). The correlation of TV-watching with other trends among the nation's emerging generations of foreign policy makers, including, for example, several years of declining Scholastic Aptitude Test scores, may be related to what some (for example, Manheim, 1984) believe to be shallow thinking about politics and a declining interest in public affairs.

[32]Rather than diversity, the popular image is that the mass media in the United States are dominated by a common set of biases and display a conformity of outlook. Spiro Agnew's claim, when he was vice president, that the mass media are dominated by "liberals" is a widely shared impression. And there is some evidence to support it. Lichter and Rothman (1981), for example, demonstrate that journalists from the nation's most influential print and electronic media share attitudes more liberal and cosmopolitan than business elites. In another study sponsored by the *Los Angeles Times* that focused not on media elites but on news and editorial staff members of over 600 newspapers, journalists were found to be markedly more liberal than other Americans, including those with similar educational and professional standing (Schneider and Lewis, 1985).

Against this background, it is interesting to note that in 1984 Ronald Reagan, the conservative Republican party candidate, was endorsed by 381 daily newspapers (circulation 18,357,512), while Walter Mondale, the more liberal Democratic party nominee, was endorsed by only 62 newspapers (circulation 7,568,369) (*Editor & Publisher*, November 3, 1984: 9). Furthermore, the *Los Angeles Times* study found that while those who write and edit news stories are overwhelmingly liberal, barely half of those who read these same newspapers could categorize them as either liberal or conservative. The study also revealed a "tendency for people to ascribe their own positions to those of their newspaper," suggesting that "readers assume that the newspaper they depend on for information shares their outlook" (Schneider and Lewis, 1985). Finally, an analysis of network and wire service coverage of the 1980 presidential campaign concludes similarly: political reporting, especially of domestic news, "reflects the canons of objectivity more often than the political opinions of the newspeople themselves" (Robinson, 1983).

has affected the opinion-media-policy linkage in important ways. Members of Congress who wish to make names for themselves (read all), for example, are induced to frame their foreign policy ideas in "one-liners" that will fit into the thirty-, sixty-, or ninety-second slots the evening news allocates to such issues. For the electorate it has meant that "a Presidential candidate without much prior international experience can come to office with a collection of half-minute clichés in his head masquerading as foreign policies" (Destler, Gelb, and Lake, 1984). And for the mass of the American people it has meant a massive infusion of foreign policy information—which most neither like nor want. Instead, owing to the fact that most who watch television news see what does not interest them as well as what does—they don't "edit" the information television journalists supply by walking away from the set or turning it off—they have become an "inadvertent audience" (Ranney, 1973).

What are the consequences? First, television may explain the decline of confidence in the nation's institutional leadership witnessed during recent decades.[33] As one well-known opinion analyst has observed, "negative news makes good video. Consequently, television presents much of the news as conflict, criticism and controversy. . . . The public responds to this large volume of polarized information by becoming more cynical, more negative, and more critical of leadership and institutions" (Schneider, 1982). Less patience with foreign policy initiatives by individuals and institutions about which Americans are cynical and distrustful may be a related consequence of exposure to American involvement in world affairs, which television brings home but which most Americans find confusing and unnecessary.

Second, being uninterested, members of the "inadvertent audience" are unlikely to have strong convictions about issues, as do those who regularly follow foreign policy issues. "[W]hen people with weak opinions are exposed to new information, the impact of that information is very strong. They form new opinions, and if the information they receive is negative or critical, their opinions will develop in that direction" (Schneider, 1982). "There is no evidence that television changes the nature of the public's concerns in the area of foreign policy," observes William Schneider (1984). "These concerns remain what they always have been: peace and strength. Television simply intensifies these concerns and creates more negative and unstable public moods."

In those instances when people do not begin with the complete absence of preconceptions, behavioral research tells us that people do not change their beliefs very easily. What they read in print and see and hear on television does not (popular myths notwithstanding) alter what they think. The reasons are mostly psychological. Beliefs are not a function of information because of the pervasive human tendency toward *selective perception*: most people most of the time search for "comfortable" information which "fits" with preexisting be-

---

[33]In the specific case of the presidency, television coverage has been shown to become increasingly negative as a president's term progresses, a finding that may help explain the decline and fall of modern presidents (Smoller, 1986).

liefs, whereas information which does not coincide with prevailing attitudes is rejected. In short, we see what we want to see, we hear what we want to hear.[34]

Selective perception is partially subconscious, stemming from the nearly universal need to maintain a stable image in the midst of often conflicting and confusing information. In the parlance of psychology, everyone seeks to maintain "cognitive balance" (Festinger, 1957), either by screening out information that runs counter to cherished beliefs or by avoiding and suppressing information which causes discomfort in failing to conform to existing, simplified images of the world. An individual subscribing to the simplistic belief that all revolutions and civil disturbances are communist inspired, for instance, is likely to reject or block out information which runs counter to that theory, such as reports that insurgency in Central America stems not from outside intervention, but from indigenous sources.

Selective perception also sometimes seems to be conscious. Many people choose to read magazines and to listen to news programs which reinforce interpretations consistent with their biases. How many people, for instance, routinely read interpretations from journals reflecting *both* liberal (for example, *The Nation*) and conservative (for example, *National Review*) perspectives? A small proportion, most studies indicate. Thus most people who care about politics and foreign policy are relatively immune to media-induced attitude change. That is *not* to say that most Americans are intellectual bigots. But the propensity for selective perception (reinforced by the related tendency toward "selective recall" of the past) renders the ability of the mass media to influence attitude change very slight.[35]

The Capacity of the Mass Media to Influence Mass Foreign Policy Attitudes Is Undermined by the Media's Vulnerability to Government Manipulation. To a considerable extent the media reflect, rather than balance, the attitudes of the government. Collusion between the media and the government, conscious and unconscious, is a persistent condition. The following describes the process:

> Government officials and the press play a game of politics and propaganda which has become as stylized as an 18th century dance. First the officials hand out privileged information to favored journalists ("U.S. intelligence flatly reported that . . ."). Then the journalists pass out the same information, with or without attribution, to their readers. Finally, pro-administration congressmen fill pages of the *Congressional Record* with the same articles to prove that the officials were right. (Draper, 1968: 89)

[34]See Paterson and McClure's *The Unseeing Eye* (1976) for an examination of the proposition that the broadcasting industry is capable of influencing public opinion. A critique of the "minimal-effects" thesis can be found in Parenti (1986). Experimental evidence that also challenges it is presented in Iyengar, Peters, and Kinder (1982).

[35]This is not meant to imply that the media have no impact on American politics, only that it is a complex and indirect one. The collection of essays in Graber's *Media Power in Politics* (1984) is a useful introduction to the broad range of issues and research questions that the media raise.

As the foregoing suggests, the media frequently operate as a conduit for the transmission of information from the governing elite to the American people rather than as a truly independent source of information about what the government is doing. For a variety of reasons (for example, dependence on government news releases, inability to obtain classified information, use of "privileged" briefings, self-censure, the fact that self-restraint is often in the media's self-interest), the mass media are frequently regarded by the government as exceedingly vulnerable to manipulation. News, in government parlance, is "manageable,"[36] and what is reported often depends on what is "leaked" by the government for public consumption rather than on what has occurred behind closed doors. In the extreme, the government effectively censors the news, as the Reagan administration did when it denied reporters permission to observe the Grenada assault force in 1983,[37] an intervention later revealed to be fraught with mistakes.

Disclosures about government lies during Watergate and in areas routinely, but liberally, defined by the government as matters of "national security" appear to have enhanced the ability of the mass media to function as a check on government control. But the fact that those abuses remained uncovered for such a long time is perplexing. Thus, whereas a more critical and aggressive posture in parts of the "fourth estate" in the wake of Vietnam and Watergate may have helped to rectify compliant tendencies, the media and the government remain intertwined to a considerable extent in a process which invites collusion.[38] Because news derived from the government itself compromises the ability of the media to oversee government actions in the foreign arena, it may be more appropriate to ask not whether the media control public

[36]The Kennedy administration in particular is often credited with having been extraordinarily successful in having the news its way. However, empirical studies of four Kennedy foreign policy crises by Kern, Levering, and Levering (1984) suggest that Kennedy's ability to dominate the news varied considerably, depending on the circumstances. Kern (1984) has also compared Carter to Kennedy, finding, not surprisingly, that Carter fared even less well than Kennedy. A number of reasons explain this, including the fact that Carter came to office "on a wave of public and press disillusionment with the strong presidency." An historical overview of the relationship between *The Press and the Presidency* is provided by Tebbel and Watts (1985), who are particularly critical of the Reagan administration's use—and abuse—of the mass media.

[37]Once information about the invasion became available, the *New York Times* (November 6, 1983, cited in Tebbel and Watts, 1985) concluded: "It has become clear that the Reagan Administration officials and military authorities disseminated much inaccurate information and many unproved assertions. They did so while withholding significant facts and impeding efforts by the journalists to verify official statements."

[38]To some extent the media seem to have accepted adversary journalism as an appropriate part of their mission, making exposure of government mistakes—and crimes—news that is "fit to print" (or show, as the case may be). General William C. Westmoreland's unsuccessful $120 million libel suit in 1984 against CBS for its documentary "The Uncounted Enemy: A Vietnam Deception" (which accused the general and his colleagues of intentionally trying to deceive the press, the public, and even the president about North Vietnamese and Vietcong strength) is a recent example of the reactions such a journalism style sometimes provokes. A final judgment was not reached in that case because the general ceased his efforts to substantiate his allegations against CBS. But the costs associated with the defense of adversary journalism may inhibit the media from pursuing it vigorously in the future.

opinion in America, but whether public attitudes are manipulated and structured by the government through the mass media.[39]

The Mass Media and Policy Makers

The foregoing casts doubt on the thesis that public attitudes are molded by what the mass media report. But the media cannot be dismissed so readily. Important qualifications must be introduced by turning attention from the influence of the media on the attitudes of ordinary citizens to its impact on the attitudes of *policy makers* and *policy influentials* (people who are knowledgeable about foreign affairs and who have access to decision makers, such as the nongovernmental members of "the establishment" described in chapter eight). The following four observations summarize available evidence on the subject.

Those Who Follow Foreign Policy Events and Who Are Attentive to Foreign Issues Derive Most of Their Information Directly from the Mass Media. American society is structured like a pyramid, with a very small proportion of people comprised of policy influentials and decision makers at the top (the "elite"), followed by a larger component comprising the "attentive public," with the bulk of the population making up the "mass public." The pyramid represents the three strata which make up the aggregate concept "public opinion." While estimates vary as to the distribution of the public among these three groups, most suggest that the elite (decision makers and policy influentials) comprise less than 2 percent of the population; the attentive public (those knowledgeable about foreign affairs but not necessarily with access to decision makers) between 5 and 15 percent; and the mass public, by definition, the rest.

The distinction among the components of "public opinion" is important in evaluating the impact of mass media on foreign policy making, because such factors as level of education, familiarity with foreign issues, and amount of information about foreign policy are important determinants of one's position within the societal pyramid as well as one's foreign policy attitudes. Television has a leveling effect in that even those who care less about foreign affairs get information about it. But those making up the elite and attentive public take advantage of a broader array of information, virtually all of it from publicly available sources provided by the mass media in the United States. Accordingly, for those concerned about foreign policy and for those actually involved in the foreign policy-making process, the impact of the mass media is potentially much greater than for the mass public, which pays little attention to such news, does not seek it, or is only inadvertently an audience for it.

---

[39]See Parenti (1986) for an examination of the proposition that the media effectively collude with the government to promote anticommunist sentiments and what Parenti calls the "Big Lie," which he says includes media and government treatment of Soviet terrorism, yellow rain, the flight of KAL 007, and the plot to assassinate the Pope.

It may appear surprising or even exaggerated to suggest that policy makers rely on the media as a primary source of information—instead of the information provided by the intelligence community, for instance—but it is an empirical tendency. The mass media provide policy makers with a basic source of information about what is happening in the world (for a variety of reasons, but especially because the press is much quicker and more readable than official reports, and because the press in the United States is often perceived to be a less biased source of information than government agencies which gather data with a purpose in mind).[40] Especially important in this respect is the prestige press. As a careful student of the subject put it:

> The most apparent way in which the press enter the policy-maker's world is by means of the daily newspaper. And the single most important newspaper is, of course, the *New York Times*. It is read by virtually everyone in the government who has an interest or responsibility in foreign affairs. . . . One frequently runs across the familiar story: "It is often said that Foreign Service Officers get to their desks early in the morning to read the *New York Times*, so they can brief their bosses on what is going on." This canard is easily buried: The "bosses" are there early, too, reading the *New York Times* for themselves. . . . The *Times* is uniformly regarded as the authoritative paper in the foreign policy field. In the words of a State Department official in the public affairs field, "You can't work in the State Department without the *New York Times*. You can get along without the overnight telegrams sooner." (Cohen, 1961: 220–221)

Other statesmen and policy influentials corroborate the observation.[41] Thus the mass media play an important role in disseminating information about foreign affairs to those interested in, and in positions of power with respect to, foreign policy making in the United States. To the extent that images of the world depend on the way they are described in the mass media, the media have potentially important input into the policy-making process.

The Mass Media May Stimulate Changes in the Elite's Attitudes Which Are Then Dispersed Throughout Society. The fact that knowledgeable and influential Americans derive most of their information about foreign affairs from the mass media does not mean they are immune to selective perception and foreign policy belief rigidity. Nor does it mean they cannot be victims of re-

---

[40]Graber (1985) illustrates the point by noting that John F. Kennedy "would read the *New York Times* before beginning his official day because stories about foreign affairs often reached him 24 hours earlier through the *Times* than through State Department bulletins. . . ."

[41]For instance, conservative writer William F. Buckley, himself no fond admirer of the news establishment of which he is a part, found himself reporting (1970) after hearing a radio bulletin that Egyptian President Gamal Abdel Nasser had died: "I slipped off to telephone *The New York Times* to see if the report was correct (one always telephones *The New York Times* in emergencies). The State Department called *The New York Times*, back in 1956, to ask if it was true that Russian tanks were pouring into Budapest." And John Kenneth Galbraith (1969b), a former American policy maker, has testified to the effectiveness of elite newspapers to gather "all the news that's fit to print": "I've said many times that I never learned from a classified document anything I couldn't get earlier or later from *The New York Times*."

ported misinformation. Because they do not receive a consistent message from the mass media, they, too, must select and choose from often contradictory information. That means that attitude changes, even among those groups, is likely to be incremental and slow.

However, attitude change may still be possible. Indeed, recent American history attests to the fact that the opinions of "the best and the brightest" can shift in response to changing circumstances and new information. Behavioral research indicates that when opinion fluctuates within the policy-making and attentive publics, it serves as a stimulus to eventual attitude change among the general populace. The classic explanation of the opinion-making and opinion-circulating process, which has received considerable scholarly treatment, is known as the "two-step flow of communications" theory, according to which "ideas often flow from radio and print to opinion leaders and from these to the less-active sections of the population" (Katz, 1957). The dynamics of attitude change are best explained, the hypothesis holds, through the crucial channel of face-to-face contact. That is not to suggest that members of the mass public actually sit down and exchange ideas with governing elites or policy influentials. Rather, it suggests that ideas become meaningful only after they have been transmitted farther down the pyramid by such opinion leaders as teachers, the clergy, local political leaders—and perhaps taxi drivers and barbers—who have an above-average interest in public affairs and occupy positions allowing them to communicate frequently with others. Thus information does not flow directly from the mass media to the general population. Rather, it is transmitted first to opinion leaders (who, incidentally, inevitably distort it) and through them to the less interested or knowledgeable in mass society. Attitude change thus stems from changes in the thinking of the policy elite and the attentive public, with society at large following sometime later. Face-to-face contacts with opinion leaders and "mobilizable"[42] Americans provide a crucial link in the incremental diffusion process. Hence, the mass media are not the primary transmitters of ideas; nor are they the primary stimulus of mass attitude change. Rather, the mass media provide information to policy influentials and those attentive to public policy which, when digested in a way that invites attitude change, is then relayed through the political system primarily through interpersonal contact.[43]

Television again challenges this view. There are few or no apparent intermediaries between evening news anchormen or women and the consumers of their messages. The two-step flow hypothesis is thus clearly overly simple. A "multistep flow" theory is preferable, for it provides a more accurate description of the opinion-making and opinion-circulating process in an age of mass electronic communication.

---

[42]Rosenau (1974) refers to such people as those—perhaps less than 1 percent of the population—whom leaders can request to perform political acts for particular reasons.

[43]In the words of Berelson and Steiner (1964), communications and the attitude change they induce "are more likely to be directed from equal to equal and from the higher-ranking members to the lower-ranking members than from the lower-ranking to the higher-ranking."

For every field of interest (politics, fashion, economics, moviegoing, etc.) there are apparently certain people who make great use of the media for information and guidance. The opinion leaders then communicate with each other, crystallizing their views into a consistent stance. Later they transmit this attitude to lesser opinion leaders, who also make use of the mass media but not so much. The recipients compare what they get from the media with what they get from their opinion leaders, then pass the combination on down the line. Eventually the message reaches that large segment of the population which makes little or no direct use of the media. (Sandman, Rubin, and Sachsman, 1972: 5)

Clearly, though, even in a multistep flow of communications, the media play a crucial role in the transmission of opinions within the political system. Hence they are pivotal in the process of opinion making and opinion diffusion. If it is true that "who mobilizes the elites mobilizes the public," the agents of mobilization are more often than not the media. The media are therefore catalysts of opinion change through the influence they may exert on the opinions of the elite. But because the process of opinion dispersion entails many steps and stages, mass opinion change in American society at large tends to be slow. Nevertheless, because there is such a process, long-term variations in public opinions are observable.

The Media: Opinion Makers or Reflectors of Policy Makers' Opinion? While the role of the media in the opinion-formation process cannot be denied, its role as an agent of change can be easily exaggerated. We would do well to recall that the mass media are part and parcel of the foreign policy-making establishment from which opinion change ultimately springs. That fact undermines the alleged independent role that the press and television might play in fomenting opinion change. Given the relationship between the mass media and the government (the mass media being dependent on the government for information, and government officials in turn comprising the media's major reference group), a congruence exists most of the time between the attitudes of the government and the views of the media which seek to scrutinize it. To be sure, conflicts between government officials and media representatives often exist, and they are likely to grow more acute as a president moves beyond his "honeymoon" period of popularity into a period of "hard choices." President Carter's comment in 1980 that "I've always been disappointed in two groups—the Iranians and the press," is a good example of the feeling every president has that his administration is being victimized by the media. But the ability of government to manage the news, combined with the media's dependence on the government to get the news, perpetuates a symbiotic (incestuous?) relationship between the two institutions.[44] The mass media are often, then, less a source of opinion change than a mirror image of government opinion.

[44]See Hess (1984) for an examination of the role of press officers and their offices in *The Government/Press Connection*.

Even the familiar news "leak," often used by competing factions within the government to fight their bureaucratic battles publicly through the media, does not alter that conclusion. Indeed, it reinforces it, since typically reporters, in addition to being required by their professional code of ethics to protect the confidentiality of "high government sources," must offer such protection in order to be assured of a news story to write or report tomorrow. It is clear from a multitude of sources, moreover, that "high government officials"—meaning White House staffers and members of the Cabinet—have often been the source of government "leaks." Polygraph tests, "ideological purity" examinations, loyalty oaths, and regulations designed to restrict the role of "background briefings," all, among other things, insisted upon by the Reagan administration at one time or another are no more likely to "fix the leaks" than was Nixon's White House intelligence group known as The Plumbers (who burglarized Democratic National Headquarters at the Watergate Hotel in 1972) a decade earlier. The "leak" is an American political "institution," a practice rooted in tradition and employed routinely.

The Media Create Foreign Policy Issues which Necessitate Action by Decision Makers. Finally, we might acknowledge again another way in which the mass media affect policy-making behavior and, ultimately, American external conduct. That is through the ability of the mass media to create foreign policy issues, described earlier as the agenda-setting function. By publicizing foreign events or international circumstances, the media draw attention to situations. Frequently that attention forces decision makers to act, rather than to ignore the situation or to choose to keep it hidden. By focusing on or ignoring some circumstance, the media "manufacture" conditions which demand a government response. Thus the media provoke decision making about issues which, had they not attracted attention, would probably have been met with apathy and indifference. As Destler, Gelb, and Lake (1984) suggest, the ability of policy makers to determine what is and what is not an important foreign policy issue may be adversely affected by the attention accorded to particular foreign policy problems by the media, especially television.

> [Television] amplifies the conflicts of the here and now. Iran becomes news when there is revolution, and it dominates our living rooms when American diplomats are held captive. Jimmy Carter certainly inflated the hostage issue and milked it for partisan gain, using the Rose Garden for cover against Teddy Kennedy. But even if he had behaved more responsibly, it is anything but clear that he could have kept things in proportion when the networks brought chanting demonstrators to us nightly and Walter Cronkite began counting the days. (Destler, Gelb, and Lake, 1984: 153)

Moreover, the media intrude into the policy-making process by defining the bounds within which policy debate takes place. The way the media treat an issue, once created, structures how it is perceived and often influences the vocabulary with which it is discussed. The effects of such input cannot, in the long run, be lightly dismissed. Theodore White captures the media's critical role in setting the agenda and shaping its content:

> The power of the press in America is a primordial one. It sets the agenda of public discussion; and this sweeping political power is unrestrained by any law. It determines what people will talk and think about—an authority that in other nations is reserved for tyrants, priests, parties and mandarins. No major act of the American Congress, no foreign adventure, no act of diplomacy, no great social reform can succeed in the United States unless the press prepares the public mind. (White, 1973: 327)

SOCIETAL SOURCES OF AMERICAN FOREIGN POLICY

By way of conclusion, we are left with the inescapable impression that the mass media play a mediating role in the foreign policy-making process. Although the mass media, through their agenda-setting and gatekeeper functions, condition the way Americans think about foreign affairs only indirectly, they affect more directly the way elite groups perceive the world. Thus they influence the course of U.S. action abroad to the extent that they are able to color the way policy makers, policy influentials, the attentive public, and opinion leaders see the world. When new information enters into the thinking of elite groups and stimulates a change in the attitudes of that stratum of American society that pays attention, then those attitudes gradually tend to affect the way the mass public thinks about foreign affairs. At the same time, the governing elite seeks to use the media to manage the view of the world that various segments of the public hold—an effort which itself attests to the perceived political importance of the media.

As we have seen, however, the impact is neither immediate nor direct. On the one hand, American diplomacy may be said to be dependent on the media in the sense that "a large proportion of diplomatic reporting consists of analysis based on the work of journalists. . . . [I]t is only a slight exaggeration to say that the mass media are the eyes and ears of diplomacy (Davison, 1976). But on the other hand, that dependency does not give the media control over U.S. foreign policy. The media enter into the policy-formation process; but they are less a source from which policy is derived than a cog in the machinery that produces policy decisions and foreign actions.

Thus, the question posed at the outset of this (and the preceding) chapters—"In what ways do societal factors influence American foreign policy?"—has invited a series of additional questions, and, inevitably, provoked a variety of answers. Examination of the potential impact of public opinion, presidential elections, and the mass media suggests that each of those societal factors does indeed intrude upon the policy-making process, and thus each serves as a source of American foreign policy. U.S. action abroad has indeed been shaped by each one of those factors, by variations in them, and by how they function in the policy-formation process. But the functions they perform explain more about the *process* of formulating American policies toward the external environment than they do about the kinds of objectives those actions are based on and the particular means chosen to realize them. The effect of the societal factors we have discussed here in generating foreign actions is rarely if ever direct; it seems, instead, they function simply as part of the context within which decisions are formulated, and in particular they operate more often as forces constraining foreign policy, thereby promoting persistence and continuity, than as forces stimulating radical departures from the past. Hence, if we assume, for example, that the anticommunist theme in American foreign policy springs naturally out of the Lockean liberal tradition described in the preceding chapter, the way in which the forces we have described in this chapter operate in the policy-making process should make clear why rapid movements away from the traditional anticommunist posture are unlikely. More generally, when we add to this the knowledge we have of the effects of the elitist foreign policy-making community and the consequences of pluralized interest-group interactions, it should not be surprising that incremental adaptations to evolving international circumstances are more characteristic of postwar American foreign policy than radical innovations.

Beyond this, however, it is difficult to isolate causal connections between *particular* societal variables and *particular* actions abroad. To pinpoint better the sources of American foreign policy decisions and initiatives, we need to turn from the consideration of factors within American society to an examination of the U.S. government from which most foreign policy initiatives spring.

SUGGESTIONS FOR FURTHER READING

ALMOND, GABRIEL A. *The American People and Foreign Policy*. New York: Praeger, 1960.

CASPARY, WILLIAM R. "The 'Mood' Theory: A Study of Public Opinion," *American Political Science Review* 64 (June 1970): 536–547.

COHEN, BERNARD C. *The Press and Foreign Policy*. Princeton, NJ: Princeton University Press, 1963.

————. *The Public's Impact on Foreign Policy*. Boston: Little, Brown, 1973.

FOSTER, H. SCHUYLER. *Activism Replaces Isolationism: U.S. Public Attitudes 1940–1975*. Washington, DC: Foxhall Press, 1983.

HOLSTI, OLE R., AND JAMES N. ROSENAU. *American Leadership in World Affairs: Vietnam and the Breakdown of Consensus*. Boston: Allen and Unwin, 1984.

MUELLER, JOHN E. *War, Presidents and Public Opinion*. New York: Wiley, 1973.

PARENTI, MICHAEL. *Inventing Reality: The Politics of the Mass Media*. New York: St. Martin's, 1986.

RANNEY, AUSTIN. *Channels of Power: The Impact of Television on American Politics*. New York: Basic Books, 1983.

RIELLY, JOHN E., ed. *American Public Opinion and U.S. Foreign Policy 1983*. Chicago: Chicago Council on Foreign Relations, 1983.

V

GOVERNMENTAL
SOURCES OF
AMERICAN FOREIGN
POLICY

10

PRESIDENTIAL PREEMINENCE IN FOREIGN POLICY MAKING

As modern bureaucracy has grown, the understanding of change and the for-mulation of new purposes have become more difficult. Like men, governments find old ways hard to change and new paths difficult to discover.

President Richard M. Nixon, 1970

In the areas of defense and foreign affairs, the Nation must speak with one voice, and only the president is capable of providing that voice.

President Ronald Reagan, 1984

There is no necessary virtue or logic in change merely for the sake of change. But when circumstances demand adaptive innovation, the capacity to under-take it becomes crucial. In the United States that capability resides foremost in the presidential foreign policy-making system. That observation forces us to ask if, as Kenneth N. Waltz (1967) contends, the presidential system is prefer-able to a parliamentary form of democratic governance, and if the ascribed ad-jectives of American institutions—"quick, pragmatic, ready, willing, and open"—aptly apply to the American practice of executive foreign policy mak-ing. It is perplexing when an incumbent president laments government's in-ability to understand change and to formulate new purposes accordingly; Nixon's observation becomes all the more rueful when we consider that nearly 3 million people work for a government that expends nearly $1 trillion annu-ally. With all that labor and all those resources, should not the understanding of change and the formulation of new purposes be the rule rather than the exception? And should not that be especially so in the area of foreign policy, since there the president is largely unencumbered by the many demands and expectations emanating from American society that characterize the making of domestic policy?

The presidential system has perhaps been more capable of adaptation to changing international exigencies than a parliamentary system. But could it be that the very size of the government—the incredibly complex organizational structures into which the millions of federal employees fit, and the maze of channels through which innovative ideas must pass before they become new policies—is itself a force working against "the understanding of change and the formulation of new purposes"? Apart from the cabinet departments, the federal roster includes over sixty different agencies and over 1,250 advisory boards and commissions. Of those, at least forty different agencies have some kind of foreign affairs responsibility. Add Congress—which often appears more like 535 separate interests than one unified body—and we can begin to understand why the very size of government fosters a process in which today's policies often turn out to be tomorrow's as well.

Consider also some simple propositions about the politics of policy making within this maze of multiple and often overlapping institutions. Money and personnel mean political power. Once you've got them, protect them. Oppose changes that would erode your sources of influence. Incremental changes at the edge are acceptable, but fundamental reorientations that would involve massive budgetary and personnel shifts are challenged.

The reasons why individuals in organizational settings protect their "fiefdoms" is the subject of chapter thirteen. In this and the two subsequent chapters we seek to describe the nature of the "fiefdoms" in the "foreign affairs government." The focus throughout these three chapters is how the structure of that part of the U.S. government concerned with foreign policy making— the governmental category—operates as a source of American foreign policy. How the United States organizes itself for the making of foreign policy, in other words, is assumed to shape the nature of American action abroad.

To guide our inquiry, we will draw on a conceptualization of the foreign policy-making process as a series of concentric circles (see Figure 10.1) suggested some years ago by Roger Hilsman (1967), himself a participant in, as well as perceptive student of, the politics of policy making. His view, in effect, bends the boxes and branches of the standard government organization chart so as to draw attention to the core, or source, of the action. Thus the innermost circle in the policy-making process consists of the president, his immediate personal advisers, and such important political appointees as the secretaries of state and defense, the director of the Central Intelligence Agency (CIA), and various under and assistant secretaries who bear responsibility for carrying out policy decisions. The most important decisions involving the fate of the nation are made, in principle, at this level.

The second circle contains the various departments and agencies of the executive branch. If we exclude from that circle the politically appointed agency

FIGURE 10.1   **The Institutional Setting: The Concentric Circles of Policy Making**

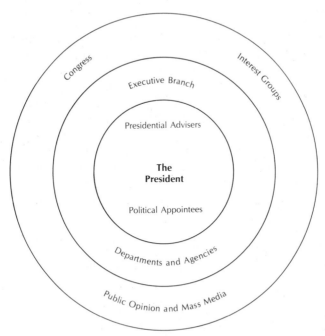

Congress

Interest Groups

Executive Branch

Presidential Advisers

The President

Political Appointees

Departments and Agencies

Public Opinion and Mass Media

SOURCE: Adapted from Hilsman, 1967: 541–544.

heads and their immediate subordinates, whom we have already placed in the innermost circle, we can think of the individuals within the second circle as the career bureaucrats who provide continuity in the implementation of policy from one administration to the next, regardless of who occupies the White House. Their primary task—in theory—is to provide top-level policy makers with the information necessary for making decisions and then to carry out those decisions.

The outermost circle is what Hilsman referred to as the "public one," consisting of Congress, domestic interest groups, public opinion, and the mass media. Collectively, the institutions, groups, and individuals at this level are least involved in the day-to-day foreign policy process.

Emphasizing this conceptualization, we will take three different approaches to describing the foreign affairs government in the subsequent chapters. First, attention will focus in this chapter on the way presidential factors, but especially the relationship between the president and his immediate group of advisers (with special reference to the National Security Council and the president's national security assistant) affect American foreign policy. In a sense, the question addressed is how particular presidential preferences combine with the generalized presidential form of government to promote what may be a distinctively American institutional approach to foreign policy making.

Second, in chapter eleven, the information-gathering and policy-implementation tasks of some of the many government organizations involved in the foreign policy-making process will be considered. If foreign policy making is primarily an executive function, then we must examine how the structural characteristics of the foreign affairs government define authority and divide the labor among those responsible for the making and execution of foreign policy. (In later chapters, particularly thirteen and fourteen, the informal mechanisms and individual behavior patterns that also determine what the government does—or doesn't do, as the case may be—will be explored.)

Finally, in chapter twelve, we will examine the governmental sources included in the third concentric circle by examining the role of Congress in foreign policy making. Here we will explore how the separation of powers—or the sharing of power by separate institutions, some would argue—is related to foreign policy outcomes. More specifically, we will look into the evolving nature of executive-congressional powers as they affect the substance of American foreign policy and the process by which it is made.[1]

FOREIGN AFFAIRS AND THE CONSTITUTION

The president's preeminent position in the foreign affairs government derives in part from the authority granted him in the Constitution. It also follows from the combination of judicial interpretation, legislative acquiescence, personal assertiveness, and custom and tradition that have transformed an otherwise coequal branch of the federal government into the most powerful office in the world.

The Constitution specifically grants the president remarkably few powers with respect to foreign affairs. Article II provides that he shall have the power, upon the advice and consent of the Senate, to make treaties and to appoint ambassadors and other public ministers and consuls, whereas a later section authorizes the president to receive ambassadors and other ministers. There is little else that deals explicitly with matters of foreign policy.[2]

---

[1]Because interest groups, the general public, and the mass media were discussed in the two preceding chapters, attention in chapter twelve to Hilsman's outermost concentric circle will be confined to Congress. This division follows naturally from the organizing framework for the examination of the sources of American foreign policy that structures this book. Whereas some have argued that Congress in particular is the object of intense "lobbying" by the nongovernmental forces elaborated in the two preceding chapters, the governmental-nongovernmental distinction is an important one conceptually. Hence Congress is treated within the governmental source category rather than the societal source category.

[2]The absence of additional constitutional provisions led Louis Henkin (1972), a leading authority on foreign affairs and the Constitution, to observe that "it seems incredible that these few meager grants support the most powerful office in the world and the multi-varied, wide-flung webwork of foreign activity of the most powerful nation in the world."

But the totality of presidential power is much greater than that governing treaties and ambassadors. The Constitution also makes the president the nation's chief legislative and executive officer and the commander in chief of its armed forces. Moreover, the courts have repeatedly conferred on the president a broadly (if ambiguously) defined foreign affairs power by making him the "sole organ" of the nation in its conduct of external affairs.

Those provisions and interpretations have combined with practice to ensure, over time, presidential supremacy in the formulation as well as execution of American foreign policy. Thus the foreign policy of the United States has come to be seen as what the president says it is. And he says what it is by concluding treaties and other executive agreements with foreign nations (held by the Supreme Court to be the supreme law of the land); by public declarations (such as the Truman, Eisenhower, Johnson, Nixon, Carter, and Reagan doctrines); by recognizing or not recognizing new governments overseas; by attending international conferences; by sending American troops here or there; by establishing military bases abroad; by encouraging or denouncing the actions of other nations, and so forth.

If the president's foreign affairs powers have turned out to be enormous, those granted Congress in the Constitution were substantial from the start. In foreign affairs Congress is authorized constitutionally to deal with the regulation of international commerce, the punishment of piracies and felonies committed on the high seas and offenses against the law of nations, and declarations of war. Congressional power to appropriate funds from the treasury and to tax and spend for the common defense and the general welfare have also proven tremendously important for the conduct of foreign affairs. Finally, the general legislative powers assigned to Congress grant it nearly limitless authority to affect the flow and form of foreign relations.[3]

The Constitution—often regarded as an open invitation for struggle between the executive and legislative branches of government—is not sufficient in itself to explain the distribution of decision-making authority over foreign affairs shown in Figure 10.1. Authority has derived as well from the ability of the president to act energetically and decisively in the crisis-ridden atmosphere that pervaded most of the post-World War II period. The widely shared consensus that the international environment demanded an active American world role also contributed to the feeling that strong presidential leadership in foreign policy was needed. Together those factors gave rise to what Arthur Schlesinger, Jr. (1973) labeled an "Imperial Presidency." Moreover, the forces giving rise to the increased power of the presidency went largely unchallenged. The Vandenburg Resolution (1949), in which Congress expressed support for a permanent American alliance with European nations (which later became NATO), and the Formosa Straits (1955), Middle East (1957), Cuban (1962), Berlin (1962), and Gulf of Tonkin (1964) resolutions, in which Congress gave the president broad congressional support for dealing with external con-

[3]For details see Henkin (1972: 67–88).

flict situations, fostered presidential supremacy by demonstrating a unity of purpose between the president and Congress. The ascendancy of presidential power in foreign policy making came about not so much because recent presidents have seized power as because Congress itself encouraged executive leadership in the postwar environment.[4]

But challenges to presidential preeminence grew in the 1960s and early 1970s, fed by discontent with executive policy in Vietnam, the Pentagon Papers, the Watergate hearings, and the Senate and House inquiries into the intelligence community. All of those revealed an abuse of executive power. In reaction, congressional authority began to be reasserted by those at the other end of Pennsylvania Avenue. Of particular concern was the question of control over American commitments and the president's war powers. The result (discussed in detail in chapter twelve) was a series of assertions of legislative authority which sought to circumscribe the executive's authority: the National Commitments Resolution (1969), the repeal of the Gulf of Tonkin Resolution (1970), the Case Act (1972), and the War Powers Act (1973), to name a few. What effect those congressional assertions have had, and will have, on the subsequent course of American foreign policy is inconclusive. No doubt they have made it more difficult for presidents to initiate war single-handedly in a far-off land. Yet none of those developments has removed, or is likely to remove, the president from his pivotal position in the foreign affairs government. Power remains concentrated in the White House.[5]

It is instructive, in this respect, that the Supreme Court has not sought to resolve the executive-congressional dispute over war powers and related issues because it considers the issues involved to be political rather than legal. The high court reaffirmed as much in 1979 when it let stand an appeals court ruling in favor of President Carter's termination without congressional approval of the United States-Taiwan mutual defense treaty. In this landmark case, four members of the court explicitly argued that the dispute between Carter and the members of Congress who brought the suit was a "political question," not a juridical one. The outcome of the continuing and perhaps inevitable presidential-congressional tug-of-war therefore will be determined at any one time largely by the resources available to each branch of government. On balance, the resources available to the president are the more formidable, if not overwhelming. Let us examine those resources in some detail from an

---

[4]Lowi observes that

Schlesinger chose the characterization *imperial* because it connotes a strong state with sovereignty and power over foreigners, as well as rank, status, privilege, and authority, and it also connotes the president's power and responsibility to do whatever he judges necessary to maintain the sovereignty of the state and its ability to keep public order, both international and domestic. The imperial presidency turns out on inspection, therefore, to be nothing more nor less than the discretionary presidency grounded in national security rather than domestic government. (Lowi, 1985b: 189)

[5]For a contrasting viewpoint, see Franck and Weisband (1979). The views of recent presidents are probably captured in Gerald Ford's lament that "We have not an imperial presidency but an imperiled presidency" (cited in *Time*, November 10, 1980).

institutional perspective before returning (in chapter twelve) to the question of executive-legislative interactions.

THE INNERMOST CIRCLE: THE PRESIDENT AND HIS ADVISERS

Executive Organization and Foreign Policy

In principle, the president's greatest resource is the vast federal executive establishment which he heads. Most federal personnel are in the executive branch of government, where collectively they bear responsibility for making and executing the full range of American domestic and foreign policies. The proportion of this vast number of employees concerned primarily with foreign affairs is difficult to determine, however. One compilation, shown in Table 10.1, puts the number of foreign affairs personnel at 36,000. It also names the sixteen federal agencies with clearly identifiable foreign policy interests and activities.[6] But the list is potentially much longer. Another study done in the mid-1970s, for example, identified thirty different federal entities with American nationals employed in international activities (Clark, 1975: 222), and in 1982 the United States Office of Personnel Management (1984: 12–13) reported a total of 131,000 civilian employees working abroad for thirty-eight executive branch departments and agencies. These compilations include such standards as the Departments of State and Defense (and "standardly" exclude the CIA!); but revealingly, they also identify some unexpected members of the foreign affairs government, including, for example, the Department of Housing and Urban Development, the Environmental Protection Agency, the Small Business Administration, and the National Aeronautics and Space Administration. Indeed, three-quarters of the agencies listed in the Office of Personnel Management tabulation are oriented primarily toward domestic policy issues.

For the most part, however, the executive departments of government, and the political appointees who head them, are at the core of the policy-making process, particularly the Departments of State and Defense. The former derives its importance from being "first among equals"[7] in the president's cabinet. The secretary of state, in principle at least, is conferred the position of the president's foremost foreign policy adviser. In part that is because the State

---

[6]As the Defense Department entry in Table 10.1 suggests, determining what proportion of the "national security establishment" should be considered a part of the "foreign affairs government" confounds not only the task of defining the latter but also of determining who matters within it. The difficulty is illustrated by the National Aeronautics and Space Administration's (NASA) space shuttle program. Although NASA is charged with the peaceful exploration of outer space and has few explicitly overseas activities, the space shuttle has enormous military potential and has been financed in part by the Defense Department.

[7]The term derives from the fact that the State Department was the first executive agency established under the Constitution in 1789.

TABLE 10.1 U.S. Government Foreign Affairs Personnel, 1984

Department or Agency	Number of Persons in Positions Related to Foreign Affairs
Department of State (U.S. citizens only)	13,500
United States Information Agency (USIA)	8,397
Agency for International Development (AID)	5,016
Arms Control and Disarmament Agency (ACDA)	170
Department of Agriculture	818
Department of Commerce	4,707
Department of Defense (persons with foreign affairs occupational specialties)	827
Department of Energy	127
Department of Labor	166
Department of the Treasury	253
Export–Import Bank	327
International Trade Commission	436
National Security Council	56
Overseas Private Investment Corporation	140
Peace Corps (permanent paid staff)	880
United States Trade Representative	131
TOTAL	35,951

SOURCE: Harry F. Young, Bureau of Public Affairs, U.S. Department of State, November 1985.

Department is the sole agency of government charged with coordinating the vast range of U.S. activities overseas; in part it is because the department houses the Foreign Service, the professional diplomatic corps of the United States. The tense international political environment of the postwar period, which has placed primary emphasis on military and defense considerations as they relate to foreign policy and national security, has made the Defense Department especially important as well. The enormous size of the Pentagon, which commands a substantial share of every annual federal budget, gives the Department of Defense clout in a policy-making environment where money and personnel mean political influence.

The importance of the State and Defense departments warrants more detailed attention; thus chapter eleven explores the way in which they are organized so as to carry out their foreign affairs responsibilities. We will also give attention there to the "intelligence community," because that community in general, and the Central Intelligence Agency in particular, plays such a central role in the foreign affairs government. Finally, chapter eleven will consider the responsibilities of some of the primarily domestic departments concerned with aspects of international economic affairs—Treasury, Commerce, Agriculture, and Labor—which have achieved importance in the foreign affairs government as a result of the proliferation of American interests in an interdependent world. But first let us focus on the president and the presidency.

The Executive Office of the President

The president is nominally "boss" of the employees who staff the executive departments and agencies of the foreign affairs government. He by no means controls them, however, a truism that led Richard Neustadt (1960) to describe the president's power as the "power to persuade." The interests of executive branch organizations are not necessarily synonymous with the interests of the president. The people who staff them have often held their positions long before any given president is elected, they are likely to hold them long after he leaves, and they frequently equate organizational survival with individual survival. To them the president often appears as a "transient meddler in their business" (quoted in Destler, 1974)—a view attributed to foreign policy professionals by an anonymous National Security Council staffer, but one unlikely to be confined to them.

If the president is viewed as a "transient meddler" in the affairs of established organizations, departmental bureaucracies are viewed from 1600 Pennsylvania Avenue as independent, unfamiliar, unresponsive, and inaccessible.

> They are suspected again and again of placing their own, congressional, or special-interest priorities ahead of those communicated to them from the White House. Even the President's own Cabinet members soon become viewed in the same light; one of the strengths of Cabinet members, namely their capacity to make a compelling case for their programs, has proved to be their chief liability with Presidents. (Cronin, 1973: 35)

For that reason, members of the cabinet have often been described as a president's "natural enemies." As a result, the importance of the president's cabinet as a collective body proffering foreign policy advice has declined to almost nothing. "That perennial loser" is the phrase one study (Allison and Szanton, 1976) used to describe the cabinet.

Presidents Carter and Reagan both pledged to involve the cabinet more intimately in key questions of policy development and implementation. Neither found the cabinet particularly useful for those purposes, however—President Reagan is even reported to have cat-napped during cabinet meetings—but Reagan did seek to build an interface between cabinet officials and his White House staff through a series of cabinet councils. Initially five councils were created in an apparent attempt not only to fulfill Reagan's campaign pledge to use the cabinet as a principle policy vehicle, but also, and more importantly, to recreate in other policy arenas what the National Security Council was believed to have accomplished in foreign and national security policy.[8]

---

[8]See Newland (1983) for an early appraisal of Reagan's design for a cabinet council system. Barger (1984) instructively observes that Reagan began almost immediately to retreat from cabinet government and turn to his personal staff for decision making.

Two issues with direct foreign policy implications that Reagan faced early in his first administration—whether to lift the grain embargo imposed on the Soviet Union by the Carter administration, as Reagan had promised during his campaign, and whether to impose import restrictions on Japanese autos—illustrated the classic dilemma "cabinet government" posed in the American presidential system of government: department chiefs become captives of the interests of the departments they administer and of the positions advanced by career bureaucrats within those agencies. Because cabinet members are necessarily advocates for the departments they head, they are often in conflict with one another and perhaps with the president himself. Although no ready organizational solution to this dilemma exists, cabinet decision making is usually the casualty. "Presidents have frequently taken office promising to use the cabinet fully; they have uniformly behaved otherwise" (Allison and Szanton, 1976).

A consequence of the erosion of cabinet policy making is that every American president since World War II has relied increasingly on his own personal staff and the Executive Office of the President for advice and assistance in the development of policies and programs. A kind of presidential subsystem within the executive branch has resulted, which has often led to differences between the presidency, on the one hand, and the established bureaucracies, on the other.

The institutionalization of the presidency began with the Executive Reorganization Act of 1939, which authorized President Roosevelt to create the Executive Office consisting of the White House Office and the Bureau of the Budget. The former unit was to house the president's personal assistants, together with their staffs, while the latter, which was created in 1921 under the jurisdiction of the Treasury Department, ensured presidential control over budgetary matters and later over the president's entire legislative program. Since 1939 the Executive Office has come to include other offices and councils as well. The lists and labels change from time to time; in the Reagan administration they included the Office of Management and Budget, the Office of Policy Development, the National Security Council, the Council of Economic Advisers, the Office of Science and Technology Policy, the Council on Environmental Quality, the Office of Administration, and the Office of the United States Trade Representative.

The growth in the number of official bodies attached to the Executive Office has been matched by growth in personnel and funds, which reached excessive proportions under President Nixon. Roosevelt never had more than eleven White House assistants; Truman never more than thirteen. The number grew to thirty-seven under Eisenhower, whereas both Kennedy and Johnson kept the number below twenty-five. In 1972, however, Nixon had forty-eight personal assistants, and the total number of permanent positions budgeted for the White House Office reached a new high of 550 (Cronin, 1984: 347). Add to that the staff in other offices and councils of the Executive Office, and the total number of White House-based employees under Nixon exceeded 2,200.[9]

Ford and Carter maintained somewhat smaller White House Office staffs than Nixon, but under Reagan the number approached 600 (Cronin, 1984: 347). In mid-1985, moreover, some 1,600 people were in the employ of Reagan's Executive Office. Furthermore, the costs of the office have grown as its functions have proliferated. During Nixon's first term alone expenditures more than doubled, growing from $31 million to $71 million. The budget request for Carter's Executive Office in his final year was in excess of $110 million. And for Reagan, it stood at $118 million in the first year of his second term.

More important than numbers of staff and dollars spent is the trend toward the concentration of decision-making authority over substantive and operational matters in the White House that the data suggest. The institutionalized presidency "has become a powerful inner sanctum of government, isolated from traditional, constitutional checks and balances" (Cronin, 1984). Whereas Roosevelt viewed his staff as channels of communication between himself and his "line" departments and agencies, for example, President Nixon held an entirely different view that led him to utilize his staff less as his "eyes and ears" throughout the government and more as an independent decision-making authority layered between himself and the rest of the executive branch. In contrast to the intent of the Executive Reorganization Act—that presidential assistants should not have power to make decisions in their own right—Nixon's staff became the center of decision making throughout the range of domestic and foreign affairs. The problem was not peculiar to Nixon, but it became glaring during his presidency. Unlike cabinet members, whose appointment required the scrutiny and confirmation of Congress, Nixon's assistants were answerable only to the president. More important, they were empowered to make decisions and issue instructions on their own, powers which often made them more influential than members of the cabinet. Those powers made Kissinger, when he was special assistant for national security affairs, more powerful than the secretaries of state or defense, and H. R. Haldeman and John Ehrlichman more powerful than domestic department heads. Carter pledged that his presidency would never operate as Nixon's had, but he too came eventually to rely heavily on a small group of White House intimates: Hamilton Jordan (chief of staff), Stuart E. Eizenstat (domestic policy

---

[9]Numbers differ depending on one's source. Polsby (1976: 55), drawing on a compilation by Representative Morris Udall, reports a total of 2,236 permanent positions in the Executive Office in 1972 and 2,206 in 1973, while Schlesinger (1973: 221), drawing on a study apparently done by the Congressional Research Service, reports the number in 1971 as "a stupefying 5,395." The discrepancy perhaps lies in the tendency of presidents to "borrow" personnel from other agencies so as to make presidential staffs (and budgets) appear smaller than they actually are. Schlesinger's figures presumably include those "seconded" personnel, while Polsby's (and Udall's) do not.

adviser), Jody Powell (press secretary), and Zbigniew Brzezinski (national security adviser). Similarly, Reagan relied heavily in his first term on a "troika" of key officials—Edwin Meese (White House counselor), James A. Baker (chief of staff), and Michael Deaver (deputy chief of staff)—and in his second term on a strong-willed chief of staff, Donald T. Regan, whom an aide described as having a corporate mentality which viewed Reagan as "chairman of the board" and Regan as "chief operating officer." In this sense each of the three presidents have followed a well established trend.

Necessity may give rise to this trend, but its consequences can be undesirable. Arthur Schlesinger, Jr., summarizes one view:

> The theory of enlarging the White House staff is to increase presidential control of the Executive Branch. In fact, . . . [b]y increasing their staffs, Presidents insert a screen between themselves and the Executive and Legislative branches and thereby reduce their own direct influence and weight of personal leadership. Large staffs, composed of ambitious and overprotective people determined to justify their existence, make work and make trouble. They cut off the President from the government and the government from the President. The staff becomes a shock absorber around the President, shielding him from reality. (quoted in the *Wall Street Journal*, January 7, 1981)[10]

Within the Executive Office, the National Security Council (NSC) is charged with foreign policy matters. It was as head of the NSC staff that Henry Kissinger rose to be more powerful than the secretaries of state or defense. Others had occupied the special assistant post in previous administrations—Robert Cutler and later Gordon Gray under Eisenhower; McGeorge Bundy under Kennedy; and Bundy and Walt W. Rostow under Lyndon Johnson. But none achieved the same level of prominence and influence in the foreign affairs government as did Kissinger. Brzezinski's dominance was less overwhelming than Kissinger's, but he, too, emerged as his boss's key foreign policy adviser. President Reagan initially sought to downgrade the national security adviser's role, but, with the exception of its first occupant, each of the men who followed in that position took on many of the trappings of their predecessors.

Presidential preferences explain in part the variations in the way different presidents have drawn on and interacted with their in-house foreign policy advisers. Simultaneously, however, it appears that all recent presidents, regardless of their initial predilections, have found it necessary to effect political control over foreign policy making by institutionalizing it within the White House. We can gain an appreciation of the way that presidential style and pressures to exert presidential control over foreign policy have led to its centralization in the White House through a historical examination of the way dif-

---

[10]See Cronin (1984) and Edwards and Wayne (1985) for additional views on current trends in the presidential staffing system.

ferent presidents have used the National Security Council and its staff. In the process we will gain an understanding of what appears to have become an endemic problem: conflict between the White House and the State Department, and between the national security adviser and the secretary of state, for control over the content of American foreign policy.

THE NATIONAL SECURITY COUNCIL: ORGANIZATION AND EVOLUTION

The National Security Council was created by the National Security Act of 1947[11] to "advise the President with respect to the integration of domestic, foreign, and military policies relating to the national security." Statutory members of the council include the president (as chairman), vice president, and secretaries of state and defense. The director of the CIA and the chairman of the joint chiefs of staff (JCS) are statutory advisers. Other participants have included the secretary of the treasury, the attorney general, the U.S. ambassador to the United Nations, the director of the Office of Management and Budget (OMB), heads of such organizations as the United States Information Agency (USIA) and the Agency for International Development (AID), and various presidential advisers and assistants, depending on the issues and presidential predilections.

The president is free to use the NSC as much or as little as he desires (understandably, since the NSC is a creation of the Congress), and its deliberations and decisions are purely advisory. As the principal formal mechanism for coordinating the vast federal structure with a view toward producing a single, coherent foreign policy, the council has nevertheless proven useful in tackling problems faced by all presidents: acquiring information; identifying issues; coping with crises; making decisions; coordinating actions; and assuring agency performance in accordance with presidential wishes.

The Early Years, 1947–1961

Although created during his administration, President Truman did not use the NSC extensively. Truman was fearful that the council might encroach on his constitutional prerogatives by imposing a parliamentary-type cabinet system over foreign policy decision making. He did not even attend NSC meetings prior to the outbreak of the Korean War in 1950, and the professional staff created to service the council remained on the periphery of Truman's relationship with his cabinet officers and departments. The effect was to emphasize the purely advisory nature of the council.

With the outbreak of the Korean War, however, Truman recognized the need for better coordination of policy and action. He therefore directed that

---

[11]The National Security Act, as amended, also created the CIA, the Department of Defense, and the Joint Chiefs of Staff. See Trager (1977) for a discussion of the National Security Act of 1947 and its subsequent meaning, as seen on the occasion of its thirtieth anniversary.

major national security policy recommendations come to him via the council. The famous NSC 68 memorandum (discussed in chapter five) is perhaps the best example of a major policy proclamation arising from Truman's NSC apparatus. By the end of his term Truman had also begun using the NSC staff for interagency planning purposes. Both developments presaged the use to which Eisenhower put the NSC.

Coming from a professional background that emphasized the need for staff work and overall coordination, former General Eisenhower took the rudiments of the NSC structure inherited from Truman and transformed them into a highly formalized system that he viewed as "the central vehicle for formulating and promulgating policy" and "the primary means of imparting Presidential direction and over-all coherence to the activities of the departments and agencies" (Clark and Legere, 1969). A planning board and an operations coordinating board, both eventually chaired by the special assistant for national security affairs, the now familiar position created by Eisenhower, became part of Eisenhower's NSC system. Those units were charged, respectively, with generating policy recommendations for consideration by the full NSC and with carrying out decisions once made.

For Truman, the National Security Council was primarily a supplementary advisory body. In contrast, "Eisenhower determined that—except in special cases of urgency—responsibility for national-security policy formulation was to run from a department, agency, or individual through the NSC mechanism and not go outside its framework" (Clark and Legere, 1969). NSC meetings dealt primarily with the development or revision of broad policies. The council did not decide what to do "tomorrow." Instead, formal council meetings were often followed by more intimate "rump" sessions, or the president would convene meetings of a select group of advisers outside the formal NSC structure to deal with urgent matters,[12] a device used extensively by President Kennedy.

Personalizing the Staff, 1961–1969

By the time Eisenhower left office the highly institutionalized and bureaucratized National Security Council system was being criticized as a "paper mill" that processed policies bearing little relevance to the real issues of the day. Critics also argued that the system tended to reduce, rather than expand, the

---

[12]These rump sessions may explain the apparent incongruity between Eisenhower's emphasis on the NSC system and the fact that Secretary of State Dulles is generally regarded as the chief architect of American foreign policy during most of the Eisenhower years. Also important is the distinction between long-range planning, which was the primary purpose of the NSC, and day-to-day control of operational matters, which increasingly fell into Dulles's hands (Hoopes, 1973a). Dulles's biographer, Townsend Hoopes, also argues that the close working ties between Eisenhower and Dulles "compromised" Eisenhower's effort to use the NSC system to "orchestrate" the activities of the various foreign policy agencies into a coordinated foreign policy.

range of alternatives available for presidential decision.[13] Eisenhower apparently believed the NSC system would bring to the surface those issues that required his decision and that once a decision was made it would be carried out. Neither happened. Interagency deliberations prior to NSC meetings often resulted in agreed-upon recommendations—agreements reached at the minimum common denominator—which were then presented to Eisenhower for ratification rather than choice. And policy positions, once decided, were often bent to fit the preferred positions of the agencies on which the president relied for implementation.

President Kennedy moved rapidly to correct the deficiencies he perceived in Eisenhower's White House-based national security system. Shortly after his election in 1960 Kennedy appointed McGeorge Bundy his special assistant for national security affairs and announced that the purpose of Bundy's staff would be *"to assist me* in obtaining advice from, and coordinating operations of, the government agencies concerned with national security" (quoted in Clark and Legere, 1969; emphasis added). He subsequently abolished the operations coordinating board and announced his intention to strengthen the role of the secretary of state in the area of interagency coordination. The planning board was also allowed to atrophy.

Some observers question whether the new president, who had a deep personal interest in foreign affairs, ever intended that the State Department assume a leadership role in the management of foreign affairs. In any event, insiders' accounts of the Kennedy administration (Hilsman, 1967; Schlesinger, 1965; Sorensen, 1965) indicate clearly that Kennedy was unhappy with the docile role assumed by Dean Rusk, Kennedy's choice as secretary of state, in an otherwise action-oriented administration. The State Department as an organization also proved too sluggish for White House officials. As one of Kennedy's top aides put it:

> The President was discouraged with the State Department almost as soon as he took office. He felt that it too often seemed to have a built-in inertia which deadened initiative and that its tendency toward excessive delay obscured determination. It spoke with too many voices and too little vigor. It was never clear to the President . . . who was in charge, who was clearly delegated to do what, and why his own policy line seemed consistently to be altered or evaded. (Sorensen, 1965: 287)

When the State Department seemed too sluggish, the White House staff stepped into the perceived vacuum—not only Bundy's staff but also other

---

[13]The hearings of the Jackson Subcommittee on National Security and International Operations of the Senate Committee on Government Operations, published in edited form in Jackson (1965), contain detailed information on both the operations and criticisms of the Eisenhower NSC system. Greenstein's (1982) analysis of the Eisenhower presidency also contains useful information on Eisenhower's NSC apparatus.

members of Kennedy's personal "team," almost all of whom were specifically recruited for his administration rather than drawn from careerists in established bureaucracies. A "situation room" (which still exists) was set up in the West Wing of the White House, which gave Bundy's staff, and through him the president, ready access to fast-breaking international events without depending on the line agencies for information. Correspondingly, concern for a comprehensive planning process such as the Eisenhower administration had developed waned.

Another of Kennedy's innovations was the use of presidentially designated interagency task forces designed to serve presidential needs rather than the agencies they represented. The 1961 Bay of Pigs fiasco, from which Kennedy learned "never to rely on the experts" (Schlesinger, 1965), contributed much to Kennedy's reliance on decision-making groups formulated for reasons other than the institutional affiliations of their members. The most celebrated was the so-called Ex Com (Executive Committee of the NSC), initially comprising some thirteen advisers on whom Kennedy relied heavily in devising a response to the installation of offensive Soviet weapons in Cuba in October 1962. Similar, but less well known, ad hoc groups were created to deal with the crises in Berlin and Laos in 1961. Other interagency groups were also set up, such as the Special Group on Counterinsurgency, headed by General Maxwell Taylor, which bore much of the policy-making responsibility for paramilitary experiments being tried in Vietnam; it was also responsible (in augmented form) for supervising operation Mongoose, a covert intelligence operation directed against Cuba (*Final Report*, IV, 1976).

The inclusion of one of Bundy's staff or another presidential assistant was a distinguishing feature of all of those interagency groups. Kennedy's national security adviser and his staff functioned much more as personal advisers than as staff members belonging to the National Security Council. The importance of the NSC as an institution declined correspondingly. Although formal meetings of the full body were held to discuss long-term policy matters, the NSC itself was far less important in ensuring presidential control over the making and execution of foreign policy than were less formal groups.

Kennedy's assassination in November 1963 brought to the White House a man with little interest and less experience in foreign affairs. But as the war in Vietnam began to heat up, Lyndon Johnson and his closest advisers devoted an increasing portion of their attention to the events unfolding in Southeast Asia—to the point that by the end of Johnson's term little else seemed to command the energies of top-level decision makers.

The style of Johnson's approach to national security matters was more akin to the informal mode of Kennedy than the institutionalized operation of Eisenhower. The NSC as a formal deliberative mechanism languished, a fact which, in the view of one of Johnson's critics, contributed to the Vietnam morass.

The decisions and actions that marked our large-scale military entry into the Vietnam War in early 1965 reflected the piecemeal consideration of interrelated issues,

. . . the natural consequence of a fragmented NSC and a general inattention to long-range policy planning. Consultation, even knowledge of the basic facts, was confined to a tight circle of presidential advisers, and there appears to have been little systematic debate outside that group. (Hoopes, 1973b: 7)

The institutional manifestation of the tight inner circle came to be known as the "Tuesday Lunch." The participants were the president, Secretaries Rusk and McNamara, the national security adviser (first McGeorge Bundy, then Walt W. Rostow, who replaced Bundy in 1966), and eventually the director of the CIA, the chairman of the joint chiefs, and the president's press secretary. Reflecting increasing preoccupation with the Southeast Asian conflict after 1965, Vietnam was the principal luncheon topic, while the organization itself reflected the president's approach to the war—tight personal control coupled with organizational flexibility.

The cost of Johnson's approach was the exclusion of subordinates on whom the president and his close circle of advisers depended for implementation of top-level decisions. Rusk and McNamara were even reluctant to discuss what happened at the Tuesday Lunch with their subordinates. "The top men grew to live in one world, having loyalty primarily to each other, and seeing problems in a context that their subordinates could not understand because they were outside the charmed circle" (Destler, 1974). Contributing to the president's tight handling of the war was his "innate tendency to sniff treason within government walls." The tendency was compounded by the increasingly vocal doubts about government policy which subordinates were suspected of having leaked to the press. "Such unhappiness below solidified the top group's sense of being embattled, both strengthening their loyalties to one another and their separation from the rest of the government" (Destler, 1974). Cut off from criticism from within, it took major policy setbacks such as the enemy's successful Tet Offensive at the end of January in 1968 and the poor showing of the incumbent president some six weeks later in the New Hampshire primary to force a reappraisal of Vietnam policy.

The role of Johnson's national security adviser changed with the appointment of Walt W. Rostow. Rostow continued to manage the flow of information to the president, to communicate presidential wishes to the bureaucracy, and to provide policy analysis and advice. But he did much less in the way of encouraging the free flow of ideas and alternatives to the president than had his predecessor. Bundy seldom allowed his personal views to color his presentation of alternatives to the president. In contrast, Rostow "was primarily a thinker and more than a bit of an ideologue, who tended to view particular events in terms of broader theoretical constructs he was most adept at developing" (Destler, 1974). The result was bureaucratic distrust of Rostow's ability to objectively present departmental viewpoints to Johnson.[14]

---

[14]Hoopes (1973b) provides an especially critical view of Rostow's role in the development of Vietnam policy.

The White House Ascendant, 1969–1981

Non-coherence is the adjective I. M. Destler uses to describe the policy-making legacy Nixon inherited from a divided and demoralized Johnson administration in January 1969. Although the outgoing administration had not been without positive achievements in foreign policy, "its policy-making institutions, formal and informal, had little that would recommend them to its successor" (Destler, 1974).

Nixon moved rapidly to recreate coherence in policy making with the NSC as the hub of the system. Nixon's promise to restore the National Security Council (of which he had been a member as Eisenhower's vice president) to a preeminent position in the foreign affairs government reflected his view that "most of our serious reverses abroad since 1960" could be attributed to "catch-as-catch-can talkfests between the President, his staff assistants, and various others" (cited in Destler, 1974).

Dr. Henry Kissinger, the noted Harvard political scientist named as Nixon's special assistant for national security affairs, was directed to establish an "Eisenhower NSC system" but "without the concurrences" (Destler, 1974). It consisted of numerous top-level interagency committees charged with developing foreign policy options for consideration by the president and the full NSC. The committees' jurisdictions covered the entire waterfront of American foreign policy, from arms control negotiations with the Soviet Union (the Verification Panel), to crisis management (the Washington Special Actions Group), to covert operations (the 40 Committee, so named because of the National Security Decision Memorandum that set it up; the group had operated in previous administrations under various names—the Special Group, the 54-12 Group, and the 303 Committee). These committees were supported by Interdepartmental Groups (IGs), typically headed by assistant secretaries of state, and an Under Secretaries Committee, chaired by the under secretary of state, whose tasks were to handle issues referred by higher-level committees and to coordinate foreign policy activities once presidential decisions were made.[15] A key feature of this elaborate committee structure was the pivotal role it assigned Kissinger: he or a member of his staff chaired nearly all of the interagency committees, which gave the national security adviser unprecedented leverage over the established bureaucratic agencies formally charged with the making and execution of American foreign policy.[16]

---

[15]The Interdepartmental Groups (IGs) and the Under Secretaries Committee (USC) were variants of similar committees created by President Johnson in 1966. Both presidents apparently had the same purpose in mind, namely, to attempt to place the State Department once again in a leadership role for purposes of coordinating foreign policy activities.

[16]Kissinger (1979) reports that creation of the Nixon NSC system, which minimized the role of the State Department (toward which Richard Nixon had an innate and deep hostility) in managing NSC business, was not "a crucial grant of power to me to the degree that was often alleged," but he does acknowledge that the outcome of the early bureaucratic struggle with the State Department "helped establish my authority early on," while the NSC organization itself "made White House control easier."

The development of the Nixon-Kissinger committee system was consistent with the preferred operating style of Richard Nixon. In contrast to Eisenhower's approach (which allowed the NSC system to focus on compromise among departments and agencies), and in contrast to the Kennedy and Johnson styles (which allowed NSC meetings to become forums for its members to advocate views), "[t]he Nixon approach was designed to bring all policy options to the table for *subsequent* consideration by the president and, above all, to maintain flexibility for the president" (Esterline and Black, 1975). By presenting options to the president, the NSC system was "very nicely suited to [Nixon's] preference for making decisions in private, like a judge who weighs evidence and alternative courses of action in lonely splendor. And solo decision-making reinforces a system in which the NSC can be the prime visible institution but the Assistant [for national security affairs] and staff the more influential one" (Destler, 1974).

The influence Kissinger achieved in part through Nixon's preferred decision-making style was enhanced by the president's trust in him. Indeed, Kissinger (1979) himself has written that "in the final analysis the influence of a Presidential Assistant derives almost exclusively from the confidence of the President, not from administrative arrangements." That confidence and the corresponding role that Kissinger played grew very rapidly in the early days of the Nixon presidency as, in Kissinger's own words, "Nixon sought to bypass the delays and sometimes opposition of the departments." Kissinger also argues cogently for why the influence of presidential advisers seems to grow over time:

> Almost all of [a president's] callers are supplicants or advocates, and most of their cases are extremely plausible—which is what got them into the Oval Office in the first place. As a result, one of the President's most difficult tasks is to choose among endless arguments that sound equally convincing. The easy decisions do not come to him; they are taken care of at lower levels. As his term in office progresses, therefore, except in extreme crisis a President comes to base his choices more and more on the confidence he has in his advisers. He grows increasingly conscious of bureaucratic and political pressures upon him; issues of substance tend to merge in his mind with the personalities embodying the conflicting considerations. (Kissinger, 1979: 40)[17]

In the particular case of Kissinger, the confidence Nixon reposed in him was reinforced by the national security adviser's spectacular diplomatic successes in the Middle East and elsewhere, which came at a time when the revelations of Watergate increasingly engulfed and paralyzed the Nixon presi-

---

[17]President Ford (1979) made a similar observation in commenting on why he eventually came to the decision he needed a chief of staff: "Because power in Washington is measured by how much access a person has to the President, almost everyone wanted more access that I had access to give."

dency. The president's efforts to expand Kissinger's power and authority under such circumstances culminated in Kissinger's appointment as secretary of state, an assignment he held concurrently with his White House role and which placed him unambiguously at the pinnacle of the foreign affairs establishment as the chief architect of American foreign policy.

As Kissinger's personal influence rose, the elaborate NSC system he created was increasingly bypassed. The decisions that led to the 1970 Cambodia incursion, for example, were a product of "catch-as-catch-can" gatherings between Nixon and his advisers outside the formal NSC framework (Destler, 1974). Other major foreign policy maneuvers engineered by the Nixon administration also evolved outside the NSC system—Kissinger's secret journey to Beijing in 1971, which led to Nixon's official visit to China the following year; the decision to place American military forces on worldwide alert during the Yom Kippur War of 1973 (Kissinger merely *announced* the decision, and did not discuss it, at an NSC meeting which he chaired in the president's absence); and a whole series of Vietnam decisions relating to the secret negotiations with the North Vietnamese in Paris. The "back channel" to the Soviet leadership that Kissinger established is perhaps his most celebrated bureaucratic end-run. It led to a breakthrough in the strategic arms negotiations with the Soviets even while formal negotiations between the two sides' delegations (the "front channel") continued (see Talbott, 1979). Nothing could have made it clearer that Nixon and Kissinger counted much more than the Nixon-Kissinger NSC system.[18]

By the time of Nixon's forced resignation in the summer of 1974, Kissinger had become indispensable. He alone among Nixon's immediate advisers was able to survive the onslaught of Watergate.[19] One of Gerald Ford's first moves on the eve of his inauguration as the first nonelected president was to ask Kissinger to remain as his secretary of state and national security adviser. In that dual capacity Kissinger continued to operate what some felt was a one-man

---

[18]Kissinger reveals that he seldom pursued even secret negotiations with foreign governments without drawing on the expertise of established departments provided through the formal NSC mechanism. In his words,

> Nixon and I could use the interdepartmental machinery to educate ourselves by ordering planning papers on negotiations that as far as the bureaucracy was concerned were hypothetical; these studies told us the range of options and what could find support within the government. We were then able to put departmental ideas into practice outside of formal channels. Strange as it may seem, I never negotiated without a major departmental contribution even when the departments did not know what I was doing. (Kissinger, 1979:47)

[19]An indication of the power he had achieved was his public threat in 1974 to resign as secretary of state unless Congress absolved him from responsibility for the wiretapping of NSC staffers and others that had occurred some years previously. Congress quickly complied. Morton H. Halperin, one of the National Security Council staff members who had been wiretapped in an effort to uncover leaks of sensitive information, pursued his case against Nixon, Kissinger, and other top Nixon advisers in the federal courts. In June 1981 the Supreme Court let stand a lower court ruling which made the former president and his aides liable to civil suit for the warrantless wiretaps.

foreign policy show, a role made more apparent because it served a president who was a relative novice in international affairs.

Over time, however, Kissinger's star and the popularity of the policies he engineered began to wane. Much of the criticism came from the right wing of the president's own Republican party—pressure which prompted Ford to drop the word détente from his vocabulary. The president also acquiesced in the inclusion of a plank in the 1976 Republican platform advanced by Ronald Reagan's supporters that was widely interpreted as a repudiation of the incumbent president's foreign policy record. Jimmy Carter, the Democratic presidential nominee, made it clear that Kissinger, his style of operation, and, perhaps, some of his policies as well, would be among the first victims of a Democratic victory.

Disagreement with Kissinger's policies surfaced within the government as well. James Schlesinger, Ford's secretary of defense, argued for increased defense spending in response to what he perceived as the growing military threat of the Soviet Union. This position was incompatible with the strategy of reducing tensions with the Soviets that Kissinger had artfully pursued for six years. Differences between Kissinger and Schlesinger appeared to be resolved in Kissinger's favor when, in the fall of 1975, Ford replaced Schlesinger with Donald Rumsfeld as defense secretary. At the same time, however, Ford also began to curtail Kissinger's one-man influence over policy making by naming Lt. General Brent Scowcroft, who had been Kissinger's immediate subordinate on the NSC staff, as the new president's assistant for national security affairs. Shortly thereafter, in the wake of Senate and House investigations into the abuse of executive power by the intelligence community, Ford began to split control of the NSC committee system by spreading responsibility for different issue areas among the national security adviser and the secretaries of state and defense. However, the subsequent history of the Ford administration indicates that Kissinger nevertheless remained the dominant, if not exclusive, influence in the foreign policy establishment.

President Carter's early designation of Zbigniew Brzezinski as assistant for national security affairs, despite the campaign attacks he had launched against Kissinger's policies and operating style, reaffirmed the determination of the White House to exercise control over the making and execution of foreign policy. Two new NSC committees were created to replace all prior ones. One was the Policy Review Committee. Chaired by a member of the cabinet chosen on the basis of which department had the greatest stake in the issue, the Policy Review Committee was given responsibility for long-term projects. Short-term projects (including covert intelligence operations and crisis management) were assigned to the Special Coordination Committee, chaired by the national security assistant, Zbigniew Brzezinski. Most important decisions appear nonetheless to have been made in less formal settings, such as the president's weekly "foreign policy breakfasts."

Carter's approach to the NSC system was once described by Brzezinski's deputy, David Aaron, as "resting somewhere between the Johnson and Nixon models.''[20] Numerous cabinet-level committees addressed a variety of important problems, but Brzezinski, unlike Kissinger before him, did not conduct all of the committee sessions, and the papers prepared for them were not always the exclusive preserve of the NSC staff. Nevertheless, Brzezinski's Special Coordination Committee eventually emerged as the most influential body within the NSC structure. Over time Brzezinski also emerged as the pivotal foreign policy adviser. Initially he was one of a "collegium" of key advisers which included Secretary of State Cyrus Vance, Secretary of Defense Harold Brown, and U.N. Ambassador Andrew Young. But Young resigned when his contacts with the Palestine Liberation Organization (in violation of established policy) were disclosed, and Vance resigned in the spring of 1980 in a dispute over the president's dispatch of a military "rescue" operations of American hostages in Iran.

The drama of Vance's resignation is underscored by the fact that it was the first time in sixty years a secretary of state had resigned because of a policy dispute with the president. Although the immediate issue was Iran, the larger issue was conflict between the secretary and the president's national security adviser. Brzezinski stressed a hard-line posture toward the Soviet Union and focused on the East-West conflict. Vance stressed détente and appeared more sensitive to North-South relations and global order issues generated by increasing transnational interdependence. Carter never seemed able to reconcile the often conflicting thrusts of his principal advisers. Perhaps no problem would have been raised if the differences between the advisers had remained private. But they were spotlighted by the media time and again as Brzezinski publicly defended policies that often appeared to differ from what the State Department said.[21] The untoward effect of such behavior was cited by Secretary Vance almost immediately after his resignation:

> Each foreign policy adviser should have a say . . . so that the President can hear the varying views and then make the final decision. However, this should be done

---

[20]George (1983b) has identified three different presidential management models: competitive, formalistic, and collegial. In the *competitive* model, the president purposely seeks to promote conflict and competition among his advisers, thus forcing problems to be brought to the president's attention for resolution and decision. Franklin Roosevelt is the only president to have clearly followed it. Johnson began by emphasizing the competitive approach but gradually moved toward a *formalistic* model. This model seeks to establish clear lines of authority and to minimize the need for presidential involvement in the politicking among cabinet officials and key advisers. A "chief of staff" is often used as a buffer between the president and cabinet heads. Nixon's approach to presidential management took the formalistic model to its extreme, but Truman and Eisenhower also followed it. Reagan likewise began with a preference for a formal, chief-of-staff operation with broad delegations of authority, but over time his approach took on some characteristics of the collegial model. Carter also embraced elements of the formalistic and collegial models. Kennedy provides the best illustration of the *collegial* model, which emphasizes teamwork and group problem solving. The president operates like the hub of a wheel with spokes connecting to individual advisers and department heads, who often act as "generalists" rather than "functional specialists" concerned only with parts of particular problems.

[21]Brzezinski was the first national security adviser to employ his own public relations officer.

within the framework of private discussion between the President and his advisers. It is wrong for this exchange to take place in public. It leads to confusion as to what the policy of the nation is. . . . The national security adviser . . . should act as a co-ordinator of the various views. But he should not be the one who makes foreign policy or who expresses foreign policy to the public. (cited in Kirschten, 1980: 817)

The White House-State Department rift did not end with Vance's departure. Senator Edmund S. Muskie was chosen as Vance's successor; but he was barely confirmed in office when Carter signed PD 59, which moved U.S. strategic doctrine in the direction of an explicit counterforce posture—and without ever consulting the new secretary of state. The subsidiary role of the State Department compared to the White House staff was affirmed once more.

Just as in previous administrations, presidential style was decisive in determining who was to play the dominant role. Carter emphasized the personal advisory role of his national security staff and, in the words of an in-house study of the Carter NSC system, "looked to his own staff for fresh ideas, new policy approaches and, in some cases, independent analysis" (NSC study by Philip A. Odeen, cited in Kirschten, 1980). Such an orientation, the study continued, emphasizes the policy-making role of the president's personal adviser at the expense of other tasks he could be expected to perform, such as managing the decision process, forcing hard choices to be made, and ensuring that once made they are implemented. Not surprisingly, Carter's emphasis on Brzezinski's personal advisory role at the expense of these other tasks "led to tensions between the Executive Office of the President and the departments" (Odeen cited in Kirschten, 1980).

Should the national security adviser be primarily a manager of the decision process or primarily a personal adviser to the president and his "resident intellectual"?

Based on the experiences of the five presidents who occupied the Oval Office in the 1960s and 1970s, "there developed a semi-articulated consensus among practitioners, scholars, and public observers as to what the national security advisers should—and should not—be doing" (Destler, 1983c).[22] If the national security adviser's activities are viewed as falling along a continuum between, on the one hand, an "inside management" role, where the adviser essentially performs the role of facilitator, and, on the other hand, a "leadership" role, which often places him in the potential position as a second secretary of state, then the thrust of this consensus is that the national security assistant should emphasize the "inside" role and eschew the "outside." Exemplary tasks associated with each role are listed in Box 10.1, which also suggests that some activities midway between the "inside" and "outside" orientations may be acceptable. (It should also be recognized, of course, that everyone may not agree with this list of "do's" and "don'ts.")

[22]See also "The National Security Adviser: Role and Accountability" (1980).

Box 10.1 The National Security Assistant: The Professionals' Job Description

YES ("Inside Management")	OK In Moderation	NO ("Outside Leadership")
Briefing the president, handling his foreign policy in-box	Discreet advice/advocacy	Conducting particular diplomatic negotiations
Analyzing issues and choices:	Encouraging advocacy by NSC staff subordinates	Fixed operational assignments
a. Ordering information/intelligence	Information and "background" communicating with press, Congress, foreign officials	Public spokesman
b. Managing interagency studies		Strong, visible internal advocacy (except of already established presidential priorities)
Managing presidential decision processes		Making policy decisions
Communicating presidential decisions and monitoring their implementation		
General interagency brokering, circuit-connecting, crisis management		

SOURCE: Destler, 1983c: 262.

The argument in favor of the insider rather than outsider orientation is essentially twofold:

> First, the assistant's performance of "outside leadership" activities preempts or undercuts other senior presidential advisers and the formally responsible institutions, particularly the State Department and its secretary. Second, it compromises the "honest broker" reputation for balance necessary to performance of the "inside management" functions, most of which (unlike the functions in the right-hand column [of Box 10.1]) are best handled from within the White House. (Destler, 1983c: 262–263)

Current History: The Reagan Administration

As presidential power passed to the nation's fortieth president in 1981, there was evidence that the new administration was sensitive to the criticism of prior presidential foreign policy management systems and of the need to redress the balance between the White House and the State Department. Indeed, Ronald Reagan had promised during his campaign to "restore leadership to U.S. foreign policy by organizing it in a more coherent way."

Reagan's choice of Alexander Haig as secretary of state was spotlighted as an indication of the new president's desire to relocate primary control over foreign policy making in the State Department. The former NATO commander had been schooled in the ways of the White House as an assistant to Henry Kissinger and later as chief of staff in the Nixon White House during its Watergate-embattled final days. Moreover, Reagan had pledged during his campaign to make the secretary of state his principal foreign policy formulator and spokesman and, implicitly, to downgrade the importance of the national security adviser's role. Haig played on the president's predilections in a lengthy memorandum submitted on inauguration day that would have assigned the secretary of state a role in foreign affairs unprecedented since the days of John Foster Dulles. However, the White House structure that was eventually established for the formulation and coordination of foreign policy reasserted the pattern of presidential primacy in foreign policy.

The Reagan framework, diagrammed in Figure 10.2, was generally patterned on a plan devised by Johnson, but never fully implemented due to the urgency of Vietnam. The cabinet-level Policy Review Committee instituted by the Carter administration was replaced by three senior interdepartmental groups (SIGs) chaired by the number two men in the Defense and State departments, acting under the direction of their agency heads, and by the director of central intelligence. Policy considerations were developed for the SIGs by interdepartmental groups headed by assistant secretaries. As their chairmanships imply, the three SIGs were responsible for conceptually distinct aspects of national security policy: foreign policy, military and defense policy, and intelligence policy.[23] In practice, of course, each is related to the others; determining the domain into which an issue falls is thus a key decision from the viewpoint of bureaucratic competition.

Reagan's NSC framework assigned that task to the office of the national security adviser, initially headed by Richard V. Allen. Allen, however, was clearly placed in a subordinate role compared to his predecessors. He not only lacked the intellectual credentials of those who preceded him; he also was denied direct access to the Oval Office, assigned instead to report to the president's White House counselor, Edwin Meese, who was given overall responsibility for developing Reagan administration policies.

Although Allen doubtless occupied a subordinate role, it matched his role conception. He offered even before assuming office that "the policy-formulation function of the nation security adviser should be offloaded to the Secretary of State." He thus opted for the "inside management" role as a facilitator rather than the "outside leadership" role, which smacks of being a second secretary of state. Even in this comparatively limited capacity, however, Allen

---

[23]Janka (1984) provides a useful description of the way the Reagan NSC system is supposed to work and the way it works in practice.

FIGURE 10.2   The Reagan National Security Council System

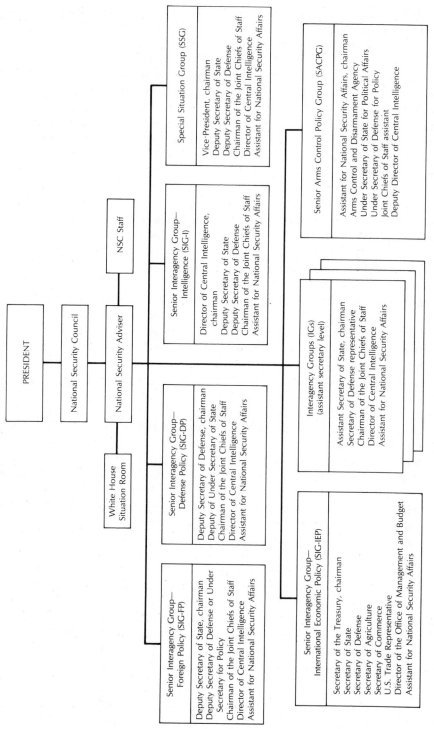

SOURCE: Adapted from Becker and Landrum, 1984: 23, and National Security Decision Directive 2, January 12, 1982.

proved inadequate. He insisted that the NSC (staff, presumably) "is not charged with formulating or implementing policy. It is charged with coordinating policy." But coordination without involvement in day-to-day bureaucratic in-fighting runs the risk of irrelevance. Moreover, Allen was unable to mediate disputes between others in the administration or to broker the competing interests of the bureaucracies involved. Allen's acceptance of $1,000 from a Japanese journalist set the stage for his replacement by William P. Clark, a former justice on the California Supreme Court. It was the first of what became many personnel changes among Reagan's key foreign policy advisers in an administration wracked by personality conflicts and internecine warfare.

The second casualty was Alexander Haig, who soon after Reagan's inauguration in 1981 claimed the role of "foreign policy vicar," only to find himself involved in a triangular competition with presidential counselor Edwin Meese and Secretary of Defense Caspar Weinberger. Weinberger consistently spelled out the guidelines of the new administration's foreign policy design in a manner normally reserved either for the secretary of state or the president himself. Furthermore, the defense secretary, a close personal friend of the president, appeared to enjoy greater influence with the National Security Planning Group, which consisted of the president's closest personal advisers and which emerged as a kind of "executive committee" of the NSC. It was Weinberger, for example, who apparently favored the decision to proceed with production of the controversial neutron bomb, while Haig, more sensitive to the concerns of the nation's European allies, reportedly urged at least a delay in the decision.

Haig's primacy was challenged further when Meese devised a plan to place control over crisis management, exercised during the Carter administration by the Special Coordination Committee headed by Brzezinski, under the jurisdiction of Vice President Bush (the Special Situation Group shown in Figure 10.2), with support provided by the staff of the National Security Council, as it had been historically, not by the Department of State.[24] Shortly thereafter, Haig provoked a confrontation with Weinberger when, at the time of the attempted assassination of the president, he declared from the White House "I am in charge here." And he subsequently found himself in conflict with almost everyone in the administration and many outside it. "Haig's peremptory, combative, 'politics of exclusion' style seemed as out of place in the Reagan administration as it had been in place under Nixon and Kissinger. . . . He seemed unable to grasp the notion that the way to build Reagan's confidence was to work with, not against, the man's trusted aides" (Destler, 1983b). Haig did have his foreign policy successes, and by and large he was the administration's key foreign policy official. But a final disagreement between Haig and others in the administration over the issue of European in-

---

[24]See Becker and Landrum (1984) for a more complete discussion of Reagan's approach to crisis management.

volvement in the trans-Siberian pipeline that would eventually bring Soviet natural gas to Western Europe led Reagan in June 1982 to accept the latest of Haig's threatened resignations. "A key reason [Reagan accepted] was that Clark now agreed with other White House aides that Haig was too volatile, too much a solo operation, for the Reagan team" (Destler, Gelb, and Lake, 1984; see Haig, 1984, for his account of this course of events).

Ironically, Judge Clark had been a source of Haig's growing influence with the White House. Although completely unschooled in foreign policy,[25] he had served for a year as Haig's deputy secretary of state and was perhaps closer to the president than any of his other advisers. Clark's appointment as national security adviser thus gave Haig "a White House man, close to the President, with whom he could deal, a Presidential connection once removed. . . . He had the added advantage of long-standing ties with Weinberger and Meese" (Destler, Gelb, and Lake, 1984).

When Clark first became national security adviser, he hewed to the "inside" description of the job, believing he could serve "as an honest broker for others, especially for the secretaries of state and defense, the director of central intelligence and others in the foreign policy bureaucracy." It took Clark "nearly a year to conclude that this idea was impractical . . . and that 'Cabinet secretaries are all parochial, so you've got to decide yourself what to do'" (Weisman, 1983).

During that year Clark enhanced the role of the NSC staff in the policy process. It grew from the thirty or so professionals Brzezinski and Allen had maintained to nearly fifty, larger than at any time since Kissinger's tenure (Destler, 1983b: 125). Policy studies were initiated by the national security assistant, and their conclusions went before the full National Security Council, which generally met at least once a week, more often than at any time since the Eisenhower years (Destler, 1983b; Janka, 1984). Clark himself enjoyed direct and frequent access to the president, thus short-circuiting the "troika" that stood between Allen and Reagan.

Clark held strongly conservative ideological convictions that led him to assume a staunchly anti-Soviet foreign policy posture. He believed, with Reagan, that the 1970s represented "a decade of neglect for the security needs of the United States": "What happened in the last decade was one of the greatest voluntary reversals of a global power relationship in the history of man," he told the Veterans of Foreign Wars in 1982. Similarly, he advocated stepped-up United States military activity in Central America and was the strongest White House voice favoring increased military spending.

By the summer of 1983, Clark was widely regarded as having become the most influential foreign policy figure in the White House and was credited

---

[25]In his Senate confirmation hearings for the position of deputy secretary of state, Clark proved ignorant of the most basic facts of international affairs, leading twenty-five senators to vote against his confirmation and Senator Charles Percy, chairman of the Senate Foreign Relations Committee, to conclude, "Never again can we accept a man who professes to have no knowledge in the area for which he has been nominated."

with having gotten Ronald Reagan more deeply involved in foreign affairs. Even as his influence rose, however, there was no visible conflict with George Shultz, who had replaced Haig as secretary of state. But as the most conservative of the president's inner circle of advisers, he did come into conflict with other, more pragmatic White House staffers, particularly Chief of Staff James Baker. The squabbling (especially on the issue of defense spending) may have contributed to Clark's sudden and unexpected departure for the Interior Department in October 1983 (even the State Department was uninformed of his decision).

Conservative supporters of Reagan saw the national security vacancy as an opportunity to urge politically conservative foreign policy approaches on the president and pressed the candidacy of U.N. Ambassador Jeane Kirkpatrick. A committed Reaganite, Kirkpatrick had been a close ally of Clark and had occupied an unusually prominent position in the Reagan foreign policy establishment (she was a regular attendee of NSC meetings, for example). Reagan chose Robert C. (Bud) McFarlane instead. Although McFarlane lacked the academic and intellectual credentials of a Kissinger or Brzezinski, he enjoyed impressive credentials as an experienced foreign affairs adviser, having served as an NSC staffer under Kissinger and Scowcroft, a member of the Senate Armed Services Committee staff, and a trouble-shooter for Secretary of State Haig. McFarlane's choice has been described as a victory for "conservative professionalism," (Destler, Gelb, and Lake, 1984), out of which emerged the picture of a national security assistant perhaps closer to the "middle position" shown in Box 10.1 than at any other time.

Clark's departure enabled Secretary of State Shultz to move toward center stage. Even while Clark was in office, where he was closely attuned to Reagan's thinking, Shultz was regarded as having superior knowledge of the substance of foreign policy. His influence grew in particular "as he identified himself increasingly with the use of military force in the Middle East and the Caribbean."

> His main governmental adversary on these issues was Defense Secretary Weinberger, buttressed by the Joint Chiefs of Staff—who were reluctant to fight anywhere unless a military action was popular and/or could be quickly concluded. McFarlane, lacking Clark's long-standing intimate ties to the President, was much less of a power. He upgraded the professional quality of routine NSC policy management, but on the big issues he was unable to force durable resolutions of the State-Defense differences. (Destler, Gelb, and Lake, 1984: 236)

Over time, however, McFarlane's influence grew, even as did Shultz's. This is unusual, since the secretary of state and the national security adviser historically have been at odds, but under Reagan they increasingly found themselves in alliance against the secretary of defense not only on the issue of the use of military force overseas but also arms control, Soviet-American relations, and other issues.

As noted earlier, McFarlane generally appeared to play the national security assistants' role close to the "consensus description" of the job. On some issues, however (like the Middle East, of special interest to McFarlane, perhaps, since he had served there as special envoy), he may have pursued his own policy preferences. According to one observer, this was because of "a long-standing feeling that the State Department bureaucracy is too intellectually constipated and divided to produce timely and creative policy recommendations" (Janka, 1984). The conclusion smacks of the reasons explaining Bundy's rise to prominence in the Kennedy administration two and half decades earlier.

Power and influence in Washington are often measured by symbols. The symbol of McFarlane's influence was his move from the White House basement into Edwin Meese's first-floor office following Meese's confirmation as attorney general early in Reagan's second term. McFarlane also is reported to have at one time enjoyed Nancy Reagan's valued approval.

McFarlane did not get along well with Donald Regan, however. He resigned in late 1985 and was replaced by his deputy, Vice Admiral John M. Poindexter. President Reagan dismissed the explanation that McFarlane had resigned due to intra-White House feuding. Press reports to the contrary were compelling nonetheless. The *New York Times* (December 4, 1985), for example, reported that the personality clashes of Regan and McFarlane were an "open secret" and that Regan felt the national security adviser was bypassing him.[26]

Early reports on Poindexter's stewardship pointed toward his ability to play the role of honest broker but questioned whether he would successfully play a leadership role on issues, like arms control, where the national security adviser is uniquely positioned to fashion compromises among otherwise contending factions in the government. Later, however, Poindexter was credited with devising the rationale leading to the April 1986 American retaliatory raid against Libya for its alleged sponsorship of international terrorism, suggesting that Poindexter, like his predecessors, would emerge as a key player in White House efforts to assert control over the making of American foreign policy.

Destler, Gelb, and Lake (1984) describe the decades-long struggle between the national security adviser and the secretary of state as a contest between

[26]Suggesting Regan's sensitivity on this issue, the *Times* reported that

One senior White House official recalled a breakfast meeting that the President held with reporters, shortly after Mr. Regan became White House chief of staff last January [1985]. At one point the President said with a laugh, "Every time the phone rings at 3 A.M. I turn over and say 'Hi, Bud.'"

The official said, "Regan visibly winced. I think he decided then and there never to let that happen again."

The *Times* also conjectured (December 5, 1985) that with McFarlane's resignation "after tense wrangles with the chief of staff, the White House now has one—and only one—focus of power in Mr. Regan." Poindexter was assured on his appointment that he would have direct access to the president, but Chief of Staff Regan was expected to become more actively involved in foreign policy.

"courtiers" and "barons," between those "in the White House who gain influence by responding to [presidents'] personal needs and their political priorities," in contrast to senior officials "in formal charge of an important domain within the presidential realm," principally a cabinet-level agency.

The trend toward concentration of power in the hands of the national security assistant suggests the courtiers have won out over the barons. "A principal cause of this power shift," Destler, Gelb, and Lake suggest, "has been the triumph of politics and ideology over foreign policy":

> Presidents use foreign policy more frequently for political reasons: Presidents increasingly head political factions committed to distinct, even ideological, policy positions, which they seek to implement once they are in office. This increases their distrust of the bureaucracy and drives them to pull policy control into their own White House. (Destler, Gelb, and Lake, 1984: 237)

And they suggest that "greater fluctuation in policy content" has been a consequence of "increased reliance on White House courtiers": "It has also made the policy process more personality-dependent, and thus more idiosyncratic, since staff aides are less constrained that Cabinet barons. It has, finally, both encouraged and enabled Presidents to seize personal control of current policy operations . . . " (Destler, Gelb, and Lake, 1984).

OTHER EXECUTIVE OFFICE FUNCTIONS: MANAGING ECONOMIC AFFAIRS

Before leaving the presidential subsystem, brief mention should be made of other units that have existed within the Executive Office and that, together with the NSC, are at the immediate disposal of the president, and thereby contribute to presidential preeminence in foreign policy making.[27]

The largest unit, with roughly 600 staff members and an annual budget in excess of $38 million, is the Office of Management and Budget (OMB). It is the sixty-year-old Bureau of the Budget "politicized and reincarnated" (Polsby, 1976) by Richard Nixon in 1970. OMB has responsibility for reviewing budgetary and other legislative requests coming from departments and agencies and for examining legislation passed by Congress before it is signed into law by the president. It also assists in devising plans for the organization and management of executive branch functions. Those tasks assign OMB a potentially critical voice in ensuring that agencies' plans and programs are consistent with presidential priorities.

Different presidents have employed different budgetary and management techniques to realize their objectives. In the early 1960s, Robert McNamara introduced planning-programming-budgeting (PPB) into the Defense Depart-

---

[27]We will return in chapter eleven to the CIA, which has roots in, but extends beyond, the Executive Office of the President.

ment as a procedure for making more informed budgetary choices and evaluating military operations. In an effort to realize greater "rationality" in the budgetary process, Lyndon Johnson later ordered that the Bureau of the Budget apply PPB throughout the government. President Nixon emphasized the concept of "management by objective," meaning the assignment of priorities to various objectives over others (which also meant choosing some programs over others). Management within that framework became advocacy of presidential interests, which facilitated not only the ongoing needs of established foreign policy bureaucracies but also ensured the availability of funds for the needs of ad hoc diplomacy (Esterline and Black, 1975).

As the 1970s wore on, concern for restraining public spending mounted. In response, Jimmy Carter implemented at the federal level zero-base budgeting (ZBB), which he had first employed as governor of Georgia. ZBB is a management technique that requires each program to be justified anew each year when money is being requested. It did not prove effective in stemming the flow of public spending, however. During the 1980s, increasingly massive federal government budget deficits and a mounting national debt therefore became key issues on the national political agenda.

By the mid-1980s, budget deficits topped $200 billion annually—and were projected to remain in the $220 to $250 billion range into the 1990s—and the national debt inched toward $1.5 trillion as the United States became a debtor nation in the international community. In this environment President Reagan turned to the Office of Management and Budget and its often controversial and outspoken director, David Stockman, to effect massive budget cuts in domestic programs alongside the administration's "supply side"[28] economics in an effort to cope with the deficit problem. Stockman did help engineer some early successes in Congress, but the problem persisted. Stockman then became a voice for cutbacks in the administration's projected defense spending increases, only to find that other players in the game had a stronger voice than OMB. When Stockman left the office early in Reagan's second term, he became critical of the political pressures that, in his view, prohibited making national economic policy rationally. His replacement was expected to play a much less visible and vocal role in setting and pursuing the administration's priorities.

Another presidential unit involved in the budgetary process is the Council of Economic Advisers (CEA), which, together with officials from OMB and the Treasury Department, makes economic forecasts on which the income and expenditures of the federal government are based. The CEA has not assumed operational responsibilities, however, serving instead exclusively as a staff

---

[28]Supply-side economics refers to the assumption that economic growth will be stimulated by reducing government spending and taxation. Supply-side economists argue that by increasing incentives in the private sector, worker productivity and employment will increase and the rate of inflation will decrease. Increased government revenues will result, which will offset any tax reductions.

arm of its "client," the president (Porter, 1983). The council itself comprises three presidentially appointed individuals, usually drawn from the ranks of the most respected academic economists, one of whom is typically assigned international responsibilities. Probably the most important function of the council is the preparation of the influential *Economic Report of the President* presented annually to Congress. More generally, the responsibility to advise the president on economic matters involves the CEA in a variety of policy considerations that can have important foreign policy implications in an economically interdependent world, considerations such as taxes, commerce, national productivity, and the balance of payments.

As a practical matter, however, the CEA historically has been oriented more toward domestic than international economic questions. That fact, coupled with Henry Kissinger's penchant for focusing on political-strategic questions, with a corresponding lack of interest in, if not ignorance about, economic matters, led President Nixon to create the Council on International Economic Policy (CIEP) in 1971. Although the CIEP did achieve some success on some issues (Destler, 1980), neither its director nor the council as a whole achieved the dominance in international economic policy making that the National Security Council and its staff has achieved in the foreign policy area, which was the apparent intent.

Neither Ford nor Carter emulated Nixon's efforts to create an Executive Office unit with responsibility for international economic affairs, but both found necessary some type of top-level coordinating mechanism to effect coherence in and control over international economic policy in the context of a changing American role in the international political economy. Ford created an Economic Policy Board (EPB), chaired by the secretary of the treasury and supported by a small professional staff, to "oversee the formulation, coordination, and implementation of all economic policy," both "national and international" (Executive Order creating the EPB, cited in Destler, 1980). Carter followed the EPB with a similarly structured Economic Policy Group. Its form and composition changed over time, but it never achieved the same degree of success as Ford's Economic Policy Board, in part because it was unable to establish the same kinds of direct links to the president. By 1979 Carter had come to rely on Ambassador Henry Owen, appointed as special representative of the president for economic summits and supported by professionals drawn from the staff of the National Security Council, to facilitate the coordination of international economic policy making (Destler, 1980).

As the foregoing makes clear, presidents generally have not sought to rely on "general purpose, formal entities" to exercise economic policy-making control (Porter, 1983). Reagan's approach to international economic affairs is consistent with this pattern. Reagan's Cabinet Council on Economic Affairs (CCEA) was given responsibility over economic policy, and the administration's NSC apparatus eventually contained a Senior Interagency Group for International Economic Policy (see Figure 10.2). The secretary of the treasury chaired both groups, which contained many of the same participants. In the case of the CCEA, staff support was provided by the White House Office of Policy Development.

Another official White House agent involved in managing foreign economic affairs is the Office of the United States Trade Representative. Headed by a presidential appointee who carries the rank of ambassador as well as membership in the cabinet (to ensure access to Congress), and dating back to the Kennedy administration, this office is responsible for directing American participation in trade negotiations with other nations, such as the Tokyo Round of Multilateral Trade Negotiations concluded in 1979. More generally, the trade representative is responsible for setting and administering overall trade policy, particularly activities and negotiations relating to the General Agreement on Tariffs and Trade (GATT), the United Nations Conference on Trade and Development (UNCTAD), and the Organization for Economic Cooperation and Development (OECD).

The trade representative's role in setting and managing trade policy was enhanced during the Carter administration as a result of his bringing the Multilateral Trade Negotiations to a successful conclusion. Robert Strauss, the former chairman of the Democratic party, served as the special representative for trade negotiations (as the position was then called); he was particularly successful not only in promoting American interests internationally but also in negotiating with important affected industries in the United States and in placating congressional concerns. As one observer put it, "Never had a special trade representative been so visible a public figure and so important a presidential adviser; never had one had comparable independent political stature; never had one displayed such dramatic virtuosity" (Destler, 1980). The result was a reorganization of the trade office in 1980 which gave it a greater voice in determining overall American trade policy. Strauss may have been unique, of course, "but he also [represented] the culmination of a trend: the movement of the special trade representative into the position of overall trade broker" (Destler, 1980) among the many government agencies necessarily involved in setting trade policy. Reinforcing this trend was the continuing internationalization of the nation's economy, which blurred further the distinction between foreign and domestic economic policy and contributed to the rise of "intermestic" policies and politics (see Cohen, 1983).

President Reagan assured Strauss's successor, William E. Brock, that a prominent role for the trade representative would remain appropriate. As the nation's once preeminent position in the global trade network deteriorated in the 1980s, however, Reagan proposed creation of a new cabinet-level trade department, which would combine the roles of policy development (exercised by the U.S. Trade Representative) and policy implementation (exercised by the Commerce Department). The proposal failed to win congressional support, however (see chapter eleven for a further discussion of this issue). It seems likely, therefore, that the White House will continue to dominate the making of trade policy, for successive administrations have attached considerable importance to trade-related issues as they bear upon the foreign and domestic interests of the nation. Congress also seems to be content with current organizational arrangements. It is pertinent to note in this context that the trade office was originally created at the behest of Congress, which felt that the State Department had given too much emphasis to foreign policy at the expense of economic policy considerations.

The record of White House efforts to coordinate foreign economic policy making is clearly a mixed one and in no way matches its mastery of foreign and national security policy making. As Destler (1980) argues, one explanation is the ambivalence various administrations have shown toward the *foreign* and *economic* aspects of the policy area. The Nixon administration adopted a laissez-faire attitude toward trade with the Soviet Union in order to promote the foreign policy goal of détente. Analogously, the Carter administration placed an embargo on grain sales to the Soviet Union in order to impose costs on the Soviet Union for invading Afghanistan. The Reagan administration, on the other hand, minimized the foreign policy aspects of the grain embargo in deciding to lift it, apparently bowing to congressional pressures and to the economic interests of the farm lobby. Such ambivalence necessarily brings one bureaucratic agency (such as the State Department) to the forefront of policy making at one time, another agency (such as the Department of Agriculture) at another. Without clear and consistent direction from the White House, interagency politics are likely to dominate the process and ultimately the outcome.

Why does the White House fail to give clear and consistent direction? Why, in other words, does it not dominate the outcome as overwhelmingly as it has come to do in national security affairs? Two intersecting lines of reasoning seem plausible.

First, although the line between foreign and economic policy is often ambiguous, ''the substance of most foreign economic policy issues relates more closely to domestic economic policy concerns than to foreign policy ones'' (Porter, 1983). One consequence is that foreign economic policy making necessarily involves many organizations whereas on national security matters the principal actors are often confined to the State and Defense departments and the White House. International economic matters typically involve a much wider network: the Department of Agriculture on food policy, the Department of Commerce on trade issues, and the Treasury Department on monetary issues. Each of those agencies, in turn, has important domestic roots and networks and often powerful congressional allies. The number of actors the White House would have to control is therefore substantial, encompassing domestic as well as foreign interests. Moreover, those interests and the goals they reflect are usually in conflict. Withholding grain from the Soviet Union can deprive American farmers of an important overseas market; lowering trade barriers on imported autos can cost Detroit assembly-line workers their jobs; manipulating the value of the dollar abroad can affect the competitiveness of American goods in overseas markets and interest rates at home. For presidents to decide among the conflicting objectives and to achieve sustained control over such diverse foreign and domestic interests apparently requires a greater expenditure of political capital than most have been willing to make. As the complex challenges of the interdependent global political economy become more potent, their management becomes more difficult and less rewarding politically.

Second, postwar presidents historically have emphasized the "high politics" of national security policy, not the "low politics" of foreign economic affairs. That emphasis reflects the perceived realities of the postwar political environment, where political and military challenges, particularly Soviet communism, are foremost. Economic issues are, understandably, treated as secondary to that overriding reality. Many of the policy problems of the 1970s seemed to challenge that pecking order, only to see it reassert itself during the 1980s, at least in the eyes of the Reagan administration's top-level foreign policy-making officials.

Because presidents are inherently political animals always with an eye toward either the next election or their place in history, no organizational framework for managing foreign economic policy is likely to be created or to endure if the president determines its activities are detrimental to his own political fortunes. And since foreigners neither vote in American elections nor write American history books (at least ones widely read by Americans), it is likely that organizational adaptations will continue to be made but that in the area of foreign economic policy—where foreign and domestic politics overlap in important and fundamental ways—domestic political interests will dominate the politics of policy making at least as often as foreign policy interests.

PRESIDENTIAL PREEMINENCE AND PRESIDENTIAL POWER

Continued and direct involvement of the White House in matters of foreign policy beyond that which any president might manage personally has doubtless become a permanent feature of the institutional setting within which American foreign policy is made and executed. The reason is especially clear in matters of "high politics": with so much at stake in the nuclear age, the president cannot afford to let someone else decide. To the extent that the United States seeks to exercise control over external problems that have grown increasingly complex, and to the extent that established departments and agencies seek to protect their own interests in coping with those problems, no one actor is fully equipped to protect the interests of the man who bears final responsibility—the president. "When things don't go well they like to blame presidents—and that's what presidents are paid for," observed John F. Kennedy. In such an environment, a personalized staff, infused with the authority and prestige that only the president and the presidency can claim, becomes an indispensable tool. For as Richard Nixon noted, presidents are chosen to make things happen.

In a larger sense, a personalized staff also serves to assist the president in his roles as ultimate decider, ultimate coordinator, and ultimate persuader. The danger, of course, is that the presidential subsystem may so cut off the president from other elements of the institutionalized foreign affairs government (or even from American society) that the ability of the president to exercise his responsibility may be impaired seriously. That appears to be precisely what happened to the Nixon presidency, to which the entire Watergate affair now stands in giant testimony. Such secrecy may be desirable from the viewpoint of managing great-power politics. But since what stimulates as well as what constrains foreign policy are much greater forces than any one or two men alone are able to manage—and since they come from domestic sources as well as from the external environment—simply playing the role of decider while ignoring the roles of coordinator and persuader may be counterproductive for the larger purposes being sought. As Henry Kissinger himself finally put it, "No foreign policy—no matter how ingenious—has any chance of success if it is born in the minds of a few and carried in the hearts of none."

There is another danger: that as ideology triumphs over policy, presidents cut themselves off from the career staff in the established foreign policy bureaucracies who are the repository of foreign policy expertise and who provide policy continuity from one administration to the next. The Reagan administration more than any other used political and ideological "trustworthiness' as a litmus for appointment to top and even middle-level staff positions. "The result," write Destler, Gelb, and Lake (1984), "has been a squandering of mainstream talent, and the substitution of elite professionals sometimes skilled more at making waves than at making government work. . . . And by weakening the bureaucracy, it has imposed on our government a painful loss of continuity."

To better understand the role that established bureaucratic organizations play in the foreign affairs government—and why presidents so often seem prone to shun them—let us next examine how they participate in the process of gathering information on which foreign policy decisions are based and in carrying them out once they are made.

SUGGESTIONS FOR FURTHER READING

BRZEZINSKI, ZBIGNIEW. *Power and Principle: Memoirs of the National Security Adviser 1977–1981.* New York: Farrar, Straus, Giroux, 1983.

DESTLER, I. M. *Making Foreign Economic Policy.* Washington, DC: The Brookings Institution, 1980.

DESTLER, I. M., LESLIE H. GELB, AND ANTHONY LAKE. *Our Own Worst Enemy: The Unmaking of American Foreign Policy.* New York: Simon and Schuster, 1984.

GEORGE, ALEXANDER L. *Presidential Decisionmaking in Foreign Policy: The Effective Use of Information and Advice.* Boulder, CO: Westview Press, 1980.

HAIG, ALEXANDER M., JR. *Caveat: Realism, Reagan, and Foreign Policy.* New York: Macmillan, 1984.

HUNTER, ROBERT E. *Presidential Control of Foreign Policy: Management or Mishap?* New York: Praeger, 1982.

KISSINGER, HENRY. *White House Years.* Boston: Little, Brown, 1979.

LOWI, THEODORE J. *The Personal President: Power Invested, Promise Unfulfilled.* Ithaca, NY: Cornell University Press, 1985.

VANCE, CYRUS. *Hard Choices: Critical Years in America's Foreign Policy.* New York: Simon and Schuster, 1983.

11

THE ROLE OF EXECUTIVE
DEPARTMENTS AND AGENCIES IN
FOREIGN POLICY MAKING

[I]t's inevitable that control over foreign policy should gravitate to the White House. It's simply impossible to shape foreign policy from the vantage point of the State Department for the very reason foreign policy is . . . an amalgam of defense, intelligence, mass persuasion, and all of these things can be coordinated from close proximity to the president.

Former Assistant for National Security Affairs Zbigniew Brzezinski, 1983

At last count some 46 agencies were running international programs, and . . . every one of them seems to have its own foreign policy agenda. This can—and often does—create an impression of chaos.

Former Foreign Service Information Officer Fitzhugh Green, 1984

Globalism is a pattern of American foreign policy. Recall from chapters four and five its manifestations: diplomatic relations with nearly every foreign government; participation in scores of international organizations; billions of dollars in military and economic assistance and in military sales; military weapons and personnel spread worldwide, with a corresponding capacity to strike militarily virtually anywhere; and trade and investment connections with the rest of the world far out of proportion to the nation's percentage of the world's population.

Whose activities are reflected in such involvements? Whose responsibility is it to protect the interests they represent? The president and the presidency are the easy answers; the executive departments and agencies of the federal

371

government, and especially the State and Defense departments, are the more accurate ones.

The distinction made in the preceding chapter between executive branch agencies (the second concentric circle of policy making) and the presidential subsystem (the innermost concentric circle) is not entirely clear-cut. The presidentially appointed heads of executive departments and agencies together with their immediate subordinates make up the innermost circle of advisers. Thus Secretaries of State Dulles, Rusk, Kissinger, Vance, and Shultz, Secretaries of Defense McNamara, Laird, Brown, and Weinberger, and Secretaries of the Treasury Simon, Blumenthal, Regan, and Baker clearly are examples of members of the inner circle as well as heads of the large, complex organizations found in the second concentric circle. Such organizations are important to those in the innermost circle because the president and the advisers closest to him depend very heavily on them and on the professional experience and expertise provided by literally thousands of career bureaucrats who carry out the day-to-day foreign affairs activities. Hence the scope and magnitude of the responsibilities of major organizations in the second concentric circle must be examined.

THE DEPARTMENT OF STATE

As the "first among equals" in the foreign affairs government, the Department of State is the executive agency bearing primary responsibility for the conduct of American foreign relations. Its activities range from negotiation of treaties and other agreements with other nations, to representing the nation in more than four dozen international organizations, to making policy recommendations and taking steps to implement them on virtually the entire range of foreign relations and interests.[1]

The State Department is organized in the typical bureaucratic pyramid, with the secretary of state perched on top of a series of lesser offices and bureaus which divide the labor within the department. As shown in Figure 11.1, that division reflects the department's orientation to the major geographic regions of the world, on the one hand, and the necessity to cope with functional problems that transcend geographic boundaries (for example, economic and business affairs, intelligence and research, and politico-military affairs) together with those arising out of the internal needs of any large government organization, on the other.

---

[1]Leacacos (1968: 42–43) provided insight some years ago into how those responsibilities translated into day-to-day routines. He noted that the department's telegraph branch handled about 4,000 messages a day, a total of 15 million words a month; that over 300 overseas phone calls went to and from the department each day; that 19 million pieces of mail were handled by the department each year; and that State Department couriers flew some 130,000 miles a year carrying department messages, while another 43,000 pouches, weighing 2 million pounds, were carried via surface transportation to U.S. overseas posts. Pringle (1977–1978: 137) further reported that State Department cable traffic increases at an annual rate of about 15 percent.

FIGURE 11.1 Department of State Organization Chart

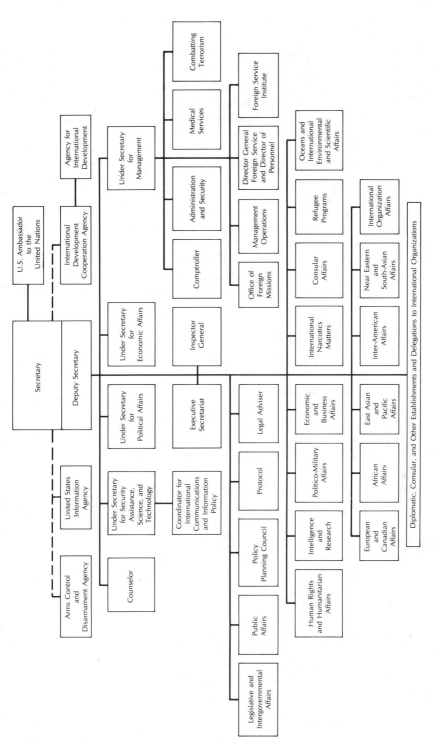

SOURCE: *The United States Government Manual, 1985–86*, 1985: 847.

As Figure 11.1 shows, three organizations that are attached to the State Department are the Arms Control and Disarmament Agency (ACDA), the United States Information Agency (USIA), and the International Development Cooperation Agency (IDCA). ACDA conducts research on arms control and disarmament policy and participates in negotiations with other nations on those subjects. USIA is responsible for the nation's public diplomacy, that is, the cultural and informational activities directed at overseas audiences (see chapter five). And the IDCA has policy responsibility for a number of activities related to economic development programs. The Agency for International Development (AID) is the principal operating arm of the IDCA.[2] AID is responsible for administering U.S. economic assistance programs in more than sixty different countries.[3] Overseas personnel of all three agencies (ACDA, USIA, and AID) are typically attached to the field mission abroad,[4] over which the State Department, usually through the person of the ambassador, bears primary responsibility.[5]

Decision-making responsibility within the State Department itself follows the hierarchical pattern of its organization chart. The most important decisions are made by the secretary, the deputy secretary, and the under secretaries who occupy the seventh floor of the State Department offices in the area of Washington, D.C., known as Foggy Bottom, and who frequently interact with the White House and other government agencies. Routine decisions, important more in the implementation than in the development of policy, are made at the levels below the seventh floor. Making such decisions begins, looking from the top down, with the regional assistant secretary who operates as "a problem manager on the periphery of significant decision-making" (Esterline and Black, 1975). Ultimately they work down to the country directors and desk officers within each regional bureau, who bear responsibility for coordinating U.S. policy toward particular countries abroad.[6] In practice the re-

---

[2]There are two other units within IDCA: the Trade and Development Program, which is responsible for promoting simultaneously the economic development of Third World countries and the sale of U.S. goods and services to them; and the Overseas Private Investment Corporation, which assists United States investors to make profitable investments in Third World countries.

[3]See Esterline and Black (1975) for an illuminating discussion of the role of AID, USIA, and the overseas field mission in the implementation of foreign policy.

[4]In 1985, the State Department was operating a network of 291 posts throughout the world—140 embassies, 11 missions, 73 consulates general, 34 consulates, 30 consular agencies, and three branch offices (*The United States Government Manual, 1985–86*, 1985: 396).

[5]For some of the important reasons discussed below, there is reason to question how effective the ambassador, or, more generally, the State Department, is in effecting control over the overseas mission. As Pringle (1977–1978) puts it, the legal mandate that the ambassador supervise the activities of other U.S. agencies attached to the field mission abroad "has usually remained in the realm of polite fiction." Even within the State Department the ambassador seems to have lost importance as modern telecommunications and travel enable Washington to handle a broad range of foreign affairs details. As one Foreign Service officer commented wryly upon resigning his post in the Moscow embassy in 1980, "We don't need an ambassador in Moscow . . . because he has nothing to do" (cited in Rubin, 1985).

[6]Rubin (1985) provides a useful description of the responsibilities associated with different levels in the State Department's bureaucratic hierarchy and of the tasks performed by the various regional and functional bureaus.

sponsibilities of the regional bureaus have been greatly diluted by the fact that several dozen federal agencies are active in foreign affairs (Warwick, 1975).[7]

The division of decision-making responsibility within the State Department has been described in these terms:

> If one reviews decision-making in the Department of State in terms of a continuum of five decision categories—minor, routine, significant, fundamental and critical—it is clear, first, that country directors are engaged principally in *minor* decision-making, although they make resource inputs [e.g., give information on and interpretations of current political developments] to routine and significant decision-making concerning "their" countries. Second, assistant secretaries are limited principally to *routine* decisions affecting their geographical areas, although they make resource inputs to significant decisions involving their areas and, occasionally, other geographical areas through inputs which propose alternative policy positions. . . . Third, few *significant* decisions are made below the level of the seventh floor, and many significant decisions—probably the bulk—are made in consequence of interactions with the White House . . . and the bureaucracies of other foreign policy agencies. Fourth, all *fundamental* and *critical* foreign policy decisions involve the White House. (Esterline and Black, 1975: 63)[8]

Within this structure the individuals who matter most are the Foreign Service officers (FSOs). Accounting (in 1985) for about 4,100 of the more than 25,000 employees of the State Department, this elite corps of professional diplomats has traditionally held the most important positions within State (outside the political appointments made by the president), both at home and abroad.

The popular image of the Foreign Service, based partly on legend as well as historical fact (see Harr, 1969; Garnham, 1975), is that of a diplomatic corps comprising upper-class men from the Northeast with degrees from Ivy League colleges. Changes in both American society and government in recent years have eroded this picture as the Foreign Service officers corps has become open to a broader geographical, educational, ethnic, and socioeconomic spectrum. "Still, if the Foreign Service is no longer a smug men's club, it is more like one than any other part of the U.S. government" (Rubin, 1985).

The corps' distinctiveness is reinforced by a personnel system that is separate from the Civil Service, of which most federal employees are a part. And because it is an elite corps, other groups, such as State's Civil Service employ-

[7]In 1985, only 30 percent of the 15,000 Americans stationed at U.S. missions abroad worked for the State Department (Spiers, 1985a: 3). The practical consequence is that a substantial proportion of State's personnel are involved in serving agencies other than their own. In 1966, 40 percent of State's total personnel was involved in providing services to other foreign affairs agencies (Leacacos, 1968: 368); by the 1970s as much as 50 percent of State's personnel was engaged in supporting other agencies (Warwick, 1975: 66. Spiers implies that these trends have continued.

[8]One must be careful not to assume from that description, which pertains more to the development than to the implementation of policy, that the State Department and other bureaucratic agencies are unimportant foreign policy actors. On the contrary, the dependence of decision makers on bureaucratic organizations for policy implementation gives such organizations considerable opportunity to shape policy to fit their preferred positions, as we shall explain in more detail in chapter thirteen.

ees, are, by definition, nonelite. This has been the source of continuing personnel problems within the State Department, for non-FSOs complain of their inferior status and their feeling of neglect within the department (Warwick, 1975).

The Foreign Service has developed a distinctive subculture and mode of operation that have important ramifications for the State Department's role in the making and execution of foreign policy. The subculture reinforces elitism and promotes respect for tradition, precedent, and conformity above all else.[9]

One characteristic of the subculture is resistance to ideas from the outside. As one officer put it, " 'The Foreign Service officer believes that his is an arcane craft which people on the outside cannot hope to understand.' We listen carefully and politely but seldom change our views" (*Diplomacy for the 70's*, 1970). Another characteristic is lack of aggressiveness in delineating State's jurisdiction within the foreign affairs government. That lack would be acceptable if other organizations were unaggressive—but they are not. Hence leadership has tended to gravitate elsewhere. Yet the norms of the Foreign Service subculture militate against a more vigorous role. Especially important are three beliefs prevalent in the subculture.

- The only experience that is relevant to the activities of the Department of State is experience gained in the Foreign Service.
- The really important aspects of the foreign affairs of the United States are the political and traditional ones—negotiation, representation, and reporting.
- Overseas operations of the kind conducted by DOD, AID, USIA, and CIA are peripheral to the main foreign policy task (Destler, 1974: 163, quoting Scott, 1969).[10]

The above beliefs led Andrew Scott (1970) to conclude that while the norms of the subculture may satisfy the short-term needs of the career service and the individuals within it, they may not necessarily satisfy the long-term needs of the Department of State or the requirements of American foreign policy.

---

[9]The State Department has encouraged women and blacks to join its ranks, but it recognizes that the problem of representativeness remains, in the words of Ronald Spiers, Under Secretary of State for Management during the Reagan administration, "a serious one." It is also the case that officers from these underrepresented groups do not always feel welcomed by their colleagues.

> The utility of diversifying the recruitment pool is precisely to broaden department culture and introduce people who may be more inclined to question, hold different perspectives, and stress other priorities. Yet these characteristics are often punished rather than valued at State. . . . Ironically, a department whose very purpose is to deal with other cultures and peoples, places a remarkably high emphasis on homogeneity and tends to regard the different as inferior." (Rubin, 1985: 240–241)

[10]Scott (1969) notes that the inability of the subculture to recognize the integral role that non-State Department agencies play in contemporary American statecraft "represents about a twenty-year lag in adjusting to foreign policy realities." Pringle (1977–1978), himself a Foreign Service officer, reports that Foreign Service promotion panels tend to penalize those who seek experience outside "the admittedly stagnant mainstream" of State Department or embassy assignments.

Within the Foreign Service itself, the subculture creates pressures to avoid rocking the boat—to avoid expressing controversial views that may be viewed as challenges to the wisdom of one's superiors, and to avoid dress and behavior that deviate from the norms of the group. Those pressures derive partly from the assignments of the typical Foreign Service officer. Viewed as a generalist rather than a specialist, the typical FSO's career pattern involves two- or three-year tours of duty both in Washington and overseas in a variety of operating and functional positions. Whether one's star is allowed to shine in an assignment to political affairs in Paris rather than budgetary affairs in Ouagadougou is thus heavily dependent on the outcome of one's evaluation by superiors.

The fiercely competitive nature of the Foreign Service has been reinforced historically by the "up-or-out" promotion system, under which an FSO has to advance beyond his or her present rank within a specified time or be "selected-out."[11] That principle, together with the exceptional importance of the efficiency rating, tends, as the department's own self-study put it, "to stifle creativity, discourage risk-taking, and reward conformity" (*Diplomacy for the 70's*, 1970).

By the late 1960s the pressures generated by the selection-out principle were aggravated by an accumulation at the top of the Foreign Service career ladder, making the Foreign Service look like an inverted pyramid with twice as many officers in the top four ranks of the service as in the bottom four ranks (Campbell, 1971). The accumulation was a direct consequence of "Wristonization," the process whereby in the mid-1950s some 1,500 to 2,500 middle-level bureaucrats were brought laterally into the Foreign Service. That disruptive and controversial move had been recommended by a study group headed by Dr. Henry Wriston, president of Brown University. The effect, according to one scholar, was to provide the Foreign Service with "a much-needed source of executive talent" (Harr, 1969). According to another, it "spread chaos and uncertainty" (Campbell, 1971).

Even more disruptive were the effects of McCarthyism. "I have in my hand a list of 205 that were known to the Secretary of State as being members of the Communist party and who, nevertheless, are still working and shaping the policy in the State Department." With those words, spoken in the winter of 1950, Senator Joseph McCarthy launched an all-out attack against suspected—but never proven—"disloyalty" in the Foreign Service. The immediate thrust was against those charged with responsibility for the "loss" of

---

[11]The selection-out principle was suspended in the early 1970s following the suicide of an FSO who had been informed he had been selected-out. In the eleven-year period prior to its suspension (1961–1971), 826 FSOs were actually selected-out, 216 on the basis of not having advanced in rank in the specified time period, 610 on the basis of low performance ratings (Clark, 1975: 206). The principle was subsequently reaffirmed in the Foreign Service Act of 1980 under which the time-in-rank principle reportedly has been vigorously enforced to reduce the "senior surplus" described below.

China. Eventually the entire corps of Foreign Service officers suffered the grueling humiliation of the security investigations engendered by an atmosphere of hysterical anticommunism. Truman's loyalty program reflected deference to McCarthyism. And unhappily for those involved, the career-shattering and head-rolling trauma continued to plague the State Department for nearly two years following the election of Eisenhower (see Hoopes, 1973a).

McCarthyism's long-term effects on the Foreign Service are testimony to its devastating impact:

> Talented officers resigned or were drummed out of the service. Field reports began to be couched in bland and roundabout language. Few dared to list Communist countries as career preferences, while East Asian specialization became a wasteland. Rumors and gossip were rampant in the corridors, reinforced by the spot visits of McCarthy's assistants. The virtues inculcated were caution, conformity, discretion, and prudence. (Warwick, 1975: 20)[12]

Extraordinary security consciousness and an elaborate system of horizontal clearances resulted. The latter in particular has made State's operating procedures among the most complex of all federal agencies. "Clearing" and "coordinating" with other comparably placed offices within the department and other agencies are necessary before an item can go up the chain of command. The result is "a most cautious way of doing business. It reflects an institutionalized desire to diffuse responsibility among many different offices and colleagues rather than to accept responsibility oneself" (Campbell, 1971).

As the effects of Wristonization and McCarthyism recede into the past, two new but analogous structural problems have emerged to plague the professional diplomatic corps. One is a bulge at the top of the Senior Foreign Service (from which the most prized positions, including ambassadorships, are chosen) as more career officers are promoted to senior ranks than can be placed in meaningful positions.[13]

---

[12]One of the certain tragedies of McCarthyism is that it robbed a later generation of decision makers of much needed expertise on Asia at the very time that the emergent Vietnam War and the China tangle demanded knowledge of that area. Thomson described the State Department's Bureau of Far Eastern Affairs (now East Asian and Pacific Affairs) as it looked in 1961 in these terms: "'FE' was notorious for its rigidity and its resistance to policy change. For the Bureau had been one of McCarthyism's central targets; and the endless Congressional and Executive Branch investigations of the early '50s had largely destroyed, through harassment and dispersal, the China career professionals of the wartime and pre-war years. . . . [B]y 1961 'FE' was a Bureau dominated by Cold Warriors and staffed largely by the cowed" (Thomson, 1972).

[13]The expectation underlying the Senior Foreign Service when created by the Foreign Service Act of 1980 was that most FSOs would retire from the corps after twenty years, leaving only a small cadre from which the highest career appointments would be made. Instead, more have been promoted than have been absorbed into productive new assignments. In 1985, for example, the Senior Foreign Service comprised 17 percent of the Foreign Service officers corps, compared to a Senior Executive Service consisting of 1 percent of the Civil Service officers of comparable grades and an even smaller fraction among the comparable military ranks (Spiers, 1985b: 35). The current surplus may in the long run turn to shortage (Steigman, 1985), but there is little question that the bloated Senior Foreign Service resulted in "a demoralizing phenomenon for those consigned to 'makework' or overcomplement status after reaching the prime of their careers" (Spiers, 1985a).

The second problem, directly related to the first, is a growing number of political appointments to top jobs from outside the Foreign Service.[14] The pattern of political appointments contributes to the "senior surplus" by reducing the opportunities available to career officers at the prime of their careers when they have the greatest potential to make meaningful contributions to American foreign policy. It reflects a profound distrust of "careerists" by "politicians," who often believe the former are not only disloyal to the latter's policies but also actively seek to undermine them. Such suspicions derive in part from State's bureaucratic subculture and from the requirement that careerists support policy, whatever it may be, objectively and without partisanship. "Since they are representing the views of the U.S. government rather than their own," Rubin (1985) observes, "FSOs are supposed to become vessels of communication, without personal views. Many of them learn to radiate blandness and to censor their own opinions. An ideal pose is to give the impression of great knowledge while revealing little of substance." Such apparent lack of conviction does not sit well with those placed in office by voters or presidents, for whom partisan loyalty and, increasingly, it seems, ideological purity are important yardsticks. Often, however, the demands political appointees make on those expected to serve them are contradictory.

> They want the career staff to be detached, but accuse it of being bland; they demand discipline, but can brand this as lack of imagination; they require experienced judgment, but may call this negativism. One FSO complains, "Presidents and their aides need scapegoats. They can't blame the administration so they blame the secretary of state and if they can't blame the secretary of state they criticize the department's staff." (Rubin, 1985: 242)

The subculture of the State Department and its interaction with related extraorganizational factors are critical in explaining why an organization that theoretically sits center stage in the foreign affairs government is in fact ill equipped to play a leadership role. "As long as the norms of the subculture prescribe organizational accommodation rather than combat, and caution rather than venturesomeness, and as long as the ideology assures members of the subculture that they are doing a good job, it is vain to expect bold and innovative policy from the Department of State" (Scott, 1969).

Two additional factors help explain State's compromised leadership role. Both are linked to the subculture but extend beyond it. One is that secretaries

---

Mention should also be made of concern within the Foreign Service for preserving its traditional structure and career patterns in a sociocultural environment where two-career families are increasingly the norm, and where the growing incidence of terrorism abroad has reduced the willingness of officers and their families to accept demanding and dangerous assignments overseas.

[14]During the Reagan administration, for example, more than 40 percent of the ambassadorships went to noncareer officials (read political appointees), compared to 27 percent for Carter and 32 percent for Nixon and Eisenhower (Perry, 1984: 21; also Spiers, 1985a), despite the fact that the 1980 Foreign Service Act specifies that ambassadorial appointments will "normally" go to career officers.

of state in the postwar era often removed themselves from the department rather than infusing the organization with the kind of vigorous leadership that might have involved it more intimately in the policy process. Secretary of State Dulles, for example, reportedly told Eisenhower he would become secretary only if he did not have to be responsible for the management of the department and the Foreign Service; in the case of Dean Rusk, time pressures, his own personality, and his preoccupation with Vietnam prevented a more effective use of State's expertise (*Diplomacy for the 70's*, 1970). The record for subsequent secretaries—Kissinger, Vance, Muskie, Haig, and Shultz—contains little to suggest they were able to bridge effectively the chasm between top officials and the careerists in such a way as to involve the latter intimately in the policy process. Kissinger took many of his NSC staffers with him to Foggy Bottom when he left the White House, and one of the hallmarks of his stewardship was the amount of time he spent out of town. Vance was apparently more popular at State "partly due to memories of his predecessor—tales of Kissinger mistreating FSOs and ashtray-throwing tantrums are legion" (Rubin, 1985)—but eventually Vance became enmeshed in a bureaucratic duel with the White House, which he ultimately lost. Alexander Haig, Reagan's first secretary of state, likewise resigned when he found himself outside the charmed circle of White House advisers in an administration otherwise known for its friction with the career staff.[15] If there is an exception, it is George Shultz, Haig's successor, whose very survival suggested he was better able than Haig to satisfy the competing demands of organization man and presidential adviser. But even he found himself under attack by right-wing Reaganites—including some former ambassadors and at least one influential U.S. senator—who sought his ouster on grounds he had become captive of the State Department's "liberal" foreign service establishment, and hence insufficiently responsive to the president's preferences and policies.

A second important reason for the State Department's inability to lead in foreign policy making is its relative lack of political resources and bureaucratic muscle in Washington's politically intense bureaucratic environment. As one Foreign Service officer (Pringle, 1977–1978) put it, although the secretary of state "is [the] most senior of cabinet members, and is charged (in theory) with responsibility for the coordination of all foreign policy activities, he presides over a bureaucratic midget." The State Department's expenditures in 1984 were $2.4 billion, compared to $240.3 billion for the Defense Department, $292.3 billion for Health and Human Services, and what is widely thought to be at least $12 billion for the intelligence community. Among the thirteen cabinet-level departments, only Commerce spends less. The State Department's 25,000 employees (many of whom are foreign nationals working in overseas field missions) likewise make it one of the smallest cabinet agencies.

---

[15]Vance's and Haig's views on the conflicts that led to their undoing are revealed in their respective memoirs, *Hard Choices* (Vance, 1983) and *Caveat* (Haig, 1984).

Increasing centralization of foreign policy making in the White House—described by three close observers as "the triumph of politics and ideology over foreign policy" (Destler, Gelb, and Lake, 1984)—has been one of the consequences of State's lack of leadership.[16] Ironically, such centralization, in turn, has further undermined State's leadership role, for it "has meant exclusion of the bureaucracy from most of the serious, Presidential foreign-policy business" (Destler, Gelb, and Lake, 1984). And both situations reflect the State Department's lack of attunement to presidential needs, especially the need to be sensitive to domestic political considerations. "Once a president comes to believe that Foggy Bottom is not attuned to politics, they are doomed to being ignored" (Gelb, 1983).

Part of the reason for the belief that the State Department is insensitive to a president's political needs is that the department necessarily represents the interests of other countries, who are its "clients," in the councils of government.[17]

> From a White House perspective, efforts to accommodate the legitimate concerns of other countries are often viewed as coming at the expense of American interests, and the accommodationists are viewed as not being tough enough. Presidents usually do not have much patience with this kind of advice, find they cannot change State's penchant for it, and soon stop listening. (Gelb, 1983: 285)

White House dominance over foreign policy is also a reaction to the State Department's lack of responsiveness. There is "a widespread feeling" within the State Department, John Kenneth Galbraith (1969a) complained to President Kennedy, "that God ordained some individuals to make foreign policy without undue interference from presidents and politicians." More specific presidential complaints are that the State Department produces bad staff work and is slow to respond, resistant to change, reluctant to follow orders, unable to lead, and incapable of putting its own house in order. Although in some respects those problems reflect internal State Department politics, they also demonstrate that the department is not unlike other large government organi-

---

[16]The State Department and the foreign affairs community generally have been the subject of literally dozens of official studies over the past three decades. Most have concluded that the State Department must assume a more assertive leadership role in the foreign affairs government. In contrast, as noted by Pringle (1977–1978), one study group, popularly known as the Murphey Commission, concluded that "State should concentrate on what it can realistically do, and then do it well. It defined this role as that of 'advocate' in two senses: making sure that the interests of friendly foreign powers are not overlooked in the hurly-burly of Washington decision-making and, perhaps more important, articulating the broader national interest as opposed to the often competing and sometimes parochial concerns of agencies like Commerce, Defense, or Agriculture." The commission's conclusion was based on the conviction that since significant foreign policy problems increasingly involve domestic concerns (and hence are sometimes referred to as "intermestic" issues), the president must necessarily be involved in the decision-making process.

[17]Rubin (1985) provides a useful discussion of the way, for example, that the Bureau of European Affairs and the Bureau of Near Eastern and South Asian Affairs "serve" their respective client states.

zations whose parochial viewpoints often lead them to put their own functions and programs ahead of broad policy issues. It is not surprising, therefore, that other government entities, the Defense Department, the CIA, the White House staff, have made more important innovative contributions to recent American foreign policy than the Department of State.

THE DEPARTMENT OF DEFENSE

During the 1960s, when White House dominance over foreign policy first began to emerge in part in response to the State Department's inability to lead (see also chapter ten), the Office of International Security Affairs (ISA) emerged as an influential Defense Department voice in the foreign affairs government.[18] Once described as the "little State Department," ISA traditionally has been organized like the State Department along both geographic and functional lines. As an arm of the secretary of defense, it was responsible for developing and coordinating Department of Defense (DOD) policies and positions in matters lying at the intersection between foreign and national security policy. Its influence in this area, and in the foreign affairs establishment generally, reached its apogee during Robert McNamara's tenure as defense secretary (1961–1967), in part because of McNamara's ability to effect civilian control over the mammoth military complex, which others had been unable to do, and in part because the principal foreign policy problem of the era—Vietnam—was also a formidable military problem. Thereafter ISA's influence waned as the constellation of forces that had sustained its influence shifted (see Piller, 1983). A 1979 reorganization created a new under secretary of defense for policy as the assistant to the defense secretary in matters relating to international security policy and political-military affairs. The move radically altered ISA's role within the Defense Department, but no other unit appears to have emerged to wield the kind of influence that it once did. The importance of the department as a whole, however, remains unambiguous, all the more so in a foreign policy-making environment where national security issues figure prominently in creating what has been dubbed a "security culture" (Hughes, 1981).

The secretary of defense together with the secretary of state and the joint chiefs of staff bear the heaviest responsibility for advising the president on matters relating to the national security of the United States. In contrast to the secretary of state, however, the defense secretary commands (nominally, at least) an organization so thoroughly interwoven into the fabric of American

---

[18]Just as Bundy's NSC staff became influential because of State's sluggishness, ISA's influence was in part a response to the sluggishness of the professional military, particularly the joint chiefs of staff (described below). Paul Nitze, whose involvement in the national security establishment spans four decades, compared ISA and the joint chiefs during the Kennedy years: "It sometimes would take them [the joint chiefs] three days to blow their nose. We [ISA] would sometimes be able to get a position together within an hour. When you get into a rapidly moving situation, when the house is burning down, every president likes to see something reasonable put forward for his consideration promptly" (cited in Piller, 1983).

social, political, and economic life that his recommendations regarding national security carry influence for their potential impact on not only the foreign environment but the domestic one as well. It is simply a matter of immensity[19] that cannot be ignored. Moreover, each of the branches of the armed forces has developed important and influential allies in Congress, particularly in the four military committees of Congress that traditionally serve as conduits for translating Pentagon requests into legislation. The military-congressional alliance has not always worked to the advantage of either the secretary of defense or the president, since the alliance has often enabled the uniformed services to fight for policies and programs (for example, weapons systems) that are at variance with the wishes of the civilian leadership.[20] The alliance has also on occasion made the defense establishment appear fragmented and divided by exacerbating interservice rivalries. Still, in the larger context of policy making, the ability of the military establishment to draw on support from influential segments of the legislative branch of government has contributed to its importance in the making of foreign policy.

Each branch of the uniformed military services is organized as a separate department within the DOD and headed by a civilian secretary appointed by the president. As suggested by the department's organization chart (Figure 11.2), the civilian secretaries operate under the control, direction, and authority of the secretary of defense (who operates under the authority of the president). As a practical matter, the responsibility and authority of the civilian secretaries of the Army, Navy, and Air Force have waned considerably during the past four decades as the power of the office of the secretary of defense has grown. Caspar W. Weinberger, President Reagan's secretary of defense, pledged to reverse that trend by involving the service secretaries more intimately in the management of Pentagon business, but it remained clear who was in charge.[21]

The senior military man within each military department is responsible for advising his civilian secretary on military matters and for maintaining the efficiency and operational readiness of the military forces under his command. Known collectively as the joint chiefs of staff (JCS), these men—the chief of staff of the Army, the chief of staff of the Air Force, the chief of naval operations, and the commandant of the Marine Corps (who heads a separate service within the Department of the Navy, as shown in Figure 11.2)—are statuto-

---

[19]The description is from Borklund (1968: 95–97), who provides interesting data on what it means to be huge. His description of DOD's headquarters will suffice to make the point; the Pentagon "is one of the largest office buildings in the world, covering, under one roof, 17½ miles of corridors running into and around 83 acres of offices, drafting rooms, tabulating sections, storerooms, laboratories, libraries, restaurants, auditoriums, dispensaries, banks, a shopping center, a printing plant, and even its own fire department." It is also interesting to note that since the Pentagon was built, DOD has outgrown its physical capacity.

[20]An interesting example was provided in 1963 when General Curtis LeMay, chief of staff of the Air Force, expressed doubt about the wisdom of concluding a nuclear test-ban treaty with the Soviet Union at precisely the time the Kennedy administration was negotiating such a treaty.

[21]See Daleski (1980) for a discussion of the role of the service secretaries in defense management.

FIGURE 11.2 Department of Defense Organization Chart

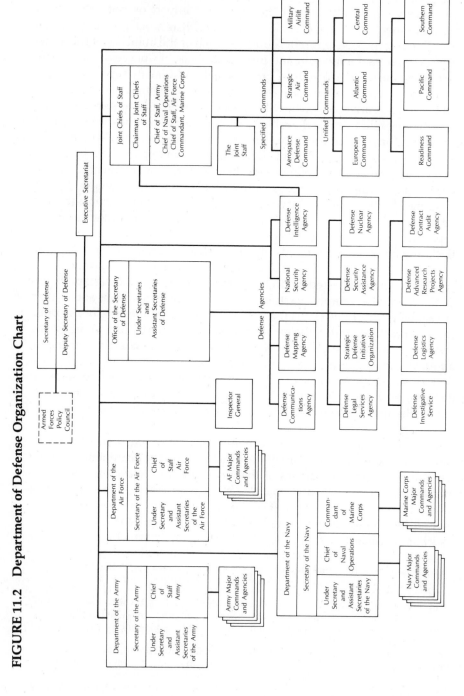

SOURCE: *The United States Government Manual, 1985–86*, 1985: 836.

rily the principal military advisers to the president, the National Security Council, and the secretary of defense.

The chairman of the joint chiefs is appointed by the president, with the advice and consent of the Senate, from among the officers of the uniformed services. The chairman takes precedence over all other officers of the armed forces. As a body, the joint chiefs are responsible, among other things, for preparing strategic plans and providing strategic and operational direction to the armed forces, and for advising the secretary of defense on military requirements as they relate to budget making, military assistance programs, industrial mobilization plans, and programs of scientific research and development.[22] They are assisted in their tasks by a joint staff comprising some 400 officers selected from each branch of the armed forces. As a practical matter, the joint chiefs have often drawn heavily on the ideas and recommendations of the staffs of each branch of the armed forces. The policy proposals of the joint chiefs have often reflected the compromises and logrolling inherent in any bureaucratic operation.

The prominence of the joint chiefs has varied over time. In the immediate postwar period, for example, President Truman used the JCS to defend major political as well as military decisions, including the NATO alliance, Truman's firing of General Douglas MacArthur, and the carrying out of "limited" war in Korea. Under Eisenhower the joint chiefs provided political support for the administration's military strategy of massive retaliation, but their overall prominence was somewhat reduced, presumably because President Eisenhower was his own best military adviser.

During the early part of Robert McNamara's term as defense secretary, a combination of President Kennedy's disenchantment with the advice of the joint chiefs at the time of the Bay of Pigs fiasco and McNamara's mastery of modern management techniques led influence within the Pentagon to gravitate toward the civilian leadership and away from the professional military. The trend was reversed during the Vietnam War, when the joint chiefs re-emerged as a voice for the military independent of the secretary of defense, as manifested by the eventual inclusion of the chairman of the JCS in President Johnson's Tuesday Lunch group (a move rumored to have been to counterbalance McNamara's increasingly dovelike stand on the war).

Nixon and Ford likewise gave the JCS a relatively prominent role, but one that again was challenged during the Carter administration. Under the tutelage of Harold Brown, the secretary's Office of Program Analysis and Evaluation, which McNamara's "whiz kids" had used to assert civilian control over the military, grew to be bigger and more powerful than at any time since the 1960s. (Brown himself was one of the original "whiz kids.") As a consequence, the secretary of defense often appeared not to advocate the military's views, or to defend them, at the White House. The joint chiefs of staff op-

[22]Kester (1982) provides a useful discussion of the role of the joint chiefs in the making of national security policy.

posed the Carter administration's decision to cancel the B-1 bomber, for example, and also its decision (later reversed) to withdraw American troops gradually from South Korea. Subsequently, the Reagan administration sought to give the joint chiefs a greater role in policy development and management, but Defense Secretary Weinberger likewise either ignored or went against the joint chiefs on such major issues as the basing mode for the MX missile and the Rapid Deployment Force.

At issue is the quality of advice that the joint chiefs provide civilian leaders (which Harold Brown once described as "worse than nothing") and, more broadly, their capacity to command the separate and powerful military services. General David C. Jones, chairman of the joint chiefs of staff from 1978 to 1982, became catalyst to a 1980s defense reform movement when, in his final testimony before Congress, he charged that "the fundamental balance of influence within the defense establishment is oriented too much toward the individual services" and concluded that "fundamental defense deficiencies cannot be solved with dollars alone." A year later, General Edward C. Meyer, chief of staff of the army, sounded a similar theme: "If we were trying to convince an enemy that we were able to go to war with a system that works like this, he would laugh." Robert W. Komer, under secretary of defense for policy in the Carter administration, predicted that "a system which is so inadequate in peacetime will perform even worse in crisis or war."[23] A 1985 study by the staff of the Senate Armed Services committee confirmed that prognosis when it blamed poor interservice coordination for the failure of the 1980 Iranian hostage rescue mission and for shortcomings in the 1983 invasion of Grenada.

Interservice rivalry and parochial interests underlie the seeming paralysis of the JCS system. "Dual-hatting" sums up much of the problem. This refers to the fact that each service chief wears two hats, one as leader of his own service, the other as a member of the joint chiefs. This requires, in the words of General John W. Vessey, successor to General Jones as chairman of the joint chiefs, that the chiefs "be able to hang their service loyalties and prejudices on the hat rack outside the Joint Chiefs' meeting room." Only in this way can they give military advice from a "national perspective." The evidence suggests they are unable to give such advice if it threatens their own service's budgets or military missions.

The problem permeates the joint staff as well. Called "purple suiters" because they are supposed to represent all of the services with impartiality (as opposed to the "green-suiters," "white-suiters," and "blue-suiters," who typically reflect the views of their respective services), members of the joint staff run the risk of being "too purple," of forgetting what the colors of their uniforms really mean to the detriment of their own careers. Because the individual services, not the joint chiefs, control promotions, money, and person-

---

[23]A particularly biting criticism came from Jeffrey Record (1984), who charged that "America's military record since Inchon has been one of persistent professional malpractice that in any other profession would constitute grounds for disbarment, denial of tenure or legal action."

nel, "few incentives exist for an officer assigned to joint duty to do more than punch his or her ticket and then get back into a service assignment" (Jones, 1984).

The problem is compounded by the fact that the senior military officers of each of the three services who make up the joint chiefs of staff do not command combat forces in the field. They are an essentially administrative unit outside the operational chain of command. The actual command of combat forces in the field rests with nine commanders-in-chief (CINCs),[24] who receive their orders from the president as commander-in-chief through the secretary of defense. The joint chiefs of staff have no independent role in this chain of command, despite its often bizzare twists and turns.

> When the Marine headquarters in Beirut was blown up [in 1983], for example, the Marine Corps commandant . . . was not responsible for security there; the Marines reported to officers offshore, who reported to "unified" commanders in London, Naples, Stuttgart and Belgium, who in turn were responsible to Defense Secretary Caspar W. Weinberger and President Reagan.
>
> In the Persian Gulf, the five-ship Middle East task force reports to an Army general in Florida who heads the Central Command. But if the task force runs into trouble, support would have to come from an aircraft carrier in the northern Arabian Sea that would take orders from an admiral in—depending on the ship—Hawaii or Virginia. If the carrier battle group could not handle the problem, the first reinforcements probably would be European-based forces controlled by an Army general outside Brussels and his deputy, an Air Force general in Stuttgart. (Hiatt, 1984b: 7)

Various proposals to correct deficiencies in the military advisory and command systems have been made, and in 1986 Congress seemed poised to make some major changes. Until then, even comparatively modest ones, like making the chairman of the joint chiefs a member of the National Security Council and placing him in the chain of command, had run into strong opposition from the military services and their congressional allies. Proponents of reform argue that the jockeying among the uniformed services results in advice so watered down to accommodate interservice differences as to be useless. Opponents counter that a more unified military system would cut civilian policy makers off from competing viewpoints. Navy Secretary John F. Lehman vigorously opposed military reform with the argument that a "general staff"—often pejoratively called a "Prussian-style general staff"—"would very seriously diminish civilian control of the military" and would be "unlikely to improve efficiency."

From Lehman's perspective, the issue of military reform is fundamentally a question of protecting bureaucratic turf. For forty years the Navy has been

---

[24]There are six geographically oriented unified commands, the Atlantic, Pacific, European, Southern, Readiness, and Central commands, and three Air Force organizations, the Strategic Air Command, the Aerospace Defense Command, and the Military Airlift Command.

the most vigorous opponent of a more integrated military which might undercut the present "services-dominated architecture." The reason appears to lie in the fact that the Navy is the most strategically independent of the three service branches, with its own air force (in naval aviation), army (the Marine Corps), and, of course, navy. In contrast, the Army, the most dependent of the three services, has been the greatest supporter of reform, and the Air Force, with some missions it cannot support without others, has been in between (Jones, 1984).

Whatever the weaknesses of the current structure of military advice, command, and coordination and their effects on the balance within DOD between the secretary of defense and the joint chiefs, more fundamental is the question of their combined influence within the policy-making process. The postwar record of American foreign policy is replete with evidence of a military approach to foreign affairs. Although Vietnam may have challenged the supremacy of the military, the security culture of the 1980s points toward a resurgence of military thinking about political problems to which Vietnam itself stands as a monument. Its manifestations are clear: unprecedented levels of peacetime military spending, military intervention in Grenada, a "peacekeeping force" in Lebanon, and "shows of force" in the Caribbean, Central America, the Persian Gulf, and elsewhere.

Military thinking is often said to dominate discussions of the means necessary to realize foreign policy goals. The reason is not that the military somehow dominates the civilian centers of power (for it does not). Indeed, during the post-Vietnam decade military professionals were usually depicted as cautious about military interventions abroad because of their sensitivity to the costs and risks involved.[25]

Instead, civilian leaders often approach international problems "in a specially tough, macho, or militaristic spirit" that stresses the use of raw military power and lets questions of strategy dominate diplomacy (Kattenburg, 1980). This viewpoint traces the roots of military machismo to the psychological reactions of individuals to the circumstances they experience in their environments and to the beliefs they maintain about those experiences (see chapter fourteen for an elaboration of the psychological dimensions of decision-making behavior). Among those beliefs and experiences shared among civilian policy makers since World War II have been a "deep respect for military effectiveness and efficiency"; a "belief in the capacity of U.S. military forces to accomplish virtually any mission"; "fear of being perceived as weak"; "fear of losing policy control to military leaders"; and a "belief that the fame of states was a game of men" (Kattenburg, 1980).

---

[25]Secretary of State Shultz, for example, was a strong Reagan administration advocate of using military force as an instrument of diplomacy, and it was the State Department that pushed for American intervention in Grenada, which the joint chiefs of staff resisted. Similarly, National Security Adviser Robert McFarlane (a retired Marine Corps lieutenant colonel) was a strong advocate of American intervention in Lebanon, and both he and Shultz favored retaliation for the October 1983 suicide truck bombing of U.S. marines in Beirut; Defense Secretary Weinberger and the joint chiefs opposed retaliation.

The propensity toward military thinking shared by virtually all postwar presidents and those on whom they have depended can also be explained by societal and external factors. Writing while the United States was still enmeshed in Vietnam, a former deputy assistant secretary of defense for international security affairs, Adam Yarmolinsky (1971), makes the case cogently. Among the factors Yarmolinsky cites as having favored military considerations and military logic is the trust the American people came to place in the judgment of professional military men. That trust, in turn, reflected Cold War antagonism toward what was perceived as aggressive Soviet expansionism. "It is hard to conceive, under the circumstances, how reasonable men in the executive branch could have developed or espoused any policies other than those emphasizing military security, enemy capabilities, and readiness for worst contingencies." In such a context deference to the military establishment "was merely one by-product of the forces that produced the policies themselves" (Yarmolinsky, 1971).

Yarmolinsky also observes that the involvement of the Pentagon and the military in foreign policy making had the effect of intertwining rationales for certain foreign policies with rationales for increased defense spending. And as defense spending increased, what Kattenburg (1980) describes as "the abundant availability and pervasiveness of all forms of military power" also increased. So, too, did domestic political support for the maintenance of the defense establishment.

The process continues. During the first Reagan administration alone, some $1 trillion was spent on national defense to support more than 3 million military and civilian employees of military agencies who came to depend directly on the military establishment for their livelihoods. To their ranks must be added the more than 850,000 people employed (in 1982) in defense-oriented industries and the tens of thousands more who depend on military contracts for their livelihoods.[26] In 1983, for example, the Defense Department spent over $140 billion for supplies, services, and construction in all of the fifty states. If to that the normal multiplier effect of government expenditures is added, the number of Americans dependent directly or indirectly on the maintenance of a large military establishment, even in peacetime, would probably reach well beyond 10 million people, or about 9 percent of the total labor force. Compare the defense sector to the sizable agricultural and construction industries, which together employed less than 8 million people in 1984. Sheer immensity thus becomes a matter of unassailable political clout. Unlike the State Department, the clientele groups (supporters of agencies who often are served by or receive benefits from the agencies) of the military establishment are not "faceless foreigners" somewhere "out there." They are members of the American electorate.

---

[26]Duchin (1983: 546) estimates that in 1977 military spending resulted in the indirect employment of 2.02 million people beyond those directly involved in defense-related agencies. See *The Defense Monitor* (September–October 1977) for a critical evaluation of the role of military spending in generating nonmilitary employment.

In the final analysis, however, even though policy makers sometimes make foreign policy decisions with an eye to their domestic consequences (recall chapter nine), the relative importance of military thinking in foreign policy making will not be determined simply by the sheer size of the military establishment, enormous as it may be, but by the way in which it is viewed by the American public in general, and civilian policy makers in particular. Call it the "martial spirit," "military machismo," or some other epithet, the correlates and consequences remain the same:

> The influence of the military establishment on domestic politics or the domestic economy may be functions of its budget or size or power, but its influence on foreign policy depends on an altogether different variable—the extent to which civilians in the executive branch, in Congress, and among the public bear in mind or forget General George C. Marshall's maxim that political problems, if thought about in military terms, become military problems. (Yarmolinsky, 1971: 133)

THE INTELLIGENCE COMMUNITY

Like the military, the intelligence community has played a prominent role in postwar American foreign policy because of the preferences of elected officials and their advisers. As Bobby Inman, former deputy director of central intelligence, observed on his retirement from government service in 1982, "every administration ultimately turns to the use of covert operations when they become frustrated about the lack of success with diplomatic initiatives and are unwilling to use military force."

The intelligence community itself is a vast complex of operating agencies and interagency and oversight committees. The agencies involved are depicted in Figure 11.3,[27] which also suggests that primary responsibility for managing the community rests with the director of central intelligence, who is also director of the Central Intelligence Agency (although, as will be seen, the director's managerial role is less overwhelming than the figure perhaps suggests). His authority is exercised through chairmanship of the National Foreign Intelligence Board (NFIB), the body made up of the principals of all the components of the intelligence community, and he, in turn, is responsible to

---

[27]The term "intelligence community" "connotes a good deal more harmony and commonality of goals and views than actually exists. Indeed, tribal and feudal metaphors often seem more appropriate in describing how the various collection, processing, and analytic organizations interact with one another and with policymakers" (Flanagan, 1985). Similarly, the visual impression conveyed by Figure 11.3 belies the complexity of the community. In one of several reorganizations undertaken during the 1970s, for example, President Nixon ordered creation of a National Cryptological Command under the auspices of the National Security Agency, which resulted in the Central Security Service consisting of the National Security Agency and units from the Army, Navy, and Air Force intelligence organizations. The 1971 reorganization also led to the creation of the Defense Mapping Agency and the Defense Investigation Service. The former combined the separate mapping, charting, and geodetic organizations of the military services, while the latter combined the various Defense Department personnel security investigatory units into a single office. See Richelson (1985) for a detailed description of the complex network of institutions that are involved in the United States's intelligence effort.

FIGURE 11.3   **The Intelligence Community**

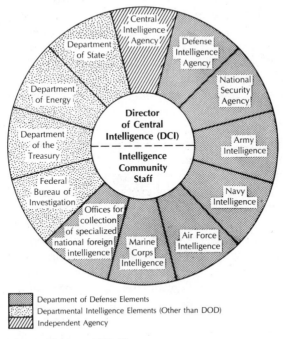

Department of Defense Elements
Departmental Intelligence Elements (Other than DOD)
Independent Agency

SOURCE: Central Intelligence Agency, 1985: 20.

the National Security Council, and through it, to the president. During the Carter administration, the director of central intelligence was also given unprecedented responsibility for creating a consolidated national intelligence budget, and he chaired the NSC Policy Review Committee, whose purpose it was to determine priority guidelines for intelligence activities, among other tasks. Advice was proffered by the National Foreign Intelligence Board, consisting of the director of central intelligence and the agencies with operating responsibilities, and oversight was provided by an Intelligence Oversight Board, with the attorney general given the task of determining the legality of intelligence operations of questionable propriety.

Under President Reagan, who reorganized the intelligence community via Executive Order 12333 in 1981, the National Foreign Intelligence Board continued to serve in a coordination and review role, and the Intelligence Oversight Board was retained, but its mandate was restricted to matters of legality, not matters of propriety.[28] Paralleling Carter's Policy Review Committee, a Senior Interagency Group-Intelligence (SIG-I) was given responsibility "to advise

[28]This is despite the fact that the 1975–1976 congressional hearings on the CIA questioned the propriety of its actions as much as their legality. "[A]pparently," write Turner and Thibault (1982), "an impression exists that less scrutiny will somehow result in better intelligence." Their

and assist the NSC in discharging its authority and responsibility for intelligence policy and intelligence matters." Reagan also revived the President's Foreign Intelligence Advisory Board (PFIAB), which Carter had abolished in 1976. Made up of citizens appointed by the president from outside the government, the PFIAB's mandate was to review the performance of those agencies involved in intelligence collection, production, and evaluation and the execution of intelligence policy. Under Reagan the board reportedly focused attention on technology transfer and counterintelligence issues (Flanagan, 1985). The House and Senate intelligence committees also performed oversight roles under both Carter and Reagan. Following earlier precedents, legislation passed in 1980 requires the president to keep Congress "fully and currently informed" of all intelligence activities.

The concern for control, legality, and oversight reflects response to revelations of abuses committed over the past quarter of a century by intelligence agencies, including illegal activities against American citizens as well as questionable operations overseas.[29] Carter's reorganization of the intelligence community in 1978, the purpose of which was to establish top-level control, direction, and coordination over this labyrinthine community, was only one in a series of similar moves undertaken in the 1970s by others. For the Central Intelligence Agency (CIA), the key intelligence institution, the result was an "identity crisis" that made the agency unsure of itself and its mission. Besides the decline in morale, the efforts may have affected adversely the willingness of intelligence officers to take risks in pursuit of their convictions about key issues and ideas out of fear they might bring further disrepute to the CIA (Turner and Thibault, 1982). Following Reagan's first election in 1980, however, a number of restrictions were lifted. The intelligence community, with the CIA at the vanguard, enjoyed a resurgence not only as a servant of American foreign policy, but also as a substitute for it in certain world regions, notably Central America and Southwest Asia.

Indicative of the new mood was the intelligence oversight legislation passed in 1980. What began in 1978 as a comprehensive bill designed to provide a statutory basis for the national intelligence activities of the United States ended up as "no more than a few fence posts around which the intelligence agencies may pass with little effort" (Johnson, 1980). The principal

---

observation is reinforced by other Reagan administration changes that dropped "requirements both for clearing sensitive collection operations with the NSC and for conducting an annual NSC review" as well as relaxation of controls designed "to constrain intrusions into the lives of Americans." See Clarke and Neveleff (1984) for a discussion of changes made during the Reagan administration in regulations governing the intelligence community insofar as they relate to the balance between the protection of civil liberties and the demands of national security.

[29]Many trace the roots of intelligence abuses to the top-secret sixty-nine-page report that Lieutenant General James Doolittle submitted to President Eisenhower in 1954, which urged the Central Intelligence Agency to become "more ruthless" than the Soviet KGB, and which asserted that "if the United States is to survive, long-standing American concepts of 'fair-play' must be reconsidered."

change was the repeal of the 1974 Hughes-Ryan Amendment, which required that covert CIA operations be reported to as many as eight congressional committees "in a timely fashion." The new law required that only the Senate and House intelligence committees be informed of covert actions. And while the law reaffirmed the principle of congressional oversight, it also permitted the president discretion to limit prior congressional notification and specifically denied Congress the right to disapprove intelligence operations.

Despite the legal restraints imposed in the oversight legislation, Congress itself subsequently concluded it had been deluded by the intelligence community. The issue was Nicaragua. For some time following the Sandinistas' rise to power in 1979, the CIA had been engaged in a "secret" effort to subvert the new government by means little short of supporting widespread warfare against the Nicaraguan regime. As part of its program designed to support Nicaraguan insurgents (often referred to as contras), the agency in 1984 supported the mining of Nicaragua's harbors—and did so without properly informing Congress as required by law, which, as noted above, obliges the intelligence community to keep Congress "fully and currently informed" of all intelligence activities, including "any significant anticipated activity." In addition, the 1982 Boland Amendment (to the 1983 appropriations act) specifically prohibited the use of CIA or Defense Department funds "for the purpose of overthrowing the Government of Nicaragua." The congressional response to the CIA's defiance of the relevant legal requirements was reminiscent of the Vietnam years. Barry Goldwater, chair of the Senate's Intelligence Committee, castigated the CIA's director for the Nicaraguan operation, and Senator Moynihan, vice chair of the committee, announced his intent to resign to "express my view that the Senate Committee was not properly briefed on the mining of Nicaraguan harbors with American mines from an American ship under American command." Congressman Norman Mineta, a member of the House intelligence committee, expressed the perennial congressional dilemma more colorfully—and perhaps more to the point: "We are like mushrooms. They keep us in the dark and feed us a lot of manure."[30]

Intelligence Operations and the Department of Defense

Apart from the administrative units which make up the intelligence community, its precise size in terms of money and personnel remains uncertain owing to the secrecy in which the community and its activities are shrouded. One widely cited estimate puts the number of personnel in the early 1970s at

---

[30]Congressional pique was fueled by revelations in October 1984 that the CIA had produced a psychological warfare manual which recommended to the contras the use of violence, perhaps assassination, to achieve their political goals in Nicaragua. Such methods were perceived to be in violation of the CIA's policies and of presidential orders as stated in Executive Order 12333. In addition to the discussion in chapter twelve, see the Senate's *Report of the Select Committee on Intelligence* (1985) for a useful synopsis of the Central American issues as viewed from a congressional perspective.

153,250, with annual expenditures slightly in excess of $6.2 billion (Marchetti and Marks, 1974: 80). Although the figures shown were "sanitized" by the CIA prior to publication, comparisons with other estimates suggest they bear some relation to reality.[31]

In the decade following publication of these data, the resources available to the intelligence community first continued a declining trend begun earlier and then later increased dramatically. *Newsweek* (October 10, 1983: 38), for example, reports that the intelligence community's budget grew 17 percent annually during the first three years of the Reagan administration, which is even faster than the Pentagon's growth, and the Senate Intelligence Committee reports that the fiscal 1985 budget "authorized the largest budget in the history of the . . . Intelligence Community" (*Report of the Select Committee on Intelligence*, 1985: 3). The figure is believed to have been about $9 billion (Taubman, 1984: 5b; *Congressional Quarterly Almanac, 1984*, 1985: 119). Of this amount the CIA is reported to have accounted for $2 billion, the National Security Agency (NSA) $4 billion, and the National Reconnaissance Office (NRO) $2.5 billion (Taubman, 1984: 5b).[32]

Personnel figures are more difficult to corroborate. Victor Marchetti and John Marks qualify their estimates of CIA personnel, for example, with the observation that the agency itself does not know how many employees it has.

> [Our estimate of 16,500] does not reflect the tens of thousands who serve under contract (mercenaries, agents, consultants, etc.) or who work for the agency's proprietary companies. Past efforts to total up the number of foreign agents have never

---

[31]The estimates by Marchetti and Marks are comparable to estimates cited by Senator William Proxmire in 1973 (cited in Esterline and Black, 1975), while those for the CIA are comparable to figures cited by Ransom (1970), perhaps the leading academic authority on the intelligence community. One of the supplementary staff reports of the Senate Select Committee to Study U.S. Intelligence Activities (the Church Committee) also cites the Marchetti and Marks estimates. The report adds an important qualifier to these data, however: "Such statistics provide some indication of the size of the immediate intelligence community within the Federal government but, of course, ignore the commitment of resources to intelligence efforts, on one hand, by front groups, proprietary organizations [e.g., Radio Free Europe and Radio Liberty], and informers, and, on the other hand, by sub-national government agencies, and other Federal entities (such as Department of Agriculture overseas attachés, National Aeronautics and Space Administration satellite launching systems, and the products of the National Weather Service). With these additional components identified, the pervasive nature of the intelligence organization begins to become more apparent" (*Final Report*, VI, 1986: 290–291).

[32]The fall and then rise of the intelligence budget became a matter of public controversy when President Reagan in 1984 asserted that "the near destruction of our intelligence capability" was partly responsible for the car bombing of the U.S. embassy in Beirut in September of that year. He later explained to Jimmy Carter, who demanded an apology for the comment, that he had not meant to suggest that "you or your Administration was responsible for the decline in intelligence-gathering capability" or for the Beirut bombing. White House press spokesman Larry Speakes later suggested that Reagan had been talking about "a decade-long trend and climate in Congress." Senator Moynihan responded that the comment "undermines—I am prepared to say betrays—almost a decade of sustained bipartisan efforts in Congress to reconstruct an intelligence community whose budgets had run down steadily through the first half of the 1970s and began to rise sharply in the second." See Pickett (1985) for a discussion of the role of Congress in the reversal during the latter part of Carter's administration of the downward trend in the intelligence community's funding.

resulted in precise figures because of the inordinate secrecy and compartmentalization practiced by the Clandestine Services [a subunit of CIA formally known as the Directorate of Operations]. (Marchetti and Marks, 1974: 58)[33]

Although difficult to pinpoint, the number of people comprising the intelligence community, like its budget, has doubtless fluctuated widely in the recent past. Bobby Inman, then deputy director of central intelligence, testified before Congress in 1982 that "the intelligence establishment was cut back sharply in the 1960s and 1970s after a major buildup in the 1950s, losing 40 percent of its personnel from 1964 to the mid-1970s." By the mid-1980s, however, previous cutbacks had been restored and probably surpassed. By then the CIA's work force was reported to have been about 19,000 (which again would appear not to include contract employees) and the National Security Agency's over 60,000 (Taubman, 1984: 5b).

The foregoing makes clear that the Defense Department is the largest executive agency in the intelligence business, consuming as it does 75 percent or more of the federal intelligence budget (see also *Final Report*, I, 1976: 328-340). The intelligence operations of the various branches of the armed services, the Defense Intelligence Agency, and the supersecret National Security Agency/Central Security Service (NSA/CSS) are the actual intelligence organizations. The latter appears to be the biggest spender.

Created by a classified presidential directive in 1952, the NSA was not even generally acknowledged as a government organization until 1957. Even today, references to it in government documents are hard to find and deficient in detail. Some sense of the magnitude of its operation is suggested by the fact that the capitol building in Washington, which houses the legislative body of the world's largest democracy, contains 718,740 square feet. In contrast, NSA's headquarters in Fort George Meade, Maryland, encompasses 1,912,000 square feet (Pett, 1984: 8-B). Moreover, its budget may be far greater than the $4 billion reported above. Signal intelligence, communications security, and cryptology—code breaking and code making—are NSA's main responsibilities. If all of the nation's military and civilian programs in these areas are combined, NSA's budget may be as high as $10 billion (Bamford, 1983: 109).

NSA's operations are extraordinarily technology-intensive, and it has developed a massive bank of computers believed to be the largest and most advanced available to any bureaucracy in the world (Burnham, 1983). In addition to "intercepting, 'traffic analyzing,' and cryptanalyzing the messages of all other nations, presumably friend as well as foe," and ensuring the security of United States messages, NSA is charged with maintaining "order and coherence among the various cryptosystems of the CIA, the State Department, the FBI, the armed services, and other governmental agencies" (Ransom, 1970).

---

[33]Other estimates of the size and expenditures of various components of the intelligence community can be found in Bamford (1983), *Newsweek* (February 6, 1978), *Newsweek* (October 10, 1983), Richelson (1985), Taubman (1983), and *U.S. News and World Report* (June 25, 1984).

The NSA operates under the direction, authority, and control of the secretary of defense.

Next in size by expenditures is the National Reconnaissance Office, whose existence was first revealed in 1973 when its name was inadvertently included in a declassified congressional document (Richelson, 1985). NRO manages the nation's satellite reconnaissance programs. It operates under the "cover" of the Air Force, which reportedly pays the bills for the extremely costly photographic and electronic reconnaissance satellites and the rockets necessary to put them into orbit. Replacing the spy planes (for example, the U-2) and spy ships (for example, the *Pueblo*) of the 1960s, reconnaissance satellites have become the single most important source of technical intelligence data gathered by the United States. Employing high-resolution and wide-angle cameras, the photographic satellites have for years provided enormous amounts of detailed information on military and related strategic developments within the Soviet Union and China, while the electronic sensing tasks of the reconnaissance satellites have been oriented toward gathering data on missile testing, on radars and the emissions of other electronic equipment, and on communications traffic (Marchetti and Marks, 1974). The intelligence gathered by reconnaissance satellites is shared throughout the intelligence community.

Like NSA, the Defense Intelligence Agency (DIA) also operates under the authority of the secretary of defense. Created by Robert McNamara in 1961, the DIA was intended to consolidate the various intelligence units of the armed services. The latter are involved in the collection of "departmental" intelligence as opposed to "national" intelligence; that is, they are involved in collecting information germane to their tactical missions. In so doing, however, their intelligence product has often been skewed in the direction preferred by their parent organizations for "budgeteering" purposes.

> Thus the air force saw the development of a "bomber gap" and then a "missile gap" which never materialized. The navy was inclined to exaggerate Soviet naval power, and the army was often found estimating a number of Russian army divisions that existed only on paper. All of these activities tended to inflate budgetary requests and fundamentally to challenge the decision-making authority of the Secretary of Defense, particularly vis-à-vis Congress. (Ransom, 1970: 103–104)

The DIA was designed to provide direct intelligence assistance to the secretary of defense and the joint chiefs of staff, an assignment that required improved coordination and management of Defense Department intelligence resources. Moreover, it was assumed that the DIA would take over many of the functions of the armed forces intelligence units. This has never happened. Although the functions assigned the DIA appear to place it in a superior position compared to the Army, Navy, and Air Force, the DIA collects little information on its own, relying instead on the service intelligence agencies for its raw intelligence data (Marchetti and Marks, 1974). The service agencies thus have continued to flourish. President Ford appeared to recognize this, for in reorganizing the intelligence community he placed the service agencies at the same level in the community's organization chart as the DIA, rather than as three separate units under the DIA as previously had been the case. The implication was that the armed forces intelligence units are relatively independent. But following the principle that bureaucracies seldom disappear, the DIA continues to exist, even though it may lack a unique role within the larger network of intelligence agencies.[34]

Intelligence Operations and the Department of State

The State Department's Bureau of Intelligence and Research (INR) is at the other end of the (estimated) expenditure spectrum from the DOD. State's intelligence functions arise naturally out of its general foreign affairs responsibilities, and much of what the department routinely does in the way of analyzing and interpreting information might be regarded as intelligence work.[35] INR is the focus of such activity as it relates to the larger intelligence community, for it is through that bureau that State makes its input into the various interagency committees that seek to guide intelligence operations. The director of the Bureau of Intelligence and Research is also the senior in-house intelligence adviser to the secretary of state.

In addition to representing the State Department within the intelligence community, the National Security Council also once assigned INR the duty of collecting, analyzing, and disseminating overt intelligence information on political, economic, cultural, and sociological developments abroad for the entire intelligence community. Despite those functions, and the otherwise important place of the State Department in the intelligence community, INR does not engage in the collection of intelligence other than through normal cable traffic and reporting from overseas posts. It depends on input from other agencies, which its small staff then turns into finished intelligence reports. Within the intelligence community, therefore, the State Department has been more a consumer than a producer of intelligence. That fact alone should lead us to expect that State is in a relatively disadvantageous position in the highly competitive intelligence establishment. The small size of its intelligence operation tends to confirm the conjecture.

---

[34]Campbell (1971) makes the scathing observation that the DIA "has not been a serious contender for influence in Washington since its founding in 1961, because much of its work has been regarded by other members of the intelligence community as sloppy and frequently inaccurate. Richelson (1985) concludes that while "abolition of the DIA has often been suggested," it is an "unlikely" outcome in part because "the DIA continues to be the prime intelligence component of the DOD with respect to strategic intelligence."

[35]Paralleling the earlier discussion of the State Department's bureaucratic subculture, Rubin (1985) observes that "Because INR is seen as a specialized and research-oriented bureau outside the policy-making chain of command, many FSOs consider an INR assignment detrimental to their careers."

Intelligence Operations and Other Departments and Agencies

The Treasury Department, the Energy Department, and the Federal Bureau of Investigation (FBI) are the remaining officially designated members of the intelligence community. All play an important role in intelligence operations, although none is concerned primarily with the collection of foreign intelligence.

Treasury's intelligence activities derive in part from the collection of foreign economic intelligence by its overseas attachés. More specific intelligence activities derive from the department's responsibilities for protecting (by the U.S. Secret Service) the president, presidential candidates, and certain foreign dignitaries; for controlling (through the Bureau of Alcohol, Tobacco, and Firearms and the U.S. Customs Service) illegal trafficking in alcohol, tobacco, firearms, and other articles entering international trade and for protecting against terrorism in international transportation facilities; and for ensuring compliance (through the Internal Revenue Service) with the Internal Revenue laws. Executing those functions has often resulted in the use of undercover personnel, paid informants, and electronic surveillance operations (*Final Report*, IV, 1976).[36]

The Department of Energy, operating through an assistant secretary for defense programs, is responsible for conducting nuclear weapons research, development, production, and surveillance programs. In the latter capacity, it is responsible for verifying compliance with treaties limiting nuclear tests and with foreign nuclear weapons technology analysis. Historically that function has involved it in monitoring nuclear explosions abroad through overseas listening posts and measuring radioactivity in the atmosphere. The department is also responsible for the overt collection of intelligence on energy policies and developments abroad that may affect the United States, and for monitoring compliance with nuclear nonproliferation policies.

The Federal Bureau of Investigation, like the Treasury Department, historically has not engaged directly in overseas intelligence operations, although it does assign agents to overseas posts. Domestic counterintelligence is the FBI's major intelligence function, and the bureau has jurisdiction in the investigation of espionage, sabotage, treason, and other internal security matters. The FBI is also responsible, in cooperation with the CIA, for counterintelligence

---

[36]Since the targets of such activities have often been American citizens, it would be inappropriate to label all of the activities as relating to the making and execution of foreign policy. As a practical matter, the line between foreign and domestic intelligence gathering is an amorphous one, which opens the intelligence community to charges of abuse. It was revealed in congressional testimony, for example, that for a time during the Nixon presidency, the Internal Revenue Service operated a Special Service Staff (SSS) initially designed to ensure that dissident groups were complying with the tax laws. By the time it was disbanded in 1973, a total of 11,458 SSS files had been generated on 8,585 individuals and 2,873 organizations. Those files were reportedly used as "a reference source for White House intelligence actors" as well as a means of identifying subjects for IRS scrutiny (*Final Report*, VI, 1976: 288–289). Alleged abuses of various intelligence agencies are detailed in *Final Report*, II, 1976; see also U.S. Commission on CIA Activities Within the United States, 1975, and various hearings of the Senate Select Committee on Presidential Campaign Activities, published in 1973.

outside the United States, and it works with the Defense Department in certain counterintelligence matters.

Although not formally designated members of the intelligence community, mention should be made of the Justice Department's Drug Enforcement Administration and of the Department of Commerce. Intelligence relating to illicit drug trafficking is a primary concern of the former. Both foreign and domestic aspects of narcotics production and trafficking fall within its jurisdiction. Technology transfer issues involve the Commerce Department. The Office of Intelligence Liaison links the department to the intelligence community in matters involving technology transfer intelligence (Richelson, 1985). Heightened national concern with drug trafficking and the protection of high-tech secrets led the CIA under William Casey also to become involved in these issues.

Central Intelligence Agency

Placing the CIA last in our discussion of executive intelligence agencies underscores the fact that the most widely known and notorious of intelligence organizations is far from the only one. Indeed, the estimates cited earlier suggest that the CIA constitutes less than 15 percent of the intelligence community. Its attention thus derives more from its reputation for "dirty tricks" and its assumption of the primary responsibility for covert political operations than from its size.

As the *central* in its name implies, the CIA was originally designed for something other than covert operations as its primary function. Successor to the World War II Office of Strategic Services (OSS), the CIA was conceived as the center of the various intelligence community activities and the coordinator of an integrated and coherent national intelligence operation. The Japanese attack on Pearl Harbor on December 7, 1941 revealed the necessity for such a centralized operation. Evidence of the impending Japanese aggression was available, but its form was so fragmented and its location so diffuse as to be useless for purposes of decision making.

The CIA was created by the National Security Act of 1947 as a subsidiary of the National Security Council with responsibilities for (1) advising the NSC on intelligence matters relating to national security; (2) making recommendations to the NSC for coordinating the intelligence activities of the various federal executive departments and agencies; (3) correlating and evaluating intelligence and providing for its dissemination; and (4) carrying out such additional services, functions, and duties relating to national security intelligence as the NSC might direct. Those responsibilities reflect the fact that the concept of a central intelligence organization evolved out of concern for the quality of intelligence analysis available to policy makers. Yet within a year of its creation, the CIA was charged with the conduct of covert psychological, political, paramilitary, and economic activities. The acquisition of a covert mission had a profound impact on the subsequent activities of the agency and ultimately on its relative political stature within the government.

The initial impetus for covert activity was provided by the increasingly hostile international political environment of the late 1940s and early 1950s. Subsequent policy directives and organizational adaptations contributed to the extensiveness of such activity. (The consequences in terms of external actions were discussed in chapter five.) Internally, the relative importance of clandestine activities within the CIA itself is documented by the fact that between 1962 and 1970, the budget of the Clandestine Services of the CIA averaged 52 percent of the agency's total budget, while roughly 55 percent of its personnel were assigned to such activities (*Final Report*, I, 1976: 121).

The years 1971 to 1975 were a transition period. Vietnam, public disclosures of CIA abuses of power (spurred in part by a more assertive Congress), and the shifting distribution of international power and officials' perceptions of the nation's role within the emergent power structure all contributed to an erosion of the foreign policy assumptions on which CIA clout within the policy-making community had come to be based. "The consensus that had existed among the press, the informed public, the Congress, and the Executive branch and that had both supported and protected the CIA broke down" (*Final Report*, I, 1976).

An outward manifestation of the crisis was a rapid succession of directors of central intelligence (DCIs)—Richard Helms, James Schlesinger, William Colby, George Bush, Stansfield Turner, and William Casey. (The latter, chief of secret intelligence in the OSS during World War II, was tapped for the CIA post after serving as Ronald Reagan's 1980 campaign manager and became the first DCI to enjoy cabinet rank.) Schlesinger and Colby, in particular, were concerned with carrying out management reforms that would enhance the CIA's communitywide role and provide improved intelligence to policy makers.[37] Colby's appointment was inopportune, however, since it coincided with public disclosures of CIA domestic spying (in violation of its foreign intelligence charter), including, for example, operation CHAOS (which was directed against domestic political dissidents from 1967 to 1974) and a massive mail rifling program conducted in partial cooperation with the FBI.

Clandestine activities also continued to be the bread and butter of the CIA. Despite reductions and reorientations, by 1975 clandestine activities still constituted 37 percent of the agency's total budget,[38] and its covert capabilities

---

[37]For details, see *Final Report*, IV (1976: 84–88) and Flanagan (1985).

[38]Johnson (1980: 145) cites a report by former CIA Director William Colby that covert actions—called "special activities" by both the Carter and Reagan administrations—consumed only 5 percent of the CIA's budget, presumably during the Carter administration. The *Wall Street Journal* (January 11, 1985: 9) used the same figure in a 1985 article in obvious reference to the Reagan administration. In both cases the figures represent such a sharp decline from the proportion reported for earlier time periods that it appears not to be comparable to them. Since covert actions constitute only one type of clandestine operation—the secret gathering of intelligence also falls into this category—the Colby figure would appear to cover only a restricted portion of the budgetary expenditure on clandestine activities.

were still intact—as illustrated by CIA activities against the Marxist Allende government in Chile (*Final Report*, I, 1976: 123). Those facts led the Senate committee examining foreign and military intelligence to conclude:

> The activities of the Clandestine Service have reflected not what the Agency can do well but what the demands of American foreign policy have required at particular times. The nature of covert operations, the priority accorded them by senior policy-makers, and the orientation and background of some DCIs have made the clandestine mission the preeminent activity within the organization. (*Final Report*, I, 1976: 124)

Allen Dulles, Richard Helms, and William Casey are known to have been intimately involved in the CIA's clandestine activities, which may cause conflicts of interest within the intelligence community and erode its credibility elsewhere in the government (Flanagan, 1985). At the same time, the coordination function implied by the *central* in CIA's name has taken a back seat. "The CIA's primary task is not to coordinate the efforts of U.S. intelligence or even to produce finished national intelligence for policy-makers," observe Marchetti and Marks (1974). "Its job is, for better or worse, to conduct the government's covert foreign policy." Correspondingly, the other activities of the agency have tended to overlap with those of other intelligence organizations. Although created in part to rectify the problem of duplication among the departmental intelligence services, the CIA has contributed to the problem rather than minimizing it by becoming yet another source of intelligence production. Moreover, the bureaucratic subculture operative in the CIA and elsewhere in the intelligence community militates against change:

> . . . intelligence officers often compartmentalize data collected by the sensitive methods of one agency and restrict dissemination to the rest of the community. This practice is rationalized by narrowly interpreting the "need-to-know" security guidelines. But the bottom line is that the bureaucratic culture underlying the American intelligence system does not now guarantee that all of what is collected is subject to community-wide, objective, and rigorous analysis. (Goodman, 1984–85: 173)

Although to date the CIA has been ineffective in communitywide coordination of the national intelligence function,[39] it has played an integral role in the various interagency groups functioning under presidential authority. Principal among those groups, of course, is the National Security Council, in which the director of central intelligence has historically been an active participant. The perceived importance of the DCI is also reflected in his inclusion in the various NSC interagency committees described in chapter 10.

As a practical matter, neither the president nor the NSC exercises control over the day-to-day management of the intelligence community. As noted ear-

---

[39]For a discussion of the coordination process in action, see the testimony in "The Role of Intelligence in the Foreign Policy Process" (1980).

lier, the DCI is formally charged with this responsibility, which has been exercised in different ways and via different institutional mechanisms historically. Under Turner and Casey, the National Foreign Intelligence Board (NFIB), the historic successor of the U.S. Intelligence Board (USIB), assisted the DCI in the production of national intelligence (as distinct from ''departmental'' intelligence, which is directly related to the missions of particular departments, such as the armed services, as noted earlier) and in establishing intelligence policy, requirements, plans, and priorities. Among his management tools in the production of national intelligence is the National Intelligence Council (NIC), consisting of a group of analysts and writers who bear special responsibility for National Intelligence Estimates (NIEs) and Special National Intelligence Estimates (SNIEs), the ''best judgments'' of the intelligence community on a particular subject.

The national foreign intelligence budget in principle gives the DCI a second important lever on his management responsibilities. In practice he has been unable to control the budget effectively. The DCI exercises independent authority only over the CIA's budget, which, as noted earlier, is a comparatively small portion of the whole pie. This has placed the DCI at a competitive disadvantage in dealing with the other intelligence agencies whose activities he in principle is to coordinate. Indeed, a congressional committee, noting that the DCI controlled ''less than 10 percent of the combined national and tactical intelligence efforts,'' described his influence over the allocation of the other 90 percent as ''limited, in effect, to that of an interested critic'' (cited in Bamford, 1983).

Ultimately, the issue is control of the intelligence community by the president, for whom the DCI is principal foreign intelligence adviser. Different presidents have approached the issue differently. President Nixon first charged the DCI with making recommendations for a consolidated national foreign intelligence budget, and he created the Intelligence Resources Advisory Committee (IRAC) to assist in that task. President Ford also sought to further enhance the DCI's role, particularly in allocation of national (as opposed to tactical or departmental) intelligence resources. Carter went farthest in enhancing the DCI's budgetary role, giving him ''full and exclusive authority over approval of the National Intelligence Program budget submitted to the President.'' To accomplish this task, the size of the intelligence community staff, which assists the DCI (as suggested in Figure 11.3), was considerably enlarged.

Not surprisingly, the other intelligence agencies were less than enthusiastic with Stansfield Turner's efforts to expand the DCI's communitywide role. They won the day when those who joined Reagan's administration with a strong penchant toward the military were able to curb the DCI's communitywide management role in favor of preserving DOD's historic independence.

The Reagan [intelligence community executive] order cast the DCI more in the role of a coordinator, rather than a manager, of Community affairs, and DCI Casey has adopted a more collegial, "board of directors" approach than his immediate predecessor. Casey reportedly relies on the advice of the National Foreign Intelligence Board, the council of leaders of the principal Community collection and production components, and uses "it more frequently to evaluate substantive issues." (Flanagan, 1985: 74)

Critics often have argued that bringing the tasks of intelligence gathering, analysis, and coordination under the authority of the head of the CIA may have a detrimental impact on the ultimate intelligence product:

> This consolidation exposes the entire intelligence community to the same political and cultural pressures, and reinforces the tendency of all elements to sway together with the mood of the moment. It has fostered a type of "group-think" where the pressures for unanimity override individual mental faculties—somewhat analogous to what occurs in a jury room. (Ellsworth and Adelman, 1979: 158)

The inability of the CIA to foresee the fall of the Shah of Iran in 1979 may have been related to the centralization of intelligence functions. As noted in a study by the House Intelligence Committee, the CIA was essentially caught in a conflict of interests: "On the one hand, the CIA had historically considered itself the Shah's booster. On the other hand, it was supposed to provide sound intelligence analysis of the Iranian political situation" (quoted in *Congressional Quarterly Almanac,* 1980, 1981). The merging of intelligence gathering and analysis in the DCI did little to enable the agency to separate its estimates of the Shah's survivability from its confidence in him, since the director of the CIA is simultaneously head of the agency that collected the information and the president's chief adviser in determining what the information means. The Iranian intelligence failure thus bore similarities to the 1961 Bay of Pigs fiasco, in which the CIA was responsible for both gathering intelligence and planning a program of action based on that information. Ultimately its commitment to the program led it to discount information that might have caused it to abandon the military option.

Iran and Cuba are only two instances of thirty or more intelligence failures investigated by Congress or the media since 1960 (Goodman, 1984–85: 162). Perhaps such failures are inevitable (Betts, 1978), but explaining why they occur is important nonetheless.

Iran and Cuba suggest that the inability of the intelligence establishment to provide policy makers with objective, timely, and accurate intelligence contributes to policy failures. Furthermore, bureaucratic culture, as we suggested earlier, doubtless contributes to intelligence shortcomings by favoring (and rewarding) some kinds of analyses more than others (Goodman, 1984–85). It is also true, however, that policy makers may disregard objective intelligence or otherwise seek to skew it to their purposes (Johnson, 1983). During the Vietnam War, for example, CIA Director Richard Helms received an estimate only thirteen days before the American military incursion into Cambodia that suggested an invasion would not deter continued North Vietnamese involvement in the war, but he did not bring it to the attention of the White House. Contrariwise, the resignation of two senior CIA analysts during the first Reagan term because, they claimed, William Casey pressured them to rewrite their Central American assessments to make them more consonant with existing United States policy points to what Senate minority leader Robert Byrd described as "a shocking use of the CIA for political purposes."[40]

A common thread running through many inquiries into intelligence operations has to do with the control of covert operations. Responsibility for approval and supervision of "special activities" during the Reagan administration rested with the National Security Planning Group, consisting of the president, the vice president, the secretaries of state and defense, the director of central intelligence, the assistant for national security affairs, and key White House advisers. Subordinates and other staff aides were apparently barred from meetings in an effort to prevent security "leaks" (a practice which may, however, also have excluded those with the professional expertise necessary to judge the wisdom of actions contemplated by senior political officials). Later, however, a secret interagency committee consisting of the deputy national security adviser, the director of the State Department's Bureau of Intelligence and Research, the under secretary of state, the under secretary of defense for policy, and the head of the CIA's Clandestine Services was established to oversee the growing number of covert operations initiated by the administration (Tyler and Ottaway, 1986). Sometimes called the "208 Committee" because it met in Room 208 of the Old Executive Office Building across from the White House, the committee reportedly assumed responsibilities akin to those of the 40 Committee, which had managed U.S. covert operations during the 1970s. Decisions of the group were ratified by the National Security Planning Group. The fact that the president actually participated in the latter's meetings made it the highest-level group ever employed for the approval of covert operations. During the Carter administration, the NSC Special Coordination Committee, headed by the national security adviser, Zbigniew Brzezinski, was responsible for this task. The committee was a successor to President Ford's Operations Advisory Group, which in turn was a refur-

---

[40]Pinpointing responsibility for political pressure to change "objective intelligence" is difficult. The foregoing example implicates William Casey, President Reagan's DCI, widely acknowledged to have abandoned the role of intelligence provider in favor of the role of policy advocate in an administration where he had close and continuing contact with the president and other key policy-making officials. In another case, it appears the White House was directly responsible for applying political pressure:

One recent CIA estimate (1983) concluded that the controversial Soviet oil pipeline to Western Europe would fail to make our allies vulnerable in any significant way to Soviet pressures, as argued by the Reagan administration. A senior staffer on the National Security Council (NSC) telephoned the CIA, complaining that "it is not helpful to have an NIE (National Intelligence Estimate) suggesting disagreement with White House policy." The thinly-veiled implication was: deep-six the estimate. When told of the call, CIA deputy director John McMahon reportedly responded with searing scatological advice for the NSC staffer. On this occasion the NIE stood. (Johnson, 1983: 183)

bished and restyled 40 Committee bearing policy-making responsibility for overseeing clandestine political operations during the Nixon administration and the early months of Ford's.

Part of the impetus for sensitivity to the need to pinpoint responsibility for covert operations came from Congress. The Hughes-Ryan Amendment to the 1974 Foreign Assistance Act (repealed in 1980) required the president to certify to Congress that an executive-approved covert action is "important to the national interests of the United States." The DCI was to inform Congress of the "Presidential Finding" in a "timely manner."[41] The process of informing Congress did not have to be completed prior to the implementation of the covert action, however. The requirement was a response to the prior concept of "plausible denial," which meant that covert operations were formulated and approved in such a manner that the president could be saved the embarrassment of a "blown" covert operation. Secretary of State Kissinger testified before Congress that from 1972 to 1974 President Nixon personally and directly approved all covert operations, and that he believed with "almost certain knowledge" that the same had been true at every period in time (House Select Committee on Intelligence cited in *Final Report*, I, 1976). Other testimony before Congress, however, indicated that "one means of protecting the President from embarrassment was not to tell him about certain covert operations, at least formally. . . . [T]he concept of 'plausible denial' was taken in an almost literal sense: 'The government was authorized to do certain things that the President was not advised of'" (*Final Report*, I, 1976). Although the concept still holds sway officially, it obviously has no practical relevance if the president himself authorizes covert operations or if they become widely known and discussed, as with the arming of Nicaraguan and Afghan rebels.

Available evidence suggests other ways top-level management of covert operations has been lax. The Senate's extensive inquiry into the intelligence community found that verbal checks by telephone rather than extensive face-to-face discussions were used to approve proposals, for example. When formal meetings and extended discussions did occur, they were directed primarily at new departures rather than thorough examinations of ongoing projects.

---

[41]In practice, the requirement meant informing the House and Senate committees on intelligence, armed services, appropriations, and foreign affairs and relations. Theoretically this meant that anywhere from roughly 45 to perhaps as many as 200 members of Congress and their staffs could be knowledgeable about impending covert actions, which is one reason why the number of committees needing to be informed was cut to only two in the intelligence oversight legislation passed in 1980. Underlying the perceived need to trim the number of committees was the belief that Congress cannot keep a secret, a matter discussed in chapter twelve.

The number of "presidential findings" submitted to Congress provides a clue to the importance of covert actions in the Reagan administration. *Newsweek* (October 10, 1983: 39) reports that the House intelligence committee was informed of two or three "findings" each year during the Carter administration, whereas less than two years into Reagan's first term it was informed of "12 to 14," of which "seven or eight" were considered "major" (defined as "any covert operation costing between $5 and $7 million—or one that is designed to undermine a foreign government"). These numbers are consistent with others reported by Leslie Gelb in the *New York Times* (June 11, 1984: 1), in which government officials indicated there was "a fivefold increase [in covert operations] since the last year of the Carter Administration to over 50 continuing operations."

During 1975, for example, the 40 Committee met nine times to discuss Angola (compared with one National Security Council meeting on the subject), and an Interagency Working Group on Angola met twenty-four times between August 1975 and January 1976 (*Final Report*, I, 1976: 55).

The Senate hearings, which took place during the Ford administration, pointed out that Ford's reorganization of the intelligence community did little to define the criteria by which covert operations were brought forth for top-level executive approval. There is no evidence that Carter's reorganization accomplished anything more, and what little is available for the Reagan administration suggests less stringency, nor more.[42] Previously, it had been the director of central intelligence who decided whether an operational program should be submitted to the 40 Committee for approval. "Political sensitivity" of the project was one criterion guiding his decision. Cost was another. Projects involving "large" sums of money—defined as $25,000 or more—were apparently more likely to be brought before the 40 Committee.

Given those rules, many clandestine political operations were outside the purview of most top-level officials. The Senate's report (*Final Report*, I, 1976: 56) indicates that 409 covert projects were approved by the 40 Committee and its predecessors between March 1955 and February 1967 (104 under Eisenhower, 163 under Kennedy, and 142 under Johnson). Contrast those numbers with a CIA study that showed that of the 550 Clandestine Services projects existing in 1962, only 86 were separately approved or reapproved by Kennedy's 40 Committee predecessor, the Special Group, during that year (*Final Report*, I, 1976: 57). Projects not receiving explicit consideration were viewed as low-risk, low-cost operations. There apparently was also a tendency by the CIA to view specific projects not reviewed by the 40 Committee as having received prior approval under broader program guidelines. In all, however, the number of specific covert operations subjected to top-level interagency scrutiny appears to have been small.[43]

---

[42]Drawing on the historical record from the inception of the CIA in 1947 through 1982, Ransom (1983) argues that "the state of relations with the Soviet Union determines the degree of accountability imposed upon intelligence operations. The greater the hostility between the U.S. and the U.S.S.R., and the stronger the consensus about threats to national security, the fewer the restrictions, audits, and controls that will be imposed upon the CIA." Thus the increase in Soviet-American tensions evident in the early 1980s "produced a domestic political climate within the United States more tolerant of the intelligence agencies" than had been true in the immediate wake of Vietnam and Watergate.

[43]It appears, moreover, that the situation persisted throughout the Carter administration:

A tendency reportedly has grown within the CIA to forward only a few broad covert action categories to the president and make in-house decisions on all the supposedly routine ones. Although these routine operations are allegedly offsprings of earlier presidential findings, this permits the agency to by-pass the White House and Congress. (Johnson, 1980: 148)

Since this was a time when external restraints on CIA activities were presumably greatest, it seems reasonable to conclude that the CIA has since used the same or similar devices to preserve its autonomy. Congressional unhappiness with the way the CIA interpreted its mandate when mining Nicaraguan ports in late 1983 (see chapter twelve) reinforces that conclusion.

In a high-risk world of push and shove, threat and counterthreat, there is no question that policy makers demand the best available information about the present and future status, capabilities, and intentions of foreign powers. Nor is there question that national security often requires policy making behind closed doors. But what are the consequences for democratic control of foreign policy making? Can a democratic society long absolve itself from responsibility for the conduct of its government officials without also running the risk of losing sight of who is serving whom, for what purpose, and in pursuit of what ideals? These questions go to the heart of a fundamental democratic dilemma: effective intelligence requires secrecy, yet democracy depends on public scrutiny of the government's exercise of power. Those responsible for the management of the intelligence community and its operations must wrestle with that dilemma.

ECONOMIC AGENCIES: AGENTS OF POLITICAL ECONOMY

The State and Defense departments are the preeminent executive departments concerned with foreign policy and national security. In a complex and interdependent world, however, their jurisdiction, particularly the former's, impinges upon, and is infringed upon by, other executive departments whose policy responsibilities spill over into international affairs. A brief look at four essentially domestically oriented departments that are also concerned with foreign economic policy provides additional evidence about the complexities of the foreign affairs government.

Department of the Treasury

Concern for the position of the U.S. dollar in the international monetary system gives Treasury a keen interest in international affairs. Its responsibilities include tax policy, tariffs, the balance of trade and payments, exchange rate adjustments, and the public debt. Those responsibilities make Treasury the principal department through which domestic and international financial and fiscal policy recommendations are formulated. Cohen (1981) describes the ascendancy of the Treasury Department to a position of power in the area of international economic policy making as "the outstanding organizational feature of U.S. international economic policy since the end of World War II." He attributes Treasury's rise to the position of "an organizational superpower" to three overarching factors: "the relative international decline of U.S. economic strength, as measured in the deterioration of the U.S. balance of payments and two subsequent dollar devaluations; the increased impact of the external sector on domestic economic management; and the increased interest in Washington in achieving a broad range of economic policy goals."

The importance of the Treasury Department has often brought the secretary of the treasury, who serves as the chief financial officer of the United

States, into the most intimate circle of presidential advisers, where he has been able to influence foreign as well as domestic policy making. The roster of influentials would take us all the way back to Alexander Hamilton. In the postwar period, it would include George M. Humphrey, Douglas Dillon, John Connally, George Shultz, William Simon, Michael Blumenthal, G. William Miller, Donald Regan, and James A. Baker.

The secretary's chairmanship of major White House economic policy coordinating bodies, such as President Reagan's Cabinet Council on Economic Affairs and President Nixon's Council on International Economic Policy, is an institutional manifestation of his position in the areas of foreign and economic policy.[44] Other key roles derive from the secretary's duties as the U.S. governor of the International Monetary Fund, the World Bank, and the Inter-American, Asian, and African development banks. Those assignments give the Treasury secretary and department a major voice in decisions regarding United States participation in, and the level of contributions to, multilateral lending institutions, which have been the focus of considerable debate in recent years,[45] as well as in the larger issues involved in the maintenance and operation of the complex international monetary system.

The office of the assistant secretary for international affairs is the main unit within Treasury through which the department's international functions are carried out. It is organized into subunits responsible for monetary affairs, developing nations, trade and investment policy, and Arabian Peninsula affairs. Through these groups the office assists the secretary of the treasury and the under secretary for monetary affairs in the formulation and execution of international financial, monetary, commercial, energy, and trade policies and programs. The office is also responsible for providing assistance to the secretary in his roles as cochair of the U.S.-Saudi Arabian Joint Commission on Economic Cooperation, the U.S.-Israel Joint Committee for Investment and Trade, the U.S.-China Joint Economic Committee and chair of the National Advisory Council on International Monetary and Financial Policies. In the past it has also played a key role in institutional arrangements and policies governing commercial ties between the United States and the Soviet Union and Eastern Europe.

Other subdivisions in the Treasury Department include the Bureau of Alcohol, Tobacco, and Firearms, the United States Customs Service, and the United States Secret Service. In carrying out their functions, each of those units performs limited intelligence activities relevant to foreign affairs, as noted earlier.

---

[44]Edwards and Wayne (1985: 259) note that the economic affairs council met as frequently as the other six cabinet councils combined and conclude that it ''had the most impact on policy within its sphere.''

[45]See Schoultz (1982) for a discussion of the decision-making structure governing United States participation in multilateral banks and an examination of its voting record in them.

Department of Commerce

Foreign economic policy is also the bailiwick of the Commerce Department insofar as it is concerned with international affairs, particularly that portion relating to the expansion and protection of American commerce abroad. Unlike the secretary of the treasury, however, the secretary of commerce and the Commerce Department as a whole historically have not been principal actors in foreign policy making. Under President Nixon, however, a succession of assertive and business-oriented commerce secretaries did come to act as principal advisers to the president on matters of international trade policy (Irish and Frank, 1975). Their assertiveness was spurred by the first combined adverse American trade and payments balances in the twentieth century; their influence was further augmented by a foreign policy strategy that gave emphasis to trade and commercial policies as mechanisms for bridging the gulf between capitalist America and the socialist states of Eastern Europe, the Soviet Union, and China. Moreover, the importance of the Commerce Department as a foreign policy actor increased as a consequence of a 1980 reorganization of the government's trade-related responsibilities. As indicated in chapter ten, the United States Trade Representative is responsible for developing and administering overall trade and investment policy. And the Commerce Department has become the principal agency with operating responsibilities in the trade area except in matters involving agricultural trade.

Specific trade responsibilities of the Commerce Department include administration of countervailing duty and antidumping statutes,[46] foreign commercial representation, implementation of the Multilateral Trade Negotiations (MTN) agreements, administration of export controls, trade policy analysis, and foreign compliance with trade agreements. Those duties are discharged by the International Trade Administration (ITA), headed by the under secretary for international trade. More generally, the ITA's charge is to promote world trade and to strengthen the position of the United States in the global network of trade and investment.

Illustrative of the way in which foreign economic affairs, which encompass issues both foreign and domestic in nature, have eroded the primacy of the traditional foreign policy agencies is the fact that the Commerce Department rather than the State Department is now responsible for U.S. commercial representation. The Foreign Commercial Service is responsible for commercial representation and trade promotion overseas. It combines some four dozen district offices in the United States with posts located in sixty-eight countries

---

[46]Countervailing duties are import taxes that offset the special advantages which imports have due to subsidies provided by the exporting nation; they are designed to place subsidized imports on the same price footing as other imports and domestic products. Dumping means selling exports for prices below those in the exporter's own domestic market. Antidumping regulations are designed to make up the difference between the exporter's price and the foreign market value when the selling price is less than the fair value.

throughout the world, thus bringing together in one organization those encouraging American firms to sell abroad and those who deal with the potential buyers of American products.

Despite the enhanced role of the Commerce Department in trade policy and promotion following President Carter's 1980 reorganization, it remains a comparatively weak actor in the councils of government. In part this reflects a historical aversion to close ties between the manufacturing sector and government bureaucrats, with the result that the department plays "more of an operational than a policymaking role" (Cohen, 1981). The distinction is in part an institutional reflection. As Commerce Secretary Malcolm Baldrige observed, "trade is the only major Cabinet function where policy is made in one department (the United States trade representative) and carried out in another (Department of Commerce)." As a result, "trade policy has to be 'brokered' among the other Cabinet departments, instead of being advocated. Yet all of those other departments act as advocates for their own interests, which sometime turn into competing interests. . . . Trade is not [actively advocated]; the brokering involved too often forces trade policy into the lowest common denominator acceptable to the rest of the executive branch. . . . [W]e end up lacking strong policy because of our institutional problems" (Baldrige, 1983).

To correct these institutional deficiencies, President Reagan in 1983 proposed creation of a Department of International Trade and Industry. Designed to eliminate the split between who makes policy and who implements it, described by Baldrige as almost unique among "our industrialized trading competitors," the proposed department would have incorporated the trade representative's office and about 20 percent of the Commerce Department into a small new department designed to focus responsibility and accountability in a single place. The implication was that a stronger trade policy might result, and it is perhaps no accident that the acronym for the proposed department—DITI—bore striking resemblance to Japan's Ministry of International Trade and Industry—MITI—after which the new agency was presumably modeled. The proposed department failed to receive the support of the 98th Congress, however, and even though Reagan revived it following his reelection, opposition within the executive branch as well as outside it seemed to doom the proposal. The result is that the Commerce Department will likely remain more of an implementer than advocate of United States trade policy.

Department of Agriculture

In 1984–85 the value of American agricultural exports stood at $31.2 billion. Although this figure was an almost 30 percent decline from the $43.8 billion peak in 1980–81—attributable to a combination of bumper crops elsewhere in the world, poor economic conditions abroad, and the high value of the dollar—American exports of particular products (such as grain and soybeans) continue to account for a substantial proportion of total world exports and domestic farm income. Those facts attest to the importance of the United States in the world marketplace and to the importance of agriculture in the domestic economy. Necessarily, therefore, the Department of Agriculture has a major stake in the administration of foreign economic policy. Particular departmental interests include promotion of the sale of agricultural commodities abroad, including the sale or distribution of surplus commodities owned by the government under Public Law 480 and the Food for Peace Program; allocation of import quotas for certain agricultural commodities; collection of information about agricultural developments overseas; and participation in international negotiations relating to world trade in agricultural products.

The Foreign Agricultural Service (FAS), operating under the authority of the under secretary for international affairs and commodity programs, is the principal subdivision of the department concerned with international affairs. Its primary purpose is promoting sales of American agricultural commodities overseas. Toward that end, it maintains agricultural counselors and attachés in seventy American embassies overseas covering 110 different foreign countries. The FAS is responsible for formulating, administering, and coordinating Agriculture Department policies and programs as they relate to multilateral conventions, such as the General Agreement on Tariffs and Trade (GATT), and for participating in negotiations involving agricultural products in such international forums as the Organization for Economic Cooperation and Development (OECD) and the Food and Agriculture Organization (FAO) of the United Nations.

The Foreign Agricultural Service is also responsible for managing Public Law 480, the Food for Peace program, which is aimed at the long-run improvement of developing nations' economies. Included under PL 480 are long-term credit sales for American dollars, whereby the government dispenses commodity surpluses purchased by the government to support the American farmer. Donations for humanitarian purposes to foreign governments, voluntary relief agencies, and international institutions, such as the World Food Program of the United Nations, are included. The Agriculture Department carries out provisions of PL 480 in cooperation with the Agency for International Development (AID).

Finally, the department's Office of International Cooperation and Development directs the department's international development and technical cooperation efforts. That task involves the department simultaneously with American universities and other domestic organizations, foreign governments, and international organizations.

Department of Labor

Gathering information, proffering advice, administering selected programs, and participating in international negotiations (especially in the International Labor Organization [ILO], the General Agreement on Tariffs and Trade, and the Organization for Economic Cooperation and Development)—those, too, are the international affairs functions of the Labor Department, but with a view toward their importance for the American wage earner rather than the agricultural, business, or financial communities. They are carried out by the Bureau of International Labor Affairs headed by the deputy under secretary for international affairs. Among other things, the department's authority traditionally has carried with it a special concern for immigrant labor. It also has involved the department with the State Department in the provision of labor attachés for assignment abroad and with the Agency for International Development in the execution of technical assistance activities overseas. The department has also borne responsibility for the administration of the trade adjustment assistance programs for workers under the Trade Act of 1974. The act provides that workers adversely affected by foreign trade competition are entitled to restitution. Payments authorized by the act, which ran into the billions of dollars during the economic slowdown of the 1970s, were greatly reduced under the Reagan administration, which targeted them for elimination.

THE POLITICS OF POLICY MAKING: RETROSPECTIVE AND PROSPECTIVE OBSERVATIONS

The executive agencies which are part of the foreign affairs government are so numerous and multifaceted that no brief description could adequately capture either the breadth of their interests or the depth of their involvement in matters of foreign policy. As a way of explicating governmental sources of American policy, however, the description provided here should demonstrate what clearly has become a distinguishing characteristic of American foreign policy making—decision making by and within a disparate set of exceedingly large and complex organizational structures. Effecting control over them and dealing with the consequences of their decisional behavior have become important parts of the way in which the president and the advisers who surround him within the innermost concentric circle of policy making seek to make American foreign policy. Hence, we will return later (in chapter thirteen) to a further examination of the characteristics and consequences of decision making by and in organizations.

The jurisdictions of the executive agencies necessarily catapult them into the forefront of the political processes through which the nation's external conduct ultimately becomes visible. Determining which are preeminent among those agencies is therefore important. On the basis of the diplomatic and historical record examined in chapters three, four and five, the Defense Department and the CIA appear to have been in a commanding political position throughout the postwar period. Certainly the stimuli coming from what was widely perceived to be a hostile external environment, which buttressed widely shared fears of Soviet communism, were important in promoting Defense and CIA influence within the policy-making community—to the point, in fact, that preferences for military might and interventionist means have become distinctive patterns of American foreign policy. The fact that the CIA often controlled the information on which policy decisions had to be based, and that both the CIA and the military often had ready alternatives available from which decision makers could choose, also contributed to their commanding political positions.

Beyond those factors, the ties between government agencies and the larger societal system within which they reside also become important in understanding who matters within the policy-making community. In fact, if we think of the institutions of government as filters through which the other source variables must ultimately pass if they are to affect foreign policy outcomes, the way in which the government agencies described in this chapter both reflect and respond to the other source categories illuminates the role they play in that process. In that context, the nongovernmental groups which government agencies serve, and with which they often are therefore identified, become important sources of agencies' political power. That fact helps explain why the State Department—which is the only agency of government that bears responsibility for the totality of American relations with other nations—has not assumed a more commanding position within the foreign affairs government. There is virtually no substantive area of foreign policy in which the State Department does not become involved. But it often lacks the political resources and domestic support to go along with its formal authority that would make it a more dominant force.

As a practical matter, the State Department is involved in the range of substantive items that are the stuff of foreign policy through its extensive consultation and coordination with other agencies. The State Department's relative lack of political resources means that in those interagency contacts that do occur, it is frequently likely to be bargaining from a position of weakness rather than strength. Our earlier discussion of the relative advantages of the Defense Department compared to the State Department is relevant here. It is also germane to State's position with regard to the economic agencies, whose importance in the policy-making process derives from the changing position of the United States in the transitional political economy discussed in chapter seven. John Franklin Campbell cogently summarizes the point:

> State speaks to a broad but weak national constituency, whereas the domestic economic departments represent narrower but more vocal special interest groups. These inherent conflicts of point of view are expressed in a complex series of interagency committees in which State is one voice among many, and generally a minor voice in the debate. The reasons for this are twofold. Business, farm, and labor lobbies bring considerable pressure to bear on the other departments of government, which by custom respond to those interests more passionately than does the Foreign Affairs Department. Second, economic policy is but one of many foreign policy concerns of State, whereas it is the central issue with the other departments concerned in the process. Treasury, not State, is the "expert" on monetary matters; Agriculture is the "expert" on U.S. farm surpluses; Commerce is the "expert" on American industry; while State speaks for a foreign policy that may seem quite remote if not abstract in comparison to these immediate home issues. State's logical domestic ally in these debates would often be the American consumer, who

is unfortunately the least organized of the actors in our interest group domestic politics. (Campbell, 1971: 220).

Congress frequently is an intimate part of the complex interagency politicking in which government agencies often become engaged. Indeed, Congress, or, more correctly, congressional committees and subcommittees, often behave much like domestic clientele groups in protecting government agencies from attack by "outsiders." "Outsiders" in this context may include those making up the presidential subsystem. The convenient alliance between certain bureaucracies and their congressional allies helps explain, for example, the political functions of bureaucratic "leaks" to the press. They become mechanisms for cuing others within the political system, such as Congress, of impending changes in policies or programs which they can then attack or defend. In the political struggle between Congress and the president, however, the president is generally in the more commanding position when it comes to foreign policy. Exploring why that is so is the subject of the next chapter.

SUGGESTIONS FOR FURTHER READING

BAMFORD, JAMES. *The Puzzle Palace.* New York: Penguin Books, 1983.

COHEN, STEPHEN D. *The Making of United States International Economic Policy: Principles, Problems, and Prospects for Reform*, 2nd ed. New York: Praeger, 1981.

FLANAGAN, STEPHEN J. "Managing the Intelligence Community," *International Security* 10 (Summer 1985): 58–95

GELB, LESLIE H. "Why Not the State Department?" pp. 282–298 in Charles W. Kegley, Jr., and Eugene R. Wittkopf, eds., *Perspectives on American Foreign Policy: Selected Readings.* New York: St. Martin's, 1983.

KINNARD, DOUGLAS. *The Secretary of Defense.* Lexington: The University of Kentucky Press, 1980.

LUTTWAK, EDWARD N. *The Pentagon and the Art of War: The Question of Military Reform.* New York: Simon & Schuster, 1984.

MAURER, ALFRED C., MARION D. TUNSTALL, AND JAMES M. KEAGLE, eds. *Intelligence: Policy and Process.* Boulder, CO: Westview Press, 1985.

RUBIN, BARRY. *Secrets of State: The State Department and the Struggle Over U.S. Foreign Policy.* New York: Oxford University Press, 1985.

YARMOLINSKY, ADAM. *The Military Establishment: Its Impact on American Society.* New York: Harper & Row, 1971.

12

THE ROLE OF CONGRESS IN FOREIGN POLICY MAKING

[I]n recent years Congresses have tended to try to curb and take away from the presidency some of the prerogatives that belong there—the handling of foreign policy and so forth—and placed restrictions on the office that in effect would have foreign policy determined by a committee of 535.

President Ronald Reagan, 1986

Congress as an institution is a conservative organization—cautious and reluctant to initiate change. It responds to old stimuli better than new. When it opposes the Executive, it is usually to protect some interest group or some aspect of the status quo rather than to initiate action. Any new things that are going on in the federal government are not going on in Congress. Sometimes a member of Congress will take the initiative, or a group of members will, but Congress as an institution will not.

Congressman Les Aspin, 1976

Few observations better capture the essence of the role of Congress in foreign policy making than the preceding one by Congressman Les Aspin. The old adage that "the president proposes, Congress disposes" implies as well that Congress plays essentially a negative role by functioning as a public critic of the executive and otherwise setting limits on permissible behavior. Advocates and detractors of increased congressional involvement in foreign policy making would doubtless contest that conclusion. Both could find evidence to support their viewpoints. Detractors in particular could cite a number of instances in the post-Vietnam era that demonstrated that, regardless of what the earlier

415

post-World War II record may have looked like, the world of the 1970s and 1980s is different, including the following:

- In 1970 Congress "repealed" the Gulf of Tonkin Resolution, which had given President Johnson, as interpreted by him, a "blank check" for prosecuting an undeclared war in Southeast Asia.
- In 1973 Congress overrode President Nixon's veto to write the War Powers Act into law, thus requiring a modicum of consultation between the president and Congress on the issue of dispatching troops abroad.
- In 1974 Congress embargoed arms sales to Turkey in retaliation for its invasion of Cyprus, despite the protests of the Ford administration.
- In 1974 Congress refused to permit the president to extend "most-favored-nation" (MFN) trade treatment to the Soviet Union by linking MFN to the emigration of Soviet Jews.
- In 1975 Congress ensured termination of American participation in the Vietnam war by denying the president authority to provide emergency military aid to the South Vietnamese government to forestall its imminent collapse in the face of communist forces.
- In 1976 Congress prohibited continued expenditures by the CIA to bolster anti-Marxist forces fighting in Angola.
- In 1976, fully twenty years after the proposal was first introduced, the Senate established a permanent intelligence oversight committee to monitor the sprawling intelligence community; the House followed suit a year later.
- In 1980 Congress passed legislation designed to establish its right to prior notice by the executive branch of covert intelligence activities abroad.
- In 1982 Congress refused to fund deployment of a new strategic weapon, the MX missile.
- In 1982 Congress prohibited the use of funds by the Defense Department and the CIA for purposes of overthrowing the government of Nicaragua.
- In 1983 Congress invoked provisions of the War Powers Act to limit the time military forces could remain in Lebanon.
- In 1984 the Senate joined the House in refusing additional funds for covert actions against the Sandinista government of Nicaragua.
- In 1986 the House refused to support a presidential request to provide additional assistance to the contras fighting the Sandinista regime.
- In 1986 Congress overrode a presidential veto to place economic sanctions on South Africa.

Most of these examples of congressional assertiveness illustrate a belief that arose during the Vietnam and Watergate periods that the "imperial presidency" needed to be curtailed—to the point that Under Secretary of State William D. Rogers lamented in 1979 that "foreign policy has become almost synonymous with lawmaking. The result is to place a straitjacket of legislation around the manifold complexity of our relations with other nations."

On the other hand, Congress has also sought on occasion to restrain presidential efforts to *limit* America's global commitments. In 1977 and 1978, for example, Congress expressed opposition to the Carter administration's decision to withdraw American troops from South Korea, and it used the occasion to reassert its right to be involved in the policy-making process. In 1978 certain conditions and reservations imposed by Congress and attached to the two Panama Canal treaties signed by the United States (turning control of the waterway over to Panama) nearly torpedoed agreements that had been negotiated under four presidents for over a decade. And in 1979, following the Carter administrations's decision to abrogate the defense treaty with the Republic of China (Taiwan) in order to normalize relations with the People's Republic of China, more than two dozen senators challenged in court the right of the president to terminate a treaty without congressional approval.[1]

There is no question that these maneuvers are manifestations of assertiveness by a coequal branch of the federal government seeking a coequal voice in foreign policy making. Although that fact has definitely colored the process whereby policy is made and implemented, on closer inspection, none of these manifestations of assertiveness does violence to the general proposition that "the president proposes, Congress disposes." Indeed, if anything, they have done more to enhance the adversary function of Congress than to augment its capacity to take the lead in foreign policy.[2] And in the process of expanding its adversarial capabilities, Congress may actually have weakened its authority relative to the president rather than strengthened it. Thus the metaphor which describes the government as the only "vehicle on earth that has two steering wheels: one for the President, one for Congress" (*The New Republic*, January 28, 1978) may perhaps have some meaning with respect to domestic policy. But in foreign affairs, it takes little skill to tell "who's driving" (the president) or, for that matter, "who's braking" (Congress). Hence, the term *initiator-respondent* continues to accurately portray executive-congressional functions and linkages in foreign policy making, despite the fact that threats to the continuation of the relationship between the two branches have arisen periodically.

The purpose of this chapter is to explore the whys and hows of the initiator-respondent label as a way of further explicating the governmental source category. We shall do so by examining those characteristics of Congress as an institution which favor its more passive role vis-à-vis the executive. Then we shall probe the role of Congress with respect to treaties, war, and money—three areas in which congressional powers as embodied in the Constitution would appear to be especially formidable—and inquire into the appropriate-

---

[1]Rogers (1979) explains part of the reason for this vehement response: "President Carter had improvidently failed to advise leadership on the Hill until a bare three hours before his recognition . . . of the People's Republic of China and his termination of the United States' diplomatic relations and defense treaty with Taiwan."

[2]See Franck and Weisband (1979) for a contrasting viewpoint, which argues that "a system of *policy codetermination*," implying "a sharing of the decision-making process" more aptly describes executive-congressional relations as they evolved in the wake of Vietnam.

[3]As the following discussion will seek to illustrate, congressional interest and involvement in the foreign policy-making process as a general rule will tend to increase in proportion to the rele-

ness of the initiator-respondent label in these special policy areas.[3] As a preface, however, the historical regard of executive-congressional interactions in foreign policy making should first be explored briefly.

PAST EXECUTIVE-CONGRESSIONAL INTERACTIONS

Although "initiator-respondent" summarizes the relationship meaningfully, its precise nature is more complex than the label conveys. Not infrequently ideas are born on Capitol Hill for which the president subsequently receives political credit when they are brought to fruition. Moreover, the picture of extensive presidential dominance appears most accurate with respect to the 1955–1965 period, with congressional assertiveness in foreign policy more characteristic of the two subsequent decades. In fact, six relatively distinct phases describe postwar executive-congressional relations.[4]

Accommodation describes the pattern of relations from roughly 1943 to 1951. The nation's goals of globalism, anticommunism, and containment of alleged Soviet expansionism were given meaning during that time in a variety of specific foreign policy initiatives and programs. Accommodation suggests that Congress participated willingly in efforts to establish an activist postwar foreign policy posture.[5] "Bipartisanship" (discussed more fully below) captures the essence of the accommodative atmosphere of the period.

Following accommodation was an approximately four-year period (1951 to 1955) which Frans Bax describes as "the phase of *antagonism*." McCarthyism fell within that period. So, too, did recriminations over who "lost" China, disenchantment with "limited" war in Korea, and the firing of a general (Douglas MacArthur) who wished to prosecute the war in other ways, growing concern over the cost of foreign aid, and probing questions about Truman's commitment of troops to Europe. Efforts by the Senate (also discussed in more detail below) to curb presidential treaty-making powers symbolized the antagonisms of the period.

---

vance of a "foreign" issue to "domestic" concerns. The domestic consequences of decisions regarding war and how money is to be spent are sufficiently great so as to thrust Congress to the fore almost instinctively. But other allegedly "foreign policy" issues—such as immigration and draft registration policy—that exert a strong domestic impact can be expected to provoke congressional participation in debate of the issue as a matter of course. Indeed, one can presume that whenever an international issue with domestic overtones is addressed, efforts by both Congress and relevant interest groups to shape policy will intensify. Thus while we concentrate attention on the role of Congress with regard to the issues of treaties, war, and money, readers should contemplate the extent to which the proposed characterizations might apply to other, less prominent issues.

[4]Bax (1977) provides the delineation of the first five phases of executive-congressional relations.

[5]That is not to say Congress unanimously supported the premises on which American postwar strategy was predicated. Despite the consensus that existed, there were some who opposed continuation of the international role the nation assumed following World War II and advocated instead a return to limited involvement globally (Robert Taft, Republican senator from Ohio, exemplified such thinking). But on the whole it is safe to label such neoisolationist sentiment a minority view.

For nearly a decade thereafter (from 1955 to 1965), the congressional role in foreign policy making can be described as one of *acquiescence*. It was in that phase that Congress passed the "area resolutions" granting the president broad congressional support for dealing with external conflict situations, as in the Middle East, Berlin, Cuba, the China straits, and Vietnam. The chief congressional function was essentially that of legitimizing presidential decisions. Congress became a partner to the national consensus supporting the containment of communism. It agreed with most of the specific foreign policy decisions made by the three presidents who held office during the period. And it participated in supporting containment by reassuring the public that presidential actions were necessary and consistent with the consensus. "On some occasions, the Congress did deliberate upon and then agree with presidential plans, but all too often the Congress simply swallowed its lingering doubts, preferring not to share the responsibility of decision with the president" (Bax, 1977).

Presidents, for their part, encouraged the acquiescent congressional role. Since the basic parameters of the containment posture were already well in place, there was little need to consult "mere congressmen." Following the massive Vietnam buildup in 1965, however, Congress was no longer content with such a docile role. The Senate Foreign Relations Committee hearings during the mid-1960s, chaired by J. William Fulbright, focused attention on what began to be perceived as a major foreign policy failure. Yet Congress refused to exercise what prerogatives might have been at its disposal to curtail presidential assertiveness. Congress was in a state of *ambiguity*.

The Cambodian incursion in the spring of 1970 transformed ambiguity into *acrimony*. During the next three years the Senate passed a variety of measures that would have curtailed the president's ability to keep or use American troops in Indochina, but the House generally failed to go along. One measure did pass both houses, however. In 1971 the Special Foreign Assistance Act proscribed the use of funds authorized or appropriated by Congress "to finance the introduction of United States ground combat troops into Cambodia, or to provide United States advisors to or for Cambodian military forces in Cambodia." Significantly, the bill was passed only *after* the spring offensive of 1970 had been completed. Subsequent congressional restrictions on the expenditure of funds were also largely symbolic. Nevertheless, Congress had begun to participate in the termination of America's role in that tragic conflict. Once direct military involvement in Vietnam ended in late March 1973, Congress pushed termination of the entire Indochina involvement by banning continued bombing of Cambodia after August 15 of that year.

The high point of congressional acrimony was reached in 1973, when the War Powers Act (discussed below) was passed over the president's veto. Thereafter congressional activism is perhaps best described as *assertiveness*. The term applies aptly to the Ford, Carter, and Reagan administrations.

Three situations which developed during the Ford administration illustrate the assertive mood of Congress: the Turkish arms embargo; the prohibition of aid to Angola; and the assertion by Congress of its right to veto major arms sales and related executive initiatives.

The event leading to the Turkish arms embargo was Turkey's invasion of Cyprus in July 1974, an effort ostensibly designed to protect Cyprus's ethnic Turkish minority from the Greek Cypriot majority. Some have argued that the successful embargo effort mounted by nonleadership elements in the House and Senate reflected the emergence of a powerful pro-Greek lobby in Congress. Others believe that consideration of the federal law requiring the termination of military aid to any recipient using American arms for other than defensive purposes overrode arguments by the Ford administration that the nation's interests and the need for a flexible foreign policy strategy toward others were paramount.[6] Certainly the acrimonious atmosphere surrounding executive-congressional relations in the wake of Vietnam influenced the congressional desire to curtail the president's prerogatives in foreign policy making:

> It was time for Congress to teach the Executive that it was not above the law, not even in the conduct of foreign relations. What was at stake was the integrity of *procedure*; and, as every old hand on Capital Hill knows, even legislators who agree on nothing else usually close ranks to protect *The Process*. (Franck and Weisband, 1979: 38)

The congressional decision in the winter of 1975–1976 to bar the use of funds "for any activities involving Angola directly or indirectly" followed a similar course. President Ford and Secretary of State Kissinger sought to retain the flexibility and latitude the executive had traditionally enjoyed in dealing with foreign policy; Congress sought a greater role in defining the executive's behavior. When the funding prohibition passed, Ford lamented: "How can the United States, the greatest power in the world, take the position that the Soviet Union can operate with impunity many thousands of miles away with Cuban troops and massive amounts of military equipment, while we refuse any assistance to the majority of the local people who ask only for military equipment to defend themselves?"[7] But from the viewpoint of Congress, other issues were also involved, including, for example, misinformation it received from the administration about the nature and extent of American involvement. The critical factor looming in the background, however, was Vietnam.

> While there were many in Congress who doubted the importance of Angola to the U.S. national interest, it was not neoisolationism, indifference to Soviet expansion,

---

[6]For an examination of the events and maneuvers surrounding the Turkish arms case, see Legg (1981) and Franck and Weisband (1979).

[7]Ford summarized his views of Congress after leaving office: "Congress has gone too far [in recent years] in many areas in trying to assume powers that belong to the president and the executive branch."

or loss of nerve that motivated Congress. Rather, it was a fear that the President had embarked on yet another war the United States could not win, and that he had done so covertly, without the Constitutionally required consent of Congress. (Franck and Weisband, 1979: 46)

The issue of congressional consent began to color American arms sales policy during the same period. As the value of foreign military sales skyrocketed during the Nixon years, Congress became concerned about providing sophisticated equipment to others, particularly Third World countries and, perhaps most of all, Arab countries opposed to Israel. In 1975 it passed a law requiring that the executive inform Congress of any sale in excess of $25 million. Congress would then have twenty days within which it could veto the sale. The dollar amount was lowered to $7 million for "major defense equipment" in 1976, and the period within which Congress could override a sale was extended to thirty days.[8] Significantly, the law stipulated that congressional disapproval need only be expressed in a concurrent resolution of the two houses of Congress, thus avoiding the threat of a presidential veto. The procedure is known as a *legislative veto*.[9]

In 1983 the Supreme Court ruled the legislative veto unconstitutional.[10] Uncertainty surrounds the applicability of the Court's decision and its long-term impact, since it was considerably less definitive than first appearances suggested.[11] Significantly, however, Congress never exercised its powers to veto major arms sales before the Court's ruling (nor since, for that matter). Nevertheless, the mere existence of the legal requirements has doubtless complicated the president's life, as President Carter learned when he sought congressional approval in 1978 of a massive arms package involving Israel, Egypt, and Saudi Arabia. The fact that Carter's victory on the issue was thought of as a major foreign policy triumph of his administration is testimony to the potential importance of congressional restraints on executive flexibility.

Carter's campaign pledges included efforts to promote human rights in other countries. They were encumbered by congressional restraints as soon as he became president. Well before his election, Congress, spurred by violations of human rights occurring in Chile following the violent overthrow of Salvador Allende, began legislating restrictions on the use of foreign aid

[8]"By mutual agreement, every president since 1976 gave Congress an extra 20 days' advance notice, during which the two branches frequently worked out deals on politically sensitive issues.

"Under the definition in use in 1985, the notice and veto provisions applied to arms sales packages totaling at least $50 million, to sales of individual weapons worth $14 million or more, and to sales of military construction services worth $200 million or more" (Congressional Quarterly, 1986a: 78).

[9]The origins of the legislative veto can be traced to the early 1930s, and it was typically used more widely in domestic than in foreign policy matters. See *Studies on the Legislative Veto* prepared by the Congressional Research Service (1980) and Fisher (1985).

[10]*Immigration and Naturalization Service v. Chadha*, 103 S. Ct. 2764 (1983).

[11]There is a substantial body of literature that addresses the Court's ruling and it implications for the role of Congress in foreign policy making. A useful sampling that focuses on the institutional impact of the Court's ruling includes Cooper (1983 and 1985), Destler (1983a), Fisher (1985), and the materials in "The U.S. Supreme Court Decision Concerning the Legislative Veto" (1983).

funds in countries where human rights were being violated (Crabb and Holt, 1984). Secretary of State Kissinger sought to ward off those restraints, arguing the need for flexibility in promoting the nation's foreign policy and in influencing the behavior of others. Carter's avowed human rights stance was more consonant with congressional concerns, but eventually he too became frustrated by the seeming intrusion of Congress into the day-to-day conduct of foreign affairs.

By the summer of 1978 Carter was complaining about restrictions on his latitude. "Global issues were fine, but the prime foreign policy actors, Carter learned, were countries and their leaders, and a certain flexibility was necessary in dealing with them" (Destler, 1981a). Carter savored his legislative victories: the Panama Canal treaties (and the implementing legislation that was nearly as difficult in coming), Middle Eastern arms deals, the sale of nuclear fuel to India, the lifting of the Turkish arms embargo, and ratification of the trade accords hammered out in the Multilateral Trade Negotiations. But in many cases the margins of victory were slim, the debate intense, and the compromises substantial. And one issue which the president initially championed—the SALT II treaty—never was brought before the full Senate for a vote; Carter found it more expedient to shelve the document.

The electoral tide that swept Ronald Reagan into office in 1981 enabled the new president to pursue vigorously his promises regarding federal fiscal policy. Some even compared Reagan's mastery of Congress to Johnson's, whose handling of the legislative branch contributed immeasurably to building his Great Society program. Curbing federal spending and mounting federal government budgets ultimately proved beyond Reagan's reach, however. And while congressional receptivity to the renewed sense of foreign policy assertiveness that Carter initiated continued under Reagan, especially with respect to military spending, the restraining influences of a Congress still willing to assert itself were not to be dismissed.

Reagan's first significant encounter with Congress's foreign policy assertiveness occurred on an arms sale issue. The Carter administration's 1978 arms package referred to earlier included the sale to Saudi Arabia of F-15 aircraft, the most sophisticated jet fighters in the American arsenal, but to secure congressional approval of the deal in the face of strong opposition by the pro-Israeli lobby, the planes were not equipped with bomb racks or air-to-air missiles. The Saudis chafed under the restrictions and repeatedly sought the additional equipment. Upon assuming office, the Reagan administration determined that the Saudis should have the equipment. It also added a startling new twist: it decided to sell Saudi Arabia advanced-technology airborne warning and control systems aircraft (AWACS). By pitting the administration against the Israeli lobby and its congressional supporters (who were able to claim a majority opposed to the sale), the decision "precipitated some of the most intense lobbying activities witnessed on a foreign policy question since World War II" (Crabb and Holt, 1984).

As expected, the Democratically-controlled House voted against the proposed sale shortly after the administration brought it before Congress. To win approval of the sale, the White House then launched an intensive campaign, which eventually focused on a handful of Senators considered maneuverable. One was Republican Senator Roger Jepsen of Iowa. A White House official described the efforts to get Jepsen to switch this way: "We just beat his brains out. We stood him up in front of an open grave and said he could jump in if he wanted to" (cited in Bard, 1985). Jepsen chose not to; he and six other Republican senators who had earlier opposed the AWACS deal decided to switch: in a dramatic 48–52 vote, the Senate rejected a resolution to disapprove the arms deal. Thus Reagan won his first major foreign policy test with Congress—but it was a victory that required the expenditure of an extraordinary amount of political capital and that was secured only after Reagan elevated the issue to that of the credibility of a presidential commitment.

Three years later, in 1984, Reagan again faced formidable opposition to a proposed arms sale. This one involved a portable antiaircraft missile called the Stinger destined for Jordan and Saudi Arabia. This time, to the surprise of many, Reagan chose not to fight.

The sale of arms to Arab states typically encounters stiff congressional opposition. In this case adverse comments about the U.S. role in the Middle East peace process by Jordan's King Hussein stiffened the opposition. Reagan then withdrew the proposal. "It was the first time in the 16-year history of direct congressional involvement in arms sales that a president had withdrawn an arms sales proposal without stating that he would resubmit it to Congress at a future date" (*Congressional Quarterly Almanac, 1984*, 1985). The precedent-setting move was followed shortly thereafter by the decision to send Stingers to Saudi Arabia under the president's emergency power, thereby bypassing Congress. It was only the second time Congress's role in a major arms sale had been circumvented by this unusual procedure.[12]

On a third important Mideast arms package, however, Reagan did fight. Saudi Arabia was again the arms recipient, and once more intensive White House lobbying was necessary to save the weapons deal. In this case the effort was directed at sustaining a presidential veto of a measure that would have blocked the $258 million sale from going forward. The president prevailed by a single vote when, in June 1986, thirty-four members of the Senate gave the president the minimum number he needed to turn around an earlier Senate decision blocking the Saudi sale. Like the 1981 decision, some senators who switched their votes indicated they had done so because of the president's argument that his ability to conduct the nation's foreign policy was at stake. Others suggested that the arms package had been changed sufficiently (by deleting Stinger missiles, some feared would fall into the hands of terrorists, as well as other weapons systems sought earlier) so that their earlier objections

---

[12]The first occurred in 1979, when the Carter administration sent military equipment to North Yemen, which was at that time involved in an intensifying war with South Yemen, headed by a Marxist-oriented government.

no longer mattered. Significantly, however, the case represented the first time that both houses of Congress had moved to block a major arms sale, thus requiring a sustained presidential veto to proceed with the sale.

Vexing as congressional assertiveness on arms sales was, Congress was even more persistent in challenging the administration's Central American policies, particularly those involving Nicaragua.[13]

In 1979 the dictatorial regime of Anastasio Somoza long supported by the United States collapsed. It was succeeded by an anti-Somoza coalition known as the Sandinista National Liberation Front (FSLN), which increasingly took on the trappings of a Marxist regime. Alarmed by what it believed to be growing Cuban and Soviet influence in Nicaragua (and in Central America generally), the Reagan administration authorized in December 1981 United States support for Nicaraguan exiles in Honduras, known as contras, who were fighting the Sandinistas. Covert CIA operations in support of the contras were designed "to disrupt arms shipments into Nicaragua and to harass what the [Reagan] executive order [authorizing covert actions by the CIA] called the 'Cuban-Sandinista support' structure in Nicaragua and elsewhere in Central America" (Congressional Quarterly, 1986b). With U.S. support the contras grew in numbers and their actions became bolder. In 1984, with CIA help, they mined Nicaraguan ports, leading the Sandinistas to bring suit against the United States in the World Court, alleging that its support of military attacks against Nicaragua violated international law. They demanded a halt to U.S. assistance to the antigovernment insurgents and compensation for the damage they had caused.

Even before the Sandinistas challenged the United States in the World Court, members of Congress had expressed growing apprehension about U.S. efforts to overthrow an internationally recognized and established government. The CIA's covert actions were initially justified on grounds of protecting Nicaragua's neighbors from the leftist regime. As knowledge of the antigovernment guerrilla operations became increasingly widespread, it became clear that the contras themselves sought nothing less than the overthrow of the Sandinista regime.

Congress moved against that objective. Even though Reagan administration officials argued that the objective was not to overthrow the Nicaraguan government but to interdict the flow of Soviet and Cuban supplied arms to leftist insurgents in El Salvador, House Democrats succeeded in December 1982 in passing the so-called Boland amendment, which prohibited the use of CIA and Defense Department funds (during fiscal 1983) for operations specifically aimed at overthrowing the Nicaraguan government.

The congressional-executive tug-of-war over Central American policy con-

[13]See the Congressional Quarterly (1986b) and Destler (1984) for accounts that focus on El Salvador, which, until the election of José Napoleón Duarte in May 1984, commanded major attention by the administration and Congress. El Salvador receded from the limelight thereafter as political events in El Salvador largely removed the causes of contention between Congress and the executive. Our subsequent discussion of U.S. policies toward Nicaragua draws on the Congressional Quarterly (1986b).

tinued throughout Reagan's first term in office and into his second. Congress repeatedly sought to thwart efforts to expand United States involvement in Central America through covert actions and direct military aid. The Democratically-controlled House, where the specter of "another Vietnam" was repeatedly raised, typically led the fight against administration proposals, only to be checked by the Republican-controlled Senate. Then, in 1984, following the mining episode that led to Nicaragua's World Court suit, the Senate joined the House in refusing to approve additional funds for covert actions against the Sandinistas. The turnabout was less a matter of conscience than a belief that the CIA had shirked its legal responsibility to keep Congress "fully and currently informed" about covert operations, as noted in chapter ten.[14] A year later, in April 1985, Congress refused to resume U.S. aid to the contras, agreeing only later to provide $27 million in nonmilitary assistance. The funds were made available through March 1986 and specifically excluded the CIA and Defense Department from participation in their distribution. As noted earlier, in April 1986 the House once again voted against a presidential request for renewal of aid to the contras.

The Reagan administration mounted an intensive lobbying campaign designed to reverse the House decision. Eventually it was successful. In June 1986 the House narrowly approved a $100 million aid package for the contras, including $70 million in military aid. The president thus prevailed over the Democratic leadership in the House, which, drawing an analogy with Vietnam, opposed military aid out of fear that it would be the first step toward direct U.S. military involvement. As House Speaker Thomas P. "Tip" O'Neill argued, "I see us becoming engaged step-by-step in a military situation that brings our boys directly into fighting."

The administration's victory in the House was widely regarded as the president's most important foreign policy victory to that point in his second term. That he had not been successful earlier in his contest with Congress over aid to the anti-Sandinista guerrillas is all the more striking given the presidential resources invested in the project.[15] Reagan on several occasions "appealed"

---

[14]Senator Barry Goldwater, chairman of the Senate Intelligence Committee, captured the mood in a pithy "Dear Bill" letter to CIA Director William Casey, in which he remarked, "I've been trying to figure out how I can most easily tell you my feelings about the discovery of the President having approved mining some of the harbors in Central America.

"It gets down to one, little, simple phrase: I am pissed off."

He continued: "Bill, this is no way to run a railroad and I find myself in a hell of a quandary. . . . The President has asked us to back his foreign policy. Bill, how can we back his foreign policy when we don't know what the hell he is doing?" (*Congressional Quarterly Weekly Report*, April 14, 1984: 833).

[15]Referring to El Salvador as well as Nicaragua, Destler usefully describes the way Congress constrained the administration's Central American policies:

It . . . trimmed, at the margins, the resources available. It . . . imposed a substantial tax on the time and energies of administration officials to extract those resources they got. It . . . forced those officials to give some attention to the values—internal reform, human rights—which the [administration's] initial . . . approach seemed to ignore. And by both legislation and public advocacy, Congress . . . increased the cost to the administration of going beyond its stated policies with Nicaragua as the clearest case. (Destler, 1984: 334).

his case to the American people by "going over the heads of Congress" in nationally televised appeals for support of his proposals. The imagery evoked by the Great Communicator called upon some of the most centrist values in the nation's foreign policy experience. The contras were variously described as "freedom fighters" and "our brothers," while those opposing aid to the insurgents were labeled "new isolationists" who, if, as alleged on another occasion, they "hide their heads in the sand and pretend the strategic threat in Nicaragua will go away . . . are courting disaster and history will hold them accountable." The president and other top administration officials described the "strategic threat" variously: "another Cuba"; "a privileged sanctuary for terrorists and subversives just two days driving time from Harlingen, Texas"; "a permanent staging ground for terrorism, a home away from home for Khadafy, and the Ayatollah, just three hours by air from the U.S. border." Ultimately, the president asked rhetorically in March 1986, "Will we give the Nicaraguan democratic resistance the means to recapture their betrayed revolution, or will we turn our backs and ignore the malignancy in Managua until it spreads and becomes a mortal threat to the entire New World?" "Those who would compromise must not compromise the freedom fighters' lives nor their immediate defensive needs," he continued. "They must not compromise freedom."

The Reagan administration's struggles with an assertive Congress contain little evidence to encourage those who prefer a return to an acquiescent or accommodative style of interactions on foreign policy matters. The historical overview given here suggests nonetheless that executive-congressional relations are cyclical. Foreign policy is not unique, however, as suggested by Figure 12.1. The figure shows the percentage of times in selected congressional votes (including votes on foreign policy items) that a position the president personally supported was also supported by Congress. It is clear from the figure that Reagan, despite his personal popularity, has not been unambiguously more effective with Congress than his predecessors. In fact, his status as a lame duck president seemed to engulf him already in 1985, as the president's ability to work his will in Congress continued the decline evident since 1981, during which the president scored a series of key legislative victories on parts of his economic program. It is also interesting to compare Reagan's legislative success with Carter's, a president widely reputed to have been unskilled in managing successfully both legislators and legislation. Although the data displayed in Figure 12.1 are fragmentary and subject to qualifications, they suggest the need to reevaluate some popular but potentially inaccurate images of the Carter presidency, which seems to fall well within the general parameters of presidential success in congressional votes as evident over the past quarter century.

Disenchantment with the Vietnam quagmire and later the Watergate abuses were the critical catalysts giving rise to congressional acrimony in the 1970s. In a larger sense, however, it wasn't just Vietnam or Watergate but rather a breakdown of the conditions on which congressional acquiescence of

FIGURE 12.1   Presidential Success on Congressional Votes, 1953–1985

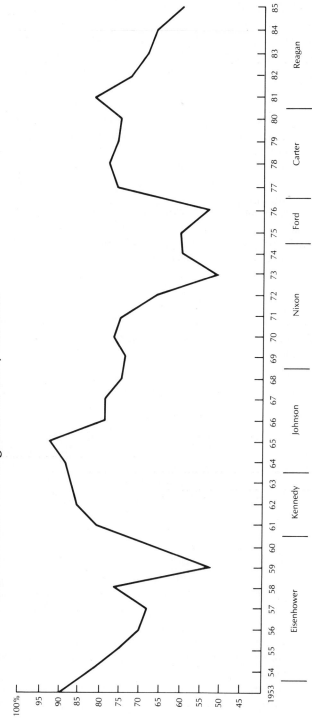

SOURCE: *Congressional Quarterly Weekly Report*, January 11, 1986: 69. Copyright © 1986 Congressional Quarterly, Inc. Reprinted with permission.

NOTE: Percentages based on votes on which presidents took a position.

the 1950s and 1960s had been based. Congressional acquiescence, as Bax (1977) argues, is possible only when two conditions are fulfilled. First, there must be substantial consensus in the nation on the general purposes of policy. Second, the specific means chosen by the president to pursue those purposes must be generally successful. That those conditions should crumble in the wake of Vietnam is significant, however. For there is a pattern here, in that an assertive congressional mood has typically coincided with, and followed, a major foreign war, much as congressional dissatisfaction in the 1950s coincided with the Korean War. The parallels with congressional activity in the post–Civil War Reconstruction era and in the post–World War I "return to normalcy" period are striking. Moreover, the general trend of congressional behavior since World War II suggests an important fact:

> Congress pays much less attention to constitutional niceties or consistency than it does to pragmatic considerations. When Congress has agreed with the general thrust of presidential policy, it has acquiesced in the use or even the enlargement of presidential power. When it has disagreed, it has asserted its own prerogatives. (Crabb and Holt, 1984: 129)

It would appear, then, that Congress, if willing, is able to effect greater control over foreign policy making than the initiator-respondent characterization suggests. Does Congress have the ability? Indeed, is it yet certain that Congress is willing?

CONGRESS AND FOREIGN POLICY

Although historically Congress has played an assertive role at one time (notably following war), and a politically necessary (if acquiescent) role at another, neither description overrides the fact that as an institution Congress is poorly equipped to compete effectively with the executive when it comes to outlining the basic features of America's conduct abroad. Three interrelated factors explain this: parochialism, organizational weaknesses, and lack of expertise.

Parochialism

Congress is more oriented toward domestic than foreign affairs. All 435 members of the House are up for reelection every two years, as is a third of the Senate. Continual preoccupation with reelection (admittedly more important on the House side than the Senate) creates pressure to attend more to parochial interests than to international concerns. The pressure is reinforced by the fact that the president has a national constituency; all 535 members of Congress have much more narrowly construed electoral bases and corresponding sets of constituency interests.

Because senators and representatives depend for their survival on satisfying the interests of their rather limited constituencies, it is natural that they see the world in those terms. Indeed, "being national-minded can be a positive hazard to a legislative career" (Sundquist, 1976). Or as former senator, and chairman of the Senate Foreign Relations Committee, J. William Fulbright, observed: "With their excessively parochial orientation, congressmen are acutely sensitive to the influence of private pressure and to the excesses and inadequacies of a public opinion that is all too often ignorant of the needs, the dangers, and the opportunities in our foreign relations" (cited in Lehman, 1976).[16] Thus a foreign policy problem viewed from the vantage point of a particular constituency may predispose a representative toward the Greek, Israeli, or Irish viewpoint, and the needs of the military begin to be weighed in terms of the industries located within a state or district. A story told by Henry Stimson about the chairman of the House Naval Affairs Committee early in the century underscores the point. "Asked one day whether it was true that the navy yard in his district was too small to accommodate the latest battleships, the chairman replied, 'That is true, and that is the reason I have always been in favor of small ships'" (Sundquist, 1976).

The president's vantage point is much different. Because he has a nationwide constituency and a government-wide perspective on foreign policy problems, he necessarily brings a much broader outlook to them. And more to the point, perhaps, he can usually afford to alienate some local or narrow interests (by closing a military base, for example) without fear of electoral retribution. He can be rewarded for thinking in terms of the long run instead of the problems of the moment. A senator or representative cannot.

The inward, home-base focus of senators and representatives typically means that interest in and attention to foreign policy issues will be short-lived, with the duration determined by how newsworthy the issue is (Crabb and Holt, 1984). In the mid-1970s the issue of controlling intelligence activities commanded considerable attention. Since then it has receded from the limelight, and most of those once heavily involved in the issue have moved on to other matters. "Summing up a conversation about attempts by Congress to restore its powers, one senator characteristically exclaimed, 'I think we've made substantial headlines—I mean headway'" (Crabb and Holt, 1984).

Parochialism is reinforced by the congressional committee system, in which the institution's real work is done. Members of Congress are motivated to serve on committees as a way of achieving such goals as reelection, influence within their chambers, good public policy, and careers beyond their present ones (Fenno, 1973; see also Smith and Deering, 1984). Although the congressional committee system may be compatible with achieving each of those goals, prospects for reelection in particular are enhanced through constituent service. Members of Congress are best able to perform such service by

---

[16]Former Under Secretary of State William D. Rogers (1979) makes a similar point: "Congress cannot resist the temptation to play low politics with high policy. With the fate of the entire House and a third of the Senate in the hands of the voters every 730 days, Congress is beholden to every short-term swing of popular opinion. The temptation to pander to prejudice and emotion is overwhelming."

gaining an assignment to a committee relevant to their constituencies' interests. The preferred means of making such assignments from the point of view of both those who get the assignments and those who make them is by taking that fact into account. The prospects for internal influence and for affecting public policy are enhanced in the process.

> Farm state members want to deal with agriculture while city people do not, so the agriculture committees are rural and proagriculture in their composition. The military affairs committees are dominated by partisans of the military, urban affairs committees by members from the cities, interior committees by proreclamation westerners, and so on. By custom, the judiciary committees are made up exclusively of lawyers. Within each committee, there is further specialization of subcommittees and of individual members. The decisions of the specialists have to be accepted by their colleagues most of the time without more than a cursory examination; a fresh and exhaustive review of every question by every member is obviously impossible. And through logrolling, the advocates of various local interobviously impossible. And through logrolling, the advocates of various local interests form coalitions of mutual support. (Sundquist, 1976: 600)

Organizational Weaknesses

The congressional committee system is representative of the fragmentation of both power and responsibility within Congress. President Truman's famous quip, "The buck stops here!" has no counterpart in Congress. On the contrary, over half of the standing committees in both the House and Senate have jurisdictions so broadly defined as to give them some kind of foreign affairs responsibility (see Table 12.1). By no means does that mean the executive branch is monolithic, as our discussion of the two preceding concentric circles of policy making should have made abundantly clear. But there is an important difference in the sense that executive branch policy debates tend to take place in private, with a single individual, the president, often making the final choice, whereas congressional debates are perforce public, with final choices made by counting yeas and nays, and with the centers of decision making being fragmented and diffuse.[17]

During the 1970s Congress undertook a number of procedural reforms that decentralized power from the committee to the subcommittee level, encouraged challenges to the seniority system, and reduced the importance of leadership positions.[18] The consequence was that it became more difficult than

[17]Smith and Deering (1984: 276–277) provide empirical data on the jurisdictional fragmentation of congressional committees based on the number of departments or agencies under each committee and the number of areas of legislative jurisdiction for each in their respective chamber rules. On the basis of these data, the House Foreign Affairs Committee has an average rank of 6.5 (among twenty-one committees) in terms of its jurisdictional fragmentation, and the Senate Foreign Relations Committee an average rank of 4.5 (among fifteen committees).

[18]As one senior national political correspondent noted wryly, "there are 165 different people in the House and Senate who can answer to the proud title 'Mr. Chairman,' having been given committees or subcommittees of their own" (Broder, 1986: 9). Cavanagh (1982–83)) explores a

TABLE 12.1 Responsibilities of Foreign Affairs Committees in the House and Senate

Senate Committee	Foreign Affairs Responsibility	House Committee
Agriculture, Nutrition and Forestry	Foreign agricultural policy and assistance	Agriculture
Appropriations	Appropriation of revenues, rescission of appropriations	Appropriations
Armed Services	Defense, national security, national security aspects of nuclear energy	Armed Services
Banking, Housing and Urban Affairs	Foreign commerce, international economic policy, export and foreign trade promotion	Banking, Finance and Urban Affairs; Energy and Commerce
Budget	Budgetary matters	Budget
Commerce, Science and Transportation	Merchant marine, marine fisheries, oceans, coastal zone management, nonmilitary space sciences and aeronautics	Merchant Marine and Fisheries; Science and Technology
Energy and Natural Resources	Energy policy, nonmilitary development of nuclear energy	Energy and Commerce; Science and Technology
Environment and Public Works	Environmental policy, ocean dumping, environmental aspects of outer continental shelf lands	Science and Technology
Finance	Revenue measures, customs, foreign trade agreements, tariffs, import quotas	Ways and Means
Foreign Relations	Relations with foreign nations, treaties, executive agreements, international organizations, foreign assistance, intervention abroad, declarations of war	Foreign Affairs
Governmental Affairs	Organization and reorganization of the executive branch, organization and management of nuclear export policy	Government Operations
Intelligence	Intelligence activities, covert operations	Intelligence
Judiciary	Immigration and naturalization	Judiciary
Labor and Human Resources	Regulation of foreign laborers	Education and Labor

NOTE: Descriptions of the foreign affairs responsibilities are derived from the jurisdictions of the Senate committees in the 99th Congress, with the corresponding jurisdictions of House committees matched to those as closely as possible. All of the committees are standing committees of the respective houses of Congress except the Intelligence committees, both of which are select committees.

ever to locate power and influence in Congress. The leadership finds it increasingly difficult to speak for the institution as a whole, and individual members of Congress from committees other than those traditionally concerned with foreign policy are able to take the initiative in defining particular issues and setting agendas. Many of the restraints on executive flexibility emerging during the 1970s (for example, the legislative veto on military sales and the Turkish arms embargo) were the product of individual initiatives taken by members of Congress outside the congressional foreign policy "establishment" (Franck and Weisband, 1979).

The rise of single-issue politics—which subjects members of Congress to evaluation not on the basis of their entire record but only their performance on particular issues—has exacerbated the problems associated with the diffusion of power.[19] Noting that the 385 committees and subcommittees of Congress are scouted by more than 1,300 registered lobbyists, one former official lamented that instead of a two-party system, Capitol Hill resembled "a 385 -party system" (cited in Crabb and Holt, 1984: 224).

The diffusion of power and sharing of responsibility within Congress means that no one is capable of speaking for the whole institution, which complicates and frustrates efforts at executive-legislative consultation and coordination. It also leads to the charge that Congress is irresponsible. When facing a skeptical electorate, for example, individual senators and representatives can always hide behind the defense that "I didn't do it; it was everyone else." Such individual unaccountability is reinforced by the congressional penchant for dealing with issues in procedural terms rather than confronting them directly. A striking illustration was provided during the Senate's consideration of the two Panama Canal treaties: "In all, senators offered 145 amendments, 26 reservations, 18 understandings, and 3 declarations—a grand total of 192 changes of one kind or another" (Crabb and Holt, 1984: 85).

The temptation to deal with matters procedurally is often irresistible. In the Panama Canal case, for example, a common procedural practice was to bill many of the proposed changes "improvements," which made it easier to vote for a politically unpopular document. In other words, procedure becomes a useful tool for coping with single-issue politics, because congressmen are able to mask the real effects of their votes and thereby deflect potential electoral criticism. They can also avoid direct confrontation with the executive by couching their opposition in procedural arguments to which the executive branch has no retort. A congressman makes the point cogently:

> If done directly, a Congressional decision—for example, to disapprove money for a new aircraft carrier—would require that more than half of all Congressmen conclude that the Navy can do with fewer carriers in the nineteen-eighties. This would

---

number of elements related to the dispersion of authority in the House since the 1960s, and Drischler (1985) provides insight into the importance of changes in Congress for the enactment of foreign affairs legislation.

[19]See Tesh (1984) for a statement "in support of 'single-issue' politics."

involve a stark confrontation with expertise that would be very uncomfortable for a Congressman. If a showdown is reached on the carrier issue, the vote is almost certain to be cloaked in procedures (motions to table, etc.) that would allow the Congressman to justify his vote, if he needed to, on a procedural question rather than on the merits of the case. The end-the-war vote in the House in 1972, for example, was in fact a motion to table, a motion to instruct the conferees to insist on the House version of the Defense Authorization bill in the light of the Legislative Reorganization Act of 1970. Nobody's constituents would ever be able to figure that one out. (Aspin, 1976: 165)

Procedure, then, is purposely used to avoid direct responsibility. This does not mean that members of Congress are incapable of performing their jobs. On the contrary, by masking the real effects of their votes in procedural gobbledygook, members of Congress may perhaps more readily take the road of conscience rather than the road of convenience. Yet there is another dimension, a lack of responsibility, that speaks less kindly. It manifests itself in the tendency of Congress to "leak" information. A glaring example occurred in the winter of 1976, when, after several years of striking a more responsible pose on foreign policy matters, the House voted not to release the controversial Pike committee report on the CIA—only to have a copy that was leaked to CBS news correspondent Daniel Schorr appear in the *Village Voice*.

Congressional leaks of information arise perhaps naturally out of the more open and public processes of Congress, but they are also related to the independence which senators and representatives prize. Hence, they are prone to seize upon opportunities placing them in the mass media's spotlight. One of the consequences is that the president often has used "executive privilege" to conceal information—particularly classified information—thereby denying Congress an effective role in policy making.

Finally, irresponsibility (of a different sort, perhaps) arises out of the very sluggishness of the legislative process. Slow, deliberative procedures may be inherent in a body charged with reconciling disparate views, but delays are accentuated in the American context by such factors as the dispersion of power and responsibility between two houses, their further fragmentation within a complex structure of committees and subcommittees, and the erosion, even absence, of party discipline.[20] "The result is that any piece of legislation must surmount an obstacle course of unparalleled difficulty. . . . [F]ew things happen quickly. Policies eventually adopted are often approved too late. . . . And in the process of overcoming the countless legislative hurdles, policies may be compromised to the point of ineffectiveness" (Sundquist, 1976). Contrast that picture with the president's proven ability to act quickly and decisively, as rapidly moving and often dangerous international events frequently seem to require. "Presidents can procrastinate too," James L.

---

[20]The rule in the Senate requiring an extraordinary majority for terminating debate (the cloture rule) is another complicating factor. As former Senate Majority Leader Robert C. Byrd put it in the context of the Senate's debate of President Carter's energy proposals: "It would be impossible for Jesus Christ to do anything without unanimous consent."

Sundquist observes, "but unlike Congress they are not compelled to by any institutional structure."

Lack of Expertise

A third organizational weakness contributing to the "respondent" relationship of Congress vis-à-vis the executive derives from the president's relatively greater command of technical expertise and from his ability to control the flow of information. This fact should be apparent from the preceding discussion of the departments and agencies comprising the second concentric circle, all of which are *executive* branch organizations. Although such organizations have the capacity to frustrate presidential dominance in foreign affairs (as we shall show in chapter thirteen), they contribute enormously to presidential supremacy over Congress. For without the willingness to create independent information-gathering capabilities on the mammoth scale of the executive branch both at home and abroad, Congress continues to depend on the executive branch to call the tune in foreign policy making. That dependence is compounded by the perceived need for secrecy in national security matters, plus the frequent necessity to act quickly. Neither contributes to independent legislative scrutiny of the executive's information or recommendations. Thus the changing character of information and intelligence in modern policy making is largely responsible for the tendency of legislative bodies such as Congress to react to executive initiative rather than to seize the initiative itself.

Congress has sought to overcome its lack of expertise in several ways. Periodically it has expanded the overseer role of the General Accounting Office as a way of better equipping itself to deal with the executive. It created the Office of Technology Assessment to evaluate scientific and technical proposals and the Congressional Budget Office to assist in analyzing budget options and preparing the annual budget resolution. Most important, perhaps, the size of the professional staff serving congressional committees and individual members of Congress has grown enormously in recent years—from less than 10,000 in 1972 to more than 21,000 in 1985, a growth rate that supports the view that since the 1960s Congress has been the fastest-growing bureaucracy in Washington (Malbin, 1980: 253, 256; Broder, 1986: 9; see also Fox and Hammond, 1977).[21]

The growth of congressional staff has had a dual impact on the foreign policy role of Congress:

A larger staff provides Congress the *means* to assert its own independent position vis-à-vis the executive branch with regard to major international questions. It also

[21]Precise figures are more difficult to establish than these numbers suggest. For example, Malbin (1980: 252) puts the total congressional staff in 1979 at 23,528, a figure which includes not only personal staff and the staff of standing committees but also select committee staff, leadership staff, staff of the House and Senate offices, joint committee staff, and staff of the support agencies (the General Accounting Office, Congressional Research Service, Congressional Budget Office, and Office of Technology Assessment). See also the *Congressional Quarterly Weekly Report*, November 24, 1979: 2,636–2,638, and Smith and Deering, 1984: 205.

supplies national legislators with a new *incentive* to become active in a field where, during an earlier period, they often had neither the interest nor the expertise to become deeply involved. (Crabb and Holt, 1984: 220–221)

To that could be added the ability of congressional staffs, in an atmosphere where knowledge is power, to tip the balance in struggles between executive agencies, and thereby to influence the direction of policy.

Committee staffs are most important because they have great influence over legislation. The technical experts filling staff roles, and the networks of communications and coalitions that have developed among them, operate as an "invisible force in American lawmaking" in steering policy (Fox and Hammond, 1977). But whether the growth of congressional staff has enhanced the ability of Congress to cope with the complex issues of foreign policy is uncertain. Clearly the increase in staff size has led to a corresponding increase in the information available to members of Congress, but that is no guarantee of better policy making. In any large organization information is often biased. Just as Congress must be wary of information provided by the executive, now it also must determine whether the information it receives from its own staffs may not be designed to serve some special interest (Malbin, 1977).

The foreign policy initiatives taken by individual members of Congress during the 1970s can be traced in many cases to activist legislative staffers. Senator Henry Jackson's initiatives on questions relating to trade and strategic arms negotiations with the Soviet Union, for example, have been attributed as much to Jackson's influential national security adviser as to the senator himself (Destler, 1985). The reasons are not hard to find. Staff assistants are typically ambitious people for whom Capitol Hill is merely a steppingstone to bigger and better things. Getting the boss's name in the news therefore serves not only the boss but also his or her aide: the more visible the boss, the more influential the aide responsible for that visibility. "In fact, a staff member typically has much stronger stakes in pushing any particular proposal than does his boss since the legislator will have a number of policy aides and a number of initiatives pending" (Destler, 1985).

Individual initiatives may promote individual careers. For Congress as a whole, they have the effect of contributing to the diffusion of power. If the phrase "385-party system" describes Congress, so does "535 power centers." From the vantage point of the executive such an amorphous congressional body is complex, and an element of unpredictability is thereby added to the nation's foreign policy. The director of a Carnegie Endowment project on executive-congressional relations put it this way: "Institutional decentralization, policy conviction, and ample staffing encourage legislators to become involved in the detail of policy. This not only takes away executive flexibility, but it also adds new uncertainty because no one can predict what Congress ultimately will do" (Destler, 1981).

Doubtless Congress has enhanced its foreign policy expertise (as has the executive), but its continuing attachment to procedure reflects its meager resources *relative* to the executive branch. "Caution," observes Congressman

Aspin, "is a prime political virtue because it is expedient." And procedure is a handmaiden of caution. That is not meant to suggest that individual members of Congress do not in some cases possess exceptional expertise on certain matters. On the contrary, the committee system and the corresponding congressional preference for allocating positions of authority according to the rules of seniority (despite challenges to it) mean that some senators and representatives often spend their entire legislative careers specializing in their committees' areas. Some congressional careers have spanned more than a quarter of a century, much longer than any postwar president has been permitted by the Constitution to remain in office. Historically, specialization by entrenched members of Congress has been especially prominent in the House and Senate Armed Services committees, where southern Democrats in particular have claimed considerable expertise on national defense issues.

At the same time the committee and seniority systems have laid the basis for development of the kinds of patron-client relationships between Congress and the foreign policy bureaucracy described in the previous chapter. Whereas such relationships often have subverted the interests of the president and the presidency, they have also been a source of congressional power with regard to the executive.

> Every Congressman of seniority has cultivated numbers of career civil servants, military, foreign service, or intelligence officers throughout those agencies dealing in his areas of committee or constituent interest. The pattern of such symbiotic relationships typically stretches over three or more administrations. For the bureaucrat, the relationship yields benefits (or protection) to his agency or bureau office, or perhaps to his job. It can assist in promotion and even such things as service academy appointments to favored sons. The Congressman of course gains access to information and an influence on the day-to-day application to policy. (Lehman, 1976: 33)

But all members of Congress cannot be experts on all matters of policy. The executive, however, can be and is. When expertise is lacking, the tendency is to look to the experts—that is, the executive. It is especially pronounced in matters of foreign policy and national security, where there is a corresponding tendency to "play it safe."[22] Moreover, members of Congress are especially ill equipped to acquire the kinds of information that would enable them to better monitor, and hence influence, decision making in times of crisis. Following the Ford administration's use of marines to rescue the ship *Mayaguez* from its Cambodian captors in May 1975, for example, the House Foreign Affairs (then the International Relations) Committee and the General Accounting Office conducted a survey of members of Congress in which 80 percent of those who responded indicated that the press was their principal source of information

---

[22]In an interesting variant on this theme, Destler (1986) argues that in the area of foreign trade policy Congress devised a number of means that enabled it "to avoid having to fix the level of import protection for individual commodities," the main result of which "was not protection for industry but protection for Congress—insulation of its members from trade pressures."

during the *Mayaguez* seizure. Three out of five members serving on congressional committees directly concerned with international military and political affairs also said the media were their principal source of information. Little wonder that one (anonymous) member of Congress cynically observed that "the actions of the United States are not secret to other nations, only to Congress and the American people" (*Congressional Quarterly Weekly Report*, November 13, 1976). Little wonder also that the role of Congress is best described as a negative one, in which Congress serves as a public critic of what the executive has already done. The same relationship characterizes the exercise of congressional powers with respect to treaties, war, and money.

THE POWERS OF CONGRESS AND FOREIGN POLICY MAKING

As indicated in the opening pages of chapter ten, congressional powers with respect to foreign policy as embodied in the Constitution would appear to be more far-reaching than those of the president. Its powers with respect to treaties, war, and money, in particular, would appear to give it a commanding position, enabling it to set overall policy much like a board of directors does in private enterprise. But the reality is quite different.

Treaties

Treaty-making powers rest in the Senate, whose advice and consent (by two-thirds vote) is necessary before the president can enter into a treaty with another country.[23] The Senate Foreign Relations Committee bears primary responsibility for conducting the hearings and investigations on which senatorial advice and consent are based. The Senate has broad responsibilities over other foreign policy matters as well, including, for example, an initial approval of presidentially appointed foreign policy officials. These functions at one time made the Foreign Relations Committee the most prestigious of all Senate committees, and hence the assignment most desired by members of the Senate. But the influence of the committee has waned since J. William Fulbright left its chairmanship in 1974.[24] Still, it remains an important base for those senators aspiring to visibility and a reputation in foreign affairs.

Despite the importance of the treaty clause of the Constitution, the precise

[23]The requirement that any treaty must receive consent by a two-thirds majority effectively concentrates power in the hands of only thirty-four of the 535 members of Congress. A practical consequence of the rule is the difficulty it presents for mobilizing sufficient support for controversial treaties. It has been observed that "Partisans and zealots can get a Senate one-third-plus-one minority on almost any controversial subject" (*The New Republic*, March 4, 1978). The two-thirds rule thus often operates more as a barrier to foreign policy change than as a facilitator of it.

[24]According to the authoritative Congressional Quarterly service, the most sought after Senate committees in recent years have been Appropriations and Finance, with Armed Services and Budget also in demand. In the House, Appropriations, Ways and Means, and Rules have been the most preferred, with Energy and Commerce, Budget, and Banking, Finance, and Urban Affairs often in demand (*Congressional Quarterly Weekly Report*, April 27, 1985: 3).

mechanism whereby senatorial advice and consent is to be proffered the president is ambiguous. The result is that from the very beginning of the Republic the provision has been open to dispute and the subject of controversy. In barest form the process works when the president (that is, his representatives) negotiates a treaty with another nation in his capacity as the nation's chief diplomat, which the Senate then merely votes up or down.[25] More likely, advice is given in written communications between the executive and the legislature or through the inclusion of members of Congress in the treaty negotiating team. The latter practice has been widespread ever since the Senate's rejection of the Versailles treaty, which would have brought the United States into the League of Nations, and which had been negotiated without senatorial representation on the Peace Commission.[26]

Consent is still established by a two-thirds vote, but the Senate has also adopted the practice of attaching reservations to treaties. These may take the form of amendments to treaties which require the executive to renegotiate the terms of the treaty with other signatory nations—a potentially serious problem, particularly with the increase in the number of multilateral treaties. Alternatively, reservations, or "conditions," may simply incorporate the Senate's interpretation of the treaty without any binding effect on parties to the treaty. Other variants are reservations that apply only to the United States. Perhaps the most important example of such reservations is the so-called Connally Amendment to the Statute of the International Court of Justice, whereby the United States reserves for itself determination of whether matters falling under the compulsory jurisdiction clause of the court are essentially within the domestic jurisdiction of the United States. As still another variant there are conditions which seek to bind presidential behavior. When the Senate Foreign Relations Committee finally approved the SALT II treaty in late 1979 (which, however, was never voted on by the full Senate), it did so with the stipulation that American defense spending be sharply increased in future years. The ability of the Senate to attach reservations to treaties does not undermine the initiator-respondent description of executive-congressional relations. But it should be apparent that the president cannot rush headlong into treaty making without at least some deference to congressional views.[27]

Historically, the Senate's record of treaty ratification has been overwhelmingly positive. During this century only six treaties have failed to receive the two-thirds vote necessary for Senate advice and consent (Congressional Research Service, 1984: 117). Only two rejections occurred in the

---

[25]Negotiations with foreign governments are normally the exclusive preserve of the executive branch. However, Senator Howard Baker made an unprecedented move when he engaged in actual negotiations with the Panamanian government while on a fact-finding trip to Panama during the course of the deliberations on the Panama Canal treaties (Crabb and Holt, 1984).

[26]Another widespread practice is that of including members of Congress on delegations to international conferences. See Riggs (1977) for an assessment of the effects of international participation on congressional attitudes.

[27]Lepper (1971), drawing on the Nuclear Test Ban treaty of 1963, provides interesting insight into the Senate's role in the treaty-making process. See also Lehman (1976) for a case study involving the Spanish military base agreements.

postwar period. Perhaps this record reflects presidential deference to congressional views. More likely, however, it reflects the substantial consensus between the president and the Congress on the appropriate role of the United States in world affairs, a consensus embodied in the concept of "bipartisanship." It is generally agreed that matters involving the nation's security should not be subjected to partisan debate or, as a popular slogan proclaims, "Politics stops at the water's edge."

The kinds of behavior assumed to be associated with bipartisanship remain ambiguous, but generally the concept presupposes broad-based agreement within American society about the appropriate role of the United States in world affairs. Deeply held anticommunist values were at the heart of such a consensus in the 1950s and early 1960s, but the Vietnam conflict opened questions about foreign policy to factional and partisan dispute. Decision makers continued in the 1970s to advocate maintenance of the same bipartisan unity of an earlier period, arguing its necessity for effectively carrying out the nation's purposes abroad. But critics raised important questions about the appropriateness of bipartisanship in an era when the value consensus that had supported the American role appeared to have broken down. James A. Nathan and James K. Oliver (1976), for example, argue that Henry Kissinger's call for continued bipartisanship during his White House and State Department tenure was understandable, based on the need he perceived for flexibility, responsiveness, and a degree of ambiguity in American national security policy—a need rationalizing the centralization of control over foreign policy and national security operations in the White House. Yet, they continue, if foreign and national security policy were subjected to partisan debate and scrutiny that need would have been challenged because, at least during the mid-1970s, the "values and substance of American national security [were] no longer self-evident to many" (Nathan and Oliver, 1976). On some issues, notably defense spending, somewhat greater partisan unity was apparent during the early phases of the Reagan administration—largely as a result of what were seen as challenging initiatives by the Soviet Union—but on other questions, such as aid to Central America, partisan disagreements persisted.[28]

If bipartisanship historically provided the support necessary for congressional acquiescence to presidentially initiated treaties, executive agreements provided a means for avoiding the necessity of securing the advice and consent of the Senate altogether.[29] For although such government-to-government agreements have essentially the same legal force as treaties, and thus become

[28]The political potency of bipartisanship is suggested by how frequently policy makers invoke the idea. Secretary of State Shultz chose the theme "Bipartisanship in Foreign Affairs" for an address before the American Bar Association in May 1985, for example, and President Reagan labeled as "bipartisan" two of his most important foreign policy commissions, those popularly known as the "Kissinger Commission," charged with devising alternative Central American policies, and the "Scowcroft Commission," concerned with the MX missile-basing mode and the larger issue of United States strategic defense policies.

[29]The term *executive agreement* has come to be used to refer to any international agreement which is not submitted to the Senate. In fact, however, even that definition is ambiguous, as we will note below.

part of the "supreme law of the land," they may be concluded without legislative scrutiny.[30] Examples of some of the more prominent recent executive agreements include the Paris peace agreement on Ending the War and Restoring Peace in Vietnam (1973); the SALT I accords (1972); and various agreements covering American military base rights in Spain, the Azores, Diego Garcia, Bahrain, and Iceland. Earlier examples include the agreements necessary to implement the Lend Lease Act of 1941, under which the United States provided war materials to its World War II allies; and the Truman plan for providing aid to Greece and Turkey in the late 1940s.

The preceding examples indicate clearly that executive agreements often cover some of the most important aspects of foreign relations. And their quantity indicates that they have been a preferred mechanism for reaching international accords. In the period from 1946 through 1985 the United States concluded over 10,100 executive agreements, compared with only 598 treaties.[31] Proportionately, then, 94 percent of all international agreements concluded by the United States since World War II have not been subjected to the formal procedures of the Senate, a proportion remarkably constant on an annual basis. Such data should not be used as an index of presidential dominance or of arbitrary executive action, since many of those agreements are based on statutory directives while others are entered into pursuant to treaty provisions. One study reports, for example, that of the over 7,000 agreements concluded with other nations between 1946 and 1976, 87 percent are so-called statutory or executive-congressional agreements, that is, agreements made pursuant to congressional legislation (Johnson and McCormick, 1977: 118). Nevertheless, the vast number of agreements made without the expressed advice and consent of the Senate indicates the enormous discretion the president has to pursue the nation's foreign policy unrestrained by constitutional checks and balances.

That executive agreements amount to an effort by a dominant presidency to evade Congress is attested to by periodic congressional attempts to block such maneuvers. One of the most sustained of those attempts occurred in

[30]See Stevens (1977), Johnson and McCormick (1977), and Johnson (1984) for useful discussions of executive agreements and of congressional efforts to curtail their use or otherwise assert greater congressional controls over them.

[31]As of March 1, 1984, 7,537 agreements were in force between the United States and other nations and international organizations. Of these, 6,571 were executive agreements, 966 treaties. Frequency counts of the number of executive agreements often differ because of the difficulty of defining exactly what constitutes an executive agreement. The following quip about a former secretary of state illustrates the problem:

> Secretary of State John Foster Dulles . . . said at the Bricker Amendment hearings that "every time we open a new privy, we have to have an executive agreement." Pointing out that with every treaty or agreement listed in the Executive Agreement Series there were numerous concomitant unlisted agreements, he estimated that about 10,000 such informal agreements accompanied the North Atlantic Treaty alone. Probably the number was picked out of the air, but Dulles was doubtless including informal understandings in letters, notes, even oral conversations, and routine transactions reflecting some element of consensus. (Henkin, 1972: 420, n. 1)

1953–1954, when Senator John Bricker proposed a constitutional amendment that would have had the effect of limiting the president's treaty-making powers. The proposal fell one vote short of the two-thirds majority necessary for Senate approval.

More recently, the congressional assault on executive prerogatives resulted in the enactment into law, in 1972, of a statute requiring the executive to submit to Congress all international agreements within sixty days of their execution. Passage of the law, which was popularly known as the Case Act, was in some sense the culmination of a process begun in the late 1960s, when the Senate Foreign Relations Committee successfully sponsored a sense-of-the-Senate (that is, without the binding force of law) National Commitments Resolution, declaring that no future commitments be made by the United States without the approval of Congress. Following that resolution, a Senate Foreign Relations Subcommittee on U.S. Security Agreements and Commitments Abroad, headed by Stuart Symington, undertook an extensive analysis of foreign commitments through which—to the surprise and chagrin of the committee—the breadth and depth of overseas commitments entered into by the executive, and without the knowledge of Congress, were unearthed.[32] In country after country a series of expressed, implied, secret, or open commitments were discovered which involved, or might involve, the United States in any number of ways in other countries. Not only were secret agreements and de facto understandings discovered, but knowledge was also gained about covert activities and paramilitary operations authorized by the executive with neither the knowledge nor approval of Congress. In case after case the Symington subcommittee found the executive tactic was to maximize the importance of American commitments in secret talks with foreign governments, but to minimize their importance at home (Irish and Frank, 1975).

The legal requirement that the executive submit to Congress the texts of all international agreements, largely a response to the secret agreements discovered by the Symington subcommittee, is one manifestation of congressional assertiveness toward a dominant presidency. But assertiveness is not equivalent to changing the balance between the president and the Congress in treaty making any more than it is in foreign policy making in general. The facts remain that the president is still the initiator of agreements with other governments and is still *not* required to get congressional advice or consent before such agreements can be concluded. Moreover, the law protects the secrecy of executive agreements by providing that the texts of agreements may be sent

[32]Again, however, some caution is required here. Proponents of the view that executive agreements provide a method of making de facto agreements without the participation of Congress overlooked the fact that by 1969:

> 97 percent of the agreements regarding the basing of U.S. personnel abroad were made pursuant to treaties approved by the Senate or statutes passed by Congress as a whole. Further, the vast majority of U.S. bases abroad had resulted from eight security treaties made with 43 countries in the period following World War II that were still in force. Major bases existed in only four countries without treaty sanction—Cuba, Morocco, Ethiopia, and Spain. (Lehman, 1976: 83)

only to the Senate Foreign Relations and House Foreign Affairs committees, under an injunction of secrecy, if the president determines that public disclosure would endanger the national security.[33] Thus the statute may have the effect of complicating the president's life, but there is serious question as to how much it has affected executive behavior. Nathan and Oliver provide a sobering post-Case Act experience:

> The habit of negotiating agreements and neglecting to inform Congress continues in spite of debate, disclosure, and legislation. In September 1975 Congress requested information from the Executive that might be pertinent to the Sinai Peace accord wherein 200 American technicians would be sent to man an area between opposing Israeli and Egyptian troops. The State Department was forced by a series of leaks to the press to acknowledge that understandings in the form of assurances regarding "the long standing U.S. commitment to the survival of Israel" had been given to the Israelis. Nevertheless, it was insisted by the State Department that these were not international agreements but merely "expressions of intent" which "leave our options open" and thus should not be made public or formally presented to the Senate for approval. (Nathan and Oliver, 1976: 489)

Another novel example of the ability of the president to side-step congressional restraints occurred in 1977. When it became apparent that the SALT II treaty would not be approved before the five-year interim SALT I accord expired, the Carter administration issued a declaration indicating that the United States would continue to abide by the terms of SALT I pending completion of the SALT II negotiations. The Soviet Union did likewise. An analogous tactic was used subsequently to ensure compliance with the signed but unratified SALT II treaty. The Reagan administration even voluntarily dismantled older nuclear submarines as the new Trident came on line rather than violate the limits on strategic weapons contained in the accord. The Soviets also publicly expressed their willingness to abide by the terms of SALT II (although the Reagan administration repeatedly castigated the Soviets for alleged violations and later used them to justify its announced intention to cease observing its provisions). Do such public announcements and tacit behavioral accommodations constitute international "agreements"?

The Case Act is directed essentially toward the question of secrecy of executive actions. It does not raise the issue of presidential authority to enter into executive agreements. Congressional efforts to cope with executive prerogatives, and with the question of the necessity of congressional approval, have been frustrated in part by the differing perspectives that the House and Senate bring to the issue (Franck and Weisband, 1979). Although both houses of Congress have shown concern for executive agreements with other countries that bypass Congress completely, the Senate is equally concerned with execu-

---

[33]As of January 1, 1986, 4,800 international agreements had been transmitted to Congress pursuant to the Case Act. Of those, 219 were transmitted under the injunction of secrecy provision of the statute (Treaty Affairs, Office of the Legal Advisor, U.S. Department of State, personal communication, April 1986).

tive agreements that spring from acts of Congress, since they bypass the ''advice and consent'' of the Senate required by the Constitution. The House, on the other hand, sees executive-congressional agreements as a vehicle for exercising a greater voice in foreign policy matters, which recently it has been prone to do. Although historically only a junior partner to the Senate in such matters, the House nearly nullified the Senate's final action on the Panama Canal treaties when it temporarily balked at passing what normally would have been routine implementing legislation. It, too, was being assertive, in this case toward that legislative arm given exclusive constitutional jurisdiction over the approval of treaties. The House, therefore, is not necessarily concerned with cutting back the president's use of executive agreements, ''but with exercising greater direct control over their content. For the House, in other words, the issue is less one of Constitutional purism than of Congressional oversight'' (Franck and Weisband, 1979).

Beyond the Case Act, little has been done to strengthen the position of Congress in relation to the executive in the treaty-making enterprise. In the meantime, the president continues to exercise leadership in making treaties and other agreements with foreign powers, and the historical record—which now covers more than seventy years of attempts to alter the treaty-making provisions of the Constitution—indicates that Congress is unlikely to enjoy much success in curbing executive independence.

War

A similar degree of caution must be used in assessing legislative war-making powers. The Constitution would appear to be clear on that issue by stating (Article I, Section 8) that ''the Congress shall have power . . . to declare war.'' Elsewhere, however (Article II, Section 2), the Constitution specifies that ''the President shall be Commander-in-Chief of the Army and Navy of the United States.'' Of the two provisions, the latter has proven the more important, for the president has used that provision to defend the stationing of troops all over the world; the provision was also used to justify American military intervention in Korea (1950–1953), Lebanon (1958), the Dominican Republic (1965–1966), and Vietnam (1965–1973, if not earlier). Yet in none of those cases was military action accompanied by a formal declaration of war.

Protracted American involvement in Korea and, in particular, Vietnam, set the stage for sharp criticism from Congress and attempts to redress the war-making balance. In the case of Vietnam, the issue was whether President Johnson had exceeded his constitutional powers by continually escalating the nation's involvement without a corresponding congressional mandate. Johnson, in turn, argued that his authority rested on the Gulf of Tonkin Resolution, passed by Congress in August 1964. By that joint resolution, the president was accorded congressional support and approval ''to take all necessary measures to repel any armed attack against the forces of the United States and to prevent further aggression.''

The meaning of the Gulf of Tonkin Resolution became the source of intense debate as the quagmire of Vietnam deepened. With hindsight, it is now generally agreed that Congress was duped by a president who controlled the information, and hence the policy.[34] At the same time, however, it should be noted that four times previously Congress had authorized the president to use armed forces to defend certain geographical areas—in the Formosa Straits Resolution (1955), the Eisenhower Middle East Doctrine Resolution (1957), the Cuban Resolution (1962), and the Berlin Resolution (1962). What seemed to differentiate the Tonkin Gulf Resolution was (1) the magnitude and duration of military involvement in Vietnam, and (2) the assertion by then Under Secretary of State Nicholas Katzenbach that the resolution was the "functional equivalent" of a declaration of war.

Katzenbach's interpretation was rejected partially with the passage of the National Commitments Resolution in 1969 and further with the repeal of the Gulf of Tonkin Resolution in 1970. More concrete steps to limit presidential war-making prerogatives were embodied in the War Powers Act passed by Congress over President Nixon's veto in 1973. That act provides that troop commitments by the president cannot extend beyond sixty days without specific congressional authorization, although this period can be extended up to ninety days if the safety of American troops is at stake. The law also provides that at any time American forces are engaged in hostilities without a declaration of war or a specific congressional authorization, Congress can direct the president to disengage such troops by a concurrent resolution of the two houses of Congress. Because such a measure would not require the president's signature to take effect, it constitutes a legislative veto of the sort the Supreme Court ruled unconstitutional in 1983. Presumably that provision of the War Powers Act is now null and void. The sixty-day limit and various consulting and reporting requirements remain intact.

In his veto message, President Nixon raised important questions about both the constitutional and practical consequences of the War Powers Act. Regarding the sixty-day limit and the concurrent resolution provisions in particular, Nixon contended that they "purport to take away, by a mere legislative act, authorities which the President has properly exercised under the Constitution for almost 200 years." They are unconstitutional, he contended, because "the only way in which the constitutional powers of a branch of government can be altered is by amending the Constitution—and any attempt to make such alterations by legislation alone is clearly without force." He also asserted that the act would "seriously undermine the nation's ability to act decisively and convincingly in times of international crisis"; that it would "undercut the ability of the United States to act as an effective influence for peace"; and that it would "give every future Congress the ability to handcuff every future President."

[34]It is now clear that the circumstances used to sell the Tonkin Resolution were well staged and the timing of the resolution carefully calculated. Kattenburg (1980) reports that a draft of the resolution "had been reposing in Assistant Secretary of State William P. Bundy's drawer for several months." For accounts of the affair, see Goulden (1969) and Austin (1971).

If the constitutionality of the War Powers Act is tested in the courts, the judiciary probably will retreat to its traditional position that the issues raised are fundamentally political, not juridical, in nature. In the meantime, even though the War Powers Act remains a monument to Congress's assertive reaction to what it believed to be an imperial presidency, it has not effectively restrained the president's determination to use force abroad—and to do so without congressional involvement. The rescue of the *Mayaguez* authorized by President Ford in 1975 and the abortive attempt to rescue American hostages in Iran authorized by President Carter in 1980 both proceeded without prior consultation between Congress and the president despite the fact that the War Powers Act specifically urges the president to consult the Congress ''in every possible instance'' prior to committing U.S. forces to hostilities or to situations likely to result in hostilities. Congressional criticism of Ford's unwillingness to consult Congress in the *Mayaguez* operation was generally muted, despite the loss of forty-one marines in a mission designed to ''rescue'' thirty-nine crewmen who had already been released by their Cambodian captors. In the case of the Iranian operation, Congress generally accepted the Carter administration's contention that the need for secrecy plus the fact that the military force was engaged in a rescue operation rather than a military exercise precluded consultation with Congress.[35]

The Reagan administration's proclivity to use military force in pursuit of political objectives inevitably presented questions about the applicability of the War Powers Act. The prior consultation issue cropped up in April 1986, for example, when United States warplanes made a surprise nighttime attack on Tripoli and Benghazi in an operation designed to impose costs on Libyan leader Muammar Qaddafi's alleged support of international terrorism. Congressman Robert H. Michel, a Republican party leader and one of the dozen or so lawmakers briefed by the White House just before the Libyan raid, expressed the sentiment that ''we really ought to have some sort of vehicle for getting Congress into the mix, so we're not left out in the cold.'' ''We are in a war,'' he continued. ''It's a new kind of war. It's a terrorist war. We're going over a threshhold, we're ploughing new ground, and we have to think what comes next.''

Concern for another, all too familiar kind of war surfaced among members of Congress in 1981, when the Reagan administration decided to send military advisers to El Salvador. Several senators and congressmen voiced concern for the parallel to what they saw as the incremental decision-making process that ultimately drew the United States into the Vietnam quagmire. Accordingly, a number of resolutions were introduced in the House and Senate asserting the

---

[35]Although the Ford administration, like Nixon's, held the view that the War Powers Act was unconstitutional, it nevertheless complied with the reporting procedures embodied in the law not only in the case of the *Mayaguez* but also earlier, when it conducted a series of rescue missions from Danang, Saigon, and Phnom Penh as United States involvement in Indochina finally came to an end. The Carter administration likewise submitted a report to Congress after the Iranian rescue mission was aborted. The administration did not contest the constitutionality of the War Powers Act (Crabb and Holt, 1984; see also Holt, 1978).

administration's move required a report under the provisions of the War Powers Act. Although the administration never conceded that point,[36] it did agree that the number of advisers would not exceed fifty-five and that they would not be assigned combat roles.[37] The numbers and rules were never written into law, but the administration continued to honor them nonetheless.[38]

The invasion of Grenada by United States forces in October 1983 again raised a number of questions about the applicability of the War Powers Act and the president's compliance with both its letter and spirit. Key congressional leaders were briefed about the invasion, but "a careful reconstruction of the sequence of events that took place immediately before and after the decision to invade had been reached clearly shows that the Reagan administration circumvented the requirements to consult with Congress before deploying the troops in Grenada" (Rubner, 1985–86). Furthermore, although the president sent a report to Congress about the invasion shortly after it began, the report claimed only to be "consistent with the War Powers Resolution." By implication, the report did not recognize the right of Congress to prior consultation. Nor did it explicitly state that U.S. troops were being introduced "into hostilities or into situations where imminent involvement in hostilities is clearly indicated by the circumstances"—language from the act describing the circumstances that would set in motion the sixty-day clock requiring termination of the deployment of U.S. troops without explicit congressional authorization. "This proved to be a crucial omission because . . . it is only the submission of a 'hostilities' report . . . that triggers the automatic sixty-day termination provision" (Rubner, 1985–86). In any event, the administration characterized the Grenada mission as a "rescue" operation, the actual conflict was of short duration, and it was enormously popular. All of these factors militated against a concerted congressional effort to assert war-making prerogatives claimed by Congress vis-à-vis the executive (see also Rubner, 1985–86).

The most serious test of the War Powers Act came during the crisis in Lebanon in the fall of 1983. American marines were first sent to Lebanon in 1982 (under the president's authority as commander in chief) in the hope that they would be there only a short time. A year later they were still in Lebanon, and questions had begun to be raised not only about the objectives of American policy but also whether American troops were subject to "imminent" hostilities that should trigger the sixty-day clock. In August 1983 the marines suf-

[36]Reagan did submit a war powers report in 1983 on the dispatch of AWACS and fighter aircraft to Sudan, where they stood by for possible use in support of Chad's defense against attacks from Libya (Crabb and Holt, 1984).

[37]The administration did, however, expand the U.S. presence elsewhere in Central America, especially in neighboring Honduras, leading some critics of the administration's policies to conclude that Reagan had violated the spirit if not the letter of his pledge not to "Americanize" the war in El Salvador.

[38]Some twenty-nine members of the House brought suit in federal court against the Reagan administration, contending it acted in violation of the War Powers Act in sending military advisers and other assistance to El Salvador. A U.S. district court in 1982 dismissed the suit, ruling that Congress and the executive, not the court, must resolve the complex question of what conditions trigger the provisions of the Act.

fered two fatalities and several casualties. Reagan submitted to Congress a report on the hostilities "consistent with . . . the War Powers Resolution" and shortly thereafter entered negotiations with Congress with a view toward securing authorization for the marine presence in Beirut. In the weeks that followed U.S. forces were drawn more actively into the civil conflict in Lebanon as a partisan rather than a neutral peace keeper. Meanwhile, negotiations between Congress and the president resulted in a compromise, passed by both houses and signed by Reagan in mid-October, which authorized the marines to stay in Lebanon for eighteen months. In signing the Lebanon resolution, however, Reagan did not concede the applicability of the War Powers Act: "I do not and cannot cede any of the authority vested in me under the Constitution as President and as Commander in Chief of the United States Armed Forces. Nor should my signing be viewed as any acknowledgment that the President's constitutional authority can be impermissibly infringed by statute."

Partisan cleavages marked the vote in Congress on the Lebanon resolution, terrorists truck bombed marine headquarters just days before the U.S. invasion of Grenada, killing some 240 marines. In the months following the Beirut tragedy members of Congress questioned the wisdom of the continued presence of marines in Lebanon, but Reagan defended his policies, often accusing Congress of wanting to "cut and run." Then, in a dramatic about-face, he announced in February that the marines would be withdrawn from Lebanon and placed on ships offshore. Not long thereafter the American presence was completely withdrawn.

Both Reagan and Secretary of State Shultz alleged that the debate over the applicability of the War Powers Act and other congressional misgivings about the American presence in Lebanon contributed to the terrorism there. As the president argued in a speech on Congress and foreign policy in April 1984, "If we are to have a sustainable foreign policy, the Congress must support the practical details of policy, not just the general goals. . . . I believe that once we established bipartisan agreement on our course in Lebanon, the subsequent second-guessing about whether to keep our men there . . . hindered the ability of our diplomats to negotiate, encouraged more intransigence from the Syrians and prolonged the violence." Shultz was more broadly critical of the War Powers Act, arguing in a speech before the Trilateral Commission that the provisions that U.S. troops must be withdrawn from conflict situations unless Congress authorizes their continued presence "practically invite an adversary to wait us out."

Jacob K. Javits, architect of the War Powers Act, wrote shortly before his death that the resolution "did not, and does not, guarantee the end of presidential war, but it does present Congress with the means by which it can stop presidential war if it has the will to act" (Javits, 1985). The historical record raises serious questions about Congress's will, the charges of Reagan and Shultz notwithstanding. Commenting on Grenada, one observer concludes that "The Grenada episode makes perfectly clear that it is not the absence of constitutional or legal powers that prevents effective enforcement of the War

Powers Resolution. Rather, in this as well as in previous cases in which the legislation had been violated, Congress was unwilling to secure strict compliance with the law because it was severely constrained by political circumstances over which it had very little control" (Rubner, 1985-86). Lebanon added a new twist to the test of will. "For many Members of Congress, it was the first occasion on which they had confronted the constitutional questions involved, at least in the context of having to vote for a specific authorization when American lives were immediately at stake," observed Frederick S. Tipson, former chief counsel to the Senate Foreign Relations Committee. Thus, faced with the first real test of its self-defined war powers, "Congress waffled" (Crabb and Holt, 1984).

The historical record also indicates that the War Powers Act has failed in its intention to redress the balance between Congress and the president because, quite simply, the president has not conceded he is bound by its provisions. Furthermore, it can be argued that the act "does not give Congress any substantial powers to check the president or any substantial new opportunities to participate in foreign policy that it did not already have or could not exercise without the resolution." But it does in effect give the president "blanket power to use military force for sixty days, without legislative authorization; in other words, this provision 'legitimizes a war-making power that heretofore had been based on customary practice and precedent' " (Lowi, 1985b).

Money

What about the power of the purse? Since Congress has the exclusive power to appropriate funds for foreign as well as domestic programs, we should expect that here, more than in any other area, Congress would assert its authority over foreign affairs. And, in some respects at least, that has been the case. The foreign aid program has been a favored target, with Congress often substantially cutting the president's foreign aid request. Part of the reason foreign aid is often the target of budget cuts is that, unlike many other areas of the budget, cuts here are unlikely to affect adversely the interests of local constituents. The aid program has also enabled Congress to scrutinize periodically the executive's conduct of foreign policy, and through such scrutiny to place a legislative stamp on certain aspects of U.S. conduct overseas. Congressional efforts over the period of several years to promote respect for basic human rights in other countries by imposing specific requirements and restrictions on foreign economic and military aid are illustrative (see Crabb and Holt, 1984, for details). Such "barnacles" (as insiders call these and other legislative restraints[39]), many of which were unrelated to congressional concern for human rights, were particularly irritating to the Carter administration:

---

[39]President Reagan and others sometimes referred to the "150 restrictions" imposed by Congress "in the last 10 years" on presidential prerogatives in foreign affairs. The number appears in fact to have originated during the Carter administration, as reported in the New York Times (September 9, 1979).

There are specific restrictions on aid to at least 30 named countries. There were general bans on aid to countries that took certain types of action—expropriating U.S. property, developing nuclear weapons, violating human rights, seizing U.S. fishing vessels, granting sanctuary to terrorists, or failing to pay U.N. dues. There were prohibitions on certain types of aid activities, such as supporting police and financing abortions. There were limits on the size and form of arms sales and the activities of U.S. military assistance teams. There were elaborate reporting requirements and tight restrictions, in law and in practice, against reallocation of aid funds among countries and projects without specific appropriations committee approval. (Destler, 1981: 170–171)

Whether such restrictions always had their intended effect is questionable.[40] Furthermore, despite specific mandates, Congress normally left a loophole, the most general of which permitted the president to ignore most restrictions if he found that the security interests of the United States were compromised. The provision of such a large loophole fits the pattern whereby Congress permits the president a degree of flexibility at the same time that it seeks to give some overall direction over foreign policy (while escaping responsibility—and criticism—for its management). Concern for a possible adverse effect on the nation's security and interests underlies such seemingly contradictory behavior. In general, however, the president, out of fear that the loopholes might be closed, has moved cautiously in taking advantage of the escape clauses Congress has provided. Thus influence is exercised by both branches of government: Congress imposes some restrictions on the nation's foreign policy, and the president retains an element of the flexibility the executive so highly prizes.

The legislative veto which Congress wrote into the War Powers Act and which was applied to other instruments of foreign policy, notably foreign military sales and certain aspects of the aid program, also served historically as a way for Congress to exert influence in dealing with the executive. This seems ironic, since the legislative veto is such a blunt instrument: Congress either says yea or nay, and if it votes against a major issue, "it destroys presidential and thus U.S. credibility" (Destler, 1981). Not surprisingly, therefore, successive administrations opposed legislative veto provisions as intruding on presidential prerogatives, even though they were "less constraining than advance prohibitions written into law" and thus did "less collateral damage because they [did] not single out particular countries for negative treatment" (Destler,

---

[40]For example, despite the congressional restraints on providing aid "to the government of any country which engages in a consistent pattern of gross violations of internationally recognized human rights," the evidence shows that, at least in Latin America in the mid-1970s, relatively more American aid was received by repressive than by nonrepressive regimes (Schoultz, 1981). Congressional use of specific requirements to gain control over executive behavior can also have detrimental effects. In 1974 Congress mandated that 70 percent of American food aid go to the world's neediest countries. South Asia was the intended target, and the law did correct an imbalance in 1974 and 1975 in the allocation of food aid. But by 1976 the legal requirement was creating a new imbalance, with more food aid pouring into Bangladesh than the country's ports and storage facilities could handle (Destler, 1980).

1985).[41] Moreover, as noted previously in discussing foreign military sales, the veto was rarely exercised. Instead it served "as a club in the closet: The threat [forced] prior consultation, information sharing, and anticipatory adjustment by an administration before it . . . made a firm decision and staked its credibility on it. The tendency [was] to press controversial proposals only when the need [seemed] urgent and then to bargain with Congress over details" (Destler, 1981).

President Carter took advantage of the conservative congressional mood following the Soviet invasion of Afghanistan to have several of the foreign aid barnacles removed. The Reagan administration pursued this tack even more forcefully as part of its drive to transform the aid program into a more immediate means of achieving American foreign policy objectives. In the case of the Clark amendment, for example, which was passed in 1976 in an effort to prevent covert assistance to anti-Marxist elements in Angola (see below), Secretary of State Alexander Haig argued that the ban was "a blatant restriction on executive authority," and the administration pushed for its repeal as a matter of principle. It was not successful until August 1985, however, but shortly thereafter it began to identify openly with various factions in the ongoing Angolan conflict by providing military equipment and other assistance.[42]

Military spending is another budgetary area in which Congress potentially can play a major role. During the 1950s and 1960s Congress often voiced its views on the defense budget by appropriating *more* for defense than was asked for by the president. But as the pattern of executive-congressional relations moved from acquiescence to ambiguity and then to acrimony, Congress began cutting administration requests substantially, much as it has done in the foreign aid area.[43] Moreover, some evidence (Kanter, 1972) suggests that

---

[41]Although the legislative veto has come to be viewed as a necessary instrument to protect Congress from the executive's usurpation of legislative prerogatives, the record shows that the executive willingly accepted legislative veto provisions in exchange for the flexibility Congress granted the president in turn. As Louis Fisher, an expert on constitutional issues, has observed,

> The Nixon administration never uttered a word of protest when the Impoundment Control Act of 1974 authorized the President to defer the spending of funds subject to a one-House veto. It wanted the authority and accepted the condition. No one in the Ford, Carter, or Reagan administrations suggested that the one-House veto over deferrals was in any way unconstitutional. (Fisher, 1985: 169)

The import of that observation is that Congress can be expected, perhaps with presidential acquiescence if not overt support, to devise new means to serve the functions served previously by the legislative veto. "We should not be too surprised or disconcerted if, after the Court has closed the door to the legislative veto, we hear a number of windows being raised and perhaps new doors constructed, making the executive-legislative structure as accommodating as before for shared power" (Fisher, 1985).

[42]See Smith (1986) for a critical view of impending United States involvement in the Angolan civil conflict in the wake of the rescinding of the ten-year-old Clark amendment prohibition.

[43]Between fiscal 1950 and fiscal 1977, Congress appropriated more than the original defense budget estimates eight times, and cut the estimates twenty times (Congressional Quarterly, 1978: 4A). Ten of the twenty cuts were made in the last ten fiscal years in the series, and they averaged over $2 billion more than the cuts made in the fiscal years prior to 1968. Again, however, there is reason to raise the flag of caution. Although Congress cut the $97.9 billion request for fiscal 1976 by 7.5 percent, the $112 billion approved by the House Budget Committee was only $1.3 billion

while the dollar magnitude of congressional changes in the Defense Department budget has been comparatively small, throughout the 1960s Congress expressed special concern about funds for the development and production of weapon systems, and it was particularly inclined to adjust presidential requests in that area following the 1968 Tet offensive in Vietnam. This "does not mean to imply that Congress makes defense policy," observed a student of Congress in the mid-1970s. "In fact, the model of executive dominance applies to the field as a whole. But [it] does suggest that even in a situation of executive dominance there is room for substantial congressional impact" (Ripley, 1975).

With some variation, these patterns continued into the 1980s. As the Reagan administration launched the most ambitious peacetime military buildup in American history—it projected a five-year defense spending plan that called for increases from $222.2 billion in fiscal 1982 to $367.5 billion in fiscal 1986—Congress was cast in the role of asking "how much is enough?" The acknowledged buildup of Soviet military forces during the 1970s created a political environment conducive to substantial spending increases, as did specific events, such as the Soviet invasion of Afghanistan, coming only a month after the seizure of American embassy personnel by Iranians in November 1979. Congress nonetheless often trimmed Reagan administration appropriation requests, particularly as concern over mounting federal government budget deficits grew. Rarely, however, did Congress target specific programs or weapons for major reductions; more often the cuts were spread so widely as to have inconsequential programmatic consequences (see Congressional Quarterly, 1983). The MX missile was, with some qualifications, an exception.

The Carter administration became convinced the MX was necessary to replace the increasingly vulnerable ICBM force made up principally of aging Minuteman III missiles. The basing modes for the projected mobile missile proved to be extraordinarily costly, however, not only financially ($30–34 billion) but also environmentally and politically (see also chapter four). The Reagan administration scrapped the mobile design in favor of "dense pack," a plan that would place the MX in fixed silos so close to one another that the blast effects created by the first incoming Soviet warheads would destroy others that followed in a manner known as "fratricide." The principal advantage of dense pack was cost; deployment of 100 MX missiles in 100 shelters was estimated to cost $22.6 billion compared to the $33.8 billion for the Carter administration's multiple protective shelter scheme (Congressional Quarterly, 1983: 90). But in December 1982 Congress refused to appropriate the funds necessary for production of the first five MX missiles. It was the first time

---

lower than the president's revised request for fiscal 1977. Three factors appear to account for the congressional penchant for less frugality—all of which sustain the proposition of executive dominance in foreign policy making: the collapse of South Vietnam in April 1975, Soviet support for radical movements in southern Africa later that year, and intelligence estimates leaked in late 1975 and published in early 1976 showing a steady rise in Soviet military spending (*Congressional Quarterly Almanac*, 1976, 1976: 979).

since the Vietnam War that Congress had denied funds for a major weapons system requested by the president (Congressional Quarterly, 1983).

Congressional skepticism about the dense-pack basing mode and about the Reagan administration's argument that the MX was necessary to enhance its bargaining strength in arms control talks with the Soviet Union were major reasons for Congress's action. But as dramatic as it was, the decision was a deferral, not an outright cancellation of the MX.[44] Indeed, the MX has proven to be remarkably durable and is a graphic illustration of the fact that Congress rarely defeats a weapons system proposed by the president. In this case the tie that Ford, Carter, and Reagan first made between the missile and the Soviet arms buildup and then, later, to arms talks with the Soviet Union enhanced its survivability. Uncertainty over nuclear security issues strengthened the presidents' hands. "There is a kind of reverence to strategic issues," Senator Gary Hart observed. "Strategic issues are of a different order, a higher order. It's survival; it's the whole ball game if things go wrong." Senator Lawton Chiles also remarked (in 1985), "I have a feeling that there are not 30 people here [the Senate] who believe that we should have MX if we could ever get to a vote . . . on the merits. But I guess we never will."

The inability of Congress to grapple effectively with the overarching issues of national security policy that the MX raises applies broadly to its treatment of the defense budget. Rather than focusing on the big picture, Congress typically engages in *micro-management*. The motivation to do so is tied directly to the factors that stimulate committee service by members of Congress, as described by a former staff member of the House Armed Services Committee:

> Things have gone too far, not in terms of getting into the knickers of the services, but in the sense that it [detailed review] consumes too much attention of representatives and senators. We don't do enough of the long term policy. But there is a natural constituency for concentration on weapons systems in the here and now. It is difficult for members to focus on the big issues because of the lack of time, because of the need to get reelected, and because of the fact that constituency service, not policy oversight, is what is necessary today to stay in office. How to get them to focus on policy, not programs, is the problem. (cited in Art, 1985: 235)

In Pentagon jargon, "policy oversight" is captured in issues of "force structure" or "force design." The consensus is that on these issues, Congress does not do well (Art, 1985). Again, the observations of a former House Armed Services Committee staff member illustrate the point,

> Members of Armed Services get into policy but only obliquely. For example, on the Lehman power projection or sea control issue. We made a decision in favor of the

---

[44]In April 1983 the Scowcroft Commission recommended deployment of 100 MX missiles in existing silos. The next month Congress approved the funds to implement the basing plan and to produce the first twenty-one missiles. A year later the missile narrowly survived an attempt to bar additional production, and in July 1985 Congress placed a cap of fifty on the total number to be deployed.

former by authorizing a 600-ship navy, but we did it this way: We justified a carrier by stating the policy behind it rather than the reverse. We did not debate which policy we needed and then determine the best weapons systems to achieve it. The members of the committee thus back into policy. We debate policy when we attack or support specific weapons systems, but it should be the other way around. We should debate policy first and then determine which systems to procure. The hearings are program focused. If you say to the committee members, ''have policy hearing first,'' you will get the big Pentagon brass there; but the members' questions are either parochial or programmatic. (cited in Art, 1985: 237)

Avoiding policy oversight may undermine the capacity of Congress as an institution to exercise the power of the purse effectively, but for individual members such avoidance is politically astute.

The only thing worse than taking on an issue that will not make a legislator look good is taking on one that will make him look bad. Most issues of general policy oversight . . . involve longstanding and fairly intractable problems, ones in which the risk of looking bad is high. The penchant for the quick fix makes legislators conservative in their choices of how they spend their political resources. To tackle an intractable problem takes both political courage and a secure incumbency. If many members possess the former, most do not believe that they enjoy the latter, even if they do. . . . Thus, the political incentives as they are structured on Capitol Hill today put the bias on the short term, the specific, the details, the programs that can be grabbed, manipulated, changed, and sold. (Art, 1985: 240)

Congressional actions on the foreign aid and defense budgets demonstrate that Congress is not unwilling to exercise its power of the purse, even if its instruments for doing so are not finely honed. Elsewhere, however, the frequency with which Congress has sought to deal with a dominant executive through its fiscal powers has been remarkably irregular. There have been examples, of course, as in the winter of 1975–1976 when the Clark amendment to the 1976 appropriations bill barred the use of funds in the bill ''for any activities involving Angola directly or indirectly.'' Congress apparently was not in the mood to accept the view that Soviet adventures in Africa required an American reaction. But historically such action was the exception rather than the rule. Indeed, the Angolan story demands attention as much for its uniqueness as for its illustration of congressional assertiveness.

More characteristic of executive-congressional relations is the fate of the much publicized Cooper-Church amendment, which sought to cut off funds for U.S. war efforts in Cambodia following Nixon's ''incursion'' into the country in the spring of 1970. The authoritative Congressional Quarterly Service (*Guide to the Congress of the United States*, 1971) described the proposal as ''a precedent-setting attempt by the Senate to use authorizations and appropriations to influence U.S. foreign affairs.'' The amendment failed. In fact, the only action taken by Congress to cut off Cambodian war funds occurred after (then known) U.S. military activity had ceased, as noted earlier in this chapter. The ultimate wording of the funding prohibition was essentially that of

Cooper-Church, but the timing was significant to the initiator-respondent proposition. The Congressional Quarterly's commentary on the entire issue of funding the war is instructive:

> The picture of the Johnson and Nixon administrations carrying on military activities in Indochina without congressional consent often has been overdrawn by critics of the war. They tended to overlook the frequent votes in Congress for appropriations to support the war. And while they often spoke of a constitutional crisis over war powers, they usually did not consider that throughout the war there was never a constitutional confrontation between a President determined to pursue the war and a Congress unwilling to appropriate the necessary funds. (*Guide to Congress,* 1976: 274)

The fate of the Cooper-Church amendment, the ultimate importance of which was largely symbolic, illustrates the difficulty inherent in getting even a majority of 535 independent-minded lawmakers to agree on a specific proposal—a prospect made all the more difficult when the proposal is at variance with the president (or, as was often true during the Carter years, when the president fails to exercise the leadership that Congress has come to expect). More generally, however, the extent to which money can be used to affect the nation's foreign policy is limited. Simply put, it is difficult to legislate foreign policy, or to equate lawmaking with foreign policy making. As Roger Hilsman (1971) points out, programs, but not necessarily policies, require appropriations. Hence, some of the most important aspects of the nation's role in world politics do not require specific and direct appropriations of money. The Nixon and Carter doctrines are excellent cases in point. Both are essentially statements of intent which created important expectations both at home and abroad quite independently of fiscal activities Congress was asked to undertake. Moreover, the division of congressional responsibility among many different committees, alongside the breakdown of party unity and the erosion of leadership in Congress, militates against a more effective use of congressional powers. This fact is nowhere more evident than in the funding process, where, within each house of Congress, authorizations for expenditures are specified by the substantive committees having jurisdiction over particular programs but the actual appropriations are made by another committee.

The Budget and Impoundment Control Act passed by Congress in 1974 was an attempt to consolidate control over the purse to some extent, for it requires Congress to specify overall spending guidelines and otherwise broadens the ability of Congress to scrutinize the president's budgetary requests. Congress is thus required to face squarely the unwelcome political task of weighing federal spending against federal income. The process may have enhanced its institutional capacity to cope with the demands of the executive branch generally, but whether it copes more effectively with the executive bureaucracy in particular, especially given the rise of single-issue politics, remains unclear. Moreover, some have argued that the budget act has merely added a new layer of fiscal authority to those already existing in Congress. The power of the appropriations committees has not been curtailed, so the argument runs, but the authority of the substantive foreign policy committees has. In other words, even though the Senate Foreign Relations and the House Foreign Affairs committees may have increased their expertise through such moves as the expansion of their staffs, their ability to translate that into a greater voice in policy making has fallen victim to purely fiscal, budgetary, and intracongressional political considerations.[45]

Even if there were not built-in impediments to the use of congressional spending powers to affect foreign affairs, the devices that the executive has developed to spend as it pleases, irrespective of congressional wishes and oversight, give the president substantial fiscal independence. One mechanism widely used by the Nixon administration is impoundment, or presidential refusal to spend money appropriated by Congress. Other mechanisms which presidents—or, perhaps more accurately, the executive—have used to get what they want include (1) discretionary funds, (2) transfer authority, (3) reprogramming, (4) "pipeline" funds, (5) excess stocks, and (6) outright budgetary trickery (Nathan and Oliver, 1976). Each enables the executive to undertake activities that may well be at variance with congressional wishes and intent. Discretionary funds, for example, are monies provided the president to deal with situations unforeseen at the time of the annual budgetary process, but they have often been used for purposes other than emergencies. Kennedy used some $500 million in discretionary funds to finance the Peace Corps during its first year in operation, for example, whereas Johnson used $1.5 billion in contingency funds embedded in the Defense Department budget to finance military operations in Southeast Asia during 1965 and 1966 (Nathan and Oliver, 1976: 495–496). Similarly, budgetary trickery was used to convert Food for Peace currencies generated in Southeast Asia to support the war effort there.

Reprogramming is another device which enhances the executive's fiscal independence. Essentially it provides executive flexibility by allowing funds within an appropriation to be moved from one purpose to another (for example, from shipbuilding to submarine construction). The device is widely used by the Defense Department. "Major reprogramming" actions require some

---

[45]A case in point was the Senate Foreign Relations Committee's authorization in 1977 of multiyear appropriations for the International Development Association (IDA), and simultaneously the Budget and Appropriations Committees' denial of a long-range commitment to the international organization (see Franck and Weisband, 1979, for details). (The IDA is an arm of the World Bank that provides long-term loans with low interest rates and long repayment schedules to developing nations.) The Carter administration had sought $3.24 billion for the so-called IDA replenishment, which still had not been funded when President Reagan assumed office. The new administration was especially hostile toward multilateral aid, but its attitudes did soften somewhat over the years. In the case of IDA, however, the decision, apparently made by Reagan himself, was to provide $750 million a year for three years, or a total of $2.25 billion. "Under the complex formula governing contributions, this effectively held the total capitalization [of the seventh IDA replenishment] at $9 billion, representing a 40-per cent cut in real terms, since other industrial-country donors were unwilling to raise their contributions without a corresponding U.S. increase" (Sewell and Contee, 1985: 111).

congressional committee oversight (but *not* approval by the whole Congress), but minor reprogramming decisions are internal Defense Department actions. Reprogramming is one of several nonstatutory control mechanisms Congress and the executive have devised to deal with contingencies that neither branch is able to anticipate in the annual budgetary cycle (Fisher, 1985). The sums involved in Defense Department decisions in particular are often substantial, however, which opens the mechanism to charges that it is but one more device used by the executive to undermine Congress's constitutional power of the purse.

Constraining the executive's flexibility in using funds appropriated by Congress was a principal purpose of the Budget Control and Impoundment Act. It specifies that if the president wishes to impound funds, there are two avenues, both subject to congressional review. Temporary spending delays, which can extend up to twelve months, are known as *deferrals;* permanent efforts to cancel budget authority are known as *rescissions.* The role of Congress in each of these executive decisions is now clear:

> Funds may be rescinded when the president decides the budget authority is not required to fulfill the objectives of a program, when he wants to terminate a program, or when the appropriated money for a program is not to be obligated [i.e., committed to that program so departments and agencies can award contracts, and so forth]. The president must send a rescission message to Congress and both houses must approve it by majority vote within 45 days of continuous session, or the proposed canceled funds must be spent. The president must also notify Congress of any delay in obligating budget authority, a deferral. Either house may overturn the deferral message by passing an ''impoundment resolution'' by simple majority in one body at any time. There is no time limit on overturning deferrals as there is with the passage of rescissions. (Ellwood and Thurber, 1981: 265)[46]

Securing congressional approval for rescissions would appear more formidable than for deferrals, and the record bears this out. Congress sustained nearly 90 percent of the deferrals reported by the president in the four fiscal years from 1977 through 1980, compared to less than half of the proposed rescissions (Ellwood and Thurber, 1981: 267). How foreign policy items fared relative to other items is unknown, but one can surmise from the preceding discussion that they were treated no differently. In the area of spending, then, it would seem again that Congress has sought to tighten politically its control in an area where it appears dominant constitutionally, but it has done so in a way that has not reduced substantially presidential flexibility.

One area in which Congress has been especially reluctant to fix leaks from the fiscal faucet is in the financing of the intelligence community. Indeed, intelligence funding remains the best-known example of dollars provided the executive by Congress which remain outside the direct control of Congress as

---

[46]Ellwood (1985) provides a useful analysis of the theory and practice of the budget process a decade after the Budget Control and Impoundment Act was signed into law.

a whole.[47] The House and Senate Intelligence committees have been empowered to authorize expenditures by the intelligence community—which presumably means that committee members know what the funding figures are—but the periodic efforts by some members of Congress to have the actual costs of intelligence operations released publicly have routinely failed. The reasons derive from the familiar—and often legitimate—concern for security. Interestingly, Congress has not even revealed an overall figure for the intelligence function, despite the fact that one CIA director indicated he was not opposed to disclosure of the amount.[48] On at least three different occasions (in 1979, 1982, and 1984) the House of Representatives specifically voted not to reveal the figure. It reasoned in its report on the fiscal 1983 intelligence authorization bill that "By itself, a single intelligence budget total would probably not harm intelligence activities or capabilities. Such a number, however, would be meaningless in a vacuum. . . . Budget disclosure might well mean more to this country's adversaries than to any of its citizens" (cited in Crabb and Holt, 1984).

Congressional reluctance to reveal the cost of intelligence activities is only one manifestation of the reluctance of Congress to curtail presidential dominance in this sensitive foreign policy area. Other examples include the House decision to override the recommendations of its own special intelligence committee and not release the Pike committee report on the CIA because, as argued by the president, it contained sensitive classified information; and the Senate decision, when it created a permanent Intelligence Committee, not to require prior congressional approval of impending covert political actions. That reticence was reaffirmed in 1980 when Congress passed new intelligence oversight legislation. Although it required the executive branch to keep the Intelligence committees "fully and currently informed" of all intelligence activities, it specifically established that the committees could not disapprove intelligence operations.[49]

[47]The Senate Select Committee on Intelligence (*Final Report*, I, 1976: 470) noted that the CIA's budget is contained within the Defense Department budget and reported that "the CIA spends approximately 70 percent more than it is appropriated, with the additional funds coming from advances and transfers from other agencies. These . . . are made with the knowledge and approval of OMB and the appropriate congressional committees. The use of advances and transfers between agencies is a common governmental practice." Although intelligence expenditures continue to be buried in the Defense Department budget, the practice of spending more than is appropriated may no longer be widespread since the charters for the House and Senate Intelligence Committees contain provisions prohibiting appropriations that have not been authorized.

[48]This was Admiral Stansfield Turner, director of central intelligence in the Carter administration who, however, did not himself reveal the sum.

[49]As noted earlier, Congress felt it had been burned by the CIA's reporting procedures in the case of the mining of Nicaraguan ports. To ensure that Congress was kept "fully and currently informed," an agreement was worked out between CIA Director William Casey and the Senate specifying that "the CIA would inform the [Senate Intelligence] committee about all activities 'planned to be undertaken as part of ongoing covert action programs.' Previously, the agency had interpreted a 1980 reporting law as requiring it to notify the committee only of overall covert operations, such as aiding the contras, and not of specific activities within those operations, such as helping the contras to mine harbors" (*Congressional Quarterly Almanac, 1984*, 1985). Casey reportedly was willing to use similar procedures to inform the House of CIA activities.

IS CONGRESS EITHER ABLE OR WILLING?

As in the area of treaties and war, then, the congressional power of the purse in practice appears less formidable than it does in principle. The reason lies in part in the basic consensus between the executive and legislative branches of government about what the United States ought to do abroad, and how it ought to do it. The challenges of an assertive Congress are significant, there-fore, for they may represent a breakdown in at least some components of the consensus on which most post-World War II U.S. foreign policy has been based. Challenge provokes debate; through debate some of the untested as-sumptions of American policy may be discarded.

Yet we cannot safely assume that congressional assertiveness will produce meaningful change in the nation's foreign relations. For the main purpose of congressional acrimony and assertiveness seems to be more to ensure Con-gress a voice in policy making than to alter fundamentally the nature of the policy itself. To assert one's powers is not necessarily the same as expanding one's area of governance. Nor does it necessarily assure responsible behavior in the sense of helping the president to devise realistic alternatives to the pol-icy problems that face the nation. In many instances in recent years Congress seems to have done quite the opposite (Destler, Gelb, and Lake, 1984).

Congress is clearly part of the exceedingly complex institutional labyrinth of American foreign policy making. In the processes whereby policy emanates from this institutional maze, however, the resources available to the president in particular, and the executive branch in general, are clearly more formidable than those available to Congress. Congress has made some strides toward coping with its structural inadequacies, notably in increasing staff expertise, but a countertrend has been the diffusion of power within Congress— to the point that "By the early 1980s Congress appeared to be more decentralized, fragmented, and resistant to unifying influences than in any previous period of American history" (Crabb and Holt, 1984). But even if Congress were able to reverse such trends, and even if senators and representatives were some-how magically able to transcend their parochial perspectives in favor of a broader picture (which is doubtful at best), the powers of the institutionalized presidency are so vastly superior to those of the legislature that Congress is far more likely to be co-opted by the wishes of the president than vice versa. That conclusion has been reinforced many times since Ronald Reagan assumed of-fice in 1981, for his detractors as well as his supporters willingly concede that he has done much to put the malaise of the 1970s behind and to infuse the na-tion with a renewed sense of national consciousness and pride. Hence, there is little that warrants a revision of the initiator-respondent view of executive-congressional relations. And, if the foreign policy-making structure is viewed as a series of concentric circles wherein "the action" is located fundamentally in the innermost circle comprising the president and his immediate circle of advisers, Congress remains relatively far removed from the center.

Many would argue that Congress functions most appropriately when it is removed from day-to-day activities. Even J. William Fulbright (1979), once an outspoken critic of presidential dominance in foreign policy making, has argued that the role of Congress is "in the authorization of military and major political commitments, and in advising broad policy directions, while leaving to the executive the necessary flexibility to conduct policy within the broad parameters approved by the legislature." But such a view should not obscure the fact that Congress is an important component of the governmental source category. As Congressman Aspin (1976) observed, Congress functions reasonably well as an avenue for the expression of constituent and other views and interests; as an overseer of government policies and resource allocations; and as a "guardian" of the processes of government. In the latter capacity, in particular, Congress is often able to shape significantly the mechanisms through which policies evolve and hence to influence the composition of the contestants who engage in the debate. The creation by Congress of the National Security Council, the Defense Department, and the CIA are cases in point.

Similarly, the actions that Congress takes in executing its negative, limit-setting functions often can shape significantly the content of debate about the goals and means of foreign policy, and inhibit the prospects for a hasty revision of them. In the final analysis, then, Congress affects most the way in which policy is debated within the executive branch; it becomes part of the ultimate decision-making process even if only by affecting the various political forces involved there. Hence, the existence of a coequal legislative branch may require even a preeminent president to defer to what often becomes a relatively public policy-making process. It is process that is perhaps unique even among democratic societies.

SUGGESTIONS FOR FURTHER READING

BAX, FRANS R. "The Legislative-Executive Relationship in Foreign Policy: New Partnership or New Competition?" *Orbis* 20 (Winter 1977): 881–904.

CRABB, CECIL V., JR., AND PAT M. HOLT. *Invitation to Struggle: Congress, the President and Foreign Policy,* 2nd ed. Washington DC: Congressional Quarterly Press, 1984.

DESTLER, I. M. "Executive-Congressional Conflict in Foreign Policy: Explaining It; Coping with It," pp. 343–363 in Lawrence C. Dodd and Bruce I. Oppenheimer, eds., *Congress Reconsidered,* 2nd ed. Washington DC: Congressional Quarterly Press, 1985.

FISHER, LOUIS. *Constitutional Conflicts Between Congress and the President.* Princeton, NJ: Princeton University Press, 1985.

FRANCK, THOMAS M., AND EDWARD WEISBAND. *Foreign Policy by Congress.* New York: Oxford University Press, 1979.

JAVITS, JACOB K. "War Powers Reconsidered." *Foreign Affairs* 64 (Fall 1985): 130–140.

JOHNSON, LOCH K. *The Making of International Agreements: Congress Confronts the Executive.* New York: New York University Press, 1984.

SPANIER, JOHN, AND JOSEPH NOGEE, EDS. *Congress, the Presidency and American Foreign Policy.* New York: Pergamon, 1981.

WHALEN, CHARLES W., JR. *The House and Foreign Policy: The Irony of Congressional Reform.* Chapel Hill, NC: University of North Carolina Press, 1982.

VI

ROLE SOURCES OF AMERICAN FOREIGN POLICY

13

THE PROCESS OF DECISION MAKING: RATIONALITY AND THE IMPACT OF BUREAUCRATIC ORGANIZATION

In so many of the *ex post facto* investigations, they [outsiders] take individual documents and assume that people sat around the table in a seminar-type discussion, having all the facts. . . . But that is rarely the case. Usually decisions are made in a very brief time with enormous pressure and uncertain knowledge.

Former Secretary of State Henry Kissinger, 1977

The process was the author of the policy.

Under Secretary of State George W. Ball, 1962

Many different people, widely dispersed throughout the government, contribute to the making of foreign policy. We have examined the offices and their overall organization, as well as the effect of both on foreign policy. Those are the superstructures of decision making—the machinery of government. Here, however, we are concerned with the *process* of decision making and how the roles associated with the networks of formal positions within the superstructure influence the behavior of the policy makers occupying those roles, and, ultimately, American foreign policy itself. Our working assumption is that the roles and the process, rather than the preferences of the individuals making the decisions or the structures within which they are made, influence the courses of action the United States pursues abroad. Furthermore, any changes in policy are assumed to result from changes in the processes through which decisions are reached.

ROLES AS A SOURCE OF FOREIGN POLICY

One way of interpreting the origins of foreign policy is to argue not that individuals are unimportant but that all individual behavior is constrained and molded by the roles individuals perform within their institutions. Both the actions and attitudes of members of the elite who perform particular tasks in the policy-making arena are greatly influenced, if not determined, by the positions they occupy.

Role theory holds that although the actual behavior of any individual can be distinguished from the role he or she assumes, each role (or position) carries with it certain expectations and demands of how it should be performed. Such pressures, including the functions of the position itself and the rules governing how each job is to be handled, encourage the individual to modify his or her attitudes and to act in accordance with the perceived requirements of the role. These images and expectations are assumed to influence the behavior of *anyone* filling a particular role; every individual acts somewhat similarly to others who have occupied the same role.

To suggest that the role one occupies influences thoughts and behavior should not be disturbing. All of us play roles in life; and unless we are hermits we find ourselves on occasion in social situations with which we have had no previous experience. We respond to such new circumstances by changing our attitudes and behavior in accordance with what we think is appropriate conduct. Witness the changes in yourself as you shift from the role of student to that of employee, or to that of new parent or even politician; you begin to act, perhaps subconsciously, in the manner you think is expected of you. Your vocabulary changes, the importance of certain ideas undergoes subtle but meaningful fluctuations, and the way you view the world, and your place within it, shifts in accordance with the role you now assume. Each of us plays a variety of roles in our life, and these roles, evidence suggests, explain and predict our attitudes and behavior.[1]

Policy makers are not immune from this phenomenon. Each role in the decision-making machinery carries with it certain expectations, obligations, rights, and images of appropriate behavior, pressures which tend to make the new occupant of an office think and act like his predecessor. Whereas an individual's style may be markedly different from that of the person who held the job previously, the individual's position on crucial issues tends to be very similar to his predecessor's position.[2] "It's an old story in Washington that where

---

[1]Examples of this propensity come readily to mind. Consider the professor who becomes the recipient of a large research grant from the Department of Defense and then ceases to write articles critical of defense spending; or take the labor organizer who is promoted to a position of authority in a major corporation and suddenly begins to see the "necessity" for "right to work" laws and for wage controls. Likewise, the general may return home from work, take off his uniform, become husband and father, and change his behavior accordingly.

[2]That a causal relationship between attitudes and roles exists for policy makers has been amply demonstrated by systematic research (for example, Lieberman, 1965; Singer, 1965). Stouffer et al. (1949) found, for instance, that people who get promoted in the armed services tend to de-

you stand depends on where you sit. That's a practical acknowledgment of the fact that people's views change as they change responsibilities,'' political journalist David Broder observed. An example: while campaigning, Jimmy Carter criticized Henry Kissinger's ''personal diplomacy'' and advocated less emphasis on private talks with foreign leaders. Yet in the first seven months in office, Carter played host to no fewer than eighteen foreign heads of state, and his secretary of state appeared to have been out of the country more often than not.[3] The discrepancy between advocated and actual behavior changed once the role was actually, rather than theoretically, performed.

Of course, it would be dangerous to lean too heavily on role theory as an explanation of policy-making behavior. Individuals do have the capacity to transcend the limits of the roles they occupy. Indeed, a forceful personality may actually redefine the role so as to extend the boundaries of permissible behavior, as Franklin Roosevelt is pictured as having done in expanding the office of the presidency and as Ronald Reagan is sometimes believed to have accomplished through his habit of taking many naps and frequent vacations— a propensity that reflected a relaxed style in an office that heretofore demanded sleepless attention to the duties of governance. Moreover, particular roles permit more than one interpretation, and some roles have boundaries so wide and elastic that individual behavior within them is almost unpredictable. Although high positions allow several interpretations—as evidenced, for example, by the contrast between the concept of the presidency held by Eisenhower and Kennedy, or by Carter and Reagan—each interpretation is, in effect, a specific role. Variations in behavior will still be systematic, depending on which role interpretation a new occupant of a policy-making position adopts.

Such alternative role interpretations are one of the ways in which the individual source category (elaborated in chapter fourteen) affects foreign policy making. For example, consider the way in which various role conceptions led each postwar president to organize and use his White House foreign policy staff somewhat differently (described in chapter ten). The consequences, as shown in particular by Johnson's approach to the Vietnam War and Nixon's insulation from the larger foreign affairs government, can be significant. Although policy makers are not their roles,[4] and may at times be given considerable leeway to act as they wish, most appear to conform to the conventional

---

velop more favorable attitudes toward the Army than those who don't, and that commissioned officers are more pro-Army than draftees. Rieselbach (1964) found that the length of service in the U.S. House of Representatives affected members' attitudes toward foreign aid; in addition, Rosenau (1980) discovered that the role requirements (that is, committee experience) of U.S. senators made a direct impact on their attitudes toward the secretary of state.

[3]On August 8, 1980, after merely two and a half months in office, Secretary of State Edmund S. Muskie reported: ''When the President asked me to become the new Secretary of State, he assured me that there would not be too much traveling. Since then I've been to Brussels and Vienna; to Venice, Ankara, and Kuala Lumpur; and to Japan—twice.''

[4]For a discussion of how certain types of people *do* tend to become their roles, see Snyder (1980).

attitudes and behaviors associated with their positions and to acquiesce to the prevailing norms associated with those positions. Conformity is especially evident in formal roles, such as those found in government positions, where norms governing performance are backed by legal obligations and sanctions and not merely social pressures.[5]

The implications of this line of reasoning for the study of American foreign policy are substantial. The proposition derived from role theory—that decision makers exhibit behavior in conformity with their roles—means that to understand the sources of American foreign policy, we should look not at individuals but at the behavior most often associated with foreign policy-making roles.

A focus on the importance of roles in decision making also enables us to deal with change in foreign policy, because policy change, when it occurs, may derive from changes in the structural characteristics of the major policy-making roles. Roles may shape goals; policy modification, in short, may be a product of role transformation. It is the decision-making system, the interlocking expectations within the foreign affairs machinery, that produces continuity and stable performance in policy. Thus, to revise the policy of the United States most effectively, the system by which decisions are made and the roles which induce those decisions must be modified.

The present chapter will investigate two interpretations of roles assumed by many to be descriptive of American decision-making procedures: the notion that American foreign policy is made by a *rational* decision process, and the rival or alternate role conception emphasizing the process of decision-making as it unfolds within large-scale bureaucratic organizations.

FOREIGN POLICY MAKING AS A RATIONAL PROCESS

The image President Carter's campaign strategists attempted to portray of their candidate when he was running for reelection in 1980 was clear. In an often-televised commercial, Carter was photographed in the Oval Office, working industriously late into the night, pouring over documents. The image conveyed was one of a deep thinker, intellectually absorbed in the tasks of the office—making the decisions that only he could make—decisions on which the nation's destiny would ultimately depend. Viewers of the footage were asked to consider whether there was anyone else as qualified—possessing the attributes of intelligence, experience, dedication, energy, and diligence—to make the formidable choices facing the country.

The message did more than attempt to sell the candidate, though. It also reinforced a popular view of the policy-making process at the nation's nerve center on Pennsylvania Avenue: that fateful decisions are made by *rational* actors engaged in orderly, contemplative processes. In this view, American for-

---

[5]Consider Watergate. Richard Nixon found that there were limits to the kinds of conduct that the system would tolerate, even from the presidency.

eign policy results from a deliberate intellectual process, in which the central figures are guided by the desire to choose what is best for the country and to select tactics that promote its national interests.

Thus, the question "Is foreign policy making rational?" actually may seem a curious one to ask. We tend, almost instinctively, to think, "How could it be otherwise?" Indeed, it is disconcerting to picture something as important as foreign policy, where the stakes are the survival of the nation and perhaps civilization itself, being produced by a process governed by incoherence, emotions, or worse. The notion of rational policy making is much more attractive. Moreover, decision makers try to cultivate public images of themselves as capable of decisiveness, unfettered by subconscious psychological drives, able to manage the stress and burden of the responsibility of the position, endowed with limitless energy, and prepared to guide the country safely through crises while pursuing what is best for the country's interests. Their efforts are frequently successful because we prefer to think of our leaders that way and to picture their decisions as the product of rational deliberation.

What is meant by the phrase "rational foreign policy," which is employed by policy makers to describe themselves and their actions and by foreign policy analysts seeking to understand that behavior? Unfortunately, there is no agreement on the meaning of the concept, and people speak of "rationality" in a variety of ways. Some, for instance, define rationality in the economist's sense of the term, as "actions chosen by the nation . . . that will maximize strategic goals and objectives" (Allison, 1971). Others simply equate rationality with "considering the evidence" (Gibson, 1960); or as behavior "that is 'correctly' designed to maximize goal achievement, given the goal in question and the real world as it exists" (Dahl and Lindblom, 1953). Most analysts would probably accept a general definition that sees rational behavior occurring when "the individual responding to an international event . . . uses the best information available and chooses from the universe of possible responses that alternative most likely to maximize his goals" (Verba, 1969).

Despite the diversity of meanings attached to the concept of rationality, and the attendant deficiencies associated with its use,[6] it is a useful tool in describing the foreign policy of nations and evaluating the processes by which those policies are formulated. To build a model premised on nonrational behavior, in which actions are derived exclusively from emotional predisposi-

---

[6]The concept of rationality as usually employed is vulnerable to a number of criticisms, including (1) the confusion between the normative recommendation as to how actors should make decisions, on the one hand, and the empirical description of the kind of process that actually takes place, on the other; (2) the dependence of the term on subjective criteria to identify instances of rational behavior; (3) the difficulty in measuring variables used in conjunction with the concept; (4) the frequent failure to distinguish the rationality of selected goals from the rationality of chosen alternatives; (5) the difficulty of dealing with nonlogical (psychological) sources of behavior; (6) the difficulty of resolving the altruism/self-interest dichotomy; (7) the inability in practice to fulfill some of the requirements of the concept, such as full information; (8) the ambiguity involved in identifying all the relevant actors in the process; and (9) the amenability of the concept to polemics, as a tool to critique others for what they have decided.

tions, subconscious impulses, and nonintellectual forces, does not seem like a useful way to proceed. Thus, in most discussions of foreign policy, the simplifying assumption is usually made that the actors are capable of purposeful, goal-seeking choice (even if at times particular decisions appear, on hindsight, as if they only could have come from individuals driven by neurotic impulses). An approach that operates from the assumption that decisions are affected more by the kind of morning conversation the decision maker had with his spouse than by what he or she thinks is not very useful (although there may be an element of truth in such approaches).

The simplifying assumption of rationality can be attractive when the nation-state is treated as a *unitary-actor*, a single entity, and is regarded as a ''decider,'' since *all* decision makers presumably go through the same rational thought processes to reach conclusions. This assumption

> allows one to consider all decision-makers to be alike. If they follow the [decision] rules, we need know nothing more about them. In essence, if the decision-maker behaves rationally, the observer, knowing the rules of rationality, can rehearse the decisional process in his own mind and, if he knows the decision-maker's goals, can both predict the decision and understand why that particular decision was made. (Verba, 1969: 225)

Academics who study decision making and advise policy makers on ways to improve their policy-formulation skills have described the perfect rationality role model as a sequence of decision-making activities involving the following intellectual steps:

1. *Problem recognition and definition.* The necessity for decisions begins when policy makers perceive the existence of a problem with which they must deal and attempt to define objectively its distinguishing characteristics. To be rational, policy makers must see the situation as it actually exists and not as they merely assume it to be. This requires an accurate image of what is occurring in the world, which in turn necessitates full *information* about the actions, motivations, and capabilities of other actors as well as the state of the international environment and transforming trends within it. The search for such information must be exhaustive; all the facts relevant to the problem must be gathered.
2. *Goal selection.* Next, rational actors must determine what their *objectives* are. How do they want the problem resolved? Rational goal selection is far from simple. It requires that values be ranked in terms of the degree to which they are preferred so that a coherent vision of the national interest emerges. This can be difficult because many interests may coexist, some of which are incompatible; national goals may be mutually exclusive or even contradictory, even though they are all preferred states for the future. Yet comprehensive rationality requires that *all* goals giving definition to the national interest must be identified and, in the terminology of policy analysis, ''prioritized'' in order to rank goals in a hierarchy from most to least preferred. For instance, rationality would require policy makers to decide which of many attractive goals—containment of communism, preservation of world order, promotion of human rights, self-

defense, enhancement of economic growth at home and abroad, facilitation of the growth of democratic institutions abroad, alleviation of hunger and human suffering, assuring adequate energy resources—should guide the nation's conduct; more importantly, they must judge which of these should receive priority. Such value clarification entails nothing less than determining what the nation's ideals and fundamental purposes should be and identifying the conditions under which they are to assume significance.

3. *Identification of alternatives.* To be rational, *all* policy alternatives (including the option of doing nothing) must then be identified. An alternative consists of an "actionable" behavioral choice to realize each of the goals given priority.

4. *Choice.* Finally, rational decision making necessitates selecting from among competing options (or sets of options) the alternative with the best prospect of achieving the desired goal. This selection requires the ability to *predict* the likely results of each possible option; the probability or success rate of each option in producing the goal must be estimated realistically. Policy choice or decision then consists of selecting that alternative most likely to succeed according to a rigorous means-ends, cost-benefit analysis.

Clearly, the requirements of the perfect rationality role model are very stringent. Nonetheless, decision makers often tend to view their own behavior in such terms or, more modestly, to argue that the processes associated with rational decision making describe how they *think* decisions *ought* to be made. For example, Theodore Sorensen (1963) described policy making in the Kennedy administration as aspiring to follow an eight-step procedure which is consistent with the model we have described:

1. Agreement on the facts
2. Agreement on the overall policy objective
3. Precise definition of the problem
4. Canvassing of all possible solutions
5. Listing of the possible consequences flowing from each solution
6. Recommendation of one option
7. Communication of the option selected
8. Provisions for its execution

In some instances the idealized version of decision making presented here may even appear to have been approximated. Graham T. Allison's classic study of the 1962 Cuban missile crisis reveals several points at which the deliberations of the key advisers concerned with the issue of Soviet missiles in Cuba resembled the perfect rationality role model. President Kennedy had charged the group, which came to be called the ExCom (Executive Committee of the National Security Council), to "set aside all other tasks to make a prompt and intensive survey of the dangers and *all possible courses of action*" (Allison, 1971). Six options were ultimately identified: do nothing; exert diplomatic pressure; make a secret approach to Castro; invade Cuba; launch a surgical air strike against the missiles; blockade Cuba. Choosing among these six implied the specification of goals. Was removal of the Soviet missiles the goal? Or did the missiles pose no serious threat to the vital interests of the United States? "Do nothing" could not be eliminated as an option until it was determined that the missiles did indeed represent a real threat to the United States. Once that determination was made, discussion focused on the surgical air strike and blockade. The latter was eventually chosen because of its presumed advantages, among which were the demonstration of firmness it permitted the United States and the flexibility with respect to further choices it allowed both parties.

Often, however, it would appear that rational decision making is more an idealized vision, a standard by which to evaluate behavior, than it is an actual description of real-world decision making. Sorensen himself has indicated how different real decision making is from the eight-step procedure identified above:

> Each step cannot be taken in order. The facts may be in doubt or dispute. Several policies, all good, may conflict. Several means, all bad, may be all that are open. Value judgments may differ. Stated goals may be imprecise. There may be many interpretations of what is right, what is possible, and what is in the national interest. (Sorensen, 1963: 19–20)

In the case of the Cuban missile crisis, explanations other than rational choice can be offered to understand the decision-making process as it unfolded. The choice also depended, for example, on the ability of different organizations to carry out the tasks considered by the ExCom and the politicking that occurred among the key advisers themselves. Thus the surgical air strike became a less satisfactory option once the Air Force admitted it could not guarantee 100 percent success in taking out the missiles. And the blockade option became more feasible once three of the president's closest and most trusted advisers (Robert McNamara, Robert Kennedy, and Theodore Sorensen) declared their opposition to the air strike.

Let us examine the impediments to rational decision making in more detail, in order to clarify why it does not describe accurately the ways in which most foreign policy decisions are reached.

Rationality and Reality: The Limits to Rational Choice

There is a noticeable lack of fit between the realities of actual decision making and the idealized version embodied in the rational decision-making model. The conditions that define rational choice are rarely met in practice. Some of the more conspicuous discrepancies follow.

Problem Recognition Is Usually Tardy. Decision makers often fail to proceed until a problem reaches crisis proportions, and they may be inclined to ignore evidence of an impending problem until it confronts them directly, for people seldom possess a sensible mental model for dealing with improbable events

(Boffey, 1983). Even in the face of overwhelming evidence, decision makers frequently appear to have been the last to recognize the existence of situations necessitating decisions and action. Think of the oil crisis or the lack of concern for the rapid depletion of energy reserves in the early 1970s. Why did policy makers wait to respond until the problems reached critical proportions? Perhaps because most people often psychologically deny the existence of troublesome problems (even when they might be partially responsible for them), avoid facing difficult decisional predicaments when they can, and discount information suggesting the necessity for decisive action.

Policy Makers Lack Sufficient Information to Define Accurately an Emergent Decisional Problem. Information is often incomplete, outdated, or unavailable. This is a somewhat paradoxical observation, since "information overload"—the availability of too much information—also is a frequent problem. Yet what information is available is often discrepant and contradictory, making it difficult to distinguish the significant from the irrelevant, or, in the idiom of communications theory, the true "signals" from mere "noise." And often, neither visible nor open to scrutiny are such critical variables as the motivations and intentions of others (see Thorson, 1984). A key factor inhibiting long-term arms control agreements between the United States and the Soviet Union, for example, is not the absence of information about weapon systems themselves but the lack of knowledge about their intended purposes. Observing the uncertainties diplomats often face in dealing with problems without sufficient information, Kissinger reflected that "when the scope for action is greatest, the knowledge on which to base such action . . . is at a minimum."

The Available Information Is Often Incorrect. The information on which decision makers base policy is screened, sorted, and rearranged by *both* the decision makers and the advisers who serve them; distortion of otherwise reliable intelligence is therefore often introduced, and different pictures of reality appear when different frames of reference are employed. Furthermore, the natural human tendency to reject unfamiliar or disturbing information is compounded by the tendency of advisers to tell their superiors what they want to hear rather then supplying them with the cold, hard facts.[7]

There Are Substantial Material and Psychological Costs Involved in the Acquisition of Information. The economical thing to do is to stop searching for *all* pertinent information and to base decisions on partial—and, one hopes, representative—information.[8] If policy makers habitually make decisions on the basis of information that is readily available instead of searching for addi-

---

[7]This observation is discussed more fully in chapter fourteen.

[8]Downs (1957), for instance, has suggested that the rational voter cannot afford to gather all the information available about all candidates prior to deciding for whom to vote: the costs involved are too high for the resultant payoff. Instead, voters tend to make such decisions with partial information, for example, the candidate's party label.

tional information that might lead to a different set of policy choices, it can be said that they are not acting in a fully rational manner. Furthermore, substantial psychological obstacles are involved in confronting objectively any evidence that demonstrates that previous decisions were mistaken. When that happens, leaders are prone to cling to prophecies already proven wrong rather than to admit error, and to search energetically for new information that justifies the past (mistaken) policy (Wilensky, 1967).

Goal Selection Is Difficult Because of Ambiguities in Defining the National Interest. In facing a policy problem, it is not sufficient to ask what goals best serve the national interest. That merely begs the question. The more difficult intellectual problem involves taking inventory of *all* possible goals, entertaining the possibility that different national goals may be incompatible, and "prioritizing" them in terms of their ability to promote the country's welfare.

Those tasks may be impossible. Identifying all the goals the nation might pursue and then choosing that goal which "best" serves the national interest may be beyond rational assessment in today's complex, interdependent world (which may be why reasonable people often differ when debating definitions of the national interest). The first step in doing good, the Greek philosopher Plato believed, is to know what is good. But identification of what is good is obscured by the fact that every goal has costs associated with it, as well as possible unanticipated consequences (especially in the long run).[9] Therefore, "rational" goal selection frequently means choosing the lesser of two evils. For instance, if a leader's goals include (1) the economic development of impoverished countries and (2) the enhancement of America's standard of living, one goal may be achieved only at the expense of the other. Or consider the goals of (1) fostering human rights throughout the world and (2) protecting American allies. Choosing the latter may entail sacrifice of the former by rationalizing support of repressive regimes.

Policy Options Tend to Be "Prepackaged" and Searching for Them Is Constrained by Time Pressures. The search for policy options is seldom exhaustive. Policy makers work constantly with overloaded agendas and short deadlines. Time for careful identification of possible courses of action and for a cool-headed assessment of their consequences is therefore typically unavail-

---

[9]Andrew Scott illustrates the kinds of unintended consequences that can result from previous foreign policy choices:

> The Bretton Woods system was designed to foster increased trade, the improvement of payments procedures, and economic development. It succeeded in accomplishing these objectives. It also "accomplished" a number of other things that were not intended—it furthered inequality between developed and less-developed nations, it contributed to the build-up of international debt, it provided the institutional framework within which an extraordinary growth of multinational enterprises took place, it tied global economic conditions to domestic and foreign policy decisions of the United States, [and] by contributing to the increase of trade it also contributed to the growth of interdependence and to the vulnerability of the global economic system to disruption. (Scott, 1979: 2–3)

able. As Kissinger (1979) observed: "There is little time for leaders to reflect. They are locked in an endless battle in which the urgent constantly gains on the important. The public life of every political figure is a continual struggle to rescue an element of choice from the pressure of circumstance."

If options are not identified, they cannot be considered, for, as Thomas Schelling asks, "How do you make a list of things you would never have thought of?" (cited in Bloomfield, 1974a). In fact, instead of identifying options themselves, decision makers usually are presented with a list of possible decisions by their advisers and by bureaucratic agencies. Such lists are invariably abbreviated. The range of choice is reduced by the elimination of "unthinkable" actions during the crucial "pre-decision-making" stage. During a crisis in particular, the pressure is intense to shorten the search for options, which often limits consideration of options to the first ones that come to mind (and ones frequently derived from prior analogous situations).

In the "Choice" Phase of the Decision Process, Goal-maximizing Options Are Rarely Selected. The assumption of rationality is nowhere more violated than in how foreign policy *choices* tend to be reached in practice. The evidence (Lindblom, 1959; March and Simon, 1958) is overwhelming that individuals, and policy makers in particular, do not choose the option or set of options which has the maximum chance of realizing desired goals. Instead, people settle for the first possibility that satisfies minimal requirements or expectations, one they believe will get them by. They engage in what Herbert Simon (1957) has labeled "satisficing" behavior whereby rather than seeking to "optimize," decision makers are content to select any "acceptable" or satisfactory course of action. According to another characterization, decision makers engage in "optional stopping": in considering options, the typical decision maker evaluates one option at a time but terminates the evaluation as soon as an option is discovered that appears to be superior to those previously considered (Slovic, Fischhoff, and Lichtenstein, 1977). Is it any wonder that people who operate in such a way are prone afterward to complain that they are dissatisfied with the results or that things did not seem to work out as well as they should? Had they acted rationally by engaging in maximizing behavior, they would have chosen the one "best" choice and therefore ultimately would find themselves less dissatisfied with decision outcomes.[10]

---

[10]It is tempting to speculate that the more important the decision, the less likely it is that the decision will be based on pure rationality (and, conversely, the more likely satisficing behavior will be exhibited). Notice how little effort is put into acquiring information, considering alternatives, and making choices for the really big life decisions one makes, like choosing a career or a marriage partner. Here people seem to slide into the path of least resistance and to settle for the first available alternative, rather than conducting a thorough search and selecting that alternative which best fulfills one's basic values. More intellectual effort and rational behavior may typically be put into buying a car or a six-pack of beer, where at least people shop comparatively and gather some information. It is worth asking if the same pattern exists in the realm of foreign policy decisions, where it appears more time, attention, and energy are given to choosing seating arrangements for a diplomatic reception than to evaluating the effectiveness of the latest weapon system proposed by the Department of Defense.

It might be added that the great difficulties of *ascertaining correctly the payoff probabilities* of each available option reduce the prospects for rational choice (and promote satisficing instead). Even in the best of circumstances—even if policy makers could obtain full information, and even if they were able to identify all the choices capable of achieving the preferred goal—the final choice would still likely be affected by "guesstimates" regarding the relative utility and efficacy of each alternative.

If the difficulty of discovering the best choice is acknowledged, then a further question is raised: "Is it advantageous to search for a 'most suitable' solution when every option involves some cost?" Perhaps the "rational" thing to do is to settle for a compromise, not an optimal solution. "Irrationality" might even be desirable (see Mandel, 1984). Problems could be dealt with *incrementally* and alternatives sought that would permit minor modifications based on what is feasible and pragmatic. Although this approach to management (termed by its proponents the "muddling-through model") is decidedly "nonrational," it may be a concession to reality. At least worth considering is whether it may be preferable to a purely rational model that promises more than can be delivered. Charles Lindblom (1959) summarizes the reasoning behind such a view by observing, "A wise policy-maker . . . expects that his policies will achieve only part of what he hopes and at the same time will produce unanticipated consequences he would have preferred to avoid. If he proceeds through a succession of incremental changes, he avoids serious lasting mistakes." Some past leaders have themselves been known to advocate this less than comprehensive approach to foreign policy making. Franklin Roosevelt, for instance, once noted that in making difficult decisions, "It is common sense to take a method and try it; if it fails, admit it frankly and try another" (cited in Perkins, 1964).

Other Restricting Factors. Still other factors diminish the accuracy of rationality as a description of the way decision makers actually perform their roles. How many policy makers, for example, have a purposeful agenda for action? Probably few actually have probed their values to the point that they are aware of, and can measure hierarchically, their *value priorities*. More often than not, when a problem arises a policy maker then devises a goal appropriate to the problem rather than allowing a predetermined hierarchy of preferences to lead to goals. Furthermore, because few if any decision makers actually consider all possible goals before selecting some, objectives may be determined more frequently by psychological needs, deference to precedent and tradition, and uncritical, subconscious acceptance of prevailing but unexamined wisdom clothed in conventional policy slogans. Letting the situation of the moment structure the kinds of objectives sought, and ignoring their long-term consequences, may be a recurrent pattern of behavior among some policy makers.

Policy makers also often disagree among themselves about the relevant facts. Consequently, they differ in their evaluations of what characterizes particular situations. Proponents and opponents of the SALT II treaty, for example, differed sharply over the issue of verifying Soviet compliance with the treaty's terms. Both sides examined the same set of data regarding U.S. intelligence and surveillance capabilities, but they reached different conclusions from the same facts. That intelligent individuals often see "reality" differently stems from people's tendency to stress different facts, to draw different inferences from the same facts, to operate from different values, and to hold different roles which influence their perceptions of a situation (Snyder, 1968).

Finally, we must acknowledge that foreign policy is made not by states but by human beings acting on behalf of the state. Hence, decision-making processes cannot be separated from psychodynamics (Kinder and Weiss, 1978; Holsti, 1976a and 1976b; Simon, 1985). Major decisions therefore may be rooted in the subconscious needs and drives of the decision maker rather than in the logic of the situation (a perspective explored in detail in chapter fourteen). The need to be liked, the desire to be popular, and the temptation to look decisive, even heroic, may interfere with rational judgment and ultimately sacrifice the nation's welfare. Decision makers also tend to be overconfident about their judgments and analytical skills, thereby overestimating their abilities in order to maintain a self-image that has been dubbed the "illusion of control" (Langer, 1975).

Personal emotional needs and passions may also lead decision makers to confuse their own goals with those of the nation. If they come to see themselves as indispensable to the welfare of the nation, they will tend to equate what is good for them with what is good for the country. When this happens, foreign policies are initiated for the purpose of maintaining or strengthening the power and popularity of the leader, possibly at the expense of America's self-interest.[11]

The foregoing review of some of the ways individuals and policy makers go about the process of making decisions in real life warrants the conclusion that the ideal requirements of rational problem solving cannot be met in practice. Preconceived notions pass for facts. Decisions are made to satisfy immediate, not long-term, needs. There is a natural reluctance to reach a decision, and a strong temptation to pass the buck. Only a small number of alternatives are usually considered and only a restricted number of consequences pondered. Full knowledge is rarely achieved, even though the volume of information may be staggering. Decisions are generally reached under conditions of "bounded rationality," with only the information regarded as most relevant to the decision being scanned. Fear of public criticism discourages decision

---

[11]Examples are numerous, and it is probably safe to regard the confusion of personal and national interests on the part of leaders as a recurrent problem. Nixon, for instance, may be interpreted (Ball, 1976) as having at times gone on foreign trips (for example, the Beijing visit of 1972) not to effect changes in the external environment or to bring about some long-cherished national goal abroad, but instead to augment his public popularity. Similarly, President Johnson is said to have consciously sought to time his negotiations abroad at the height of the Vietnam War so as to diffuse criticism of his policies at home and to divert attention from protest demonstrations.

makers from making choices that deviate far from tradition and precedent. And often before a final decision is reached or announced, a favored, orthodox alternative is advanced and information is gathered that might justify the preferred option (that is, a decision is reached first and reasons found to support it only later). The result is not rationality, with each step taken leading logically to the next in a value-maximizing way, but something that appears quite different—a haphazard, trial-and-error, seat-of-the-pants, decision-making process conducted in a rush, based on "gut it out," best-guess calculations, and influenced strongly by the social context of the process (see Anderson, 1986). The process thus looks decidedly indecisive and more improvisational than rational. Indeed, we must conclude that in foreign policy decision making, the "degree of rationality . . . bears little relationship to the world in which officials conduct their deliberations" (Rosenau, 1980).[12]

What are the implications of such a conclusion? If comprehensive rationality is not an accurate description of decision-making behavior, and if, indeed, even the notion of planning in foreign policy can be questioned (Bloomfield, 1978), then we are forced to reject depictions of American foreign policy making as being based purely on rational calculations. For it is simply inaccurate to think of the nation's actions as the response of public officials laden with exceptional skills and cognitive powers, untiring in the collection of accurate information on which to base decisions, and logical in the derivation of conclusions designed to maximize the national interests of the country. The image does not fit with the facts.

But having said all that, we nevertheless can assume that policy makers aspire to rational decision-making behavior, which they may even occasionally approximate. Indeed, as a working proposition, it is useful to assume rationality in analyzing how the decisional process *should* work as well as in discussing some aspects of the conduct of foreign policy.

> Officials have some notion, conscious or unconscious, of a priority of values; . . . they possess some conceptions, elegant or crude, of the means available and their potential effectiveness; . . . they engage in some effort, extensive or brief, to relate means to ends; and . . . therefore, at some point they select some alternative, clear-cut or confused, as the course of action that seems most likely to cope with the immediate situation. (Rosenau, 1980: 304–305)

Administrative Theory and Foreign Policy Rationality

Before we accept the notion that the less-than-rational decision-making style of policy makers is responsible for the many problems besetting the United States in world affairs, we should probe a competing thesis: that the foreign policy machinery of the United States enhances the rationality in decision making to which decision makers aspire, even if they do not always realize the

---

[12]Oneal (1983) argues that the rational-actor model is often judged against unrealistic standards because its postulates are impossible to meet. See also Holsti (1976a) and A. Rowe (1974).

ideal. For it is not possible for one, two, or a few officials to make the foreign policy of a superpower like the United States, with its incredibly varied interests. Hence, some kind of bureaucracy is necessary; there is neither sufficient time to cover all pressing matters of the day nor the resources to gather the necessary information without the support of large organizations. They make other contributions as well, thereby perhaps enhancing the kind of rational decision-making process that would otherwise be lacking (see Goodsell, 1983). Let us briefly examine these contributions so that we might shed light on the role behaviors associated with the machinery of foreign policy making.

The idea that modern bureaucracy—by virtue of the roles it creates—enhances the prospects for rationality in decision making has a long intellectual tradition, going back to the seminal theoretical work on bureaucracies by the German scholar Max Weber (1864–1920). His hypothesis was that bureaucratic decision making produces the highest degree of efficiency and the best form of administration. Applying his theory to American foreign policy, it may be postulated that large-scale bureaucratic organizations contribute to rational decision making in a number of ways:

- Administrative efficiency increases in bureaucracies because of specialization. Structured on the principle of division of labor, bureaucracies make each individual in the machinery a specialist, even an expert, at his job. Efficiency is also enhanced by the division of labor between agencies as well as within them, as, for example, in the separation of diplomatic and defense responsibilities between the State and Defense departments.

- Efficiency increases in large-scale organizations because authority is distributed hierarchically, and the jurisdictions of decision makers are fixed. A chain of command facilitates the implementation of orders by assigning responsibility for different tasks to different people. It is easier to get things done when everyone has a clear notion of who is subordinate to whom, of who has authority over whom, and what role is to be performed by each cog in the machinery. Precious time does not have to be devoted to deciding who has the power to decide. The "formalization" of authority in hierarchically organized bureaucracies also enhances control, speed, clarity of policies, certainty, and security, and diminishes pressures from special pleaders (Stewart, 1972).

- Rational administrative and decision-making procedures derive from rules specifying how each major function or task is to be performed and indicating the appropriate behavior attached to each major role. Hence, rather than deliberating about the best method for handling a problem, the bureaucrat can concentrate on mastering those methods. Rules reduce the incidence of capricious decision making and also make for consistency by providing officials with rituals and precedents.

- Bureaucratic reliance on a system of records, managed by reference to written documents systemically gathered and stored, aids rational decision making. The often hazy memory of the typical decision maker is replaced by objective, hard information. Keeping records facilitates intelligence retrieval, provides a data bank of past decisions, and increases the amount of information available for making future decisions.

- In principle, bureaucracies recruit personnel on the basis of achievement and aptitude, rather than on the basis of ascriptive criteria such as wealth, sex, ethnicity, or family background. To the extent that model recruitment behaviors are practiced, the best and brightest will indeed be chosen.

- Similarly, rationality in policy making is presumed to increase in bureaucracies because people are promoted and compensated on the basis of merit according to regularized processes. Again, to the extent that achievement criteria govern who is "selected up" and who is "selected out" (rather than criteria such as longevity, personal characteristics, ingratiation, or repayment for favors to superiors), decision-making responsibility is placed in the hands of the most competent. Morale, effort, and dedication to duty will also increase.

- Rationality in decision making is enhanced because organizations operate from a value system predicated not on "transcendental values" but on "pragmatic operationalism," built on respect for consultative management, cooperative effort, task orientation, empirical fact, and expertise. Bureaucracies are therefore staffed by technocrats "who fly no flags, and who are completely bored by ideological considerations" (Katz and Kahn, 1966).

- Large bureaucracies are pluralized, which presumably increases rationality because pluralism encourages consideration of a large number of alternatives. With authority divided among competing agencies, with each agency protective of its own interests, the odds are increased that a variety of policy proposals will be articulated before decisions are reached, and "multiple advocacy" (George, 1972) will maximize the probability that many options will be identified. When policy decisions come from a political process involving interagency bargaining, greater effort is put into defending positions and considering multiple courses of action. The process of negotiation (including the accommodation and compromise required to reach a consensus) also enhances communication and prevents any one actor from making a major policy decision unilaterally. In short, multiple advocacy increases rationality by encouraging consideration of competing positions.

- The administrative norms of bureaucracies allow some specialists the luxury of engaging in *forward planning*, determining in advance the objectives to be accomplished in meeting long-term needs and identifying the means by which the goals might be attained. Unlike the president, whose role requires that attention be focused on the crisis of the moment, bureaucracies can consider the future, and not merely the present.

These hypotheses suggest just some of the major contributions organized group decision making can make to rational foreign policy choice. What emerges from the portrayal above is a picture of the policy process that appears more rational than the one previously described. As one student summarized this view, for complex and large societies:

> a bureaucratic form of organization may be indispensable. The advantages of bureaucratic organizations are great. Bureaucracy can operate like a machine with great precision and speed in accordance with calculable rules, by experts without regard to persons, with a minimum of friction, and with continuity. Individuals may come and go, but the organization continues. (Lorch, 1978)

Before jumping to the conclusion that bureaucratic decision making is a modern blessing which brings out the best in government, we would do well to note that the role-induced behavior described here is an ideal characterization, much like the rational role model itself. It tells us how (that is, the roles by which) decision making *should* occur, according to organization theory. It does not tell us how American foreign policy making in bureaucratic structures *does* occur. Probing the empirical reality of organizational behavior and evaluating the linkage between bureaucratic decision making and the outcomes it produces thus requires consideration.

THE CASE AGAINST BUREAUCRACIES: CHARACTERISTICS OF FOREIGN POLICY MAKING BY ORGANIZATIONS

In principle, bureaucracies exist to help the president carry out his policies. In practice, the president is dependent on those comprising the foreign affairs government to get things done. Thus, as Henry Kissinger advised, "to understand what the government is likely to do, one has to understand the bureaucratics of the problems."

What are some of the consequences of the dependency of the presidency on the bureaucracies created to serve it? Is presidential power over American foreign policy diminished rather than enhanced by such dependence? Are foreign policy bureaucracies "ruling servants," in control of policy by virtue of their power to impede? Indeed, does the bureaucracy rule while the president merely reigns?

Those troublesome questions have been raised by the recurrent complaints of past presidents that they were unable to control the government they were elected to run (see Box 13.1). The subordinates working the foreign affairs machinery have often appeared insubordinate; rather than helping to get things done, they have opposed presidential directives, and the chief executive consequently has been frustrated in gaining effective control of foreign policy. Most presidents have complained, at one time or another, about their lack of real authority and about the time they have had to expend, not in dealing with other nations, but in trying to persuade and coerce their own bureaucracy to go along with policy decisions.

Although it is perhaps an exaggeration to speak of the "bureaucratic captivity" of the president, the president is heavily reliant on the bureaucracy for information, for the identification of problems, for advocacy of solutions, and most importantly, for the implementation of presidential orders (see Smith and Clark, 1985). The president's leeway in controlling and redirecting the nation's foreign policy is constrained to a considerable extent by the powers and role of the foreign affairs government.

And it is constrained by the sheer size of the federal bureaucracy. The U.S. government is substantial in size. It consists of a work force of roughly 3 mil-

---

BOX 13.1 Bureaucratic Agencies: Policy Servants or Policy Saboteurs? Some Perspectives

---

"You know, one of the hardest things in a government this size is to know that down there, underneath, is that permanent structure that's resisting everything you're doing."

President Ronald Reagan, 1985

"I thought I was used to all sorts of back-knifing from my years in private industry, but I wasn't prepared for this [level as head of the State Department]. Why, down here they literally search your back for soft spots."

Secretary of State George Shultz, 1985

"There is nothing more frustrating for a President than to issue an order to a Cabinet officer, and then find that, when the order gets out in the field, it is totally mutilated. I have had that happen to me, and I am sure every other President has had it happen."

President Gerald Ford, 1980

"I underestimated the inertia and the momentum of the Federal bureaucracy. . . . It is difficult to change."

President Jimmy Carter, 1977

"The fact is that most of the problems [ascribed to President Carter's foreign policy] had more to do with lousy execution than with bad initial policy."

Former State Department official Hodding Carter, III, 1981

"To a degree, the needs of bureaucrats and President are incompatible. The better one is served, the worse will be the other."

Former presidential adviser Richard E. Neustadt, 1963

---

lion civilians and another 2.2 million military personnel. Those bureaucrats are firmly ensconced in roughly 2,000 separate but overlapping government agencies; presidents come and go, but bureaucrats abide. Moreover, the officials at the top, those presumably responsible for the nation's foreign policy, are relatively few in number: among the over 3 million federal civil servants, only about 3,300 are policy makers (that is, individuals appointed by the president and capable of being fired by him). The consequence of such a massive superstructure is that foreign policy decisions necessarily stem from fragmented centers of authority and from the choices made by many individuals within the government, most of whom are beyond the immediate reach of elected public officials. As Woodrow Wilson put it in a timeless description,

"Nobody stands responsible for the policy of government . . . a dozen men originate it; a dozen compromises twist and alter it; a dozen offices put it into execution."

Major Attributes of Bureaucratic Behavior

What are the characteristics and policy consequences of the decision roles played by bureaucratic agencies? At least eight attributes of administrative decision making are important to an understanding of bureaucratic behavior.[13] Each is discussed below.

Parochialism. Each agency in the federal government—and every administrative unit within it—is often assumed to share three distinct characteristics with every other: it seeks to pursue its own purposes, to promote its own power, and to enhance its own position in the government hierarchy.

To pursue its own purposes, a bureaucratic organization first must protect its jurisdictional territory. Thus organizations are motivated by the desire to protect their own self-interests, and they define issues and take stands on them in a manner perceived to promote those interests. As James M. Fallows, President Carter's chief speech writer, once observed, "The chief force motivating most top bureaucrats, Cabinet secretaries, and even some White House aides is job security—you can predict a bureaucrat's reaction to almost any issue by the way it will affect their job or fiefdom. That's what comes first."

The parochial tendency of bureaucratic organizations is natural to government departments "since each has, by definition, less than government-wide responsibilities and hence less than a society-wide constituency. And to a degree such parochialism is useful, for the department head must retain credibility with his constituency (and the congressional committees responsible to it) if he is to be effective" (Destler, 1980). Yet the consequences of bureaucratic parochialism can be detrimental to the larger interests of the government the bureaucracies ostensibly serve. Indeed, "since a public bureaucracy is concerned with special and limited aspects of public policy, to a degree it resembles the ordinary private pressure group" (Freeman, 1965).

Given the inherently parochial orientation of public bureaucracies, "[a]n endemic problem of government organization is to build counterweights to parochialism" (Destler, 1980). In part the centralization of control over foreign policy making in the White House is a response to that problem. But the task is made more difficult by the tendency of bureaucratic organizations to promote their power and position in the government hierarchy.

[13]The inventory of characteristics that follows summarizes the so-called "bureaucratic politics" model of foreign policy decision making. For useful statements of the assumptions of this model, see Allison (1971), Caldwell (1977), Rosati (1981), Oneal (1982 and 1983), Townsend (1982), and C. Hermann (1983); for a critique, see Krasner (1983).

Competitiveness. Bureaucratic parochialism breeds interagency competition. Far from being neutral or impartial administrators, desiring only to carry out presidential orders and seeking only to maximize the country's national interests, organizations comprising the foreign affairs government frequently take policy positions designed to maximize their own influence relative to that of other agencies. As a former deputy assistant defense secretary and National Security Council staff member noted, organizations take stands on issues which advance their interests and maneuver to protect them against other organizations and senior officials, including the president (Halperin, 1971).[14] Their behavior is due in part not to any intentional maliciousness, but instead to the understandable confusion between organizational and national interests. Many officials come to believe that the welfare of their agency is crucial to the country's security, and that the nation's interests are identical to the agency's.[15]

> National security managers have a personal investment in the health and aggrandizement of their own bureaucratic organizations. They equate the national interest and their organization's interest as a matter of course. They will fight to maintain an obsolete air base, build redundant weapons systems, proliferate arms around the world by certifying that the nation's ''vital interests'' are at stake when it is merely their own budgets. (Barnet, 1972: 122)

The result of contention over policy among competing groups is policy arrived at, all too frequently, through bargaining guided by self-interest rather than a rational consideration of the issues involved. That does not mean that heads of bureaucratic agencies are incapable of putting the nation's interests ahead of those of their organization. Although struggle among bureaucracies often characterizes the policy-making debate, considerations of what is best for the country dominate the rhetoric. The cynic might argue that such verbiage simply camouflages selfish parochial concerns. But regardless of the motivation, the incidence with which agency officials propose policies that blatantly benefit their own agency is remarkable.[16]

---

[14]One example of interagency competition emerged in the summer of 1977 between the Defense Department and the Energy Department over the issue of control of nuclear weapons development. When the Energy Department was created, it assumed control over nuclear weapons research as the successor to the Energy Research and Development Administration, which in turn was preceded by the Atomic Energy Commission (abolished in 1974). The latter two agencies reflected the outcome of a continuing debate going back to 1946 over whether nuclear research and weapons production should be under civilian or military control. At stake in the recent round of that controversy was not only Energy Secretary, and former Defense Secretary, James Schlesinger's continuing involvement in national security questions, but also control over several research and test sites, 30,000 employees, and over $1 billion annually.

[15]Bureaucrats act as they do in part because their world view is shaped by their training within organizations where they work. Foreign Service officers, for example, are prone by virtue of their training to recommend that the nation confer and negotiate to settle its international problems, just as military officers, by virtue of their training, are likely to emphasize military solutions to political problems.

[16]In 1962, for example, on the issue of rescinding a promise to give Great Britain the Skybolt missile, the position of the Defense Department was defined by the budgetary strains involved;

The reasons for such intragovernmental politics and competitive fighting are numerous. Kissinger (1969) suggests one: "The decision-maker will always be aware of the morale of his staff. . . . [He] cannot overrule it too frequently without impairing its efficiency. . . . Placating the staff then becomes a major pre-occupation of the executive." Another reason is that most heads of agencies are not only tied *to* their own organization but also *by* it in the sense that they are dependent on it for their own political influence in the policy process: "A Secretary of a Federal Department almost invariably becomes more the agent of the permanent bureaucracy under his command than a free agent, mainly because he must rely upon the permanent officials for expert information and analysis" (MacMahon, 1951). Thus, caught in the middle between higher level executives and the career personnel of an agency, the typical agency head must try to satisfy both. The pressures encourage competition with other agencies for scarce resources and power. Policy success in such an atmosphere tends very quickly to be defined less in terms of national interests than in terms of organizational interests.

Task Expansion and Imperialism. Because they are driven by the desire to protect and promote their own influence, bureaucratic agencies seek to enlarge their budgets and staffs, both absolutely and in relation to other agencies with which they are in competition. Size is a sign of security, expansion an indicator of importance and power, and, to some extent, prestige and influence can be conferred only by growth. Other things being equal, larger bureaucracies have greater access, greater credibility, greater resources, greater durability—and greater influence. (Such organizations probably have more enemies as well!) Thus, a principal goal of most organizations is the maintenance and enhancement of the organization's "health," defined in terms of growth in budget and personnel. Correspondingly, career bureaucrats' candid list of the criteria by which their success is judged would have to include such things as salary, number of people under their command, location of their office, and distance between their office and the parking lot. Somewhere in that list a concern for the promotion of the nation's interest would presumably be included.

Although it is commonplace to note that bureaucracies grow, there is an equally important feature of that behavioral law. Not only have bureaucratic agencies sought to increase their size (and budget) when the opportunity has arisen, many also attempt to enlarge their prerogatives and functional

---

the Air Force interpreted the idea as a threat to one of its missions—the manned bomber; the secretary of state viewed the proposal as potentially disruptive of close American-British relations; the State Department's Bureau of European Affairs saw in the proposal a chance to seduce Great Britain out of the strategic weapons business; and the president wanted to reconcile such conflicts and avoid congressional action against Skybolt's cancellation. Thus, in each case the major agencies involved sought to deal with the issue in a manner beneficial to its own interest. The consequence was competition among those involved for acceptance of their preferred definition of the national interest (see Halperin, 1971; and Neustadt, 1970).

powers. That is, bureaucratic organizations have a marked tendency to expand, whenever possible, the conception of their tasks (but always to preserve their original mission). As Herbert Hoover noted long ago, "Bureaucracy is ever desirous of spreading its influence and its power."

The *raison d'être* of administrative organizations is the acknowledged value of having various tasks or functions performed by independent units. Administrative theory maintains that decision making will be improved by such a division of labor, in which clearly differentiated functions are performed by experts specializing in particular roles. This was the reasoning behind the formation in 1947 of a separate Central Intelligence Agency whose ostensible purpose was to coordinate the gathering of foreign intelligence, and for the creation in 1961 of the Agency for International Development to specialize in the administration of foreign aid and technical assistance.

Practice, however, frequently has not conformed to theory. Because bureaucracies tend to be imperialistic, in many instances they have sought to assume the tasks assigned to and performed by other agencies. That inclination provides one reason why the Council on International Economic Policy created by President Nixon did not become an effective coordinator of economic policy making: it became another competitor in the jockeying for a piece of the policy action among those whose activities needed coordination. Bureaucratic imperialism also explains why so many different agencies are independently involved in gathering roughly the same intelligence information (for example, the State Department, the Defense Department, the CIA, the FBI, and the Treasury Department, among others), and why the three military services have found it "absolutely essential" that each develop its own capabilities in areas where the other services specialize (as evidenced by the Army's accumulation of more support aircraft than the Air Force). The result: instead of a bureaucratic division of labor, functions are often duplicated.

Endurance. Bureaucracies are not only imperialistic; they are also survival-oriented. To speak of "the bureaucratization of American foreign policy" is to refer to the empirical fact that both the number and size of administrative units responsible for making foreign policy have increased enormously over the past forty years. Units are more often created or added to than phased out or cut back.[17] Once created, they usually persist, even in the face of great adversity.[18]

---

[17]As a demonstration of their survivability, Kaufman (1976) has shown that of 175 organizations extant in 1923, fully 148 (nearly 85 percent) were still active in 1973.

[18]The reasons for the endurance of federal agencies are varied. Kaufman's (1976) list of the important ones remains relevant:

1. Most administrative agencies are established by law or are accorded statutory recognition (as opposed to being established merely by departmental or presidential directive). Since laws are hard to change, organizational survivability is enhanced.
2. Laws are hard to change in part because they reflect the presence of congressional allies. But even after the original allies pass from the scene, "committee staffs tend to develop possessive and protective attitudes toward them."
3. Even without powerful legislative allies, federal agencies tend to be protected by the enormity of the federal budget. Agencies' budgets usually are added to each year, rather than

Bureaucratic growth and imperialism often carry with them the proliferation of functional units. Bureaucratic endurance contributes to the problem, because organizational reforms often result in the creation of *new* agencies to coordinate the activities of existing organizations. The result is not streamlining, but the addition of new layers to a burgeoning bureaucracy. Secretary of the Navy John Lehman illustrated the problem by lamenting in 1985: "it would be impossible for me or anyone to accurately describe to you the system with which, and within which, we must operate. There are thousands upon thousands of officers and entities and bureaus that have been created over the years to deal episodically with aspects of defense."

Secrecy and Exclusiveness. Organizational exclusiveness refers to the propensity of bureaucratic agencies to seek to minimize interference from and penetration by external groups, including elected officials as well as other government agencies. In a world where knowledge is power, the common device for promoting organizational exclusivity is to hide inner workings—and policy activities—from others and to retain information until its release is politically advantageous in the competition with others. Since many agency endeavors fail and none can please everyone, bureaucracies are naturally prone to hide information about themselves that can hurt their reputation and public image. Conversely, bureaucratic secrets are "leaked" selectively for propaganda purposes when disclosure is assumed to produce benefits. Thus, each agency attempts to keep its proceedings secret[19] as a maneuver against interference or as a method of concealing its activities from present or potential enemies, including the president, who might use such knowledge to publicly attack its operations.[20]

Attitudinal Conformity. Also characteristic of bureaucratic behavior is the pervasive tendency of individuals to adopt the outlook and beliefs prevailing in the bureaucracy. Every bureaucracy tends to develop, over time, a shared

---

calculated anew from a base of zero. Once an agency receives an appropriation, the sheer momentum of the budgetary process tends to protect that appropriation from one year to the next.

4. The fact that presidents and cabinet officers typically pass from the scene far more rapidly than do most agencies or their congressional allies makes federal agencies immune and insulated from efforts from the top to control them.

5. Administrative agencies are typically "active, energetic, persistent participants" in the game of politics. Job preservation, the fact that the reputations of agency leaders are linked to their organizations' fate, and "the mysterious forces of organizational loyalty and commitment to program" are all powerful ingredients in organizational preservation.

6. Preservation is enhanced further by the clientele groups which administrative agencies serve. When trouble arises, those groups and outside supporters can be expected to marshall political support on behalf of an agency.

7. When threats to an agency surface, support can also be expected from the professional and trade associations outside a particular agency with whom the dominant occupational group within that agency is identified—whether lawyer, doctor, or professional soldier.

[19]For a probing look at the advantages—and dangers in a democracy—of government secrecy in the realm of foreign affairs, see Franck and Weisband (1974).

[20]"There are no secrets in Washington," President Kennedy once observed, "except things I need to know."

"mind set," or dominant way of looking at reality, which few of its members are able to resist.

A number of factors serve to promote that phenomenon, which has come to be known as "groupthink" (Janis, 1972), rendering it nearly universal. The ubiquity of attitudinal conformity in foreign policy bureaucracies is due partly to the recruitment process. Homogeneity of outlook is reinforced because the process of selection and self-selection brings together individuals who already share many basic attitudes. One study (Harr, 1969) notes, for instance, that the Foreign Service sought "young people they consider most like the successful officers already in the system." Trouble-makers, free thinkers, people who are inclined to "rock the boat" or "make waves" are not welcomed; instead, those subscribing to the dominant values of the organization are preferred.[21]

Once an individual enters the confines of a bureaucracy, socialization reinforces the pressures to conform to prevailing beliefs. Recruits are quickly educated into their role and the acceptable attitudes that go with it, including traditional patterns of behavior, a new and often esoteric vocabulary, and "standard operating procedures." Those who fail to act in accordance with agency standards are punished. Nonconformity can result in loss of influence or, in the extreme, unemployment. On the other hand, those who conform to peer-group attitudes, who are perceived as team players, are rewarded. Indeed, the cynic might argue that promotions are awards given to bureaucrats for accepting organizational myths.

At the very least, the development of an institutional mind set discourages creativity, dissent, and independent thinking, and thereby undermines rational policy making. Moreover, attitudinal conformity all too often breeds decision making by attention to ritual and precedent. Specialization detracts from an individual's ability to focus on overall goals, and emphasis on routines and operational rules makes the rituals and procedures more valued than the goals they are designed to achieve. Self-evaluations made by the Department of State, for instance, routinely identify pressures to conform and stifled creativity as persistent problems.

Deference to Tradition. Attitudinal conformity is reinforced by the fact that decision making in complex organizations is conducted according to *rules*. Norms govern the general behavior of decision makers, and decisions are made in accordance with specific standard procedures. Rather than invent a new way to deal with a problem, the bureaucrat defers to tradition. The behavior emanating from bureaucracies thus becomes patterned, ritualized, and invariant over time. As Frankel (1969) commented on this characteristic: "A man comes to an assignment, and he is told what policy is. He must find a

---

[21]Some organization theorists have noted that *new* units within administrative agencies recruit ideologues and risk takers, whereas old ones recruit cautious, security-conscious personnel who are more likely to be motivated to protect their stakes in the present scheme of things rather than to express their policy preferences and attempt reform. An example of the former was the State Department's Bureau of Human Rights under Carter.

way to navigate through the storms, to resist the pressures of people and events, and to turn over the policy to his successor in the same condition in which it was when he received it from his predecessor." In the case of the State Department, that characteristic has been dubbed by a former State Department officer and National Security Council staffer as the "curator mentality" (cited in Destler, 1974).

Reliance on Historical Analogies. When confronted with what appears to be a new, unusual, or even unique situation, decision makers, and particularly bureaucrats, tend to search history (typically impressionistically) for parallels that suggest options for dealing with the problem. Respect for precedent and routine has a conservative effect, hindering change and thus preserving previous patterns. That tendency helps account for the continuity of American foreign policy over long periods of time. It is often argued, for example, that the "Munich" analogy was drawn on by a generation of policy makers as evidence that it is impossible to appease aggressors. The analogy refers to the 1938 agreement between Great Britain and France, on the one hand, and Nazi Germany, on the other, to allow Germany to annex a large part of Czechoslovakia in return for what British Prime Minister Neville Chamberlain called "peace in our time." In fact, war broke out in Europe a year later, with the apparent lesson that an aggressor cannot be stopped short of fighting him.[22]

As an inventory of the salient characteristics of group decision making, the preceding is far from complete. Other attributes that describe the behavior of bureaucracies could certainly be identified, and other aspects of decision making by group methods become relevant under particular conditions and in response to certain kinds of issues.[23] What the preceding brief survey suggests, however, can be stated in a single general proposition: the attributes of the decision-making system clearly influence the behavior of those who occupy institutionally defined decision-making roles. In the section that follows, we will shift our attention to some of the major consequences of those attributes for the kinds of policies the government chooses to pursue beyond the nation's boundaries.

POLICY CONSEQUENCES OF ORGANIZATIONAL DECISION MAKING

What features of American foreign policy emerge as a result of the characteristics of bureaucracies? What properties of policies are traceable to the organizational decision-making process? Answers to those questions can be found by

[22]As discussed in chapter nine, some have also argued that the Munich generation has since been replaced with a Vietnam generation less inclined to use military power to respond to aggression, regardless of where it may occur.

[23]See Simon (1957) for an excellent review of these other characteristics and Hummel (1977) for a critique and synthesis of the bureaucratic experience.

observing some of the conspicuous repercussions of the bureaucratic policy-making process.

Bureaucratic Competition and Foreign Policy Inertia

As described in earlier chapters, a major feature of American foreign policy has been the resistance of its grand vision to change during the postwar era. Key assumptions have remained consistent and intact; similarly, reactions to external events have conformed to long-established precedents. When changes have occurred, they have more often been incremental deviations from the past than radical new departures.

The reasons for the seeming lack of innovation in policy are many. They include the constraints on change imposed by the international environment, by domestic society, and by the separation of powers within the federal government. But bureaucratic factors also partly explain why most policy areas have changed so slowly, departing from tradition only slightly in nuance and style while leaving key value assumptions and actions intact, and why foreign policy has seemed so "gradualist." The overwhelming complexity of the foreign affairs machinery, with its entrenched and competing bureaucracies, limits what members of the decision-making elite can do and casts doubt on Washington's capacity to act expeditiously. The fact that policy is formulated and implemented by a large number of individuals situated in a complex institutional arrangement reduces the probability of obtaining consensus and taking decisive action. Bureaucrats in charge of the different agencies usually disagree: they want different policies, and they define the situation differently because of their differing vantage points. The result is that policy formulation often boils down to a tug of war among competing agencies, a political game with high stakes, in which differences are settled at the minimum common denominator. As Henry Kissinger described the process:

> Each of the contending factions within the bureaucracy has a maximum incentive to state its case in its most extreme form because the ultimate outcome depends, to a considerable extent, on a *bargaining process*. The premium placed on advocacy turns decision-making into a *series of adjustments among special interests*—a process more suited to domestic than to foreign policy. This procedure neglects the long-range because the future has no administrative constituency and is, therefore, without representation in the adversary proceedings. Problems tend to be slighted until some agency or department is made responsible for them. . . . The outcome usually depends more on the pressures or the persuasiveness of the contending advocates than on a concept of over-all purpose. (Kissinger, 1969: 268; emphasis added)

In addition, decisive action and policy innovation are also discouraged by the policy-making process, it can be argued, because the political nature of policy formation results in policy incrementalism: bureaucratic decision making naturally tends to slice problems into smaller components and to deal

with them in a piecemeal fashion. Such an approach avoids making fundamental or far-reaching choices. It also avoids the possibility of offending a
large segment of the many constituencies involved in the decision. And it
skirts the necessity of rationally assessing a whole spectrum of goals and the
range of alternative means for achieving them.

Inertia in American foreign policy is also reinforced by some of the characteristics of bureaucratic behavior we have previously discussed, including the
conservative impulse and built-in preference for the status quo; the inclination
among career officials to "go along in order to get along" (which brings about
"groupthink" and encourages acceptance of prevailing policies); and the effects of the sheer size of the foreign affairs government on policy change. On
this last point it might be argued that the larger and more complex the institutional machinery for foreign policy making, the greater will be the probability
that inertia will govern policy, and the greater will be the force of that inertia.

Another obstacle to change in foreign policy stems from the fact that bureaucracies typically are involved in the administration of programs reflecting
the consequences of *prior* decisions. Most bureaucrats therefore see their role
as being loyal, even unquestioning, implementors of other people's policies
rather than as being the creators of their own.[24] The greater the loyalty and
dedication to specific administrative tasks, the greater tends to be the commitment to the policy being implemented. "[T]o try and believe in what one is
doing, . . . to see broader problems in narrow terms derived from one's own
specific activities," is a natural part of a bureaucrat's role, and because change
itself is always challenging, it is natural for many of the players in the game to
react to the threats posed by resisting change. The result, however, is that
"the information and judgments bureaucrats provide for use in the making of
policies tend to be strongly biased in favor of the continuation, rather than the
modification, much less the reversal, of existing policies. . . . Thus a bureaucracy inevitably comes down heavily on the side of established policies and
strongly resists change" (Reischauer, 1968). Some bureaucrats, of course,
fight inertia, and in some areas of domestic policy, innovation has been engineered by bureaucratic agencies (see Britan, 1981). But such efforts are rare,
and tend to be screened out before they reach the ultimate decision makers.

Bureaucratic Sabotage of Presidential Foreign Policy Initiatives

However appealing (or discomforting) the notion that the foreign policy of the
United States is little more than what the president says it is, at best the notion is only partially accurate. The president alone does not make foreign policy. As previously discussed, policy must not only be pronounced but carried
out. For that task the chief executive must turn to his bureaucracy. Hence,

---

[24]Loyalty to others' policies is reinforced by the bureaucracy's hierarchical chain of command,
which makes it psychologically and politically difficult to tell superiors that their policy and orders are mistaken. For an illustration of the consequences of this "to get along, go along" bureaucratic syndrome in the context of the Vietnam War, see Blachman (1973).

what the various executive agencies of government choose to enact becomes the foreign policy of the United States; external policy is what is *done, not* just what is *said*.

When we recall that bureaucracies are by nature exclusive, parochial, and interested primarily in protecting their own power and authority, it comes as no great surprise to learn that few agencies are willing or likely to carry out cheerfully presidential directives that they perceive to be harmful to their organizations. When personally threatened, bureaucrats are inclined to put themselves first and to defend their own welfare. The result: the foreign affairs machinery is often intractable, capable of disloyalty to the president it ostensibly serves, and obstructive to top-level executive policy proposals. And since change, or the prospect of change, is often threatening (because policy change almost invariably entails some redistribution of influence in the government hierarchy), bureacratic agencies are inclined to resist it and to respond disobediently. Thus bureaucracy can serve as a brake on policy innovation simply by refusing to act promptly in response to higher level directives.

Bureaucratic recalcitrance has been recurrent. Nearly every president has complained on occasion that his bureaucracy has undercut his policy by refusing to carry out orders expeditiously. Witness the observation of President Truman prior to General Eisenhower's succession to the White House: ''He'll sit here and he'll say, 'Do this! Do that!' *And nothing will happen.* Poor Ike—it won't be a bit like the Army. He'll find it very frustrating.'' Or reflect on President Kennedy's observation that giving the State Department an instruction was like dropping it in the dead-letter box.

Most often, bureaucratic nonresponsiveness and inaction manifest themselves as lethargy. The machinery of agencies routinely grinds slowly, and sometimes appears motionless.[25] The norm appears to be procrastination, which can easily be interpreted as intentional when in fact it is often inadvertent. It simply takes time to get things moving, and delay is routine in getting even the simplest requests completed (see Box 13.2). An impatient president can easily mistake the crawling pace for insubordination, even sedition (in part because the effect of abrogating policy decisions is the same). But we would do well not to confuse everyday bureaucratic inaction with planned foot dragging; the differences between slothful protraction and disobedient noncompliance are substantial.

But then again, willful bureaucratic sabotage is not a mere figment of leaders' imaginations, and it can take several forms. Bureaucracies can withhold or slant vital information. They can provide advice showing reasons why recommendations for policy innovation will not work, and they can circulate that advice to those in a position to challenge the policy change (such as Congress). They can discreetly contact pressure groups capable of mobilizing op-

---

[25]To quote the tongue-in-cheek characterization of James H. Boren, founder of the International Association of Professional Bureaucrats: ''One must always remember that freedom from action and freedom from purpose constitute the philosophical basis of creative bureaucracy.''

BOX 13.2 Bureaucratic Lethargy in Action

Once upon a time in Camelot, Robert F. Kennedy was commuting daily through the Virginia countryside and was irritated to see a road sign directing any passing motorist to CIA headquarters at Langley. He complained to his brother the President. "Get somebody to take that sign down," JFK ordered an aide. A call went out to the Interior Department. Days passed. Nothing happened. Bobby repeated the complaint. JFK repeated his order. Again, nothing happened. Finally, exasperated, the President short-circuited the bureaucratic chain of command and put in a direct call to the man in charge of signs in the Virginia suburbs. "This is Jack Kennedy," he said, looking at his watch. "It's 11 o'clock in the morning. I want that sign down by the time the Attorney General goes home tonight, and I'm holding you personally responsible." He returned the receiver, still smoking, to its cradle. "I now understand," he said, "that for a President to get something done in this country, he's got to say it three times."

SOURCE: *Newsweek*, January 26, 1981: 41.

position against a directive the bureaucrats find intolerable. Or they can delay policy implementation by demanding time to study the problem thoroughly (that is, to death)—a tactic known as "paralysis by analysis"—or by complexifying it into incomprehensibility (that is, by violating the kiss principle: "Keep It Simple, Stupid!"). And, of course, bureaucracies can buck a presidential directive by interpreting it in such a way that it can be administered differently than proposed or with a change in emphasis. The result, of course, is the absence of a change in the country's foreign policy. It has been said in this context that bureaucracies never change the course of the ship of state; they just adjust the compass.

Sometimes bureaucratic sabotage can be direct and immediate, as President Kennedy discovered in the midst of the 1962 Cuban missile crisis. While the president sought to orchestrate American action and bargaining, his bureaucracy in general, and the Navy in particular, was in fact controlling events by doing as it wished. The bureaucracy was

> choosing to obey the orders it liked and ignore or stretch others. Thus, after a tense argument with the Navy, Kennedy ordered the blockade line moved closer to Cuba so that the Russians might have more time to draw back. Having lost the argument with the President, the Navy simply ignored his order. Unbeknownst to Kennedy, the Navy was also at work forcing Soviet submarines to surface long before Kennedy authorized any contact with Soviet ships. And despite the President's order to halt all provocative intelligence, an American U-2 plane entered Soviet airspace at the height of the crisis. When Kennedy began to realize that he was not in full control, he asked his Secretary of Defense to see if he could find out just what the

Navy was doing. McNamara then made his first visit to the Navy command post in the Pentagon. In a heated exchange, the Chief of Naval Operations suggested that McNamara return to his office and let the Navy run the blockade. (Gelb and Halperin, 1973: 256)

Another example of bureaucratic disobedience occurred during the tense period *preceding* the Cuban missile crisis in 1962. President Kennedy had come to the conclusion, in March 1961, that Jupiter missiles in Turkey should be removed. They were obsolete, Kennedy observed, and they served only to exacerbate Soviet fears of encirclement and possible American attack from just beyond the Soviet border. The president therefore instructed the State Department to negotiate withdrawal of the American missiles. But Turkish officials were displeased with the proposal, and the State Department came to the conclusion that the politically astute thing to do was to comply with the Turkish request that the missiles stay. The president, however, was convinced that the benefits of removing the missiles far outweighed the costs and reiterated his command. Kennedy then "dismissed the matter from his mind," Robert Kennedy (1971) reported, because "[t]he President believed he was President and that, his wishes having been made clear, they would be followed and the missiles removed." But to his amazement and chagrin, President Kennedy discovered during the missile crisis months later that the State Department had failed to carry out his instructions—the missiles were still in Turkey. Because the crisis with the Soviets centered, in part, on the existence of American weapons on the periphery of the Soviet Union, the president was, needless to say, angry at this blatant sabotage of presidential policy.

Incidents like those illustrate the extent to which bureaucratic agencies perceive themselves to be free to act as they see fit. The consequence of bureaucratic intransigence is a marked lack of initiative in policy making and, at times, what appears to be a rudderless ship of state in foreign affairs. Bureaucratic inactivity may either abrogate or veto policy change, thus contributing to continuity in American foreign policy.

At another level, the chief executive and the bureaucracies created to serve him may be natural enemies even in the crucial realm of broad foreign policy conceptions and goals. Because most upper echelon career officials have been in their positions for years, sometimes even decades, they have been socialized into accepting long-held assumptions about American foreign policy that may be as deeply entrenched as the bureaucracies for whom they work. Those fundamental assumptions—about the nature of communism, the need for globalism, the utility of force, and other themes that have defined American foreign policy for four decades—have become almost conventional wisdom and are regarded as unworthy of further reexamination in bureaucratic settings. But presidents intermittently come to power with fresh ideas about foreign policy essentials—and with plans to implement new departures. The inevitable result is a clash between politicians and bureaucrats, between new and old, between policy innovation and policy continuity, with the former

---

BOX 13.3 President Versus Bureaucracy: An Insider's Look at the State Department's Reaction to Jimmy Carter

Since the Georgia team had little built-in expertise in foreign affairs, it acquiesced in the appointment of some State Department officials who had more loyalty to their résumés than to Carter.

Moreover, the permanent bureaucracy at State has watched Presidents come and go and is not much moved by each new Administration's inevitable exercises in rediscovery of the obvious. . . . Some of the older generation of diplomats openly didn't and don't believe in the efficacy or wisdom of such notions as campaigns for human rights or restraint in arms sales abroad. They have used arms as the sweetener with recalcitrant client states for so long that they see them as irreplaceable tools of the diplomatic trade. As for human rights concerns, there are those at State who believe that torture is not something that gentlemen discuss, publicly or privately. They fully expected that most of the new initiatives would soon be dropped, and they did everything they could to see that the day of abandonment came sooner rather than later. . . . [T]he career Foreign Service obstructors of the new policies often made more converts among the appointees than the newcomers were able to convert to the President's policies.

SOURCE: Hodding Carter, III, "Life Inside the Carter State Department," *Playboy* 28 (February 1981): 96ff.

more frequently the loser and the latter the victor. President Carter's experience with the State Department (see Box 13.3) suggests once again that the failure to change foreign policy can be attributed in part to a bureaucracy's reluctance to accept and support a new administration's new ideas.

Preventing Bureaucratic Sabotage

To acknowledge the "bureaucratic captivity" of American foreign policy is to run the danger of exaggerating its influence. While presidents often fail to appreciate the extent to which their policies are in the grip of the bureaucracies, presidents are, nevertheless, not powerless in dealing with bureaucratic disloyalty and obstruction. They have resources at their disposal to handle even the most recalcitrant agency. Some control tactics deserve scrutiny.

First, consider the strategy employed by the "master" at managing the federal bureaucracies, Franklin Roosevelt. His approach defies easy characterization but may be termed, for lack of a better label, "planned disorganization and confusion." An astute politician, Roosevelt anticipated the policy implementation problems he would encounter and sought to address them through a divide-and-rule posture. Roosevelt's strategy has been described thus:

[H]e deliberately organized—or disorganized—his system of command to insure that important decisions were passed on to the top. His favorite technique was to keep grants of authority incomplete, jurisdictions uncertain, charters overlapping. The result of this competitive theory of administration was often confusion and exasperation on the operating level; but no other method could so reliably insure that in a large bureaucracy, filled with ambitious men eager for power, the decisions, and the power to make them, would remain with the President. . . . Franklin allowed no one to discover the governing principle. (Schlesinger, 1958: 527)

In short, Roosevelt sought to control policy by denying control to those around him.

A second approach may be termed the "Kissinger solution." It is rather blunt but highly effective: punish the disobedient agency by excluding it from future decision making or circumvent it by setting up a smaller, substitute unit. Removing a bureaucracy from influence by bypassing or omitting it during important policy deliberations, especially on issues that vitally concern it, can have salutary reforming effects. Such a manipulative tactic can sometimes modify organizational behavior and transform a hostile agency into a submissive, compliant one, less intent on opposing presidential policy every time its own parochial interests are at stake.[26]

A third tactic is one Kennedy was gifted at employing: causing disturbance *within* a recalcitrant agency by skipping the normal chain of command and dealing directly with officials at lower echelons of authority. By upsetting standard operating procedures and going through unusual channels of communication, Kennedy was able to obtain needed information and to avoid bureaucratic bottlenecks.[27]

Nixon suggested yet a fourth strategy for obtaining obedience from uncooperative bureaucracies. It is described best by his words to George Shultz when the latter was director of OMB:

You've got to get us some discipline, George. You've got to get it, and the only way you get it, is when a bureaucrat thumbs his nose, we're going to get him. . . . They've got to know, that if they do it, something's going to happen to them, where anything can happen. I know the Civil Service pressure. But you can do a lot there. There are many unpleasant places where Civil Service people can be sent. (cited in Aberbach and Rockman, 1976: 457)

[26]Isolation from policy influence by denying access to the "magic circle" of power may also have been a tactic employed by President Reagan in his effort to control the State Department and to contain the open feud that erupted between Secretary of State Alexander Haig and Secretary of Defense Caspar Weinberger. Exasperated by the lack of attention and authority he felt were due him, Haig resigned, protesting that "At times it seems that the secretary of state is nothing but an errand boy." (For his account of his experiences in the corridors of power in the Reagan administration, see Haig, 1984.)

[27]Another Kennedy tactic was to encourage the voluntary resignation of a recalcitrant official by hinting that he or she was no longer in favor, a strategy described thus: Kennedy "would plant newspaper reports that the official was planning to resign. After reading a sufficient number of these reports, the official would grasp what was happening and turn in his resignation" (Berkley, 1978).

The punitive approach incorporates a number of related tactics, from dismissal or forced resignation to reassignment of the insubordinate to a lesser position or an undesirable location. As we have already noted, it can cause problems, since it is difficult to fire personnel. (Removal proceedings are time consuming and personally unpleasant, and the president who becomes involved in "administrivia" at this level risks ridicule for his meanness and for his misguided sense of priorities.) Moreover, it is often difficult to identify the individual responsible for the insubordination among the faceless bureaucrats within government. (John Roche, a Johnson policy adviser, once suggested to the chief executive that he "fire the s.o.b." who had sabotaged one of the president's pet programs. "Fire him!" screamed Johnson. "I can't even find him!") And geographic exile—removing the victim by reassignment to an intolerable location—may precipitate a costly "appeals" case, thus risking adverse publicity and, possibly, retaliatory acts. That is why, perhaps, the more common approach is to remove the obstructionist employee by giving him or her a promotion or special assignment to a prestigious-sounding but meaningless position.

Although dismissal or forced resignation of a career civil servant remains exceedingly difficult, an intransigent bureaucrat may be "squeezed" from a position of responsibility even while retaining employment. That is, the victim may be "layered over" by assigning others to perform his or her duties or by hiring someone new and more compliant to do the same tasks. "Layering" can be expensive and contributes to the growth of government, but the practice is not uncommon.[28]

The punitive approach assumes that obdurate individuals are at fault, not the processes that create incentives for disloyalty. The belief is that changing the people will solve the problem and get the bureaucracy moving. George Kennan once said, "Let me control personnel and I will ultimately control policy. For the part of the machine that recruits and hires and fires and promotes people can soon control the entire shape of the institution" (cited in Campbell, 1971). In practice, however, those presidents who have carefully picked their "own" people and instructed them to get their agencies to obey executive orders often have discovered that instead "their" people have, in Nixon aide John Ehrlichman's words, "married the natives." Typically, cabinet officers come to see their role as spokesmen for the departments they run instead of servants of the presidents who appointed them.

A fifth solution to bureaucratic intransigence is available, one that attacks causes instead of symptoms. Carter proposed it when he sought to regain control of government by reorganizing it: "We must give top priority to a drastic and thorough revision and reorganizing of the federal bureaucracy." The

[28]Insiders report that this tactic was used by Nixon's national security adviser, Henry Kissinger, to exclude from power Richard V. Allen. Allen later became Ronald Reagan's first national security adviser, but was squeezed out of the position when he clashed openly with other Reagan appointees.

approach, advocated by Carter in his 1976 campaign for office, was also pursued by Nixon, Johnson, Truman, and Reagan.

There have been many attempts at reorganization.[29] Symptomatic of the magnitude of the problem—and indicative of why solutions are improbable—is the fact that calls for reorganization are seldom calls for the demolition of existing and powerful bureaucracies. As noted earlier, entrenched bureaucracies have usually perfected their tactics for survival. (As former Secretary of State James F. Byrnes noted, ''[T]he nearest thing to immortality on Earth is a government bureau.'') Evidently reorganization (or even what Secretary of the Navy John Lehman termed ''de-organization''—not greater centralization and unification of authority, but decentralization and greater accountability) is not a final solution, as Reagan and others have learned.

A related approach stressed by Carter is reform of the Civil Service and the regulations governing civil servants' employment. Carter accomplished a major change in 1978 with the Civil Service Reform Act, which put some 7,000 top bureaucrats into a Senior Executive Service, entitling them to earn bonuses (which previously were virtually automatic) for outstanding job performance, but separating them from specific job tenure (a virtual guarantee of permanent employment). The reform permits the chief executive and cabinet officers to shift upper-middle management personnel into different assignments and, where deemed necessary, to replace those not moving quickly enough or in the right direction.[30] Although this innovation does not mean that hereafter the upper echelon of the bureaucracy necessarily will be responsive to presidential orders, it does augment considerably the president's ability to make the bureaucracy more manageable.

President Reagan continued the endeavors of his predecessors to control the federal bureaucracy. His campaign rhetoric made his posture clear. He echoed the sentiment of recent presidents by running against the government he was seeking to run, by berating its size, and by promising to reduce, reorganize, and streamline it. ''Government is not the solution, it is the problem,'' Reagan said in his first inaugural speech.

The efficacy of Reagan's approach is difficult to estimate, in part because he largely failed to practice what he preached. Big government got bigger un-

[29]In the area of foreign policy, one of the reorganization studies was the Murphy Commission (*Commission on the Organization of the Government for the Conduct of Foreign Policy*, 1975), which found that nearly 200 official or semi-official reports had dealt with some aspect of U.S. government foreign policy organization in the 37 years since the Brownlow Report, which resulted in the creation of the Executive Office of the President (Treat, 1974). Since the 1950s over thirty reorganization studies have been undertaken on the management of public diplomacy alone (Adelman, 1981: 915).

[30]Describing the set of problems the reforms hoped to correct, Carter said: ''It's become impossible to reward good service, to give promotions and salary increases to those who really do an outstanding job. It's almost impossible to discharge or demote someone who occupies a position in the federal government and refuses to do [his or her] job.''

The counterpart to the Senior Executive Service in the foreign policy area is the Senior Foreign Service. As described in chapter eleven, however, it has not proven to be an answer to many of the State Department's own personnel problems.

der Reagan: federal spending went up, not down, as budget outlays as a percent of the GNP rose to peacetime records. Moreover, while reductions in force for some agencies were implemented, for others expansion occurred; the Defense Department added nearly 58,000 new civilian employees between 1980 and September 1983, for example (*U.S. News and World Report*, January 30, 1984: 9). Overall, at the end of 1984 the number of civilian employees in the U.S. government stood at 2,960,000, an *increase* over previous levels (*U.S. News and World Report*, December 10, 1984: 73).

More instructively, the Reagan approach to the "problem" of government may be described best as an attempt to *redistribute* the budget, personnel, and policy authority of various agencies. Reagan sought to control the bureaucracy by infiltrating it with political operatives and by requiring them to pass a "censorship" test with respect to their ideology and behavior to gain a top government post (see Barber, 1985). The number of political appointees increased by a third, from roughly 2,200 to more than 3,300 (Struck, 1985: 31). Presumably, the practice of patronage would purchase obedience and loyalty from those whose jobs depended on the president—for these are the only personnel who can easily be relieved of their duties. In the area of domestic policy, Reagan's "New Federalism" program to shift power to the states promised to have lasting effects, for better or for worse (see Richter, 1986). But in the area of foreign and defense policy, the effort and need, in the words of Navy Secretary Lehman, "to roll back the accretion of layers of centralized bureaucracy and restore a crisper accountability," appears to remain as elusive as ever. Indeed, whether the federal bureaucracy can be made to perform the role of problem solver rather than problem maker remains a problem. The capacity of the foreign affairs government for responsiveness and for taking direction apparently is as much in doubt as ever.

The existence of these—and other, though often ineffectual—methods for presidents to deal with uncooperative bureaucracies means that although agencies in the foreign affairs government can block presidential proposals, none is likely to practice sabotage for long without inviting repercussions. Bureaucratic disobedience nevertheless persists in the foreign policy-making process, serving to diminish the prospects for policy innovation and rapid change.

Compartmentalized Policy Making and Foreign Policy Fragmentation

We tend to think of American foreign policy as goal directed, with the nation pursuing a consistent set of objectives in the world arena. According to that comforting image, there is fundamental agreement on the goals the country should pursue abroad. The government accordingly devotes its energies to realizing those goals as interpreted by the president and his staff. But if we recall that each bureaucracy in the foreign affairs government has its *own* definition of proper goals, we find another consequence of foreign policy making by groups—competing foreign policies.

Foreign policy tends to lack cohesion in part because the "facts" governing the interpretation of any situation are colored by the position a policy maker holds. Where one sits shapes one's vision and version of reality. And because facts are less important than what is perceived, different policy makers often differ about the nature of the circumstances confronted and about what the United States should do to meet the challenges posed. The compartmentalized division of labor in the foreign affairs government therefore often produces friction and debate between the bureaucratic units involved and, on occasion, culminates in efforts by one unit to undermine those of the others. When such contests become public, American foreign policy looks as if it were working at cross-purposes and has no clear sense of mission.

Consider, for example, the events during the final days of the Shah's rule in Iran, events that set the stage for a takeover of the American embassy and the confinement of American embassy personnel. Whether the disaster could have been averted is likely to remain an open question. But it is clear that the U.S. response to the unfolding drama was clouded by a quarrel that developed between the National Security Council staff in Washington and the State Department representatives in Teheran, a quarrel rooted in how different the relevant "facts" looked to those in the field compared to those in the White House. Those divergent views, and the interagency bickering and struggle they produced, led to the tragic outcome in Iran, which no American policy maker sought (see Box 13.4). From that perspective, the tendency of American foreign policy makers to pursue competing strategies stems from their inclination to define the national interest differently, based on the differing positions from which they operate in a far-flung, compartmentalized system of policy making.

The fact that American foreign policy is incohesive and uncoordinated is due also to the inherently political nature of foreign policy making. Policy decisions and the ordering of international priorities result from negotiations among the various administrative units in the foreign affairs government. Policy is determined by interagency competition, sometimes without the benefit of interagency coordination. Because foreign policy decisions come from fragmented centers of authority, with each center pursuing its own vision of the proper goals of the nation, the overall policy of the country is itself often fragmented.

Bureaucratic struggle helps to explain why the United States can find itself taking contradictory positions rather than common postures on a particular problem. Policy inconsistency was evident, for instance, in the American response to the Laotian situation in 1960, when the State Department and the CIA found themselves giving aid to opposing armies. The pursuit of inconsistent policies is also apparent in the call for arms reductions by the Arms Control and Disarmament Agency while the Defense Department ships arms abroad.

A good illustration of how bureaucratic competition can lead to policy in-

---

BOX 13.4   The Drama of Interagency Policy Debate: An American Ambassador's Account of the Route to the Iranian Disaster

---

William H. Sullivan, the former American ambassador to Iran, reports:

> [W]hen the State Department advanced the view that the shah's regime would not survive, there were many others in the Washington bureaucracy, particularly on the National Security Council (where the revolt was simplistically believed to be an Islamic revolution), who attributed State's perception, and by indirection that of the embassy, to an expression of wishful thinking on the part of those whose vision was blurred by their zeal for human rights. . . . [This] division of perceptions within the Washington bureaucracy . . . extended to the . . . instructions that were sent to the embassy or, more often, to the abscence of any instructions whatsoever . . . [and] embassy reports were apparently received with divided conclusions. . . . In this pernicious atmosphere, U.S. policy formulation broke down. By November 1978 [national security adviser] Brzezinski began to make his own policy and established his own embassy in Iran. . . . It soon became apparent that my [critical] views were no longer welcome at the White House.

Sullivan's recommendation that, upon the shah's departure from power in his country, the United States should not cast its fate with the Bakhtiar government was ignored. The former ambassador felt that the Bakhtiar government

> was a chimera the shah had created to permit a dignified departure, that Bakhtiar himself was quixotic and would be swept aside by the arrival of Khomeini and his supporters in Teheran. . . . By this time my exchanges with Washington had become increasingly acerbic [and] the reply I received [from Washington] contained an insulting aspersion upon my loyalty and instructed me, in no uncertain terms, to support Bakhtiar no matter what reservations I had.

As history records, the Ambassador's dire predictions proved correct even while Brzezinski's policy prevailed, and Iran fell into chaos. The revolution was then underway, and American personnel became its target. But the ambassador sought to negotiate with the revolutionaries to prevent the Americans' capture. His words describe the sequence of events that, from his perspective, sealed the fate of the United States and insured that disaster would result:

> Well into the night, I worked with our contacts among the revolutionaries to arrange for the extraction of these Americans from the bunker in which they were trapped. Just as I was at the point of achieving their rescue, I received a telephone call in the clear over the international circuit from Washington relaying a message from Brzezinski who asked whether I thought I could arrange a military coup against the revolution. I regret that the reply I made is unprintable.

SOURCE: Excerpted from Sullivan, 1980: 177ff.

consistency is provided in this disturbing account by a former American official:

> The Agency [CIA] supported Indonesian rebels against Sukarno while State was trying to work with Sukarno. It supplied and emboldened the anticommunist Chinese guerrillas in Burma over the protests of the Burmese Government and the repeated protestations of the State Department in Washington and our ambassador in Burma that we were doing no such thing. In Vietnam, too, CIA and State have worked at cross-purposes.
>
> But the [CIA] has not confined its activities to unstable countries. It has meddled elsewhere, to the consternation of the State Department and friendly governments. In the mid-1950s, its agents intruded awkwardly in Costa Rica, the most stable and democratic country in Latin America. While the Agency was trying to oust José Figueres, the moderate socialist who became the Costa Rican President in a fair election in 1953, the State Department was working with him and our ambassador was urging President Eisenhower to invite him to the United States to enhance his prestige. So it went the world around. (Simpson, 1967: 103)

Bureaucratic Pluralism and Foreign Policy Making by Compromised Solution

The ability of members of the policy-making elite to effectively control the nation's actions abroad is undermined by the fragmented nature of the policy-making system. Most decision makers find themselves playing the role of "power broker," attempting to reconcile conflicting demands from various segments of the competing bureaucracy. As the ultimate decision maker, the president often finds himself choosing among agreed-upon bureaucratic solutions rather than selecting policies from alternative recommendations and turning to the bureaucracy to implement them.

That image does not conform to the usual way most people (including inexperienced presidents) visualize the policy-making process. According to the popular vision, presidents formulate policies rationally and direct the nation's affairs abroad. A more realistic image is one in which few, if any, of the decisions that either the president or the executive branch makes are decisive or final. Policy may be only a collection of loosely related, or even unrelated, actions. It may sometimes be an unstable, internally inconsistent compromise. In either case policy is a result of the political process of accommodation.

Seen in this way, the chief executive is placed in the position of serving as an arbitrator of interagency disputes. Policy making then becomes a set of decisions made to settle jurisdictional struggles; policy recommendations emerge as a result of conflict[31] among competing elite policy makers and the

---

[31]Addressing the senior officials of the State Department at the beginning of the Kennedy administration, for example, Secretary of State Dean Rusk noted that "the process of government has sometimes been described as a struggle for power among those holding public office." This

agencies they head. The decision the president makes must reconcile those divergent claims in order to maintain a modicum of harmony within the government he presumably leads. In many ways the president is a captive of the government there to serve him. His chief task is to govern by managing his own bureaucracy. It is that aspect of policy making that led Grant McConnell (1962) to say of President Kennedy that ''perhaps his greatest achievement lay in holding the diverse elements of his administration together and creating a facade of unity in government.'' The problems dominating presidential thinking, therefore, are how to get the bureaucracy to do what is needed and how to prevent its rebellion. As Theodore Lowi (1967) concluded, ''Somehow a President must try to make a ministry out of what is at best a coalition.''

How does the process of pluralistic policy formulation affect the content of American foreign policy? If the chief executive acts as neither creative thinker nor spokesman for his own view, but instead as negotiator among competitive and parochial agencies, then his overpowering incentive is to do little or nothing in the way of taking on extra burdens. The status quo has a natural ally in a fragmented system of authority, especially when that system is well entrenched. The chief executive is rewarded for taking the middle of the road—the compromise position—between conflicting extremes. And compromise, we can assume, generally is not conducive to policy innovation.

If we see foreign policy formulation from the perspective of the role any president must play, the reasons for foreign policy continuity become apparent. From that vantage point, the decisional situation is ripe for compromise, incrementalism, and caution. Think of what the president faces on a daily basis. He is surrounded by advisers, including members of his cabinet, who so interpret their jobs as to make maximum claims on their agencies' behalf. Having heard from one agency the extreme of one side of the policy dispute, and then the other extreme from another agency, the president must forge the terms of settlement.

But look at the atmosphere in which he must make a choice. ''The President . . . has to operate in a world populated with countervailing organizations which believe his every move is of concern to them, and must therefore be cleared with them'' (Cleveland, 1959). The struggle among competing viewpoints must be permitted to recur on a regular basis, and all contestants must attempt to remain friends. The situation encourages the participants to make maximum claims as bargaining points, but all expect a compromise settlement, in part because the president must give everyone something if he hopes to elicit their cooperation. Thus the president is driven by the politicized circumstances to satisfy most groups somewhat, rather than a few agencies fully; to keep future options open by appearing neutral and hedging

---

remark suggests the reasoning behind one of Dean Acheson's more memorable observations. When asked by a former colleague in the State Department to name the quality he thought most necessary in a secretary of state, Acheson, without hesitation, is reported to have replied ''the killer instinct.''

rather than by allowing the opposition to become adamant or allied; and to deal in increments and adjustments, inching toward fundamental goals step by step, gaining a little but also losing a little. Permitting foes to save face is also an important part of this game. Because policy making on those terms is a constant struggle, with much give and take and much adjustment, and because bureaucratic forces remain relatively constant in their distribution and effects, policy outcomes tend to be stable. Consequently, one is inclined to agree with Roger Hilsman (1971) that many of the problems in American foreign policy may "stem not from the concentration of power, but at least in part from its diffusion. The very profusion of so many centers of power makes building the kind of consensus necessary for positive measures a formidable task." Because bureaucratic routines are usually the product of long-established bargains, reflecting distributions of power and influence, disruptions in those routines are unlikely unless the distributions of power and influence themselves are changed, a rare occurrence.

Some Other Effects of Group Decision Making

The preceding analysis has attempted to identify some basic consequences of policy making by organizational procedures. Certainly that list is incomplete. Without going into detail, it might be noted that decision making by and within organizations tends to promote several other kinds of behavior. One effect is decision making, particularly at the top, by *ad hoc procedures*. Decision makers are preoccupied with the immediate rather than the long range; they tend to confront issues only after they have reached crisis proportions. As a result, American policy often fails to reflect a general sense of purpose. Instead of adhering to a master strategy or plan of action based on an explicit sense of the interests of the United States, American policy appears to be a passive reaction to the decisions of others or to issues only as they arise. As one State Department official described decision making in the Carter administration: "Adhocracy gone mad seemed too often to be the order of the day, with policy careening from crisis to crisis with no more certain guide than the decisions of the moment" (Carter, 1981). The picture is not very attractive, suggesting as it does policy by improvisation instead of planning.

But the picture needs to be contemplated, for it forces us to see the ideal of rational decision making in light of the reality of its bureaucratic counterpart. Rather than choices being made in the context of predetermined goals, we find trial-and-error policy making consisting of adaptive responses to problems as they surface. The result is an inertial tendency to keep doing what is presently being done as long as it appears to be working within acceptable limits. At most, existing policy is modified only slightly. Policy persistence and continuity are inevitable results of such ad hoc procedures.

Another consequence of bureaucratic behavior related to the first is the inclination toward *decision avoidance*. Most of us think of presidents as decisive people of action. Certainly it is the image they try to project. Some even manage to live up to it. Recall Harry Truman: "The greatest part of the President's job is to make decisions—big ones and small ones . . . The President—whoever he is—has to decide. He can't pass the buck to anybody. No one else can do the deciding for him. That's his job" (Truman, 1966).

Unfortunately, relatively few presidents live up to Truman's vision. Many manage not to decide. And some have been quite proficient at passing the buck.[32] The psychological incentives for dealing with problems by ignoring them, or stretching the time to reach a decision to the limit, are enormous. Refusing to take direct action, to let the force of momentum determine policy outcomes instead, has the virtue of permitting the policy maker to escape responsibility for the consequences, particularly in the realm of foreign policy where the wrong decision can mean the difference between life and death for millions.[33] It is quite natural, under such conditions, for even the most responsible individual to seek refuge from the burden of decision making by simply denying the existence of the problem requiring a decision. Even crisis conditions may deter a decision. Crisis situations can "often lead . . . to decisions not to act or to discussions that never result in a decision. The surprise quality of the situation makes less likely the existence of preparations appropriate for coping with it" (Hermann, 1969b).

Still another possible effect of decision making by group methods is the so-called *risky-shift* phenomenon. In contrast to what was argued above, it can be assumed that under some circumstances, the decisions made by groups may actually entail greater risks than those that individual members would have made had they been acting alone. Groups, in other words, may be more inclined to take dangerous, bold, and aggressive actions than individuals. The reasoning, which is an outgrowth of the "groupthink" concept discussed above, is that people deciding in groups are prone to reinforce and support each other's extreme positions, especially when there is an *esprit de corps* among members of a policy-making group. They desire to appear assertive, and they are reluctant to appear overly cautious or, worse, fearful.[34] Thus, people act differently together than when they act alone, so the reasoning goes, and one of the ways they act differently is by reaching shift-to-risk decisions.

[32]As Gelb and Halperin (1973) note, "Presidents are, in the eyes of bureaucrats, notorious for putting off decisions or changing their minds. They have enough decisions to make without looking for additional ones. In many cases, all the options look bad and they prefer to wait."

[33]For an incisive analysis of the manner by which policy may evolve from the inertia of previous decisions and a fait accompli from the depths of the bureaucracy, see Schilling (1973), "The H-Bomb Decision: How to Decide Without Actually Choosing."

[34]Barnet (1972) comments on this: "One of the first lessons a national security manager learns . . . is that toughness is the most highly prized virtue. Some of the national security managers of the Kennedy-Johnson era, looking back on their experience, talk about the 'hairy chest syndrome.' The man who is ready to recommend using violence against foreigners, even where he is overruled, does not damage his reputation for prudence, soundness, or imagination, but the man who recommends putting an issue to the U.N., seeking negotiations, or, horror of horrors, 'doing nothing,' quickly becomes known as 'soft.'" Case in point: President Johnson had the habit of addressing his resident-dove adviser Bill Moyers: "Well, here comes Mr. Stop-the-Bombing."

Part of the basis for the phenomenon is psychological. Most people conform to peer-group pressures, and groups, it has been argued, are usually dominated by their most neurotic (and reckless) member. "Madness," Friedrich Nietzsche observed, "is the exception in individuals but the rule in groups." Part of the reason also undoubtedly stems from the willingness of people to sacrifice themselves for others and to take chances on behalf of others that they would not normally take when acting merely for themselves. And part of the reason can be attributed to the fact that decisions by groups are shared: risky alternatives are more likely because no member of the group making the risky decision can be held personally responsible for proposing a policy which produces failure.

Regardless of the reasons, however, the idea is sobering. It suggests that there may be a built-in incentive in the bureaucratic system against the exercise of caution. Although the general effect of bureaucracies is to encourage caution and restraint, when policy making becomes centralized in the hands of a small group, as it is prone to do when the nation faces an external threat, that penchant for caution may be overcome and even reversed (we shall have more to say in chapter fifteen about decision making in crisis situations).

Yet another product of decision making in large, complex organizations is the increased likelihood of *unmanaged policy initiatives.* Increases in organizational size reduce the ability of the foreign affairs machinery to maintain strict control over the behavior of subordinates through a clear chain of command. Many individuals in such an environment occasionally have the opportunity to act unilaterally, often in an unauthorized manner. "In the intricate sticky webs of paperwork, the principle of accountability flutters and expires. Responsibility gets diffused; finally it disappears. Everyone is responsible; therefore no one is responsible. It is 'the system'" (Kilpatrick, 1985). If policy making is really determined at the implementation stage, and not at the declaratory stage (the stage when the president or his staff proclaims the policy), then what government officials actually do serves best to define the policy. In a sense, then, every bureaucrat has the opportunity to be a policy maker. The debate over who has authority to control the nuclear missiles on U.S. submarines, Navy personnel or only the president (see Meyer, 1984), illustrates that the issue of command and control is not a trivial one.

A revealing case in point occurred during the Vietnam War. After President Nixon finally declared a cessation of the bombing over North Vietnam in 1972 in the hope of encouraging bargaining concessions from the North Vietnamese, General John D. Lavelle of the Air Force took it upon himself to order hundreds of pilots to attack North Vietnamese territory, and he persisted in his decision to drop the bombs over a three-month period in clear violation of the president's official policy. To the North Vietnamese, not surprisingly, the president's policy proclamation mattered little: American policy had not changed.

Finally, we might note *the dehumanization of foreign policy* associated with the organizational apparatus for the making of foreign policy. The proposition is that the cruelest and most inhumane features of recent American foreign policy behavior have been caused not by evil men, but by the institutions in which evil behavior is sometimes bred. The nature of bureaucratic decision making within bureaucratic settings, in other words, accounts for the inhumane decisions that have been reached there—and not deficiencies of those who work in those settings.

Proponents of that thesis note that contemporary American foreign policy is formulated by a process that rewards specialization but discourages the humanitarian from playing an important role. Foreign policy is produced by an army of technocrats—individuals who only know how to perform certain specific tasks but who feel no responsibility for anything beyond the narrow confines of their job. More often than not they give unquestioning loyalty to their agency without doubting its motives. They are prevented, by the nature of the bureaucratic policy-making process, from grasping the overall content of the policy. And they are punished for evaluating the ethics of what they are doing. Even the managers, the agency heads, are isolated from the policy product; a manager's true product is management.

Additionally, it has been noted that the size of the foreign affairs machinery prevents even the most sensitive from taking responsibility for foreign actions; decisions are shared, so that assigning credit—or blame—for what the United States does abroad becomes a hopeless task. Without responsibility for policy initiatives, few policy makers are prompted to accept the fact that they had a hand in producing foreign actions which, on a personal level, they would regard as morally repugnant or socially harmful. The system may cause immoral behavior because incentives limiting the range of choice are absent. It was the anonymity of the policy-making process, critics note, that gave us Vietnam. Indeed, a reading of *The Pentagon Papers* (1971) gives the impression that no one was to blame for the way the war was prosecuted: it was the faceless bureaucratic system, and not people, that produced the product.

Though it is difficult to substantiate the hypotheses just laid out, they are worth entertaining as possible explanations of some actions toward other countries. The following thought-provoking argument of what happens to states when their foreign policies emanate from ''the activities of thousands of human beings organized into bureaucratic structures'' is chilling. The argument contends that one of the consequences of the bureaucratic revolution in American policy making is what is termed ''bureaucratic homicide'' waged abroad, the essential characteristic of which is a division of labor:

> In general, those who plan do not kill and those who kill do not plan. The scene is familiar. Men in blue, green, and khaki tunics and others in three-button business suits sit in pastel offices and plan complex operations in which thousands of distant human beings will die. The men who planned the saturation bombings, free fire zones, defoliation, crop destruction, and assassination programs in the Vietnam War never personally killed anyone.

The bureaucratization of homicide is responsible for the routine character of modern war, the absence of passion, and the efficiency of mass-produced death. Those who do the killing are following standing orders. . . . An infantryman, aware that even old men, women, and children will shoot or lay booby traps for foreigners who burn their village, sprays machine-gun fire randomly into a crowd of cowering "Vietcong sympathizers." . . . [T]he man who does the killing or terrorizing on behalf of the United States has been sent by others—usually men he has never seen and over whom he has no control.

The complexity and vastness of modern bureaucratic government complicates the issue of personal responsibility. At every level of government the classic defense of the bureaucratic killer is available: "I was just doing my job!" The essence of bureaucratic government is emotional coolness, orderliness, implacable momentum, and a dedication to abstract principle. Each cog in the bureaucratic machine does what it is supposed to do.

The Green Machine, . . . the military establishment, kills cleanly, and usually at a distance. America's highly developed technology makes it possible to increase the distance between killer and victim and hence to preserve the crucial psychological fiction that the objects of America's lethal attention are less than human. For the bureaucratic killer destruction is almost hygienic provided one does not have to lay hands on his victim. (Barnet, 1972: 13–14)

THE AMERICAN PROCESS OF DECISION MAKING: A BALANCE SHEET OF CREDITS AND DEBITS

The preceding discussion raises some grave doubts about the proposition that American foreign policy is the end product of a logical chain of reasoning. Although the official histories one is likely to read in a high-school civics text make everything that happened sound rational, the memoirs of past participants in the decision-making process—including presidents—and an objective treatment of the diplomatic record create quite a different impression. To people there at the time, as well as to many who subsequently have probed past events, those happenings often did not look orderly or rational. At times they seemed more like scenes stolen from the theater of the absurd. To some, the American process of foreign policy decision making has contributed to its recurrent failures (Etheredge, 1985); to others, the decisional process has made the United States its "own worst enemy" (Destler, Gelb, and Lake, 1984).

How valid is the villain image of foreign policy-making procedures and the corollary hypothesis that the decision-making process within large-scale organizations is characterized by malaise? The symptoms are numerous. Let's recall some of them: bureaucracies constantly driven to expand the boundaries of their own power; bureaucracies that are parochial, defining objectives in light of their own needs, values, and traditions; agencies that reward blind loyalty and pursue fierce interagency competition; institutions which promote the obedient, unimaginative, and cautious, but ostracize the questioner, the doubter, and the reformer; organizations that require decisions on the basis of ritual and precedent; agencies whose main mission in life is to grow; machinery that avoids risk and honors the status quo; groups composed of "yes-men" intolerant of divergent viewpoints; a government of technocrats; bureaucracies with lives, policies, and purposes of their own, intent on doing whatever they were assigned initially to do regardless of their present usefulness; institutions resisting control from above while perfecting it from within; and decision making by mechanical procedure rather than by reflection. The words commonly associated with bureaucracies are not flattering: red tape, backlogs, waste, foulups, overstaffing, overpaid and underworked workers, duplication, special interests. "Bureaucrat" has never been a word commanding respect; to many it's a term of derision.

Recall as well some of the policy consequences of such decision-making procedures and structure: policy inaction; policy sabotage; policy by compromise; policy governed by inertia and incrementalism, where continual nibbling becomes a substitute for a good bite; policy based on biased, self-serving information and oversimplifications, which makes decision makers captives of their advisers; policy by delay; policy devoid of an image of a preferred future, content to deal only with the present and to try to "get by" or "muddle through" when it comes to the future; a process that strips leaders of real authority and encourages them to try to be everything to everyone instead of leading; a process where major policy may occasionally percolate upward from the decisions of people at the bottom of the machinery; a process that can promote policies insensitive to human needs, or to life itself; one that deals with methods of handling problems instead of programs for preventing them; and of course methods of implementation so notoriously sluggish that *bureaucracy* and *red tape* are practically synonymous.

Few of us can fail to recognize some of those symptoms in contemporary American foreign policy. Many of the things that are wrong, and that go wrong, are clearly attributable to the way the government organizes itself for the making of foreign policy decisions and the kinds of role-induced behavior that organizations promote. "We overorganize, overman, overspend, and underaccomplish," was the way former Deputy Secretary of Defense David Packard described his department's performance—and his words seem to describe well the way most people think of bureaucratic performance in general. The problem resides, so it seems, in the institutional arrangements and sheer size of the government itself and the consequent impact on the behavior of those individuals who populate the foreign affairs government. Correspondingly, the policy of the United States abroad is often weakened by the policy-making process itself.

But such a conclusion may be an overstatement, indeed a caricature, of the impact of large-scale organizations on the making of American foreign policy. This picture must be offset by the one in our preceding discussion of the advantages of modern bureaucracy. That explication suggested that the foreign affairs bureaucracy of the United States provides more than liabilities. "Bureaucrat" need not be a dirty word. In fact, the conduct of diplomacy would not be possible without a modern bureaucracy and the kind of organizational support that it alone can provide. For no president could successfully manage foreign policy without the assistance of a large bureaucracy.

Often the assistance of America's foreign affairs government has proven invaluable. One example perhaps makes the point. India and China, a critical neutral and a (then) proclaimed adversary, went to war during the Cuban missile crisis. Because President Kennedy was necessarily preoccupied with events in Cuba, the bureaucracy had to act—almost unilaterally—to protect American interests in South Asia. The important message is that the actions taken were judged successful (in contrast with the 1971 India-Pakistan war when President Nixon and Secretary of State Kissinger were in charge). Incidents such as that suggest that the image of the bureaucracy-as-enemy can easily be overdrawn and may often be simply inaccurate. Some kind of bureaucracy is necessary; it can often be beneficial to effective policy making. The question, therefore, is not whether to have foreign policy made in a group context, but rather how to make that context more responsive to prevailing needs.

Indeed, it is *not* the huge size of the bureaucracy that alone makes it appear that officials are continually tripping over each other (although that is part of the problem). Nor is the propensity for the policy-making system to stumble and blunder due merely to self-serving people (although they contribute to the problem as well). It is at least partly the formidable challenges posed by today's complex and threatening world environment that make bureaucratic government so necessary even while it looks to some so inept. "Inveighing against big government," observes syndicated columnist George Will, "ignores the fact that government, though big, is often too weak." What may be needed is more government, not less (Alperovitz and Faux, 1984) Bureaucratic government, though deficient in many respects, is nonetheless indispensable to the functioning of a great power. The solution, therefore, is not to do away with bureaucratic government. It is to subdue it, to run it efficiently, and to shape its power to national purposes. For that, leadership is required.

In the final analysis, then, bringing out the best that the foreign affairs bureaucracy has to offer (and preventing the worst that it can produce) rests with the president and his principal advisers. The kind of leadership exercised by the president can affect the kinds of behavior expected of those who occupy roles in the foreign affairs machinery. Or can it? Can presidents make a difference? Or was the great sociologist Max Weber correct when he argued, "In a modern state the actual ruler is necessarily and unavoidably the bureaucracy"? To address that question, we must turn to consider yet another potential source of American foreign policy: individual leaders.

SUGGESTIONS FOR FURTHER READING

ALLISON, GRAHAM T. *Essence of Decision: Explaining the Cuban Missile Crisis*. Boston: Little, Brown, 1971.

ANDERSON, PAUL A. "What Do Decision Makers Do When They Make a Foreign Policy Decision?" Forthcoming in Charles F. Hermann, Charles W. Kegley, Jr., and James N. Rosenau, eds., *New Directions in the Study of Foreign Policy*. London: Allen and Unwin, 1986.

BARNET, RICHARD J. *Roots of War: The Men and Institutions Behind U.S. Foreign Policy*. Baltimore: Penguin, 1972.

DESTLER, I.M., LESLIE H. GELB, AND ANTHONY LAKE. *Our Own Worst Enemy: The Unmaking of American Foreign Policy*. New York: Simon and Schuster, 1984.

GELB, LESLIE H., AND MORTON H. HALPERIN. "The Ten Commandments of the Foreign Affairs Bureaucracy," pp. 505–516 in Steven L. Spiegel, ed., *At Issue: Politics in the World Arena*, 4th ed. New York: St. Martin's, 1977.

HERMANN, CHARLES F. "Bureaucratic Constraints on Innovation in American Foreign Policy," pp. 390–409 in Charles W. Kegley, Jr., and Eugene R. Wittkopf, eds., *Perspectives on American Foreign Policy*. New York: St. Martin's, 1983.

JANIS, IRVING L. *Groupthink: Psychological Studies of Policy Decisions and Fiascoes*, 2nd ed. Boston: Houghton Mifflin, 1983.

KRASNER, STEPHEN D. "Are Bureaucracies Important? A Re-examination of Accounts of the Cuban Missile Crisis," pp. 410–423 in Charles W. Kegley, Jr., and Eugene R. Wittkopf, eds., *Perspectives on American Foreign Policy*. New York: St. Martin's, 1983.

SIMON, HERBERT A. *Administrative Behavior: A Study of Decision-Making Processes in Administrative Organizations*, 2nd ed. New York: Macmillan, 1957.

SNYDER, RICHARD C., H. W. BRUCK, AND BURTON SAPIN, eds. *Foreign Policy Decision-Making: An Approach to the Study of International Politics*. New York: Free Press, 1962.

VII

INDIVIDUALS AS SOURCES OF AMERICAN FOREIGN POLICY

14

LEADER CHARACTERISTICS AND FOREIGN POLICY PERFORMANCE

One of the most unsettling things for foreigners is the impression that our foreign policy can be changed by any new president on the basis of the president's personal preference.

Former Secretary of State Henry Kissinger, 1979

To some extent, a president is a prisoner of historical forces that will demand his attention whatever his preference in policy objectives.

Former presidential adviser Joseph A. Califano, 1975

Picture a president of the United States sitting alone in the White House, wrestling with a crisis that affects the very survival of the nation, possessing the power by virtue of his position to unleash incredible destruction. Assume that this individual is impulsively competitive, prone to act brashly to attract attention, inclined to take risks to exploit opportunities, motivated by the view that the world is a jungle and that it is appropriate to claw and scratch in a struggle for survival and power, distrustful of others, contemptuous of his adversaries, and a man of quick temper. Assume also that this same man is driven by a fear of failure stemming from his low self-esteem, a fear overcome in the past by dramatic and successful actions which restored his self-confidence. How is such a man likely to respond to the crisis he faces? It is hard to imagine that his response will not be affected to a significant degree by his uniquely individual characteristics—by his background, his beliefs, and his personality traits—and that the destiny of the nation will therefore also not be so affected. Indeed, to understand why the United States acts the way it does in world affairs, it would appear obvious that we must take into account the characteristics of those whose responsibility it is to act on behalf of the United States.

This chapter focuses on individuals as a source of foreign policy. It looks at the leaders themselves, the people who occupy the decision-making roles at the highest echelons of government and who thereby act for the nation. From that perspective, the actions of the United States abroad are thought to originate in the idiosyncracies of particular members of the decision-making elite. Their personal aspirations, their convictions, their anxieties, and their experiences and memories are all variables that shape the external conduct of the nation.

INDIVIDUALS AS A SOURCE OF FOREIGN POLICY

It is indisputable that individuals, and not countries, act. Therefore, insight into the characteristics of those who make the decisions affecting the foreign behavior of the nation is crucial. Foreign policy decisions are often made by a remarkably small number of individuals, most conspicuous of whom is the president. "The management of foreign affairs," Thomas Jefferson once declared, is "executive altogether"; similarly, Harry Truman revealingly exclaimed, "I make American foreign policy"; and Justice Sutherland of the Supreme Court went so far as to interpret the president as the sole organ of the federal government in the field of foreign affairs.[1]

Given the prominence and power of the presidency in the foreign policy-making process, it is inviting to think of foreign policy as being caused exclusively by the whims and wishes of a powerful official leadership.[2] There is a natural tendency to personalize government by identifying a policy with a leader's name, even though, as we have noted in the preceding chapters, American foreign policy is relentlessly the product of a collective decision-making process. "There is properly no history, only biography," Ralph Waldo

---

[1]*United States* v. *Curtiss-Wright Export Corporation*, 299 U.S. 304 (1936).

[2]Scholars and the public at large are not the only ones who think that the character, values, and personality of the leaders are the crucial, perhaps decisive, determinants of a country's foreign policy. Leaders themselves tend to operate from this assumption: "Policymakers always make certain assumptions about the personalities of their counterparts, consciously or unconsciously, and such assumptions influence their behavior" (Wendzel, 1980).

Henry Kissinger, himself a highly successful diplomatic negotiator, warned against placing too much reliance on personalities when discussing Soviet-American relations during a commencement address at the University of South Carolina (1985):

[There is] a profound American temptation to believe that foreign policy is a subdivision of psychiatry and that relations among nations are like relations among people. But the problem [of reducing tension with the Soviet Union] is not so simple. Tensions that have persisted for 40 years must have some objective causes, and unless we can remove these causes, no personal relationship can possibly deal with it. We are doing neither ourselves nor the Soviets a favor by reducing the issues to a contest of personalities.

Emerson asserted in a statement that dramatizes the importance most people attach to the role of individuals as movers of history. With regard to American foreign policy, this "great man theory" equates American action with the preferences and initiatives of its highest elected officials. Names of presidents are attached to policies as if the men were synonymous with the nation itself, and all successes and failures in foreign affairs are attributed to the administration in which they occur. New leaders are assumed to make a difference. In fact, the view that leaders' differences matter is reinforced by the efforts of each new administration to distinguish itself from its predecessor and to highlight policy departures in order to convey the impression that it is distinctive. The media's tendency to label presidential actions "new" abets those efforts. Hence policy is seen as the product of leadership behavior, and policy fluctuations are thought of as caused by innate differences among the primary decision makers. By extension, if American foreign policy is little more than the predispositions of the leadership, then Truman's "doctrine," Eisenhower's "massive retaliation," Kennedy's "frontiersmanship," Nixon's "détente," and Carter's "human rights initiative" were simply products of the leaders whose names they bear.

There is yet another reason for thinking of American foreign policy in terms of the idiosyncratic characteristics of individuals. By looking at individuals, attention is drawn to the psychological dimension of human conduct. Perceptions, personal needs, and drives are all important determinants of the way people act. Correspondingly, decision makers' inner traits affect their behavior and influence the manner in which they respond to various situations. Indeed, the cognitions and responses of decision makers are determined not by "the 'objective' facts of the situation . . . but . . . [by] their 'image' of the situation," that is, they "act according to the way the world appears . . . not necessarily according to the way it 'is'" (Boulding, 1959). That principle suggests the importance of individual factors, and especially images, as forces shaping foreign conduct. Such perceptions, psychologists inform us, are not simple reflections of what is being observed (see Kelman, 1965; Falkowski, 1979; Jönsson, 1982a). Instead, they are influenced by the memories, values, needs, and beliefs the observer brings to the situation. The perceptions of all individuals are to some extent biased by personality predispositions and inner drives, as well as by prior experiences and future expectations. What occurs in decision makers' heads is therefore important.

Such reasoning invites consideration of the potential impact of leadership characteristics on policy making and policy outcomes. As we shift attention from the way issues are debated to the debaters themselves, we must ask if contrasts among decision makers make a difference in policy—in content as well as in style. Is the type of person elected to or selected for policy-making positions a variable affecting the behavior of the nation abroad? Do the particular personal qualities of the people holding positions of power make a difference in determining the course the nation charts for itself in foreign affairs? Or would others holding those positions during the same period have acted similarly? Do changes in leadership promote changes in foreign policy? If so, in what ways, and under what conditions? To this set of questions we now turn.

SOME INSIGHTS INTO LEADERSHIP CHARACTER

No two individuals are identical; every person differs in some significant way from every other. Thus, it is not surprising that personal diversity has characterized the major figures in recent American foreign policy. Compare "give 'em hell" Harry Truman, soft-spoken Ike Eisenhower, charismatic Jack Kennedy, tricky Dick Nixon, "down home" Jimmy Carter, and, most recently, Hollywood "Dutch" Reagan.

Nevertheless, the differences in personality of policy elites are often simply a matter of degree and may mask important similarities. The relevant question, therefore, is not how different the individuals who make American foreign policy are, but, instead, what impact a leader's peculiar traits have on his foreign policy decisions. Although it is difficult to generalize about that question, it is easily demonstrated that the personal characteristics of individuals may often directly influence their behavior as foreign policy makers, since in-depth case studies of particular decision makers abound, especially in the era of "the personal president" (Lowi, 1985a).[3] Most studies probe the life history of public officials for the purpose of describing their psychological makeup and world view. Almost invariably, psychobiographies of leaders assume that their personalities are determined by such factors as early childhood experiences, relationships with parents and peers, and their self-concept. Such background factors are presumed to mold the leaders' personalities, structure their belief systems, affect their decision styles, and influence their subsequent adult and policy-making behavior.

Personal Characteristics and Foreign Policy Behavior

Exemplary of such studies is Alexander and Juliette George's (1964) classic analysis of Woodrow Wilson, which discusses the psychological consequences of President Wilson's stern and often punitive childhood. The Georges demonstrate that Wilson's inability to please his rigid father during childhood created an all-consuming need in later life to attain self-esteem. That need accounts for most of Wilson's policy conduct as president; Wilson strove for idealistic feats of one sort or another as a way of compensating for his fear of failure and rejection. Most notable in that regard were Wilson's political battles over the League of Nations, behavior which can be explained, the Georges contend, by Wilson's overwhelming need to attain a puritanic "state of grace."

---

[3]The studies by Barber (1985), Donovan (1985), and Stoessinger (1985) provide insights on the personalities and beliefs of the postwar presidents that are particularly relevant to the management of foreign policy.

Another illustrative psychobiography is Arnold A. Rogow's (1963) examination of the life of the first American secretary of defense, James Forrestal. A driven, compulsive man, Forrestal's career path shows that he became increasingly obsessed by paranoid fantasies. He not only feared what he regarded as the Soviet menace, but distrusted his own friends and coworkers as well. His career came to a tragic end with suicide.

Other recent case studies illustrate perhaps more vividly the possible relationship between a leader's psychological profile and his policy behavior. Consider, for instance, the elements of President Kennedy's personality that may have been instrumental in the decisions he made during the Cuban missile crisis. According to one (admittedly controversial) interpretation (Mongar, 1974), Kennedy suffered most of his life from a neurotic conflict between an overpowering fear of failure, on the one hand, and an overwhelming need for assistance, on the other. The first stemmed from his inability to compete successfully with his older brother (Joe, Jr.), a son given unfair advantage in a contrived competitive family environment. Joe, Jr., was introduced by his father to friends as a future president of the United States, and his mother held him up as a model for the other children, especially Jack, and gave him a free hand in disciplining them. In that atmosphere it became impossible for Jack to attain an equal portion of attention, recognition, and affection from his parents: "No matter how hard he tried, Jack could neither conquer his older brother nor equal his competitive triumphs outside the family arena." Consequently, the younger Kennedy lacked self-assurance and feared failure. To overcome those psychological problems, he "hit upon the strategy of feigning helplessness as a way of avoiding the costs of competitive failure." He experienced a succession of childhood illnesses which permitted him to avoid fruitless competition, and he resorted to "the manipulation of fantasy to protect his [preferred self-] image of greatness." Thus the need for assistance was deeply ingrained as a defense mechanism to protect him from his fears of failure.

Maturity, however, helped young Jack Kennedy to moderate some of those psychological attributes. As his personality took shape, Kennedy exhibited tendencies reflecting a continued need to prove his personal worth, including the search for adventure, restlessness, intellectualism, and the open acceptance of difficult tasks. In style, his personal needs were reflected in his habit of disarming criticism "by modestly calling attention to minor shortcomings. This witty self-derision, which reflected a merciless introspection, undermined criticism early and at the same time elicited reassurance and support from other people."

What sorts of decisions can be expected from a man possessing those background characteristics and inner personality conflicts? Thomas Mongar suggests that many of Kennedy's words and actions as president are explicable in terms of his unresolved inner conflicts. The Cuban missile crisis, for example, became a "game," an opportunity to recover self-esteem; Kennedy's actions were made for psychotherapeutic reasons rather than for strategic reasons, such as preventing a change in the nuclear balance of power. Mongar suggests, moreover, that the risks were not trivial. When asked about the probability of nuclear war and the destruction of civilization resulting from U.S. actions, Kennedy coolly replied "about 50-50." And every time a major crisis occurred, Kennedy's response, Mongar argues, was colored by his psychological needs.

Is Kennedy's situation unique, or do other policy makers respond to foreign policy situations in terms of their own emotions and personality needs? Consider the example of Henry Kissinger, a decision maker whose "story refutes the myth that individuals are of little importance in the world politics of the nuclear age. . . . Indeed, history may show that Henry Kissinger was the most powerful individual in the world in the 1970s" (Isaak, 1975).

That could hardly have been predicted twenty years earlier. Kissinger's childhood was remarkable, far from the usual route to positions of power: escape from Nazi persecution in his native Germany; study in high school at night while working all day; service in the Army as a draftee; college at Harvard; and then, college professor and presidential foreign policy adviser, culminating in his appointment as the first Jewish secretary of state.

Did Kissinger's background and training influence his later thinking and behavior?[4] Isaak thinks so, arguing that ideas formed at an early age were resurrected to deal with analogous personal and national problems later in life. In particular, Kissinger's inherent pessimism and his lack of faith in progress (stemming from early experiences) are hypothesized to have affected Kissinger's image of world affairs. Words unfamiliar to other foreign policy analysts, like *ambiguity, irony, paradox, nuance,* and *tragedy,* punctuated his writings; "[i]nstinctively he knew that truth in the modern nuclear age was more a question of constant change, indeterminancy, and relativity, than of fixed boundaries, roles, and unambiguous situations and positions. Yet, even so, he longed to know the limits of knowledge and his own limits . . ." (Isaak, 1975).

Personally insecure, yet egocentric, Kissinger felt that historical uncertainty is the dominant theme in international affairs. As a decision maker, he consistently acted on the assumption that people are limited in what they can do, and that because of the complexity of life many imponderable factors make history move. Ironically, however, the principle of uncertainty which supported his pessimistic world view may have been the source of his successes, for Kissinger's achievements may be attributed in part to his ability to use ambiguity, negotiated compromise, and secrecy—as well as public relations strategies ingeniously devised to enhance his image—in his conduct of diplomacy.[5]

---

[4]See Montgomery (1975) and Walker (1977) for overviews of Kissinger's world view and "operational code" and an assessment of their impact on Kissinger's policy performance. See also Starr (1980 and 1984) and Stuart and Starr (1981–1982) for excellent surveys of literature dealing with Kissinger's belief system and his behavior as a policy maker.

[5]Woodward and Bernstein (1979) provide a less than flattering glimpse of this man who otherwise was successful as a diplomat. They note the alienation of Kissinger from his own staff,

Then, too, much of Kissinger's posture toward international affairs can be traced to his assumptions about interpersonal relations as those were shaped by the distinctive nature of his past. His *realpolitik* outlook—stressing the expectation of conflict between states, not collaboration, the need to increase power relative to one's adversaries, the inadequacy of moralism as a basis for interaction with others, and distrust of others' motives—finds a counterpart in the "lessons" he derived from his personal experiences during the crucial formative period of his political awakening. Could it be that Kissinger's disdain as a foreign policy strategist for moralism—and his corresponding tendency to ask not, "What is right and what is wrong?" but "Who is strong and who is weak?"—was rooted in the views he formed in his youth in an uncertain environment?

The preceding case studies show the varied personalities of those who have risen to positions of power, the impact of their needs, background, and prior experience on their subsequent outlook, and also how the way in which foreign policy decisions are made and implemented may be molded by the predispositions individuals bring with them into decision-making roles. We can probe the latter hypothesis further by examining the relationship between presidential character and policy performance.

Presidential Character and Policy Performance

When we move from observation of individuals to *types* of leaders, we can propose some generalizations about the relation between the character of leaders and the kind of performance they may be expected to exhibit while occupying policy-making roles. Here the most incisive work has been conducted by James David Barber (1985), who has focused attention on categories or classes of leadership, with special reference to recent American presidents. Based on in-depth analysis, Barber places each chief executive into a two-dimensional classification scheme according to the personal traits and leadership styles he exhibits.

Specifically, Barber suggests that presidents can be understood best by noting the energy they put into the job (active or passive) and their personal satisfaction with their presidential duties (negative or positive). The first dimension captures the decision maker's image of his job and its duties and responsibilities. Active presidents are movers and shakers, energetically engaged in the tasks of leading, eagerly attentive to the responsibilities of leadership, and comfortable with the task of implementing new policies and programs. Conversely, passive presidents prefer to steer an even course, to maintain existing arrangements; in short, to slide and glide with events and

---

which became over time increasingly "disillusioned with both the Kissinger policies and his personality. . . . He seemed to thrive on trouble, hysteria, fright, uncertainty. He raged at his secretaries. He appeared to take pleasure in humiliating his aides." And he was judged unable "to manage either personal relationships or staff organization." For another highly critical appraisal, see Hersh (1983).

prevailing circumstances. The second dimension reflects a president's level of contentment with his job, an important dimension given the observed reluctance of some presidents to relate favorably to the office they hold. Such negative types, Barber notes, tend to have had childhood experiences that make them dutifully accept but not enjoy the demands that go with holding power. Thus each president fits into one of four categories: passive-negative (Coolidge, Eisenhower); passive-positive (Harding, Taft, Reagan); active-negative (Wilson, Hoover, Johnson, Nixon); and active-positive (F. Roosevelt, Truman, Kennedy, Ford, Carter). Barber distinguishes among the tendencies represented by these categories thus:

> Active-positive Presidents want most to achieve results. Active-negatives aim to get and keep power. Passive-positives are after love. Passive-negatives emphasize their civic virtue. The relation of activity to enjoyment in a President thus tends to outline a cluster of characteristics, to set apart the adapted from the compulsive, compliant, and withdrawn types. (Barber, 1985: 10)

Obviously, Barber would contend presidents with active-positive characters are best equipped to lead the nation in its domestic and foreign policies and to meet challenges and crises. Active-positives are self-respecting and happy, open to new ideas, and able to learn from their mistakes; their energies are no longer consumed with conquering the developmental traumas associated with youth but instead are directed outward toward achievement. As policy makers, therefore, active-positives have the greatest capacity for growth and flexibility.

The value of Barber's analysis lies in its ability to demonstrate that the behavior of leaders with similar skills and values can be quite different, depending on the type of character possessed. The nature of a leader's inner self, and especially his degree of self-confidence and self-esteem, can be crucial factors. Also of value is Barber's demonstration that psychic attributes developed during childhood and youth affect the careers and performance of all decision makers. Truman, for example, an active-positive president, is described by Barber as having taken "massive initiatives at a time when such initiatives seemed unlikely, given the circumstances of his accession to office, his own qualifications, and the condition of the country." The implication, of course, is that these initiatives, many of which were in the foreign policy area (for example, the Truman Doctrine, the Marshall Plan, NATO, and the Korean intervention), were taken as a consequence of Truman's character. Kennedy, too, is credited (Mongar's analysis notwithstanding) with having handled the Cuban missile crisis in the way that he did as a consequence of his active-positive orientation. That orientation entails the capacity to learn from experience, including such disastrous experiences as the Bay of Pigs fiasco of April 1961. By October 1962, Kennedy showed that he had learned. "In command, in the assessment of information, in the technique of consultation, and in the empathy with his opponent, clearly John Kennedy had grown. He was, at that point, a professional president" (Barber, 1985).

In contrast to Truman and Kennedy, Richard Nixon was an active-negative president. "The danger in his Presidency," Barber wrote while Nixon was still in the White House, "is the same as the danger Wilson, Hoover, and Johnson succumbed to: rigid adherence to a failing line of policy." Nixon's decision to widen the Vietnam War by invading Cambodia in the spring of 1970 illustrates the tendency. The decision was made without the urging of his advisers, and the tone and content of the speech in which the president announced his decision to the American people "flabbergasted" his defense secretary, Melvin Laird. Indeed, to many in Washington,

> the process by which the President had decided and acted was . . . as scary as the invasion itself. As the story of the crisis decision-making came out—the fact that senior State Department officials had been suddenly cut off from key cablegrams, that military orders were issuing directly from the White House, and especially the nearly complete isolation of the President from Congressional opinions as he stepped out beyond his most sanguine military advisors—the President's judgment as a professional came into question. (Barber, 1977: 439)

Extreme isolation, as we have noted previously, ultimately came to characterize—and destroy—the Nixon presidency. In a sense, isolation became an expression of Nixon's individual interpretation of his presidential role, an interpretation, Barber would argue, that in turn reflected Nixon's character:

> To see in President Nixon the character of Richard Nixon—the character formed and set early in his life—one need only read over his speech on the Cambodian invasion, with its themes of power and control, its declaration of independence, its self-concern, its damning of doubters, and its coupling of humiliation with defeat. (Barber, 1977: 441)

How did Jimmy Carter fit into this pattern? Noting that Carter came to Washington full of high expectations at a time of low hopes, Barber places the energetic, "up and at 'em" Carter in the active-positive category and once predicted that Carter would enjoy life in the Oval Office, that he would find that it could be fun. But Barber's diagnosis also warned that Carter's troubles would spring "from an excess of an active-positive virtue: the thirst for results."

With hindsight, it is now apparent that the excess of active-positive virtue of which Barber warned may have contributed to the demise of the Carter presidency. It seems that Carter's character eventually led him, impatiently, to pursue too many goals simultaneously—a penchant which lent credibility to the frequent charges that he was inconsistent and indecisive, that he lacked a clear sense of priorities, and that he abandoned policy objectives almost as soon as they were announced in favor of still newer objectives, which then also were shelved. Carter's eagerness for results—rooted in his temperament—was said to have been induced by hyperactivity, which produced not the success that was sought but the failure that was dreaded because there was no follow-through. Critics and friends alike laid much of the blame for his policy failures and unsuccessful reelection bid to those self-defeating tendencies; few linked them to the president's lack of effort (his energy and drive were remarkable), to deficiencies in natural intelligence, or even to improper intentions and motives.

What values, personality traits, and personal experiences of Ronald Reagan have most shaped his reactions and perceptions, and given definition to his presidency? Although there has been much speculation about those attributes of Reagan which separate him from his recent predecessors (see Glad, 1983; Hermann, 1983; Reeves, 1985; and Dallek, 1984), no clear conclusions have emerged. Many speculations focus on the following facts about Reagan:

- The oldest candidate ever elected to the presidency
- The only president with theatrical experience and a show business career
- The first divorced man to become president
- The survivor of an assassination attempt
- An individual whose childhood is said to have been affected profoundly by the alcoholism of his father and his closeness to his mother
- A multimillionaire whose closest friends are extremely wealthy
- A leader, like Jimmy Carter, inexperienced in the ways of government on the Potomac and unfamiliar with the conduct of foreign diplomacy

There is no general agreement on the significance of those facts. Nor does an obvious pattern emerge when they are put into context with other elements of Reagan's prior record, personal convictions, emotional needs, and fundamental attitudes. "What makes it difficult to sort out Reagan's operative world view," observed Barber (1981) on the day of Reagan's first inauguration, "is his peculiar way with rhetoric. Obviously, it dominates his political style." But although his way with words may hide his true feelings, his character, in Barber's view, would be revealed by his past actions and experiences:

> Reagan's way of being a politician is held together by his character, his orientation toward his own experience. . . . [H]e is basically "a passive person," a take-it-easy type. And, as everyone has noticed, he is an optimist, a booster, a smiler, a genial fellow. In my jargon, that combination makes Reagan a "passive-positive," that is, "the receptive, compliant, other-directed character whose life is a search for affection as a reward for being agreeable and cooperative rather than personally assertive." (Barber, 1981: 8)[6]

---

[6]Although Reagan has often revered Franklin Delano Roosevelt as his childhood hero (Barber, 1985: 473), he has repeatedly stated that "silent" Cal Coolidge and Ike Eisenhower—both passive-negatives—are his role models. Reagan subsequently did prove to resemble in important ways those he selected as his role models (especially Eisenhower; see Greenstein and Wright, 1981). If Reagan is indeed more a passive-negative than he is a passive-positive, then this character type would predict that he will be most handicapped by his lack of experience, his inflexibility, and his tendency to stress vague principles and procedural solutions, and that he would show a

Barber singled out other aspects of Reagan's character to support inclusion of the president in the passive-positive category. One is Reagan's pronounced sentimentality, captured by his romantic infatuation with the past and his nostalgic need to recover the presumed order and simplicity of the good old days. Another is his lack of a coherent ideology and awareness of the need for one. According to Barber, "His conservatism is an attitude, not a theory"; it "has been circumstantial, not visceral"—which explains why his policy decisions have veered to the center and displeased those on the political right who expected their philosophy and program to be carried out. The absence of a coherent ideology may also be hidden by a rigid simple "black and white" outlook uninterested in facts and unaffected by them (see Glad, 1983; Lewis, 1984; Kaiser, 1984; Dallek, 1984).

A third characteristic of Reagan's passive-positive character is his apparent need to avoid close contact with others, to distance himself from others in order to escape intimacy. He has been described as a "loner" and a "privacy freak." This may explain a fourth trait: a pronounced tendency to delegate authority and responsibility to his staff and to depend on his advisers' decisions for guidance. Even during crises, Reagan "has been described by his own aides as 'uninvolved in the planning process,' 'secluded,' and 'disconcertedly disengaged'" (McElvaine, 1984).

Finally, Reagan's life has been spent playing roles. Thirty years of show business as an actor following scripts written by others may have fostered that penchant, but it is a disposition that is part of Reagan's character. "So much of our profession is taken up with pretending, with interpretation of never-never roles, that an actor must spend at least half his waking hours in fantasy," Reagan has written. That experience may have colored Reagan's conception of the presidency, for, as he once revealingly commented: "Politics is just like show business. You have a hell of an opening, coast for a while and then have a hell of a close." These propensities in combination portray a president whose decisions do not spring from cogitation; rather, a "laid back," easy manner has been characteristic of the way President Reagan has borne the burdens of office. At the top of a government conceived of following, ideally, a laissez-faire philosophy, Ronald Reagan has been "remarkably disengaged from the substance of his job" (*Time*, February 6, 1984).

Barber predicted at the time of Reagan's inauguration that if Reagan performed as president according to this assessment of his character, Reagan could ultimately prove "dangerous":

> [As a passive-positive,] the good news is that Reagan is definitely no Nixon. . . . There is no hatred in him, no vindictiveness, no grudges, no desire to get back at anybody. The worry of that is his type's tendency to drift, particularly with

---

tendency to withdraw from conflict, feel politically ineffectual, and be plagued by self-doubt. These, indeed, were some of the propensities often ascribed to Reagan's behavior while in the Oval Office (see Barber, 1985).

forces in the close-up environment. The danger is confusion, delay, and then impulsiveness. If tragedy comes to Ronald Reagan, it will be because he wants to be liked too much. . . . Having taken on a sentimental president, now we must live with him. The odds are small that . . . he will emerge pleased with his presidential role. He is a nice guy who finished first, soon to discover that not everyone is a nice guy. (Barber, 1981: 8).

With the benefit of hindsight, President Reagan's performance in the White House does not lend itself to easy interpretation. The study of presidential personality and character "at a distance" (see Hermann, 1983) is difficult, especially in a case where the correspondence between a president's words and his actions are, "to put it mildly, loosely knit" (Barber, 1985). Reagan has been enigmatic, because his statements and actions have often been inconsistent. It has been difficult to disentangle the rhetoric of Reagan "the actor" from the convictions of Reagan the decider, Barber concludes, especially to the extent that David Broder was accurate in his assessment that "It is apparently President Reagan's belief that words cannot only cloak reality but remake it."

Barber's approach to the classification of types of leaders has proven useful in efforts to assess the impact of the man on the performance of his foreign policy role. But while his categorizations have gained popularity, his is not the only way of addressing questions about the impact of individual differences on the kinds of decisions and policies that are formulated. John Stoessinger has provided another, which looks exclusively at the nexus between the personalities of leaders and their foreign policy behavior.[7] Stoessinger believes, with considerable justification, that there are two basic personality types among decision makers in the twentieth century—*crusaders* and *pragmatists*. He characterizes the first type in this way:

> The crusader tends to make decisions based on a preconceived idea rather than on the basis of experience. Even though there are alternatives, he usually does not see them. If the facts do not square with his philosophy, it is too bad for the facts. Thus, the crusader tends toward rigidity and finds it difficult, if not impossible, to extricate himself from a losing posture. He does not welcome dissent and advisers will tend to tell him what he wants to hear. He sets out to improve the world but all too often manages to leave it in worse shape than it was before. (Stoessinger, 1985: xiii)

Pragmatists, on the other hand, come closer to fitting the model of the rational decision maker described in chapter thirteen. A pragmatist seeks facts, welcomes advice, accepts criticism, considers alternatives, and searches foremost for the flexibility in foreign policy that permits adjusting policy to new realities, changing its course where necessary, but never inflicting damage on

---

[7]See Wilkenfeld et al. (1980). For a discussion of the epistemological and analytic problems analysts confront in dealing with this topic, and for useful illustrations, see Elms (1976).

his self-esteem in the process. Not surprisingly, Stoessinger feels that the country has been served best in matters of foreign policy when pragmatists have held the reins of power; but this conclusion does not argue that pragmatists never make mistakes:

> They often do. But as a general rule, such mistakes are more easily reversible than those of the crusaders. It is also true that a pragmatist may lack an overall blueprint or design for American foreign policy. But this does not mean that the pragmatic mind is unable to conceive a general philosophy. The crucial difference is this: the pragmatist always tests his design against the facts of his experience. If the design does not hold up against the facts, the design will have to change. The crusader, on the other hand, tends to sacrifice unwelcome facts on the altar of a fixed idea. (Stoessinger, 1985: 317–318)

Looking at the record of contemporary American diplomatic history in that light, Stoessinger is able to discern both types of foreign policy leaders in recent American history. Among the leaders that probably belong in the category of crusaders are Woodrow Wilson, John Foster Dulles, General Douglas MacArthur, Lyndon B. Johnson, and Richard Nixon, whose policies generally ended in failure. Among the pragmatists were Harry Truman, John F. Kennedy, and, to some extent, Henry Kissinger—leaders whose policies on the whole succeeded in making practical accommodations to the exigencies of the times in which they held power. Jimmy Carter is depicted as falling somewhere between the crusader and the pragmatist, and Franklin D. Roosevelt is held up as the ideal—unique in combining the qualities of the two basic personality types in a way that tempered a concern with ideals by an overriding concern with doing what worked. Finally, Ronald Reagan is characterized as a "nice guy, Teflon president." His desire to be liked and to be a hero were overriding. But it was his theatrical talents that enabled him to avoid paying the political costs for his often excessive efforts "to imbue the foreign policy of the United States with his personal convictions." His errors did not "stick" to his presidency. Nonetheless, Reagan stands as "the classic crusader":

> President Reagan's foreign policy was based on deeply held ideological convictions: of these, the most important was anti-communism. . . . Communism [to him] was still a monolithic evil force that would bully, lie, and cheat its way to world conquest. During his first term, the President did not seek to correct this devil image with new facts. He surrounded himself with like minded men. Not only did he choose not to visit Soviet Russia, but he was content to receive a series of one-page "mini-memos" summarizing foreign and defense problems and a foreign policy paper of ten pages or more once a month. Facts would only confuse these powerful convictions, rooted deeply in Ronald Reagan's past. . . . Ronald Reagan's shallow knowledge of history and foreign policy thus snared him into several serious mistakes, but he was never trapped as Lyndon Johnson was. The crusader and the actor inhabited his soul in equal measure. (Stoessinger, 1985: 312, 314)

The implication of Stoessinger's reasoning and reading of history is that the decision maker who governs American foreign policy best is the one whose personality and decision-making style meet the needs of the time and whose pragmatic realism predominates over the compulsion to play the role of crusading evangelist. (There is a parallel here between Barber and Stoessinger, in that Barber regards the active-positive character as best able to meet emergent challenges.) That conclusion, of course, is not beyond dispute, but few can consider either Barber's or Stoessinger's interpretations without sensing that past leaders have undoubtedly left their imprint on history, as Stoessinger would say, ''for better or for worse.''

PERSONALITY TRAITS AND FOREIGN POLICY ORIENTATIONS

An analogous approach to assessing the impact of idiosyncratic factors on American foreign policy is to investigate the relation between clusters of personal traits and the foreign policy orientations that tend to be associated with them. The approach assumes the existence of different types of decision makers, differentiated by the kinds of traits they manifest in international affairs, and argues that such traits help explain differences in the kinds of policies ultimately chosen.

The number of available classifications of personality traits is large. Unfortunately, most are based almost exclusively on empirical studies of representative segments of the entire population instead of elites. Nevertheless, ten types of personalities, which represent clusters of traits, may be regarded as important in foreign policy-making circles:[8]

- *The Nationalist.* Nationalism is a state of mind that gives primary loyalty to one nation-state, to the exclusion of other possible objects of affection (such as other countries, family, or extranational entities like the United Nations or a religion). Nationalists glorify their own nation and exaggerate its virtues, while denigrating others. Because nationalists develop an ego involvement with their state, they tend to defend its right to superiority (Stagner, 1971).

- *The Militarist.* Militarism is an attitude syndrome defining the individual's orientation toward aggressive behavior. The ''militarist'' accepts a view that leads to hostility and to the use of force as the means to an end. Interestingly, research offers little support for the often popular impression that aggressiveness is rooted in human nature (Kelman, 1965; Maslow, 1966). On the contrary, an individual's predisposition toward aggressiveness is a learned trait.

[8]Useful elaborations of the personality types discussed below can be found in Stagner (1971), McClosky (1958), Levinson (1957), Palmer, Stern, and Gaile (1974), Kreml (1977), Rokeach (1960), Hermann with Milburn (1977) and Hopple (1982). Note that the categories are based on individuals' attitudes, motives, decision styles, personalities, role perceptions, beliefs, and values; the approach assumes that all of those factors are interrelated in the delineation of types of dispositions.

- *The Conservative.* Psychologists use the concept to denote a cluster of interrelated personality characteristics rather than a political philosophy. Attributes of the conservative personality include hostility and suspicion, rigidity and compulsiveness, intolerance, and perceptual and judgmental inflexibility. Included is the inclination to condemn weakness and imperfection in others and to blame the disadvantaged for the misfortunes that befall them. Lacking compassion, the conservative has a need to discern hierarchy and rank and to resolve self-doubts by identifying people who are inferior ("I'm OK—you're so-so"). The conservative is said to greet new ideas not with curiosity but with fear. Conservative dispositions are found most often among the uninformed, the poorly educated, the less intelligent, and among those who are socially isolated yet conforming, submissive, and wanting in self-confidence (McClosky, 1958).

- *The Pragmatist.* Expediency, intellectualism, impatience, eagerness, ambition, detachment, experimentalism, and tough-minded bravado are characteristic of a pragmatic temperament. "Pragmatists are interested in what works; their prime criterion of value is success. It is the very definition of pragmatism to turn away from a belief in fixed principles toward the truth of concrete results" (Miroff, 1976). Pragmatists' need for control overwhelms their fear of power; indeed, they are drawn to it, tempted by it, and willing to exercise it to get things done, even at the expense of ideals and morality. Indeed, as Miroff's (1976) profile of John F. Kennedy demonstrates, the dispassionate rational pursuit of solutions promising results enables pragmatists to sacrifice higher principles and values and to rationalize the sacrifice with the classic excuse that "the ends justify the means."

- *The Paranoid.* The affliction known as paranoia is regarded as a psychoneurotic disorder characterized by excessive suspicion, fear, and distrust of others. Paranoids believe that people are out to "get" them, and their expectation becomes the driving force behind their behavior. Normally, we do not expect politicians to manifest such symptoms regularly. But under stressful conditions otherwise stable officials tend to display some characteristics of the disorder, the effects of which can impair the performance of their roles. The case of the first secretary of defense, James Forrestal, is an example (Rogow, 1963). A dogmatic sense of certainty, superiority, and self-confidence are aspects of the paranoid temperament that coexist alongside distrust and fear of deception (as psychobiographies of classic paranoids, Adolf Hitler and Joseph Stalin, reveal). The tendency of some Americans holding positions of power to think conspiratorially has provoked inquiry into *The Paranoid Style in American Politics* (Hofstadter, 1965), as one classic work on the subject is titled. Paranoids occasionally tend to fear foreigners as well as their own countrymen.

- *The Machiavellian.* Deriving its name from the philosopher to the prince of Florence in Renaissance Italy, Machiavellianism is a personality syndrome emphasizing strategy and manipulation over principle and sentiment. The need to acquire power, and to exercise it effectively, dominates the Machiavellian's attention above all other values; indeed conventional morality, love for and empathy toward others, and ideological goals may all be sacrificed if they interfere with the ability to manipulate others, for it is the cold exploitation of others that gives greatest satisfaction to the Machiavellian. Politicians who display that syndrome are motivated most by the desire to win and by the fear of losing; they seek to exercise influence for the satisfaction, prestige, and arousal of emotions in others it provokes, and not for the sake of demeaning opponents or to carry out a policy program. Because taking advantage of others is their primary motive, Machiavellians provoke competition and take risks in order to create opportunities for gaining concessions from others (Christie and Geis, 1970). The trait is strongly associated with the psychological need for power (McClelland, 1975).

- *The True Believer.* Fanatic, ideologue, and crusader are words often associated with true believers. They are the joiners of mass religious, political, or ideological movements. Whether militant Christians, nationalists, communists, or fascists, true believers share with others of like mind the need to join a cause and to sacrifice themselves for its advancement. Their willingness is not animated by the power of ideas, for crusaders will join any movement that fulfills their need for something to worship and perhaps for which to die. The need to join a cause—any cause—is rooted in personal frustration, low self-esteem, a sense of humiliation, a craving for status, and a search for control of one's life. Adherents seek to lose themselves in a glorified mass movement and to regain a sense of personal worth by identifying totally with the doctrine or group, the status and power of which will confer status and power on them. Because true believers need to believe in the absolute truth and virtue of the movement they choose, they are motivated to coerce people to their way of life and to compete with all other movements outside it. For instance, fanatical patriots who place their country above everything else (including themselves) are intolerant of foreigners and seek to spread their nation's way of life worldwide. The definitive work on the mentality of true believers remains Hoffer (1951).

- *The Authoritarian.* Authoritarianism is a constellation of dispositions including the propensity to conform and to adhere to conventional values while condemning those who violate such values. It entails the tendency to identify with, and submit uncritically to, leaders of in-groups, coupled with a tendency to dominate those who, to the authoritarian, appear weak or inferior. Authoritarians think in terms of stereotypes. They see themselves as victimized by a hostile social environment, they are cynical about other people's motives, and they value force and order (Adorno et al., 1950; Palmer, Stern, and Gaile, 1974).

- *The Antiauthoritarian.* In contrast to the above, antiauthoritarianism refers to a partially integrated attitude syndrome exhibited by those who are against order and power, who tend to express their impulses, and who are introspective. Antiauthoritarians tend to embrace left-wing political views emphasizing idealism, optimism, and a preference for change (Kreml, 1977).

- *The Dogmatist.* The dogmatic personality has a closed mind. For all intents and purposes dogmatists are prisoners of past attitudes who form an opinion and refuse to modify it despite evidence to the contrary. They are unreceptive to forming new images, to tolerating ambiguity and inconsistent information or contradictory images. Perceptual inflexibility is particularly endemic, as is attachment to one-sided authority figures. Established doctrines are important to the dogmatist; hence, dogmatism is associated with rigidity (Rokeach, 1960).

The personality syndromes described above are meant to be examples. The categories are neither exhaustive nor mutually exclusive (and, indeed, some are associated with others). Other attitudes and traits relevant to policy making could easily be identified. For example, Harold Lasswell (1930) examined politicians' attitudes and dispositions displayed while in office and identified three types of figures: the agitator, the administrator, and the theorist. Similarly, Jeane Kirkpatrick (Reagan's first ambassador to the United Nations) has differentiated four types of (women) politicians: the leader, the personalizer, the moralizer, and the problem solver (Kirkpatrick, 1974).

Typing personality traits is important because the categories provide tools for explaining leaders' behavior and for making predictions. Predictions are possible (though not always accurate) because the traits possessed by a leader influence his or her response to international events (Pruitt, 1965). It has also been demonstrated that personality traits can operate as a prime determinant of foreign policy attitudes. Some illustrations of the more firmly substantiated findings may suffice to indicate how a leader's traits may affect views taken toward international affairs.

Nationalism and Foreign Aggressiveness

Nationalistic traits tend to be associated with a willingness and predisposition to engage in foreign conflict: the more nationalistic the policy maker, the more warlike and aggressive the person's foreign policy orientation will tend to be. Leaders maintaining strong attachments to their nation are prone to feel hostility, loathing, and toughness toward foreigners. They frequently accept foreign policy conflict and international competition as inevitable and therefore appropriate. Nationalists oppose policies that transcend national borders, such as support for international law, arms control, and international organizations. Also opposed are policies such as foreign aid, if given largely for altruistic reasons. On the other hand, nationalists tend to favor policies that promote their nation's interests and welfare over others, such as tariff controls and ''buy American'' incentives; and they seek policies that accentuate differences between their country and others, such as strict immigration controls. In general, nationalists advocate national self-interest over any other principle of foreign policy.

Authoritarianism and Policy Consistency

Authoritarians have a tendency to form and to maintain attitudes in conformity with the kind of groups of which they are a part. They reject new information running counter to prior images, and they search for information that reinforces and justifies existing beliefs. Such individuals base actions on opinion and affections rather than facts and inquiry. Once committed to a position, they are reluctant to change it. With respect to foreign policy, the goals of a state controlled by an authoritarian individual (for example, Germany under Hitler) are unlikely to show significant change. The reason is that the behavior of authoritarians is governed by the psychological need for consistent images and by an intolerance for ambiguity and fear of diversity. Their emphasis on protocol and rule-based, routinized procedures reinforces consistency in policy positions. States run by authoritarian personalities are thus not inclined toward innovation in their foreign policy thinking. Consistency also has been shown between authoritarianism and isolationist foreign policy attitudes, Cold War thinking, and opposition to conciliation in international affairs (Rosenberg, 1967; Levinson, 1957; and Lane, 1955).

Conservatism and Isolationism

The conservative personality holds a pessimistic view of both human nature and the human prospect and accordingly sees inequality between nations as an inevitable, if not preferable, feature of international affairs. Foreigners are seen as outsiders, as threats, and as suspicious. The conservative personality (as contrasted to the political creed) thus tends to think that the best way to deal with other nations is to avoid them. The association between the conservative personality and foreign policy isolationism has been noted in the reluctance of both isolationists and conservatives

> to become involved with others or to assume responsibility for them. They oppose the rearranging of institutions for the purpose of correcting imbalances or promoting social and economic equality. They resist legislation that might interfere with a man's (or a nations's) autonomy and the disposition of his property, and they are, for the most part, inhospitable to social change. There is in both conservatism and most forms of isolationism the . . . same implicit belief that one's own good fortune—and, by extension, the nation's good fortune—is part of the natural order of things. (McClosky, 1967: 84)

Isolationism is also closely correlated with aversive (tending to avoid, shut out, deny) dispositions rather than appetitive (tending to embrace, reach out, accept) temperaments. Generally, isolationism occurs most frequently among the members of the general population than among the leaders of American society, with isolationist attitudes greatest among the less educated segments of society (McClosky, 1967; Wittkopf, 1984).

These illustrations barely scratch the surface in describing the correlation between types of personality traits and foreign policy beliefs.[9] The danger with such correlations, however revealing, is that they tempt one to assume that they can be used safely to predict the behavior of each individual. The correlations, however, describe relationships based on large aggregations (collectivities) and do not necessarily hold for each individual in the group. But if we want to anticipate the foreign policy orientation of a particular leader, we

---

[9]By way of further illustration, Hermann (1978) advances, among others, the following propositions: (1) "The more dogmatic the head of state, the less likely his government is to change its position on a well-established policy"; (2) "The more Machiavellian the head of state, the more face-to-face foreign policy interactions his government will have"; and (3) "The greater the head of state's need for achievement, the more cooperative behavior his government will initiate." For other statements of the relationship between the personality of leaders and their foreign policy behavior, see also Hermann (1974, 1976, 1980, and 1983).

can classify him or her by ostensible traits and then predict the expected foreign policy orientation as long as we recognize the limitations of this approach. Worth considering, then, is the assumption that the traits of leaders influence the way they view other nations and, correspondingly, how they want their nation to respond to other nations.

An Example: John Foster Dulles and the Soviet Union. Former Secretary of State John Foster Dulles serves as a useful example of the impact of personality traits on policy postures. According to a now classic treatment of the subject (Holsti, 1975), the source for Dulles's behavior toward the Soviet Union resided in his belief system, rather than in overt Soviet behavior. The major components of that belief system included the following assumptions: (1) while the Russian people were basically "good," the Soviet leaders were irredeemably "bad"; (2) Soviet national interest was "good" in the same sense that, like the national interest of all countries, it sought only to enhance and preserve the Soviet state; however, atheistic international communism was implacably "bad"; and (3) the Soviet state was "good" whereas the Communist Party was "bad." Dulles's perception of the Soviet Union, Ole R. Holsti concludes, "was built on the trinity of atheism, totalitarianism, and communism, capped by a deep belief that no enduring social order could be erected upon such foundations."

What were the sources of Dulles's belief system? We can assume that it stemmed in part from his childhood experiences, his relationship with his parents and his peer groups, and his psychological needs and personal predispositions—in short, from his basic personality. Some of those influences were crucial in the determination of his image. Dulles came from a celebrated, well-connected elite background that boasted two previous secretaries of state. His father was a stern Presbyterian minister, which presumably accounts for the moralistic, evangelic attitude Dulles assumed toward most objects in his environment. Of those who see the purpose of policy as the pursuit of moral values, John Foster Dulles has been classified as the most unabashed moralist ever to sit in the office of the secretary of state (Barnet, 1972). This may help to explain his belief that the Cold War was basically a moral, rather than a political, conflict. His moralistic and spiritual upbringing also explain his hatred of the Soviet leadership: they were bad ("insincere," "immoral," and "brutal") because their creed was "Godless." The clash was between two universal faiths, and because one was nonreligious, no compromise could be made.

Other aspects of Dulles's background may be hypothesized to have affected his later outlook. For instance, Dulles's early training and practice in business law may have inculcated an aggressive "can do" attitude, "an inspired ability to calculate risks and gamble on them," and a habit of mind that "carried over into his diplomacy, where countries 'were all instinctively rivals and opponents of his own client, America' " (Barnet, 1972). Moreover, his establishment credentials and elitist background may have affected his personal outlook. Richard Barnet, drawing on Richard Goold-Adams's study of Dulles, speculates that Dulles was:

> never in touch with people who knew hunger, poverty, or personal failure. Believing in addition that everyone must make the most of themselves in life and that those who do not have something wrong with them, he never seriously tried to understand the people whose misfortune it is to get left on the bottom rungs of the ladder. (Barnet, 1972: 59)

A self-described conservative with a strong authoritarian bent, John Foster Dulles showed some of the distinguishing characteristics of those personality types. His attitude toward the weak and poor is indicative of his conservative mind: adversity and poverty are the fault and character weaknesses of the victim and serve as a measure of the worth of the person or nation suffering from them. His authoritarianism as secretary of state was legendary: back your superior, buck your subordinates. As Barnet (1972) notes, Dulles "demanded what he called 'positive loyalty' from all employees of the State Department, but he felt none himself toward subordinates who were unjustly attacked by McCarthy" (for their alleged, but not verified, communist sympathies).

How did those attitudes and personality traits affect Dulles's actions toward the Soviet Union during his tenure as secretary of state? Holsti's evidence suggests that Dulles's rigid, doctrinaire belief system predetermined his reactions to the Soviets. It led him to distort information so as to reduce any discrepancies between his knowledge and his perceptions when dealing with the Soviets. Dulles's image of the Soviet Union—which is akin to what Kissinger (1962) termed as "inherent bad faith" model—was at the core of his belief system (see Stuart and Starr, 1981–1982, for a comparative evaluation of this model as it applies to Dulles, Kennedy, and Kissinger himself). Dulles interpreted the very data that might have led him to alter his belief system in such a way as to preserve it because his strong psychological need for image maintenance led him to reject any information that conflicted with his preexisting belief that the Soviet Union could not be trusted. He saw friendly initiatives from the Soviets as attempts at deception rather than as efforts at tension reduction. He reinterpreted cooperative acts in an analogous light: "In the case of the Soviet [plans to make cuts in their armed forces], these were attributed to necessity (particularly economic weakness), and bad faith (the assumption that the released men would be put to work on more lethal weapons). In the case of the Austrian State Treaty,[10] he explained the Soviet agreement in terms of frustration (the failure of its policy in Europe), and weakness (the system was on the point of collapse)" (Holsti, 1975). Thus, according to Dulles's image, the Soviets could do only harm and no good. If they acted cooperatively, it was either because they were dealing from a posi-

---

[10]The Austrian State Treaty, initiated by the Soviet Union, called for the peaceful withdrawal of Soviet and American occupation forces from Austria in return for the promise that the Austrians would maintain a policy of neutrality in the East-West dispute.

tion of weakness or because they were trying to deceive the United States into a position of unpreparedness. When they did anything bad, it supported Dulles's prior image that the Soviets were incapable of virtuous behavior. The policies of John Foster Dulles toward the Soviet Union during the Cold War, it is safe to say, were reflections of that negative image.

Part of the reason why Dulles's image was so inflexible and why Dulles was so unwilling to accept any uncomfortable information, it has been suggested, was that Dulles believed in himself and therefore was not receptive to unwelcome advice form those he regarded as his inferiors. Holsti notes that Dulles's closed image of the Soviet Union was in part due to his unique personal disposition:

> Dulles placed almost absolute reliance on his own abilities to conduct American foreign policy. He felt, with considerable justification, that his family background and his own career had provided him with exceptional training for the position of Secretary of State. Intensive study of the Marxist-Leninist classics added to his belief that he was uniquely qualified to assess the meaning of Soviet policy. This sense of indispensability carried over into the day-to-day operations of policy formulation, and during his tenure as Secretary of State he showed a marked lack of receptivity to advice. (Holsti, 1972: 231)

John Foster Dulles's image of the Soviet Union may thus be seen as a product of his attitudinal characteristics and personality traits—almost to the exclusion of other possible explanatory factors. The Dulles example thus makes a convincing case for the influence of individual variables on policy behavior.

Other Examples. Other examples supporting the conclusion that personality may influence foreign policy behavior come readily to mind. There was, for instance, LBJ's intense need to be loved, his drive to feel that he was in control of his fate, and his subsequent penchant during the Vietnam War to surround himself with advisers who provided him with what he wanted to hear—that his popularity with the American people was enduring, and that the war was going well (Kearns, 1976).[11] Or take Henry Kissinger's need for personal acceptance, his reputed distrust of democratic foreign policy, and his intolerance of dissent, and note in turn his insistence on secrecy, his ''taste for solo performances,'' and his preference for going it alone and for substituting private for public diplomacy.

---

[11]Equally evident was Johnson's immense ego involvement with affairs of state, which led him, like other presidents, to ''personify'' the policies he devised for the nation and to think of himself as the embodiment of the nation itself. Stoessinger (1985) illustrates what we term the ''personalization'' of foreign policy by quoting Johnson's statements regarding his Vietnam policies: ''By 1965, Johnson was speaking of 'my Security Council,' 'my State Department,' 'my troops.' It was *his* war, *his* struggle; when the Vietcong attacked, they attacked *him*. On one occasion, a young soldier, escorting him to an army helicopter, said: 'This is your helicopter, sir.' 'They are *all* my helicopters, son,' Johnson replied.'' Says Kearns (1976), ''The White House machinery became the President's psyche writ large.''

Or consider Harry Truman, a president who drew "confidence and strength from the office of the Presidency rather than from any particular belief in himself" and who "was prone to back up his subordinates to an extent that was indiscriminate" (DeRivera, 1968). Truman was a decisive person who expected loyalty and respect. Hence when he was confronted with blatant insubordination from General Douglas MacArthur (an authoritarian who wanted to call the shots and expand the war with the communists in Asia), it is understandable why the president was able to deal with this insubordination so decisively once he made up his mind ("You're fired!"). Able to give loyalty himself, Truman expected and demanded it from others.

President Eisenhower's personality illustrates the difficulties sometimes encountered with this genre of research. His style does not lend itself to interpretation, because his low-key approach produced results that were not initially recognized as a part of his design. Revisionists have come to reevaluate his presidency and to see strength and command where previously historians had seen almost indifference. Eisenhower's personality may have contributed to his "hidden hand" approach to management and its quiet effectiveness (see Greenstein, 1982).

And the perplexing case of Richard Nixon lingers. Some of Nixon's conduct, both in and out of office, appears explicable only in terms of his private conflicts and emotional problems. One psychoanalytic probing (Abrahamsen, 1977) diagnosed Nixon as a disturbed personality, at war with himself since his unhappy childhood (described as a succession of traumatic events and parental conflicts). Those conflicts persisted into adulthood, making Nixon unstable, indecisive, and, above all, self-consciously unsure of himself. That, David Abrahamsen contends, accounts for Nixon's obvious discomfort in the White House, his inability to maintain warm relationships with anybody, his paranoid distrust of those around him, his self-absorption, and his competitive, adversarial approach to his political opponents. It also accounts for his penchant for aggressive behavior. By conquering and destroying, in order to become the "victor," Nixon could remove, temporarily, his self-doubts and submerge his private conflicts. But those personal problems may have attracted Nixon unconsciously to failure, because inwardly he felt inadequate and suspected that he did not deserve better. The tragedies of Vietnam and Watergate may have resulted from decisions motivated by such personal factors, Abrahamsen has concluded.

Examples such as the ones above certainly suggest that with respect to particular types of decisions, and in specific kinds of circumstances, individual factors help to explain why the United States acts abroad in the manner it does. Or do they?

LIMITS ON THE EXPLANATORY POWER OF INDIVIDUAL FACTORS

The preceding discussion supposes that variations in American foreign policy can be traced to personal differences of leading decision makers. As compelling as that argument might be—whether attractively or disturbingly so—it ignores the fact that individuals are only one of several sources of American foreign policy, any one of which would appear to limit severely the effect of individuals.

When Are Individual Variables Powerful Explanatory Factors?

Under what conditions, in other words, are leaders' personal characteristics influential? In general, the impact of personality on attitudes and behavior in the international sphere may be said to increase only under certain circumstances, particularly the following:

1. *The higher the individual is in the decision-making structure.* The higher one climbs in the hierarchy of the foreign policy establishment, the more one's personality shows (Hermann, 1974; Snyder and Robinson, 1961; Palumbo, 1969). By inference, personality attributes have a greater impact on foreign policy as one's position of responsibility rises.

2. *The more ambiguous and complex the decision-making situation.* The nature of the circumstance confronting the decision maker, as he perceives it, is important. People have a tendency to respond to bewildering and uncertain situations psychologically and emotionally, rather than rationally and calmly. As Levinson (1964) and others have demonstrated, situations that are not clear-cut tend to be dealt with in terms of psychological drives and ideological beliefs. Many foreign policy situations are ambiguous, which makes nonlogical factors especially potent in explaining the reactions of policy makers. At least four types of situations tend to be especially ambiguous: new situations, where the individual has had little previous experience and few familiar cues to assist in the definition of the situation; complex situations, involving a large number of different factors; contradictory situations, which include many inconsistencies and incompatibilities; and situations devoid of social sanctions, which permit freedom of choice because societal definitions of appropriate options are unclear (DiRenzo, 1974).

3. *The greater the self-confidence and ego of the individual.* Decision makers' self-image, or degree of self-confidence and perceived ability to control events, however subjective, is crucial. Leaders vary considerably in their self-esteem and perceived political efficacy. Most theoretical work assumes that a people's belief in themselves and their own ability leads them to make decisions in terms of their peculiar values and psychological needs (for example, Abrahamsen, 1977; De-Rivera, 1968). Conversely, when such traits are absent, "leaders" governed by self-doubt will undermine their own capacity to lead and innovate. (From that perspective, leaders are not imprisoned by their bureaucracies, public opinion, and circumstances as much as by their own internal impulses and self-images.)

4. *The greater the personal involvement of the individual in the situation.* When people believe their own interests and welfare to be at stake in a situation, they tend to respond in terms of their private needs and psychological drives. They cease to appear cool and rational and begin to act emotionally. Compare student behavior when mechanically taking class notes during a lecture with behavior when called upon to recite or when negotiating with a professor over an exam grade. Likewise, when policy makers assume personal responsibility for the direction of policy (and permit their egos to become involved in outcomes), reactions are frequently made in terms of emotional considerations. Contrast President John-

son's behavior with respect to Vietnam in 1963 (cautious) with his behavior in 1968 (excited, compulsive), by which time the war had become "his war." The way in which personality factors intrude in the policy process can readily be seen.

5. *The less information available to the decision maker.* In the absence of pertinent information regarding a situation, policy makers tend to respond in terms of their base attitudes and their gut likes or dislikes for the relevant foreign nations involved. "The more information an individual has about international affairs, the less likely is it that his behavior will be based upon non-logical influences," notes Sidney Verba (1969). Ample information reduces the probability that decisions will be based on psychological drives and personal needs.

6. *The more recent or dramatic the assumption of power.* When an individual first enters office, the formal requirements of the role are least likely to circumscribe what he can do. That holds true especially for newly elected presidents, who routinely are allowed a "honeymoon" period during which they are relatively free of criticism and extraordinary pressure. So, too, cabinet officials and other top-level officials usually experience a brief period during which their personal freedom is great and their decisions encounter little resistance. Moreover, when a leader comes to office following a dramatic event (a landslide election or the assassination of a predecessor), "the new high-level political leader can institute his policies almost with a free hand. Constituency criticism is held in abeyance during this time" (Hermann, 1976). Accordingly, personal factors are likely to have a greater impact on policy.

Thus, while interpretations of American conduct in light of individual idiosyncrasies are useful in some circumstances, they can be misleading in others. Innate drives and personal predispositions are not all-powerful determinants of foreign policy behavior in all contexts. Rather, they vary in terms of the nature of the concrete decision, the psychological posture assumed by the decision maker toward the situation, and his subjective definition of its importance.

We can carry such reasoning one step further and suggest a corollary hypothesis: personal characteristics of leaders tend to be relatively potent determinants of decision-making behavior when those decisions center on broad, abstract conceptions of policy and strategy relating to the nation's basic goals. That is, unlike occasions when a policy maker is asked to find a pragmatic solution to a specific problem, when attention focuses on doctrinal and ideological issues, the decision maker is likely to respond primarily in terms of value preferences, fundamental beliefs, and inner needs.

Consider the divergent postures assumed by past presidents on the issue of containing communism. In the specific context of Indochina, where five different presidents were confronted with the necessity of deciding if and how a "war" with communism should be waged, personality became a visible influence on how each reacted. One analyst and former policy planner illustrates the point:

Truman was obdurate, tough, and determined to demonstrate these traits in his policies. . . . [H]e felt challenged by the rise of communism in Southeast Asia and became determined to arrest it. Eisenhower, far more at ease in the office, accustomed to high command, and not in need of establishing his credentials as a tough leader with the Congress, was relatively relaxed and more aloof. He alone among the five presidents involved was able to absorb a defeat to communism in Indochina [that of the French] and to provide such a defeat with a domestic appearance of success by way of gradually increasing U.S. responsibility in Southeast Asia. . . . Kennedy was sophisticated, eager, and daring to the point of adventurousness. He accordingly did not shy away from undertaking new commitments. . . . Johnson suffered from the combination of an enormous inferiority complex in regard to handling affairs of state, and an enormous feeling of superiority, experience, and self-confidence in handling and manipulating the movers, shakers, and sleepers in American politics. His inferiority complex . . . put him in wholly unwarranted awe of the national security and foreign affairs expert advisers he inherited from Kennedy [and] the intellectuals who surrounded him. . . . Accordingly, Johnson accepted the ill-conceived scenarios of the graduated escalation school of thought in regard to Vietnam. . . . Finally, Nixon's negative manipulative traits of a highly insecure (proto-paranoid) but extremely ambitious power-seeker . . . led him to deceive the public into believing he was withdrawing from Vietnam when in fact he was not only continuing but intensifying the war. . . . [H]e managed also to convince the public that he was turning defeat in Vietnam into standoff . . . by changing the most fundamental premise of American foreign policy, namely, the coequation in the U.S. public's mind of American security with the defeat of communism everywhere. (Kattenburg, 1980: 227)

One cannot read the above account without deriving the impression that for five different presidents, personality factors influenced significantly the approach they took toward the same basic problem, namely, how best to react to perceived communist activity in Southeast Asia. Though the problem was roughly the same, the reactions were generally divergent.

In addition to the argument that personal predispositions influence policy when the focus is abstract principles, another proposition that should be considered is that individual factors become especially powerful determinants of foreign policy under conditions of national crisis.[12] During such times decision making tends to be centralized and handled exclusively by the top leadership. The situation is ambiguous and threatening. Elites become highly involved in the determination of policy and tend to perceive themselves responsible for its outcome. And crucial information is likely to be unavailable. At such times the personality of the individual may be the determining factor, especially because the usual barriers to decisive action tend not to be there. In a situation that simultaneously challenges the will of a nation and the self-esteem of the decision maker, the decision processes in the political system could easily become fused with the psychodynamic processes of the personality of the executive; and the resolution of a policy crisis under such cir-

---

[12]It is not an accident that the great leaders of history have customarily arisen during periods of extreme challenge. The moment may make the person, rather than the person the moment, in the sense that crisis can liberate a gifted leader from the constraints that normally would inhibit his or her capacity to engineer change.

cumstances could depend ultimately on the outcome of a personal, emotional crisis (DiRenzo, 1974).[13]

It is instructive to note in this context that the influence of personality on the decisions of American foreign policy makers has been found to be especially strong when the use of force has been involved (Etheredge, 1978). Conversely, under more routine circumstances, the personalities of decision makers are decidedly less influential. The interesting question is, therefore, how different are the personalities of those in the decision-making elite?

Do Policy-Making Elites and Politicians Have Similar Personality Profiles?

In terms of background and experience, the people who have made up the foreign policy establishment for the past four decades have been as a group remarkably homogeneous. Recall from chapter eight the similar characteristics, backgrounds, and experiences of those who have managed the foreign policy of the United States for almost half a century. But even with such homogeneous characteristics, is it not possible that the personality predispositions of elite decision makers are sufficiently heterogeneous as to be a source of variation in their decision-making behaviors and foreign policy orientations?

Apart from what we have already discussed, the empirical evidence pertinent to the question is unfortunately scant. What is available suggests that even in terms of their personality predispositions, members of the decision-making elite are similar. Several considerations support that observation.

It is commonly assumed in the United States that positions of power and prestige command respect and honor and therefore are naturally desired by nearly everyone. ("In America, anyone can grow up to be President.") But are they? The answer is clear: only a small proportion of the American public even seeks or desires to make it to the top. Moreover, those who do become involved or active politically constitute a very small portion of the citizenry.

What we find when we look carefully at those who make foreign policy is that they possess a distinctive set of shared personal characteristics which set them apart from the average person. Participation in politics and political aspiration may be functions of personality, with the consequence that those who seek positions of power share psychological traits that make them more like one another and less like "average" Americans.

By convention, those who are attracted to political careers are thought to possess an instinct for power. Thus political leaders are presumed to be motivated by the desire to acquire influence over others. It is also clear that political leaders themselves choose to play the role of leader; that is, they select themselves by choosing to participate and electing to climb the ladder to the corridors of power. What are the reasons for their choice? The classic psycho-

---

[13]We will return in chapter fifteen to a more thorough discussion of decision making in crisis situations.

logical interpretation sees ''political man'' attempting to overcome poor self-images: ''The power seeker . . . pursues power as a means of compensation against deprivation. *Power is expected to overcome low estimates of the self,* by either changing the traits of the self or of the environment in which it functions'' (Lasswell, 1974). Accordingly, politicians seek positions of power that confer attention and that command deference, respect, and status, in order to overcome their personal sense of inadequacy and to reduce their insecurity. Erich Fromm has argued in a similar vein that ''the lust for power is rooted in weakness and not in strength, and that fundamentally this motive is a desperate attempt to gain secondary strength where genuine strength is lacking'' (DiRenzo, 1974).

The suggestion here is that policy makers are power-hungry individuals who may claim they are attracted to political life in order to do good and serve the public while, in fact, subconsciously they seek leadership to compensate for their personal insecurities and to build their own self-esteem by holding power over others. That interpretation conforms to the conventional view of the personalities of presidential aspirants. As Bruce Buchanan describes it:

> Recent national experience—and common sense—tell us that those who make the final presidential sweepstakes are men of near fanatical personal ambition who show themselves willing to sacrifice health, family, peace of mind, and principle in order to win the prize. To the question, ''What price success?'' presidential candidates are near-unanimous in responding: ''Any price.'' (Buchanan, 1978: 154)[14]

Unfortunately, however, identification of the idiosyncratic characteristics of politicians other than the power instinct is difficult. Leaders are alike, presumably, in the similarities of their personalities and their need and desire for power.[15] But beyond that observation, it is difficult to draw safe conclusions.

Generalizations about similarities in the *response* of people to the acquisition of power are less risky, perhaps. For if the motives that drive individuals to seek positions of authority are mixed, their reactions to the privileges and ascribed importance of the office are relatively patterned. Those with power, whether conferred by election or appointment to high positions in the foreign affairs government, tend to become personally absorbed in the roles they play, to let their egos and identity become involved with it, and to become intoxicated with the sense of power, purpose, and importance they derive from the experience. After all, they find themselves making history, attended by press and public. Even the most self-assured individuals can easily confuse personal identity with the role played and to mistake the power conferred by the position for personal power. The next step is for leaders to exaggerate their

---

[14]This kind of preoccupation with personal success,'' adds Buchanan (1978), ''is neither characteristic of, nor does it favor the prospects of, moderate or temperate people. Rather it suggests that aggressive types—some positive, some negative—will prevail.''

[15]Even that finding must be qualified by cognizance of the existence of ''power seekers'' in other occupations as well.

own importance in the overall scheme of things: to think that they have made things happen when in fact things have happened only because of the power they control, and to assume that, being powerful, they are indispensable. John Kenneth Galbraith characterizes the human tendency of individuals playing roles to become the masks they wear and to perceive themselves as synonymous with their roles thus:

> [M]embers of bureaucracy enjoy power not by personal right but from association. An official of the Pentagon or the State Department is dispensing authority that derives not from his personal qualities but from the majesty and power of the United States. There is interesting proof of the point in the life style of . . . an American ambassador to a country of more than marginal consequence [who] is accorded considerable deference by most people, including himself, until the day he retires. Then he disappears. . . . It was the United States . . . that made the man important and not, unhappily, any quality of the man himself. This fact, not surprisingly, quite a few organization men fail to grasp. In consequence, they parade the power under the impression it is their own. The contrast between the biggest authority and the smallest man is an unpleasant thing to see. (Galbraith, 1973: 315)

The point Galbraith makes is important in understanding the alleged influence of individuals on the nation's destiny: the office can make the person as much as the person can make the office. People become elite only because they occupy elite positions and not because, as they sometimes assume, they are inherently special. In that respect the impact of the office on the office-holder makes those in the foreign policy elite more alike than different.

Do Individuals Make a Difference?: Psychological Limits on Radical Policy Innovation

> In a sense, I had known that "power" might feel like this, just as I had known, before I ever had a drink, that whiskey goes to the head. The taste of power, or whatever it was that I tasted that first day, went to my head too, but not quite as I had been warned it would. I had come into the office with projects and plans. And I was caught in an irresistible movement of paper, meetings, ceremonies, crises, trivialities. There were uncleared paragraphs and cleared ones, and people waiting for me to tell them what my plans were, and people doing things that had nothing to do with my plans. I had moved into the middle of a flow of business that I hadn't started and wouldn't be able to stop. There were people in place to handle this flow, and established machinery in operation to help me deal with it. The entire system was at my disposal. In a word, I had power. And power had me. (Frankel, 1969: 5–6)

That recollection of a new policy maker's first day in the office sheds light on the impact acquisition of authority can have on individuals and their outlook. The policy-making system can influence the behavior of those who work within it.[16] Although we cannot speak precisely about what makes a politician a politician, our discussion in the previous chapter documented the similarity of outlook among those who occupy roles within the foreign affairs government—regardless, by implication, of the idiosyncratic variations among the individuals themselves and their projects and plans. As individuals enter new groups, they tend to conform to the prevailing and preexisting views of that group. They find as they struggle to obtain positions of power that they must ''go along to get along.'' Moreover, they tend to be rewarded for accepting the views of their superiors and predecessors. The pressures for conformity to prevailing attitudes can be enormous, and few are able to resist their influence.[17] Those who challenge majority beliefs are often purged or ostracized. It is thus little wonder that initiates to policy-making roles tend to adopt the attitudes and assumptions of their superiors and to mouth the same expressions and clichés of those within their immediate circle.

This psychological aspect of human behavior—the tendency of individuals to accept the views of those with whom they interact frequently—is sobering. It may be that situations, not personalities, determine behavior, since (1) situations mold the behavior of individuals, and (2) certain types of situations elicit certain uniform behaviors regardless of the different kinds of personalities involved in the situation. Most of us tend to behave differently when in different groups and when engaged in different activities. That is not to sug-

[16]Zbigniew Brzezinski, President Carter's national security adviser, describes these influences thus:

> To succeed at the top in government you need strong nerves and a thick skin. Public officials today are so exposed that they're subjected to continuous criticism from within the government and outside it—and a lot of it tends to be ad hominem—so a thick skin is an absolute prerequisite.
>
> You are also continuously under pressure. If you are at the very top in the White House, you are working 15 to 16 hours a day in 5-to-7 minute fragments, occasionally interspersed with sessions of up to an hour that shift from topic to topic, from event to event. That imposes enormous strains.
>
> When the pressure is high, it's essential to be very low-key and to cool everybody's moods rather than contribute to a heightened sense of anxiety and tension. . . .
>
> It's important not only to have control over your emotions but also over your schedule and work habits. That means discriminating about what you want to do and, once you have made that decision, acting expeditiously. Never let your desk be cluttered or your briefcase overflow.
>
> Beyond that, it's crucial to come into government with a larger perspective of what you wish to accomplish, with clear priorities because, once in office, you tend to be so overwhelmed by events that it is very easy to lose perspective and get absorbed in specifics. You can become increasingly responsive to situations rather than using your power to shape situations and to define outcomes. (*U.S. News and World Report*, May 20, 1985: 65)

[17]The classic research on the tendency of most individuals to conform to the perceived will of the majority was conducted by Asch (1951), who demonstrated that people often yield to group images even when they are perceived to be contrary to fact. This disturbing tendency indicates that independent judgment is often nonexistent in many decision-making situations, but especially in those, like those involving foreign policy, in which decisions are routinely made in groups. See Janis (1972) for a discussion of this phenomenon in the context of foreign policy making.

gest that we lose our identity; we remain the person(s) we are. But different situations tend to bring out different aspects of our personality and may make us behave in unusual, perhaps embarrassing, ways.

Although an especially strong personality might cope better than most in resisting what group pressures and social demands can do to his or her behavior in certain roles, all people—because they are human—are inclined to adapt themselves and sometimes their personalities to their roles or positions (see Lieberman, 1965), each of which has certain expected ways of behaving and attitudes associated with it and each of which is governed to a large extent by a preexisting set of decision norms (see Kegley, 1986b) embedded in and reinforced by the force of a social process within an institutional structure (see Anderson, 1986). Every occupant of those roles tends to conform to the rituals, vocabulary, and beliefs defined by them.[18] That applies to the office of the presidency as well. In fact, the formal and informal norms of that office in particular—the demands of the job, its constitutional obligations, and public pressures—may permit less freedom of individual expression than almost any other. "Both its prominence and its symbolic functions," concludes David Truman (1951), "make the presidential office a more important molder of its incumbents than any other in the nation."[19]

Given this perspective, it is therefore not difficult to hypothesize still another reason for persistence and continuity in postwar American foreign policy: the individuals who through time became part of the policy-making establishment accepted the prevailing image of the world and bent their behavior, and ultimately their beliefs, to that of their predecessors. As James Rosenau (1980) concluded, "Even the President must function within narrowly prescribed limits, so much so that it would be easier to predict the behavior of any President from prior knowledge of the prevailing state of that role than from data pertaining to his past accomplishments, orientations, and experiences." There are definite limits to what individual leaders can do and the amount of change they can accomplish. The external environment, soci-

---

[18]Haney and Zimbardo summarize a decade of research on this phenomenon by noting that:

If there has been one important lesson coming from all the research in social and personality psychology in the past few years, it is that situations control behavior to an unprecedented degree. It is no longer meaningful, as it once was, to talk in terms of personality "types," of persons "low in ego strength," or of "authoritarians"—at least it is not meaningful if we wish to account for any substantial portion of an individual's behavior. . . . Rather, we must look to the situation in which the behavior was elicited and is maintained if we hope ever to find satisfactory explanations for it. The causes of behavior we have learned are more likely to reside in the nature of the environment than inside the person. And although the operation of situational forces can be subtle and complex in the control of behavior, it can also be extremely powerful. . . . Research . . . seems to indicate that . . . [i]n "real life" we are often faced with a situation or role which demands behavior of a certain kind and, over a period of time, our beliefs are likely to change in a way consistent with this situation or role behavior. (Haney and Zimbardo, 1973: 40–42)

[19]"The historical consistency of the president's responsibilities," writes Buchanan (1978), "produces a like consistency in the kinds of exposures he will encounter as he goes about the business of performing his functions."

etal factors, governmental characteristics, and role-induced constraints—all serve to limit available policy choices and hence the range of permissible action abroad. The result has been a set of policy prescriptions that shows incredible durability despite changing international circumstances. The names of the actors may have changed over the course of four decades, but the song has remained the same.

Additional Restraints on Individual Initiative and Policy Innovation

If the constraints discussed above are not enough, other considerations properly falling within the individual source category also narrow the range of alternatives available to decision makers. Among them are the following:

1. the tendency of policy makers, like the general public, to maintain preexisting images and to perceive new information selectively so as to preserve their perceptual models of reality;
2. the propensity of policy makers to avoid decision-making responsibilities altogether by relying on reassuring illusions and rationalizations (see Janis, 1980);
3. the impact of "organizational norms, routines, and standard operating procedures [which] may . . . constrain the manner in which issues are defined, the range of options that may be considered, and the manner in which executive decisions are implemented by subordinates" (Holsti, 1976b), with the result that policy continuity is the essential product of group decision making;
4. the legacy of past policies—in the form of treaties signed with other countries, previous budgetary decisions, prior commitments, and the like—which may reduce considerably the range of available choice and limit changes in existing policy to only incremental revisions (see Burns, 1978);
5. the tendency of decision makers to feel subjective, if subconscious, loyalties toward pet programs (and the people associated with them), with the result that they are often reluctant to withdraw support from them despite their diminishing utility;
6. the tendency for acquiescent personalities (people who are "team players") to make it to positions of power and for "rugged individualists," those who are reformers and innovators, to be systematically selected out;
7. the preference of individuals for incremental change, which is encouraged by the tendency of most to focus attention on familiar experiences and to shy away from the unfamiliar;
8. the desire of most officials to be "loved" and respected together with their concern for earning a "place in history," which promote policy definition in terms that are least likely to be threatening or destabilizing and that appeal to the conservative sentiments of the majority;
9. the fact that the difficulty of making policy choices and the need for predictability encourage policy makers to reach decisions through routinized procedures and in accordance with the established rules of a "decision regime" (Kegley, 1986b) and by reference to the "operational codes" they develop (see George, 1969; Walker and Falkowski, 1984);
10. the probability that length in service will encourage conservatism, for, as President Nixon said in 1972, "It is inevitable [that] when an individual has been in

a Cabinet position or, for that matter, holds any position in government, after a certain length of time he becomes an advocate of the status quo; rather than running the bureaucracy, the bureaucracy runs him.''

When those psychological and circumstantial restraints on policy initiatives are added to the many domestic and external factors discussed in the preceding chapters, it is not hard to comprehend why foreign policy appears to change so little.[20]

The above psychological constraints on policy-making innovation do not comprise an exhaustive list. Other idiosyncratic factors also decrease the likelihood that any leader will inaugurate fundamental policy change. The range of viable choices is likely to be circumscribed. Most leaders will be influenced by their political party identification, and such variables as family, status, age, and experience, as we have already suggested, will in all probability make a difference in how a leader defines policy goals. So, too, will the health of the official, as a reading of FDR's behavior while he was seriously ill (in fact, close to death) at the Yalta Conference will illustrate.[21] All such factors act to constrain rather than to liberate. Thus these political and psychological considerations tend to restrain the way in which American foreign policy is shaped by leaders.

THE QUESTIONABLE UTILITY OF THE ''GREAT MAN'' THESIS

The interpretation at the beginning of this chapter articulated a potentially powerful source of change in American foreign policy: since so much authority is concentrated in the hands of so few, it is logical to assume that the members of the decision-making elite in charge of foreign policy can, with relative ease, choose to revise, indeed, revolutionize, the policies of the nation abroad. Change the people in charge, it is assumed, and the policy itself will often change in turn. By extension, when the character of the leadership changes, a change in American behavior toward other countries may be anticipated, according to this reasoning.

The theory and evidence summarized in this chapter force one to question the utility of this ''great man'' theory of American foreign policy.[22] At the very

---

[20]As Seabury (1973) noted, ''Change, as it occurs, does so in acts of renewing, repairing, or improving existing relationships or commencing new ones that correspond to familiar patterns. Diplomacy . . . thus normally resembles more the act of gardening than of bulldozing.''

[21]Cronin (1980) is dubious about anyone's ability to fill the modern presidency's role without falling victim to its pressures: ''If we concede that in part the office does make the man, we must admit also that time in office often unmakes the man.''

[22]The terminology is borrowed from the timeless ''great man'' versus ''Zeitgeist'' debate. At the core of the controversy is the perhaps unanswerable question of whether the times must be conducive to the emergence of great leaders, or whether, instead, great people would have become famous leaders regardless of when and where they lived. For a discussion, see Greenstein (1969).

least, that theory appears much too simple an explanation of American action abroad. Attributing great variation in foreign conduct to a single source (the characteristics of the individuals who make the policy), the "great man" theory seeks to explain everything and succeeds in explaining little.

Why? To recapitulate, we find that the people who make American foreign policy are not that different from one another after all. Only certain types of people seek positions of power, and top leaders are recruited from similar backgrounds and rise to the top in similar ways. Consequently, they have in common many attitudes and personality characteristics. Moreover, once in office, their behaviors, for a variety of psychological reasons, have a pronounced tendency to be shaped by the positions they occupy, and they see their options differently from within the system than they did outside of it. They often find themselves conforming to the behavioral habits and beliefs of their peers and predecessors and responding to the pressures imposed by the office. The situational context of the decision-making setting elicits similar policy responses from diverse personalities. The result: different individuals often carry out the same sort of policies as their predecessors and respond to international events in consistent and patterned ways. As a group, elites' behavior tends to be governed by repetition and regularity. The activities of most policy makers have thus been marked by a propensity for incremental change, for perpetuation of established routines of thought and action, and for preservation of established policies.

These factors in combination invite the conclusion that, even though the president and his immediate circle of advisers constitute one of the most powerful institutions in the world, and even though, in principle, they have the resources to bring about prompt and immediate change by the decisions they make, the fact is that those powers are seldom exercised. The consequence: decisions are seldom innovative or radical. The leadership is a prisoner of powerful political and psychological forces; it is constrained both materially and subconsciously from initiating basic changes. Personal characteristics thus serve to influence the style with which decisions are reached and carried out. But that style rarely makes a serious modification in the actual foreign conduct of the nation. American foreign policy is highly patterned because, as Holsti (1973) puts it, "Names and faces may change, interests and policies do not."

Those observations lead to the conclusion that the amount of foreign policy change any particular leader is likely either to seek or to effect in the foreseeable future is not great. The basic policies of the United States have become established and have developed a life and durability of their own. Indeed, Henry Kissinger's cogent comment in 1976 may retain its pertinence as the next occupant of the Oval office is determined: "The essential outlines of U.S. policy will remain the same no matter who wins the U.S. Presidential election." The highly institutionalized foreign affairs government and the psychological constraints on those who propel the system's machinery create severe limits on what any one individual can do. The real alternatives are few in number, and made fewer by the viable range of choice. Under normal circumstances, most leaders cannot be expected to transcend these obstacles to radical policy innovation. Individual factors are indeed an important source of influence on American foreign policy, but we must conclude that other kinds of variables turn out to be more potent.

SUGGESTIONS FOR FURTHER READING

BARBER, JAMES DAVID. *The Presidential Character: Predicting Performance in the White House*, 3rd ed. Englewood Cliffs, NJ: Prentice-Hall, 1985.

BUCHANAN, BRUCE. *The Presidential Experience: What the Office Does to the Man.* Englewood Cliffs, NJ: Prentice-Hall, 1978.

DALLEK, ROBERT. *Ronald Reagan: The Politics of Symbolism.* Cambridge, MA: Harvard University Press, 1984.

DERIVERA, JOSEPH H. *The Psychological Dimension of Foreign Policy.* Columbus, OH: Charles E. Merrill, 1968.

DIRENZO, GORDON J., ed. *Personality and Politics.* Garden City, NY: Doubleday-Anchor, 1974.

ETHEREDGE, LLOYD S. *A World of Men: The Private Sources of American Foreign Policy.* Cambridge, MA: MIT Press, 1978.

HERMANN, MARGARET G., WITH THOMAS W. MILBURN, eds. *A Psychological Examination of Political Leaders.* New York: Free Press, 1977.

ISAAK, ROBERT A. *Individuals and World Politics*, 2nd ed. North Scituate, MA: Duxbury, 1981.

STOESSINGER, JOHN G. *Crusaders and Pragmatists: Movers of Modern American Foreign Policy*, 2nd ed. New York: W. W. Norton, 1985.

VIII

PATTERN AND PROCESS IN AMERICAN FOREIGN POLICY

15

THE SOURCES OF CHANGE AND CHANGELESSNESS IN AMERICAN FOREIGN POLICY: A SYNTHESIS AND INTERPRETATION

Looking back over the years since World War II, the really surprising thing about this country has been the basic stability of American foreign policy. There has been a continuity that, in fact, nobody could have expected.
Correspondent and presidential adviser Henry Brandon, 1983

In the field of foreign affairs, . . . a new direction is evident. We are acting to restore confidence in American leadership through a more robust defense of U.S. ideals and interests and a more realistic approach to the dangers and opportunities of the international situation.
Secretary of State Alexander M. Haig, 1981

As the opening chapters of this book have demonstrated, one of the most striking characteristics of post-World War II foreign policy has been the extent to which persistence and continuity have been its hallmarks. Although eight different presidents have occupied the Oval Office during this period, the defining characteristics of foreign policy—captured in the themes of globalism, anticommunism, and containment—have proven to be remarkably resilient. Reliance on military strength and a propensity to become involved in the affairs of others have also remained paramount. Those patterns are persistent in the images and values that define the nation's general orientation toward international problems and that describe the means through which it has sought to cope with a series of emergent, momentous challenges emanating from abroad.

549

What accounts for such policy persistence and continuity? Answers to that question were provided in the previous discussion of the five sources of foreign policy: the external, societal, governmental, role, and individual factors. Within each of those "master variables," forces operate in favor of change as well as continuity. Yet together the interaction of these source categories more often than not has produced in the policy-making process incremental rather than radical departures from the past. American foreign policy has changed and is changeable; but change has unfolded in a gradual, piecemeal manner. Our characterization of American foreign policy, therefore, emphasizes evolution rather than revolution. It draws attention to the presence of trends as opposed to sharp reversals; it highlights the facts that interruptions in the general thrust of foreign policy tend to be ephemeral and that the postwar premises underlying American foreign policy, always under challenge, nevertheless tend to reassert themselves and to persist.

But is it appropriate to argue that American foreign policy will continue to be marked by continuity? Or is it preferable to draw attention to those forces that may stimulate new patterns, and not simply marginal adjustments to old patterns? The purpose of this chapter is to provide tentative answers to those questions and to explain why policy innovation or nonincremental change tends to be so unusual. In particular, we shall elaborate on the themes of change and changelessness as a way of linking the pattern of American foreign policy to the process by which it is articulated and implemented. In so doing, we will examine how the sources of American foreign policy come together to produce policy outcomes, which so often appear to be little more than slight deviations from the past.

EXPLAINING FOREIGN POLICY: THE SOURCES OF A CONSISTENT POSTWAR PATTERN

Former Secretary of State Henry Kissinger spoke revealingly not only for himself but also for the United States and the two presidents he served when he reflected:

> I have participated in the conduct of American foreign policy during a period of fundamental change. As always in such times, that policy emerged from an amalgam of factors: objective circumstances, domestic pressures, the values of our society and the decisions of individual leaders. The relative weight to be given to each can be left to historians. But their mix shaped a profound transition in our nation's foreign policy. The trauma of Vietnam transformed our international perceptions; the nightmare of Watergate brought into question the validity of our domestic institutions. These upheavals coincided with radical alterations in the international environment. We have had to cope . . . with an increasingly complex and turbulent world in which America must seek to achieve its principles and its purpose under circumstances greatly at variance with traditional attitudes. (Kissinger, 1977b: 6)

Kissinger's rumination shows a policy maker's awareness of the potency of interacting variables in influencing the course of American foreign policy.

Moreover, it serves to stimulate thinking about the central theoretical question to which this book is addressed: What accounts for American foreign policy? Are those influences in some way linked to the stability of postwar American foreign policy? Might they also serve as forces of change? Let us briefly review the material covered in previous chapters as a way of providing answers to those questions. At the same time, some tentative answers to the questions of whether each of the explanatory variables previously discussed is of equal importance and whether their rank in order of importance varies with time and circumstances will be offered.

In chapter two, the sources of American foreign policy were visually depicted as a funnel of causality (see Figure 2.1), in which external, societal, governmental, role, and individual sources combine as inputs into the foreign policy-making process to explain the outputs of that process, namely, the foreign policy of the United States. After describing the substance of postwar American foreign policy, that is, its historic pattern, the subsequent chapters then treated each of those major sources in turn, demonstrating how each independently serves to influence the prospects for policy continuity (or change). The presentation began with the most complex set of interrelated variables, the external environment, and worked from there through societal, governmental, role, and individual explanations of foreign policy outcomes. The concepts of inputs and outputs and the order of presentation are illustrated in Figure 15.1, which recasts the "funnel of causality" shown in Figure 2.1.

As Figure 15.1 shows, the sources of American foreign policy can be thought of as the outcome of a series of interrelated factors, each one of which (except the largest, the external environment) is "nested" within a larger and more complex set of variables. In the same framework we can view individual decision makers as being constrained as well as stimulated by their roles, roles defined largely by the policy-making positions within the foreign policy-making structure. Those governmental variables are cast within the larger framework of American society, which in turn operates within an even larger international environment comprising a host of other nations, nonstate actors, and global trends and issues to which the United States as a global actor responds.

Let us review briefly the influence of each of those source categories so that some observations about their relative potency in explaining American external behavior may be reached.

Do Individuals Make a Difference?

Change the people who make the policy, and the policy itself will probably change, so one view has it. However, perusal of this theory and corresponding evidence in the previous chapter has shown us that this tenet is not persuasive. Kissinger's hypothesis that it really doesn't make a difference who is elected president—the essential outlines of foreign policy will remain the same regardless—appears more cogent. Why? As we have seen, the system recruits the same types of individuals into positions of power. And top-level

FIGURE 15.1 The Hierarchy and Interrelationship of Sources of Foreign Policy

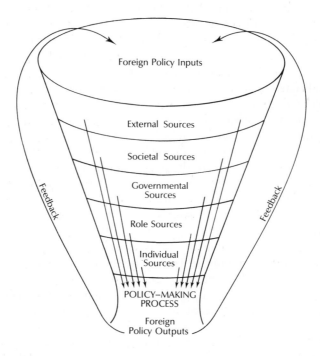

decision-making posts are frequented by many of the same individuals over time, according to a revolving-door principle. Moreover, once in office individuals tend to be shaped by, more than they are able to shape, the roles they occupy. As a result, individual differences tend to be canceled out: new decision makers act like and reach the same kinds of decisions as their predecessors. Although changes in personnel often produce changes in style, rhetoric, and tactics, such surface changes should not be mistaken for fundamental changes in values and images that give rise to new foreign policy objectives and strategies. In short, radical departures from ongoing policy trends are not likely to stem from changes in personnel. The individual factor is too weak to be a force for policy change. Whereas policy change may be stimulated by action initiated by single individuals, individuals are not likely to be successful in augmenting change without reinforcement from other sources.

The Organizational Network

American foreign policy is decreed, executed, and implemented by a complex collection of individuals organized in government institutions. That fact makes role and governmental variables potentially powerful in influencing American foreign policy. The process itself affects the final decisions that are reached and how they are carried out; it has, in other words, a force of its own that shapes the kinds of decisions that are reached.

What is known about the process? To begin with, we can review the kinds of behavior that are bred by the roles and government structures of the institutional environment, behavior that was summed up in President Kennedy's description of Washington—"Southern efficiency, Northern charm." The process encourages delay, punishes taking a stand, rewards marking time, and spreads responsibility so that no one is blamed for failures. Among the salient characteristics of behavior in the institutional setting are bureaucratic parochialism (bureaucratic agencies pursue their own narrowly defined purposes); bureaucratic competitiveness (they seek to enhance their power and position within the government hierarchy); and attitudinal conformity (they discourage creativity, dissent, critical thinking, and long-range planning; reward conservatism, rigidity, timidity, and crisis management). In addition, bureaucratic behavior is conditioned by intragovernmental politics. Because competing and often imperialistic bureaucracies want different things, policy formulation frequently results from a bargaining process, a tug of war in which differences among competing actors are resolved through compromises, so that ultimately policy gravitates toward the lowest common denominator. In such an environment, decisions are made not on the basis of the substance of issues, but rather on how the decisions will affect the interests of bureaucratic organizations. And top-level policy makers cannot afford to do otherwise, for they depend on those organizations to carry out their decisions.

Other aspects are also detrimental to efficiency. The huge size of the institutional apparatus alongside its penchant for growth is one complication. The fragmentation of power within the multiple channels of this institutional maze is another. Finally, the institutional setting also splinters authority and divides the labor in the making and execution of foreign policy. In so doing, it decentralizes power and diminishes the political influence and control of each of those involved in the policy-making process relative to the others. Thus, while the president and the institutionalized presidency predominate in a federal structure of three presumably coequal branches of government, the presidency's control over foreign policy formulation and implementation is partial. The presidency is surrounded by the departments and agencies of the executive branch, which simultaneously enhance the preeminence of the president as the chief executive officer and limit his ability to act in an unrestrained manner. Among those departments and agencies power and influence are differentially distributed, with the result that policy execution and coordination are often compromised. That postwar American foreign policy has often appeared counterproductive may be the price of this inelegant policy-making structure (see Destler, Gelb, and Lake, 1984).

The widely shared perception in the postwar era of a hostile international environment (with Soviet communism at its forefront) contributed to the corollary belief in the efficacy of military and clandestine solutions to political problems. Those perceptions in turn gave rise to an immense peacetime military establishment and sprawling intelligence community, both of which achieved substantial political clout in a policy-making environment where money and personnel mean influence. Once acquired, such political clout has been self-perpetuating, because those with relatively greater influence are more often likely to win intragovernment political battles. Since winning means choosing the option most consonant with one's organizational goals, interests, and expertise, a cycle was set into motion that helps to explain why today's policies so often look like yesterday's.

President Reagan's campaign pledge to liberate the people from the government implied his appreciation of the importance of role and governmental variables in the formulation of policy. He recognized that meaningful redirection of policy was unlikely to occur without major reforms in (and, from Reagan's perspective, reductions in the size of) the organizations designed to carry out presidential decisions. But the record indicates instead the power of these roles and institutional forces. Policy makers, and especially the career bureaucrats so needed in a complex, advanced industrial society, have continued to behave in the customary, predictable ways associated with their positions.

Whether future administrations place emphasis on reduction of the size of government (as with Reagan) or on reorganization of it, the result is likely to be periodic feather ruffling rather than massive reshuffling of organizational responsibilities. The penchant to infiltrate this structure with large numbers of political appointees, especially evident during Reagan's tenure, has not had a visible impact on the government's foreign policy performance.

We may conclude that role and governmental variables are likely to remain powerful. Roles determine probable behavior, and government structures influence the kinds of roles that exist. The impact of those factors has undoubtedly grown as the problems with which the government grapples have become more complex, and the foreign affairs government has become increasingly layered, enlarged, and duplicative in function. Those facts alone makes efforts to reduce the influence of role and governmental factors over American foreign policy improbable.

The American People

Societal variables must also be taken into account. Such important if relatively permanent characteristics as the geographical size, economic productivity, military preparedness, and political culture of the United States exert an impact on American foreign policy. So, too, do the more volatile societal sources of foreign policy, such as public opinion, elections, the mass media, and interest groups. Any assessment of foreign policy that fails to give attention to such societal variables would necessarily be incomplete, because clearly the United States acts the way it does abroad partly as a consequence of the kind of country it is. That is true because America's superpower status derives from the nation's characteristics as a whole. It is also true because individuals—including decision makers—are products of the American political culture, which shapes attitudes before, during, and after the assumption of power, teaching individuals how to perceive, judge, and act. American society provides resources that decision makers might tap in order to cope with the international environment (capabilities which, in economic and military terms, have been varied, rich, and virtually limitless during much of the postwar era). Forces within American society also help to delimit the alternatives from which decision makers actually choose, thereby helping to define the limits of permissible options (options which have largely been rationalized in liberal precepts and buttressed by concern for wealth, power, status, moral virtue, self-determination, and freedom for the world's peoples).

We also know, however, that decision makers are not simply shaped by societal forces—they also shape them. That is clearly the case with public opinion, which can be characterized as uninformed about and uninterested in international affairs, as highly unstable in the short run and subject to shifts in "mood" in the long run, and as nationalistic and fearful of things foreign. Coincidental with those characteristics is a permissiveness regarding foreign policy and an instinctive tendency to be acquiescent to government initiatives and supportive of existing policies and leadership. The net result is that government officials influence opinion as much as they respond to it. There are exceptions, of course. Moreover, public opinion serves as a constraint on policy innovation in the sense that the fixed images ascribed to the public limit policy makers' thinking about policy innovation. More often, however, public opinion is something to be shaped by decision makers rather than followed by them. Not surprisingly, therefore, over time there is a strong correspondence between the foreign policy of the nation and the preferences held by the public about that policy.

Decision makers' ability to manipulate public opinion in the direction of their preferred policies is enhanced by an electoral system that does not measurably shape the nation's foreign policy goals. Voter behavior is not influenced strongly by the foreign policy preferences to which voters subscribe. Decision makers may act *as though* voters make choices on the basis of their policy preferences, but preferences held about foreign policy are often indistinguishable from other preferences that might motivate voter behavior.

Nor do the mass media substantially alter the proposition that decision makers lead and the public follows. Situated midway between decision makers and the public, the media would appear to play two roles simultaneously: that of shaping public preferences and that of critically evaluating what decision makers do. Again, however, the evidence paints quite a different picture. The mass media do not determine public preferences on foreign policy matters because most people (and the mass media, too, for that matter) are habitually inattentive to foreign affairs, because most public attitudes are relatively impervious to new information the media might provide, and because the mass media are characterized by diversity and heterogeneity. The media do, however, help to define agendas by telling people what to think *about* and by providing the basic information which a generally passive public filters and shapes into a general image of world affairs.

The influence of the media is mediated by a multiple-step communications flow. The mass media provide information to (and define agendas for) those concerned with and attentive to foreign issues and events and also those involved in foreign policy making. If attitude changes occur among those small, select groups, then they are also likely to be filtered through various opinion leaders to much larger segments of American society. Hence the mass media play a role in shaping popular attitudes or preferences that is neither direct nor immediate. Television is a partial exception to this generalization, having created an inadvertent audience for a vast amount of foreign policy information which most Americans neither seek nor want.

When changes in attitudes occur, whose preferences do they reflect? More often than not, they are the preferences of members of the policy-making elite. The mass media themselves are part of the foreign policy-making establishment from which opinion change must ultimately derive because the mass media are dependent upon the government for information. It is not surprising, therefore, to find at times considerable congruence between the attitudes and preferences of government officials and those of the mass media assigned to scrutinize the government's behavior, even during periods when investigative and advocacy journalism prevail.

Nor do interest groups and political action committees change the picture substantially. The mere presence of numerous interest groups should not be taken to mean they are effective in exercising influence in the policy-making process. Several factors explain why: the fact that interest groups are generally more interested in domestic than foreign affairs, that the public is generally impervious to persuasion by interest-group efforts, that during crisis situations top-level decision makers are free to act (and to mold opinion) largely unconstrained by interest-group pressures, and that the occasions for group influence are relatively small in number (usually when the issues at stake are outside the public limelight). Indeed, while interest groups often seek to constrain policy makers, their ability to do so is usually limited by the importance of the issue: the more important the issue, the less likely it is that they will be influential. And because they often seek to inhibit policy innovation, interest groups committed to preserve the status quo are generally more successful than those that seek to bring about policy changes. That characterization appears to be even more true with the rise of single-issue politics. Even here, however, we must be careful not to overstate the importance of interest-group activity, for members of the policy-making elite retain a substantial capacity to influence interest groups.

The foregoing reflects primarily the pluralist model of interest-group activity, which emphasizes the countervailing forces of competing groups whose efforts have the effect of constraining policy makers, thereby promoting policy continuity and militating against policy innovation. By way of contrast, the elitist model of policy making sees consistency in foreign policy as emanating not from competition among groups, but rather from the common backgrounds, activities, and orientations of the governmental and nongovernmental members of the "establishment." From this perspective, foreign policy is of the elite, by the elite, and for the elite. As a variation on that perspective, the military-industrial complex is a specialized segment of American society, which is alleged by some to foster a policy posture toward the rest of the world that satisfies its own parochial and often profit-motivated interests in the perpetuation of a globalist containment strategy resting on fear of Soviet communism.

Precisely because so many people have a stake in the perpetuation of present military postures and expenditures, defense policy has become a not-easily-broken "national-economic addiction" (Kennan, 1977). The privileged few who make American foreign policy are unlikely to propose policy changes that would erode others' benefits from which they themselves often derive their power. From that perspective, the patterns identified as characterizing postwar American foreign policy—globalism, anticommunism, containment, military might, and interventionist means—are not likely to be challenged by forces within American society. That observation stems from the fact that "the national interests pursued by a nation or stated by its official leaders are simply the interests of the dominant groups or classes. It is this transmutation of private interests into national interests that is the essence of the elitist tradition" (Berkowitz, Bock, and Fuccillo, 1977).

In the final analysis, then, the societal factor as a source of American foreign policy provides important insight into the continuity that has characterized that policy since World War II. None of what has been said is inconsistent with the proposition that foreign policy has changed and is changeable. What it all points to, however, is change that rarely occurs in other than piecemeal fashion. Slow, halting, and incremental changes provide remedial adjustments to evolving circumstances without requiring fundamental reevaluations of the untested assumptions upon which conventional definitions of "the national interest" rest.

The International Environment

The very existence of an external environment over which nation-states have no absolute control gives rise to the need for foreign policy. But how important is the external environment in the process whereby everyday decisions are made about how to cope with it? "Not very" is, at least in some respects, the most valid description of most foreign policy making as it has unfolded on an everyday, routine basis. Throughout most of the postwar era the United States has depended much less on the state of the world than the state of the world has depended on it. It was this largely hospitable global setting that made possible the U.S. role of global policeman and the corresponding imposition of *Pax Americana*. In effect, the capabilities that give rise to the superpower status of the United States coupled with the nation's willingness to use those capabilities in pursuit of its foreign policy objectives have done much to create the kind of international environment that currently exists.

That situation is changing, as in fact it has been changing since the end of the nation's atomic monopoly in 1949. We have moved from a time in the immediate postwar years when the United States was the only superpower through a period of tight bipolarity to what might now be thought of as a bipolycentric international distribution of power. The most outward manifestation of those shifts has been a relative decline in American "power potential" in relation to other nations. The growing power of the Soviet Union, the perceived adversary of the United States, is the most obvious example (and one that incidentally is closely tied to the maintenance of a large peacetime military arsenal whose purpose has shifted from compellence to deterrence). But we also noted in chapter six the growing power potential of Japan and Western European nations. Closely related to those shifts has been growth in the number and importance of nonmilitary issues, and an increase in global interdependence, over which the United States has found it has no final control. And on the Soviet side, the rift between Moscow and Beijing has given rise to triangular politics, in which the United States has found cooperation with one or the other of its communist adversaries to be as useful as confrontation.

To that picture must be added the increasing number of intensely nationalistic Third World nations whose interests and objectives are often dissimilar from those of the United States. During the period of tight bipolarity and the peak of the Cold War, the widely shared anticommunist perceptions of American policy makers led the United States to compete with the Soviet Union for the allegiance of those nations in a variety of different ways (for example, through economic and military aid). The anticommunist stand was also responsible for the postwar instances of military intervention—as in Korea, Lebanon, the Dominican Republic, Vietnam, and Grenada, and for the use of covert operations to pursue this policy goal. It continues today to be at least part of the motivation underlying the massive armaments trade in which the United States is engaged and a stimulant to its frequent use of force short of war.

At the same time that the world is characterized by an ever widening gap between rich and poor, the 1990s promise that the Third World nations will play an increasingly important role in international politics not simply as objects of Soviet-American competition, but as independent forces capable of making demands on Western industrial nations. The role played by nonstate actors and the expanded autonomy afforded their actions—as illustrated by the increasing frequency of international terrorist activity—introduce another dimension to the global environment with which the United States must deal. In this sense, too, the world has become more complex, thereby inhibiting the ability of the United States to follow its own preferences unrestrained by the demands of others. The increased salience of transnational problems (as illustrated by population growth, food scarcities, trade, debt, environmental degradation, energy, and terrorism as international issues) are indicative simultaneously of growing interdependence and the diminished ability of any one nation to accomplish its goals single-handedly in the complex world environment. The global scenarios that might unfold by the turn of the century will confront the United States with extraordinary challenges and will challenge prevailing American policy, making the international environment a potentially powerful source for policy adaptations.[1]

To the extent that varied and often profoundly shifting international conditions become salient in the perceptions and cognitions of top-level decision makers and the career bureaucrats who implement their policies, the international environment as a cluster of trends has perhaps the greatest potential for modifying the fundamental assumptions on which postwar American foreign policy has been based. Correspondingly, it may also call for new directions in the American response to the world. Although we cannot assume that the global environment exercises a direct causal impact on the policies of the United States, it can be argued that the external environment serves as a stimulus to foreign policy innovation, setting the decision-making process in motion, if only in a psychological sense. It is only partially true that policy makers spend their time deciding issues: the international system as well determines the nature of issues they decide. At a minimum, the global environment operates as a set of changing conditions continuously asserting themselves, thereby producing incentives for any nation to adjust to changing requirements. Shifting global conditions and "issue cycles" (Vasquez and Mansbach, 1983) can pull even a great power in the direction of accommodation to new realities, for those who resist accommodation may be endangered. As Edmund Burke warned in the last century, "A state without the means of some change is a state without the means of its preservation."

A COMPARATIVE ASSESSMENT OF THE SOURCES OF AMERICAN EXTERNAL BEHAVIOR

The elements that help determine the course of policy are myriad. Five major source categories, all interacting and in flux, have been posited to affect the rate of change in American foreign conduct. Most of them work to sustain continuity in foreign policy, and collectively, the five factors operate largely to make policy change, when it occurs, come slowly and incrementally. Policy innovation amounts more often than not to remedial adjustments devoid of fun-

---

[1]Consider the picture portrayed by the U.S. government's study of the global future: "If present trends continue, the world in 2000 will be more crowded, more polluted, less stable economically, and more vulnerable to disruption than the world we live in now. Serious stresses involving population, resources, and environment are clearly visible ahead. Despite greater material output, the world's people will be poorer in many ways than they are today" (*The Global 2000 Report to the President*, 1980). See Editorial Research Reports (1986) for a discussion of threats to global resources and the sometimes human resourcefulness in meeting the challenges those threats pose.

damental reevaluations of the untested assumptions on which those policies often rest.

But how important are the source categories in comparison with each other? What is their relative impact? It bears repeating that our responses to those questions must necessarily be tentative. The policy-making process combines many causal factors, the recipe for which defies precise definition. But the preceding discussion suggests a ranking of the relative potencies of the source categories of American foreign policy, as follows: (1) role, (2) governmental, (3) societal, (4) external, and (5) individual.

In essence that ranking[2] of the relative importance of the explanations of policy outcomes provides the skeleton of a crude theory of foreign policy making. Important caveats will be added to this framework in the next two sections of this chapter.[3] But first let us note what the theoretical interpretation forwarded here contends and how it might organize thinking about the influences that shape American foreign policy.

The interpretation advanced suggests that continuity (and discontinuity) in foreign policy is caused more by role variables than by any other factor. Individual variables are the least powerful sources, with governmental, societal, and external factors—in that order—playing an intermediate role. Hence our interpretation holds that continuity in American foreign policy is most explicable by reference to the powerful characteristics of role-induced behavior within the policy-making system. Note also, therefore, that if change is to come, it is most likely to come from a dramatic shift in the roles policy makers play. The same logic holds for the other source categories, so that we are provided with the outlines of a theory able to account not only for the factors that

---

[2]The ranking proposed here is strikingly similar to the one Rosenau (1966) proposed in his original pre-theoretical formulation. Our only difference is that we have switched the relative positions of the governmental and societal source categories. That switch is explained by the extraordinarily close association between role and governmental variables; roles determine probable behavior of individuals, and government structures mold the kinds of roles that exist. Hence, in an advanced industrial and highly bureaucratized society like the United States, there is an intimate and often indistinguishable link between the institutions of foreign policy making and the role-induced behaviors of individuals within them.

In his subsequent work, Rosenau (1973; see also 1984 for Rosenau's latest statement of the pre-theory's origins and modifications) dropped the distinction between the institutional and role factors by reconceptualizing governmental variables as "the role requirements built into policy-making positions." From that new perspective, the governmental factor would be considered an intervening variable in the sense that it is through this complex network that the demands and supports giving rise to decision making on the part of those in positions of authority in foreign affairs must ultimately pass. Thus the institutional setting would not be considered a source of foreign policy per se, but rather a set of structures that serve "as a filter through which the values that underlie individual, role, societal, and systemic [external] variables must pass" (Rosenau, 1980). Hence, our own conclusions about the relative potencies of the sources of American foreign policy are more consistent with Rosenau's subsequent thinking than with his original pre-theoretical formulation. Ease of exposition, however, persuaded us to treat the sources of American foreign policy as five in number, rather than four, with one additional intervening variable.

[3]Rosenau's (1966) original pre-theory also appended caveats to his ranking of the source categories by introducing the concepts of issue-areas and of penetrated political systems. We will briefly touch on the issue-area below but do not find the concept of penetrated political systems necessary in our effort to understand the process by which American foreign policy is made.

inhibit policy change, but also for those that enhance the prospects for policy innovations.

The pre-theoretical ranking has other uses as well. It raises questions as well as posits partial answers about what matters most. Ranking the source categories stimulates thinking about the causal impact that other combinations might produce. The ranking itself is overly simple, postulating, as it does, a general theory about the factors that affect the overall course of policy, its direction, and rate of change.

Indeed, it is more realistic to assume that *all* the factors affect foreign policy outcomes in very complex ways, and that the precise balance among them will shift depending on an almost infinite set of conditions. This complexity should be acknowledged, and the multitude of ways in which different factors may combine with one another should be considered. For example, the relative weight assigned to the five sources may be different with respect to American policy toward a particular actor (the Soviet Union) than it is for others (Japan, Israel, NATO, the United Nations). A whole host of circumstantial factors might influence these weightings (for instance, are they different in election years?). Nonetheless, by asking which source categories predominate over the others, inferences about the relative potencies of each can be reached because the sources provide the categories with which theorizing about the determinants of foreign policy can commence. Moreover, efforts to construct a theory by ranking the source categories invite consideration of the conditions under which any hypothesized ranking might not hold.

CRISIS: AN INTERVENING VARIABLE?

Conditions of crisis affect the behavior of individuals and induce them to engage in actions they would not otherwise perform. Crises change the way people and governments make decisions and influence the kinds of decisions reached. They thus present situations that may upset "business as usual" and thereby serve to influence the relative potency of the variables that are the sources of foreign policy.

According to one authoritative academic perspective (Hermann, 1972b), a foreign policy crisis may be thought of as "a situation that (1) threatens high-priority goals of the decision-making unit [for example, foreign policy makers], (2) restricts the amount of time available for response before the decision is transformed, and (3) surprises the members of the decision-making unit by its occurrence."

When such a situation arises, how do decision makers proceed? And what happens to the way in which decisions are reached? Charles Hermann (1969b: 416–417) has offered the following hypotheses about decision making in situations characterized by surprise, limited response time, and perceived threats to high-priority goals:

1. The highest level of government officials will make the decision(s) (because of the perceived threat to national goals or interests).

2. Bureaucratic procedures usually involved in foreign policy making will be side-stepped (because the high ranking of decision makers enables them to commit the government to action without the normal deference to bureaucracies).
3. Information about the situation is at a premium (because time limits the ability of decision makers to acquire new information).
4. The basis for selecting among alternatives is often something other than information about the immediate situation (for example, because of the short time, analogies with prior situations may provide the basis for decision).
5. Personal antagonisms among policy makers will remain subdued (because of the felt need for ultimate consensus), although substantive disagreements among them about what to do may occur.
6. Extreme responses are encouraged (because of limited information and the enhanced importance of the personalities of decision makers).
7. Substantial energy following the decision is devoted to gaining support for it from allies and others (because of the uncertainty surrounding the outcome of the decision).

Considerable evidence drawn from in-depth case studies of particular crises and from experimental research supports those hypotheses.[4] The most important finding for our purposes is that crisis situations encourage the centralization of foreign policy making by giving rise to the formation of ad hoc decision-making groups. Crises assign a dominant position to members of the decision-making elite either as individuals or collectively. Perhaps those are the situations President Kennedy had in mind when he reminisced: "The day before my inauguration President Eisenhower told me, 'You'll find that no *easy* problems ever come to the President of the United States. If they are easy to solve, somebody else has solved them.' I found that hard to believe, but now know it is true."

The consequence of ad hoc decision making is that bureaucratic procedures are short-circuited and authority for the decision is redistributed from the usual centers of power in government. Hence, one of the greatest role-induced constraints on decision makers is circumvented. Moreover, crises tend to force decision makers to reorder their priorities. "Crisis alters organizational plans and objectives by disrupting the regular schedule of activities." As a result of crisis, "personnel assignments are reallocated and top-level decision-makers focus their attention exclusively on the crisis, postponing action on other matters that may originally have had a higher priority on their scale of values" (Robinson, 1972). In the context of the Cuban missile situation, many of the decision makers also were "relieved" of their organizational affiliations. Assigned the role of "skeptical generalists," "[t]hey were charged with examining the policy problem as a whole, rather than approaching the issues in the traditional bureaucratic way whereby each man confines his re-

---

[4]See especially Paige's (1968) study of the Korean decision; Allison's (1971) analysis of the Cuban missile crisis; Falkowski's (1978) evaluation of the performance of various presidents and secretaries of state during crises; and the interpretations of crises and threats in Hermann (1972a), McGowan and Kegley (1980), Lebow (1981), and Brecher and Wilkenfeld (1982).

marks to the special aspects in which he considers himself to be an expert and avoids arguing about issues on which others present are supposedly more expert than he'' (Janis, 1972). Finally, evidence from the Korean and Cuban situations suggests that domestic political implications of the crisis situation or intended action are not given their usual explicit attention (Paige, 1972). That is not to say that domestic politics are unimportant.[5] But it does suggest that the societal factor is a less potent explanation of foreign policy outcomes in crisis situations than in, say, general (for example, the Nixon Doctrine) or administrative (for example, whether to recognize a new government) decision situations.

All this means that crisis conditions are unique—that they upset existing decision-making structures and routines, and that they affect the kinds of options that might be seized by opening the door to new initiatives. In short, *crises are opportunities for foreign policy innovation*. Hence, crises, which erupt from external disturbances, can be viewed as potential turning points, which have the capacity to transform the nation's policies.[6] Under such circumstances— and ignoring the external source category for a moment—the relative potency of the (four) explanatory source categories might be altered as follows: (1) individual, (2) role, (3) governmental, and (4) societal.

Again the ranking should be considered as suggestive rather than conclusive. Generally, however, the thinking it reflects is as follows. The individual factor is most potent because of the impetus toward ad hoc decision making by small collectivities that crises engender, and because the responsibility for determining the existence of a crisis situation typically remains in the hands of the chief policy maker, the president, whose personal characteristics can exert a crucial, even decisive, impact. Role factors are next in importance since, despite circumvention of the usual bureaucratic constraints, decision makers still occupy policy-making roles with the attendant responsibility for protecting the interests of the nation. The governmental factor again is closely related to the role factor. In this instance the presidential form of government as it has evolved over time ensures that the executive branch of government will bear primary, probably exclusive, responsibility for dealing with crises. Last in importance is the societal factor. The conditions of short time and surprise (to which we might add secrecy) preclude active involvement by interest groups, the mass media, the attentive public, and so forth (although nongovernmental

[5]Allison (1971) points out that one of the factors giving rise to the perception of the 1962 Cuban situation as a crisis was President Kennedy's feeling that Khrushchev had reneged on his promise not to complicate the president's delicate domestic political situation at the time of the forthcoming congressional elections, in the context of which the president's Republican opponents were calling for sterner measures against Castro's Cuba.

[6]Some historians, for example, have interpreted the Cuban missile crisis as the point at which the nation's foreign policy turned away from the instinct toward nuclear brinkmanship; others see it as the impetus for détente, since it sparked realization of the mutuality of Soviet and American interests. An analogous policy-transforming event occurred with President Carter's definition of the Soviet invasion of Afghanistan as a crisis and with his subsequent call for a reorientation of American foreign policy in response to what he labeled ''the most serious threat to peace since the Second World War.''

members of the elitist foreign policy ''establishment'' may be, on occasion, directly involved). Hence the societal factor will become important only to the extent that decision makers take it into account.

Most difficult to place is the external source category. Its ranking varies, depending on how one conceptualizes a crisis. Crises may be viewed as ''situational variables'' that serve as stimuli to foreign policy decisions, where the decisions themselves are the responses to those stimuli occurring in the external environment (Hermann, 1969a). That perspective would suggest that the external source category is the most important explanation of foreign policy, because it is the external environment that sets in motion the decision-making process that ultimately generates behavior.

In the decision-making process itself, however, the external environment may be somewhat less important. As argued in chapters six and seven, global circumstances help to shape foreign policy options by defining what is possible and probable. But the external environment, and the constraints and opportunities it provides, become relevant to the realization of foreign policy objectives only insofar as decision makers perceive them. In other words, because policy ultimately derives from what policy makers choose, policy makers themselves must perceive the external environment as affecting their choices if the external factor is to be accorded substantial potency in accounting for foreign policy outcomes.

Against that background it is important to recall the pattern of foreign policy described in part two. It is a pattern that suggests very little in the way of constraints—with the possible exception of the need to avoid nuclear war—imposed by the external environment. To be sure, concern for ''world opinion'' and maintaining the support of allies are threads that run through the diplomatic record of the postwar era. In general, however, it would appear that even in an atmosphere punctuated by periodic crises, the external environment placed few constraints on what was perceived to be possible to achieve abroad. Vietnam stands as giant testimony to the danger of this view—and may continue to restrain the options available for consideration in the future.[7] But the important point is that even in crisis situations the external environment would appear not to be more important than the individual factor in determining foreign policy behavior.

So it does matter who is elected or who is appointed to top-level foreign policy positions—at least in crisis situations. Sensitivity to the characteristics of the president and the men and women who surround him is thus an important way to gauge the future of American foreign policy. Such characteristics are not the only things to be aware of, but neither can they be as lightly dismissed as previously suggested.

[7]Congressional fear about U.S. involvement in Angola during the winter of 1975–1976 leading to ''another Vietnam'' is perhaps a case in point, as were the El Salvadorian situation in the early 1980s and the abiding hesitancy of the Reagan administration to expand the level of the American involvement in the Nicaraguan situation in the mid-1980s.

Although crisis situations are occasions that invite policy change, it is questionable whether crises do in fact produce such results. Suspicions that crises may cause disturbances but not real changes in policy are aroused when we note how endemic crises are to international politics. One compilation (Hazlewood, Hayes, and Brownell, 1977) identified as crises over 230 incidents between 1946 and 1975 that in most instances related in some way to U.S. military interests or assets. Hence, the recurrent nature of international crises was made evident; indeed, they erupted an average of eight times annually during this thirty-year period. Nevertheless, there had been continuity in American foreign policy throughout that period. Thus crises did not lead to transitions in the overall pattern of foreign policy as theorized. On the contrary, this evidence suggests the proposition that *whereas crises do indeed present opportunities for policy innovation, the opportunities are seldom seized*. Rather than stimulating new departures, crises more often tend to be "managed" in a way that keeps existing policy intact and preserves the assumptions on which it is based. The propensity for American foreign policy to bounce from one crisis to another—without change in orientation, appears to continue (Oberdorfer, 1983). The reasons are complex.

One of the ironies of crisis situations is that although they remove many of the impediments to policy innovation, the limited time frame within which decisions must be reached precludes careful deliberation of all available alternatives as well as long-range planning. It also inhibits an exhaustive search for complete information on the matter at hand.

In the absence of full information, decision makers reason by analogy. Those analogies provide guidelines for policy actions (May, 1973). When faced with the Soviet pressures on Iran, Turkey, and Greece, which ultimately led to the Truman Doctrine, for example, the Truman administration came to view those events as analogous to developments prior to World War II (especially the Manchurian, Italo-Ethiopian, and Czechoslovakian crises). In the case of the Vietnam embroilment, several inferred historical parallels contributed to American involvement—the "loss" of China, the French defeat at Dienbienphu in Vietnam, concern for the success of communist-inspired wars of national liberation, Korea, and communist behavior in the Quemoy-Matsu, Berlin, and Cuban crises.[8]

---

[8]The important question, then, is how well decision makers are able to use the past. Ernest May is skeptical: "Policy-makers ordinarily use history badly. When resorting to an analogy, they tend to seize upon the first that comes to mind. They do not search more widely. Nor do they pause to analyze the case, test its fitness, or even ask in what ways it might be misleading. Seeing a trend running toward the present, they tend to assume that it will continue into the future, not stopping to consider what produced it or why a linear projection might prove to be mistaken" (May, 1973).

May speaks kindly of Kennedy's imaginative thinking about historical analogies at the time of the Cuban missile crisis, and especially Kennedy's awareness of the dangers of fallacious historical inference. Even in that instance, however, one might be skeptical, for Kennedy, too, relied on historical analogies to guide his response. In his announcement to the nation of the presence of Soviet missiles in Cuba, for example, Kennedy branded the Soviet move a provocative and unjus-

The tendency of decision makers to rely on historical analogy suggests that even in crisis situations decision makers are not completely free of anything other than their personal preferences. Nor are the seemingly all-powerful role constraints within which they normally operate completely absent. Whereas role expectations are perhaps less potent in crises than in other situations, decision makers nevertheless remain confined by them. Among the primary role constraints under which they operate are existing policy goals, consisting of the commitments, practices, and orientations of their predecessors. In fact, faced with the perceived need to do something, decision makers in crises will be especially sensitive to prior commitments, practices, and orientations if for no reason other than that the high-priority goals threatened by crisis situations are embedded within existing policy goals. The tendency to equate successful crisis management with the restoration of precrisis conditions may also be operative.

Nor can we completely dismiss the role constraints of bureaucratic institutions. Howard Lentner's (1972) study of personnel in the State Department's Operations Center, for example, observes that middle-level watch officers in the center play a critical role in selecting and filtering information about potential or actual crisis situations before it is passed on to higher level decision makers. That enables watch officers to ''subtly but surely affect the outcome'' (Hermann, 1972a). More generally, Graham Allison devoted fully a third of his study of the Cuban missile crisis to an explication of the role of bureaucratic organizations in crises. The thrust of his argument is that what bureaucratic organizations can and cannot do limits the range of alternatives from which decision makers can choose in coping with crisis, a premise based on the truism that decision makers ultimately depend on bureaucracies to implement their decisions. Because bureaucracies carry out their tasks according to standard operating procedures, and because the limited time available in crisis situations precludes development of new procedures to deal with new problems, the existing repertoires of bureaucratic organizations effectively define the range of choice available to decision makers. In the case of the Cuban missile crisis, for example, the fact that the Air Force could not guarantee 100 percent accuracy in obliterating Soviet missiles ultimately removed the ''surgical air-strike'' from the list of available action alternatives.

It would also be inappropriate to ignore completely external and societal constraints. Even if we regard crisis as the exogenous variable that requires a foreign policy decision, in the actual decision phase of a specific crisis situation international considerations can be expected to be accounted for in calculations of costs and benefits. Again in the case of the Cuban missile crisis, where decision makers' estimates of the probability of success of each alternative and of the likely reactions of allies, adversaries, and nonaligned nations to

---

tified change in ''the status quo, which cannot be accepted by this country if our courage and our commitment are ever to be trusted again by either friend or foe. The 1930's taught us a clear lesson: aggressive conduct, if allowed to go unchecked and unchallenged, ultimately leads to war.''

each alternative brought the external environment into the decision-making calculations.

Such implicit calculations are likely to be more pronounced than considerations of domestic political consequences, particularly because decision makers can usually count on broad-based support for the actions they initiate. But that does not mean that all of those forces subsumed under the societal source category will be inoperative in crisis situations. The public, the mass media, and interest groups (at least according to the pluralist model) may not be directly involved (but certainly interested—to the extent the crisis is public knowledge) in the interplay of forces leading to decisions. But to the extent that decision makers are drawn from the same political culture, usually from a relatively limited pool of elite members of the "establishment," and go through similar socialization processes, societal factors, too, will place constraints on decision makers' ability to choose courses of action solely on the basis of their personal predispositions.

In the final analysis, then, we can posit that the individual source category is perhaps the most potent explanation of foreign policy outcomes in crisis situations, but it is not the only one. Even crisis situations are affected by constraints imposed by the confluence of explanatory factors. More often than not, whereas the advent of an international crisis enhances dramatically the prospects for policy innovation, crises typically have been managed in such ways as to preserve the parameters of existing policy rather than to alter them.

AN ADDITIONAL CAVEAT: ISSUES AND ISSUE-AREAS

The preceding discussion of the operation of the policy-making process in crisis situations suggests something of the difficulty in assessing the relative influence and importance of the sources of foreign policy. Meaningful and empirically valid generalizations do not come easily because of the large number of factors that intervene in the policy-formation process.

Although many confounding factors exist which can alter the hypothesized ranking of our source categories,[9] the effects of issues stand out in particular. Let us briefly consider their potential impact on our hypothesized ranking of the source categories.

Foreign policy, as we have used the term in this volume, refers to the goals that a nation's officials seek to attain abroad, the values that give rise to those objectives, and the means (instruments) whereby the nation pursues them. Although attention has been given to particular substantive aspects of the nation's objectives with regard to the external environment (particularly in part two), generally speaking we have not been concerned with the substantive issues and the responses of decision makers to them that make up the day-to-

---

[9]The relationship between the source categories, on the one hand, and foreign policy behavior, on the other, may also be affected by changes in *situations*. See Brady (1978) for a discussion of that analytic perspective.

day work of government. In a sense, then, what has been provided is a macrotheoretic view (a theory of the broad general aspects of policy considered as a whole) of the sources of American foreign policy. Using that perspective, we are able to gain considerable insight into the forces that contribute to persistence and continuity in American foreign policy as it has been defined.

But we also know that from the perspective of the work of government, foreign policy is a multifaceted, issue-focused phenomenon. At that level, one easily gains the impression that the broad terms *persistence* and *continuity* do not describe all substantive aspects of foreign policy equally well. Instead, policy with respect to one cluster of issues, such as immigration policy, may be in a state of flux, whereas in another area, such as support of the NATO alliance, persistence and continuity are apt descriptions. Hence, it is appropriate to think of different clusters of issues, or issue-areas, as manifesting differential rates of change over the same period.

And over longer periods of time, it may be that what is defined in the United States as a "critical" foreign policy issue is subject to cyclical variation, with moods determining the degree and length of time in which any particular issue receives attention (Vasquez, 1985). If the salience of an issue peaks and declines in a cyclical fashion, but never remains salient for an extended period of time, then the sources of American foreign policy would also be expected to vary in their relative influence depending on the phase of the cycle at any particular point in time. For instance, how the sources interact to shape American foreign policy would be different during those periods when perceived threats to national security assume prominence on America's foreign policy agenda than during a stage in which energy scarcities or trade deficits became the preoccupations of the moment.

Presumably, the five source factors themselves also contribute to the cyclical swings in the attention given to discrete foreign policy issues. Whereas the five source categories serve collectively in the long run to promote stability in the assumptions underlying postwar American foreign policy, they also may stimulate in the shorter run cyclical changes in the attention particular foreign policy issues tend to receive. Thus there is continuity in the premises of American foreign policy but a cyclical variation in the salience of particular foreign policy issues.

Several examples illustrative of both these short- and long-term processes come readily to mind. We have seen, for instance, that American strategic doctrine has undergone since World War II a fundamental shift from compellence to deterrence, while the nation's commitment to a strong defense posture has remained constant. Similarly, American support for human rights was momentarily awakened in the late 1970s, only to have waned recently, while globalism as a diplomatic orientation has remained intact. With respect to international institutional development, American policy again shows ambivalence, with a clear trend away from support for many transnational organizations (the United Nations, the World Court, UNESCO) but an apparent renewed interest in strengthening the institutional mechanisms through which America's trade problems might be alleviated. The picture that emerges is one of uneven change, with historical continuity in some areas and discontinuity in others. Issues are given only episodic attention.

Turning from issue-cycles to issue-areas, an attempt to develop a complete set of theoretical propositions about issue-areas and foreign policy making (propositions that would define issue-areas in a conceptually and empirically valid way, specify connections among them, and delineate relationships between issue-areas and the sources of foreign policy) is beyond the scope of this book.[10] Yet at least two ideas can be inferred from the issue-area concept that are related to the theme of change and changelessness in foreign policy. One has to do with the relative potency of the source categories; the other with relationships between different issue-areas.

The core idea of the issue-area concept is simple: policies determine politics. That means that the specific issue or policy at stake will determine who will become involved in the process of policy making.[11] If different individuals, groups, or institutions become involved in one set of specific policies but not in another, the effect could be to alter our hypothesized ranking of the source categories in terms of their potency in influencing foreign policy outcomes. Consider, for example, the differences between the processing of a "routine" foreign policy decision, such as whether to recognize a newly arrived military government in a small African state, as compared with a "nonroutine" situation, such as the prosecution of a limited war like Vietnam. In the first case, foreign policy decision makers would normally be allowed to make their own final choices. But in the latter, where the issues more intimately touch the daily lives of Americans, we would expect the matter to be processed much like a domestic issue. In the former case the issue engages a relatively small proportion of the total political system—primarily the specialized foreign affairs government (or perhaps the elitist foreign policy "establishment"). In the latter the societal factor will rise in potency as a larger number of individuals, groups, and institutions both within and outside government become active and attempt to influence the ultimate policy outcome. Because the resources and relationships of many Americans are intimately linked to a nation's prosecution of war, we would expect large segments of the general public, the attentive public, the mass media, and so forth to attempt to influence the government's choice of means and ends in such conflict situations.

If we extend that logic to a more general range of substantive questions, we can hypothesize that matters falling into a category called "noncrisis military-

[10]An especially persuasive case for the empirical utility of the issue-area concept is provided in Ripley and Franklin's (1984) *Congress, the Bureaucracy, and Public Policy*. Theoretical arguments relevant to the concept can be found in Rosenau (1966, 1967); Lowi (1964, 1967, and 1972); Zimmerman (1973); Mansbach and Vasquez (1981); and Underdal (1979).

[11]Note that for a particular actor, an issue will become a factor only when a problem is defined as an issue that needs resolution. Thus, issues are relevant only when they are recognized as such by decision makers.

security issues'' will generally be processed by the foreign affairs government (that is, both role and governmental sources will predominate), with little consideration given to other factors except perhaps the external source category. Included here would be questions of whether to deploy troops to country A, withdraw them from country B, and replace outmoded weapons system X with system Y.

An alternative generalized set of substantive questions might be labeled simply ''economic.'' In those the foreign affairs government would still be critically important, but the societal category would probably supersede the external in importance. Many issues usually thought of as falling under the rubric of ''foreign economic policy'' would fit here (such as the Reagan administration's push to weaken substantially the Foreign Corrupt Practices Act of 1977, which prohibited American businesses from bribing foreign officials and others in order to win export contracts). Military-security issues insofar as they relate to domestic resources and relationships would also fit. Included, for example, would be questions relating to the procurement of new weapons systems and the related question of initial prime contract awards. Those stand in contrast to ''routine'' decisions to continue funding an ongoing weapons system, which are typically made in an incremental fashion. In short, some combination of considerations relating to ''routine-nonroutine,'' ''military-security'' and ''economic policy'' issues would help to account for variations in the relative potency of the sources of American foreign policy when we move beyond (or below) the macrotheoretic view of policy construed in its broadest sense.

A second line of reasoning growing out of the issue-area concept is that we should be sensitive to the effects that change in one issue-area might have on other issue-areas. In the long run, variation in any one component of American foreign policy—however gradual—has implications for other components. Continuity in any one area of policy (for example, economic issues) may retard the rate of change in other areas (for example, the issue of American troops in Europe). Conversely, significant discontinuity in a particular area may increase the prospects for change in other areas. The history of one phase of American efforts to contain Soviet influences illustrates some of these interconnections. Détente was more than the simple relaxation of tensions: accommodations in the military-security sphere were linked inextricably to shifts in the diplomatic and the economic spheres. The 1972 wheat deal was tied to SALT, and both were tied to the level of diplomatic consultation evolving at least since creation of the ''hot line'' in 1963. Conversely, but still to the point, some critics (for example, Pisar, 1977) argue that President Carter's push for human rights in the Soviet Union, which was vigorously opposed by Soviet leaders, impeded progress in achieving long-term Soviet-American agreements on limiting strategic arms. With the inauguration of Reagan, there was still a marked interaction between developments in the military, diplomatic, and economic spheres of Soviet-American relationships, as indicated by the administration's expressed (but largely unrealized) preference for a ''linkage'' approach to American foreign policy toward the Soviet Union and its willingness to remove barriers to trade with the Soviets while at the same time confronting them in the military-political sphere.

Change in any one part of American foreign policy may not stimulate change immediately in others; however, over time significant change in one issue-area may substantially affect others. Thus a dramatic change in any one issue-area may generate substantial amounts of change in other issue-areas as adjustments to the new circumstances engendered by the original policy change are made. The dramatic rate of increase in the price of oil during the OPEC decade, for example, which was tied to the rapid growth of domestic energy consumption since World War II, may be said to have stimulated major changes in the American posture toward the dangerous political situation in the Middle East.

The point is that the different issue-areas that make up American foreign policy may contain within them the seeds of change. The overall pattern may be one of persistence and continuity, but altered conditions in any one issue-area may ultimately stimulate change in another. The result may be adaptation to changing circumstances or conditions in the overall approach of the United States to its external environment. Or, conversely, it may be a cycle of attention and neglect of particular issues in foreign policy.

In addition to shifts within issue-areas, change in foreign policy might be generated by fundamental changes within one or some combination of the five source categories that have been conceptualized as influences on foreign policy. Despite the fact that the source categories examined in this text have served to promote historically observable persistence and continuity, we can hypothesize that policy change, if it is to occur, will occur if there is significant and fundamental change in one or more of the five sources.

But what are the prospects for change in American foreign policy generated by changes in the sources of it? Have domestic and international circumstances changed so substantially throughout the 1980s that they are now exerting pressures for the revision of underlying assumptions? If so, will policy makers respond to the changes and challenges with new adaptive orientations? Or will they, instead, reaffirm the pattern of American foreign policy behavior so dominant since World War II? Our concluding chapter will probe this set of questions about the probable future of American foreign policy.

SUGGESTIONS FOR FURTHER READING

HERMANN, CHARLES F., ed. *International Crises: Insights from Behavioral Research*. New York: Free Press, 1972.

HERMANN, CHARLES F., CHARLES W. KEGLEY, JR., AND JAMES N. ROSENAU, eds. *New Directions in the Study of Foreign Policy*. Boston: Allen and Unwin, 1986.

ROSENAU, JAMES N. "A Pre-theory Revisited: World Politics in an Era of Cascading Interdependence," *International Studies Quarterly* 28 (September 1984): 245–305.

ROSENAU, JAMES N. "Paradigm Lost: Five Actors in Search of the Interactive Effects of Domestic and Foreign Affairs," *Policy Sciences* 4 (December 1973): 415–436.

VASQUEZ, JOHN A. "Domestic Contention on Critical Foreign Policy Issues: The Case of the United States," *International Organization* 39 (Autumn 1985): 606–643.

VASQUEZ, JOHN, A., AND RICHARD W. MANSBACH. "The Issue Cycle: Conceptualizing Long-Term Global Political Change," *International Organization* 37 (Spring 1983): 257–280.

WILKENFELD, JONATHAN, GERALD W. HOPPLE, PAUL J. ROSSA, AND STEPHEN J. ANDRIOLE. *Foreign Policy Behavior.* Beverly Hills, CA: Sage, 1980.

ZIMMERMAN, WILLIAM. "Issue Area and Foreign Policy Process: A Research Note in Search of a General Theory," *American Political Science Review* 67 (December 1973): 1204–1212.

16

AFTER REAGAN: THE FUTURE OF AMERICAN FOREIGN POLICY

> The Soviet Union is the focus of evil in the modern world.
>
> *President Ronald Reagan, 1983*

> Over the last thirty-five years, the evolution of the international system was bound to erode the predominant position the United States enjoyed immediately after World War II. . . . [I]n this disorderly world, the loss of American predominance puts an even greater premium on consistency, determination, and coherence in the conduct of our foreign policy. We have less margin for error than we used to.
>
> *Secretary of State George P. Shultz, 1984*

The past half century of world politics has been one of accelerating change, continual turbulence, and frequent crises. Yet, despite this turmoil, American foreign policy has displayed a remarkable degree of continuity, durability, and stability. The world has changed dramatically, but the assumptions underlying the American approach to it have resisted fundamental change.

As the evidence and opinion summarized in previous chapters of this book have revealed, American foreign policy since the end of World War II has evolved only slowly and incrementally in its response to global changes and challenges. While modest adjustments in America's orientation toward the world beyond its borders are detectable, far more evident is a consistency of outlook and a singularity of purpose. The fundamental assumptions that American leaders have made about the nature of international realities and the appropriate place and position of the United States within the world they define have remained largely intact. To project American power throughout the globe, to oppose the spread of communism, to contain the expansion of Soviet influence, and to rely on extensive military might and intervene in the affairs of others to achieve these objectives have consistently been the ends and means of American foreign policy since Hiroshima. No postwar administration has seriously challenged the *realpolitik* assumptions undergirding the emphasis American foreign policy has repeatedly placed on those premises.

That conclusion is nowhere more apparent than in an assessment of the Reagan administration's foreign policy approach. Its policies have been marked by the same kinds of conflicts, contradictions, and inconsistencies evident in the policies of its predecessors. This ostensible inability to pursue a stable direction has led many observers—beginning with Alexis de Tocqueville in the nineteenth century—to conclude that democratic government is inherently ill suited to the conduct of foreign policy in an often intractable and threatening global environment. When, however, our horizons are cast beyond the headlines of the day and we probe beneath the smiles, the handshakes, and the hassles that routinely engulf America's foreign policy managers as they seek to cope with a world of rapid change, it is clear that globalism, anticommunism, containment, military might, and interventionism have retained their import as the most definitive aspects of the postwar pattern of American foreign policy. The Reagan presidency infused these themes with new vitality and elevated them to new levels of prominence. Its record thus enables us to probe the basic, long-term tendencies in American foreign policy as a way of projecting its future.

In speculating about the future of American foreign policy, we will review and elaborate on the experience of the Reagan administration's efforts to reaffirm and extend the entrenched pattern of postwar American foreign policy thinking. This examination will allow us to consider both the extent to which, and how, Reagan's embrace of an established policy was affected by the five sources of foreign policy analyzed in previous chapters. Does the Reagan experience suggest that the path chosen was to some extent predetermined—with options foreclosed and new departures inhibited while the preservation of previous approaches was encouraged? If so, does the collective force of these sources structure what any administration is likely to do and limit what it can hope to change, even if conventional policy assumptions, however treasured, have become obsolete? Or might future administrations find that the sources of American foreign policy provide opportunities for policy innovation as well as limits? Let us review the record before advancing some predictions.

THE REAGAN ADMINISTRATION'S FOREIGN POLICY: PRINCIPLE VERSUS PRAGMATISM

Ronald Reagan is the most ideologically oriented president to have occupied the White House in the post–World War II era. He is arguably a symbol of the national turn toward the political right as much as he is a cause of it. Regardless, Washington's key policy-making roles have come to be occupied by those subscribing to conservative political values in greater proportion than at perhaps any other time in the preceding half century.

Ronald Reagan's orientation toward foreign policy stems from a few easily identified, innate feelings that have been the driving force of his entire career in public life. Since he first stepped onto the national political stage in support of Barry Goldwater's conservative Republican candidacy for the presidency in 1964, Ronald Reagan has held to the simple proposition that the United States has no more important mission to fulfill than defending the cause of freedom around the world. It is a belief infused with the messianic spirit characteristic of the long heritage of American involvement in world affairs. "I have always believed that this anointed land was set apart in an uncommon way, that a divine plan placed this great continent here between the oceans to be found by people from every corner of earth who had a special love of faith and freedom," exclaimed the president in 1982 and on other occasions since. Globalism and anticommunism as preferred foreign policy orientations flow naturally from and reinforce such beliefs. The president's conservative philosophy is likewise a source of his innate anti-Sovietism: "Reagan's foreign policy is less a response to the outside world than another expression of his struggle to defeat values and trends that challenge conservative truths. The enemy or problem everywhere abroad is Soviet Russia or left-wing totalitarianism opposing conventional American ideals" (Dallek, 1984).

Ronald Reagan proved he was not above pragmatism, however. Shortly after his first election, one observer suggested that beneath the outward charm of the Great Communicator, there were two Ronald Reagans: "Ronald the Radical" and "Ronald the Reasonable." Ronald the Radical "is the doctrinaire true believer and conservative zealot who stokes up right-wing audiences with generous helpings of red meat, whose ideology has a sharp and well-defined edge, and who has longed for the day when the principles he has espoused can be brought to fruition in the Presidency" (Baker, 1981). The strong anticommunist and anti-Soviet overtones of the Reagan administration originate in the conservatism of Ronald the Radical, as suggested above. A vigilant foreign policy posture backed by superior military might are natural outcomes of anticommunism and anti-Sovietism. Against this background, Reagan's relentless drive to augment the nation's military capabilities to enable it figuratively to "stand tall" on the world's stage is understandable.

In contrast to Ronald the Radical,[1] Ronald the Reasonable is, according to the same observer, "the thoroughgoing pragmatist who dwells in the realm of

---

[1]"Ronald the Radical" is a caricature, to be sure, for politicians cannot prosper within the American polity if they deviate too far from the political mainstream—as Barry Goldwater and George McGovern both learned through their abortive runs at the White House. There has been considerable discussion among journalists and scholars as to whether Reagan has helped to create a political spectrum in which conservative values will become more mainstream than has been the case at least since the onset of Franklin Roosevelt's New Deal in the 1930s. At issue is whether the Republican party is replacing the Democratic party as the majority party in the country. Ladd (1985) provides a useful introduction to some of the data and ideas bearing on the proposition that a *partisan realignment* may be unfolding.

the practical and achievable rather than the ideal and optimal.'' Rather than being a blunt-spoken ideologue, Ronald the Reasonable is ''the recognizable half-loaf politician who practices the arts of compromise and builds a consensus around essentially centrist programs and incrementalist policies'' (Baker, 1981).

In the foreign policy arena, globalism, anticommunism, containment, military might, and interventionism have long been centrist values. The record of the Reagan regime demonstrates unequivocally that these elements making up the administration's world view were approached with that combination of ideological purity and political practicality which Reagan himself embodied. That conclusion is based not only on the way in which the administration approached and acted on each of these thematic foreign policy premises, but also in the way it was shaped by and responded to the multiple sources of American foreign policy—the external, societal, governmental, role, and individual variables that collectively determine the direction of the nation's external conduct.

GLOBALISM

From the beginning the Reagan administration continually reaffirmed its commitment to an internationalist posture for the United States. Priority was given to projecting American power abroad, to demonstrating the nation's resolve to retain its global influence, to protecting its interests everywhere, and to tightening the American grip on developments worldwide. Responding to the view of Jimmy Carter and many others that the ascendance of new centers of power in an interdependent world had eroded the nation's ability to exercise influence, Reagan summarized the view of his administration by asserting (January 27, 1981), ''We hear it said that we live in an era of limits to our powers. Well, let it also be understood, there are limits to our patience.'' By implication, the missionary, crusading role of the country, which had fallen into disrepute in the wake of the Vietnam War and the Watergate Affair, was restored; the United States once again perceived itself as responsible for redeeming the world and managing global affairs.

Although Reagan's enthusiasm and ambitious activism seemed to differ markedly from Carter's vacillation and reluctance to act assertively, it is clear with hindsight that both administrations shared similar globalist assumptions. Both endorsed the belief expressed by Zbigniew Brzezinski that the American ''commitment to international affairs on a global scale [has] been decided by history. It cannot be undone, and the only remaining relevant question is what its form and goals will be'' (Brzezinski, 1970).

Conceptually, the Reagan administration's hearty push for an activist American foreign policy represented more an attack on the alleged retreat of American power than it did an attack on the Carter administration's rhetorical emphasis on moralistic ideals (most notably in its human rights stance) in its practice of internationalism. During the 1970s elements suggesting the rise of a neoisolationist mood surfaced. That mood was a reaction to the strain that an unrestrained internationalist foreign policy had placed on the Republic and to the possibility that America's hegemonic position relative to others had begun to decline, perhaps irreversibly. A contraction of the scope of America's global interests and involvements appeared to some to be inevitable, and the challenge (at least as perceived by the Carter administration) became how to accommodate the nation to this deteriorating reality without jeopardizing U.S. security. Lost was any exhilaration about the possibilities of power.

The Reagan administration greeted this alleged retreat of American power and diplomatic presence with repugnance. It rejected the view that the United States was, in a phrase (Nuechterlein, 1985), "overcommitted" and the accommodative disengagement it implied. It effectively repealed the Nixon Doctrine, which had acknowledged the diminished capacity of the Untied States either to control global developments everywhere or to assume responsibility for them, believing instead that no corner of the global system lay outside American interests and that no issue on the global agenda should be left unattended if it touched in any way the security interests of the United States.

> The Reagan philosophy . . . represented a radical departure from the foreign policies of the previous decade. Presidents Nixon, Ford and Carter had consistently, albeit in different ways, conducted foreign policies that were adjusting to the changed world. Each pursued an active diplomacy to compensate for the diffusion of international power that had become so evident by the late 1960s. Ronald Reagan reversed the logic: Washington's policies should not have to adjust to the world—a strong reassertive America could make the world adjust to Washington. (Gelb and Lake, 1985: 466)

The Reagan administration's assertive, global activism was consistent with its ideological conservatism. In another sense, however, American involvement in world affairs may no longer be reversible, globalism no longer a matter of choice. Instead, globalism may now be a necessity created by the cumulative impact of decisions made over the previous forty years, regardless of the ideological lens through which different administrations might view the world.

The Reagan brand of globalism is different, however. For three decades following World War II the responsibility for world affairs that the United States took upon itself was consistent with an internationalist orientation that supported international institutions, respect for the rule of (international) law, and economic interdependence, among other things. Globalism meant internationalism, which implied support for multilateralism, not unilateralism.

The Reagan administration shifted the emphasis. Today it is the United States, a chief architect and long-time supporter of the United Nations, which is among its most outspoken critics and niggardly financial backers. The United States has withdrawn from the United Nations Educational, Scientific and Cultural Organization (UNESCO) and has threatened to withdraw from several other U.N. agencies. Relations with the World Bank group, the major international lending agencies in the world, have often been strained, and those with the major regional organizations (such as the Organization of American States) are floundering, with external challenges and internal dissent converging behind America's retreat from multilateralism. The administration continues to profess support for the principle of free trade underlying postwar economic internationalism but selectively violates it. International law is transgressed when Nicaraguan ports are mined and then flouted with the announcement that any attempt by the World Court—which the United States also helped to found—to bring the United States to task for its behavior in this case or others like it will be ignored. The president of the United States warns against placing too much faith in treaties in general—and in those with the Soviet Union in particular—and the Law of the Sea Convention, negotiated by three administrations in the largest multilateral negotiating forum in history, is rejected. And while a majority of Americans approved the invasion of Grenada, ''it was left to British prime minister Margaret Thatcher to remind the White House: 'Whether I like or dislike a regime, I do respect other people's boundaries. *We* uphold international law' '' (Hughes, 1985–86).[2]

Global activism remains a tenet of American foreign policy. But egged on by the highest echelons of government, the values embodied in the ''international ethos''—peace, collective security, freedom, justice, dignity, growth, progress, and respect for the opinions of humankind—have, in the words of the president of the Carnegie Endowment for International Peace, Thomas L. Hughes, ''pretty well exhausted themselves in mainstream American political life. Traditional internationalist themes are no longer significant outlets for political idealism in the United States. Instead, they are the objects of derision and contempt'' (Hughes, 1985–86; compare Shultz, 1985). International institutions are now perceived to be obstacles—not, as in the past, tools—to the promotion of American foreign policy goals. Accordingly, multilateralism has been challenged by global unilateralism.[3]

---

[2]These and other ideas regarding the Reagan administration's retreat from multilateralism are explored in greater detail in Hughes (1985–86), from whom the foregoing is in part drawn. Garten's (1985) overview of Reagan administration foreign economic policy provides much additional supporting evidence for the retreat-from-multilateralism proposition, and Krauthammer's (1985b) analysis of the sources of this transition is insightful.

[3]Reflecting sensitivity to the charge of pursuing a go-it-alone foreign policy, John Poindexter, Reagan's national security adviser, rejected what he labeled ''global isolationism'' in a May 1986 speech, insisting that ''The most secure peace . . . is the kind that is protected not by a distant superpower but by the efforts of free peoples working together on problems that affect them directly. . . . America wants to cooperate with others because that's what works—because that is the best way of protecting the peace and freedom that serve both our interests and theirs.''

In fact, the administration had reason to wonder whether its allies shared that conviction. Speaking before the British Parliament in 1982, Reagan echoed themes from Britain's wartime Prime Minister Winston Churchill when he urged upon the Western nations a ''crusade for freedom.'' However, the United States found itself without allied support for its policies opposing the sale of energy technology to the Soviet Union, countering the alleged supply of Soviet and Cuban weapons to pro-Marxist forces in Nicaragua and El Salvador, and the isolation of Libya, accused of having engaged in ''armed aggression against the United States'' by supporting Palestinians who butchered more than a dozen travelers in terrorist attacks in Rome and Vienna during the 1985 Christmas holidays. Later, when the United States retaliated militarily against alleged Libyan-

ANTICOMMUNISM

Anticommunism has been a persistent and dominant theme of American foreign policy throughout the postwar decades. During much of that time discussions of American national interests and conceptions of American foreign policy were couched routinely in the language of ideology—of opposition both to the communist world view and to what was perceived to be its global expansionist tendencies. Indeed, the record of diplomatic pronouncements by American statesmen during this period is testimony to the tenacity of the anticommunist theme. American foreign policy has focused on the communist threat to the exclusion of other potentially important issues and problems that seemed to have no direct bearing on the competition between capitalism and communism.

The hold of anticommunist thinking on the making of American foreign policy was never stronger than during Reagan's occupation of the White House. The administration chose to view nearly every international development through the prism of anticommunist ideology; every event that threatened to disturb the global status quo was traced to the revolutionary activities of a supposedly coordinated communist movement. Whether an uprising by the left against their oppressors or rightist terrorism by nationalists pursuing national causes, the interpretation was the same: communism was responsible.

Behind the propensity to ascribe inordinate power to the force of communist states was a Manichean world view (see Glad, 1983). Communism—the perceived "focus of evil in the modern world"—was seen as the source of the world's afflictions, a force which, in Reagan's view, it was America's duty not just to contain, but to eliminate. Confronting that evil has given American foreign policy its primary purpose.

From this stance it is but a short step to accepting repressive regimes that deny freedom to their own people but voice opposition to Marxist principles. Thus administration spokesmen in the early 1980s dismissed the denial of basic rights to people in South Africa, Argentina, Chile, the Philippines, Haiti, El Salvador, and elsewhere as beyond the purview of American concern. Dictators were once again embraced by the United States. As Carl Rowan, former head of the United States Information Agency, observed (March 8, 1981), "The message is clear to the dictators and would-be tyrants of the world. If you claim to be anticommunist, the Reagan administration is not going to give you any trouble." As in the past, an unintended product was reinforcement of unpopular, often undemocratic governments in other nations, which laid the basis for eventual domestic strife often backed by leftists and for a virulently anti-American posture among those who perceived themselves victimized by U.S.-backed regimes—the very outcomes most feared. The generally positive

---

sponsored terrorism, the Thatcher government in Britain, in what proved a controversial decision, provided support for U.S. warplanes, but France refused them overflight privileges.

role the United States played in the removal from power of Ferdinand Marcos in the Philippines and Jean-Claude Duvalier in Haiti, widely regarded as tyrannical exploiters of their own people, stand out so clearly precisely because they differ so markedly from the general rule.

A closely related area of concern was United States relations with governments embracing socialism and Marxism. The reassertion of anticommunism in American foreign policy was elevated to the status of a new principle: the Reagan Doctrine. The Doctrine sought to take American foreign policy beyond the confines of the Truman Doctrine to the next logical level: U.S. policy would no longer merely defend states threatened by communist insurgency; hereafter it would also actively assist anticommunist "freedom fighters" everywhere. As Reagan announced in his State of the Union address in early 1985: "We must not break faith with those who are risking their lives on every continent from Afghanistan to Nicaragua to defy Soviet-supported aggression and secure rights which have been ours from birth. . . . Support for freedom fighters is self-defense." In encouraging anticommunist insurgencies by supporting resistance forces and liberation movements active in communist states and Marxist-dominated regimes in developing countries, the Reagan administration threatened to make concrete the empty rhetoric of the Dulles era, during which "roll back" of the "iron curtain" was sometimes threatened. To roll back the gains of Soviet imperialism, the Reagan Doctrine revised the containment resolution by moving from a defensive to an offensive foreign policy orientation. "In effect," Krauthammer (1986) observed, "ten years after Vietnam, a coherent policy reasserting the return of active American intervention in the world has been formulated."

A number of troublesome consequences may be associated with this aggressive approach. First, it undermines the moral basis of American foreign policy. By engaging in the very conduct believed to be so unprincipled when practiced by America's adversaries, it erodes the distinction between the United States and the Soviet Union and jettisons the U.S. claim to the high moral ground in world politics. Second, a defeat for communism is not necessarily a victory for democracy. As one observer put it, "in any situation the simple fact that insurgents are battling a Soviet-supported government is not a good enough reason to support them" (Solarz, 1985). Placing an opportunistic tyrant into power, albeit an anticommunist one, does not promote America's professed interest in the creation of democratic institutions throughout the world. Third, if freedom is a universal right, it invites foreign intervention against dictatorial regimes supported by the United States as well as those supported by the Soviet Union. Those who would deny others' freedoms come from the right as well as the left of the political spectrum. Finally, the dangers of such an aggressive approach are not inconsequential. The assertive practice of anticommunism poses the risk of escalation to open hostility with a militarily potent Soviet Union.

In principle, the Reagan Doctrine is universal in scope. In practice, it has been supplied selectively. CIA-supplied covert aid to the rebels fighting the

Soviet-backed Marxist regime in Afghanistan is an open secret. Nicaragua was subjected to a trade embargo, and nonmilitary support (and projected military aid) of the counterrevolutionaries seeking to topple the Sandinista regime was a matter of public policy. But in Mozambique the United States openly sided with the Marxist regime, even asking Congress to support "nonlethal" military aid to help the Marxist government defeat a non-Marxist insurrection, presumably in an effort to demonstrate the rewards of cooperation with the United States. In Angola U.S. aid to anti-Marxist forces was not forthcoming until 1986, and then in circumstances that led critics to question sharply the wisdom of the decision (see Solarz, 1986); in Kampuchea only $5 million was approved for the noncommunist resistance forces opposing Vietnamese troops there; and in Ethiopia, where a variety of Marxist and non-Marxist insurgent forces had for a decade sought to overthrow the Marxist government of a country once firmly within the Western camp, no known United States effort to assist their cause militarily was made. (The government, on the other hand, benefited from American food aid designed to cope with widespread famine in Ethiopia.) In Poland, the very heartland of the communist camp, nothing was done to exploit the crisis of 1981–1982 as a way of rolling back communism and doing in the evil empire. Nowhere is the contrast between principle and practice more glaring. Whereas the Reagan Doctrine speaks of the need to promote freedom on a universal basis, apparently Soviet colonialism is to be dismantled only at the periphery, where the costs and risks are modest. "This gap between the doctrine's universal aspirations and its particular applications is a source of frustration to its more ardent advocates; to others it is cause for relief" (Rosenfeld, 1986). Thus, whereas the Reagan administration's rhetorical support of "freedom fighters" is grounded in the president's belief that this period is "a critical turning point in the struggle between totalitarianism and freedom" (May 17, 1985), staunch conservatives could still conclude, as did Norman Podhoretz (1984), that "Mr. Reagan's foreign policy is indistinguishable from Mr. Carter's."

CONTAINMENT

For decades rivalry with the Soviet Union has dominated American diplomacy, coloring all aspects of its foreign policy. That focus has been challenged by some policy makers. It has also been challenged by the rise of important new issues in world politics, which either do not involve the Soviet Union directly or require cooperation with it. Issues such as arms control, the North-South split, energy and food security, balance-of-trade and payments deficits, and resurgent Third World nationalism have all demanded attention and, in the view of some, have stimulated the need for reordering the foreign policy priorities of the United States.

The Carter administration sought to bring those challenges and new issues into the national spotlight, but its emphasis on relations with the Soviet Union was uninterrupted. Although President Carter believed that cooperation with the Soviet Union was possible, he described the essence of the Soviet-centric thrust of American foreign policy and the containment foreign policy strategy that sustains it in an address at the U.S. Naval Academy in 1978: "We must realize that for a very long time our relationship with the Soviet Union will be competitive."

Initially the Reagan administration refused to take advantage of opportunities to collaborate in areas where American and Soviet interests intersected, and almost daily the United States went to new lengths to reinforce an unremittingly militant, confrontational posture toward the Soviet Union. The bitter antagonism characteristic of U.S.-Soviet relations from the end of World War II until the 1962 Cuban missile crisis was again evident, and some of the toughest language in recent history was used.

Behind the effort to project (for domestic as well as foreign consumption) the image of a resolute and unswerving policy toward the Soviets stood the conviction that the Soviet Union was a menace. "The Soviet Union underlies all the unrest that is going on," declared an alarmist Ronald Reagan in December 1980, adding, "If they weren't engaged in this game of dominoes, there wouldn't be any hotspots in the world." The hostility underlying that view was revealed later, when Reagan branded the Soviet Union as "an evil empire." In granting the Soviet Union "most favored enemy" status, the Reagan administration through its verbal assaults expressed its fears while simultaneously reaffirming a belief that has undergirded American foreign policy for decades. Secretary of State Haig expressed the position in this way: "A major focus of American policy must be the Soviet Union . . . because Moscow is the greatest source of international insecurity today . . . and the greatest danger to world peace."

Early in his first administration Reagan added another novel twist to old formulations of the anticommunist threat with the argument that communism may be a transitory historical phenomenon whose time had passed. Speaking at Notre Dame University in May 1981, Reagan argued:

> The years ahead will be great ones for our country and for the cause of freedom. The West will not contain communism; it will transcend communism. We will not bother to denounce it. We'll dismiss it as a sad, bizarre chapter in human history whose last pages are even now being written.

A few weeks later the president branded communism an "aberration—it's not a normal way of living for human beings," while his secretary of state, Alexander Haig, charged that the Soviet Union was suffering from "spiritual exhaustion" and showing "clear signs of historic decline."

The administration's purpose in downgrading Soviet communism appeared to be to change its image in the eyes of other nations. By boasting of the virtues of the American way of life, the administration also gave its blessing to the long-standing tendency of the United States to pursue its foreign policy objectives with a crusading, self-righteous, zeal. Yet critics wondered about the wisdom of laying down so bold a challenge to the nation's historic adversary. Might not the Soviet Union eventually react with a more aggressive posture in order to prove the fallacy of the administration's charge that it was weak? The dangers of provoking the Soviet bear, they warned, were all the more ominous since, whatever its other weaknesses might be, the Soviet Union had managed to build enormous military power.

If the goal of containing the Soviet Union was unoriginal, the means selected to accomplish the task were likewise unimaginative. Two tactics were outlined. First, the administration pledged to resurrect Henry Kissinger's "linkage" strategy, meaning that U.S. behavior toward the Soviet Union would be tied directly to Washington's assessment of Moscow's activities anywhere in the world and that cooperation on such issues as arms control, trade expansion, and the like would be contingent on the willingness of the Soviet Union to curb what Washington saw as its expansionist appetite. Second, it proposed to confront Soviets with preponderant military strength.

Linkage was somehow still born. Negotiations were eventually begun with the Soviets on controlling both strategic and intermediate-range nuclear forces—although the primary impetus, it seems, was growing domestic fear of the administration's warlike posturing. And these were suspended in 1983 with the Soviet walk-out after the NATO allies proceeded with deployment of the very intermediate-range forces about which the Soviets had hoped to strike a bargain. Secretary of State Shultz and Soviet Foreign Minister Gromyko agreed in early 1985 to commence new arms control negotiations, but it took the Geneva Summit initiative in November 1985 (and the promise of two subsequent summits) to infuse the arms control process with the prospect of meaningful progress once more. That step was not linked to Soviet aggression in Afghanistan and elsewhere, however. Early in 1981, in fact, the administration lifted the grain embargo placed on the Soviet Union by the Carter administration without gaining any Soviet concessions. And two years later it refused to retaliate against the Soviet Union for shooting down a Korean civilian airliner (killing all of its nearly 300 passengers) by abrogating a new grain agreement concluded only a week before. Furthermore, the administration endorsed the provisions of SALT II (even dismantling older nuclear submarines to remain within its limits) at the same time that it publicly castigated the Soviets for violating that treaty and threatened to take the United States beyond its limits. The overriding interest in pursuing a new arms accord signaled Reagan's apparent desire to avoid being stigmatized by historians as the first American president since Truman to fail to reach an agreement on the control of nuclear weapons with the Soviets. Ronald the Reasonable was nowhere more apparent, as the boundaries defining linkages were expediently relaxed.

Besides linkage, the second strategy for restraining the Soviets was to meet their perceived threat by challenging them with force and with the risk of devastation. The essence of that cowboy spirit, especially prevalent in Reagan's first term in office, was captured in Defense Secretary Caspar W. Weinberger's claim (May 14, 1981) that ''we have to be prepared . . . to exploit the aggressor's weaknesses, wherever we might find them.'' Conflict with the Soviet Union was not to remain localized. If the Soviets were to attack in the Middle East, for example, the United States might choose to respond in any number of other locales should American superiority permit it. Fortunately, that proposition was not put to the test, but the belief that the administration's rearmament program (about which more is said below) had successfully moderated Soviet behavior was underscored by Reagan's assessment (December 2, 1985) of the Geneva summit: ''The progress we made at Geneva was possible only because in the past five years we have been determined to make America stronger.''

The Reagan administration's approaches toward the containment of Soviet influence were paths that had been beaten before. New intensity marked their application rhetorically, but practice suggested much greater selectivity. Reagan's approaches nonetheless perpetuated still another aspect of the ''troubled coexistence'' (Ulam, 1985) in Soviet-American relations: even after decades of intense and highly dangerous competition, each superpower ''remains indifferent to the effect of its moves on the other, and eager to blame the other for all that goes wrong'' (Hoffmann, 1980).

MILITARY MIGHT AND INTERVENTIONIST MEANS

To address what is fundamentally a political problem—namely, the containment of Soviet influence—the Reagan administration turned to an extraordinary extent to reliance on military power, as the foregoing suggests. It reiterated a familiar and dominant tenet of American thinking about the best way for the country to cope with its most basic foreign policy problems: that defense policy is an adequate substitute for foreign policy. As Under Secretary of Defense Fred C. Iklé put it, ''[M]ilitary strength is . . . the backbone of diplomacy.'' The president himself articulated the belief shortly after his first election: ''The only thing the cause of peace has to fear is fear itself. We must build peace upon strength. Only if we are strong will peace be strong.''

The contours of Reagan's militant orientation toward foreign policy problems were defined sharply. The most expensive peacetime expansion of the military budget in American history was launched. Reagan increased defense spending by 50 percent (in constant dollars) in his first five years in office; more than $1 trillion was spent on defense (a figure that not so coincidentally amounted to the level by which the national debt increased during that same period). That represented a ''military tax'' of more than $16,000 on each of the nation's 62 million families.

Those who remembered how vehemently Reagan had campaigned against what he labeled the Democratic opposition's proclivity to ''throw money at social problems'' were struck by the absence of clear objectives or a coherent plan for how his own defense allocation was to be spent. The initiative took on the appearance of a large pool of money in search of a policy. As one critic argued:

> Defense has become the one public problem to be solved by continued budget increases. In any other policy matter—health, housing, transportation—a prescription to increase the federal budget indefinitely by seven per cent a year without demonstrating the specific need for or utility of the items purchased would not be taken seriously. The defense budget is peculiarly susceptible to such a gross approach because neither generals nor legislators really know how much is enough. (Barnet, 1981: 52)

If there was a plan, it evolved piecemeal. The administration first placed primary emphasis on its desire to upgrade the land-based missile leg of the nation's strategic triad. To close the "window of vulnerability" to Soviet nuclear attack at first seemed a preoccupation and a rationale, but then receded from attention.

Deployment of the MX missile, dubbed "Peacekeeper" by the administration, was thought to be the anewer to the vulnerability of the Minuteman III fixed-base missile force central to the "window of vulnerability" metaphor. But no basing mode was ever devised that would make the new missile less vulnerable to Soviet attack and thus able to survive a potential Soviet first strike, than was the Minuteman, and the fifty that Congress finally seemed willing to approve were only half what the administration sought. The MX was thus unable to close the gap between the theory of the window of vulnerability and the reality of what the MX could (or could not) accomplish. The Scowcroft Commission had recommended development of a single-warhead mobile missile. The MX would become a bargaining chip in negotiations with the Soviets and an effort would be made to convince them to embrace a similar path to the mutually beneficial goal of maintaining stable deterrence. But that approach was undercut when the president proposed to Soviet General Secretary Mikhail Gorbachev during the 1985 Geneva summit that mobile missiles be banned. Emphasis by then turned to the "Star Wars" Strategic Defense Initiative, a perhaps impossible quest to remove the threat of nuclear annihilation through extremely costly and as yet unknown and untried military technology. Meanwhile, the "window of vulnerability" will remain wide open well into the future.

The administration's unilateralist and militant thrust was also apparent in its approach to the Third World, whose importance was viewed primarily in terms of its role in the East-West conflict. Support for multilateral institutions was cut, with preference given to bilateral aid and solo performances, like the Caribbean Basin Initiative and expanded support for Central America, where more aid was disbursed between 1981 and 1983 than in the preceding eighteen years (Garten, 1985: 553). Furthermore, an increasing proportion of the economic aid package was in the form of security supporting assistance, while military aid and the sale of arms to those perceived to need them or otherwise willing to pay for them remained consistent priorities. The purpose of arms sales abroad, as articulated by Under Secretary of State James L. Buckley, was to "complement and supplement our own defense efforts and serve as a vital and constructive instrument of American foreign policy." Arms transfers would also be used as instruments to "face up to the realities of Soviet aggrandizement."

In conformity with the martial thrust of Reagan's foreign policy, the administration expressed little hesitation about conveying its apparent willingness to employ military instruments to protect American interests overseas. "Those who choose to live by the sword can expect to die by it," warned Reagan's first ambassador to the United Nations, Jeane Kirkpatrick. The threat that the administration would use force to get its way was consistent with past policy, but the renewed willingness to speak and act that way affected the diplomatic atmosphere. The mining of Nicaraguan harbors in early 1984 and the snatching of an Egyptian airliner from the night skies over the Mediterranean in 1985 following the terrorist capture of the Italian liner *Achille Lauro*, acts believed by many to contravene international law, also colored the diplomatic atmosphere. So, too, did the administration's hints that it believed a nuclear war might be winnable. At the same time, the capacity of the United States to wage extended conventional war worldwide began to be restored; concern for developing counterinsurgency capabilities was renewed; the Carter Doctrine, which pledged the use of military force if necessary to maintain a free flow of oil from the Persian Gulf region, was reaffirmed; the frequency with which military force short of war was used as an instrument of political persuasion increased sharply; and the CIA was "unleashed" from restraints placed earlier on its covert activities abroad. The use of military force against Grenada in 1983 and Libya in 1986 showed that the administration was prepared to act on its threats (even if the targets hardly demonstrated American resolve or provided evidence of U.S. might).[4] In all of these ways the Reagan team sought to demonstrate that the "Vietnam syndrome" had been cast aside—that the United States had lost its aversion to military and other forms of intervention that had developed in the wake of the Southeast Asian tragedy.

Ambiguity marked the administration's behavior nonetheless. U.S. Marines were airlifted to Beirut to participate in a multilateral peace-keeping force, and the president declared after a terrorist bombing that killed many of them that the Marines were there to protect "vital interests" of the United States. But when their mission, while never clear, seemed to become unattainable, they were conveniently withdrawn (just before the prime 1984 presidential primary election season).

---

[4]Reagan's predecessor, Jimmy Carter, might be remembered by history as the first president since Herbert Hoover not to send American troops into combat, although eight American servicemen did lose their lives in 1980 during the ill-fated mission designed to rescue American hostages in Teheran.

The withdrawal of the Marines seemed consistent with a "lesson of Vietnam" learned by at least some: "if we can't win, get out." That is a less bold interventionist thrust than might otherwise be ascribed to the Reagan administration. It is consistent with the Weinberger defense doctrine, one of the very few enunciations of national security policy made since Reagan's election in 1980. In a speech on "The Uses of Military Power" in late 1984, Secretary of Defense Weinberger, drawing on the lessons of Korea and Vietnam, suggested that United States military forces should be committed to combat only when vital interests are at stake, when the political and military objectives are clearly defined, when the United States has "the clear intention of winning," and when the support of Congress and the American people is assured. Those are difficult requirements to meet, which is perhaps why the Pentagon was often seen as the home of the doves in the Reagan administration, with the hawks in the White House and the State Department. The irony is that the military tools available to the Pentagon had grown dramatically even while their use was approached cautiously. "It seems as if Secretary Weinberger believes that having more American arms will speak for itself, deter challenges and obviate the need to actually use force in the first place," observed Gelb and Lake (1985).

The conflict between hawks and doves, and the ambivalence in the administration's otherwise strident posture, is illustrated in the dilemma posed by terrorism and those believed to sponsor it, particularly Libya.

Since coming to office in 1981, Reagan was committed to containing Libyan radicalism and Libyan-sponsored terrorism. Navy war planes downed two Libyan jets in 1981 that had challenged the right of the United States to fly over the Gulf of Sidra. AWACS electronic surveillance aircraft were used in 1983 to monitor Libyan threats to Chad and the Sudan. A trade embargo was placed on Libya and its financial assets frozen in retaliation in January 1986, for its alleged complicity in the Rome and Vienna airport massacres the previous month (in that context Reagan described Libyan leader Colonel Muammar Qaddafi as "flaky" and branded him a "barbarian"). But military intervention was slow to follow.[5] Not until the administration claimed to have the "smoking gun" following a terrorist bombing of a West Berlin discotheque later that year did the administration act.

Weinberger and Secretary of State Shultz openly feuded about the wisdom of military action. Shultz, who felt especially strongly about terrorism, preferred the military option, while Weinberger, concerned about practical questions as well as larger strategic issues, opposed it. *Inaction* has a natural ally in a nation with multiple interests, each of which are protected by powerful bureaucratic organizations. An important lesson of five years of failed efforts to

---

[5]Iran was implicated in the 1983 truck bombing of Marine headquarters in Beirut. Other than adding Iran to the list of nations that have "repeatedly provided support for acts of international terrorism," however, little is known to have been done to retaliate against the Khomeini regime. See Lake (1985) for a comparative assessment of the Carter and Reagan records in connecting means to objectives in their treatment of radical regimes.

deal with Qaddafi is that "it demonstrates the pitfalls of trying to conduct an assertive foreign policy in a democracy with diverse bureaucratic and foreign policy interests" (Kemp, 1986). In the real world, interventionism is an instrument of policy that may be set aside in the face of other realities, even by an administration committed to the view that "it could make the world adjust to Washington."

Putting aside the sources for hesitation and restraint in the Reagan administration's actual diplomatic practice, the principles it espouses reaffirm a cluster of deeply instilled American beliefs: strength produces peace, might yields influence, weapon superiority can both deter and compel, the capacity to destroy is the capacity to control, the price of military preparedness is never too high, and political problems are susceptible to military solutions.

THE SOURCES OF CONTINUITY IN AMERICAN FOREIGN POLICY

What forces reinforced so strongly the postwar version of American foreign policy embraced by the Reagan administration? Are those forces so potent as to preclude the possibility of reorienting American foreign policy in a world seemingly in constant flux? Or can there be found in the changing circumstances of world and American domestic politics the kinds of stimuli necessary to accommodate American foreign policy to emergent international circumstances?

The balance sheet on forces now at work at home and abroad yields no sure conclusions. Even when we move beyond the rhetoric and deeds of the Reagan administration, there is little on the horizon that leads one to believe the patterns of globalism, anticommunism, containment, military might, and interventionism will not be perpetuated well into the future. The world views of the nation's leaders, Republican and Democrat alike, are clearly compatible with the interests and values that have made those tenets so durable. Furthermore, the combination of internal and external factors that influence American foreign policy appear destined to interact with one another in such a way that departures from past foreign policy patterns, if they occur at all, will be infrequent, modest, and short lived. While the forces that influence foreign policy are thus likely to restrain a future administration's excesses, the prevailing world view is also likely to promote continuity with the past rather than encourage deviations from it.

Any administration's foreign policy reflects the character of the man sitting in the innermost sanctuary of American power, the Oval Office. A future president's *individual* qualities, whatever they may be, are likely to influence the style of future policy. But this effect is also likely to be temporary, as the pressures of the office begin to take their toll on even the most cherished of the president's policies and programs. Ronald Reagan demonstrates the pattern.

Although the most ideologically motivated of all recent presidents and more popular than most, even he found it necessary to bend to the force of competing political pressures and to act as a pragmatic politician, as noted in the preceding discussion. The art of successful presidential leadership may be reinforced by personal qualities, but it is ultimately secured by a capacity for flexibility, not ideological purity or idiosyncratic flair.

Reagan also makes clear that the president is not the personification of the state. A newly elected president's capacity to accomplish goals—is limited by the constraints imposed by *role* factors. The priorities and policies of his predecessors, the actions and preferences of the individuals he selects to implement policy, and his own role conception will all reduce the prospects for fundamental change.

The profiles of those selected for foreign policy-making roles historically have been strikingly similar. As the nation's political and economic center of gravity continues to shift to the South and West, members of the liberal Eastern "establishment," who have guided American foreign and defense policy for more than four decades, may be less in evidence in subsequent administrations, but the players selected to manage the nation's external relations will tend to share the sentiments of the president who alone has the power to appoint them. Presumably, this can give a president some room for maneuver and control in foreign affairs.

It is instructive to note that the selection of key personnel on the basis of their ability to be loyal team players was the Reagan administration's approach to overcoming potential bureaucratic intransigence—before it could develop. But loyalty to the president's formulations of the national agenda did not prevent the inevitable struggle for power among ambitious men and women. True to role theory, the president's players fought repeatedly and openly among themselves, compromising the day-to-day effectiveness, coherence, and consistency of the country's foreign policy. The resignations of three national security advisers and one secretary of state—all in frustration—dramatized the extent of the in-fighting and its untoward consequences. The intense and prolonged battle between Secretary of State Shultz and Secretary of Defense Weinberger over the administration's policies toward the Soviet Union, arms control, and terrorism, among others, demonstrated that even the most ideologically homogeneous administration is prone to turn the policy-making process into a battleground. Policy innovation is not a characteristic product of such conflict-ridden processes. Nor is it likely that a new administration will be able to escape the syndrome; as in the past, bureaucratic battles and sabotage will continue to undermine the ability of the United States to chart a new foreign policy course.

A new president's success will also be circumscribed by the nature of the *government* he or she is elected to run. The elaborate, overlapping bureaucratic machinery of the foreign affairs government is resistant to streamlining, management, and coordination. Often this is for good reason. As one observer put it in commenting on Reagan's vow to "get government off the backs of people":

> Bureaucrats do not climb onto the backs without a boost from interest groups and members of Congress. They do not write regulations because they are malevolent but because someone wants those rules on the books. . . . Congress, in the interest of appearing responsive to public revulsion with large and complicated government, may tinker a little here and streamline a little there, but the basic structure of alliances will remain intact. (Baker, 1981: 160)

Nevertheless, to a considerable extent, the governmental machinery is beyond presidential control.

> Presidents operate on the brink of failure and in ignorance of when, where, and how failure will come. They do not and cannot possibly know about even a small proportion of government activity that bears on their failure. They can only put out fires and smile above the ashes. They don't know what's going on—yet they are responsible for it. And they feed that responsibility every time they take credit for good news not of their own making. (Lowi, 1985b: 190)

Add to this an independent-minded Congress with a propensity to act as much as an obstacle to than as an initiator of new departures in foreign policy, and it is clear that the prospect that American foreign policy will move boldly in new directions is remote at best.

Ultimately, a new president's ability to work his will in Congress on foreign and domestic matters alike will be influenced by the support his policies enjoy among the American people. For just as Congress provides different federal bureaucracies with influential friends and allies, its generally parochial viewpoint makes it particularly sensitive to pressures from constituents. Indeed, the potential influence of *societal* forces in a globally interdependent world is especially potent, for under such circumstances foreign policy is often little more than an extension of domestic policy. Different groups within American society are driven to attempt to influence the shape of foreign policy, and presidents are tempted to take foreign policy positions primarily for their public impact, for in a highly politicized domestic environment presidents are inclined to resist everything but temptation. Politics does not stop at the water's edge.

Reagan's 1984 reelection is illustrative. It was fundamentally a personal victory; evidence demonstrates that many Americans who voted for the incumbent president did not approve of many of his specific policies. That experience illustrates once again that even for a president who enters office with an electorate favorably disposed toward him and his avowed objectives, American society will still provide formidable obstacles to radical policy innovation. Single-issue special-interest groups and political action committees will continue to press their causes; and public opinion, always potentially fickle, may be expected to turn sharply against a president when the costs of ambitious and disruptive new programs begin to be felt. When that occurs, organized interests within American society will turn with renewed vigor to an assertive if parochial Congress for protection from the threats they perceive to their welfare. The status quo, accordingly, has a strong ally in the influences emanating from American society. The paradox exists that whereas the American public clearly desires and rewards presidential leadership, the forces comprising the American political culture in conjunction with its fragmented, pluralistic political system thwart the exercise of presidential leadership.

But the public "mood" is prone to cyclical trends and dissensus. It seems committed permanently to neither internationalism nor isolationsism. Rather, it has vacillated between periods in which global internationalism has received support, followed, predictably, by periods of public support for American retrenchment and withdrawal from the responsibilities of an active involvement in the world. Moreover, American "thinking about world affairs . . . has oscillated between an idealistic commitment to a world order yet to be shaped and a periodic swing toward fascination with realpolitik" (Brzezinski, 1983).

Together these sometimes discordant strains, both evident in the 1980s, point toward potentially divergent future paths as the costs and rewards of global involvement are weighed. Some will find the interventionist thrust of the Reagan administration palatable; others will recoil from it. Among those who "learned" from Vietnam, for example, Krauthammer (1985a) suggests that "right isolationists" (like Secretary of Defense Weinberger and the joint chiefs of staff in the Reagan administration) will support interventionism only when a compelling case can be made that United States national interests are directly threatened. On the other hand, "left isolationists," he argues, continue to support interventionist goals, but with an emphasis on human rights and applications short of force.[6]

The potential impact of societal variables on American foreign policy making is nowhere more apparent than in the lesson that even Reagan had to learn: that guns and butter, military spending and economic prosperity, are incompatible in the long run; one can only be obtained at the expense of the other.

Initially Reagan sought both. Supply-side Reaganomics promised to stimulate economic growth by reducing government spending and the level of taxation. Simultaneously, sharply higher defense spending (accomplished in a shrinking budget by increasing the defense share of the total federal pie) promised to reverse the deterioration of the United States' strategic and conventional military balance vis-à-vis the Soviet Union. But the budget was not trimmed as the deepest and most prolonged economic recession since the Great Depression of the 1930s curtailed tax revenues and as defense spending

---

[6]Although Krauthammer uses "isolationism" to describe these competing thrusts, they are conceptually analogous to the accommodationist and hard-line internationalist values discussed in chapter nine.

climbed. Simultaneously, interest rates soared as government borrowing to meet ever mounting budget deficits forced them higher; the value of the dollar rose to new heights as foreign investors clamored to take advantage of the stability and high returns the American market promised; and American industrial and agricultural workers threatened by less expensive foreign imports or dependent on overseas markets for their products found themselves unemployed or facing foreclosure. Yet the market-oriented philosophy of the conservative Reagan regime made it recoil from intervening either at home or abroad to ease their plight. Meanwhile, federal deficits continued to mount. By fiscal 1985 interest on the federal debt was costing $179 billion annually, the government's single largest continuing obligation.

Taxes became an issue in the 1984 presidential campaign. Mondale pledged to raise them; Reagan pledged not to. And both promised a strong defense.

By the time of the election the economy had staged a remarkable recovery. Stimulated by mounting government deficits and gradually declining interest rates, the Gross National Product (GNP) grew at a rate of 6 percent or better in 1983 and 1984, unemployment declined, and inflation receded sharply (Garten, 1985: 539). The red ink continued to flow, however, and gradually the mounting federal deficits overwhelmed the issues and promises the presidential contenders had made earlier.

Although Reagan was the first president since the Korean War to succeed in increasing defense spending more than three years consecutively, he, too, hit the "limit" in his second term as pressure for the containment of his ambitious spending programs became overwhelming. In a rare show of congressional-executive unanimity on a keenly partisan issue, Reagan in December 1985 signed into law what was popularly known as the Gramm-Rudman-Hollings amendment (to legislation raising the national debt ceiling to over $2 trillion, so named because of three senators who were its principal architects). It provided mandatory and declining targets for the federal deficit with a view toward producing a balanced federal budget in fiscal year 1991. It also set mandatory cuts in the event Congress and the president could not agree on means to reach the deficit-reducing targets. Importantly, the amendment stipulated that defense spending must share half of the mandatory cuts, should they be imposed.

By signing the legislation, Reagan seemed to acknowledge the guns versus butter tradeoff: that one can only be had at the expense of the other. It also clearly reflected the president's conclusion that history would judge him by the deficit issue—adversely, unless something dramatic was implemented.

Considerable uncertainty surrounded Gramm-Rudman-Hollings, and in 1986 the Supreme Court ruled a key provision of the deficit-reduction law unconstitutional. Congress showed a subsequent inclination to implement the basic features of the legislation's intent. Whether defense spending would experience the congressional ax remained problematic, however. Even before the Supreme Court's ruling, the perquisites of "national security" might have been used to exempt the Pentagon's budget from sharing deficit-reducing cuts equally with domestic programs. The Court's action renewed defense-spending advocates' opportunities to do so. But there is no gainsaying the symbolic importance of the deficit-reduction legislation. Reagan was forced to compromise on one of the most important tenets of his conservative political philosophy and public political posture: the belief that the cause of freedom around the world could be protected only by American willingness and ability to fund a preponderant military capability.

How freedom is best protected and promoted is, of course, a matter of opinion. Other nations who help to make up the *external* environment, which also stimulates and constrains American foreign policy, do not always share the views of the United States. Many of the nation's closest allies did not subscribe to the basic principles that motivated the Reagan administration's foreign and domestic policies:

> They don't think every disruptive development in the world is caused by the Kremlin's decision. They don't think government controls are the main obstacle to economic growth. They don't think that turning the world over to private enterprise and individual initiative is a universal solution. Reiteration of these ideological themes creates new domestic political problems made in America for every allied leader. (Hughes, 1981: 15)

Interestingly, few global developments (whether a consequence of American behavior or of trends independent of American influence) fit neatly into the East versus West, communism versus capitalism mold that was the essence of the Reagan administration's world view. The Reagan administration nevertheless persisted in responding to events in terms that often bore little relation to the priorities and outlook of other nations. Third World nations, for instance, found that the agenda for a New International Economic Order so prominent in the 1970s was unable to animate an administration that viewed developing nations primarily as "targets of opportunity" for Soviet expansionism. And this despite the growing importance of Third World nations to the United States both as a source of needed imports and as a market for American exports.

Political economy issues were principal among those often separating the Reagan administration from other Western nations. "At a time when interdependence among nations was growing rapidly, the Administration seemed quite willing to ignore the impact of its policies on the rest of the world" (Garten, 1985). But the impact was often profound—and resented. Former West German Chancellor Helmut Schmidt set the tone and defined the issues in a broadside against the administration's role—or lack thereof—insofar as it related to the unprecedentedly high volume of the U.S. dollar in the mid-1980s:

> Profligate American fiscal policy, caused by inadequate taxes and a grossly inflated military budget, combines with a low savings rate to result in massive borrowing,

much of which comes from the rest of the world's taking advantage of preposterously high American interest rates. These rates produce an overvalued dollar that feeds protectionism and crushes debtors in the third world and at home. Everywhere, the high dollar destabilizes financial institutions and discourages serious investment—the latter desperately needed in Europe to transform the old industrial base. The whole situation grows politically and economically intolerable. The world's richest country cannot go on sustaining its prosperity by borrowing from the rest of the world. (Calleo, 1985: 14)

Only blindness to United States interdependence with the rest of the world could explain such insensitivity. Interdependence is a fact of America's international life nonetheless, and it continues to grow more complex. Consider, for example, the following evidence:

By 1984, 12.5 percent of America's GNP could be related to traded goods and services, and some estimates showed that 70 percent of total U.S. production of goods was exposed to international competition. Forty percent of American farmland was devoted to exports. One sixth of all jobs in the manufacturing sector depended on sales abroad. Half of the after-tax profits of U.S. corporations came from overseas subsidiaries. The nine largest U.S. banks had foreign exposure in the Third World alone of close to 200 percent of their primary capital base. (Garten, 1985: 542–543)

Figures such as these are closely correlated with the relative decline of American power in the postwar period, a reality denied by the administration's belief that ''a strong reassertive America could make the world adjust to Washington'' (Gelb and Lake, 1985). The United States maintains unmatched military strength and doubtless continues to exercise preponderant power in international politics and to have a disproportionate influence over international outcomes (Russett, 1985). In this sense one can easily agree with Henry Brandon's facile conclusion that ''The presumed retreat of America never happened.'' But that conclusion ignores the decline of the material base of the United States relative to others, whether measured in terms of its proportion of total world product, its dependence on foreign resource supplies, its strategic superiority, its conventional military capabilities, its leadership in science and technology, and the like. The relative erosion of the material base has made it more difficult for the United States to exercise leverage over the global system as a whole (Keohane and Nye, 1977). Alexander Haig underscored the predicament posed by the deteriorating position of the United States in the global system (February 18, 1985): ''The idea that the United States, acting alone in an interdependent world, can somehow renew the mythical golden era of the immediate postwar years when [the United States] seemed invulnerable to international political or economic developments is a dangerous illusion.''

The Reagan administration was also unusually insensitive to the ''planetary predicament,'' a host of global conditions described by one observer as widespread insecurity, poverty, alienation, injustice, ecological spoilation, and economic inequality (Beres, 1984). Clearly many of these challenges do not fit well with a foreign policy agenda that defines American interests almost exclusively in terms of military security and the means of enhancing it. Nor do they fit comfortably with a globalist vision that embraces anticommunism and anti-Sovietism as overriding values. Other issues derived from the unfolding trends in world politics could be added to the list of challenges to American foreign policy thinking, ranging from the dispersion of military power to the challenge of alien ideas, from the need for alternative energy technologies to the desecration of the earth's delicate ecosystem, from the demands of industrializing and postindustrial societies to non-fuel resource scarcities, from the pressures of burgeoning populations to the constraints of stagnant and steady-state economies, and from the requirement that the level of international debt be contained to the need for massive investments and capital to stimulate future economic growth. Those trends and the potential transformations they may entail pose perhaps the greatest challenges to the next phase of American foreign policy. Former Secretary of State Dean Acheson once noted, ''there are fashions in everything, even in horrors . . . and just as there are fashions in fears, there are fashions in remedies.'' To the extent that that telling aphorism is true, global trends and issues are inclined to pull American foreign policy away from the approach advocated with such singularity by the Reagan administration and toward others more sensitive to the complexities that appear to perplex the world so relentlessly.

THE PROBLEMATIC FUTURE

Harper's Magazine characterized the setting for American foreign policy thus:

> It is a gloomy moment in the history of our country. Not in the lifetime of most men has there been so much grave and deep apprehension; never has the future seemed so incalculable as at this time. The domestic economic situation is in chaos. . . . Prices are so high as to be utterly impossible. The political cauldron seethes and bubbles with uncertainty. Russia hangs, as usual, like a cloud, dark and silent, upon the horizon. It is a solemn moment. Of our trouble no man can see the end.

That statement, written not in the 1980s, but in 1847, is disconcerting. It depicts circumstances both today and nearly 150 years ago that convey the impression that trend is destiny, that yesterday's problems are likely to remain tomorrow's, and that, therefore, the capacity of the United States to chart a foreign policy course for a more promising future is questionable. By implication, the statement also suggests, to our despair, that *new* global challenges may be beyond the nation's ability to manage and that, in conjunction with the durability of those *old* troubles, the United States is somehow doomed by declining opportunities and diminishing expectations.

But the shape of America's future is not predetermined by powerful, invisible forces. Trend is *not* destiny. The nature of the world that today's youth will inherit will be influenced by how today's American foreign policy makers respond to the many problems facing the nation. The adequacy of their response will rest on the accuracy of their assumptions about global realities and about the country's appropriate role in the world.

As before, the issue is whether the conventional assumptions that have guided American foreign policy making since World War II are warranted. Although reaffirmed and reinforced during the Reagan years, their appropriateness, given the prevailing international climate, is still destined to be tested and reevaluated in an environment necessitating hard choices.

Reagan's efforts to expand the logic of *realpolitik* underlying American foreign policy is certain to undergo questioning, for it is uncertain whether that approach is wise or foolish. (The perseverance over time of the same ideas may attest either to their continuing wisdom or to their adherents' inability to recognize new circumstances, for assumptions that withstand the test of time tend to be classified by later historians as either constructive wisdoms or destructive myths.) The consequences that surface in the waning days of the millennium will determine how future generations will judge the Reagan administration's policies.

Less uncertain than the wisdom of the premises underlying Reagan's orientation is the influence of the forces acting on American foreign policy making. The factors that collectively define the policy-making process will give direction to the policy pattern that emerges. Indeed, the process—more so than the individuals involved in it—will parent the policy. For the process will provide not only stimuli to the efforts of Reagan's successor(s) to cope with the external environment but also constraints on his (or her) ability to implement the design chosen. "All of [the nation's past presidents], from the most venturesome to the most reticent, have shared one disconcerting experience: the discovery of the limits and restraints—decreed by law, by history, and by circumstance—that sometimes can blur their clearest designs or dull their sharpest purposes," noted Emmet John Hughes (1972). "I have not controlled events, events have controlled me" was the conclusion that President Lincoln reached.

It is unlikely that circumstances will permit America's forty-first president to be an exception. The job is difficult, the constraints enormous, the number of problems devoid of simple solutions staggering. The inclination to look to the future with a vision inspired by the past will no doubt be compelling. It will be difficult to pull away from the prevailing pattern that has defined American foreign policy so consistently for almost fifty years. "The really surprising thing about [the United States]," noted Henry Brandon in 1983, "has been the basic stability of American foreign policy. There has been a continuity that, in fact, nobody could have predicted."

Now, however, we *can* predict that policy continuity will persist. The assumptions made by American policy makers in the immediate aftermath of World War II have proven to be remarkably resilient ever since, even in the face of turbulent global changes. Perhaps our changing times call for a new American foreign policy, but past policy has the force of momentum behind it, and that force is powerful. The outlines of American foreign policy are therefore unlikely to be disturbed. Little will change after Reagan.

SUGGESTIONS FOR FURTHER READING

ANDERSON, WILLIAM D., AND STERLING K. KERNEK. "How 'Realistic' is Reagan's Diplomacy?" *Political Science Quarterly* 100 (Fall 1985): 389–409.

BERES, LOUIS RENÉ. *Reason and Realpolitik: U.S. Foreign Policy and World Order.* Lexington, MA: Heath, 1984.

CONGRESSIONAL QUARTERLY. *U.S. Foreign Policy: The Reagan Imprint.* Washington, D. C.: Congressional Quarterly, Inc., 1986.

FEINBERG, RICHARD E. *The Intemperate Zone: The Third World Challenge to U.S. Foreign Policy.* New York: Norton, 1983.

HOFFMANN, STANLEY. *Dead Ends: American Foreign Policy in the New Cold War.* Cambridge, MA: Ballinger, 1983.

KRAUTHAMMER, CHARLES. *Cutting Edges: Making Sense of the Eighties.* New York: Random House, 1985.

LENG, RUSSELL J. "Reagan and the Russians," *American Political Science Review* 78 (June 1984): 338–355.

ROSENFELD, STEPHEN S. "The Guns of July," *Foreign Affairs* 64 (Spring 1986): 698–714.

SHULTZ, GEORGE P. "New Realities and New Ways of Thinking," *Foreign Affairs* 63 (Spring 1985): 705–721.

APPENDIX
A CHRONOLOGY OF SELECTED
DIPLOMATIC EVENTS, 1945–1986

ROOSEVELT ADMINISTRATION

1945   United States rejects Soviet request for $6 billion reconstruction loan

Churchill, Roosevelt, and Stalin sign Yalta Agreements, including a provision for the Soviet treaty with Chiang Kai-shek of China

United States recognizes Soviet control of Outer Mongolia

United States approves transfer of Kurile Islands to Soviet Union

Romanian government turns pro-Soviet

Arab League Pact signed in Cairo

Last of 1,050 German V-2 rockets falls on Britain

Franklin D. Roosevelt dies; Vice President Harry S Truman succeeds

TRUMAN ADMINISTRATION

1945   VE Day (German surrender to Allied forces in Europe), May 8

Truman cancels Lend Lease allocations and shipments to the Allies

Truman sends Harry Hopkins to Moscow to discuss postwar settlement

Conference on United Nations Charter held in San Francisco

U.S. Senate approves United Nations Charter by a vote of 80-2

West recognizes Polish government

Truman informs Joseph Stalin that American scientists have successfully detonated world's first atomic bomb

Potsdam Conference (led by Stalin, Truman, and Churchill) is held

United States drops atomic bomb on Hiroshima, August 6

Soviet Union declares war on Japan and sends troops into Manchuria

United States drops atomic bomb on Nagasaki, August 9

Chiang Kai-shek and Molotov sign treaty of friendship between China and the Soviet Union

Soviet-Polish treaty recognizes Oder-Neisse line as Poland's western border
Ho Chi Minh declares independent Vietnam Republic
VJ Day (Japan surrenders to Allied forces), August 14
Council of Foreign Ministers meets in London
Iranian rebellion, supported by Soviet arms, erupts
Civil war continues in China
Nuremberg War Crimes Tribunal convenes in Germany
Big Three meet at Moscow Conference; Secretary of State Byrnes agrees to
    recognize Romanian and Bulgarian satellite governments
Yugoslavia is declared a Federated People's Republic

1946   People's Republic of Albania proclaimed
Soviet Union protests British role in Greek civil war
Armistice in Chinese civil war reached on George C. Marshall's initiative
Mao's communists and Chiang's Nationalists resume Chinese civil war
United States protests the postwar presence of Soviet troops in Iran
United States leads U.N. involvement in Iranian crisis over Soviet protest
Winston Churchill delivers militantly anti-Soviet "Iron Curtain" speech in
    Fulton, Missouri
Soviets withdraw troops from Iran
Council of Foreign Ministers (twenty-one nations) convenes Paris Peace
    Conference
General Lucius Clay stops reparations to Soviet zone of Germany
Baruch Plan to destroy atomic weapons and place control of nuclear energy
    in international hands rejected by Soviets
United States grants independence to the Philippines
United States joins UNESCO
Truman tells Congress China got $602,045,000 since VJ Day, and aid will
    continue
United States protests Soviet economic exploitation of Hungary
James F. Byrnes outlines U.S. policy for German war recovery in Stuttgart
    speech
United States backs Turkey as Soviet Union seeks influence over Turkish
    Straits
Nuremberg Tribunal concludes; ten Nazis sentenced to death; others sen-
    tenced to life imprisonment
Japan's wartime leaders imprisoned or hung following Tokyo trials
United States signs treaty of friendship and commerce with China
Iran crushes autonomy of Azerbaijan with U.S. aid
Yugoslavia shoots down U.S. aircraft
Soviets agree to troop exit from Trieste and arms inspection
Treaties at New York Foreign Ministers conference confirm U.S. recognition
    of Soviet control in southeastern Europe
United States and Britain begin joint administration of their occupation
    zones in Germany
Bulgaria is declared a People's Republic
War breaks out in Vietnam

1947   United States charges violation of Yalta agreement following the communist
    victory in supposedly rigged Polish elections
France and the United Kingdom sign a fifty-year Treaty of Alliance and
    Mutual Assistance at Dunkirk

United States abandons efforts to mediate between Chinese Nationalists and Communists

Truman pledges aid to Greece and Turkey; outlines the Truman Doctrine

Big Four Foreign Ministers conference held in Moscow reaches no agreement

Hungarian ruling party smashed by communists

United Nations makes United States trustee for Pacific islands

European Recovery Program (Marshall Plan) called for by Secretary of State George C. Marshall

Under Soviet pressure, Poland and Hungary decline Marshall Plan assistance

Kennan's "X" article, based on 1946 telegram sent from Moscow, published, proposing U.S. containment of Soviet communism

Congress passes National Security Act creating Defense Department, National Security Council, and Central Intelligence Agency

United States proposes peace treaty for Japan to make Japan a stronghold against communism in the Far East

Soviet Union charges United States with war threat

India proclaimed independent and partitioned into India and Pakistan

Marshall refers Korean independence question to U.N. General Assembly

Crisis erupts in Kashmir (which is claimed by both India and Pakistan)

GATT (General Agreement on Tariffs and Trade) treaty signed in Geneva by twenty-three countries in effort to reduce world trade barriers

Rio Pact for collective defense of Western Hemisphere concluded, committing the U.S. and Latin American republics to aid one another to resist military aggression

Comintern revived by Soviet Union and greatly expanded as Cominform

Romania becomes a People's Republic following the abdication of King Michael

1948 United States announces European reconstruction will occur without Soviet collaboration

Mohandas Gandhi assassinated in India

Communist coup occurs in Czechoslovakia

Juan Peron wins Argentinian presidency despite U.S. displeasure

Brussels Treaty, signed by Belgium, France, Luxembourg, the Netherlands, and the United Kingdom, calls for economic, social, and cultural cooperation among signatories

Soviet Union refuses to meet in Allied Control Council because of Western obstruction in Germany

Organization of European Economic Cooperation established to determine disbursement of Marshall Plan funds

Organization of American States (OAS) created to replace the Pan American Union

Israel declares independence

President Truman extends de facto recognition to independent Republic of Israel; war between Israel and the Arab League erupts

U.S. Foreign Assistance Act provides military aid to Chiang Kai-shek's Chinese Nationalists

Vandenberg Resolution pledges U.S. support for Brussels Treaty and defense agreements in Europe

Soviet Union stops road and rail traffic between Berlin and the West; airlift begins

Yugoslavia's Marshal Tito breaks with Cominform; seeks policy of neutrality in East-West dispute

Rebellion in Malaya begins

Separate North and South Korean governments established

Truman elected president

Representatives of Brussels Treaty powers, Canada, and United States open negotiations in Washington on creation of North Atlantic defense treaty

Universal Declaration of Human Rights adopted by U.N. General Assembly

1949   Point Four program recommended in Truman's inaugural address promises aid to developing countries

COMECON (Council for Mutual Economic Assistance) is initiated for Soviet assistance in Europe

Philippine insurgency is led by Huk rebels

United States launches guided missile to record height of 250 miles

Israel admitted to United Nations

The negotiating powers invite Denmark, Iceland, Italy, Norway, and Portugal to adhere to the North Atlantic Treaty

Soviet Union protests that prospective North Atlantic Treaty Organization (NATO) is contrary to U.N. charter

NATO formed with signing of North Atlantic Treaty; first U.S. alliance concluded in peacetime

The London Ten-Power Agreement sets up the Council of Europe

Berlin blockade is lifted; separate East and West German governments established

French install Bao Dai as head of Vietnamese puppet government

United States withdraws occupation forces from South Korea

Vietnamese state established with capital at Saigon

Soviet Union acquires atomic bomb

Nationalists flee mainland China for the island of Formosa

Joint Chiefs of Staff advise no U.S. occupation of Formosa but agree to send large staff

State Department issues China White Paper placing blame for Nationalists' defeat by communists on Nationalists themselves

Mao Tse-tung unifies mainland China and proclaims People's Republic of China

U.S.S.R. and satellites (and Yugoslavia) recognize People's Republic of China

Greek civil war ends in communist defeat

Truman approves Mutual Defense Assistance Act for aid to countries vulnerable to communist pressure

Truman and Shah of Iran declare United States-Iranian solidarity

India recognizes Communist China

1950   Britain extends diplomatic recognition to Communist China

Truman announces U.S. will take no military measures to protect Formosa

Acheson in National Press Club speech reaffirms ''hands-off'' policy for Formosa

United States announces intention to build hydrogen bomb

Soviet Union begins eight-month boycott of U.N. Security Council

Senator Joseph McCarthy claims State Department is riddled with communists and communist sympathizers

Far Eastern Economic Assistance bill assures continued aid to Formosa

Soviet Union and China sign thirty-year Mutual Aid Pact

National Security Council issues Memorandum No. 68

United States, Britain, and France issue Tripartite Declaration promising protection of Israel's boundary lines

United States gives France military assistance to fight Vietnamese rebels

North Korean forces invade South Korea on June 25 and capture Seoul; U.S. troops enter Korea with orders to defend Formosa and prevent Chiang's forces on Formosa from attacking mainland China; Chiang offers 30,000 troops for Korea

Chiang and MacArthur meet on Formosa

McCarran Act passed by Congress over presidential veto; calls for severe domestic restrictions of communists

U.S. forces invade North Korea; South Korean troops cross thirty-eighth parallel

Greece and Turkey accept North Atlantic Council invitation to be associated with Mediterranean defense planning

General Dwight D. Eisenhower named by North Atlantic Council to be Supreme Allied Commander of Europe

Communist China's forces occupy Tibet

Tibet appeals to United Nations but China rejects U.N. appeal for ceasefire

China enters Korean War

U.N. General Assembly passes the Uniting for Peace Resolution

1951   U.N. General Assembly accuses China of aggression in Korea

United States stations troops in NATO countries

House Minority Leader Joseph W. Martin discloses MacArthur letter endorsing use of Chiang's troops to open second front on Chinese mainland

Truman recalls General Douglas MacArthur; prevents U.S. invasion of mainland China

Ending Senate testimony, Marshall says Chinese Nationalists were beaten by communists because of poor officers, lack of public support, and "the character of government"

Treaty establishing European Community for Coal and Steel signed

Dr. Mohammed Mossadegh nationalizes Anglo-Iranian Oil Company

Ex-Secretary of Defense Louis Johnson testifies that it was Acheson who recommended U.S. intervention in Korea and that no high military figures in Washington opposed the intervention

Philippines and United States sign mutual security pact

McCarran's Internal Security subcommittee begins hearings on "subversive" influences in U.S. foreign policy

$307 million aid program to Nationalist China is proposed by the Truman administration

ANZUS Pact is signed by Australia, New Zealand, and United States

Mutual Security Act passed calling for U.S. assistance throughout the world

Korean truce line (thirty-eighth parallel) accepted at United Nations

1952   Franco-German crisis erupts over administration of Saar region

Soviet Union creates three-mile buffer zone on East German border

Greece and Turkey join NATO

United States decides to double Military Assistance Advisory Group on Formosa

European Defense Community established; falters after a few months

Cyprus begins fight for independence

Gamal Abdel Nasser emerges as strong man following ouster of Egyptian monarchy

Britain successfully completes first atomic test

United States explodes first hydrogen bomb at Eniwetok Atoll

National Security Agency created by a classified presidential directive

Dwight D. Eisenhower elected president

Truman considers using atomic bomb on Moscow and Leningrad to prompt a Soviet agreement on Korea

Fulgencio Batista seizes power in Cuba

EISENHOWER ADMINISTRATION

1953 Eisenhower announces end of neutralization of Formosa, thereby unleashing Chiang Kai-shek to attack Chinese mainland

Secretary of State John Foster Dulles reveals goal of "liberating" Eastern Europe, promising to "roll back" the Iron Curtain

Chinese Nationalists attack Communist Chinese mainland

Treaty of friendship and collaboration between Greece, Turkey, and Yugoslavia signed in Ankara

Stalin dies; next three years marked by a power struggle between Malenkov, Molotov, and Khrushchev

Eisenhower administration suggests use of nuclear weapons to fill manpower gaps in European rearmament

Vietnamese rebels attack Laos

Soviet Union extends diplomatic recognition to the German Democratic Republic (East Germany)

Soviet tanks crush riots in East Berlin

Korean armistice signed at Panmunjom

Congressional resolution supports "liberation" of Eastern Europe; Dulles threatens resumption of Korean War

Soviet Union announces possession of hydrogen bomb

Shah of Iran regains power from Mossadegh through CIA-designed coup with British assistance

Pact of Madrid signed allowing U.S. naval bases in Spain

United States and South Korea sign mutual defense treaty

Eisenhower proposes "atoms for peace" plan at United Nations

1954 Secretary of State John Foster Dulles proclaims policy of deterrence through massive retaliation

British, French, U.S., and Soviet foreign ministers meet in Berlin; Soviets reject German reunification

United States tests hydrogen bomb at Bikini Atoll

Inter-American conference in Caracas passes anticommunist declaration

Soviet Union begins aid program to gain influence in the Third World

U.S.-Japanese defense agreement reached

U.S. Congress creates Food for Peace Program

Dulles proposes Anglo-American military intervention in Vietnam

Geneva Conference on Korea and Indochina opens

Nasser becomes prime minister of Egypt

Dien Bien Phu falls to Vietnamese communists

France, Britain, and U.S. reject Soviet bid to join NATO

U.S. Central Intelligence Agency helps conservative military officers overthrow a reform-minded Guatemalan government

Geneva Conference results in armistice and partition of Vietnam; U.S. supports Geneva Accords terminating French rule in Indochina

French National Assembly decides against ratification of the treaty setting up the European Defense Community (EDC)

Senator McCarthy attempts to prove communist infiltration of the U.S. Army in nationally televised hearings; Senate formally censures and condemns McCarthy

Algerian war for independence from France begins

Southeast Asia Treaty Organization (SEATO) created

Quemoy-Matsu crisis erupts; Dulles declares U.S. is prepared to use atomic bomb on mainland China

Italy, Yugoslavia, Britain, and the United States sign a Memorandum of Understanding ending the Trieste dispute

Paris agreements signed; Federal Republic of Germany (West Germany) invited to join NATO and rearm

The U.S., which sent the Navy into the Formosa Straits at the outbreak of the Korean War, signs a mutual defense treaty with Nationalist Chinese on Taiwan

1955   U.S.S.R. ends the state of war with Germany

Signing of Baghdad Pact between Iraq and Turkey; Iran, Pakistan, and the United Kingdom join the Pact later in the year

Eisenhower pledges U.S. forces will remain in Europe as long as necessary

Opening at Bandung of the first conference of the ''nonaligned'' countries of Asia and Africa

West Germany joins NATO

Warsaw Pact formed (U.S.S.R., Albania, Bulgaria, Czechoslovakia, East Germany, Hungary, Poland, and Romania)

Soviet Union agrees to Austrian State Treaty; Soviet and American occupation forces evacuate Austria

United States and China initiate ambassadorial-level talks in Geneva in an effort to reconcile differences

Formosa crisis develops; Eisenhower pledges defense of Taiwan

Opening in Geneva of the first conference on the peaceful uses of atomic energy

Ngo Dinh Diem announces suspension of elections in South Vietnam

U.S. military advisers sent to South Vietnam

U.S.S.R. signs a treaty with the Pankow regime of the Soviet occupied zone of Germany, granting it the prerogatives of a state

1956   Soviet Premier Nikita Khrushchev establishes power position with attack on Stalin's policies at the Twentieth Communist Party Congress

Pravda announces the dissolution of Cominform

United States offers aid to rebellious East European countries

United States withdraws offer of assistance in Aswan Dam project; accuses Nasser of playing West against Soviet Union

Seventy nations, including United States and Soviet Union, sign statute of International Atomic Energy Agency

Nasser nationalizes Suez Canal

Israel launches military action against Egyptian troops in Sinai Peninsula

Britain and France intervene in Egypt by occupying Suez Canal area

Hungarian revolution suppressed by Soviet forces

Japan admitted to United Nations

Eisenhower reelected president

Britain, France, and Israel agree to cease-fire and withdrawal from Suez

1957 Eisenhower Doctrine pledges U.S. aid to Middle Eastern countries resisting communist takeovers

United States agrees to supply Britain with guided missiles

Signing of the Treaties of Rome establishing the European Economic Community and Euratom

United States agrees to continue military support of Saudi Arabia in return for lease of Dhahran airfield

United States military aids King Hussein of Jordan

United States accedes to the Baghdad Pact as an associate member

Britain explodes hydrogen bomb in central Pacific

Syria expels U.S. embassy officials for allegedly plotting coup; U.S. expels Syrian ambassador in retaliation

Soviet Union develops ICBM capability

Defense Early Warning System (DEW line) completed by United States with Canadian cooperation

U.N. General Assembly condemns the Soviet intervention in Hungary

Soviet Union launches Sputnik I and II, first earth satellites

International Atomic Energy Agency established with headquarters in Vienna

1958 European Economic Community (Common Market) and European Atomic Community come into existence

United States launches its first satellite, Explorer I

Khrushchev replaces Marshal Bulganin at the head of the Soviet government

Mao Tse-tung announces "Great Leap Forward" to promote Chinese industrialization and agricultural production

Egypt and Syria form United Arab Republic with Nasser as president

U.N. convenes Law of the Sea Conference

United States removes last ground troops from Japan

Soviet Union announces a unilateral suspension of all nuclear arms tests

Vice President Richard Nixon confronts protesters on South American tour

European Parliamentary Assembly meets for the first time in Strasbourg

Khrushchev visits Beijing

Iraq's army executes a bloody and successful coup; Iraq allies itself with United Arab Republic

U.S. Marines land in Lebanon; Soviet Union protests intervention

U.S. nuclear submarine *Nautilus* establishes the first link between the Atlantic and the Pacific, passing beneath the North Pole

China bombards Quemoy; United States pledges to defend the island

Khrushchev refuses to back China in Formosan crisis

Soviet Union protests U.S. violation of its air space

Soviet Union offers United Arab Republic assistance for building Aswan Dam

Soviet Union announces desire to terminate the four-power agreement on the status of Berlin

Charles de Gaulle elected President of the French Republic

1959   Fidel Castro assumes control of Cuba

An Anglo-Greek-Turkish Conference decides that Cyprus will become independent

Revolt in Tibet; Dalai Lama flees country

Iraq withdraws from Baghdad Pact

Civil War widens in Laos

OAS members reiterate principle of nonintervention at Santiago Conference

Vice President Nixon and Soviet Premier Khrushchev hold their "kitchen debate" about the relative merits of their countries' systems

United States denounces Soviet activity in Laos

Baghdad Pact becomes the Central Treaty Organization (CENTO), formed to defend the Middle East

Khrushchev visits the United States for Camp David meetings

Khrushchev proposes to U.N. General Assembly that total world disarmament be achieved within four years

Members of European Free Trade Association ("The Seven") ratify treaty

Inter-American Development Bank formed

Antarctic Treaty prohibits any military use of the region

1960   U.S. signs Treaty of Mutual Assistance with Japan

France becomes fourth nation to acquire atomic weapons

Soviet Deputy Premier Anastas Mikoyan visits Cuba

The United Nations ten-nation Disarmament Committee starts negotiations in Geneva

American U-2 aircraft, piloted by Francis Gary Powers, is shot down over Soviet territory; Khrushchev cancels U.S. tour over incident

Military coup in Turkey

The communist states withdraw from the United Nations disarmament negotiations in Geneva

China resumes shelling of Quemoy

United States denounces Soviet presence in Cuba

Congo crisis erupts; U.N. peace-keeping forces intervene

U.S. Navy sent to Nicaragua and Guatemala to guard against Cuban threat

Soviet Union calls for ouster of U.N. Secretary General and substitution of "troika" system

Khrushchev disrupts U.N.'s twenty-fifth anniversary session by pounding his shoe on table

John F. Kennedy elected president

United States develops submarine-launched ballistic missile (SLBM)

Organization of Petroleum Exporting Countries (OPEC) formed

United States and Canada join members of the OEEC to form the Organization for Economic Cooperation and Development (OECD)

1961   United States breaks relations with Cuba

KENNEDY ADMINISTRATION
Kennedy proclaims need to ''strengthen our military tools''
Kennedy proposes Alliance for Progress
Patrice Lumumba is killed; Soviets threaten unilateral action in the Congo
Union of South Africa leaves British Commonwealth
United States calls SEATO to action in Laos
Soviet Union agrees to Laotian cease-fire and peace talks
Soviet Union launches first man, Major Yuri Gagarin, into space
U.N. General Assembly condemns apartheid in South Africa
Invasion of Cuba at the Bay of Pigs by CIA-trained exiles fails
Alan Shepard becomes the first American in space
Rafael Trujillo, Dominican Republic dictator, assassinated; CIA involvement
    alleged
Kennedy and Khrushchev confer at Vienna summit conference
Syria secedes from the United Arab Republic
Soviet Union supports construction of the Berlin Wall; United States mobi-
    lizes for second Berlin airlift
Congress passes Foreign Assistance Act
Peace Corps made permanent U.S. agency
United States and Soviet Union resume nuclear weapons testing
United States launches a radio-reflector satellite
United States sends 500 military advisers to Vietnam
Cuba is declared a socialist republic based on Marxism-Leninism
Albania and Soviet Union break diplomatic relations
India seizes Portuguese Goa
1962 U.S. Trade Expansion Act signed
Additional U.S. military personnel enter Vietnam as advisers
OAS votes to expel Cuba
Indonesian insurgency erupts against Dutch rule
Soviet Union releases U-2 pilot Francis Gary Powers
United States sends 5,000 troops to Thailand during Laotian crisis
Laos agreement signed in Geneva
U.S. astronaut John Glenn becomes the first American to orbit the earth
Seventeen-nation disarmament conference convenes in Geneva
Peruvian coup prompts Kennedy to break diplomatic relations and suspend
    economic aid
France recognizes Algerian independence
U-2 photographs reveal Soviet missile sites in Cuba
Pro-Nasser revolutionaries overthrow monarchy in Yemen
Sino-Indian border clash occurs
U.S. Navy blockades Cuba to prevent missile installation
Soviet Union refuses to remove missiles from Cuba
Kennedy and Khrushchev end war threat by reaching agreement over Cu-
    ban missile crisis; U.S. blockade is lifted
1963 President de Gaulle of France objects to admitting Britain into the Common
    Market
U.S. thwarts effort to let Beijing replace Chinese Nationalist delegation at
    the United Nations
Ten thousand additional U.S. military personnel sent to Vietnam

Egypt, Syria, and Iraq discuss unity but with no agreement

OAU (Organization of African Unity) Charter adopted in Addis Ababa

"Hot Line" agreement establishes direct communication link between
United States and Soviet Union

Kennedy speech at American University urges end to Cold War

Signing of the first Yaoundé Convention (between the European Economic
Community and seventeen African countries)

Signing of Limited Nuclear Test Ban Treaty prohibits nuclear tests in atmosphere, in outer space, and under water

China lays claim to Soviet-occupied territory

President de Gaulle announces France will not sign Limited Test Ban Treaty

South Vietnamese President Ngo Dinh Diem is assassinated in Vietnam
with CIA involvement

Operation "Big Lift": 14,500 American troops are flown from the United
States to Germany in record time to demonstrate the U.S.'s ability to
reinforce NATO forces in Europe in emergency

Kennedy assassinated; Lyndon B. Johnson succeeds to presidency

JOHNSON ADMINISTRATION

Military leaders oust Dominican Republic President Juan Bosch; rebellion
erupts

Greek-Turkish conflict in Cyprus becomes armed confrontation

Kennedy Round of Multilateral Trade Negotiations begins

1964 France recognizes Beijing government

Panamanians riot over American occupation of Canal Zone; disturbances
lead to breaking of diplomatic relations

Soviet-Romanian rift develops

United Nations peace-keeping force in Cyprus (UNFICYP) created

Group of 77 formalized to pursue the objectives of Third World countries

OAS members impose trade sanctions on Cuba

Gulf of Tonkin Resolution permits increased U.S. involvement in Vietnam

United Nations Conference on Trade and Development (UNCTAD) convenes in Geneva

Aleksei Kosygin replaces Khrushchev as Soviet premier; Leonid Brezhnev
replaces Khrushchev as party secretary

United States uses jets to bomb Ho Chi Minh Trail in Laos

People's Republic of China explodes its first atomic bomb

Insurgencies against Portuguese rule erupt in Angola and Mozambique

Johnson elected president

1965 United States escalates war by bombing North Vietnam and introducing
125,000 additional American combat troops

World's first commercial satellite, *Early Bird*, launched by the United States;
successfully tested as first global communications system for telephone,
television, and telegraphic communications

Kashmir crisis culminates in war between India and Pakistan

Soviet and East German authorities block land access to Berlin when West
German Parliament holds plenary session in West Berlin's Congress Hall

United States intervenes militarily in Dominican Republic

Indonesian army crushes attempted coup; over 500,000 are slain

Rhodesia issues unilateral declaration of independence; Britain imposes oil embargo on Rhodesia

1966   Indira Gandhi, Jawaharlal Nehru's daughter, becomes prime minister of India

Coups occur in Nigeria and Syria; in Ghana government of Kwame Nkrumah removed by military coup

France removes its armed forces from NATO military command

Civil war erupts in Uganda

International days of protest held against U.S. policy in Vietnam

United States begins bombing Hanoi-Haiphong area of North Vietnam

Johnson links American action in Vietnam to Truman Doctrine

Chou En-lai visits Romania

European Economic Community establishes Common Agricultural Policy (CAP)

China announces its first guided missile nuclear weapon test (its fourth atomic experiment)

Manila Conference held; United States pledges to continue Vietnam War until "just peace" reached

Unmanned Surveyor I makes successful lunar landing

"Cultural Revolution" introduced in China in effort to purge society of bourgeois elements

Agreement reached at United Nations on the first international treaty governing space exploration

1967   United States and Soviet Union among over sixty nations that sign treaty governing exploration and use of outer space

U.S. deploys multiple warhead missiles; U.S.S.R. develops this capability in 1968

Soviet Union and United States increase commercial and cultural exchanges

Johnson and Vice President Nguyen Cao Ky of Vietnam confer at Guam

United States lends Bolivia military support against Cuban insurgency led by Che Guevara

Arab-Israeli Six-Day War erupts; Suez Canal closed (until June 1975)

Formation of ASEAN (Association of South-East Asian Nations); members include Indonesia, Malaysia, the Philippines, Singapore, and Thailand (Brunei joined the Association in 1984)

Johnson and Kosygin meet for Glassboro summit

Biafra rebels against Nigerian rule, leading to bitter civil war

de Gaulle, on a state visit to Canada, makes his "Free Quebec" speech supporting French Canadian separatist movement

Proclamation of the People's Republic of South Yemen

King Hussein of Jordan visits Soviet Union

Che Guevara dies in Bolivian ambush

1968   North Korea seizes U.S. intelligence vessel *Pueblo* within or near its jurisdictional waters

Vietcong launch Tet offensive, a major setback for the United States

American troops massacre Vietnamese civilians at My Lai

Johnson announces he will not run for reelection; asks for peace settlement in Vietnam

Martin Luther King, Jr., leader of civil rights movement and winner of 1964 Nobel Peace Prize, assassinated

Vietnam peace talks commence in Paris

French President de Gaulle visits Romania

Leaders of Czech Communist Party endorse policy of resisting pressure from Soviet Union

Haiti charges United States with bombing its capital

Nuclear Nonproliferation Treaty signed at the United Nations

Soviet, Polish, East German, Bulgarian, and Hungarian troops invade Czechoslovakia to quell "Prague's Spring"

U.S. ambassador to Guatemala is killed by terrorists

Robert F. Kennedy is assassinated

Treaty prohibiting Nuclear Weapons in Latin America enters into force

Violent antiwar demonstrations occur outside Democratic National Convention in Chicago

Albania formally withdraws from Warsaw Pact

Congress passes Foreign Military Sales Act

Peru nationalizes U.S. oil interests

Richard M. Nixon narrowly elected president; promises "secret" plan to end Vietnam War

NATO warns Soviet Union and denounces its intervention in Czechoslovakia

Crew of *Pueblo* released by North Korea

NIXON ADMINISTRATION

1969 Nixon supports strategic arms talks; recommends deployment of antiballistic missiles (ABMs) to enhance U.S. bargaining position

Secret U.S. bombing of Cambodia begins

National security adviser Henry Kissinger issues National Security Study Memorandum 39 which results in a U.S. policy more favorable to white African regimes

Sino-Soviet border clashes erupt along Ussuri River and on Damansly Island

Nixon calls for "Vietnamization" of war in Southeast Asia; announces reduction of U.S. troops in Vietnam

French President de Gaulle resigns; Georges Pompidou replaces him

Military clash develops between El Salvador and Honduras

United States decides to test MIRVs; Soviet Union tests SS-9

National Commitments Resolution passed by U.S. Senate

First withdrawal of U.S. troops from Vietnam achieved; 75,000 sent home by year's end

Nixon signals new line toward Beijing by allowing American tourists to bring home $100 worth of Chinese-made goods

Apollo II, launched from Cape Kennedy, lands on the moon; Neil Armstrong becomes the first man to step on the moon

Signing of the second Yaoundé Convention

North Korea shoots down American reconnaissance plane over Sea of Japan

Nixon Doctrine proclaimed

Ho Chi Minh, president of North Vietnam, dies

Violence in Northern Ireland breaks out between Protestants and Catholics

Nixon suspends Seventh Fleet's nineteen-year-long patrol of Formosa Straits

First round of SALT talks held in Helsinki, Finland

Church amendment bars involvement of U.S. ground troops in Laos and Thailand

1970   Albania and People's Republic of China conclude trade agreement
First NATO communications satellite launched from Cape Kennedy
United States invades Cambodia
Student protests against Vietnam War result in four killings by National
    Guard at Kent State University; 448 American universities close or go on
    strike
Gulf of Tonkin Resolution repealed by U.S. Senate
United States offers plan for cease-fire in Arab-Israeli fighting
Soviet Union and West Germany sign treaty affirming a permanent border
    between East and West Germany
Soviet Union and West Germany sign friendship treaty in Moscow
Civil war expands in Cambodia
Nasser dies; Anwar Sadat becomes president of Egypt
Salvador Allende, a socialist, elected president of Chile
U.S. force strength in Vietnam reduced below 400,000
Treaty on normalization of relations between the Federal Republic of Ger-
    many and Poland signed in Warsaw

1971   Seabed Arms Control Treaty signed
Second NATO communications satellite launched from Cape Kennedy
Canada and People's Republic of China exchange diplomatic envoys; new
    era of U.S.-China relations begins as China hosts U.S. table-tennis team
India-Pakistan war erupts following crisis in Bengal; Bengal becomes inde-
    pendent, renamed Bangladesh
The *New York Times* begins publication of the *Pentagon Papers*
President Nixon declares that a bipolar world has given way to a five-power
    world
Kissinger secretly visits China to arrange Nixon visit
Nixon inaugurates New Economic Policy (NEP), effectively suspending the
    1944 Bretton Woods Agreement and convertibility of American dollar
United States and Soviet Union reduce risk of nuclear war by reaching ''ac-
    cidents measures'' agreement
People's Republic of China admitted to United Nations
Violence worsens in Northern Ireland
SALT talks continue in Vienna
Fighting in Indochina spreads to Laos and Cambodia; United States con-
    ducts large-scale bombing raids against North Vietnam; U.S. planes bomb
    Vietcong supply routes in Cambodia

1972   Britain, Denmark, and Ireland reach agreement to enter Common Market,
    effective 1973
Nixon visits People's Republic of China, issues Shanghai Communiqué
    committing Washington and Beijing to pursuing normalization of rela-
    tions
Lon Nol takes control of Cambodian government
Britain assumes direct control of Northern Ireland
United States and Soviet Union sign Biological Weapons Convention
Nixon orders Haiphong Harbor mined and widens air war against Vietnam
United States returns Okinawa to Japan
Nixon visits Soviet Union and signs interim agreement on SALT and the
    ABM Treaty; first peacetime visit to the Soviet Union of an American
    president

Four-Power Agreement on Berlin signed by France, United Kingdom, United States, and Soviet Union

"Watergate" affair begins as District of Columbia police arrest five men breaking into Democratic National Headquarters in the Watergate complex

United States and Vietnam resume Paris peace talks

Soviet Union quietly arranges to buy massive amounts of U.S. grain

Egyptian President Sadat expels all Soviet advisers and technicians

Japan recognizes People's Republic of China and begins trade relations

Palestinians kill eleven Israeli athletes and six others in Munich Olympic Village

Philippine President Ferdinand Marcos declares martial law in response to alleged "communist rebellion"

Nixon reelected president in a landslide victory

SALT II talks begin in Geneva

Talks begin in Helsinki for Conference on Security and Cooperation in Europe (CSCE)

"Basic Treaty" signed by East and West Germany

Paris peace talks cease; United States resumes heavy bombing of North Vietnam on Christmas

1973   Cease-fire agreement signed in Paris by Secretary of State William Rogers, providing for withdrawal of U.S. troops from Vietnam within sixty days

United States devalues dollar for second time in fourteen months

United States and China open liaison offices in each other's capitals

United States and Soviet Union sign cooperative agreement to prevent nuclear war

Conference on Security and Cooperation in Europe (CSCE) begins

Allende, Chile's socialist president, killed in military coup that topples his government; CIA allegedly involved

Algiers summit of nonaligned nations begins

Juan Peron elected president of Argentina

East and West Germany establish diplomatic relations

Yom Kippur War between Israel and its Arab adversaries begins

Arab members of OPEC (Organization of Petroleum Exporting Countries) impose oil embargo on Western supporters of Israel

Founding session of the Trilateral Commission is held in Tokyo

Vienna talks on Mutual and Balanced Force Reductions (MBFR) in Europe begin

War Powers Act passes in Congress over Nixon's veto

United Nations Conference on Law of the Sea convenes; 157 nations begin negotiating comprehensive Law of the Sea Treaty

Tokyo Round of Multilateral Trade Negotiations begins

OPEC announces the doubling of the price of crude oil by the six Persian Gulf members

1974   Military coup in Ethiopia places Marxist regime in power

Cuba sends troops to Yemen

OAPEC (Organization of Arab Petroleum Exporting Countries) oil embargo is lifted

Military coup in Lisbon leads to end of Portuguese rule in Africa; Guinea-Bissau and Mozambique gain independence

India explodes its first nuclear device

Group of 77 secures passage of the Declaration on the Establishment of a New International Economic Order (NIEO)

Kissinger persuades Syria and Israel to agree to cease-fire on the Golan Heights

Congress passes Nelson amendment to Foreign Military Sales Act, enabling Congress to block arms sales to particular nations

United States and Soviet Union sign ABM Protocol Treaty on limitation of antiballistic systems and Threshold Test Ban Treaty limiting underground nuclear tests

Turkish-Greek conflict erupts when Turkey invades Cyprus following coup there

Resignation of the military regime in Athens, Greece; Karamanlis, returning from exile, is named prime minister

Juan Peron dies; Isabel, his wife and vice president, assumes power in Argentina

Impeachment hearings for Nixon held; Nixon resigns and Gerald Ford becomes president

FORD ADMINISTRATION

Greece withdraws its military from NATO integrated structure in protest over Turkish involvement in Cyprus (Greek forces were reintegrated in 1980)

Ford pardons former President Nixon for any criminal offenses committed while in office; widespread domestic protest ensues

Hughes-Ryan amendment requires CIA to report its covert operations to Congress

U.S. Trade Act provides most-favored-nation status to Soviet Union and other communist nations; Jackson-Vanick amendment places conditions on that status unacceptable to Soviets

Ford-Brezhnev meeting in Vladivostok results in arms agreement

Ford grants limited amnesty to Vietnam draft evaders and military deserters

Arab League endorses Palestine Liberation Organization (PLO) as sole legitimate representative of the Palestinian people

United States suspends all military aid to Turkey following Turkish invasion of Cyprus

1975 U.S.-Soviet trade agreement nullified

Vietnam launches a full-scale invasion of its former ally, Cambodia

Signing of the first Lomé Convention (European Economic Community and forty-six African, Caribbean, and Pacific [ACP] countries)

United States lifts ten-year-old embargo on arms sales to Pakistan and India

Senate publishes report of CIA plots to assassinate foreign leaders

Civil war widens in Lebanon

Cambodia falls to insurgents; Lon Nol regime ousted, replaced by Pol Pot

Last American soldiers leave South Vietnam as Saigon falls to North Vietnamese and Vietcong

Mayaguez seized by Cambodia; over forty U.S. Marines killed in rescue operation

Civil war intensifies in Angola

U.S.-Soviet spacecraft linkup achieved

Final act of the Conference on Security and Cooperation in Europe signed in Helsinki

United Nations General Assembly brands Zionism "a form of racial discrimination" over strong U.S. and Israeli protests

South Vietnam merges with North Vietnam

Biological Weapons Convention enters into force

Cuban armed intervention in Angola and other parts of Africa condemned by the United States

Ford visits China but Taiwan question remains obstacle to improved U.S.-Chinese relations

Egypt and Israel reach agreement providing for Israeli withdrawal from Sinai and creation of U.N. buffer zone

1976 Angola falls to military forces of Cuba and Angolan insurgents

Group of 77 proposes an integrated Programme for Commodities and "Common Fund" at UNCTAD IV meetings in Nairobi

Isabel Peron ousted from power in Argentina and placed under arrest

Kissinger tours Africa; Rhodesian compromise introduced

U.S.-Soviet Underground Nuclear Test Accords signed

Syria sends 30,000 "peace-keeping" troops into Lebanon under auspices of Arab League

U.S. ambassador to Lebanon slain

Israeli commando raid at Entebbe Airport in Uganda rescues 103 hijacked passengers

Mao Tse-tung dies; Hua Guofung emerges from political infighting to become new Chinese leader

Jimmy Carter elected president

CARTER ADMINISTRATION

1977 President Carter grants limited amnesty to Vietnam War draft evaders and military deserters

Carter pledges a phased withdrawal of U.S. troops from South Korea

Carter administration proclaims that countries guilty of human rights violations will face reductions in U.S. foreign aid

Argentina, Brazil, El Salvador, and Guatemala reject U.S. military aid in reaction to U.S. attacks on their human rights practices

Fighting breaks out in Zaire; 2,000 troops invade from neighboring Angola; United States sends aid to Zaire

Moscow charges that U.S. human rights stance constitutes interference in the Soviet Union's internal affairs

Menachem Begin becomes prime minister in Israel; pledges never to negotiate "liberated" territory

Talks begin in Paris to normalize relations between the United States and Vietnam

Spain holds first elections in thirty-eight years; Communist Party legalized

Carter cancels development of the B-1 bomber; proposes development of cruise missile instead

U.S. diplomats take up residence in Cuba for the first time in sixteen years

Carter and Panamanian President General Omar Torrijos sign Panama Canal treaties

Vietnam is admitted to the United Nations

Soviet Union agrees to join United States in adhering to existing SALT pact while SALT II negotiations continue

Carter withdraws United States from International Labor Organization; first U.S. withdrawal from a U.N. organization since that organization's founding

United States prohibits export of military and police equipment to South Africa

U.N. Security Council unanimously votes arms embargo against South Africa

Somalia breaks relations with Cuba, expels all Soviet advisers and renounces 1974 friendship treaty with Moscow

Egyptian President Sadat makes historic two-day visit to Israel for meetings with Israeli Prime Minister Begin and a speech before the Israeli Parliament; other Arab states break relations with Egypt in protest

President Carter proclaims Iran to be "an island of stability in one of the more troubled areas of the world"

1978   Kampuchea (Cambodia) breaks relations with Vietnam after fighting along border breaks out

Ethiopian army, aided by Soviets and Cubans, captures Somali stronghold of Jijiga

Israeli armed forces retaliate for PLO terrorist raid by invading and taking control of southern Lebanon

Carter announces postponement of production of neutron bomb, but says U.S. will test the weapon

Marcos wins landslide victory in first elections held in Philippines since 1972; widespread election fraud reported

Senate consents to ratification of two Panama Canal treaties to turn canal over to Panamanians by year 2000

Overthrow of President Daud of Afghanistan by procommunist Armed Forces Revolutionary Council

Sino-Japanese peace treaty signed

Camp David summit reaches "Framework for a Peace Treaty" between Egypt and Israel

Vietnam withdraws request to United States for war reparations; United States announces intention to establish full diplomatic relations with Vietnam

United States and Soviet Union sign convention prohibiting hostile uses of environmental modification techniques

Karol Cardinal Wojtyla of Poland becomes Pope John Paul II following death of John Paul I; furthers communications between Catholic Church and Eastern European leaders

China walks out of negotiations with Vietnam as hostilities erupt between them

Shah of Iran orders military takeover amidst widespread protests against his regime

Carter ends three-year arms embargo against Turkey

Soviet Union announces testing of neutron bomb as well as decision not to put it into production

1979

Carter administration announces establishment of full diplomatic relations with Beijing and renunciation of mutual-defense treaty with Taiwan

Deng Xiaoping visits the U.S., first top-ranking Chinese Communist leader to come to Washington

Kampuchea National United Front for National Salvation takes Phnom Penh and six other provinces with help of 100,000 Vietnamese troops

Shah leaves Iran; Ayatollah Ruhollah Khomeini returns from exile and seizes power from Prime Minister Shahpur Bakhtiar

Soviets deploy 10,000 troops in disputed islands north of Japan

Communist China invades Vietnam as "punishment" for the presence of Vietnamese troops in Kampuchea

Israeli Prime Minister Begin and Egyptian President Sadat sign a formal peace treaty in Washington, DC

China allows 1950 Soviet friendship treaty to expire

Reports show Pakistan acquiring nuclear weapons capability; United States cuts military and economic aid to Pakistan

Tanzanian forces end Idi Amin's eight-year rule in Uganda

United States military personnel withdraw from Taiwan

European Economic Community launches European Monetary System

Europeans vote in first direct election of 410-member European Parliament

Carter-Brezhnev summit in Vienna leads to signing of SALT II

Announcement of Vietnam's admission to COMECON

First U.S. Trident II missile launched

Nicaraguan dictator Antonio Somoza resigns; Managua overtaken by Sandinista rebels as National Guard surrenders

Central Treaty Organization (CENTO) dissolved following withdrawal of Iran, Pakistan, and Turkey

Treaty on exploitation of moon's riches agreed upon by U.N. Committee on Peaceful Uses of Outer Space

Brezhnev offers unilateral withdrawal of 20,000 troops and 1,000 tanks from East Germany

Carter announces decision to deploy MX missile system in the western United States

El Salvador President Carlos Humberto Romero ousted by military in bloodless coup

Iranian students seize over sixty hostages in U.S. embassy in Teheran; demand Shah's return as condition of release

United States freezes Iranian assets; Iranians release five women and eight black hostages

NATO ministers agree to install 572 U.S. medium-range missiles in Western Europe

Vietnamese invasion of Kampuchea

Signing of the second Lomé Convention between the European Community and fifty-eight ACP countries

Soviet troops enter Afghanistan, engineer coup, and install Babrak Karmal as prime minister

Islamic fundamentalists seize Grand Mosque in Mecca

Panama Canal Act returns Canal Zone to Panamanian jurisdiction, leaving canal under U.S. operation through 1999

1980   President Carter orders the embargo of grain sales to the Soviet Union in retaliation for the invasion of Afghanistan

United States announces sale of $280 million in defensive arms to Taiwan

Consular convention and three economic agreements complete process of normalizing U.S. relations with the People's Republic of China

President Carter announces that the United States is willing to sell weapons to the People's Republic of China

Carter asks Senate to table consideration of SALT II in light of Soviet invasion of Afghanistan

Soviet Union says NATO decision to deploy Pershing and cruise missiles in Europe ends chances for East-West talks on theater nuclear forces

Carter says United States will defend Persian Gulf oil fields (Carter Doctrine); calls for draft registration

Canada's embassy in Iran smuggles six hidden U.S. embassy employees out of Iran

United States obtains access to military facilities in Oman, Kenya, and Somalia

U.N. Security Council Resolution 465 censures Israel for its settlements in territory occupied since the June 1967 war; Carter disavows U.S. affirmative vote

New elections in Rhodesia bring Robert Mugabe to power; Rhodesia becomes independent, renamed Zimbabwe

Carter breaks diplomatic relations with Iran

American mission to rescue hostages in Iran aborted, eight die; Secretary of State Vance resigns in disagreement over mission

Marshal Tito of Yugoslavia dies

Common Market foreign ministers agree to sanctions against Iran

United States and fifty-nine nations boycott Moscow Olympics over Soviet presence in Afghanistan

Shah of Iran dies while in exile in Egypt

Israel annexes East Jerusalem

Presidential Directive 59 gives Soviet military targets priority over cities in case of U.S. nuclear attack against Soviet Union

Polish Solidarity workers' strike wins right to form independent unions; Soviet Union threatens military intervention to end Polish liberalization

Iraq-Iran war begins as Iraq invades ninety square miles of Iran in controversy over Shatt al Arab waterway

Reintegration of Greek forces into the integrated military structure of NATO

Boatlift brings 125,000 Cuban refugees to United States

Ronald Reagan wins electoral landslide to become fortieth president

Trial of ''Gang of Four'' opens in China as criticisms of Mao Tse-tung's policies mount

United States rejects Brezhnev proposal for joint nonintervention in Persian Gulf

NATO warns Soviet Union against Polish intervention

1981   Greece becomes the tenth member of the European Economic Community

Replacement of the European unit of account (EUA) by the European currency unit (ECU)

REAGAN ADMINISTRATION

Fifty-two American hostages released by Iran after 444 days in captivity as Reagan is inaugurated

Secretary of State Haig announces that "international terrorism will take the place of human rights" in the foreign policy concerns of the United States

United States promises military assistance to combat insurgency in El Salvador

Reagan administration announces its intention to send twenty more advisers and $25 million in military equipment to support President Duarte of El Salvador; U.S. halts aid to Nicaragua

Attempted assassination of President Reagan

Nonaligned nations call for withdrawal of Soviet troops from Kampuchea and Afghanistan

Zimbabwe announces diplomatic ties with Soviets

Rightist coup fails in Spain

United States sends fifty-four military advisers to El Salvador

Space shuttle *Columbia* returns from successful maiden flight

United States announces deal to sell Saudi Arabia sophisticated, radar-equipped aircraft; Israel protests

United States lifts Soviet grain embargo

Socialist candidate François Mitterand becomes president of France

Pope John Paul II wounded in assassination attempt

Gulf Cooperation Council established by Bahrain, Kuwait, Saudi Arabia, Qatar, Oman, and the United Arab Emirates

United States casts sole vote against a U.N. World Health Organization (WHO) proposal to limit sale of infant formula in Third World

Israeli jets destroy Iraq's nearly completed atomic reactor

United States and China announce joint monitoring of Soviet missile development from China

Chinese Communist Party ends era of Mao Tse-tung by announcing that Great Leap Forward was ridden with mistakes and was followed by the "catastrophic" Cultural Revolution

Saudi Arabia proposes eight-point peace plan which names East Jerusalem as capital of independent Palestinian state

Reagan announces the United States will construct and stockpile the neutron bomb (though not deploy it to Europe)

U.S. fails to win a majority for its proposals at the U.N. Law of the Sea Conference

U.S. Navy jets shoot down two Soviet-built Libyan fighter planes over Mediterranean Sea; United States warns Libya against further provocation

Secretary of State Alexander Haig in Beijing indicates U.S. willingness to sell arms to China, but relations are strained by disagreement over American weapons deliveries to Taiwan

United States accuses North Korea of "lawlessness" in firing surface-to-air missile over international air space at American spy plane

United States and Soviet Union announce negotiations on limiting medium-range missiles in Europe

Haig meets Soviet Foreign Minister Andrei Gromyko officially for first time at United Nations; warns Soviets to change their pattern of international behavior

China makes a comprehensive peace proposal to Taiwan; offers to let rival Nationalist leaders participate in governing China and to retain "a high degree of autonomy" if it unites with the mainland

Taiwan rejects China's peace feeler

Egyptian President Sadat assassinated; succeeded by Vice President Hosni Mubarak

Heads of forty-one Commonwealth nations issue declaration decrying "the slide from détente to confrontation between the superpowers"

Papandreou becomes first Socialist prime minister of Greece

General Jaruzelski replaces Kania as leader of the Polish United Workers Party

Twenty-two-nation Cancún summit on North-South relations convenes

Ninety-three nonaligned nations issue a report describing the United States as the only threat to world peace and prosperity

President Reagan's remark that he could envision a nuclear war limited to Europe unleashes storm of protests

Secretary of State Haig suggests the possibility of NATO use of nuclear weapons

Reagan wins congressional approval of sale of Airborne Warning and Control Systems (AWACs) to Saudi Arabia despite substantial opposition

Reagan proposes to withdraw emplacement of a new generation of American nuclear weapons in Europe in return for the dismantling of Soviet theater nuclear missiles; Soviets reject proposal

Polish government imposes martial law; Reagan administration retaliates with economic sanctions against Poland and the Soviet Union

1982 Soviet Union presented with U.S. "zero-option" arms control proposal

Reagan informs Congress of his desire to resume development of chemical weapons

President Reagan announces Caribbean Basin Initiative

Law of the Sea Treaty approved by U.N.; U.S. announces it will not sign the treaty

The British Falkland Islands are captured by Argentine forces; Britain breaks diplomatic relations and sends a naval task force to the South Atlantic

President Reagan pledges U.S. support for Great Britain in its war with Argentina over the Falkland Islands

British land troops on the Falklands; less than a month later, Argentine forces surrender at Port Stanley

Nicaragua signs $166 million aid agreement with the Soviet Union

Reagan bans all imports of Libyan oil

United States launches campaign against alleged Soviet and Cuban-backed military buildup in Nicaragua

Temporary freeze on deployment of Soviet SS-20 missiles announced by Brezhnev

Haig accuses Soviet Union of widespread use of chemical warfare agents

Morocco agrees to U.S. use of Moroccan air bases during emergencies in the Middle East

Spain becomes sixteenth member of NATO and first nation to join since 1955

U.S. negotiator Paul Nitze and Soviet negotiator Kvitsinsky reach an informal agreement on nuclear weapons in Europe during a "walk in the woods"; both governments reject plan

Israel invades Lebanon and surrounds the PLO by laying seige to West Beirut

Columbia carries the space shuttle's first commercial and military cargo into space

British, American, and Soviet talks on comprehensive test ban discontinued by Reagan administration

Japan announces plans to increase military spending by 60 percent over the next four years

United States imposes embargo on technical equipment for construction of pipeline between Siberia and ten West European countries; EEC protests U.S. ban

Reagan permits U.S. farmers to increase exports of grain to the Soviet Union, claiming that this is not inconsistent with the gas pipeline ban

U.S. Marines land in Lebanon as participants in multinational peace-keeping force (including British, French, and Italian troops)

Reagan administration agrees to reduce weapons sales to Taiwan as long as Beijing seeks peaceful solution of the Taiwan issue

United States assists Mexico avoid debt default with a multibillion dollar aid plan; U.S. banks extend repayment schedule until early 1983

President Reagan calls for "self-government by the Palestinians of the West Bank and Gaza in association with Jordan" and a "freeze" on Israeli settlements in occupied areas and an "undivided" Jerusalem; Israel rejects plan

Pentagon papers claiming a "winnable" nuclear war strategy are leaked, causing outrage in Europe

Lebanese President Bashir Gemayel assassinated in bomb explosion; brother Amin Gemayel elected as successor

Lebanese Christian forces enter Palestinian refugee camps and massacre several hundred people

Poland's "most-favored-nation" trade status suspended by the United States in response to the Polish government's ban on the Solidarity union

Soviet President Leonid Brezhnev dies; Yuri Andropov becomes General Secretary of the Communist Party of the Soviet Union

Indira Gandhi asks the Soviet Union for assistance in building several nuclear power stations

1983   United States lifts embargo on arms sales to Guatemala

The Warsaw Pact proposes a nonaggression agreement with NATO

OPEC members fail to reach agreement on policy, amidst decline of world oil prices

United States and Honduras hold joint war games, the largest to date in Central America

President Reagan delivers "Star Wars" speech calling on the scientific community "to give us the means of rendering . . . nuclear weapons impotent and obsolete"

The International Monetary Fund substantially increases its capacity to extend new loans to its major debtors

Soviet Union proposes a nuclear free zone in Central Europe

United States embassy in Beirut bombed, killing seventeen Americans

Agreement reached between Israel and Lebanon for withdrawal of Israeli forces from Lebanon

Pope John Paul II visits Poland, meets General Jaruzelski and Solidarity union leader Lech Walesa; Polish government later officially ends martial law

Reagan endorses efforts of the Contadora Group (Mexico, Colombia, Panama, and Venezuela) to negotiate for peace in Central America

United States intervenes to slow rapid rise of dollar's value in world currency markets

United States and France respond to Libyan attack on Chad by providing aircraft and supplies to Chad and the Sudan

Benigno Aquino, a prominent Philippine opposition leader, is assassinated on return to Manila from the United States

Flight 007, a Korean Air Lines Boeing 747 passenger plane, is shot down by the Soviet Union after it strays into Soviet airspace

Solidarity leader Walesa of Poland is awarded the Nobel Peace Prize

Suicide truck bomb attack against U.S. peace-keeping forces in their compound at Beirut airport kills 241 Marine and Navy personnel

United States invades Grenada

Raul Alfonsin elected president of Argentina, ending eight years of military rule

Controversial new South African constitution approved allowing for limited political participation by Indian and mixed-blood racial groups

PLO leader Yasser Arafat and loyal PLO forces are evacuated from northern Lebanon to several Middle Eastern nations

Syria shoots down two U.S. Navy jets during a raid on Syrian antiaircraft positions

United States informs UNESCO that it intends to withdraw from the agency in one year

West Germany deploys U.S. Pershing II missiles

1984 Rev. Jesse Jackson secures release of downed Navy flier Lt. Robert Goodman from Syria

Terrorist group Islamic Holy War assassinates Malcolm Kerr, president of American University of Beirut

Chinese Premier Zhao Ziyang journeys to Washington, setting the stage for President Reagan's April visit to China

Abdul Khan, Pakistan's nuclear science chief, claims Pakistan can produce nuclear weapons

U.S. Marines in Beirut begin withdrawal to offshore ships; other nations participating in multinational force withdraw their troops shortly thereafter

Soviet leader Yuri Andropov dies; Konstantin Chernenko becomes General Secretary of the Communist Party of the Soviet Union and President of the Soviet Union

William Wilson is appointed first U.S. ambassador to the Vatican since 1867

Rising unrest in Chile causes government to impose state of emergency

José Duarte wins Salvadoran national elections, defeating Roberto D'Aubuisson for the presidency

The CIA mines the main Nicaraguan port

Reagan visits China; meets with leader Deng Xiaoping to sign agreements on economic and technological relations

Andrei Sakharov, Nobel Peace Prize laureate and Soviet dissident, begins hunger strike to protest Soviet treatment

Summit meeting in London; heads of state and government of the seven major industrialized countries issue a declaration on East-West relations and arms control

The Soviet Union withdraws from the summer Olympic Games in Los Angeles; several pro-Soviet governments follow suit

The Indian army attacks the Sikh's holy shrine, the Golden Temple of Amritsar, killing Sikh leader Jarnail Bhindranwale and over 550 people

Britain and China reach agreement on the future of Hong Kong; transfer of control to China is to be made in 1997 with Hong Kong retaining economic, legal, and educational freedoms

Mexico and international banks agree to reschedule Mexico's $48 billion public sector obligations

Lebanese terrorist group Hizballah cited by United States as being responsible for attacks on U.S. forces in Lebanon

Prime Minister Indira Gandhi of India is assassinated by Sikh bodyguards; Rajiv Gandhi, her son, succeeds her

Ronald Reagan is reelected by record electoral margin

China and the Soviet Union agree to sign four new cooperation agreements, signaling a significant thawing in Sino-Soviet relations

1985 Desmond Tutu, the 1984 Nobel Peace Prize winner, becomes the first black Anglican Archbishop of Johannesburg, South Africa

United States launches the first space shuttle mission designed exclusively for military purposes

PLO leader Yasser Arafat and Jordan's King Hussein reach agreement on a framework for peace

Soviet leader Konstantin Chernenko dies; Mikhail Gorbachev becomes General Secretary of the Communist Party of the Soviet Union

The United States and Soviet Union begin news arms control negotiations in Geneva, encompassing defense and space systems, strategic nuclear forces, and intermediate-range nuclear forces

Conference of eighty Asian and African countries held in Bandung, Indonesia

Israel pulls out of Tyre, the last major Lebanese city under Israeli occupation, thus completing the second of a three-phrased withdrawal

President Reagan visits the Bitburg cemetery where Nazi soldiers are buried, provoking protests by Jewish leaders and others

Reagan announces that the United States will continue to honor the unratified 1979 SALT II treaty

U.S.-funded Radio Marti begins broadcasts to Cuba; Fidel Castro breaks a

U.S.-Cuba immigration pact and threatens to end his cooperation on hijackings

TWA airliner is hijacked by Shi'ite Muslims; thirty-nine American hostages are released after being held for seventeen days in Beirut

Soviet leader Gorbachev further consolidates his power, moving Andrei Gromyko to the ceremonial post of president

South African President Botha declares states of emergency in response to widespread and intense rioting against apartheid

United States and China sign a nuclear cooperation agreement during Chinese President Li's visit to Washington

President Reagan meets in Geneva with Gorbachev to discuss arms control and the future of Soviet-American relations

Palestinians hijack Italian cruise liner *Achille Lauro,* killing one American and holding others hostage for fifty-one hours

U.S. Navy fighter planes force Egyptian airliner carrying four fleeing Palestinian hijackers to land in Sicily

South Africa experiences severe race rioting

Israel proposes an international framework for Middle East peace talks in response to King Hussein's U.N. speech calling for talks with Israel

PLO leader Yasser Arafat renounces terrorist acts outside Israeli-occupied territories

Philippine President Ferdinand E. Marcos, bowing to U.S. pressure, promises presidential election

Prime Ministers Garret FitzGerald of Ireland and Margaret Thatcher of Britain sign a treaty giving Ireland an advisory role in Britain's violence-torn province of Northern Ireland

Terrorists hurl hand grenades and fire into crowds of holiday travelers in twin attacks on the Israeli airline El Al at the Rome and Vienna international airports

1986   U.S. officially withdraws from membership in UNESCO

Spain and Portugal join the European Economic Community

The U.S. space shuttle *Challenger,* with a crew of six astronauts and the first civilian crew member, explodes seventy-four seconds after liftoff

President-for-life of Haiti, Jean-Claude Duvalier, abdicates and flees the country

Philippines President Ferdinand Marcos is overthrown by Corazon Aquino by means of nonviolent opposition; Aquino inaugurated as new president and Marcos evacuates to Hawaii

U.S. Senate approves the international treaty outlawing genocide thirty-seven years after it was first sent to the Senate for ratification by President Harry Truman

United States orders the Soviet Union to cut its U.N. staff by a third, citing national security reasons

Reagan orders a military attack against Libya and Muammar Qaddafi, the alleged sponsor of state terrorism

OPEC nations condemn U.S. bombing of Libya, but reject an appeal by the Libyan oil minister for an oil embargo against the U.S.

United States indicates it will dismantle submarine to remain within SALT II limits, but announces intention to exceed them later in year

Soviet nuclear reactor at Chernobyl explodes, emitting radiation over Western Europe and threatening a meltdown of the reactor core

Kurt Waldheim, former U.N. secretary-general and candidate for president of Austria, is accused of complicity in World War II atrocities as Nazi officer

Leaders of seven major Western industrialized nations meet in Tokyo with international terrorism a prime topic of discussion

South Africa attacks three border states (Mozambique, Zambia, Zimbabwe); U.S. condemns South African action

New Zealand withdraws from the ANZUS defense pact in support of its antinuclear policies; U.S. terminates its obligation to New Zealand

The World Court rules against the United States on its involvement in Nicaragua; U.S. ignores decision

Radical students march against Chun Doo Hwan, South Korea's president

Crisis in South Africa grows more violent; pressure for economic sanctions mounts

U.S. House of Representatives reverses itself, agreeing to $100 million in aid to counterrevolutionaries opposing Nicaraguan Sandinista regime

U.S. military joins Bolivia in war on international drug trafficking

Reagan administration effectively reaffirms South African policy of "constructive engagement"; Congress resumes pressure for economic sanctions

Bishop Desmond Tutu condemns U.S. South African policies, saying "I think the West . . . can go to hell"

U.S. and Soviet officials agree to meet to discuss U.S. avowed intention to abandon SALT II arms limits

Citing "irrefutable evidence" linking Libya to terrorist attacks against Americans in Germany, President Reagan orders a military attack against Libya and Muammar Qaddaffi, the alleged sponsor of state terrorism

The Soviet Union cancels a meeting between Foreign Minister Eduard Shevardnadze and Secretary of State George Shultz

Representatives of the OPEC nations convene in order to condemn the U.S. bombing of Libya, but reject an appeal by the Libyan oil minister for an OPEC embargo against the U.S.

President Reagan gives speech on U.S. South African policy: South African Bishop Desmond Tutu rejects the speech as "nauseating"

The House of Representatives votes to give President Reagan full support for the Contras in Nicaragua

The Senate Appropriations Committee approves $100 million in military and other aid for the Contras

U.S. arrests Soviet physicist posted with the Soviet mission to the U.N. on charges of espionage

Thirty-five-nation conference on security-building measures and disarmament in Europe convenes

Summit meeting of the Non-Aligned Movement held in Harare, Zimbabwe

U.S. journalist Nicholas Daniloff imprisoned by the Soviet Union on charges of espionage

Egyptian President Mubarak and Israeli Prime Minister Peres hold summit meeting in Alexandria, Egypt, after accord on Taba Strip

Philippine President Aquino and President Reagan meet in Washington

Negotiations resume on strategic and medium-range nuclear weapons and on President Reagan's Strategic Defense Initiative

U.S. Secretary of State George Shultz meets Soviet Foreign Minister Eduard Shevardnadze for discussions on whether a Reagan-Gorbachev summit is possible in the coming months

NATO and Warsaw Pact negotiators meet to discuss mutual and balanced force reductions (MBFR) and conventional-arms cutbacks in Europe

The Common Market and COMECON hold talks in Geneva aimed at increasing cooperation; the talks represent a resumption of a dialogue broken off in March 1981

East-West security pact signed by the thirty-five states participating in the 1975 Helsinki Accords allowing all participating states to have the automatic right to send military observers to watch large maneuvers and exercises in any other state anywhere in Europe

The European Community and COMECON hold talks in Geneva, resuming dialogue broken off in 1981

U.S. House of Representatives overrides presidential veto of sanctions against South Africa

U.S. journalist Nicholas Daniloff, imprisoned by the Soviet Union on charges of espionage, is released

Soviet Union spurns U.S. offer to sell wheat at subsidized prices

GATT nations meet in Punta del Este to plan new round of global trade negotiations

President Reagan and Soviet leader Gorbachev agree to hold summit in Iceland*

---

*This chronology includes events through September 30, 1986.

REFERENCES

ABERBACH, JOEL D., AND BERT A. ROCKMAN. (1976) "Clashing Beliefs Within the Executive Branch: The Nixon Administration Bureaucracy," *American Political Science Review* 70 (June): 456–468.

ABRAHAMSEN, DAVID. (1977) *Nixon vs. Nixon: An Emotional Tragedy.* New York: Farrar, Straus and Giroux.

ABRAHAMSSON, BERNHARD J. (1975) "The International Oil Industry," pp. 73–88 in Joseph S. Szyliowicz and Bard E. O'Neill (eds.), *The Energy Crisis and U.S. Foreign Policy.* New York: Praeger.

ACHESON, DEAN. (1969) *Present at the Creation.* New York: Norton.

ACKLEY, RICHARD T. (1976) "Strategic Arms Limitation: The Problem of Mutual Deterrence," pp. 221–245 in William W. Whitson (ed.), *Foreign Policy and U.S. National Security.* New York: Praeger.

ADDO, HERB. (1981) "Foreign Policy Strategies for Achieving the New International Economic Order: A Third World Perspective," pp. 233–253 in Charles W. Kegley, Jr., and Pat McGowan (eds.), *The Political Economy of Foreign Policy Behavior.* Beverly Hills, CA: Sage.

ADELMAN, KENNETH L. (1981) "Speaking of America: Public Diplomacy in Our Time," *Foreign Affairs* 59 (Spring): 913–936.

ADLER, SELIG. (1957) *The Isolationist Impulse.* New York: Abelard-Schuman.

ADORNO, THEODORE W., ELSE FRENKEL-BRUNSWIK, DANIEL J. LEVINSON, AND R. NEVITT SANFORD. (1950) *The Authoritarian Personality.* New York: Harper.

ALLISON, GRAHAM T. (1971) *Essence of Decision: Explaining the Cuban Missile Crisis.* Boston: Little, Brown.

ALLISON, GRAHAM T., AND PETER SZANTON. (1976) "Organizing for the Decade Ahead," pp. 227–270 in Henry Owen and Charles L. Schultze (eds.), *Setting National Priorities: The Next Ten Years.* Washington, DC: Brookings Institution.

ALMOND, GABRIEL A. (1960) *The American People and Foreign Policy.* New York: Praeger.

ALPEROVITZ, GAR. (1985) *Atomic Diplomacy: Hiroshima and Potsdam—The Use of the Atomic Bomb and the American Confrontation with Soviet Power,* rev. ed. New York: Penguin.

——. (1970) *Cold War Essays.* Garden City, NY: Doubleday-Anchor.

——. (1965) *Atomic Diplomacy.* New York: Simon and Schuster.

ALPEROVITZ, GAR, AND JEFF FAUX. (1984) "Think Again: What We Need Is More Government, Not Less," *The Washington Post National Weekly Edition* (October 22): 23.

ALSOP, JOSEPH, AND DAVID JORAVSKY. (1980) "Was the Hiroshima Bomb Necessary? An Exchange," *The New York Review of Books* 27 (October 23): 37–42.

AMBROSE, STEPHEN E. (1985) *Rise to Globalism: American Foreign Policy Since 1938.* New York: Penguin.

AMIN, SAMIR. (1974) *Accumulation on a World Scale: A Critique of the Theory of Underdevelopment.* New York: Monthly Review Press.

ANDERSON, PAUL A. (1986) "What Do Decision Makers Do When They Make a Foreign Policy Decision?" forthcoming in Charles F. Hermann, Charles W. Kegley, Jr., and James N. Rosenau (eds.), *New Directions in the Study of Foreign Policy.* London: Allen and Unwin.

ANDERSON, WILLIAM D., AND STERLING J. KERNECK. (1985) "How 'Realistic' Is Reagan's Diplomacy?" *Political Science Quarterly* 100 (Fall): 389–409.

ANGELL, ROBERT C. (1969) *Peace on the March.* New York: Van Nostrand Reinhold.

ANJARIA, S. J. (1986) "A New Round of Global Trade Negotiations," *Finance and Development* 23 (June): 2–6.

ART, ROBERT J. (1985) "Congress and the Defense Budget: Enhancing Policy Oversight," *Political Science Quarterly* 100 (Summer): 227–248.

ASCH, S. E. (1951) "Effects of Group Pressure Upon the Modification and Distortion of Judgment," pp. 177–190 in Harold Guetzkow (ed.), *Groups, Leadership and Men.* Pittsburgh: Carnegie.

ASHER, HERBERT B. (1984) *Presidential Elections and American Politics.* Homewood, IL: Dorsey.

ASHLEY, RICHARD K. (1984) "The Poverty of Neorealism," *International Organization* 38 (Spring): 255–286.

ASPIN, LES. (1976) "The Defense Budget and Foreign Policy: The Role of Congress," pp. 115–174 in Franklin A. Long and George W. Rathjens (eds.), *Arms, Defense Policy, and Arms Control.* New York: Norton.

ATKINSON, RICK, AND FRED HIATT. (1985) "Oh, That Golden Safety Net: The Pentagon Never Met a Defense Contractor It Wouldn't Bail Out," *The Washington Post National Weekly Edition* (April 22): 6–8.

AUSTIN, ANTHONY. (1971) *The President's War.* Philadelphia: Lippincott.

AVERY, DENNIS. (1985) "U.S. Farm Dilemma: The Global Bad News Is Wrong," *Science* 20 (October 25): 408–412.

AYITTEY, GEORGE B. N. (1986) "The Real Foreign Debt Problem," *The Wall Street Journal* (April 8): 30.

AZAR, EDWARD E., AND THOMAS J. SLOAN. (1973) *Dimensions of Interaction: A Source Book for the Study of the Behavior of 31 Nations From 1948 Through 1973.* Pittsburgh: University Center for International Studies, University of Pittsburgh.

BABER, ASA. (1981) "What You're Not Supposed to Know About the Arms Race," *Playboy* 28 (June): 138ff.

BACHRACH, PETER. (ed.) (1971) *Political Elites in a Democracy.* New York: Atherton.

BAILEY, THOMAS A. (1969) *A Diplomatic History of the American People.* New York: Appleton-Century-Crofts.

BAKER, ROSS K. (1985) "The Second Reagan Term," pp. 133–156 in Gerald M. Pomper, Ross K. Baker, Charles E. Jacob, Scott Keeter, Wilson Carey McWilliams, and Henry A. Plotkin, *The Election of 1984: Reports and Interpretation.* Chatham, NJ: Chatham House.

———. (1981) "Outlook for the Reagan Administration," pp. 142–169 in Gerald Pomper, Ross K. Baker, Kathleen A. Frankovic, Charles E. Jacob, Wilson Carey McWilliams, and Henry A. Plotkin, *The Election of 1980: Reports and Interpretations.* Chatham, NJ: Chatham House.

BALDRIGE, MALCOLM. (1983) "At Last, Hope for Coherent Policy," *The New York Times* (June 19): 2F.

BALL, DESMOND. (1985) "Can Nuclear War Be Controlled?" pp. 270–277 in Charles W. Kegley, Jr., and Eugene R. Wittkopf (eds.), *The Nuclear Reader.* New York: St. Martin's.

———. (1983) *Targeting for Strategic Deterrence.* Adelphi Papers Number 185. London: International Institute for Strategic Studies.

BALL, GEORGE. (1984a) "Foreign Policy: A Tragedy of Errors," *Bulletin of the Atomic Scientists* 40 (June/July): 4–7.

———. (1984b) "White House Roulette," *The New York Review of Books* 31 (November 8): 5–11.

———. (1982) *The Past Has Another Pattern: Memoirs.* New York: Norton.

———. (1976) *Diplomacy for a Crowded World: An American Foreign Policy.* Boston: Atlantic-Little, Brown.

———. (1962) "Lawyers and Diplomats," *Department of State Bulletin* 47 (December 31): 990.

BAMFORD, JAMES. (1983) *The Puzzle Palace.* New York: Penguin.

BANKS, ARTHUR S. (ed.) (1979) *Political Handbook of the World, 1979.* New York: McGraw-Hill.

BARAN, PAUL. (1968) *The Political Economy of Growth.* New York: Monthly Review Press.

BARBER, JAMES DAVID. (1985) *The Presidential Character,* 3rd ed. Englewood Cliffs, NJ: Prentice-Hall.

———. (1981) "Reagan's Sheer Personal Likability Faces Its Sternest Test," *The Washington Post* (January 20): 8.

———. (1977) *The Presidential Character,* 2nd ed. Englewood Cliffs, NJ: Prentice-Hall.

BARD, MITCHELL. (1985) "The Water's Edge and Beyond: Defining the Boundaries of Domestic Influence on U.S. Middle East Policy." Paper delivered at the Annual Meeting of the American Political Science Association, New Orleans, August 29–September 1.

BARGER, HAROLD M. (1984) *The Impossible Presidency: Illusions and Realities of Executive Power.* Glenview, IL: Scott, Foresman.

BARITZ, LOREN. (1985) *Backfire: A History of How American Culture Led Us into Vietnam and Made Us Fight The Way We Did.* New York: William Morrow.

BARNABY, FRANK, AND RONALD HUISKEN. (1975) *Arms Uncontrolled.* Cambridge, MA: Harvard University Press.

BARNET, RICHARD J. (1981) "The Search for National Security," *The New Yorker* 57 (April 27): 50–52ff.

———. (1972) *Roots of War: The Men and Institutions Behind U.S. Foreign Policy.* Baltimore: Penguin.

BARNET, RICHARD J., AND RONALD E. MÜLLER. (1974) *Global Reach: The Power of the Multinational Corporations.* New York: Simon and Schuster.

BAX, FRANS R. (1977) "The Legislative-Executive Relationship in Foreign Policy: New Partnership or New Competition?" *Orbis* 20 (Winter): 881–904.

BECKER, HAROLD S. (1982) "Conflict and Accommodation: The Future of the Balance of Power," *The Futurist* 16 (June): 21–25.

BECKER, STEPHEN E., AND J. MICHAEL LANDRUM. (1984) "Survey and Appraisal of Current Crisis Management." Newport, RI: Center for Advanced Research, Naval War College.

BENNETT, W. LANCE. (1980) *Public Opinion in American Politics.* New York: Harcourt Brace Jovanovich.

BERELSON, BERNARD, AND GARY STEINER. (1964) *Human Behavior: An Inventory of Scientific Findings.* New York: Harcourt Brace and World.

BERES, LOUIS RENÉ. (1984) *Reason and Realpolitik: U.S. Foreign Policy and World Order.* Lexington, MA: Heath.

BERKLEY, GEORGE E. (1978) *The Craft of Public Administration.* Boston: Allyn and Bacon.

BERKOWITZ, MORTON, P. G. BOCK, AND VINCENT J. FUCCILLO. (1977) *The Politics of American Foreign Policy.* Englewood Cliffs, NJ: Prentice-Hall.

BERNSTEIN, CARL, AND BOB WOODWARD. (1974) *All the President's Men.* New York: Warner.

BERRY, JEFFREY M. (1984) *The Interest Group Society.* Boston: Little, Brown.

BETTS, RICHARD K. (1978) "Analysis, War and Decision: Why Intelligence Failures Are Inevitable," *World Politics* 31 (October): 61–89.

BHAGWATI, JAGDISH N. (1984) "Introduction," pp. 1–18 in Jagdish N. Bhagwati and John Gerard Ruggie (eds.), *Power, Passions, and Purpose.* Cambridge, MA: MIT Press.

BLACHMAN, MORRIS J. (1973) "The Stupidity of Intelligence," pp. 328–333 in Morton H. Halperin and Arnold Kanter (eds.), *Readings in American Foreign Policy.* Boston: Little, Brown.

BLAKE, DAVID H., AND ROBERT S. WALTERS. (1983) *The Politics of Global Economic Relations*, 2nd ed. Englewood Cliffs, NJ: Prentice-Hall.

_____. (1976) *The Politics of Global Economic Relations*. Englewood Cliffs, NJ: Prentice-Hall.

BLECHMAN, BARRY M. (1984) "Do Negotiated Arms Limitations Have a Future?" pp. 121–128 in Charles W. Kegley, Jr., and Eugene R. Wittkopf (eds.), *The Global Agenda*. New York: Random House.

BLECHMAN, BARRY M., AND STEPHEN S. KAPLAN, WITH DAVID K. HALL, WILLIAM B. QUANDT, JEROME N. SLATER, ROBERT M. SLUSSER, AND PHILIP WINDSOR. (1978) *Force Without War*. Washington, DC: Brookings Institution.

BLOCK, FRED L. (1977) *The Origins of International Economic Disorder*. Berkeley: University of California Press.

BLOOMFIELD, LINCOLN P. (1978) "Planning Foreign Policy: Can It Be Done?" *Political Science Quarterly* 93 (Fall): 369–391.

_____. (1974a) *The Foreign Policy Process: Making Theory Relevant*. Beverly Hills, CA: Sage.

_____. (1974b) *In Search of American Foreign Policy*. New York: Oxford University Press.

BOBROW, DAVIS B. (1982) "Uncoordinated Giants," pp. 23–49 in Charles W. Kegley, Jr., and Pat McGowan (eds.), *Foreign Policy: USA/USSR*. Beverly Hills, CA: Sage.

BOFFEY, PHILIP M. (1983) "'Rational' Decisions Prove Not To Be," *The New York Times* (December 6): 1–17.

BOGDANOWICZ-BINDERT, CHRISTINE A. (1985/86) "World Debt: The United States Reconsiders," *Foreign Affairs* 64 (Winter): 259–273.

BORKLUND, C. W. (1968) *The Department of Defense*. New York: Praeger.

BOULDING, KENNETH E. (1959) "National Images and International Systems," *Journal of Conflict Resolution* 3 (June): 120–131.

BOYD, RICHARD W. (1972) "Popular Control of Public Policy: A Normal Vote Analysis of the 1968 Election," *American Political Science Review* 66 (June): 429–449.

BRADY, LINDA P. (1978) "The Situation and Foreign Policy," pp. 173–190 in Maurice A. East, Stephen A. Salmore, and Charles F. Hermann (eds.), *Why Nations Act*. Beverly Hills, CA: Sage.

_____. (1977) "Planning for Foreign Policy," *International Journal* 32 (No. 4): 829–848.

BRECHER, MICHAEL, AND JONATHAN WILKENFELD. (1982) "Crisis in World Politics," *World Politics* 34 (April): 380–417.

BRESLAUER, GEORGE W. (1983) "Why Détente Failed: An Interpretation," pp. 319–340 in Alexander L. George (ed.), *Managing U.S.-Soviet Rivalry*. Boulder, CO: Westview.

BREWER, GARRY D., AND PAUL BRACKEN. (1984) "Who's Thinking About National Security?" *Worldview* 27 (February): 21–23.

BREWER, THOMAS L. (1980) *American Foreign Policy*. Englewood Cliffs, NJ: Prentice-Hall.

BRITAN, GERALD M. (1981) *Bureaucracy and Innovation: An Ethnography of Policy Change.*" Beverly Hills, CA: Sage.

BRODER, DAVID S. (1986) "Who Took the Fun Out of Congress?" *The Washington Post National Weekly Edition* (February 17): 9–10.

BRODY, RICHARD. (1984) "International Crises: A Rallying Point for the President?" *Public Opinion* 6 (December/January): 41–43, 60.

BRONFENBRENNER, URIE. (1975) "The Mirror Image in Soviet-American Relations," pp. 161–166 in William D. Coplin and Charles W. Kegley, Jr. (eds.), *Analyzing International Relations*. New York: Praeger.

BROWN, HAROLD. (1983) *Thinking About National Security: Defense and Foreign Policy in a Dangerous World*. Boulder, CO: Westview.

BROWN, LESTER R. (1978) *The Twenty-Ninth Day*. New York: Norton.

_____. (1974) *By Bread Alone*. New York: Praeger.

_____. (1972) *World Without Borders*. New York: Vintage Books.

BROWN, LESTER R., EDWARD C. WOLF, LINDA STARKE, WILLIAM U. CHANDLER, CHRISTOPHER FLAVIN, SANDRA POSTEL, AND CYNTHIA POLLOCK. (1985) *State of the World 1985*. New York: Norton.

BROWN, SEYOM. (1977) "A Cooling-off Period for U.S.-Soviet Relations," *Foreign Policy* 28 (Fall): 3–21.

BROWNSTEIN, RONALD, AND NINA EASTON. (1983) *Reagan's Ruling Class*. New York: Pantheon.

BRUCAN, SILVIU. (1984) "The Global Crisis," *International Studies Quarterly* 28 (March): 97–109.

BRZEZINSKI, ZBIGNIEW. (1983) *Power and Principle: Memoirs of the National Security Adviser 1977–1981*. New York: Farrar, Straus and Giroux.

———. (1972) "How the Cold War Was Played," *Foreign Affairs* 52 (October): 181–209.

———. (1970) *Between Two Ages: America's Role in the Technetronic Era*. New York: Viking.

BUCHANAN, BRUCE. (1978) *The Presidential Experience: What the Office Does to the Man*. Englewood Cliffs, NJ: Prentice-Hall.

BUCKLEY, WILLIAM F. (1970) "On The Right," *National Review* (October 24): 1124–1125.

BUNCE, VALERIE. (1981) *Do New Leaders Make A Difference?* Princeton, NJ: Princeton University Press.

BUNDY, MCGEORGE, GEORGE F. KENNAN, ROBERT S. MCNAMARA, AND GERALD SMITH. (1982) "Nuclear Weapons and the Atlantic Alliance," *Foreign Affairs* 60 (Spring): 753–768.

BURCH, PHILIP H., JR. (1980) *Elites in American History: The New Deal to the Carter Administration*. New York: Holmes and Meier.

BURGESS, JOHN. (1985) "The Rearming of Japan: Applying Money and Discipline," *The Washington Post National Weekly Edition* (August 26): 17–18.

BURKI, SHAHID JAVED. (1983) "UNCTAD VI: For Better or for Worse?" *Finance and Development* 20 (December): 16–19.

BURNHAM, DAVID. (1983) "The Silent Power of the N.S.A.," *The New York Times Magazine* (March 27): 60ff.

BURNS, JAMES MACGREGOR. (1984) *The Crisis of American Leadership*. New York: Simon and Schuster.

———. (1978) *Leadership*. New York: Harper and Row.

CALDWELL, DAN. (ed.) (1985) *Soviet International Behavior and U.S. Policy Options*. Lexington, MA: Lexington Books.

———. (1977) "Bureaucratic Foreign Policy Making," *American Behavioral Scientist* 21 (September–October): 87–110.

CALIFANO, JOSEPH A., JR. (1975) *A Presidential Nation*. New York: Norton.

CALLEO, DAVID P. (1985) "New Prescriptions for Old Ailments," *The New York Times Book Review* (December 7): 14–15.

CAMPBELL, ANGUS, PHILIP E. CONVERSE, WARREN E. MILLER, AND DONALD E. STOKES. (1960) *The American Voter*. New York: Wiley.

CAMPBELL, JOEL AND LEILA CAIN. (1965) "Public Opinion and the Outbreak of War," *Journal of Conflict Resolution* 9 (September): 318–329.

CAMPBELL, JOHN FRANKLIN. (1971) *The Foreign Affairs Fudge Factory*. New York: Basic Books.

CANNON, LOU. (1985) "The Great Delegator Has Some Pressing Command Decisions to Make," *The Washington Post National Weekly Edition* (May 27): 27.

CAPORASO, JAMES A. (1978) "Dependence and Dependency in the Global System." Special issue of *International Organization* 32 (Winter): 1–300.

CAREY, OMER L. (ed.) (1969) *The Military-Industrial Complex and U.S. Foreign Policy*. Pullman: Washington State University Press.

CARNESALE, ALBERT. (1985) "Special Supplement: The Strategic Defense Initiative," pp. 187–205 in George E. Hudson and Joseph Kruzel (eds.), *American Defense Annual 1985–1986*. Lexington, MA: Heath.

CARR, E. H. (1939) *The Twenty-Years' Crisis 1919–1939: An Introduction to the Study of International Relations*. London: Macmillan.

CARTER, HODDING, III. (1982) "The Interventionist Drums Are Still Beating," *The Wall Street Journal* (September 9): 27.

———. (1981) "Life Inside the Carter State Department," *Playboy* 28 (February): 96ff.

CASPARY, WILLIAM R. (1970) "The 'Mood Theory': A Study of Public Opinion," *American Political Science Review* 64 (June): 536–547.

CAVANAGH, THOMAS E. (1982–83) "The Dispersion of Authority in the House of Representatives," *Political Science Quarterly* 97 (Winter): 623–637.

CENTRAL INTELLIGENCE AGENCY. (1985) *Factbook on Intelligence*. Washington, DC: Central Intelligence Agency.

———. (1980) "International Terrorism in 1979." A Report Prepared by the National Foreign Assessment Center. Washington, DC: Director of Public Affairs, Central Intelligence Agency (April).

CENTRE ON TRANSNATIONAL CORPORATIONS. (1983) *Transnational Corporations in World Development: Third Survey*. New York: United Nations.

CHACE, JAMES. (1978) "Is a Foreign Policy Consensus Possible?" *Foreign Affairs* 57 (Fall): 1–16.

CHILDS, HAROLD L. (1965) *Public Opinion: Nature, Formation, and Role*. Princeton, NJ: Van Nostrand.

CHRISTIE, RICHARD, AND FLORENCE L. GEIS. (1970) *Studies in Machiavellianism*. New York: Academic Press.

CLAIRMONTE, FREDERICK, AND JOHN CAVANAGH. (1982) "Transnational Corporations and Global Markets: Changing Power Relations," *Trade and Development: An UNCTAD Review* 4 (Winter): 149–182.

CLARK, JAMES W. (1975) "Foreign Affairs Personnel Management," pp. 181–222 in *Commission on the Organization of the Government for the Conduct of Foreign Policy*, Vol. 6, Appendix P. Washington, DC: Government Printing Office.

CLARK, KEITH C., AND LAURENCE J. LEGERE. (eds.) (1969) *The President and the Management of National Security: A Report by the Institute for Defense Analyses*. New York: Praeger.

CLARKE, DUNCAN L., AND EDWARD L. NEVELEFF. (1984) "Security, Foreign Intelligence, and Civil Liberties: Has the Pendulum Swung Too Far?" *Political Science Quarterly* 99 (Fall): 493–513.

CLAUSEN, A. W. (1984) "Priority Issues for 1984." World Bank press release, January 26. Remarks prepared for delivery before the European Management Forum, Davos, Switzerland.

CLEVELAND, HARLAN. (1982) "U.S. Foreign Policy: Illusions of Powerlessness and Realities of Power," *Atlantic Community Quarterly* 20 (Summer): 143–152.

———. (1959) "Dinosaurs and Personal Freedom," *Saturday Review* 42 (February 28): 12–14ff.

CLOTFELTER, JAMES. (1973) *The Military in American Politics*. New York: Harper and Row.

CLYMER, ADAM. (1985a) "Perception of America's World Role Ten Years After Vietnam: Assertiveness Caused by Reagan, Trust and Sex." Paper presented at the Annual Meeting of the American Political Science Association, New Orleans, August 29–September 1.

———. (1985b) "Polling Americans," *The New York Times Magazine* (November 10): 37ff.

COHEN, BERNARD C. (1983) "The Influence of Special-Interest Groups and the Mass Media on Security Policy in the United States," pp. 222–241 in Charles W. Kegley, Jr., and Eugene R. Wittkopf (eds.), *Perspectives on American Foreign Policy*. New York: St. Martin's.

———. (1973) *The Public's Impact on Foreign Policy*. Boston: Little, Brown.

———. (1963) *The Press and Foreign Policy*. Princeton, NJ: Princeton University Press.

———. (1961) "Foreign Policy Makers and the Press," pp. 220–228 in James N. Rosenau (ed.), *International Politics and Foreign Policy*. New York: Free Press.

———. (1959) *The Influence of Non-Governmental Groups on Foreign Policy*. Boston: World Peace Foundation.

COHEN, ELIOT A. (1984) "Constraints on America's Conduct of Small Wars," *International Security* 9 (Fall): 151–181.

COHEN, IRA S. (1975) *Realpolitik: Theory and Practice*. Belmont, CA: Dickenson.

COHEN, STEPHEN D. (1981) *The Making of United States International Economic Policy*. New York: Praeger.

COMMAGER, HENRY STEELE. (1983) "Misconceptions Governing American Foreign Policy," pp. 510–517 in Charles W. Kegley, Jr., and Eugene R. Wittkopf (eds.), *Perspectives on American Foreign Policy*. New York: St. Martin's.

_____. (1965) "A Historian Looks at Our Political Morality," *Saturday Review* 48 (July 10): 16–18.

Commission on the Organization of the Government for the Conduct of Foreign Policy. (1975) Washington, DC: Government Printing Office.

COMMISSION ON TRANSNATIONAL CORPORATIONS. (1979) "Supplementary Material on the Issue of Defining Transnational Corporations," U.N. Doc. E/C.10/58, United Nations Economic and Social Council (March 23). New York: United Nations.

COMMITTEE ON THE BUDGET, U.S. HOUSE OF REPRESENTATIVES. (1984) *A Review of President Reagan's Budget Recommendations, 1981–1985* (August 2). Washington, DC: Government Printing Office.

CONGRESSIONAL QUARTERLY. (1986a) *The Middle East*. Washington, DC: Congressional Quarterly, Inc.

_____. (1986b) *U.S. Foreign Policy: The Reagan Imprint*. Washington, DC: Congressional Quarterly, Inc.

_____. (1984) *Trade: U.S. Policy Since 1945*. Washington, DC: Congressional Quarterly, Inc.

_____. (1983) *U.S. Defense Policy*. Washington, DC: Congressional Quarterly, Inc.

_____. (1980a) *President Carter 1979*. Washington, DC: Congressional Quarterly, Inc.

_____. (1980b) *U.S. Defense Policy*. Washington, DC: Congressional Quarterly, Inc.

_____. (1978) *U.S. Defense Policy*. Washington, DC: Congressional Quarterly, Inc.

Congressional Quarterly Almanac, 1984. (1985) Vol. 40. Washington, DC: Congressional Quarterly, Inc.

_____, *1980*. (1981) Vol. 36. Washington, DC: Congressional Quarterly, Inc.

_____, *1979*. (1980) Vol. 35. Washington, DC: Congressional Quarterly, Inc.

_____, *1976*. (1976) Vol. 32. Washington, DC: Congressional Quarterly, Inc.

_____, *1973*. (1974) Vol. 29. Washington, DC: Congressional Quarterly, Inc.

CONGRESSIONAL RESEARCH SERVICE. (1984) *Treaties and Other International Agreements: The Role of the United States Senate*. Prepared for the Committee on Foreign Relations of the United States Senate. 96th Congress, 2nd Session. Washington, DC: Government Printing Office.

_____. (1980) *Studies on the Legislative Veto*. Prepared for the Subcommittee on Rules of the House Committee on Rules, U.S. House of Representatives. 96th Congress, 2nd Session. Washington, DC: Government Printing Office.

_____. (1976) *United States/Soviet Military Balance: A Frame of Reference for Congress*. Committee Print, Senate Committee on Armed Services. 94th Congress, 2nd Session. Washington, DC: Government Printing Office.

CONWAY, M. MARGARET. (1985) *Political Participation in the United States*. Washington, DC: CQ Press.

COOPER, JOSEPH. (1985) "The Legislative Veto in the 1980s," pp. 364–389 in Lawrence C. Dodd and Bruce I. Oppenheimer (eds.), *Congress Reconsidered*. Washington, DC: CQ Press.

_____. (1983) "Postscript on the Congressional Veto: Is There Life After Chadha?" *Political Science Quarterly* 98 (Fall): 427–429.

COPLIN, WILLIAM D., PATRICK J. McGOWAN, AND MICHAEL K. O'LEARY. (1974) *American Foreign Policy*. North Scituate, MA: Duxbury Press.

CORSON, WILLIAM R. (1977) *The Armies of Ignorance: The Rise of the American Intelligence Empire*. New York: Dial Press.

COX, ARTHUR MACY. (1976) *The Dynamics of Détente*. New York: Norton.

CRABB, CECIL V., JR. (1982) *The Doctrines of American Foreign Policy*. Baton Rouge: Louisiana State University Press.

_____. (1976) *Policy Makers and Critics: Conflicting Theories of American Foreign Policy*. New York: Praeger.

CRABB, CECIL V., JR., AND PAT M. HOLT. (1984) *Invitation to Struggle*. Washington, DC: CQ Press.

CRAIG, PAUL P., AND JOHN A. JUNGERMAN. (1986) *Nuclear Arms Race*. New York: McGraw-Hill.

CRONIN, THOMAS E. (1984) "The Swelling of the Presidency: Can Anyone Reverse the Tide?" pp. 345–359 in Peter Woll (ed.), *American Government: Readings and Cases*. Boston: Little, Brown.

_____. (1980) "The Presidency and its Paradoxes," pp. 111–123 in Harry A. Baily, Jr. (ed.), *Classics of the American Presidency*. Oak Park, IL: Moore.

_____. (1973) "The Swelling of the Presidency," *Saturday Review of the Society* 1 (February): 30–36.

CROZIER, BRIAN, DREW MIDDLETON, AND JEREMY MURRAY-BROWN. (1985) *This War Called Peace*. New York: Universe Books.

DA GAMA PINTO, CLARENCE. (1983) "Who Sells What To Whom?: Reagan's High-Powered Arms Transfer Policy Keeps U.S. Exports at Record Levels," *South* 34 (August): 15–16.

DAHL, ROBERT, AND CHARLES LINDBLOM. (1953) *Politics, Economics and Welfare*. New York: Harper and Row.

DALESKI, RICHARD J. (1980) *Defense Management in the 1980s*. Washington, DC: National Defense University.

DALLEK, ROBERT. (1984) *Ronald Reagan: The Politics of Symbolism*. Cambridge, MA: Harvard University Press.

_____. (1983) *The American Style of Foreign Policy: Cultural Politics and Foreign Affairs*. New York: Knopf.

DAVISON, W. PHILLIPS. (1976) "Mass Communication and Diplomacy," pp. 388–403 in Gavin Boyd, James N. Rosenau, and Kenneth W. Thompson (eds.), *World Politics*. New York: Free Press.

Department of Defense, Annual Report, Fiscal Year 1979, Harold Brown, Secretary of Defense, February 2, 1978. (1978) Washington, DC: Department of Defense.

DERIVERA, JOSEPH H. (1968) *The Psychological Dimension of Foreign Policy*. Columbus, OH: Merrill.

DESTLER, I. M. (1986) "Protecting Congress or Protecting Trade?" *Foreign Policy* 62 (Spring): 96–107.

_____. (1985) "Executive-Congressional Conflict in Foreign Policy: Explaining It, Coping With It," pp. 343–363 in Lawrence C. Dodd and Bruce I. Oppenheimer (eds.), *Congress Reconsidered*, 2nd ed. Washington, DC: CQ Press.

_____. (1984) "The Elusive Consensus: Congress and Central America," pp. 319–335 in Robert S. Leiken (ed.), *Central America*. New York: Pergamon.

_____. (1983a) "Dateline Washington: Life After The Veto," *Foreign Policy* 52 (Fall): 181–186.

_____. (1983b) "The Evolution of Reagan Foreign Policy," pp. 117–158 in Fred I. Greenstein (ed.), *The Reagan Presidency*. Baltimore: The Johns Hopkins University Press.

_____. (1983c) "The Rise of the National Security Assistant," pp. 260–281 in Charles W. Kegley, Jr., and Eugene R. Wittkopf (eds.), *Perspectives on American Foreign Policy*. New York: St. Martin's.

_____. (1981) "Congress as Boss?" *Foreign Policy* 42 (Spring): 167–180.

_____. (1980) *Making Foreign Economic Policy*. Washington, DC: Brookings Institution.

_____. (1974) *Presidents, Bureaucrats, and Foreign Policy: The Politics of Organizational Reform*. Princeton, NJ: Princeton University Press.

DESTLER, I. M., LESLIE H. GELB, AND ANTHONY LAKE. (1984) *Our Own Worst Enemy: The Unmaking of American Foreign Policy*. New York: Simon and Schuster.

DE TOCQUEVILLE, ALEXIS. (1969) (Originally published in 1835) *Democracy in America*. New York: Doubleday.

DEUTSCH, KARL W. (1974) *Politics and Government*. Boston: Houghton Mifflin.

_____. (1953) "The Growth of Nations: Some Recurrent Patterns of Political and Social Integration," *World Politics* 5 (January): 168–195.

DEUTSCH, KARL W., AND RICHARD L. MERRITT. (1965) "Effects of Events on National and International Images," pp. 132–187 in Herbert C. Kelman (ed.), *International Behavior*. New York: Holt, Rinehart and Winston.

DEVINE, DONALD J. (1972) *The Political Culture of the United States*. Boston: Little, Brown.

Diplomacy for the 70's: A Program of Management Reform for the Department of State. (1970) Washington, DC: Department of State.

DIRENZO, GORDON J. (ed.) (1974) *Personality and Politics*. Garden City, NY: Doubleday-Anchor.

DOLBEARE, KENNETH M. (1974) *Political Change in the United States*. New York: McGraw-Hill.

DOLBEARE, KENNETH M., AND PATRICIA DOLBEARE. (1971) *American Ideologies*. Chicago: Markham.

DOLBEARE, KENNETH M., AND MURRAY J. EDELMAN. (1985) *American Politics*, 5th ed. Lexington, MA: Heath.

_____. (1981) *American Politics*, 4th ed. Lexington, MA: Heath.

_____. (1974) *American Politics*. Lexington, MA: Heath.

DOMHOFF, G. WILLIAM. (1984) *Who Rules America Now?* Englewood Cliffs, NJ: Prentice-Hall.

_____. (ed.) (1980) *Power Structure Research*. Beverly Hills, CA: Sage.

_____. (1979) *The Powers That Be: Processes of Ruling Class Domination in America*. New York: Vintage Books.

_____. (1971) "Who Made American Foreign Policy, 1945–1963?" pp. 95–114 in Douglas M. Fox (ed.), *The Politics of U.S. Foreign Policy Making*. Pacific Palisades, CA: Goodyear.

DONOVAN, HEDLEY. (1985) *Roosevelt to Reagan*. New York: Harper and Row.

DONOVAN, JOHN C. (1974) *The Cold Warriors: A Policy-Making Elite*. Lexington, MA: Heath.

DOUGHERTY, JAMES E., AND ROBERT L. PFALTZGRAFF, JR. (1986) *American Foreign Policy: FDR to Reagan*. New York: Harper and Row.

DOWNS, ANTHONY. (1957) *An Economic Theory of Democracy*. New York: Harper and Row.

DRAPER, THEODORE. (1968) *The Dominican Revolt*. New York: Commentary.

DRISCHLER, ALVIN PAUL. (1985) "Foreign Policy Making on the Hill," *Washington Quarterly* 8 (Summer): 165–175.

DROZDIAK, WILLIAM. (1984) "Hungary Leads Moscow's Satellites on a Quiet Quest for Détente," *The Washington Post National Weekly Edition* (September 19): 16.

DUCHIN, FAYE. (1983) "Economic Consequences of Military Spending," *Journal of Economic Issues* 17 (June): 543–553.

DULLES, JOHN FOSTER. (1952) "A Policy of Liberation," *Life* (May 19): 19ff.

_____. (1939) *War, Peace and Change*. New York: Harper and Row.

DYE, THOMAS R. (1986) *Who's Running America? The Conservative Years*. Englewood Cliffs. NJ: Prentice-Hall.

_____. (1983) *Who's Running America? The Reagan Years*. Englewood Cliffs, NJ: Prentice-Hall.

_____. (1979) *Who's Running America? The Carter Years*. Englewood Cliffs, NJ: Prentice-Hall.

_____. (1978) "Oligarchic Tendencies in National Policy-Making: The Role of the Private Policy-Planning Organizations," *Journal of Politics* 40 (May): 309–331.

DYE, THOMAS R., AND JOHN W. PICKERING. (1974) "Government and Corporate Elites," *Journal of Politics* 36 (November): 900–925.

DYE, THOMAS R., AND L. HARMON ZEIGLER. (1981) *The Irony of Democracy*, 5th ed. Monterey, CA: Duxbury Press.

_____. (1970) *The Irony of Democracy*. Belmont, CA: Wadsworth.

EASTERBROOK, GREGG. (1986) "Ideas Move Nations," *The Atlantic Monthly* 257 (January): 66–80.

EASTON, DAVID. (1953) *The Political System*. New York: Knopf.

EDITORIAL RESEARCH REPORTS. (1986) *Earth's Threatened Resources*. Washington, DC: Congressional Quarterly, Inc.

EDWARDS, GEORGE C., III, AND STEPHEN J. WAYNE. (1985) *Presidential Leadership*. New York: St. Martin's.

EHRLICH, PAUL R., JOHN HARTE, MARK A. HARWELL, PETER H. RAVEN, CARL SAGAN, GEORGE M. WOODWELL, JOSEPH BERRY, EDWARD S. AYENSU, ANNE H. EHRLICH, THOMAS EISNER, STEPHEN J. GOULD, HERBERT D. GROVER, RAFAEL HERRERA, ROBERT M. MAY, ERNST MAYR, CHRISTOPHER P. MCKAY, HAROLD A. MOONEY, NORMAN MYERS, DAVID PIMENTEL, AND JOHN M. TEAL. (1983) "Long-Term Biological Consequences of Nuclear War," *Science* 222 (December 23): 1293–1300.

EHRLICH, PAUL R., CARL SAGAN, DONALD KENNEDY, AND WALTER ORR ROBERTS. (1985) *The Cold and the Dark: The World After Nuclear War*. New York: Norton.

EISENHOWER, DWIGHT D. (1963) *The White House Years: Mandate for Change 1953–1956*. Garden City, NY: Doubleday.

EKIRCH, ARTHUR A., JR. (1966) *Ideas, Ideals, and American Diplomacy*. New York: Appleton-Century-Crofts.

ELAZAR, DANIEL J. (1972) *American Federalism: A View from the States*. New York: Crowell.

———. (1970) *Cities of the Prairie*. New York: Basic Books.

ELDER, ROBERT E. (1960) *The Policy Machine*. Syracuse, NY: Syracuse University Press.

ELLSWORTH, ROBERT F., AND KENNETH L. ADELMAN. (1979) "Foolish Intelligence," *Foreign Policy* 36 (Fall): 147–159.

ELLWOOD, JOHN. W. (1985) "The Great Exception: The Congressional Budget Process in an Age of Decentralization," pp. 315–342 in Lawrence C. Dodd and Bruce I. Oppenheimer (eds.), *Congress Reconsidered*, 3rd ed. Washington, DC: CQ Press.

ELLWOOD, JOHN W., AND JAMES A. THURBER. (1981) "The Politics of the Congressional Budget Process Re-examined," pp. 246–271 in Lawrence C. Dodd and Bruce I. Oppenheimer (eds.), *Congress Reconsidered*, 2nd ed. Washington, DC: CQ Press.

ELMS, ALAN C. (1976) *Personality in Politics*. New York: Harcourt Brace Jovanovich.

EMMANUEL, ARGHIRI. (1972) *Unequal Exchange: An Essay on the Imperialism of Trade*. New York: Monthly Review Press.

EPSTEIN, JOSHUA M. (1983) "Horizontal Escalation: Sour Notes of a Recurrent Theme," pp. 649–660 in Robert J. Art and Kenneth N. Waltz (eds.), *The Use of Force*. Lanham, MD: University Press of America.

ERIKSON, ROBERT, AND NORMAN LUTTBEG. (1973) *American Public Opinion*. New York: Wiley.

ERIKSON, ROBERT, NORMAN LUTTBEG, AND KENT L. TEDIN. (1980) *American Public Opinion*, 2nd ed., New York: Wiley.

ESTERLINE, JOHN H., AND ROBERT B. BLACK. (1975) *Inside Foreign Policy: The Department of State Political System and Its Subsystems*. Palo Alto, CA: Mayfield.

ETHEREDGE, LLOYD S. (1985) *Can Governments Learn? American Foreign Policy and Central American Revolutions*. New York: Pergamon.

———. (1978) *A World of Men: The Private Sources of American Foreign Policy*. Cambridge, MA: MIT Press.

ETZIONI, AMITAI. (1984) "Military Industry's Threat to National Security," *The New York Times* (April 6): A35.

FAGEN, RICHARD R. (1975) "The United States and Chile: Roots and Branches," *Foreign Affairs* 53 (January): 297–313.

———. (1960) "Some Assessments and Uses of Public Opinion in Diplomacy," *Public Opinion Quarterly* 24 (Fall): 448–457.

FALKOWSKI, LAWRENCE S. (ed.) (1979) *Psychological Models in International Politics*. Boulder, CO: Westview.

———. (1978) *Presidents, Secretaries of State, and Crises in U.S. Foreign Relations*. Boulder, CO: Westview.

FALLOWS, JAMES. (1983) "Immigration: How It's Affecting Us," *The Atlantic* 252 (November): 45–52.

———. (1982) *National Defense*. New York: Vintage Books.

FARNSWORTH, ELIZABETH. (1974) "Chile: What Was the U.S. Role? More Than Admitted," *Foreign Policy* 16 (Fall): 127–141.

FEIS, HERBERT. (1970) *From Trust to Terror: The Onset of the Cold War, 1945–1950*. New York: Norton.

———. (1966) *The Atomic Bomb and the End of World War II*. Princeton, NJ: Princeton University Press.

FELD, WERNER J. (1979) *International Relations: A Transnational Approach*. Sherman Oaks, CA: Alfred.

———. (1972) *Nongovernmental Forces and World Politics*. New York: Praeger.

FELDSTEIN, MARTIN. (1985) "American Economic Policy and the World Economy," *Foreign Affairs* 63 (Summer): 995–1008.

FENNO, RICHARD F., JR. (1973) *Congressmen in Committees*. Boston: Little, Brown.

FERGUSON, THOMAS, WITH JOEL ROGERS. (1986) "The Myth of America's Turn to the Right," *The Atlantic* 257 (May): 43–53.

FESTINGER, LEON. (1957) *A Theory of Cognitive Dissonance*. Evanston, IL: Row, Peterson.

Final Report of the Select Committee to Study Governmental Operations with Respect to Intelligence Activities. (1976) U.S. Senate, 94th Congress, 2nd Session, Books I–VI. Washington, DC: Government Printing Office.

FISHER, LOUIS. (1985) *Constitutional Conflicts between Congress and the President.* Princeton, NJ: Princeton University Press.

FLANAGAN, STEPHEN J. (1985) "Managing the Intelligence Community," *International Security* 10 (Summer): 58–95.

FOOD AND AGRICULTURE ORGANIZATION OF THE UNITED NATIONS. (1982) *FAO Trade Yearbook, 1981.* Rome: Food and Agriculture Organization of the United Nations.

"Food 1983." (1983) *UN Chronicle* 20 (January): 65–72.

FORD, DANIEL. (1985) "The Button-I," *The New Yorker* 61 (April 1): 43–91.

FORD, GERALD R. (1979) *A Time to Heal.* New York: Harper and Row.

Foreign Military Sales, Foreign Military Construction Sales and Military Assistance Facts. (1985) Washington, DC: Defense Security Assistance Agency.

Foreign Military Sales and Military Assistance Facts. (1980) Washington, DC: Defense Security Assistance Agency.

Foreign Military Sales and Military Assistance Facts. (1975) Washington, DC: Defense Security Assistance Agency.

FORSYTHE, DAVID P. (ed.) (1984) *American Foreign Policy in an Uncertain World.* Lincoln: University of Nebraska Press.

FOSSEDAL, GREGORY A. (1985a) "Sanctions For Beginners: When They Work and When They Don't," *The New Republic* 193 (October 21): 18–21.

_____. (1985b) "The Military-Congressional Complex," *The Wall Street Journal* (August 8): 22.

FOX, HARRISON W., JR., AND SUSAN WEBB HAMMOND. (1977) *Congressional Staffs: The Invisible Force in American Lawmaking.* New York: Free Press.

FRANCK, THOMAS M. (1985) *Nation Against Nation: What Happened to the U.N. Dream and What the U.S. Can Do About It.* New York: Oxford University Press.

FRANCK, THOMAS M., AND EDWARD WEISBAND. (1979) *Foreign Policy by Congress.* New York: Oxford University Press.

_____. (eds.) (1974) *Secrecy and Foreign Policy.* New York: Oxford University Press.

_____. (1972) *Word Politics: Verbal Strategy Among the Superpowers.* New York: Oxford University Press.

FRANK, ANDRE GUNDER. (1969) *Latin America: Underdevelopment or Revolution.* New York: Monthly Review Press.

FRANK, CHARLES R., JR., AND MARY BAIRD. (1975) "Foreign Aid: Its Speckled Past and Future Prospects," *International Organization* 29 (Winter): 133–167.

FRANK, ROBERT S. (1973) *Message Dimensions of Television News.* Lexington, MA: Lexington Books.

FRANKEL, CHARLES. (1969) *High on Foggy Bottom.* New York: Harper and Row.

FREE, LLOYD A., AND HEDLEY CANTRIL. (1968) *The Political Beliefs of Americans.* New York: Simon and Schuster.

FROMAN, CREEL. (1984) *The Two American Political Systems: Society, Economics, and Politics.* Englewood Cliffs, NJ: Prentice-Hall.

FULBRIGHT, J. WILLIAM. (1979) "The Legislator as Educator," *Foreign Affairs* 57 (Spring): 719–732.

GADDIS, JOHN LEWIS. (1983) "Containment: Its Past and Future," pp. 16–31 in Charles W. Kegley, Jr., and Eugene R. Wittkopf (eds.), *Perspectives on American Foreign Policy.* New York: St. Martin's.

_____. (1982) *Strategies of Containment: A Critical Appraisal of Postwar American National Security Policy.* New York: Oxford University Press.

_____. (1972) *The United States and the Origins of the Cold War, 1941–1947.* New York: Columbia University Press.

GALBRAITH, JOHN KENNETH. (1973) "The Decline of American Power," pp. 311–350 in Lloyd C. Gardner (ed.), *The Great Nixon Turnaround.* New York: New Viewpoints.

_____. (1970–1971) "The Plain Lessons of a Bad Decade," *Foreign Policy* 1 (Winter): 31–45.

_____. (1969a) *Ambassador's Journal*. Boston: Houghton Mifflin.

_____. (1969b) "The Power of the Pentagon," *The Progressive* 33 (June): 29.

GALLUP, GEORGE H. (1984) *The Gallup Poll: Public Opinion 1983*. Wilmington, DE: Scholarly Resources.

GALLUP, GEORGE, JR. (1985) *The Gallup Poll: Public Opinion 1984*. Wilmington, DE: Scholarly Resources.

GAMSON, WILLIAM A., AND ANDRE MODIGLIANI. (1971) *Untangling the Cold War*. Boston: Little, Brown.

GANS, HERBERT J. (1979) *Deciding What's News*. New York: Vintage Books.

GARDNER, LLOYD C. (1984) *A Covenant with Power: America and World Order from Wilson to Reagan*. New York: Oxford University Press.

_____. (1976) *Imperial America*. New York: Harcourt Brace Jovanovich.

_____. (1974) *American Foreign Policy: Present to Past*. New York: Free Press.

_____. (1970) *Architects of Illusion: Men and Ideas in American Foreign Policy, 1941–1949*. Chicago: Quadrangle Books.

GARNHAM, DAVID. (1975) "Foreign Service Elitism and U.S. Foreign Affairs," *Public Administration Review* 35 (January/February): 44–51.

GARTEN, JEFFREY E. (1985) "Gunboat Economics," *Foreign Affairs*. Special issue *America and the World 1984* 63 (No. 3): 538–559.

GARTHOFF, RAYMOND L. (1985) *Détente and Confrontation: American-Soviet Relations from Nixon to Reagan*. Washington, DC: Brookings Institution.

GASTIL, RAYMOND D. (1984) *Freedom in the World: Political Rights and Civil Liberties, 1983–1984*. Westport, CT: Greenwood Press.

GATI, CHARLES. (ed.) (1974) *Caging the Bear: Containment and the Cold War*. New York: Bobbs-Merrill.

GELB, LESLIE H. (1983) "Why Not the State Department?" pp. 282–298 in Charles W. Kegley, Jr., and Eugene R. Wittkopf (eds.), *Perspectives on American Foreign Policy*. New York: St. Martin's.

_____. (1976) "What Exactly is Kissinger's Legacy?" *The New York Times Magazine* (October 31): 13ff.

GELB, LESLIE H., AND MORTON H. HALPERIN. (1973) "The Ten Commandments of the Foreign Affairs Bureaucracy," pp. 250–259 in Steven L. Spiegel (ed.), *At Issue: Politics in the World Arena*. New York: St. Martin's.

GELB, LESLIE H., AND ANTHONY LAKE. (1985) "Four More Years: Diplomacy Restored," *Foreign Affairs*. Special issue *America and the World 1984* 63 (no. 3): 465–489.

GEORGE, ALEXANDER L. (ed.) (1983a) *Managing U.S.-Soviet Rivalry: Problems of Crisis Prevention*. Boulder, CO: Westview.

_____. (1983b) "Presidential Management Styles and Models," pp. 466–493 in Charles W. Kegley, Jr., and Eugene R. Wittkopf (eds.), *Perspectives on American Foreign Policy*. New York: St. Martin's.

_____. (1972) "The Case for Multiple Advocacy in Making Foreign Policy," *American Political Science Review* 66 (September): 751–785.

_____. (1969) "The Operational Code: A Neglected Approach to the Study of Political Decision-Making," *International Studies Quarterly* 13 (June): 190–222.

GEORGE, ALEXANDER L., AND JULIETTE L. GEORGE. (1964) *Woodrow Wilson and Colonel House: A Personality Study*. New York: Dover.

GERGEN, DAVID. (1985) "Pentagon Follies," *U.S. News and World Report* (June 3): 76.

GERSHMAN, CARL. (1980) "The Rise and Fall of the New Foreign-Policy Establishment," *Commentary* 70 (July): 13–24.

GIBSON, QUENTIN. (1960) *The Logic of Social Enquiry*. London: Routledge and Kegan Paul.

GILPIN, ROBERT. (1984) "The Richness of Tradition of Political Realism," *International Organization* 38 (Spring): 287–304.

GLAD, BETTY. (1983) "Black-and-White Thinking: Ronald Reagan's Approach to Foreign Policy," *Political Psychology* 4 (March): 33–76.

The Global 2000 Report to the President. (1980) Vol. 1: Entering the Twenty-First Century. Washington, DC: Government Printing Office.

GOLDMANN, KJELL. (1973) "East-West Tension in Europe, 1946–1970: A Conceptual Analysis and a Quantitative Description," *World Politics* 26 (October): 106–125.

GOLDMANN, KJELL, AND JOHAN LAGERKRANZ. (1977) "Neither Tension Nor Détente: East-West Relations in Europe, 1971–1975," *Cooperation and Conflict* 12 (No. 4): 251–264.

GOLDSTEIN, MARTIN E. (1984) *America's Foreign Policy: Drift or Decision.* Wilmington, DE: Scholarly Resources.

GOODMAN, ALLAN E. (1984–85) "Dateline Langley: Fixing the Intelligence Mess," *Foreign Policy* 57 (Winter): 160–179.

_____. (1975) "The Causes and Consequences of Détente, 1949–1973." Paper presented at the National Security Education Seminar, Colorado College, Colorado Springs, Colorado, July.

GOODSELL, CHARLES T. (1983) *The Case For Bureaucracy: A Public Administration Polemic.* Chatham, NJ: Chatham House.

GOODWIN, JACOB. (1985) *Brotherhood of Arms: General Dynamics and the Business of Defending America.* New York: Times Books.

GOULDEN, JOSEPH C. (1969) *Truth Is the First Casualty: The Gulf of Tonkin Affair.* Chicago: Rand McNally.

GRABER, DORIS A. (1985) *Mass Media and American Politics.* Washington, DC: CQ Press.

_____. (ed.) (1984) *Media Power in Politics.* Washington, DC: CQ Press.

GRAEBNER, NORMAN A. (1984) *America As A World Power: A Realist Appraisal from Wilson to Reagan.* Wilmington, DE: Scholarly Resources.

GRAY, COLIN S., AND KEITH PAYNE. (1980) "Victory Is Possible," *Foreign Policy* 39 (Summer): 14–27.

GREENBERG, EDWARD S. (1985) *Capitalism and the American Political Ideal.* Armonk, NY: Sharpe.

GREENSTEIN, FRED I. (1982) *Hidden Hand Presidency: Eisenhower as Leader.* New York: Basic Books.

_____. (1969) *Personality and Politics.* Chicago: Markham.

GREENSTEIN, FRED I., AND ROBERT WRIGHT. (1981) "Reagan . . . Another Ike?" *Public Opinion* 3 (December/January): 51–55.

GREGG, ROBERT W., AND CHARLES W. KEGLEY, JR. (eds.) (1971) *After Vietnam: The Future of American Foreign Policy.* New York: Doubleday-Anchor.

GRIFFITHS, FRANKLYN. (1984) "The Sources of American Conduct: Soviet Perspectives and Their Policy Implications," *International Security* 9 (Fall): 3–50.

Guide to Congress. (1976) Washington, DC: Congressional Quarterly, Inc.

Guide to the Congress of the United States. (1971) Washington, DC: Congressional Quarterly, Inc.

GURTOV, MELVIN. (1974) *The United Against the Third World.* New York: Praeger.

HAIG, ALEXANDER M., JR. (1984) *Caveat: Realism, Reagan, and Foreign Policy.* New York: Macmillan.

HALBERSTAM, DAVID. (1979) *The Powers That Be.* New York: Knopf.

_____. (1972) *The Best and the Brightest.* New York: Random House.

HALPERIN, MORTON H. (1971) "Why Bureaucrats Play Games," *Foreign Policy* 2 (Spring): 70–90.

HAMMOND, PAUL Y., DAVID J. LOUSCHER, MICHAEL D. SALOMONE, AND NORMAN A. GRAHAM. (1983) *The Reluctant Supplier: U.S. Decisionmaking for Arms Sales.* Cambridge, MA: Oelgeschlager, Gunn and Hain.

HANEY, CRAIG, AND PHILIP ZIMBARDO. (1973) "Social Roles, Role-Playing, and Education," *Behavioral and Social Science Teacher* 1 (No. 1): 24–45.

HANSEN, ROGER D. (1980) "North-South Policy—What's the Problem?" *Foreign Affairs* 58 (Summer): 1104–1128.

_____. (1976) *The U.S. and World Development: Agenda for Action 1976.* New York: Praeger.

HANSON, ALLEN C. (1984) *USIA: Public Diplomacy in the Computer Age.* New York: Praeger.

HARR, JOHN ENSOR. (1969) *The Professional Diplomat.* Princeton, NJ: Princeton University Press.

HARRIS, JOHN B., AND ERIC MARKUSEN. (1986) "Nuclear Weapons and Their Effects," pp. 24–26 in John B. Harris and Eric Markusen (eds.), *Nuclear Weapons and the Threat of Nuclear War.* San Diego: Harcourt Brace Jovanovich.

HARTZ, LOUIS. (1955) *The Liberal Tradition in America*. New York: Harcourt Brace and World.

HATHAWAY, DALE E. (1983) "The Internationalization of U.S. Agriculture," pp. 81–111 in Emery N. Castle and Kent A. Price (eds.), *U.S. Interests and Global Natural Resources*. Washington, DC: Resources for the Future.

HAZLEWOOD, LEO, JOHN J. HAYES, AND JAMES R. BROWNELL, JR. (1977) "Planning for Problems in Crisis Management: An Analysis of Post-1945 Behavior in the U.S. Department of Defense," *International Studies Quarterly* 21 (March): 75–106.

HEILBRONER, ROBERT L. (1977) "The Multinational Corporation and the Nation-State," pp. 338–352 in Steven L. Spiegel (ed.), *At Issue: Politics in the World Arena*. New York: St. Martin's.

———. (1968) "Counter-Revolutionary America," pp. 241–259 in Irving Howe (ed.), *A Dissenter's Guide to Foreign Policy*. Garden City, NY: Doubleday-Anchor.

HENKIN, LOUIS. (1972) *Foreign Affairs and the Constitution*. Mineola, NY: Foundation Press.

HENRY, JAMES S. (1986) "Where the Money Went," *The New Republic* 194 (April 14): 20–23.

HERBERS, JOHN. (1976) *No Thank You, Mr. President*. New York: Norton.

HERKEN, GREGG. (1982) *The Winning Weapon: The Atomic Bomb in the Cold War, 1945–1950*. New York: Vintage Books.

HERMANN, CHARLES F. (1983) "Bureaucratic Constraints on Innovation in American Foreign Policy," pp. 390–409 in Charles W. Kegley, Jr., and Eugene R. Wittkopf (eds.), *Perspectives on American Foreign Policy*. New York: St. Martin's.

———. (1982) "Instruments of Foreign Policy," pp. 153–174 in Patrick D. Callahan, Linda P. Brady, and Margaret G. Hermann (eds.), *Describing Foreign Policy Behavior*. Beverly Hills, CA: Sage.

———. (ed.) (1972a) *International Crises: Insights from Behavioral Research*. New York: Free Press.

———. (1972b) "Some Issues in the Study of International Crisis," pp. 3–17 in Charles F. Hermann (ed.), *International Crises: Insights from Behavioral Research*. New York: Free Press.

———. (1969a) *Crises in Foreign Policy*. Indianapolis: Bobbs-Merrill.

———. (1969b) "International Crisis as a Situational Variable," pp. 409–421 in James N. Rosenau (ed.), *International Politics and Foreign Policy*. New York: Free Press.

HERMANN, MARGARET G. (1983) "Assessing Personality at a Distance: A Profile of Ronald Reagan," *Mershon Center Quarterly Report* 7 (Spring): 1–8.

———. (1980) "Explaining Foreign Policy Behavior Using Personal Characteristics of Political Leaders," *International Studies Quarterly* 24 (March): 7–46.

———. (1978) "Effects of Personal Characteristics of Political Leaders on Foreign Policy," pp. 49–68 in Maurice A. East, Stephen A. Salmore, and Charles F. Hermann (eds.), *Why Nations Act*. Beverly Hills, CA: Sage.

———. (1976) "When Leader Personality Will Affect Foreign Policy: Some Propositions," pp. 326–333 in James N. Rosenau (ed.), *In Search of Global Patterns*. New York: Free Press.

———. (1974) "Leader Personality and Foreign Policy Behavior," pp. 201–234 in James N. Rosenau (ed.), *Comparing Foreign Policies*. New York: Sage/Halsted Press.

HERMANN, MARGARET G., CHARLES F. HERMANN, AND JOE D. HAGAN. (1986) "How Decision Units Shape Foreign Policy Behavior," forthcoming in Charles F. Hermann, Charles W. Kegley, Jr., and James N. Rosenau (eds.), *New Directions in the Study of Foreign Policy*. London: Allen and Unwin.

HERMANN, MARGARET G., WITH THOMAS W. MILBURN. (eds.) (1977) *A Psychological Examination of Political Leaders*. New York: Free Press.

HERSH, SEYMOUR. (1983) *The Price of Power: Kissinger in the Nixon White House*. New York: Summit Books.

HESS, STEPHEN. (1984) *The Government/Press Connection*. Washington, DC: Brookings Institution.

HESS, STEPHEN, AND MICHAEL NELSON. (1985) "Foreign Policy: Dominance and Decisiveness in Presidential Elections," pp. 129–154 in Michael Nelson (ed.), *The Elections of 1984*. Washington, DC: CQ Press.

HIATT, FRED. (1984a) "Despite All the Spending, Fewer Units Are Combat-Ready," *The Washington Post National Weekly Edition* (March 19): 29.

———. (1984b) "The War Within The Pentagon," *The Washington Post National Weekly Edition* (August 6): 6–7.

HIATT, FRED, AND RICK ATKINSON. (1985) "The Defense Boom: Uncle Sam Is a Cream of a Customer," *The Washington Post National Weekly Edition* (April 29): 19–22.

HILSMAN, ROGER. (1971) *The Politics of Policy Making in Defense and Foreign Affairs.* New York: Harper and Row.

_____. (1967) *To Move a Nation.* New York: Doubleday.

HOFFER, ERIC. (1951) *The True Believer.* New York: Harper and Brothers.

HOFFMANN, STANLEY. (1984) "Détente," pp. 231–262 in Joseph S. Nye, Jr. (ed.), *The Making of America's Soviet Policy.* New Haven, CT: Yale University Press.

_____. (1983) *Dead Ends: American Foreign Policy in the New Cold War.* Cambridge, MA: Ballinger.

_____. (1980) "The Crisis in the West," *The New York Review of Books* 27 (July 17): 41–48.

_____. (1978) *Primacy or World Order: American Foreign Policy Since the Cold War.* New York: McGraw-Hill.

_____. (1968) *Gulliver's Troubles: Or the Setting of American Foreign Policy.* New York: McGraw-Hill.

HOFSTADTER, RICHARD. (1965) *The Paranoid Style in American Politics and Other Essays.* New York: Knopf.

HOLMES, JACK E. (1985) *The Mood/Interest Theory of American Foreign Policy.* Lexington: University Press of Kentucky.

HOLSTI, OLE R. (1976a) "Foreign Policy Decision-Makers Viewed Psychologically: 'Cognitive Process' Approaches," pp. 120–144 in James N. Rosenau (ed.), *In Search of Global Patterns.* New York: Free Press.

_____. (1976b) "Foreign Policy Formation Viewed Cognitively," pp. 18–54 in Robert Axelrod (ed.), *Structure of Decision: The Cognitive Maps of Political Elites.* Princeton, NJ: Princeton University Press.

_____. (1975) "The Belief System and National Images: A Case Study," pp. 22–23 in William D. Coplin and Charles W. Kegley, Jr. (eds.), *Analyzing International Relations.* New York: Praeger.

_____. (1973) "Foreign Policy Decision-Makers Viewed Psychologically." Paper presented at the Conference on the Successes and Failures of Scientific International Relations Research, Ojai, California, June 25–28.

_____. (1972) "Cognitive Dynamics and Images of the Enemy," pp. 227–242 in Samuel A. Kirkpatrick and Laurence K. Pettit (eds.), *The Social Psychology of Political Life.* Belmont, CA: Duxbury Press.

HOLSTI, OLE R., AND JAMES N. ROSENAU. (1984) *American Leadership in World Affairs.* Boston: Allen and Unwin.

_____. (1983) "A Leadership Divided: The Foreign Policy Beliefs of American Leaders, 1976–1980," pp. 196–212 in Charles W. Kegley, Jr., and Eugene R. Wittkopf (eds.), *Perspectives on American Foreign Policy.* New York: St. Martin's.

_____. (1980) "Does Where You Stand Depend on When You Were Born? The Impact of Generation on Post-Vietnam Foreign Policy Beliefs," *Public Opinion Quarterly* 44 (Spring): 1–22.

_____. (1979a) "America's Foreign Policy Agenda: The Post-Vietnam Beliefs of American Leaders," pp. 231–268 in Charles W. Kegley, Jr., and Patrick J. McGowan (eds.), *Challenges to America: United States Foreign Policy in the 1980s.* Beverly Hills, CA: Sage.

_____. (1979b) "Vietnam, Consensus, and the Belief Systems of American Leaders," *World Politics* 32 (October): 1–56.

HOLT, PAT M. (1978) *The War Powers Resolution.* Washington, DC: American Enterprise Institute.

HOOPES, TOWNSEND. (1973a) *The Devil and John Foster Dulles: The Diplomacy of the Eisenhower Era.* Boston: Little, Brown.

_____. (1973b) *The Limits of Intervention.* New York: McKay.

HOPPLE, GERALD. (ed.) (1982) *Biopolitics, Political Psychology and International Politics.* New York: St. Martin's.

HOROWITZ, DAVID. (1971) "The Cold War Continues, 1945–1948," pp. 42–74 in Michael Parenti (ed.), *Trends and Tragedies in American Foreign Policy.* Boston: Little, Brown.

_____. (ed.) (1969) *Corporations and the Cold War.* New York: Monthly Review Press.

_____. (1965) *The Free World Colossus.* New York: Hill and Wang.

HOUGHTON, NEAL D. (ed.) (1968) *Struggle Against History: U.S. Foreign Policy in an Age of Revolution.* New York: Washington Square Press.

HOVLAND, C.I., IRVING JANIS, AND HAROLD H. KELLEY. (1953) *Communications and Persuasion.* New Haven, CT: Yale University Press.

HOWARD, MICHAEL E. (1981) "On Fighting A Nuclear War," *International Security* 35 (Spring) 3: 3–17.

HUFBAUER, GARY CLYDE, AND JEFFREY J. SCHOTT. (1985) "Economic Sanctions and U.S. Foreign Policy," *PS* 18 (Fall): 727–735.

HUGHES, BARRY B. (1978) *The Domestic Context of American Foreign Policy.* San Francisco: Freeman.

HUGHES, EMMET JOHN. (1972) *The Living Presidency.* New York: Coward, McCann and Geoghegan.

HUGHES, THOMAS L. (1985–86) "The Twilight of Internationalism," *Foreign Policy* 61 (Winter): 25–48.

――――. (1981) "Up from Reaganism," *Foreign Policy* 44 (Fall): 3–23.

HUMMEL, RALPH P. (1977) *The Bureaucratic Experience.* New York: St. Martin's.

IMMERMAN, RICHARD H. (1982) *The CIA in Guatemala: The Foreign Policy of Intervention.* Austin: University of Texas Press.

INSEL, BARBARA. (1985) "A World Awash in Grain," *Foreign Affairs* 63 (Spring): 892–911

International Economic Report of the President. (1977) Washington, DC: Government Printing Office.

International Economic Report of the President. (1976) Washington, DC: Government Printing Office.

INTERNATIONAL MONETARY FUND. (1983) *World Economic Outlook.* Washington, DC: International Monetary Fund.

IRISH, MARIAN, AND ELKE FRANK. (1975) *U.S. Foreign Policy: Context, Conduct, Content.* New York: Harcourt Brace Jovanovich.

ISAAK, ALAN C. (1985) *Scope and Methods of Political Science,* 2nd ed. Chicago: Dorsey.

――――. (1975) *Scope and Methods of Political Science,* 2nd ed. Homewood, IL: Dorsey.

ISAAK, ROBERT A. (1977) *American Democracy and World Power.* New York: St. Martin's.

――――. (1975) *Individuals and World Politics.* North Scituate, MA: Duxbury Press.

IYENGAR, SHANTO, MARK D. PETERS, AND DONALD R. KINDER. (1982) "Experimental Demonstrations of the 'Not-So-Minimal' Consequences of Television News Programs," *American Political Science Review* 76 (December): 848–858.

JACKSON, HENRY M. (1965) *The National Security Council: Jackson Subcommittee Papers on Policy-Making at the Presidential Level.* New York: Praeger.

JACOBSON, HAROLD K. (1984) *Networks of Interdependence: International Organizations and the Global Political System.* New York: Knopf.

JANIS, IRVING. (1980) "In Rescue Planning, How Did Carter Handle Stress?" *The New York Times* (May 18): E21.

――――. (1972) *Victims of Groupthink: A Psychological Study of Foreign-Policy Decisions and Fiascoes.* Boston: Houghton Mifflin.

JANKA, LES. (1984) "The National Security Council and the Making of American Middle East Policy," *Armed Forces Journal International* 122 (March 1984): 84–86.

JAVITS, JACOB K. (1985) "War Powers Reconsidered," *Foreign Affairs* 64 (Fall): 130–140.

JOHNSON, LOCH K. (1984) *The Making of International Agreements.* New York: New York University Press.

――――. (1983) "Seven Sins of Strategic Intelligence," *World Affairs* 146 (Fall): 176–204.

――――. (1980) "Controlling the Quiet Option," *Foreign Policy* 39 (Summer): 143–153.

JOHNSON, LOCH K., AND JAMES M. McCORMICK. (1977) "Foreign Policy by Executive Fiat," *Foreign Policy* 28 (Fall): 117–138.

JONES, DAVID C. (1984) "What's Wrong with the Defense Establishment," pp. 272–286 in Asa A. Clark, IV, Peter W. Chiarelli, Jeffrey S. McKitrick, and James W. Reed (eds.), *The Defense Reform Debate.* Baltimore: The Johns Hopkins University Press.

JONES, JOSEPH MARION. (1964) *The Fifteen Weeks.* New York: Harcourt, Brace and World.

JÖNSSON, CHRISTER. (1984) *Superpower: Comparing American and Soviet Foreign Policy.* London: Frances Pinter.

_____. (1982a) *Cognitive Dynamics and International Politics*. New York: St. Martin's.

_____. (1982b) "The Ideology of Foreign Policy," pp. 91–110 in Charles W. Kegley, Jr., and Pat McGowan (eds.), *Foreign Policy: USA/USSR*. Beverly Hills, CA: Sage.

JULIEN, CLAUDE. (1973) *America's Empire*. New York: Random House.

KAHAN, JEROME H. (1975) *Security in the Nuclear Age*. Washington, DC: Brookings Institution.

KAISER, ROBERT G. (1984) "Your Host of Hosts," *The New York Review of Books* 31 (June 28): 38–41.

KANTER, ARNOLD. (1972) "Congress and the Defense Budget 1960–1970," *American Political Science Review* 66 (March): 129–143.

KATTENBURG, PAUL. (1980) *The Vietnam Trauma in America Foreign Policy, 1945–75*. New Brunswick, NJ: Transaction Books.

KATZ, DANIEL, AND ROBERT L. KAHN. (1966) *The Social Psychology of Organizations*. New York: Wiley.

KATZ, ELIHU. (1957) "The Two-Step Flow of Communications," *Public Opinion Quarterly* 21 (Spring): 61–78.

KAUFMAN, HERBERT. (1976) *Are Government Organizations Immortal?* Washington, DC: Brookings Institution.

KEARNS, DORIS. (1976) *Lyndon Johnson and the American Dream*. New York: Harper and Row.

KEENY, SPURGEON M., JR., AND WOLFGANG K. H. PANOFSKY. (1981) "MAD vs. NUTS: Can Doctrine or Weaponry Remedy the Mutual Hostage Relationship of the Superpowers?" *Foreign Affairs* 60 (Winter): 287–304.

KEETER, SCOTT. (1985) "Public Opinion in 1984," pp. 91–111 in Gerald M. Pomper, Ross K. Baker, Charles E. Jacob, Scott Keeter, Wilson Carey McWilliams, and Henry A. Plotkin, *The Election of 1984: Reports and Interpretations*. Chatham, NJ: Chatham House.

KEGLEY, CHARLES W., JR. (1986a) "Assumptions and Dilemmas in the Study of Americans' Foreign Policy Beliefs: A Caveat," *International Studies Quarterly* 30 (December): forthcoming.

_____. (1986b) "Decision Regimes and Foreign Policy Behavior," forthcoming in Charles F. Hermann, Charles W. Kegley, Jr., and James N. Rosenau (eds.), *New Directions in the Study of Foreign Policy*. London: Allen and Unwin.

KEGLEY, CHARLES W., JR., T. VANCE STURGEON, AND EUGENE R. WITTKOPF. (1986) "Structural Terrorism: The Systemic Sources of State Sponsored Terrorism," forthcoming in Michael Stohl and George A. Lopez (eds.), *The Foreign Policy of Terror*. Westport, CT: Greenwood Press.

KEGLEY, CHARLES W., JR., AND EUGENE R. WITTKOPF (eds.). (1985a) *The Nuclear Reader: Strategy, Weapons, War*. New York: St. Martin's.

_____. (1985b) *World Politics: Trend and Transformation*, 2nd ed. New York: St. Martin's.

_____. (eds.) (1984) *The Global Agenda: Issues and Perspectives*. New York: Random House.

_____. (eds.) (1983) *Perspectives on American Foreign Policy: Selected Readings*. New York: St. Martin's.

_____. (1982a) *American Foreign Policy: Pattern and Process*, 2nd ed. New York: St. Martin's.

_____. (1982b) "The Reagan Administration's World View," *Orbis* 26 (Spring): 223–244.

_____. (1982–83) "Beyond Consensus: The Domestic Context of American Foreign Policy," *International Journal* 38 (Winter): 77–106.

_____. (1981) *World Politics: Trend and Transformation*. New York: St. Martin's.

_____. (1979) *American Foreign Policy: Pattern and Process*. New York: St. Martin's.

KELLY, MICHAEL, AND THOMAS H. MITCHELL. (1984) "Transnational Terrorism and the Western Elite Press," pp. 282–289 in Doris A. Graber (ed.), *Media Power in Politics*. Washington, DC: CQ Press.

KELMAN, HERBERT C. (ed.) (1965) *International Behavior*. New York: Holt, Rinehart and Winston.

KEMBLE, PENN. (1985) "Why Democrats Should Emphasize Foreign Policy," *Public Opinion* 8 (February/March): 15, 56–58.

KEMP, GEOFFREY. (1986) "Why Everybody Talks About Qaddafi but Nobody Does Anything," *The Washington Post National Weekly Edition* (January 27): 21–22.

KEMPE, FREDERICK. (1983) "Terrorist Attacks Grow But Groups Are Smaller and Narrower Focus," *The Wall Street Journal* (April 19): 1, 19.

KENDE, ISTVAN. (1978) "Wars of Ten Years (1967–1976)," *Journal of Peace Research* 15 (no. 3): 227–241.

_____. (1971) "Twenty-Five Years of Local Wars," *Journal of Peace Research* 8 (no. 1): 5–22.

KENNAN, GEORGE F. (1985) *American Diplomacy*. Chicago: University of Chicago Press.

_____. (1984) "Soviet-American Relations: The Politics of Discord and Collaboration," pp. 107–120 in Charles W. Kegley, Jr., and Eugene R. Wittkopf (eds.), *The Global Agenda: Issues and Perspectives*. New York: Random House.

_____. (1977) *The Cloud of Danger*. Boston: Little, Brown.

_____. (1976) "The United States and the Soviet Union, 1917–1976," *Foreign Affairs* 54 (July): 670–690.

_____. (1967) *Memoirs*. Boston: Little, Brown.

_____. (1954) *Realities of American Foreign Policy*. Princeton, NJ: Princeton University Press.

_____. (1951) *American Diplomacy, 1900–1950*. New York: New American Library.

_____. ("X"). (1947) "The Sources of Soviet Conduct," *Foreign Affairs* 25 (July): 566–582.

KENNEDY, ROBERT F. (1971) *Thirteen Days*. New York: Norton.

KEOHANE, ROBERT O., AND JOSEPH S. NYE, JR. (1985) "Two Cheers for Multilateralism," *Foreign Policy* 60 (Fall): 148–167.

_____. (1984) "Complex Interdependence, Transnational Relations, and Realism: Alternative Perspectives on World Politics," pp. 245–260 in Charles W. Kegley, Jr., and Eugene R. Wittkopf (eds.), *The Global Agenda: Issues and Perspectives*. New York: Random House.

_____. (1977) *Power and Interdependence*. Boston: Little, Brown.

_____. (1975) "International Interdependence and Integration," pp. 363–414 in Fred I. Greenstein and Nelson W. Polsby (eds.), *International Politics. Handbook of Political Science*, Vol. 8. Reading, MA: Addison-Wesley.

_____. (eds.) (1971) "Transnational Relations and World Politics," *International Organization* 25 (Summer): 329–349ff.

KERN, MONTAGUE. (1984) "The Press, the Presidency, and International Conflicts: Lessons from Two Administrations," *Political Psychology* 5 (March): 53–68.

KERN, MONTAGUE, PATRICIA W. LEVERING, AND RALPH B. LEVERING. (1984) *The Kennedy Crises*. Chapel Hill, NC: University of North Carolina Press.

KESTER, JOHN G. (1982) "The Role of the Joint Chiefs of Staff," pp. 527–545 in John F. Reichart and Steven R. Sturm (eds.), *American Defense Policy*. Baltimore: The Johns Hopkins University Press.

KEY, V. O. (1961) *Public Opinion and American Democracy*. New York: Knopf.

KILPATRICK, JAMES J. (1985) "An Overstuffed Bureaucracy," *The State* (Columbia, SC), (April 23): 8A.

KINDER, DONALD R., AND JANET A. WEISS. (1978) "In Lieu of Rationality: Psychological Perspectives on Foreign Policy Decision Making," *Journal of Conflict Resolution* 22 (December): 707–735.

KINDLEBERGER, CHARLES P. (1977) "U.S. Foreign Economic Policy, 1776–1976," *Foreign Affairs* 55 (January): 395–417.

KINSLEY, MICHAEL. (1985) "Reagan's Selective Aversion to Terrorism," *The Wall Street Journal* (March 28): 33.

KIRKPATRICK, JEANE J. (1984) "Human Rights and Foreign Policy," *USA Today* 112 (January): 17–20.

_____. (1974) *Political Women*. New York: Basic Books.

KIRSCHTEN, DICK. (1980) "Beyond the Vance-Brzezinski Clash Lurks an NSC Under Fire," *National Journal* 12 (May 17): 814–818.

KISSINGER, HENRY. (1979) *White House Years*. Boston: Little, Brown.

_____. (1977a) *American Foreign Policy*, 3rd ed. New York: Norton.

_____. (1977b) "Remarks by the Honorable Henry A. Kissinger, Secretary of State, Before the National Press Club, Washington, D.C., January 10, 1977." State Department Press Release. January 11, No. 3.

_____. (1974a) *American Foreign Policy*, expanded ed. New York: Norton.

_____. (1974b) "Statement on U.S.-Soviet Relations," News Release of the Bureau of Public Affairs, Department of State, Office of Media Service. Special Report September 19, No. 6.

_____. (1973) "Secretary Kissinger at *Pacem in Terris*," News Release of the Bureau of Public Affairs, Department of State, October 10.

_____. (1969) "Domestic Structure and Foreign Policy," pp. 261–275 in James N. Rosenau (ed.), *International Politics and Foreign Policy*. New York: Free Press.

_____. (1964) *A World Restored*. New York: Grosset and Dunlap.

_____. (1962) *The Necessity of Choice*. Garden City, NY: Doubleday.

_____. (1957) *Nuclear Weapons and Foreign Policy*. New York: Harper and Row.

KLARE, MICHAEL T. (1985) "Gunboats, Force Projection and Military Doctrine: Superpowers Take Aim at the Third World," pp. 201–208 in *Third World Affairs 1985*, edited by the Third World Foundation for Social and Economic Studies in London. Boulder, CO: Westview.

_____. (1984) *American Arms Supermarket*. Austin: University of Texas Press.

KLINGBERG, FRANK L. (1983) *Cyclical Trends in American Foreign Policy Moods: The Unfolding of America's World Role*. Lanham, MD: University Press of America.

_____. (1979) "Cyclical Trends in American Foreign Policy Moods and Their Policy Implications," pp. 37–55 in Charles W. Kegley, Jr., and Patrick J. McGowan (eds.), *Challenges to America: United States Foreign Policy in the 1980s*. Beverly Hills, CA: Sage.

_____. (1952) "The Historical Alternation of Moods in American Foreign Policy," *World Politics* 4 (January): 239–273.

KOLKO, GABRIEL. (1969) *The Roots of American Foreign Policy*. Boston: Beacon Press.

_____. (1968) *The Politics of War*. New York: Random House.

KRASNER, STEPHEN D. (1985) *Structural Conflict: The Third World Against Global Liberalism*. Berkeley: University of California Press.

_____. (1983) "Are Bureaucracies Important? A Re-examination of Accounts of the Cuban Missile Crisis," pp. 390–409 in Charles W. Kegley, Jr., and Eugene R. Wittkopf (eds.), *Perspectives on American Foreign Policy*. New York: St. Martin's.

KRAUTHAMMER, CHARLES. (1986) "The Poverty of Realism," *The New Republic* 194 (February 17): 14–22.

_____. (1985a) *Cutting Edges: Making Sense of the Eighties*. New York: Random House.

_____. (1985b) "Isolation, Left and Right," *The New Republic* 192 (March 4): 18–25.

_____. (1983) "From OPEC to ODEC," *The New Republic* 189 (November 28): 19–21.

KREML, WILLIAM P. (1977) *The Anti-Authoritarian Personality*. Oxford, Eng.: Pergamon Press.

KRIESBERG, LOUIS, AND ROSS KLEIN. (1980) "Changes in Public Support for U.S. Military Spending," *Journal of Conflict Resolution* 24 (March): 79–110.

KRIESBERG, LOUIS, HARRY MURRAY, AND ROSS A. KLEIN. (1982) "Elites and Increased Public Support for U.S. Military Spending," *Journal of Political and Military Sociology* 10 (Fall): 275–297.

KWITNY, JONATHAN. (1985) *Endless Enemies: The Making of An Unfriendly World*. New York: Congdon and Weed.

LADD, EVERETT CARLL. (1985) "On Mandates, Realignments, and the 1984 Presidential Election," *Political Science Quarterly* 100 (Spring): 1–25.

LAFEBER, WALTER. (1983) *Inevitable Revolutions: The United States in Central America*. New York: Norton.

_____. (1976) *America, Russia, and the Cold War 1945–1975*. New York: Wiley.

LAKE, ANTHONY. (1985) "Wrestling with Third World Radical Regimes: Theory and Practice," pp. 119–145 in John W. Sewell, Richard E. Feinberg, and Valeriana Kallab (eds.), *U.S. Foreign Policy and the Third World*. New Brunswick, NJ: Transaction Books.

LANE, ROBERT E. (1955) "Political Personality and Electoral Choice," *American Political Science Review* 49 (March): 173–190.

LANGER, E. J. (1975) "The Illusion of Control," *Journal of Personality and Social Psychology* 32 (no. 6): 311–328.

LASKI, HAROLD J. (1947) "America—1947," *The Nation* 165 (December): 641–644.

LASSWELL, HAROLD D. (1974) "The Political Personality," pp. 38–54 in Gordon J. DiRenzo (ed.), *Personality and Politics*. Garden City, NY: Doubleday-Anchor.

———. (1962) "The Garrison State Hypothesis Today," pp. 51–70 in Samuel P. Huntington (ed.), *Changing Patterns of Military Politics*. New York: Free Press.

———. (1930) *Psychopathology and Politics*. Chicago: University of Chicago Press.

LEACACOS, JOHN P. (1971–1972) "Kissinger's Apparat," *Foreign Policy* 5 (Winter): 2–27.

———. (1968) *Fires in the In-Basket: The ABC's of the State Department*. Cleveland: World.

LEBOW, RICHARD NED. (1981) *Between Peace and War: The Nature of International Crisis*. Baltimore: The John Hopkins University Press.

LECKIE, ROBERT. (1968) *The Wars of America*. New York: Harper and Row.

LEDEEN, MICHAEL. (1985) *Grave New World: The Superpower Crisis of the 1980s*. New York: Oxford University Press.

LEE, JONG R. (1977) "Rallying Around the Flag: Foreign Policy Events and Presidential Popularity," *Presidential Studies Quarterly* 7 (Fall): 252–256.

LEGG, KEITH R. (1981) "Congress as Trojan Horse? The Turkish Embargo Problem, 1974–1978," pp. 107–131 in John Spanier and Joseph Nogee (eds.), *Congress, the Presidency and American Foreign Policy*. New York: Pergamon.

LEHMAN, JOHN. (1976) *The Executive, Congress, and Foreign Policy: Studies of the Nixon Administration*. New York: Praeger.

LEIBERSON, STANLEY. (1971) "An Empirical Study of Military-Industrial Linkages," *American Journal of Sociology* 76 (January): 562–584.

LELOUP, LANCE T. (1986) *Politics in America*. St. Paul, MN: West.

LENG, RUSSELL, J. (1984) "Reagan and the Russians," *American Political Science Review* 78 (June): 338–355.

LENS, SIDNEY. (1970) *The Military-Industrial Complex*. Philadelphia: Pilgrim Press.

———. (1964) *The Futile Crusade*. Chicago: Quadrangle.

LENTNER, HOWARD H. (1972) "The Concept of Crisis as Viewed by the United States Department of State," pp. 112–135 in Charles F. Hermann (ed.), *International Crises: Insights from Behavioral Research*. New York: Free Press.

LEPPER, MARY MILLING. (1971) *Foreign Policy Formulation: A Case Study of the Nuclear Test Ban Treaty of 1963*. Columbus, OH: Merrill.

LEVINSON, DANIEL J. (1964) "Idea Systems in the Individual and in Society," pp. 297–318 in George K. Zollschan and Walter Hirsch (eds.), *Explorations in Social Change*. Boston: Houghton Mifflin.

———. (1957) "Authoritarian Personality and Foreign Policy," *Journal of Conflict Resolution* 1 (March): 37–47.

LEWIS, ANTHONY. (1984) "Vacuum at the Top," *The New York Times* (October 18): A27.

LEWIS, JOHN P., AND VALERIANA KALLAB. (eds.) (1983) *U.S. Foreign Policy and the Third World: Agenda 1983*. New York: Praeger.

LICHTER, S. ROBERT, AND STANLEY ROTHMAN. (1981) "Media and Business Elites," *Public Opinion* 4 (October/November): 42–46, 59–60.

LIEBERMAN, SEYMOUR. (1965) "The Effects of Changes in Roles on the Attitudes of Role Occupants," pp. 155–168 in J. David Singer (ed.), *Human Behavior and International Politics*. Chicago: Rand McNally.

LINDBLOM, CHARLES E. (1959) "The Science of Muddling Through," *Public Administration Review* 19 (Spring): 79–88.

LIPSET, SEYMOUR MARTIN. (1985) "Feeling Better: Measuring the Nation's Confidence," *Public Opinion* 8 (April/May): 6–9, 56–58.

LIPSET, SEYMOUR MARTIN, AND WILLIAM SCHNEIDER. (1983) "The Decline of Confidence in American Institutions," *Political Science Quarterly* 98 (Fall): 379–402.

LISKA, GEORGE. (1978) *Career of Empire: America and Imperial Expansion over Land and Sea*. Baltimore: The Johns Hopkins University Press.

LITWAK, ROBERT S. (1984) *Détente and the Nixon Doctrine: American Foreign Policy and the Pursuit of Stability, 1969–1976*. New York: Cambridge University Press.

Lorch, Robert S. (1978) *Public Administration.* St. Paul, MN: West.

Louscher, David J. (1977) "The Rise of Military Sales as a U.S. Foreign Assistance Instrument," *Orbis* 20 (Winter): 933–964.

Lovell, John P. (1970) *Foreign Policy in Perspective.* New York: Holt, Rinehart and Winston.

Lowi, Theodore J. (1985a) *The Personal President.* Ithaca, NY: Cornell University Press.

_____. (1985b) "Presidential Power: Restoring the Balance," *Political Science Quarterly* 100 (Summer): 185–213.

_____. (1979) *The End of Liberalism.* New York: Norton.

_____. (1972) "Four Systems of Policy, Politics, and Choice," *Public Administration Review* 32 (July/August): 298–310.

_____. (1967) "Making Democracy Safe for the World," pp. 295–331 in James N. Rosenau (ed.), *Domestic Sources of Foreign Policy.* New York: Free Press.

_____. (1964) "American Business, Public Policy, Case Studies and Political Theory," *World Politics* 16 (July): 677–715.

Luckham, Robin. (1984) "Militarisation and the New International Anarchy," *Third World Quarterly* 6 (April): 351–373.

Luttwak, Edward N. (1985) *The Pentagon and the Art of War.* New York: Simon and Schuster.

MacMahon, Arthur W. (1951) "The Administration of Foreign Affairs," *American Political Science Review* 45 (September): 836–866.

Magastadt, Thomas M. (1984) "Understanding George Kennan," *Worldview* 27 (September): 7–10.

Magdoff, Harry. (1969) *The Age of Imperialism.* New York: Monthly Review Press.

Maggiotto, Michael A., and Eugene R. Wittkopf. (1981) "American Public Attitudes Toward Foreign Policy," *International Studies Quarterly* 25 (December): 601–631.

Malbin, Michael J. (1980) *Unelected Representatives.* New York: Basic Books.

_____. (1977) "Congressional Committee Staffs: Who's in Charge Here?" *The Public Interest* 47 (Spring): 16–19.

Malone, Gifford D. (1985) "Managing Public Diplomacy," *Washington Quarterly* 8 (Summer): 199–213.

Mandel, Robert. (1984) "The Desirability of Irrationality in Foreign Policy Making: A Preliminary Model," *Political Psychology* 5 (December): 643–660.

Mandelbaum, Michael. (1986) "The Luck of the President," *Foreign Affairs.* Special issue *America and the World 1985* 64 (no. 3): 393–412.

Mandelbaum, Michael, and William Schneider. (1979) "The New Internationalisms: Public Opinion and American Foreign Policy," pp. 34–88 in Kenneth A. Oye, Donald Rothchild, and Robert J. Lieber (ed.), *Eagle Entangled: U.S. Foreign Policy in a Complex World.* New York: Longman.

Manheim, Jarol B. (1984) "Can Democracy Survive Television?", pp. 131–137 in Doris A. Graber (ed.), *Media Power in Politics.* Washington, DC: CQ Press.

Manning, Robert. (1983) "The Global Reach of the Superpowers," *South* 34 (August): 9–14.

Mansbach, Richard W., and John A. Vasquez. (1981) *In Search of Theory: A New Paradigm for Global Politics.* New York: Columbia University Press.

Mansbach, Richard W., Yale H. Ferguson, and Donald E. Lampert. (1976) *The Web of World Politics.* Englewood Cliffs, NJ: Prentice-Hall.

March, James G., and Herbert M. Simon. (1958) *Organizations.* New York: Wiley.

Marchetti, Victor, and John D. Marks. (1974) *The CIA and the Cult of Intelligence.* New York: Knopf.

Maslow, Abraham H. (1966) "A Comparative Approach to the Problem of Destructiveness," pp. 156–159 in Janusz K. Zawodney (ed.), *Man and International Relations: Contributions of the Social Sciences to the Study of Conflict and Integration,* Vol. I. San Francisco: Chandler.

Mastny, Vojtech. (1979) *Russia's Road to the Cold War.* New York: Columbia University Press.

May, Ernest R. (1984) "The Cold War," pp. 209–230 in Joseph S. Nye, Jr. (ed.), *The Making of America's Soviet Policy.* New Haven, CT: Yale University Press.

_____. (1973) *"Lessons" of the Past.* London: Oxford University Press.

MAYNES, CHARLES WILLIAM. (1986) "Lost Opportunities," *Foreign Affairs.* Special issue *America and the World* 64 (no. 3): 413–434.

_____. (1983) "U.S. Can't be Sole Policeman for All Threats to Free World," *The State* (Columbia, SC) (August 17): p A21.

MCCLELLAND, DAVID C. (1975) *Power: The Inner Experience.* New York: Irvington.

MCCLOSKY, HERBERT. (1967) "Personality and Attitude Correlates of Foreign Policy Orientation," pp. 51–109 in James N. Rosenau (ed.), *Domestic Sources of Foreign Policy.* New York: Free Press.

_____. (1958) "Conservatism and Personality," *American Political Science Review* 52 (March): 27–45.

MCCLOSKY, HERBERT, AND JOHN ZALLER. (1984) *The American Ethos: Public Attitudes Toward Capitalism and Democracy.* Cambridge, MA: Harvard University Press.

MCCOMBS, MAXWELL E., AND DONALD L. SHAW. (1972) "The Agenda-Setting Function of Mass Media," *Public Opinion Quarterly* 36 (Summer): 176–185.

MCCONNELL, GRANT. (1962) *Steel and the Presidency.* New York: Norton.

MCCORMICK, JAMES M. (1985) *American Foreign Policy and American Values.* Itasca, IL: Peacock.

MCELVAINE, ROBERT S. (1984) "Do We Really Want an 'Active President'?" *The Washington Post National Weekly Edition* (July 2): 28.

MCGOVERN, GEORGE S. (1980) "Seize the Initiative," *Foreign Policy* 39 (Summer): 3–5.

MCGOWAN, PATRICK J. (1975) "Meaningful Comparisons in the Study of Foreign Policy," pp. 52–58 in Charles W. Kegley, Jr., et al. (eds.), *International Events and the Comparative Analysis of Foreign Policy.* Columbia: University of South Carolina Press.

MCGOWAN, PATRICK J., AND CHARLES W. KEGLEY, JR. (eds.) (1980) *Threats, Weapons and Foreign Policy.* Beverly Hills, CA: Sage.

MCNAMARA, ROBERT S. (1984) "Time Bomb or Myth: The Population Problem," *Foreign Affairs* 62 (Summer): 1107–1131.

MELANSON, RICHARD A. (1983) *Writing History and Making Policy: The Cold War, Vietnam and Revisionism.* Lanham, MD: University Press of America.

MELMAN, SEYMOUR. (1974) *The Permanent War Economy.* New York: Simon and Schuster.

MENNIS, BERNARD. (1971) *American Foreign Policy Officials.* Columbus: Ohio State University Press.

MERELMAN, RICHARD M. (1984) *Making Something of Ourselves: On Culture and Politics in the United States.* Berkeley: University of California Press.

MEYER, JOHN W., AND W. RICHARD SCOTT. (1983) *Organizational Environments: Ritual and Rationality.* Beverly Hills, CA: Sage.

MEYER, LAWRENCE. (1984) "The Navy's Very Own Nuclear Button," *The Washington Post National Weekly Edition* (October 15): 6–7.

MILBRATH, LESTER W. (1967) "Interest Groups and Foreign Policy," pp. 231–252 in James N. Rosenau (ed.), *Domestic Sources of Foreign Policy.* New York: Free Press.

MILES, RUFUS E., JR. (1985) "Hiroshima: The Strange Myth of Half a Million American Lives Saved," *International Security* 19 (Fall): 121–140.

MILLER, ARTHUR. (1983) "Is Confidence Rebounding?" *Public Opinion* 6 (June/July): 16–20.

MILLER, ARTHUR H., WARREN E. MILLER, ALDEN S. RAINE, AND THAD A. BROWN. (1976) "A Majority Party in Disarray: Policy Polarization in the 1972 Election," *American Political Science Review* 70 (September): 753–778.

MILLETT, ALLAN R., AND PETER MASLOWSKI. (1984) *For the Common Defense.* New York: Free Press.

MILLS, C. WRIGHT. (1956) *The Power Elite.* New York: Oxford University Press.

MIROFF, BRUCE. (1976) *Pragmatic Illusions: The Presidential Politics of John F. Kennedy.* New York: McKay.

MODELSKI, GEORGE. (1962) *A Theory of Foreign Policy.* New York: Praeger.

MONGAR, THOMAS M. (1974) "Personality and Decision-Making: John F. Kennedy in Four Crisis Decisions," pp. 334–372 in Gordon J. DiRenzo (ed.), *Personality and Politics.* Garden City, NY: Doubleday-Anchor.

MONROE, ALAN D. (1979) "Consistency Between Public Preferences and National Policy Decisions," *American Politics Quarterly* 7 (January): 3–19.

MONTGOMERY, JOHN D. (1975) "The Education of Henry Kissinger," *Journal of International Affairs* 29 (Spring): 49–62.

MOON, BRUCE. (1985) "Consensus or Compliance? Foreign Policy Change and External Dependence," *International Organization* 39 (Spring): 297–329.

MORGENTHAU, HANS J. (1985) *Politics Among Nations,* revised by Kenneth W. Thompson. New York: Knopf.

———. (1983a) *In Defense of the National Interest.* Lanham, MD: University Press of America.

———. (1983b) "Defining the National Interest—Again," pp. 32–39 in Charles W. Kegley, Jr., and Eugene R. Wittkopf (eds.), *Perspectives on American Foreign Policy.* New York: St. Martin's.

———. (1969) "Historical Justice and the Cold War," *The New York Review of Books* 13 (July 10): 10–17.

MORRIS, DESMOND. (1969) *The Human Zoo.* New York: Dell.

MORSE, EDWARD L. (1986) "After the Fall: The Politics of Oil," *Foreign Affairs* 64 (Spring): 792–811.

MOSSBERG, WALTER S. (1983) "Some Congressmen Treat Military Budget As Source of Patronage," *The Wall Street Journal* (April 15): 1, 22.

MUELLER, JOHN E. (1973) *War, Presidents and Public Opinion.* New York: Wiley.

———. (1971) "Trends in Popular Support for the Wars in Korea and Vietnam," *American Political Science Review* 65 (June): 358–375.

MUNRO, DANA. (1964) *Intervention and Dollar Diplomacy in the Caribbean.* Princeton, NJ: Princeton University Press.

NATHAN, JAMES A., AND JAMES K. OLIVER. (1976) *United States Foreign Policy and World Order.* Boston: Little, Brown.

"The National Security Adviser: Role and Accountability." (1980) *Hearings Before the Committee on Foreign Relations, United States Senate.* 96th Congress, 2nd Session, April 17. Washington, DC: Government Printing Office.

NELSON, STEPHAN D. (1974) "Nature/Nurture Revisited," *Journal of Conflict Resolution* 18 (June): 285–335.

NEUSTADT, RICHARD E. (1970) *Alliance Politics.* New York: Columbia University Press.

———. (1960) *Presidential Power.* New York: Wiley.

NEUSTADT, RICHARD E., AND ERNEST R. MAY. (1986) *Thinking in Time: The Uses of History for Decision Makers.* New York: Free Press.

NEWLAND, CHESTER A. (1983) "A Mid-Term Appraisal—The Reagan Presidency: Limited Government and Political Administration," *Public Administration Review* 43 (January/February): 1–21.

NICHOLLS, DAVID. (1974) *Three Varieties of Pluralism.* New York: St. Martin's.

NICHOLS, JOHN SPICER. (1984) "Wasting the Propaganda Dollar," *Foreign Policy* 56 (Fall): 129–140.

NIE, NORMAN H., SIDNEY VERBA, AND JOHN R. PETROCIK. (1976) *The Changing American Voter.* Cambridge, MA: Harvard University Press.

NIEBUHR, REINHOLD. (1947) *Moral Man and Immoral Society.* New York: Scribner.

NOGEE, JOSEPH L. (1975) "Polarity: An Ambiguous Concept," *Orbis* 28 (Winter): 1193–1224.

NUECHTERLEIN, DONALD E. (1985) *America Overcommitted: United States National Interests in the 1980s.* Lexington: University Press of Kentucky.

NYE, JOSEPH S., JR. (ed.) (1984) *The Making of America's Soviet Policy.* New Haven, CT: Yale University Press.

NYE, JOSEPH S., JR., AND ROBERT O. KEOHANE. (1971) "Transnational Relations and World Politics: An Introduction," *International Organization* 25 (Summer): 329–349.

OAKLEY, ROBERT B. (1986) Address Before the Conference on Terrorism, Tourism and Traveler Security (February 13). Washington, DC: Government Printing Office.

———. (1985) "International Terrorism: Current Trends and the U.S. Response," U.S. Department of State Current Policy No. 706, May 15. Washington, DC: Department of State.

OBERDORFER, DON. (1984) "The U.S. Is Quietly Courting Moscow's European Satellites," *The Washington Post National Weekly Edition* (September 24): 16.

———. (1983) "From Crisis to Crisis: Making Up a Foreign Policy," *The Washington Post National Weekly Edition* (December 5): 6–7.

O'BRIEN, CONNOR CRUISE. (1977) "Liberty and Terrorism," *International Security* 2 (Fall): 56–67.

OGENE, F. CHIDOZIE. (1983) *Interest Groups and the Shaping of Foreign Policy: Four Case Studies of U.S. African Policy.* New York: St. Martin's.

OGLESBY, CARL, AND RICHARD SHAULL. (1967) *Containment and Change.* New York: Macmillan.

O'KEEFE, BERNARD J. (1983) *Oil and World Power.* New York: Penguin.

O'LEARY, MICHAEL K. (1967) *The Politics of American Foreign Aid.* New York: Atherton.

OLIVER, RICHARD P. (1971) "Employment Effects of Reduced Defense Spending," *Monthly Labor Review* 94 (December): 3–11.

ONEAL, JOHN R. (1983) "The Appropriateness of the Rational Actor Model in the Study of Crisis Decision Makers." Paper presented at the annual meeting of the American Political Science Association, Chicago, Illinois, September 1–4.

———. (1982) *Foreign Policy Making in Times of Crisis.* Columbus: Ohio State University Press.

ORNSTEIN, NORMAN J., AND SHIRLEY ELDER. (1978) *Interest Groups, Lobbying and Policymaking.* Washington, DC: CQ Press.

OSGOOD, ROBERT E. (1953) *Ideals and Self Interest in America's Foreign Relations.* Chicago: University of Chicago Press.

OSTROM, CHARLES W., JR., AND BRIAN L. JOB. (1986) "The President and the Political Use of Force," *American Political Science Review* 80 (June): 541–566.

OSTROM, CHARLES, W., JR., AND DENNIS M. SIMON. (1985) "Promise and Performance: A Dynamic Model of Presidential Popularity," *American Political Science Review* 79 (June): 334–358.

OYE, KENNETH A. (1983) "International Systems Structure and American Foreign Policy," pp. 3–32 in Kenneth A. Oye, Robert J. Lieber, and Donald Rothchild (eds.), *Eagle Defiant: United States Foreign Policy in the 1980s.* Boston: Little, Brown.

OYE, KENNETH A., ROBERT J. LIEBER, AND DONALD ROTHCHILD. (eds.) (1983) *Eagle Defiant: United States Foreign Policy in the 1980s.* Boston: Little, Brown.

OYE, KENNETH A., DONALD ROTHCHILD, AND ROBERT LIEBER. (eds.) (1979) *Eagle Entangled: U.S. Foreign Policy in a Complex World.* New York: Longman.

PAARLBERG, ROBERT L. (1980) "Lessons of the Grain Embargo," *Foreign Affairs* 59 (Fall): 144–162.

PACKENHAM, ROBERT A. (1973) *Liberal America and the Third World.* Princeton, NJ: Princeton University Press.

PAGE, BENJAMIN I., AND RICHARD A. BRODY. (1972) "Policy Voting and the Electoral Process: The Vietnam War Issue," *American Political Science Review* 66 (September): 979–995.

PAGE, BENGAMIN I., AND ROBERT Y. SHAPIRO. (1983) "Effects of Public Opinion on Policy," *American Political Science Review* 77 (March): 175–190.

PAIGE, GLENN D. (1972) "Comparative Case Analysis of Crises Decisions: Korea and Cuba," pp. 41–55 in Charles F. Hermann (ed.), *International Crises: Insights from Behavioral Research.* New York: Free Press.

———. (1968) *The Korean Decision.* New York: Free Press.

PALMER, MONTE, LARRY STERN, AND CHARLES GAILE. (1974) *The Interdisciplinary Study of Politics.* New York: Harper and Row.

PALUMBO, DENNIS J. (1969) "Power and Role Specificity in Organization Theory," *Public Administration Review* 29 (May/June): 237–248.

PARENTI, MICHAEL. (1986) *Inventing Reality.* New York: St. Martin's.

———. (1981) "We Hold These Myths to be Self-Evident," *The Nation* 232 (April 11): 425–429.

———. (1980) *Democracy for the Few,* 3rd ed. New York: St. Martin's.

———. (1974) *Democracy for the Few.* New York: St. Martin's.

———. (ed.) (1971) *Trends and Tragedies in American Foreign Policy.* Boston: Little, Brown.

———. (1969) *The Anti-Communist Impulse.* New York: Random House.

PARKINSON, C. NORTHCOTE. (1972–1973) "The Five Other Rules," *Foreign Policy* 9 (Winter): 108–116.

PATERSON, THOMAS G. (1979) *On Every Front: The Making of the Cold War.* New York: Norton.

PATTERSON, THOMAS E., AND ROBERT D. MCCLURE. (1976) *The Unseeing Eye.* New York: Putnam.

Peleg, Ilan. (1980) "Military Production in Third World Countries," pp. 209–230 in Patrick J. McGowan and Charles W. Kegley, Jr. (eds.), *Threats, Weapons, and Foreign Policy.* Beverly Hills, CA: Sage.

The Pentagon Papers as Published by The New York Times. (1971) Toronto: Bantam Books.

Perkins, Francis. (1964) *The Roosevelt I Knew.* New York: Harper and Row.

Perry, Jack. (1984) "The Foreign Service Is in Real Trouble, But It Can Be Saved," *The Washington Post National Weekly Edition* (January 16): 21–22.

Peterson, Sophia. (1971) "International Events, Foreign Policy-Makers, Elite Attitudes, and Mass Opinion." Paper presented at the annual meeting of the International Studies Association, San Juan, March 17–20.

Petras, James F., and Robert LaPorte, Jr. (1972) "Can We Do Business with Radical Nationalists? Chile: No," *Foreign Policy* 7 (Summer): 132–158.

Pett, Saul. (1984) "Spy vs. Spy," *The State* (Columbia, SC) (April 22): 1–B, 8–B.

Pickett, George. (1985) "Congress, the Budget, and Intelligence," pp. 157–179 in Alfred C. Maurer, Marion D. Tunstall, and James M. Keagle (eds.), *Intelligence: Policy and Process.* Boulder, CO: Westview.

Pierre, Andrew J. (1984) "The Politics of International Terrorism," pp. 84–92 in Charles W. Kegley, Jr., and Eugene R. Wittkopf (eds.), *The Global Agenda: Issues and Perspectives.* New York: Random House.

_____. (1982) *The Global Politics of Arms Sales.* Princeton, NJ: Princeton University Press.

Piller, Geoffrey. (1983) "DOD's Office of International Security Affairs: The Brief Ascendancy of an Advisory System," *Political Science Quarterly* 98 (Spring): 59–78.

Pincus, Walter. (1985a) "The Military's New, Improved 'Revolving Door,'" *The Washington Post National Weekly Edition* (March 18): 33.

_____. (1985b) "A Tough Arms Control Team," *The Washington Post National Weekly Edition* (October 7): 6–7.

Pirages, Dennis. (1978) *The New Context for International Relations: Global Ecopolitics.* North Scituate, MA: Duxbury Press.

Pisar, Samuel. (1977) "Let's Put Détente Back on the Rails," *The New York Times Magazine* (September 25): 31ff.

Podhoretz, Norman. (1984) "Reagan, Man of Peace," *The New York Times* (June 13): 23.

Polsby, Nelson W. (1984) *Political Innovation in America: The Politics of Policy Initiation.* New Haven, CT: Yale University Press.

_____. (1976) *Congress and the Presidency.* Englewood Cliffs, NJ: Prentice-Hall.

Pomper, Gerald M. (1968) *Elections in America: Control and Influence in Democratic Politics.* New York: Dodd, Mead.

Popkin, Samuel, John W. Gorman, Charles Phillips, and Jeffrey A. Smith. (1976) "Comment: What Have You Done for Me Lately? Toward An Investment Theory of Voting," *American Political Science Review* 70 (September): 779–805.

Porter, Roger B. (1983) "Economic Advice to the President: From Eisenhower to Reagan," *Political Science Quarterly* 98 (Fall): 403–426.

Powers, Thomas. (1979) *The Man Who Kept the Secrets: Richard Helms and the CIA.* New York: Pocket Books.

Prewitt, Kenneth, and Alan Stone. (1973) *The Ruling Elites: Elite Theory, Power, and American Democracy.* New York: Harper and Row.

Pringle, Peter, and William Arkin. (1983) *SIOP.* New York: Norton.

Pringle, Robert. (1977–1978) "Creeping Irrelevance at Foggy Bottom," *Foreign Policy* 29 (Winter): 128–139.

Proxmire, William. (1970) *Report from Wasteland.* New York: Praeger.

Pruitt, Dean G. (1965) "Definition of the Situation as a Determinant of International Action," pp. 393–432 in Herbert C. Kelman (ed.), *International Behavior.* New York: Holt, Rinehart and Winston.

Puchala, Donald J. (1985) "The United States and Its Allies: An End of Western Consensus?"

Paper presented to "The Future of the Western Community" conference at the University of South Carolina, October 3–5.

———. (ed.) (1983) *Issues Before the 38th General Assembly of the United Nations, 1983–1984.* New York: United Nations Association of the United States of America.

QUESTER, GEORGE H. (1982) *American Foreign Policy: The Lost Consensus.* New York: Praeger.

———. (1971) *Nuclear Diplomacy.* New York: Dunellen.

RAI, KUL B. (1980) "Foreign Aid and Voting in the UN General Assembly, 1967–1976," *Journal of Peace Research* 17 (no. 3): 269–277.

RANNEY, AUSTIN. (1983) *Channels of Power.* New York: Basic Books.

RANSOM, HARRY HOWE. (1983) "Strategic Intelligence and Intermestic Politics," pp. 299–319 in Charles W. Kegley, Jr., and Eugene R. Wittkopf (eds.), *Perspectives on American Foreign Policy.* New York: St. Martin's.

———. (1970) *The Intelligence Establishment.* Cambridge, MA: Harvard University Press.

RASER, DINA. (1985) *The Pentagon Underground.* New York: Times Books.

RAYMOND, GREGORY A. (1975) "Comparative Analysis and Nomological Explanation," pp. 41–51 in Charles W. Kegley, Jr., Gregory A. Raymond, Robert M. Rood, and Richard A. Skinner (eds.), *International Events and the Comparative Analysis of Foreign Policy.* Columbia: University of South Carolina Press.

RECORD, JEFFREY. (1984) "Why America's Military Has Joined the Ranks of the Losers," *The Washington Post National Weekly Edition* (February 13): 23–24.

REEVES, RICHARD. (1985) *The Reagan Detour.* New York: Simon and Schuster.

REICH, ROBERT B. (1985) "How Much Is Enough?" *The New Republic* (August 12 and 19): 33–37.

REISCHAUER, EDWIN O. (1968) "Redefining the National Interest: The Vietnam Case." Paper delivered at the annual meeting of the American Political Science Association, Washington, DC, September 2–7.

Report of the Secretary of Defense Caspar W. Weinberger to the Congress on the FY 1987 Budget, FY 1988 Authorization Request and FY 1987–1991 Defense Programs, February 5, 1986. (1986) Washington, DC: Government Printing Office.

Report of the Secretary of Defense Caspar W. Weinberger to the Congress on the FY 1986 Budget, FY 1987 Authorization Request and FY 1986–90 Defense Programs, February 4, 1985. (1985) Washington, DC: Government Printing Office.

Report of Secretary of Defense Harold Brown to the Congress on the FY 1982 Budget, FY 1983 Authorization Request and FY 1982–1986 Defense Programs, January 19, 1981. (1981) Washington, DC: Government Printing Office.

Report of the Select Committee on Intelligence. (1985) U.S. Senate, 98th Congress, 2nd Session. Washington, DC: Government Printing Office.

REUTLINGER, SHLOMO. (1985) "Food Security and Poverty in LDCs," *Finance and Development* 22 (December): 7–11.

RICHELSON, JEFFREY T. (1985) *The U.S. Intelligence Community.* Cambridge, MA: Ballinger.

RICHTER, ALBERT J. (1986) "The President and Intergovernmental Relations," pp. 72–88 in Robert Jay Dilger (ed.), *American Intergovernmental Relations Today.* Englewood Cliffs, NJ: Prentice-Hall.

RIELLY, JOHN E. (ed.) (1983) *American Public Opinion and U.S. Foreign Policy 1983.* Chicago: Chicago Council on Foreign Relations.

———. (ed.) (1979) *American Public Opinion and U.S. Foreign Policy 1979.* Chicago: Chicago Council on Foreign Relations.

———. (ed.) (1975) *American Public Opinion and U.S. Foreign Policy 1975.* Chicago: Chicago Council of Foreign Relations.

RIESELBACH, LEROY N. (1973) *Congressional Politics.* New York: McGraw-Hill.

———. (1966) *The Roots of Isolationism.* Indianapolis: Bobbs-Merrill.

———. (1964) "The Demography of the Congressional Vote on Foreign Aid, 1939–1958," *American Political Science Review* 58 (September): 577–588.

RIGGS, ROBERT E. (1977) "One Small Step for Functionalism: UN Participation and Congressional Attitude Change," *International Organization* 31 (Summer): 515–539.

RIPLEY, RANDALL B. (1975) *Congress: Process and Policy.* New York: Norton.

RIPLEY, RANDALL B., AND GRACE A. FRANKLIN. (1984) *Congress, the Bureaucracy, and Public Policy.* Homewood, IL: Dorsey.

ROBINSON, JAMES A. (1972) "Crisis: An Appraisal of Concepts and Theories," pp. 20–35 in Charles F. Hermann (ed.), *International Crises: Insights from Behavioral Research.* New York: Free Press.

_____. (1967) *Congress and Foreign Policy-Making.* Homewood, IL: Dorsey.

ROBINSON, MICHAEL JAY. (1983) "Just How Liberal is the News? 1980 Revisited," *Public Opinion* 6 (February/March): 55–60.

ROCKMAN, BERT A. (1984) *The Leadership Question: The Presidency and the American Political System.* New York: Praeger.

_____. (1981) "America's Departments of State: Irregular and Regular Syndromes of Policy Making," *American Political Science Review* 75 (December): 911–927.

RODGERS, HARRELL R., JR., AND MICHAEL HARRINGTON. (1981) *Unfinished Democracy.* Glenview, IL: Scott, Foresman.

ROGERS, WILLIAM D. (1979) "Who's in Charge of Foreign Policy?" *The New York Times Magazine* (September 9): 44–50.

ROGOW, ARNOLD A. (1963) *James Forrestal: A Study in Personality, Politics, and Policy.* New York: Macmillan.

ROKEACH, MILTON. (1960) *The Open and Closed Mind: Investigations into the Nature of Belief Systems and Personality Systems.* New York: Basic Books.

"The Role of Intelligence in the Foreign Policy Process." (1980) *Hearings Before the Subcommittee on International Security and Scientific Affairs of the Committee on Foreign Affairs, House of Representatives.* 96th Congress, 2nd Session, January 28, February 8, 11, 20. Washington, DC: Government Printing Office.

ROSATI, JEREL A. (1981) "Developing a Systematic Decision-Making Framework: Bureaucratic Politics in Perspective," *World Politics* 33 (January): 234–252.

ROSECRANCE, RICHARD N. (ed.) (1976) *America as an Ordinary Country: U.S. Foreign Policy and the Future.* Ithaca, NY: Cornell University Press.

ROSEN, STEVEN. (ed.) (1973) *Testing the Theory of the Military-Industrial Complex.* Lexington, MA: Heath.

ROSENAU, JAMES N. (1984) "A Pre-theory Revisited: World Politics in an Era of Cascading Interdependence," *International Studies Quarterly* 28 (September): 245–305.

_____. (1980) *The Scientific Study of Foreign Policy.* New York: Nichols.

_____. (1974) *Citizenship Between Elections.* New York: Free Press.

_____. (1973) "Paradigm Lost: Five Actors in Search of the Interactive Effects of Domestic and Foreign Affairs," *Policy Sciences* 4 (December): 415–436.

_____. (1967) "Foreign Policy as an Issue-Area," pp. 11–50 in James N. Rosenau (ed.), *Domestic Sources of Foreign Policy.* New York: Free Press.

_____. (1966) "Pre-Theories and Theories of Foreign Policy," pp. 27–92 in R. Barry Farrell (ed.), *Approaches to Comparative and International Politics.* Evanston, IL: Northwestern University Press.

_____. (1963) *National Leadership and Foreign Policy.* Princeton, NJ: Princeton University Press.

_____. (1961) *Public Opinion and Foreign Policy.* New York: Random House.

ROSENBAUM, WALTER A. (1975) *Political Culture.* New York: Praeger.

ROSENBERG, MILTON J. (1967) "Attitude Change and Foreign Policy in the Cold-War Era," pp. 278–334 in James N. Rosenau (ed.), *Domestic Sources of Foreign Policy.* New York: Free Press.

_____. (1965) "Images in Relation to the Policy Process: American Public Opinion on Cold War Issues," pp. 277–336 in Herbert C. Kelman (ed.), *International Behavior.* New York: Holt, Rinehart and Winston.

ROSENFELD, STEPHEN S. (1986) "The Guns of July," *Foreign Affairs* 64 (Spring): 698–714.

ROSSITER, CALEB. (1984) *The Bureaucratic Struggle for Control of U.S. Foreign Aid.* Boulder, CO: Westview.

ROTH, WILLIAM V., JR. (1984) "Let Civilians Buy Weapons For the Spineless Military," *The Washington Post National Weekly Edition* (June 11): 24.

ROTHSTEIN, ROBERT L. (1979) *Global Bargaining: UNCTAD and the Quest for a New International Economic Order.* Princeton, NJ: Princeton University Press.

ROWE, ALAN J. (1974) "The Myth of the Rational Decision Maker," *International Management* 29 (August): 38–40.

ROWE, EDWARD T. (1974) "Aid and Coups d'Etat: Aspects of the Impact of American Military Assistance Programs in the Less Developed Countries," *International Studies Quarterly* 18 (June): 239–255.

ROWEN, HOBART. (1985a) "Big Government Gets Bigger," *The Washington Post National Weekly Edition* (February 4): 5.

———. (1985b) "Those Chinese Capitalists," *The Washington Post National Weekly Edition* (January 7): 5.

RUBIN, BARRY. (1985) *Secrets of State: The State Department and the Struggle Over U.S. Foreign Policy.* New York: Oxford University Press.

RUBINSTEIN, ALVIN Z., AND DONALD E. SMITH. (1985) *Anti-Americanism in the Third World.* New York: Praeger.

RUBNER, MICHAEL. (1985–86) "The Reagan Administration, the 1973 War Powers Resolution, and the Invasion of Grenada," *Political Science Quarterly* 100 (Winter): 627–647.

RUSSETT, BRUCE. (1985) "The Mysterious Case of Vanishing Hegemony," *International Organization* 39 (Spring): 207–231.

———. (1984) "Dimensions of Resource Dependence: Some Elements of Rigor in Concept and Policy Analysis," *International Organization* 38 (Summer): 481–499.

———. (1982) "Defense Expenditures and National Well-being," *The American Political Science Review* 76 (December): 77–96.

———. (1975) "The Americans' Retreat from Power," *Political Science Quarterly* 90 (Spring): 1–21.

———. (1972) "The Revolt of the Masses: Public Opinion on Military Expenditures," pp. 299–319 in Bruce M. Russett (ed.), *Peace, War, and Numbers.* Beverly Hills, CA: Sage.

———. (1970) *What Price Vigilance?* New Haven, CT: Yale University Press.

RUSSETT, BRUCE, AND DONALD R. DELUCA. (1981) " 'Don't Tread on Me': Public Opinion and Foreign Policy in the Eighties," *Political Science Quarterly* 96 (Fall): 381–399.

SABATO, LARRY J. (1984) *PAC Power: Inside the World of Political Action Committees.* New York: Norton.

SAGAN, CARL. (1983–1984) "Nuclear War and Climatic Catastrophe: Some Policy Implications," *Foreign Affairs* 62 (Winter): 257–292.

SAID, ABDUL A. (ed.) (1981) *Ethnicity and U.S. Foreign Policy.* New York: Praeger.

SAMPSON, ANTHONY. (1977) *The Arms Bazaar.* New York: Bantam Books.

SANDERS, JERRY W. (1984) "Security and Choice," *World Policy Journal* 1 (Summer): 677–722.

———. (1983) *Peddlers of Crisis: The Committee on the Present Danger and the Politics of Containment.* Boston: South End Press.

SANDMAN, PETER M., DAVID M. RUBIN, AND DAVID B. SACHSMAN. (1972) *Media.* Englewood Cliffs, NJ: Prentice-Hall.

SCHELL, JONATHAN. (1984) *The Abolition.* New York: Knopf.

———. (1982) *The Fate of the Earth.* New York: Avon Books.

SCHELLING, THOMAS C. (1966) *Arms and Influence.* New Haven, CT: Yale University Press.

SCHILLER, HERBERT L., AND JOSEPH D. PHILLIPS. (eds.) (1972) *Super State: Readings in the Military-Industrial Complex.* Urbana: University of Illinois Press.

SCHILLING, WARNER R. (1973) "The H-Bomb Decision: How to Decide Without Actually Choosing," pp. 240–260 in Morton H. Halperin and Arnold Kanter (eds.), *Readings in American Foreign Policy.* Boston: Little, Brown.

SCHLESINGER, ARTHUR M., JR. (1984) "In the National Interest," *Worldview* 27 (December): 5–8.

———. (1983a) "Pretension in the Presidential Pulpit," *The Wall Street Journal* (March 17): 26.

———. (1983b) "Foreign Policy and the American Character," *Foreign Affairs* 62 (Fall): 1–16.

_____. (1977) "America: Experiment or Destiny?" *American Historical Review* 82 (June): 505–522.

_____. (1973) *The Imperial Presidency.* Boston: Houghton Mifflin.

_____. (1967) "Origins of the Cold War," *Foreign Affairs* 46 (October): 22–52.

_____. (1965) *A Thousand Days: John F. Kennedy in the White House.* Boston: Houghton Mifflin.

_____. (1958) *The Coming of the New Deal.* Boston: Houghton Mifflin.

SCHLESINGER, STEPHEN, AND STEPHEN KINZER. (1983) *Bitter Fruit: The Untold Story of the American Coup in Guatemala.* New York: Anchor.

SCHMIDT, WILLIAM E. (1983) "Poll Shows Lessening of Fear that U.S. Military is Lagging," *The New York Times* (February 6): 1.

SCHNEIDER, BARRY R. (1985) "Invitation to a Nuclear Beheading," pp. 278–289 in Charles W. Kegley, Jr., and Eugene R. Wittkopf (eds.), *The Nuclear Reader.* New York: St. Martin's.

SCHNEIDER, WILLIAM. (1984) "Public Opinion," pp. 11–35 in Joseph S. Nye, Jr. (ed.), *The Making of America's Soviet Policy.* New Haven, CT: Yale University Press.

_____. (1982) "Bang-Bang Television: The New Superpower," *Public Opinion* 5 (April/May): 13–15.

SCHNEIDER, WILLIAM, AND L. A. LEWIS. (1985) "Views on the News," *Public Opinion* 8 (August/September): 6–11, 58–59.

SCHOULTZ, LARS. (1982) "Politics, Economics, and U.S. Participation in Multilateral Development Banks," *International Organization* 36 (Summer): 537–574.

_____. (1981) "U.S. Foreign Policy and Human Rights Violations in Latin America: A Comparative Analysis of Foreign Aid Distributions," *Comparative Politics* 13 (January): 149–170.

SCHULZINGER, ROBERT D. (1985) *The Wise Men of Foreign Affairs: The History of the Council on Foreign Relations.* New York: Columbia University Press.

SCOTT, ANDREW M. (1979) "Science and Surprise: The Role of the Inadvertent in International Affairs." Paper presented at the annual meeting of the International Studies Association/South Athens, Georgia, October 4–6.

_____. (1970) "Environmental Change and Organizational Adaptation: The Problem of the State Department," *International Studies Quarterly* 14 (March): 85–94.

_____. (1969) "The Department of State: Formal Organization and Informal Culture," *International Studies Quarterly* 13 (March): 1–18.

SEABURY, PAUL. (1973) *The United States in World Affairs.* New York: McGraw-Hill.

SEGAL, AARON. (1984) "The Half-Open Door: Principles Clash with Pragmatism in U.S. Immigration Policies," *The Asian Wall Street Journal* (March 15): 10.

SEMMEL, ANDREW K. (1983) "Evolving Patterns of U.S. Seccurity Assistance 1950–1980," pp. 79–95 in Charles W. Kegley, Jr., and Eugene R. Wittkopf (eds.), *Perspectives on American Foreign Policy.* New York: St. Martin's.

_____. (1977) "The Elite Press, The Global System, and Foreign News Attention," *International Interactions* 4 (no. 4): 317–328.

SERFATY, SIMON. (1978) "Brzezinski: Play It Again, Zbig," *Foreign Policy* 32 (Fall): 3–21.

SEWELL, JOHN W., AND CHRISTINE E. CONTEE. (1985) "U.S. Foreign Aid in the 1980s: Reordering Priorities," pp. 95–118 in John W. Sewell, Richard E. Feinberg, and Valeriana Kallab (eds.), *U.S. Foreign Policy and the Third World: Agenda 1985–86.* New Brunswick, NJ: Transaction Books.

SEWELL, JOHN W., RICHARD E. FEINBERG, AND VALERIANA KALLAB. (eds.) (1985) *U.S. Foreign Policy and the Third World: Agenda 1985–86.* New Brunswick, NJ: Transaction Books.

SEWELL, JOHN W., AND THE STAFF OF THE OVERSEAS DEVELOPMENT COUNCIL. (1980) *The United States and World Development: Agenda 1980.* New York: Praeger.

_____. (1979) "Can the North Prosper Without Growth and Progress in the South?" pp. 45–76 in Martin M. McLaughlin and the Staff of the Overseas Development Council, *The United States and World Development: Agenda 1979.* New York: Praeger.

_____. (1977) *The United States and World Development: Agenda 1977.* New York: Praeger.

SHAFER, MICHAEL. (1982) "Mineral Myths," *Foreign Policy* 47 (Summer): 154–171.

SHERRY, MICHAEL. (1977) *Preparing for the Next War.* New Haven, CT: Yale University Press.

SHERWIN, MARTIN J. (1973) "The Atomic Bomb and the Origins of the Cold War," *American Historical Review* 78 (October): 945–968.

SHULTZ, GEORGE P. (1985) "New Realities and New Ways of Thinking," *Foreign Affairs* 63 (Spring): 705–721.

_____. (1984) "Power and Diplomacy in the 1980s," U.S. Department of State Current Policy No. 561, April 3.

SIGELMAN, LEE. (1979) "Rallying to the President's Support: A Reappraisal of Evidence," *Polity* 11 (Summer): 542–561.

SIGMUND, PAUL E. (1974a) "The 'Invisible Blockade' and the Overthrow of Allende," *Foreign Affairs* 52 (January): 322–340.

_____. (1974b) "Chile: What Was the U.S. Role? Less than Charged," *Foreign Policy* 16 (Fall): 142–156.

SIMON, HERBERT A. (1985) "Human Nature in Politics: The Dialogue of Psychology with Political Science," *American Political Science Review* 79 (March): 293–304.

_____. (1957a) *Administrative Behavior.* New York: Macmillan.

_____. (1957b) *Models of Man.* New York: Wiley.

SIMPSON, SMITH. (1967) *Anatomy of the State Department.* Boston: Houghton Mifflin.

SINGER, J. DAVID. (ed.) (1965) *Human Behavior and International Politics.* Chicago: Rand McNally.

_____. (1963) "Peace Research, Peace Action," *Bulletin of the Atomic Scientists* 19 (January): 13–17.

SIVARD, RUTH. (1985) *World Military and Social Expenditures 1985.* Washington DC: World Priorities.

_____. (1983) *World Military and Social Expenditures 1983.* Washington, DC: World Priorities.

_____. (1982) *World Military and Social Expenditures 1982.* Leesburg, VA: World Priorities.

SLOCOMBE, WALTER B. (1985) "Strategic Forces," pp. 77–94 in George E. Hudson and Joseph Kruzel (eds.), *American Defense Annual 1985–1986.* Lexington, MA: Heath.

SLOVIC, PAUL, BARUCH FISCHHOFF, AND SARAH LICHTENSTEIN. (1977) "Behavioral Decision Theory," *Annual Review of Psychology* 28: 1–39.

SMALL, MELVIN. (1980) *Was War Necessary? National Security and U.S. Entry into War.* Beverly Hills, CA: Sage.

SMITH, STEVE, AND MICHAEL CLARK. (eds.) (1985) *Foreign Policy Implementation.* London: Allen and Unwin.

SMITH, STEVEN S., AND CHRISTOPHER J. DEERING. (1984) *Committees in Congress.* Washington, DC: CQ Press.

SMITH, WAYNE S. (1986) "A Trap in Angola," *Foreign Policy* 62 (Spring): 61–74.

SMOLLER, FRED. (1986) "The Six O'Clock Presidency: Patterns of Network News Coverage of the President," *Presidential Studies Quarterly* 16 (1): 31–49.

SMYSER, W. R. (1985) "Refugees: A Never-Ending Story," *Foreign Affairs* 64 (Fall): 154–168.

SNYDER, MARK. (1980) "The Many Me's of the Self-Monitor," *Psychology Today* 13 (March): 32–40ff.

SNYDER, RICHARD C. (1968) "Introduction," pp xi–xxv in Glen D. Paige, *The Korean Decision, June 24–30.* New York: Free Press.

SNYDER, RICHARD C., AND JAMES A. ROBINSON. (1961) *National and International Decision-Making.* New York: Institute for International Order.

SOLARZ, STEPHEN J. (1986) "When to Intervene," *Foreign Policy* 63 (Summer): 20–39.

_____. (1985) "Six Questions for the Reagan Doctrine: Next Stop, Angola," *The New Republic* 193 (December 2): 18–21.

SORENSEN, THEODORE C. (1965) *Kennedy.* New York: Harper and Row.

_____. (1963) *Decision-Making in the White House: The Olive Branch or the Arrows.* New York: Columbia University Press.

SPANIER, JOHN. (1985) *American Foreign Policy Since World War II.* New York: Holt, Rinehart and Winston.

_____. (1981) *Games Nations Play,* 4th ed. New York: Holt, Rinehart and Winston.

_____. (1975) *Games Nations Play,* 2nd ed. New York: Praeger.

SPERO, JOAN EDELMAN. (1985) *The Politics of International Economic Relations*, 3rd ed. New York: St. Martin's.

———. (1981) *The Politics of International Economic Relations*, 2nd ed. New York: St. Martin's.

SPIEGEL, STEVEN L. (1985) *The Other Arab-Israeli Conflict*. Chicago: University of Chicago Press.

SPIERS, RONALD I. (1985a) "Managing the State Department," address before the Carnegie Endowment for International Peace and the American Foreign Service Association, United States Department of State, Bureau of Public Affairs, Current Policy No. 747, September 26.

———. (1985b) "Thinning the Soup," *Foreign Service Journal* 62 (March): 34–37.

STAGNER, ROSS. (1971) "Personality Dynamics and Social Conflict," pp. 98–109 in Clagett G. Smith (ed.), *Conflict Resolution: Contributions of the Behavioral Sciences*. Notre Dame, IN: University of Notre Dame Press.

STARR, HARVEY. (1984) *Henry Kissinger: Perceptions of International Politics*. Lexington: University Press of Kentucky.

———. (1982) "Détente or 'Two Against One'? The China Factor," pp. 185–212 in Charles W. Kegley, Jr., and Pat McGowan (eds.), *Foreign Policy: USA/USSR*. Beverly Hills, CA: Sage.

———. (1980) "The Kissinger Years: Studying Individuals and Foreign Policy," *International Studies Quarterly* 24 (December): 465–495.

Statistical Abstract of the United States, 1984. (1984) Washington, DC: Government Printing Office.

Statistical Abstract of the United States, 1980. (1980) Washington, DC: Government Printing Office.

STEEPER, FREDERICK T., AND ROBERT M. TEETER. (1976) "Comment on 'A Majority Party in Disarray,'" *American Political Science Review* 70 (September): 806–813.

STEIGMAN, ANDREW L. (1985) "From Surfeit to Shortage," *Foreign Service Journal* 62 (September): 32–34.

STEVENS, CHARLES J. (1977) "The Use and Control of Executive Agreements: Recent Congressional Initiatives," *Orbis* 20 (Winter): 905–931.

STEWART, ROSEMARY. (1972) *The Reality of Organizations*. New York: Anchor Books.

STILLMAN, EDMUND, AND WILLIAM PFAFF. (1966) *Power and Impotence: The Failure of American Foreign Policy*. New York: Random House.

STIMSON, HENRY L., AND MCGEORGE BUNDY. (1947) *On Active Service in Peace and War*. New York: Harper and Row.

STOCKHOLM INTERNATIONAL PEACE RESEARCH INSTITUTE. (1977) *World Armaments*. Stockholm: Stockholm International Peace Research Institute.

———. (1976) *Armaments and Disarmament in the Nuclear Age*. Atlantic Highlands, NJ: Humanities Press.

STOESSINGER, JOHN G. (1985) *Crusaders and Pragmatists: Movers of Modern American Foreign Policy*. New York: Norton.

STOHL, MICHAEL, AND GEORGE A. LOPEZ. (eds.) (1984) *The State as Terrorist: The Dynamics of Governmental Violence and Depression*. Westport, CT: Greenwood Press.

STONE, ALAN, AND RICHARD P. BARKE. (1985) *Governing the American Republic*. New York: St. Martin's.

STRANGE, SUSAN. (1971) "The Politics of International Currencies," *World Politics* 23 (January): 215–231.

STOUFFER, SAMUEL A., EDWARD A. SUCHMAN, LELAND C. DEVINNEY, SHIRLEY A. STAR, AND ROBIN M. WILLIAMS, JR. (1949) *The American Soldier: Adjustment During Army Life*. Princeton, NJ: Princeton University Press.

STRUCK, MYRON. (1985) "A Bumper Crop of Plums: Political Appointments are Proliferators," *The Washington Post National Weekly Edition* (May 20): 31.

STUART, DOUGLAS, AND HARVEY STARR. (1981–1982) "The 'Inherent Bad Faith Model' Reconsidered: Dulles, Kennedy, and Kissinger," *Political Psychology* 3 (Fall/Winter): 1–33.

STUPAK, RONALD J. (1976) *American Foreign Policy: Assumptions, Processes, and Projections*. New York: Harper and Row.

SULLIVAN, WILLIAM H. (1980) "Dateline Iran: The Road Not Taken," *Foreign Policy* 40 (Fall): 175–186.

SUNDQUIST, JAMES L. (1976) "Congress and the President: Enemies or Partners?" pp. 583–618 in Henry Owen and Charles L. Schultze (eds.), *Setting National Priorities: The Next Ten Years.* Washington, DC: Brookings Institution.

SUSSMAN, BARRY. (1985) "The 'Porcupine Theory': Explaining Contradictory Opinions," *The Washington Post National Weekly Edition* (August 5): 37.

_____. (1984) "On Central America, Reagan Is Consistently Unpersuasive," *The Washington Post National Weekly Edition* (May 14): 37.

SWOMLEY, JOHN W., JR. (1970) *American Empire: The Political Ethics of Twentieth-Century Conquest.* New York: Macmillan.

TALBOTT, STROBE. (1984a) *Deadly Gambits.* New York: Knopf.

_____. (1984b) *The Russians and Reagan.* New York: Vintage Books.

_____. (1979) *Endgame.* New York: Harper and Row.

TAUBMAN, PHILIP. (1984) "Secret Budgets Become a Public Issue," *Gainesville Sun* (September 30): 5B.

_____. (1983) "Casey and His CIA on the Rebound," *The New York Times Magazine* (January 16): 20–21ff.

TAUBMAN, WILLIAM. (ed.) (1973) *Globalism and Its Critics.* Lexington, MA: Heath.

TAYLOR, CHARLES L., AND MICHAEL C. HUDSON. (1972) *World Handbook of Political and Social Indicators*, 2nd ed. New Haven, CT: Yale University Press.

TAYLOR, PHILLIP. (1984) *Nonstate Actors in International Politics: From Transregional to Substate Organizations.* Boulder, CO: Westview.

TEBBEL, JOHN, AND SARAH MILES WATTS. (1985) *The Press and the Presidency.* New York: Oxford University Press.

TEMPEST, RONE. (1983) "We Are the Servants of Destruction," *The State* (Columbia, SC) (July 31): B1, B9.

TESH, SYLVIA. (1984) "In Support of 'Single-Issue' Politics," *Political Science Quarterly* 99 (Spring): 27–44.

THEOHARIS, ATHAN. (1970) *The Yalta Myths.* Columbia: University of Missouri Press.

THOMPSON, KENNETH W. (ed.) (1984) *Moral Dimensions of American Foreign Policy.* New Brunswick, NJ: Transaction Books.

_____. (1960) *Political Realism and the Crisis of World Politics.* Princeton, NJ: Princeton University Press.

_____. (1958) "The Limits of Principle in International Politics," *Journal of Politics* 20 (August): 437–467.

THOMSON, JAMES C., JR. (1972) "On the Making of U.S. China Policy, 1961–69: A Study in Bureaucratic Politics," *The China Quarterly* 50 (April/June): 220–243.

THORSON, STUART J. (1984) "Intentional Inferencing in Foreign Policy," pp. 280–310 in Donald A. Sylvan and Steve Chan (eds.), *Foreign Policy Decision Making.* New York: Praeger.

TILLEMA, HERBERT K. (1973) *Appeal to Force: American Military Intervention in the Era of Containment.* New York: Crowell.

TILLEMA, HERBERT K., AND JOHN R. VAN WINGEN. (1982) "Law and Power in Military Intervention," *International Studies Quarterly* 26 (June): 220–250.

TOWNSEND, JOYCE CAROL. (1982) *Bureaucratic Politics in American Decision Making: Impact on Brazil.* Washington, DC: University Press of America.

TRAGER, FRANK N. (1977) "The National Security Act of 1947: Its Thirtieth Anniversary," *Air University Review* 29 (November–December): 2–15.

TREAT, JOHN D. (1974) "Survey of Previous Reports on Organizational Reform in the Foreign Affairs Community." Washington, DC: Commission on the Organization of the Government for the Conduct of Foreign Policy.

TRUMAN, DAVID B. (1951) *The Governmental Process.* New York: Knopf.

TRUMAN, HARRY S. (1966) *Public Papers of the Presidents of the United States, Harry S. Truman, 1952–53.* Washington, DC: Government Printing Office.

TUCHMAN, BARBARA W. (1984) *The March of Folly: From Troy to Vietnam.* New York: Knopf.

TUCKER, ROBERT W. (1971) *The Radical Left and American Foreign Policy.* Baltimore: The Johns Hopkins University Press.

———. (1968) *Nation or Empire.* Baltimore: The Johns Hopkins University Press.

TUGWELL, REXFORD GUY. (1971) *Off Course: From Truman to Nixon.* New York: Praeger.

TULLOCK, GORDON. (1974) "A Neoclassical View of Postwar Europe," pp. 181–190 in Louis J. Mensonides and James A. Kuhlman (eds.), *The Future of Inter-Bloc Relations in Europe.* New York: Praeger.

TURNER, STANSFIELD, AND GEORGE THIBAULT. (1982) "Intelligence: The Right Rules," *Foreign Policy* 48 (Fall): 122–138.

TWENTIETH CENTURY FUND. (1984) *What Price PACs?: Report of the Twentieth Century Fund Task Force on Political Action Committees.* New York: Twentieth Century Fund.

TYLER, PATRICK E., AND DAVID B. OTTAWAY. (1986) "Reagan's Secret Little Wars," *The Washington Post National Weekly Edition* (March 31): 6–7.

ULAM, ADAM B. (1985) "Forty Years of Troubled Coexistence," *Foreign Affairs* 64 (Fall): 12–32.

———. (1983) *Dangerous Relations: The Soviet Union in World Politics, 1970–82.* New York: Oxford University Press.

———. (1974) *Expansion and Coexistence: Soviet Foreign Policy, 1917–1973.* New York: Praeger.

UNDERDAL, ARILD. (1979) "Issues Determine Politics Determine Policies: The Case for a 'Rationalistic' Approach to the Study of Foreign Policy Decision-Making," *Cooperation and Conflict* 14 (no. 1): 1–9.

UNGAR, SANFORD J. (1986) "U.S. Aid to Sivimbi in Angola Would Be a Major Blunder," *The Washington Post National Weekly Edition* (February 10): 23–24.

———. (ed.) (1985a) *Estrangement: America and the World.* New York: Oxford University Press.

———. (1985b) "Our Foreign Policy Elite: Is It Mostly Irrelevant?" *The Washington Post National Weekly Edition* (February 11): 36.

The United States Government Manual, 1985–86. (1985) Washington, DC: Government Printing Office.

———. *1980–1981* (1980) Washington, DC: Government Printing Office.

UNITED STATES OFFICE OF PERSONNEL MANAGEMENT. (1984) *Federal Workforce Statistics: Biennial Report of Employment by Geographic Area,* December 31, 1982. Washington, DC: Government Printing Office.

UNITED STATES INTERNATIONAL TRADE COMMISSION. (1985) *42nd Quarterly Report to the Congress and the Trade Policy Committee on Trade Between the United States and the Nonmarket Economy Countries During January–March 1985.* Washington, DC: International Trade Commission.

———. (1983) *33rd Quarterly Report to the Congress and the Trade Policy Committee on Trade Between the United States and the Nonmarket Economy Countries During 1982.* Washington, DC: International Trade Commission.

———. (1981) *24th Quarterly Report to the Congress and the Trade Policy Committee on Trade Between the United States and the Nonmarket Economy Countries During July–September 1980.* Washington, DC: International Trade Commission.

U.S. ARMS CONTROL AND DISARMAMENT AGENCY. (1985) *World Military Expenditures and Arms Transfers 1985.* ACDA Publication 123 (August). Washington, DC: Government Printing Office.

———. (1980a) *Arms Control 1979.* Washington, DC: Government Printing Office.

———. (1980b) *World Military Expenditures and Arms Transfers 1969–1978.* Washington, DC: Government Printing Office.

———. (1978) *World Military Expenditures and Arms Transfers 1967–1976.* Washington, DC: Government Printing Office.

———. (1976) *World Military Expenditures and Arms Transfers 1965–1974.* Washington, DC: Government Printing Office.

———. (1975) *World Military Expenditures and Arms Trade 1963–1973.* Washington, DC: Government Printing Office.

U.S. BUREAU OF THE CENSUS. (1985) *Highlights of U.S. Export and Import Trade,* Report FT 990, December 1985. Washington, DC: Government Printing Office.

_____. (1978) *Highlights of U.S. Export and Import Trade, Report FT 990*, December 1978. Washington, DC: Government Printing Office.

U.S. DEPARTMENT OF THE ARMY. (1969) *Special Forces Operation: U.S. Army Doctrine.* Washington, DC: Government Printing Office.

U.S. DEPARTMENT OF COMMERCE. (1978) *Selected Trade and Economic Data of the Centrally Planned Economies*, December 1977. Washington, DC: Government Printing Office.

U.S. DEPARTMENT OF STATE. (1985a) *Atlas of NATO.* Washington, DC: Government Printing Office.

_____. (1985b) "Combatting International Terrorism," *Current Policy*, No. 667, U.S. Department of State (March 5). Washington, DC: Department of State.

_____. (1983a) *Atlas of United States Foreign Relations.* Washington, DC: Government Printing Office.

_____. (1983b) "International Security and Development Program." Special Report No. 108, April 4. Washington, DC: Department of State.

_____. (1983c) *Security and Arms Control: The Search for a More Stable Peace.* Washington, DC: Government Printing Office.

U.S. Overseas Loans and Grants and Assistance from International Organizations, Obligations and Loan Authorizations, July 1, 1945–September 30, 1984. (1985) Washington, DC: Agency for International Development.

U.S. Overseas Loans and Grants and Assistance from International Organizations, Obligations and Loan Authorizations, July 1, 1945–September 30, 1979. (1980) Washington, DC: Agency for International Development.

U.S. Overseas Loans and Grants and Assistance from International Organizations, Obligations and Loan Authorizations, July 1, 1945–July 30, 1975. (1976) Washington, DC: Agency for International Development.

"The U.S. Supreme Court Decision Concerning the Legislative Veto." (1983) *Hearings Before the Committee on Foreign Affairs, United States House of Representatives.* 98th Congress, 1st Session, July 19–21. Washington, DC: Government Printing Office.

VAN DEN HAAG, ERNEST. (1985) "The Busyness of American Foreign Policy," *Foreign Affairs* 64 (Fall): 113–129.

VANCE, CYRUS. (1983) *Hard Choices: Critical Years in America's Foreign Policy.* New York: Simon and Schuster.

VASQUEZ, JOHN A. (1985) "Domestic Contention on Critical Foreign Policy Issues: The Case of the United States," *International Organization* 39 (Autumn): 606–643.

_____. (1983) *The Power of Power Politics.* New Brunswick, NJ: Rutgers University Press.

VASQUEZ, JOHN A., AND RICHARD W. MANSBACH. (1983) "The Issue Cycle: Conceptualizing Long-Term Global Political Change," *International Organization* 37 (Spring): 257–280.

VERBA, SIDNEY. (1969) "Assumptions of Rationality and Non-Rationality in Models of the International System," pp. 217–231 in James N. Rosenau (ed.), *International Politics and Foreign Policy.* New York: Free Press.

VON HOFFMAN, NICHOLAS. (1981) "Know Thy President," *The New York Review of Books* 28 (June 25): 24–28.

WALKER, STEPHEN G. (1977) "The Interface Between Beliefs and Behavior: Henry Kissinger's Operational Code and the Vietnam War," *Journal of Conflict Resolution* 21 (March): 129–168.

WALKER, STEPHEN G., AND LAWRENCE S. FALKOWSKI. (1984) "The Operational Codes of U.S. Presidents and Secretaries of State: Motivational Foundations and Behavioral Consequences," *Political Psychology* 5 (June): 237–266.

WALTZ, KENNETH N. (1971) "Opinions and Crisis in American Foreign Policy," pp. 47–55 in Douglas M. Fox (ed.), *The Politics of U.S. Foreign Policy Making.* Pacific Palisades, CA: Goodyear.

_____. (1967) *Foreign Policy and Democratic Politics.* Boston: Little, Brown.

_____. (1964) "The Stability of a Bipolar World," *Daedalus* 93 (Summer): 881–909.

WARWICK, DONALD P. (1975) *A Theory of Public Bureaucracy: Politics, Personality, and Organization in the State Department.* Cambridge, MA: Harvard University Press.

WEEDE, ERICH. (1983) "Extended Deterrence by Superpower Alliance," *Journal of Conflict Resolution* 27 (June): 231–254.

———. (1978) "U.S. Support for Foreign Governments, or Domestic Disorder and Imperial Intervention, 1958–1965," *Comparative Political Studies* 10 (January): 497–527.

WEIGLEY, RUSSELL F. (1973) *The American Way of War: A History of United States Military Strategy and Policy.* New York: Macmillan.

WEINBERG, ARTHUR. (1935) *Manifest Destiny.* Baltimore: The Johns Hopkins University Press.

WEISBAND, EDWARD. (1973) *The Ideology of American Foreign Policy: A Paradigm of Lockian Liberalism.* Beverly Hills, CA: Sage.

WEISMAN, STEVEN R. (1983) "The Influence of William Clark," *The New York Times Magazine* (August 14): 17–21ff.

WEISSBERG, ROBERT. (1976) *Public Opinion and Popular Government.* Englewood Cliffs, NJ: Prentice-Hall.

WELCH, WILLIAM. (1970) *American Images of Soviet Foreign Policy.* New Haven, CT: Yale University Press.

WENDZEL, ROBERT L. (1980) *International Relations: A Policymaker Focus.* New York: Wiley.

WESTON, RUBIN F. (1972) *Racism in U.S. Imperialism.* Columbia: University of South Carolina Press.

"White House Tapes and the Mintutes of the Cuban Missile Crises." (1985) *International Security* 10 (Summer): 164–203.

WHITE, RALPH K. (1968) *Nobody Wanted War: Misperception in Vietnam and Other Wars.* Garden City, NY: Doubleday.

WHITE, THEODORE H. (1973) *The Making of the President, 1972.* New York: Atheneum.

WILENSKY, HAROLD L. (1967) *Organizational Intelligence: Knowledge and Policy in Government and Industry.* New York: Basic Books.

WILKENFELD, JONATHAN, GERALD W. HOPPLE, PAUL J. ROSSA, AND STEPHEN J. ANDRIOLE. (1980) *Foreign Policy Behavior.* Beverly Hills, CA: Sage.

WILLIAMS, WILLIAM APPLEMAN. (1980) *Empire as a Way of Life.* New York: Oxford University Press.

———. (1972) *The Tragedy of American Diplomacy,* 2nd ed. New York: Delta.

WINIK, JAY. (1985) "Toward a Post-NATO Europe," *The Wall Street Journal* (August 27): 30.

WITTKOPF, EUGENE R. (1986) "On the Foreign Policy Beliefs of the American People: A Critique and Some Evidence," *International Studies Quarterly* 30 (December): forthcoming.

———. (1985) "Elites and Masses: Another Look at Attitudes Toward America's World Role." Paper presented at the annual meeting of the American Political Science Association, New Orleans, August 29–September 1.

———. (1984) "Public Attitudes Toward American Foreign Policy in the Post-Vietnam Decade." Paper presented at the annual convention of the International Studies Association, Atlanta, March 28–31.

———. (1981) "The Structure of Foreign Policy Attitudes: An Alternative View," *Social Science Quarterly* 62 (March): 108–123.

———. (1973) "Foreign Aid and United Nations Votes," *American Political Science Review* 67 (September): 868–888.

WITTKOPF, EUGENE R., AND MICHAEL A. MAGGIOTTO. (1983a) "Elites and Masses: A Comparative Analysis of Attitudes Toward America's World Role," *Journal of Politics* 45 (May): 303–334.

———. (1983b) "The Two Faces of Internationalism: Public Attitudes Toward American Foreign Policy in the 1970s—and Beyond?" *Social Science Quarterly* 64 (June): 288–304.

WOLFERS, ARNOLD. (1962) *Discord and Collaboration.* Baltimore: The Johns Hopkins University Press.

WOODWARD, BOB, AND CARL BERNSTEIN. (1979) *The Final Days.* New York: Simon and Schuster.

World Development Report 1985. (1985) New York: Oxford University Press for the World Bank.

World Development Report 1984. (1984) New York: Oxford University Press for the World Bank.

World Development Report 1983. (1983) New York: Oxford University Press for the World Bank.

YALEM, RONALD J. (1972) "Tripolarity and the International System," *Orbis* 15 (Winter): 1051–1063.

YANKELOVICH, DANIEL, AND LARRY KAAGAN. (1981) "Assertive America," *Foreign Affairs.* Special issue *America and the World 1980* 59 (no. 3): 696–713.

YARMOLINSKY, ADAM. (1971) *The Military Establishment: Its Impact on American Society:* New York: Harper and Row.

———. (1970–1971) "The Military Establishment (Or How Political Problems Become Military Problems)," *Foreign Policy* 1 (Winter): 78–97.

YARMOLINSKY, ADAM, AND GREGORY D. FOSTER. (1983) *Paradoxes of Power: The Military Establishment in the Eighties.* Bloomington: Indiana University Press.

YERGIN, DANIEL. (1978) *Shattered Peace: The Origins of the Cold War and the National Security State.* Boston: Houghton Mifflin.

———. (1977) "Politics and Soviet-American Trade: The Three Questions," *Foreign Affairs* 55 (April): 517–538.

ZELIKOW, PHILLIP D. (1986) "The United States and the Use of Force: A Historical Summary," forthcoming in George Osborn et al. (eds.), *Vietnam: Did It Make A Difference?* Baltimore: The Johns Hopkins University Press.

———. (1984) "Force Without War 1975–82," *Journal of Strategic Studies* 70 (March): 29–54.

ZIMMERMAN, WILLIAM. (1973) "Issue Area and Foreign Policy Process: A Research Note in Search of a General Theory," *American Political Science Review* 67 (December): 1204–1212.

INDEX